Interpretations of American History

PATTERNS AND PERSPECTIVES

VOLUME II SINCE 1877

FIFTH EDITION

EDITED BY
Gerald N. Grob
George Athan Billias

THE FREE PRESS
A Division of Macmillan, Inc.
NEW YORK
Collier Macmillan Publishers
LONDON

The Free Press
A Division of Macmillan, Inc.
866 Third Avenue, New York, N. Y. 10022

Collier Macmillan Canada, Inc.

Printed in the United States of America

printing number

3 4 5 6 7 8 9 10

Library of Congress Cataloging-in-Publication Data

Interpretations of American history.

Contents: v. 1. To 1877—v. 2. Since 1877.
    1. United States—History.   2. United States—
Historiography.   I. Grob, Gerald N.
II. Billias, George Athan
E178.6.I53   1986   973   86–18369
ISBN 0–02–911850–6 (v. 1)
ISBN 0–02–911890–5 (v. 2)

For Brad & Sharon

CONTENTS

old Bernstein

PREFACE TO THE FIFTH EDITION

This collection of essays is designed to provide supplementary readings for American history survey courses. Reflecting our philosophy of teaching history, the work is based on four major assumptions. First, that the approach to history should be conceptual rather than narrowly factual. Second, that students should be exposed to both recent scholarship and older and more traditional interpretations. Third, that students should be given brief historiographical introductions in order to appreciate more fully the assigned selections. And finally, that the selections themselves should be intellectually stimulating and interesting reading assignments.

To meet the challenge posed by our first assumption, we have chosen selections that are broadly conceptual in nature. In each case these selections represent an interpretation that illuminates either a different problem or period. Despite the different issues or ages presented, one theme is self-evident in all the selections: the view of American history has been a constantly changing one.

Generally speaking, new interpretations in American history have arisen for two reasons. First, the perspective of American historians of a given generation has often been shaped by the sweep of events in the everyday world—by developments outside the scholar's study. Scholars have tended to reflect in their writings, either explicitly or implicitly, the problems and predilections of the period in which they live. Each succeeding generation has rewritten America's past in part to suit the felt needs of its own time. In our historiographical introductions we have tried to show how the contemporary concerns of the age in which the historian is writing has shaped starting assumptions, the gathering of evidence, and the interpretation of events. From the 1960s to the mid-1980s, for example, the consciousness of many American historians has been influenced by sweeping social changes related to changing perceptions of race, sex, poverty, ethnicity, war, as well as by certain economic and technological developments. It is not surprising, therefore, to find a discussion of these same notions appearing in the writings of recent scholars on earlier periods of American history.

The second reason why the picture of America's past is constantly changing results from the internal intellectual changes within the historical profession itself. These changes have taken place within the scholar's study, so to speak. History, like most academic disciplines, has developed a built-in tendency toward self-generating change. When scholars sense that they have reached the outermost limits in applying what has become an accepted interpretation, they do one of two things: they either introduce major revisions to correct the prevailing point of view, or they strike off in a completely new direction. Some selections in these volumes, therefore, represent the writings of scholars seeking to revise existing traditional interpretations. Other articles reflect the exciting work of a current generation of American scholars who have written over the past twenty-five years what has been called the "new history."

The "new history" may be described as different in terms of both methodology and subject matter. It is more analytical and conceptual in its approach and emphasizes narrative history less. It borrows more from the insights of the other social sciences—psychology, sociology, anthropology, and political science. It tends to rely more on the newer techniques of historical inquiry, such as quantification, computer technology, model-building, and psychohistory. The "new history" is more interested in groups than individuals, and it often focuses on the inarticulate masses who left behind few written records rather than on elites who left traditional literary sources. It stresses more the material forces at work in history—demography, geography, technology, and economics—and somewhat less the power of ideas. It emphasizes certain institutions involved in the socialization of individuals, such as the family, schools, factories, prisons, and aylums.

One of the main aims of the "new history" is to analyze the social structure of America and the changes that structure has undergone over time. In studying the processes of social change, those writing the "new history" have examined changes in social stratification, shifts in the accumulation and distribution of wealth, the role of vertical and horizontal mobility, and the social origins of different groups within society.

The so-called "old history," by way of contrast, concerned itself more with traditional subjects—political events, wars, diplomacy, revolutions, intellectual movements, and the more standard institutions of society. Its method was usually narrative in approach, although it never eschewed interpretation. Its cast of characters tended to hail more from the elites in society—the rulers, politicians, and important public figures. There was often a greater emphasis placed on the role of individuals. And the stress was often more upon an idealist than a materialist approach to history.

The fact of the matter is, however, the "old" and "new" history do not constitute mutually exclusive categories. Some traditional historians have used the insights of the "new history," have been interested in mass movements, and have resorted to quantification. By the same token certain "new historians" have simply applied new methods to old subjects. Nevertheless, the degree of emphasis and intent between the two groups of scholars is sufficiently different to warrant making a distinction between the "old" and the "new" history.

To answer the needs of our third assumption, we have written chapter-length introductions to accompany each set of selections. These long introductions will enable students to approach the readings with greater ease and familiarity because of the historiographical context that has been provided.

Lastly, we have searched for scholars who write with a literary flair. Much of the most exciting work in American history has been done by scholars who possess a lively literary style and present their findings in spirited prose. Students will discover the richness of history when they read in these pages the selections written by Perry Miller, Bernard Bailyn, Gordon S. Wood, Joyce Appleby, Richard P. McCormick, Stanley Elkins, Lawrence W. Levine, Samuel P. Hays, Arthur M. Schlesinger, Jr., John Hope Franklin, C. Vann Woodward, Alfred D. Chandler, Nancy F. Cott, and Carl N. Degler, among others.

In preparing a work of this nature, acknowledgments are in order to a number of generous individuals who helped us. We wish to thank first those scholars who gave permission to reprint the selections appearing in these pages. We thank also colleagues who made insightful comments on previous editions and contributed to the final shape of the fifth edition: Francis Couvares, Amherst College; Ronald Petrin, Oklahoma State University; Milton M. Klein, professor emeritus, University of Tennessee; and Ronald P. Formisano, Clark University.

Certain scholars read specific chapters in which they are experts and saved us from some errors: Nancy Cott, Yale University; Nathan Huggins, Harvard University; Peter Onuf, Worcester Polytechnic Institute; James Hoopes, Babson College; and Douglas Little and Theo von Laue of Clark University.

Other members of the Clark University community made a special contribution to these volumes. Friends in the secretarial pool—Terry Reynolds, Rene Baril, Karen Shepardson, and Roxanne Rawson—cheerfully typed and retyped numerous drafts of chapters. Mary Hartman and Irene Walch, reference librarians at the Robert Hutchings Goddard Library, deserve particular thanks for their time-consuming labors on our behalf. And Trudy Powers, secretary of the Clark History Department, assisted in the preparation of these volumes.

To others to whom we owe a very special debt, we have dedicated these two volumes.

GERALD N. GROB
GEORGE ATHAN BILLIAS

☆ 1 ☆

Introduction

"Every true history is contemporary history." Thus wrote Benedetto Croce, the great Italian philosopher and historian, over a half century ago. By his remark Croce meant that history—as distinguished from mere chronicle—was meaningful only to the degree it struck a responsive chord in the minds of contemporaries who saw mirrored in the past the problems and issues of the present.

Croce's remark has special relevance to the writing of American history. Every generation of American scholars has reinterpreted the past in terms of its own age. Why is this so? One compelling reason, no doubt, has been the constant tendency of scholars to reexamine the past in light of the prevailing ideas, assumptions, and problems of their own day. Every age has developed its own climate of opinion—or particular view of the world—which, in turn, has partially conditioned the way it looks upon its own past and present. Thus, each succeeding generation of Americans has rewritten the history of the country in such a way as to suit its own self-image. Although there were others reasons for this continual reinterpretation of American history, the changing climate of opinion more than any other single factor caused historians to recast periodically their view of the past.

Changing interpretations arose also from the changing nature of American historians and their approach to the discipline. The writing of history in America, broadly speaking, has gone through three distinct stages. In the first stage—the era of Puritan historians during the seventeenth century—historical writing was dominated by ministers and political leaders of the Puritan colonies who sought to express the religious justification for their New World settlements. The second stage—the period of the patrician historians—saw the best history being written by members of the patrician class from the early eight-

eenth century to the late nineteenth century. Patrician historians—
often gentlemen of leisure with private incomes—normally had little
or no connection with the church or other formal institutions, as had
the Puritan historians. They were stirred to write history by a strong
sense of social responsibility that characterized the class from which
they sprang, and by a personal conviction that each individual had a
moral obligation to employ his best talents for the betterment of mankind. Their works, as a general rule, reflected the ideology and preconceptions of their class. Although they were amateur scholars for
the most part, many patrician writers succeeded in reaching a high
level of literary distinction and accuracy. The third stage—the period
of the professional scholars—began during the 1870s and may properly
be called "the age of the professional historians." These scholars qualified as professionals on several counts: they were specifically trained
for their craft; they supported themselves by full-time careers of teaching, writing, and research at colleges and universities; and they looked
to their professional group to set the standards of achievement by
which historical studies were evaluated. Their work has been characterized by constant revisionism: they attempted to correct one another, to challenge traditional interpretations, and to approach old historical problems from new points of view.[1]

During each of these three stages of historical writing, the intellectual milieu in America was distinctly different. In the seventeenth
century the best histories were written by Puritan ministers and mag-
istrates who saw history as the working out of God's will. Theirs was
a Christian interpretation of history—one in which events were seen
as the unfolding of God's intention and design. Borrowing the concept
of a Chosen People from the ancient Hebrews, they viewed the colonization of America in Biblical terms. They cast the Puritans in the
same role as the Jews in the Old Testament—as a regenerate people
who were destined to fulfill God's purpose. New England became for
them New Canaan—the place God had set apart for man to achieve a
better way of Christian living. Massachusetts, therefore, was more than
simply another colony. In the words of John Winthrop, it was to be a
"city upon a hill"—a model utopia to demonstrate to the rest of the
world that the City of God could be established on earth along the lines
set forth in the New Testament.

The major theme of most Puritan historians, whether they were
ministers or lay leaders, was the same: to demonstrate God's special
concern for His Chosen People in their efforts to build a New Canaan.

---

[1]John Higham *et al.*, *History* (Englewood Cliffs, N.J., 1965), pp. 3–5.

New England's history served their purposes best because it was here that God's mercy could be seen more clearly than in any other part of the globe. To the Puritans, New England's history was one long record of the revelation of God's providence toward His people. Their disasters as well as their triumphs were seen only in relation to God, and the setbacks they suffered were viewed as evidence of God's wrath and displeasure.

Of all the Puritan histories, William Bradford's *Of Plimouth Plantation* was, perhaps, the preeminent work of art. Written in the 1630s and 1640s while Bradford was governor of the colony, this book recounted the tale of the tiny band of Pilgrims who fled first to Holland and then to the New World. No other narrative captured so perfectly the deep feeling of religious faith of New England's early settlers. None illustrated better the Puritan ideal of a plain and simple literary style, or mastered so well the rhythms of Biblical prose. Yet like most Puritan literature it was written during the few spare moments that Bradford could find from his more important activities as a governor of a new community in the wilderness.

The patrician historians of the eighteenth century replaced the Puritan historians when the church ceased to be the intellectual center of American life. The Christian theory of history with its emphasis on supernatural causes increasingly gave way to a more secular interpretation based upon the concepts of human progress, reason, and material well-being. Influenced by European Enlightenment thinkers, American historians came to believe that man, by use of his reason, could control his destiny and determine his own material and intellectual progress in the world.

The patrician historians were profoundly influenced also by ideas derived from the writings of Sir Isaac Newton. This seventeenth-century English scientist, by applying a rational, mathematical method, had arrived at certain truths, or "natural laws," concerning the physical universe. Newton's systematization of scientific thought led many men to conclude that the same mathematical-scientific method could be employed to formulate similar natural laws in other fields. In order to develop a theory of history in keeping with Newtonian thought, writers began to postulate certain natural laws in the field of history. Thus, patrician historians abandoned the Christian theory in which God determined the events for a view of the universe in which natural laws were the motivating forces in history.

This shift from a Christian interpretation of history to a more secular approach was reflected in the change of leaders among American historians. Minister-historians were increasingly replaced by members of the patrician class—political leaders, planter-aristocrats, merchants, lawyers, and doctors.² In the eighteenth century, for example, America's outstanding historians included Thomas Hutchinson, member of the Massachusetts merchant aristocracy and royal governor of that colony; William Smith of New York, doctor, landowner, and lieutenant governor of that colony; and Robert Beverley and William Byrd of Virginia, who were planter-aristocrats, large landowners, and officeholders. Most of these men possessed a classical education, a fine private library, and the leisure time in which to write. With the growth of private wealth and the opening up of new economic opportunities, more members of the upper classes were in a position to take up the writing of history as an avocation.³

The reaction against the Christian interpretation of history was particularly evident in the writings of Thomas Jefferson. In his *Notes on the State of Virginia,* first published in 1785, Jefferson stressed reason and natural law instead of divine providence as the basis for historical causation. Jefferson believed also that men were motivated by self-interest, and he employed this concept as one means of analyzing the course of historical events. As he wrote in his history of Virginia, "Mankind soon learn to make interested uses of every right and power which they possess, or may assume."

Jefferson's history showed the impact of yet another major influence—nationalism—which affected historical writing after 1776. As author of the Declaration of Independence, Jefferson felt a fierce, patriotic pride in the free institutions that emerged from the Revolution. He was convinced that America as a democratic nation was destined to pave the way for a new era in world history. A whole new generation of patrician historians sprang up after the Revolution, writing in a similar nationalistic vein—David Ramsay, Mercy Otis Warren, Jeremy Belknap, and Jared Sparks. They likewise contrasted America's free institutions with what they considered to be Europe's corrupt and decadent institutions.

During the first three quarters of the nineteenth century, the writing of history continued to be dominated by patrician historians. The influence of the romantic movement in the arts with its heightened appreciation of the past, emphasis upon pictorial descriptions, and stress upon the role of great men, caused history to be viewed increasingly as a branch of literature. Many outstanding literary figures—Washington Irving, Francis Parkman, Richard Hildreth, William H. Prescott, and John Lothrop Motley—wrote narrative histories about America, other lands, and other times, in a romantic style calculated

---

²Harvey Wish, *The American Historian* (New York, 1960), p. 25.
³Higham, *History,* p. 3.

to appeal to a wide reading public. Such authors were often part of an Anglo-American literary culture, for many English historians were writing in the same vein.

America's patrician historians, however, were not always content to provide only a colorful narrative. Writing within a developmental framework, they sought to reveal some of the underlying principles which they believed lay behind the rational evolution of historical events. For the most part, their writings reflected certain assumptions that were common to many historians on both sides of the Atlantic in the first half of the nineteenth century—the idea that history was essentially the story of liberty; that man's record revealed a progressive advance toward greater human rights down through the ages; and that peoples of Anglo-Saxon origin had a special destiny to bring democracy to the rest of the world.

Many of these American historians, influenced by the pronounced nationalism of the period, used such broad assumptions within a chauvinistic framework. They felt a responsibility to help establish the national identity of the new United States. Thus, they employed history as a didactic tool to instruct their countrymen along patriotic lines and presented America's story in the best light possible. Running through their writings were three basic themes: the idea of progress—that the story of America was one of continuous progress onward and upward toward greatness; the idea of liberty—that American history, in essence, symbolized the trend toward greater liberty in world history; and the idea of mission—that the United States had a special destiny to serve as a model of a free people to the rest of mankind in leading the way to a more perfect life. The last theme, in effect, was nothing more than a restatement of the idea of mission first set forth by the Puritan historians.

George Bancroft, the most distinguished historian of the mid-nineteenth century, organized his history of the United States around these three themes. After studying in Germany in the 1820s, Bancroft returned to America determined to apply Teutonic ideas of history to the story of his own country. Bancroft believed in the progressive unfolding of all human history toward a future golden age in which all men would eventually achieve complete freedom and liberty. This march of all mankind toward a greater freedom was in accordance with a preordained plan conceived by God. One phase of God's master plan could be seen in the way that a superior Anglo-Saxon people developed a distinctive set of democratic institutions. The United States, according to Bancroft, represented the finest flowering of such democratic institutions. American democracy, then, was the fruition of God's plan, and the American people had a unique mission in history to spread democracy throughout the rest of the world. Such was the central theme of Bancroft's famous twelve-volume work, *History of the United States from the Discovery of the American Continent*, written between 1834 and 1882.

Francis Parkman, a patrician historian from New England, held many views similar to those of Bancroft. Writing about the intercolonial wars in his *France and England in North America*, Parkman portrayed the American colonists as democratic Anglo-Saxons of Protestant persuasion whose superior qualities enabled them to conquer authoritarian-minded French Catholics in Canada. But in many other ways the two writers were quite different. Parkman was more representative of the gentlemen-historians of the nineteenth century who, being drawn from the upper classes, usually reflected an aristocratic bias in their writings, advocated a conservative Whig philosophy, and were distrustful of the American masses. Bancroft, on the other hand, eulogized the common man and was a Jacksonian in politics; his history was distinctly democratic in outlook.

By the 1870s two profound changes began to influence the writing of American history. The first was the change in leadership from amateur patricians to professional historians. Until the last quarter of the nineteenth century, American history had been written almost exclusively by men who had received no special training as historians—except, of course, for a few individuals like Bancroft. From this point on, however, the writing of history was dominated by professionally trained scholars educated in the universities of America and Europe. Professionalization in the field was made possible by developments in higher education as graduate schools appeared in increasing numbers in America to train college history teachers. In the last three decades of the century, this trend proceeded at a rapid rate: the Johns Hopkins University, the first institution devoted to graduate study and research, began its activities in 1876; the American Historical Association was founded in 1884; and the *American Historical Review* made its appearance in 1895.

The advent of professional historians brought about a marked transformation in the field. No longer was historical writing to be vested mainly in the hands of amateurs—though it should be emphasized that many patrician historians had been superb stylists, creative scholars, and researchers who made judicious use of original sources. Nor would historians be drawn almost exclusively from the patrician class in the Northeast, particularly from New England. Professional scholars came from all walks of life, represented a much broader range of social interests than the patricians, and hailed from different geographic regions. Finally, instead of being free-lance writers, as many patricians had been, professionals made their living as teachers in colleges and universities.

The second major development affecting the writing of American history was the emergence of a new intellectual milieu that reflected the growing dominance of novel scientific ideas and concepts. Influenced by Darwinian biology and its findings in the natural sciences, historians began to think of history as a science rather than as a branch of literature. Why couldn't the historian deal with the facts of history in much the same way that the scientist did with elements in the laboratory? If there were certain laws of organic development in the scientific field, might there not be certain laws of historical development? What historian, wrote Henry Adams, with "an idea of scientific method can have helped dreaming of the immortality that would be achieved by the man who should successfully apply Darwin's method to the facts of human history?"[4]

The first generation of professional historians—who held sway from about 1870 to 1910—was best exemplified by two outstanding scholars, Henry Adams and Frederick Jackson Turner. Henry Adams, a descendant of the famous Adams family that contributed American presidents, statesmen, and diplomats, turned to history and literature as his avocation after his hopes for high political office were dashed. In 1870 he was invited to Harvard and became the first teacher to introduce a history seminar at that institution. Adams pioneered in training his students in the meticulous critical methods of German scholarship, and searched for a time for a scientific philosophy of history based on the findings in the field of physics. His nine-volume history of the United States during the administrations of Jefferson and Madison was destined to become one of the classics of American historical literature. Although he left Harvard after a few years, his career symbolized the transformation from patrician to professional historian and the changing intellectual climate from romanticism to a more scientific approach in the writing of American history.

While Henry Adams was attempting to assimilate history and physics, Frederick Jackson Turner—perhaps the most famous and influential representative of the scientific school of historians in the first generation of professional historians—was applying evolutionary modes of thought to explain American history. Born and reared in a frontier community in Wisconsin, Turner attended the University of Wisconsin, received his Ph.D. from the Johns Hopkins University, and then went on to a teaching career first at Wisconsin and later at Harvard. Like Adams, Turner believed that it was possible to make a science out of history; he attempted, therefore, to apply the ideas of Darwinian evolution to the writing of history. Turner emphasized the

---

[4]Henry Adams, "The Tendency of History," *Annual Report of the American Historical Association for the Year 1894* (Washington, D.C., 1895), p. 19.

concept of evolutionary stages of development as successive frontier environments in America wrought changes in the character of the people and their institutions. As one frontier in America succeeded another, each more remote from Europe than its predecessor, a social evolutionary process was at work creating a democratic American individualist. The unique characteristics of the American people—their rugged individualism, egalitarianism, practicality, and materialistic outlook on life—all resulted from the evolutionary process of adapting to successive frontier environments. Turner's famous essay, "The Significance of the Frontier in American History," written in 1893, remains a superb statement of one approach that was employed by the scientific school of historians.

Between 1910 and 1945 a second generation of professional scholars—the Progressive historians—came to maturity and helped to transform the discipline by introducing new ideas and methodologies. Many of them were influenced by the Progressive movement of the early 1900s—a period when the future of American democracy appeared to be threatened by new economic and social forces arising from the rapid industrialization of American society. Rejecting the views of the older and more conservative patrician historians, the Progressive scholars viewed history as an ideological weapon that might explain the present and perhaps help to control the future. In sympathy with the aims and objectives of the Progressive movement between 1900 and 1920, these scholars continued to write history from a Progressive point of view even after the decline of the Progressive movement following World War I.

Unlike the New England patrician historians of the nineteenth century, the Progressive scholars tended to hail more from the Midwest and South. These Progressives complained that in the past American history had been presented mainly as an extension of the history of New England. American civilization, they argued, was more than a transplanted English and European civilization that had spread out from New England; it had unique characteristics and a mission all its own. But while the Progressive historians were as nationalistic as the patrician school, their nationalism was different in nature. The patricians had conceived of nationalism as a stabilizing force, preserving order and thus assuring the continued ascendancy of the aristocratic element in American life. The Progressives, on the other hand, considered nationalism a dynamic force. To them the fulfillment of democracy meant a continued and protracted struggle against those individuals, classes, and groups who had barred the way to the achievements of a more democratic society in the past.

In changing the direction of American historical writing, Progressive scholars drew upon the reform tradition that had grown out of the effort to adjust American society to the new demands of an urban-centered and industrialized age. This tradition had originated in the 1890s and reached maturity in the early part of the twentieth century with the Progressive movement. Drawing upon various sources, the adherents of the Progressive movement rejected the idea of a closed system of classical economic thought which assumed that certain natural laws governed human society. Society, these reformers maintained, was open-ended and dynamic; its development was determined not by immutable laws, but by economic and social forces that grew out of the interaction between the individual and his environment.

Reacting against the older emphasis upon logic, abstraction, and deduction, these reformers sought a meaningful explanation of human society that could account for its peculiar development. Instead of focusing upon immutable laws, they began viewing society and individuals as products of an evolutionary developmental process. This process could be understood only by reference to the past. The function of the historian, then, was to explain how the present had come to be, and then to try and set guidelines for future developments. As a result of this approach, history and the other social sciences drew together, seeking to explain the realities of social life by emphasizing the interplay of economic, technological, social, psychological, and political forces.

History, according to its Progressive practitioners, was not an abstract discipline whose truths could only be contemplated. On the contrary, historians had important activist roles to play in the construction of a better world. By explaining the historical roots of contemporary problems, historians could provide the knowledge and understanding necessary to make changes which would bring further progress. Like the Enlightenment *philosophes*, historians could reveal prior mistakes and errors and thus liberate men from the chains of tyranny and oppression of the past. When fused with the social sciences history could become a powerful tool for reform. "The present has hitherto been the willing victim of the past," wrote James Harvey Robinson, one of the greatest exponents of Progressive history; but "the time has now come when it should turn on the past and exploit it in the interests of advance."[5]

Clearly, the sympathy of this school lay with change and not with the preservation of the status quo. Committed to the idea of progress, they saw themselves as contributing to a better and more humane world for the future. Consequently they rejected the apparent moral neutrality and supposed objectivity of the scientific school in favor of

---

[5]James Harvey Robinson, "The New History," *The New History: Essays Illustrating the Modern Historical Outlook* (New York, 1912), p. 24.

a liberal philosophy of reform. In so doing they rewrote much of American history, greatly widening its scope and changing its emphasis. Instead of focusing on narrow institutional studies of traditional political, diplomatic, and military history, they sought to delineate those determinant forces that underlay human institutions. In their hands American history became a picture of conflict—conflict between polarities of American life: aristocracy versus democracy; economic "haves" versus "have-nots"; politically overprivileged groups versus those underprivileged; and between geographical sections, as the East versus West. In short, the divisions were between those dedicated to democratic and egalitarian ideals and those committed to a static conservatism.

Believers in inevitable progress, the Progressive historians assumed that America was continually moving on an upward path toward an ideal social order. Not only was American society growing in affluence, but in freedom, opportunity, and happiness as well. The primary determinant of progress was the unending conflict between the forces of liberalism and those of conservatism. Thus all periods in American history could be divided into two clear and distinct phases: periods of active reform and periods of conservative reaction. As Arthur M. Schlesinger, Sr., wrote in 1939: "A period of concern for the rights of the few has been followed by one of concern for the wrongs of the many."[6]

Turner, a transitional figure beween the scientific and Progressive historians, with Charles A. Beard and Vernon L. Parrington, best presented the Progressive point of view. After his epochal essay on the frontier in 1893—an essay that emphasized unity rather than conflict—Turner's interest turned elsewhere, particularly to the idea of sectional conflict. From the late 1890s until his death in 1932, he elaborated and refined his sectional conflict hypothesis. Turner and his students attempted to understand not only how a section came into being, but also the dynamics of conflict that pitted the East against West, North against South, labor against capital, and the many against the few. Under Turner's guiding hand American scholars wrote a series of brilliant monographs as well as broad interpretive studies that emphasized the class and sectional divisions in American society. Although a few favored the conservative side, the overwhelming majority of historians made clear their preference for democratic liberalism and progress.

While Turner was developing and elaborating his sectional approach, Charles A. Beard was applying the hypothesis of an overt class

---

[6]Arthur M. Schlesinger, Sr., "Tides of American Politics," *Yale Review* 29 (December 1939):220.

conflict to the study of American institutions. His *An Economic Inter-pretation of the Constitution*, written in 1913, was perhaps the most influential historical work of the twentieth century. Beard attempted to demonstrate that the Constitution, far from representing a judicious combination of wisdom and idealism, was actually the product of a small group of propertied individuals who were intent upon establishing a strong central government capable of protecting their interests against the encroachments of the American masses. In a series of books climaxed by *The Rise of American Civilization* in 1927, Beard argued that American history demonstrated the validity of the class conflict hypothesis between "haves" and "have-nots." Time and again, he showed the paramount role that economic factors played in determining human behavior. Fusing his ardent faith in progress with a qualified economic determinism, Beard made clear that his sympathies lay with the forces of democracy as opposed to those of reaction and privilege.

The culmination of the Progressive interpretation came with the publication of Vernon L. Parrington's *Main Currents in American Thought*. Using literature as his vehicle, Parrington portrayed American history in clear and unmistakable terms. The two central protagonists of Parrington's work were Jefferson and Hamilton. Jefferson stood for a decentralized agrarian democracy that drew its support from the great masses of people. Hamilton, on the other hand, represented a privileged and aristocratic minority seeking to maintain its dominant position. American history, according to Parrington, had witnessed a continual struggle between the liberal Jeffersonian tradition and the conservative Hamiltonian one. Underlying Parrington's approach was one major assumption that had also governed the thought of Turner and Beard, namely, that ideology was determined by the materialistic forces in history. Like Turner and Beard, Parrington clearly preferred the forces of reform and democracy, but there were times when he was much less certain of their eventual triumph than his two intellectual companions.

The Progressive point of view generally dominated the field of American historical scholarship down to the end of World War II. Class and sectional conflict, Progressive historians implied, was a guarantor of progress. Even during those eras in American history when the forces of reaction triumphed—as in the post–Civil War period—their victory was only temporary; ultimately the forces of progress and good regrouped and thereby gained the initiative once again. Such an approach, of course, led to broad and sweeping interpretive syntheses of American history, for the basic framework or structure was clear and simple, and the faith of historians in the ultimate triumph of good over evil remained unquestioned.

Beginning in the 1930s, however, some American scholars began

to question the idea of progress that was implicit in this view. The rise
of Nazism in the 1930s and 1940s, and the menace of communism in
the 1950s and 1960s, led to a questioning of older assumptions and
generalities. How, some asked, could one subscribe to the optimistic
tenets of liberalism after the horrors of Auschwitz, Buchenwald, Hiroshima, Nagasaki, and the threat of modern totalitarianism? Indeed,
had not American historians, through their own optimistic view of
history and their faith in progress, failed to prepare the American people for the challenges and trials that they would face during the middle
of the twentieth century? Parrington himself had recognized as early
as 1929 that the Progressive faith was under attack by those who did
not subscribe to its basic tenets. "Liberals whose hair is growing thin
and the lines of whose figures are no longer what they were," he wrote,
"are likely to find themselves today in the unhappy predicament of
being treated as mourners at their own funerals. When they pluck up
heart to assert that they are not yet authentic corpses, but living men
with brains in their heads, they are pretty certain to be gently chided
and led back to the comfortable armchair that befits senility. Their
counsel is smiled at as the chatter of a belated post-Victorian generation that knew not Freud, and if they must go abroad they are bidden
take the air in the garden where other old-fashioned plants—mostly of
the family *Democratici*—are still preserved."[7]

Following the end of World War II, a third generation of professional
historians appeared on the scene to challenge the Progressive point of
view. They were sometimes called neoconservatives because they
seemed to hark back to the conservative historical position that had
prevailed prior to Turner and Beard. Their rise was partly a result of
pressures—both external and internal—upon the historical profession
in the postwar era.

External pressures resulting from changing political conditions in
the world at large brought about a major change in the mood of many
Americans. Some neoconservative historians reflected, either consciously or unconsciously, an outlook that prevailed in the United
States as the nation assumed the sober responsibility of defending the
world against the threat of communism. During the Cold War era,
when the country felt its security endangered from abroad, these scholars wanted, perhaps, to present an image to the rest of the world of an
America that had been strong and united throughout most of its history. Hence, the neoconservative scholars pictured American history
in terms of consensus rather than conflict.

---

[7]Vernon L. Parrington, *Main Currents in American Thought*, 3 vols. (New York,
1927–1930), 3:401.

Internal pressures within the profession itself likewise brought changes. Particular points of view expressed in any academic discipline seem to have an inner dynamism of their own. After subscribing to a given interpretation for a time, scholars often sense that they have pushed an idea to its outermost limits and can go no farther without risking major distortion. A reaction inevitably sets in, and revisionists begin working in a different direction. Such was the case of the Progressive interpretation of history. Having written about American history from the standpoint of conflict and discontinuity, scholars now began to approach the same subject from an opposite point of view—that of consensus and continuity.

One way this new group of scholars differed from the Progressives was in their inherent conservatism. Progressive historians had had a deep belief in the idea of progress. Neoconservative historians, on the other hand, often rejected progress as an article of faith. Skeptical of the alleged beneficial results of rapid social change, they stressed instead the thesis of historical continuity.

Given their emphasis on continuity the neoconservatives were less prone to a periodized view of American history. Progressive scholars had seen American history in terms of class or sectional conflicts marked by clearly defined turning points—the Revolution, the Constitution, the Jeffersonian era, the Jacksonian period, the Civil War, and so forth. These periods represented breaks, or discontinuities, from what had gone on before. For the Progressives, American history was divided into two distinct phases that followed one another in a cyclical pattern: periods of reform or revolution when the popular and democratic forces in society gained the upper hand and forced social changes, and periods of reaction and counterrevolution, when vested interests resisted such changes. For the neoconservative scholars, however, the enduring and unifying themes in history were much more significant. To them the continuity of common principles in American culture, the stability and longevity of institutions, and the persistence of certain traits and traditions in the American national character represented the most powerful forces in history.

Consensus, as well as continuity, was a characteristic theme of the neoconservative historians. Unlike the Progressives, who wrote about the past in terms of polarities—class conflicts between rich and poor, sectional divisions between North and South or East and West, and ideological differences between liberals and conservatives—the neoconservatives abandoned the conflict interpretation of history and favored instead one that viewed American society as stable and homogeneous. The cement that bound American society together throughout most of its history was a widespread acceptance of certain principles and beliefs. Americans, despite their differences, had always agreed on the following propositions: the right of all persons in society to own private property; the theory that the power of government should always be limited; the concept that men possessed certain natural rights that could not be taken from them by government; and the idea of some form of natural law.

One of the foremost neoconservative historians writing in the 1950s was Louis Hartz. In *The Liberal Tradition in America,* Hartz took issue with those Progressive historians who had viewed the American Revolution as a radical movement that fundamentally transformed American society. America had come into being after the age of feudalism, Hartz claimed, and this condition had profoundly shaped its development. Lacking a feudal past, the country did not have to contend with the established feudal structure that characterized the *ancien régime* in Europe—a titled aristocracy, national church, national army, and the like. Hence, America was "born free" and did not require a radical social revolution to become a liberal society—it was one already. What emerged in America, according to Hartz, was a unique society characterized by a consensus upon a single tradition of thought—the liberal tradition. The absence of a feudal heritage enabled the liberal-bourgeois ideas embodied in the political principles derived from John Locke to flourish in America almost unchallenged. "The ironic flaw in American liberalism," wrote Hartz, "lies in the fact that we have never had a conservative tradition."[8]

What, then, of the "conservatives" in American history about whom the Progressive scholars had written? When viewed within the context of comparative history, Hartz said, American conservatives had much more in common with their fellow American liberals than with their European counterparts. Many of the presumed differences between so-called American conservatives and liberals was in the nature of shadowboxing rather than actual fighting, he concluded, because both groups agreed on a common body of liberal political principles. The Federalists, for example, were not aristocrats but whiggish liberals who misunderstood their society—they misread the Jeffersonian Democrats as being "radicals" rather than recognizing them as fellow liberals. What was true of the Federalists and Jeffersonians held for the other political confrontations in American history; if measured in terms of a spectrum of thought that included European ideologies, the American conflicts took place within the confines of a Lockean consensus.

Daniel J. Boorstin, another major neoconservative historian, also offered a grand theory which pictured American history in terms of continuity and consensus. Boorstin, like Hartz, stressed the unique-

[8]Louis Hartz, *The Liberal Tradition in America* (New York, 1955), p. 57.

ness of American society, but he attributed this development to other causes. A neo-Turnerian, Boorstin postulated an environmental explanation of the American national character. To him the frontier experience was the source of America's conservatism.

In two books written in the 1950s—*The Genius of American Politics* and *The Americans: The Colonial Experience*—Boorstin denied the significance of European influences and ideas upon American life. Boorstin's premise was that the Americans were not an "idea-centered" people. From the very beginning Americans had abandoned European political theories, European blueprints for utopian societies, and European concepts of class distinctions. Americans concerned themselves instead with concrete situations and the practical problems experienced by their frontier communities. Thus they developed little knack for theorizing or any deep interest in theories as such. The "genius of American politics" lay in its emphasis on pragmatic matters— its very distrust of theories that had led to radical political changes and deep divisions within European societies.[9]

The American way of life which evolved during the colonial period, wrote Boorstin, set the pattern for the nation's later development. That pattern placed a premium on solutions to practical problems, adaptations to changing circumstances, and improvisations based upon pragmatic considerations. Lacking a learned class or professional traditions, the colonists were forced to create their own ways of doing things in the areas of education, law, medicine, science, diplomacy, and warfare. During this process the "doer" dominated over the "thinker" and the generalist over the specialist. Over the course of time this nontheoretical approach developed into a distinctive American life-style—one characterized by a naive practicality that enabled Americans to unite in a stable way of life and to become a homogeneous society made up of undifferentiated men sharing the same values.

The "cult of the 'American Consensus,'" as one scholar called it, made the nation's past appear tame and placid; it was no longer a history marked by extreme group conflicts or rigid class distinctions.[10] The heroes in America's past—Jefferson, Lincoln, Wilson, and Franklin D. Roosevelt—became less heroic because there occurred no head-on clash between individuals on the basis of ideology since all Americans shared the same middle-class Lockean values. Conversely, the old vil-

---

[9]Daniel J. Boorstin, *The Genius of American Politics* (Chicago, 1953), and *The Americans: The Colonial Experience* (New York, 1958). Boorstin further elaborated on his views in two more volumes: *The Americans: the National Experience* (New York, 1965), and *The Americans: The Democratic Experience* (New York, 1973).

[10]John Higham, "The Cult of the 'American Consensus': Homogenizing Our History," *Commentary* 27 (February 1959): 93–100.

lains—Hamilton, Rockefeller, and Carnegie—became less evil and were portrayed as constructive figures who contributed much to their country. The achievements of the business community in particular were glorified. Without the material achievements of American entrepreneurs, according to some scholars, the United States could not have withstood the challenges to democracy during World War I and World War II. The underdogs in American history—the reformers, radicals, and working class—were presented as being less idealistic and more egocentric as neoconservative scholars sought to demonstrate that the ideology of these elements in society was no less narrow and self-centered than that of other elements. The "cult" of the neoconservatives continued into the 1960s—though "cult" was perhaps too strong a term, and implied a unanimity rarely found in the historical profession.

Besides Boorstin and Hartz, other neoconservative scholars published specialized studies which revised the Progressive point of view in virtually every period of American history. The neoconservative trend, marked by a new respect for tradition and a de-emphasis on class conflict, brought many changes in American historiography: the revival of a sympathetic approach to the Puritans; the treatment of the American Revolution as a conservative movement of less significance; the conclusion that the Constitution was a document faithfully reflecting a middle-class consensus; the favorable, if not uncritical, attitude toward the founding fathers of the new republic; the diminution of the traditional ideological differences between Hamiltonianism and Jeffersonianism; the consensus interpretation of the Jacksonian era; the enhanced reputation of America's business tycoons; a renewed appreciation of such controversial political leaders as Theodore Roosevelt; the inclination to play down the more radical aspects of the Progressive and New Deal periods; the predisposition to support the correctness of America's recent foreign policy; and the tendency to view American society as being satisfied, unified, and stable throughout most of the nation's history. Implicit in the neoconservative approach was a fear of extremism, a yearning to prove that national unity had almost always existed, and a longing for the security and way of life America presumably had enjoyed before becoming a superpower and leader of the free world.

During the decades of the 1960s and 1970s the assumptions and conclusions of the neoconservative historians were rudely overturned by two major developments. First, the mood of the American people shifted markedly as the seemingly placid decade of the 1950s was succeeded by tumultuous events in America's foreign and domestic affairs. Second, within the historical profession itself a reaction to the neoconservative point of view led to the rise of many revisionist interpretations. The result was a pronounced fragmentation in the field of American historiography.

The prevailing mood among the American people shifted dramatically in the 1960s and 1970s because of a series of shattering events on the domestic scene. Gone were the complacency, national self-confidence, optimism, and moral composure that seemed to have characterized the 1950s. Many historians were stirred by the great social upheavals that undermined previously held assumptions. A marked trend toward racial divisions within American society appeared with the newfound militancy among blacks during the civil rights movement. The resulting hostility to integration among many whites showed that American society was hardly as homogeneous as had been previously believed. At the same time, an increased tendency toward violence during the urban riots in the 1960s indicated that Americans were not always committed to the idea of peaceful compromise. President Kennedy's assassination in 1963 followed by that of Martin Luther King and Robert Kennedy revealed that the United States was as vulnerable to political terrorism as other societies. There was also a renewed awareness of poverty with the economic downturn in the 1970s, and some scholars began voicing doubts about the supposed social mobility within American society, the virtues of technological change, and the benefits of economic growth.

The appearance of numerous social-protest movements during those two decades also made many American historians more conscious of the importance of minority groups in the nation's past. Having witnessed protest movements by the blacks, the poor, and the women's liberation movement, some scholars took a greater interest in black history, women's history, and in protest groups like the Populists and IWW. Generally speaking, historians became more sympathetic to the role of the underdog in American history.

Changes in America's foreign affairs during these decades similarly had a profound effect on the writing of history. The Vietnam War, above all, divided the American people. Students participated in large-scale antiwar demonstrations, and college campuses were transformed into centers of political protest and activism. Many intellectuals grew disenchanted with the government's military policy and became increasingly suspicious of the political establishment in general. The Vietnam War also exposed the dangers of what one historian termed "the imperial presidency." President Nixon and the Watergate scandal revealed further the threat posed to constitutional government by this concept of the presidency. As some historians grew more critical of America's foreign policy, they began to question the credibility of the government both in the present and past.

During the course of the 1960s and 1970s scholars were affected also by sweeping intellectual changes within the historical profession itself. Some began by challenging the traditional approach to history— one that assumed the discipline was separate and self-contained. Acting on the premise that the other social sciences—psychology, sociology, anthropology, and political science—could contribute to the study of history, they turned more to an interdisciplinary approach. In doing so, these historians applied concepts, laws, and models from other social sciences in order to understand the conduct of individuals and social groups in the past. This interdisciplinary approach could hardly be called new for it had been employed during the first half of the twentieth century. Still, there was a stronger tendency among scholars to apply social science techniques during these two decades.

A second major development was the use of new methodological approaches to the study of history. Some historians began relying more on quantitative techniques in their efforts to derive scientifically measurable historical data to document their studies. Other scholars turned to a comparative history approach—comparing entire societies or segments of societies—to illuminate the American past. Quantitative and comparative history were but two of a number of methodological approaches which were employed with greater frequency in the 1960s and 1970s.

It was within this general context that there arose a significant challenge to the neoconservative historians in the 1960s from a group of younger radical scholars known as the New Left. Like the older Progressives, these historians sought to fuse historical scholarship with political activism, and might be called neo-Progressives. Unlike the neoconservatives who emphasized consensus, continuity, and stability, the New Left saw social and economic conflict as the major theme in American history. Of all historians, the individuals identified with the New Left were the most disenchanted with the course of events in recent American history. As a result they presented a radical critique of American society and took a more jaundiced view of the American past.

These scholars reinterpreted American history along more radical lines and insisted that their colleagues pay far greater attention to the lower classes and minority groups of all kinds. Members of the New Left were exceedingly critical in particular of those neoconservative scholars who tended to celebrate the virtues and achievements of the American people. Because the neoconservatives had excluded conflict in their interpretation, the New Left argued, the American people were unprepared to cope with the social upheavals that occurred in the 1960s. These younger historians declared that the resort to violence by social groups to achieve their goals was a theme that had deep roots in the American past. The New Left historians sought to create a "usable past"—a history that would account for the country's social problems, such as racism, militarism, economic exploitation, and imperialism, and would serve as the basis for reforming American society. American history had too often been written from "the top down"— that is, from the point of view of elites and the articulate like Washington, Lincoln, and Franklin D. Roosevelt. History, they argued, should be written "from the bottom up," a perspective which would reflect the concerns of the common people, the inarticulate masses, and nonelites. Viewing history in this way, scholars would discover the radicalism inherent in the American past.

In their treatment of America's foreign policy, for example, the New Left developed a much more critical interpretation than previous historians. America from its beginnings, they argued, had been an aggressive, expansionist, and imperialist nation. It expanded first at the expense of the Indians, and then later at the expense of its weaker neighbors like Mexico. The United States turned subsequently to an overseas imperialist foreign policy based on its need for foreign markets, raw materials, and investment opportunities. This expansionist foreign policy had global ramifications, the New Left claimed. America had played a major role in precipitating two world wars and was primarily responsible for bringing about the Cold War. The Vietnam War, according to the New Left, was simply a logical extension of America's aggressive and expansionist foreign policy.

The New Left view of American history never attained the importance or cohesion of either the Progressive or the neoconservative interpretation. One reason was that few Americans were prepared to accept either the analyses or the solutions proposed by these radical historians. Another was that the American withdrawal from Vietnam and the economic downturn of the 1970s brought a halt to most radical protest movements. Although New Left scholarship failed to develop the potential many had expected of it, some of its insights and concerns were absorbed by nonradical historians seeking to break out of the mold and limitations of the neoconservative approach of the 1950s.

A more significant challenge to both the older school of Progressive historians and the neoconservatives came from the "new social historians" who transformed the writing of American history from the 1960s to the mid-1980s. Generally speaking, the major focus of these scholars was on America's social structure and the changes that this structure underwent over time. The "new social historians" claimed they differed from the older and more traditional historians in at least four ways: their approach to history; the subject matter in which they were interested; the nature of their evidence; and the methodologies that they used.[11]

Their approach to history, the "new social historians" claimed, was more analytical. Traditional historians, they argued, had written descriptive, narrative history, and usually depicted historical events in isolation from broader conceptual considerations. The "new social historians" claimed that social, political, and economic events were inevitably related to changes in America's social structure, and that these events could be traced back to that structure in an analytical way.

The "new social historians" argued also that the traditional historians had made generalizations based on vague and limited evidence. Historical evidence, they said, should be more precise and approached in a more scientific manner. Numerical evaluations expressed in such phrases as "some," "many," and a "few" were no longer acceptable. Such evidence whenever possible should be set forth in quantitatively verifiable terms in order to provide a greater degree of precision. Moreover, evidence of this sort should be used to test in a systematic way broad conceptual hypotheses about human behavior advanced by other social science disciplines.

As regards subject matter, the "new social historians" charged that traditional historians had focused narrowly on political events, diplomacy, revolutions, and wars. The new scholars claimed that they studied a much broader spectrum of human affairs—they were interested in analyzing the entire span of human social experience. Thus they focused more on social groups than on individuals, and on the masses rather than on certain elites, such as politicians or prominent people. They concentrated more on the ordinary doings of ordinary people and sought to capture the perspective of events "from the bottom up"—so to speak.

The emphasis of the "new social historians" was also more on subjects that stressed the material basis of existence. They were concerned more with material forces operating in history—determinants such as demography, geography, economics, and technology—and less with matters of ideology. Institutions concerned with the socialization of individuals—the family, schools, factories, prisons, and asylums—were more apt to draw their attention. Their greatest interest, perhaps, was in the processes of social change, in mobility both geographical and social. Such a materialistic approach, they claimed, would lead to a much richer synthesis of historical understanding of events.

The "new social historians" also applied different methodologies

---

[11]The term "new social historians" was used to distinguish these scholars from an older generation of social historians—scholars who had written descriptive and narrative history dealing with the manners and mores of the common people that was sometimes termed "pots and pans history."

in their studies. To reconstruct meaningful patterns of behavior about the inarticulate masses they borrowed methodologies used in the other behavioral sciences, such as psychology, sociology, and anthropology. At the same time they resorted to different methodological techniques such as the use of computers, model-building, and theories of psychoanalysis.

Several important influences affected the rise of the "new social history" in America. First, French scholars since the 1930s had been moving away from narrow political and institutional studies and raising new questions as well as employing novel methodologies. The most significant outlet for the work of these European scholars was the *Annales*, a French publication. The aim of this distinguished journal was to break down the traditional disciplinary barriers and to create a new and more unified approach to the understanding of the totality of human experience. Under the editorship of Lucien Febvre and Marc Bloch, the *Annales* became the leading journal in creating the new field of social history. Continuing such innovative studies after World War II, the *Annales* increasingly served scholars employing quantitative techniques or resorting to multidisciplinary approaches. Slowly but surely the influence of the French scholarship made itself felt in England and the United States.

A second influence in shaping the "new social history" was the proliferation of work in the behavioral and social sciences in America following World War II. Behavioral science methodologies were increasingly applied in other fields to attack certain contemporary social problems. Such issues included race relations, sexism, family problems, child-rearing, patterns of social and geographical mobility, crime, and the bettering of educational and job opportunities. American historians inevitably began to examine the historical roots and antecedents of these same social problems and to study them with the aid of insights derived from other disciplines.

A third influence were the powerful protest movements that swept through American society during the troubled decades of the 1960s and 1970s. Scholars shifted their focus to the history of social groups that heretofore had been largely invisible in American history—blacks, Indians, women, and the poor as well as many others. By becoming visible in the public eye, such social groups became more visible to historians. Scholars responded by writing history that was directly relevant to the expressed needs of these social movements. Thus the civil rights movement stimulated a new found interest in black history, the women's liberation movement gave rise to more women's history, and the antiwar movement brought about a sweeping revision of American diplomatic history.

The fourth and final major influence was the increased use of computers and the application of new quantitative techniques. These permitted the "new social historians" to analyze historical evidence from heretofore unusable sources. Before the advent of computers scholars had found it difficult, if not impossible, to handle and analyze massive amounts of data. Historians, for example, had been unable to make much use of manuscript census schedules, which form the basis of published federal and state censuses. These census schedules, which provided information about individuals and households in the past, had remained unused for the most part because of problems encountered in reducing a mass of discrete information to usable data. Computers made it possible to collect and manipulate these data, while new quantitative techniques enabled researchers to analyze the information in more meaningful ways. New quantification techniques that made use of computers also made it possible to pose and answer historical questions in different ways.

Although the "new social historians" were loosely united in their desire to examine the American social structure and changes within that structure, they did not constitute a coherent coalition of scholars. Instead they were fragmented into separate groups divided along many different lines. Some approached the discipline differently in terms of subject matter and studied a major area in the field, such as the "new economic history" or the "new labor history." Others studied an old subfield (community studies), a new subfield (women's studies or black history), or a narrow specialty (history of medicine). Still others were so-called cliometricians employing quantification techniques. Some were structuralists who sought to identify historical causes by studying structures more than the role, acts, and motives of individuals. Others were distinctly different by virtue of their use of methodologies derived from the behavioral sciences. Another group approached history from a Marxist or quasi-Marxist orientation and were greatly influenced by the writings of two English historians, Eric Hobsbawn and Edward P. Thompson. Such eclecticism led to the charge that history had become so fragmented as to be incoherent as a separate discipline. History, it was said, was "a discipline in crisis."

The fragmentation of American history so evident in the "new social history" was accompanied by the continuation of four old approaches to the discipline that continued along more traditional lines. First, as previously mentioned, the old Progressive tradition was carried on after World War II by a group of scholars known as the neo-Progressives. These historians, who included among them the populist-oriented New Left, continued to approach American history in ways similar to the old Progressive interpretation.

A second development along similar lines was the continuation of the work of the older intellectual historians, like Perry Miller, into the post–World War II era by those termed the "new intellectual historians." Many of them employed the new concept of ideology advanced by Clifford Geertz, a cultural anthropologist. Geertz insisted on viewing ideology in a new way, as a cultural system—a set of symbols, values, and beliefs that enables members of a society to give meaning and find order in their political and social lives. Ideology, in Geertz's terms, reflected the way of life of an entire society, not just the status and thought of a particular group or class. Puritanism was viewed in such terms by scholars like Kenneth Lockridge in his study of Dedham, Massachusetts. The "republican synthesis" postulated by J. G. A. Pocock, discussed later in this volume, was also in this mode. The same was true of the free-labor ideology in Eric Foner's thesis regarding the antebellum North, and Eugene Genovese's plantation ideology in the slave South. This new approach to ideology changed the older tradition by insisting more on the primacy of the social structure when dealing with ideas.[12]

A third development—comparative history—likewise represented an extension of an older tradition. Comparative historians usually studied the histories of two or more countries in search of similarities and differences in national experiences. Their approach was often transnational in character in hopes of shedding light on the origins and destiny of the modern world. At other times they compared ideas and concepts like democracy, nationalism, and imperialism to discover to what extent these concepts operated the same or differently within diverse historical settings.

A fourth and final development was what one historian has termed the "emerging organizational synthesis." This hypothesis presupposed the triumph of a new bureaucratic ideology based on the needs and values of large-scale management in the American economy. In some accounts this mentality arose as an inevitable response to the modernization and centralization of American society in the nineteenth century. It provided a framework of belief appropriate for living in a mature industrial state where business, labor, and government were all organized on a national scale. Its practitioners were scholars such as Robert Wiebe, Alfred Chandler, Louis Galambos, and Samuel P. Hays. These scholars emphasized that the behavior of individuals might be better understood when seen within such an organizational context.[13]

---

[12]Daniel J. Singal, "Beyond Consensus: Richard Hofstadter and American Historiography," *American Historical Review* 89 (1984):998–1001.

[13]*Ibid.*, 1001.

What is the status of American history, and just where does the field stand in the mid-1980s? Fragmentation has had the greatest impact upon the discipline in recent years. Part of the problem has been the intense specialization within the field. The "new social history" has become a loose coalition of scholars in subdisciplines investigating a wide variety of discrete problems rather than a community of scholars—a community who were agreed on what was worth investigating and how results were to be evaluated. To be sure, greater specialization resulted in new areas of research, led to new methodologies, and produced more sophisticated interpretations. But at the same time overspecialization has posed a problem for those scholars seeking to maintain coherence and integrity within the discipline as a whole.

Quantification likewise has led to greater fragmentation. The issue was not over quantification as a technique per se, as one scholar noted, but rather a profound epistemological question regarding the meaning of reality itself. On one side, there were the materialists who sought to prove their theories by statistical exactness, replicable precision, and generalized knowledge. On the other were the antimaterialists who sought to restore the role of the individual in history or to discover meaning through intuitive, personal study of *mentalités*—i.e., the study of popular beliefs, customs, sentiments, and modes of behavior within society.[14]

Another reason for fragmentation was the existence of two other broad competing sets of historians—the radicals and the social scientists—who sometimes overlapped with the groups of scholars already discussed. At issue between them were two different paradigms of historical understanding. The radicals—social democrats of varying persuasions—were highly critical of American society and skeptical of its presumed liberalism. They distrusted also the use of computers as conservative instruments created by what they called America's ruling class. The social scientists, on the other hand, relied more upon statistical methods, serial data, and computer analysis. But what was significant in separating these two groups were four important issues: the nature of American society regarding its liberalism or conservatism; the source and scope of theories of history to be applied; the proper methods of evaluating data and drawing conclusions; and the role that moral judgments should play in the writing of history.[15]

---

[14]Robert Swierenga, "Historians & Computers: Has the Love Affair Gone Sour," *O.A.H. Newsletter* (November 1984).

[15]Robert Berkhofer, "The Two Histories: Competing Paradigms for Interpreting the American Past," *O.A.H. Newsletter* (May 1983).

The effort on the part of certain scholars to turn history more in the direction of the social sciences likewise had led to some fragmentation. More traditional scholars, however, successfully resisted such attempts. Many of them rejected this move on the grounds that a dangerous reductivism was inherent in the social science approach.

The process of fragmentation was exacerbated, moreover, by the tendency of historians to apply methodologies borrowed from the other behavioral sciences. Social theories from the other disciplines—psychology, sociology, and increasingly of late anthropology—often enabled historians to gain new insights. But at the same time such methodologies were derived from certain behavioral sciences that were themselves in intellectual disarray. Thus fragmentation in other disciplines sometimes added to the problems historians encountered in their own profession.

Despite the evidence of ideological diversity within the historical profession, there were a few signs that suggested a more fruitful reconceptualization might take place within the discipline some time in the future. One was the greater focus in the "new social history" on various subordinate social groups—blacks, women, Indians, immigrants, and workers—and less emphasis on more elite groups—mostly whites, males, and those in more established positions in society. This change in focus brought about a better balance in American history by incorporating into the story social groups that had been relatively neglected heretofore. It has emphasized also the ties, values, and experiences of family, sisterhood, fraternity, and sense of community that bound together these subordinate social groups and provided them with a sense of group consciousness. What needs to be explored now is a new agenda: the relationship of these groups and their connection with public life and society as a whole. Such an approach would seek to establish why some groups and certain of their values were represented—or underrepresented—in public life.[16]

A second sign has been the call for a return to narrative history voiced by two leading historians in America, Bernard Bailyn and Lawrence Stone. Both called upon scholars to emphasize more narrative effect, readability, and the human interest side of history in their writings in order to rouse and hold the interest of readers. Too often, they argued, historians had sacrificed reader interest to emphasize the apparent precision of quantification, the scientific claims of some new methodology, or the technical aspects of some kind of economic or

---

[16]Thomas Bender, "Making History Whole Again," *New York Times Book Review* (October 6, 1985).

materialistic determinism. Both Bailyn and Stone were committed to the innovative contributions of "the new social history," but suggested that scholars review the emphasis on narrative as one means of meeting the current crisis in the historical profession.[17]

To return, then, to the question: What is the status of American history? The answer is that the discipline is characterized by both creativity and chaos. Scholars have been more creative in the post–World War II period—in terms of analytical approaches, new methodologies, and technical expertise—than at any other time in American history. This exciting advance, however, was achieved at considerable cost. The chaos inevitably accompanying change has given rise to the charge that history was a discipline in crisis. At the same time, chaos within the profession has led to a diminished audience as the general public lost interest in American history written by serious scholars. Hopefully the American people will turn again in the future to the reading of American history. They should remember the old dictum: those who fail to study the past and to learn from it are doomed to repeat their mistakes.

---

[17]Bernard Bailyn, "The Challenge of Modern Historiography," *American Historical Review* 87 (February 1982):1–24; Lawrence Stone, *The Past and the Present* (Boston, 1981).

☆ 2 ☆

The American Businessman

INDUSTRIAL INNOVATOR OR ROBBER BARON?

For many students of American history, the problems of war and peace appear to be the dominant ones in the years from 1850 to 1877. Yet during this same period the country was undergoing an industrial and urban transformation that inevitably resulted in profound changes in the structure of American society. Few individuals or institutions remained unaffected by the forces at work, and the nation as a whole was destined to experience fundamental changes which enabled it to emerge as a leading world power by the close of the nineteenth century. "The old nations of the earth," Andrew Carnegie observed in 1886 with considerable pride, "creep on at a snail's pace; the Republic thunders past with the rush of the express. The United States, [in] the growth of a single century, has already reached the foremost rank among nations, and is destined soon to outdistance all others in the race. In population, in wealth, in annual savings, and in public credit; in freedom from debt, in agriculture, and in manufactures, America already leads the civilized world."[1] Industrial growth and the accumulation of wealth, Carnegie suggested, would lay the cornerstone of a better America: Ultimately, material progress would lead to spiritual and intellectual progress.

Although this new burst of industrialism gave the United States one of the highest standards of living in the world, it was not always

---

[1] Andrew Carnegie, *Triumphant Democracy* (New York, 1886), p. 1.

27

greeted with unrestrained enthusiasm. To some the new industrialism was destroying the very traits that had given America immunity from class strife, internal divisions, and rivalries that had long plagued Europe. Others feared the greed and ugliness that accompanied the industrial transformation. Walt Whitman, in "Democratic Vistas," summed up the opposition: "The depravity of the business classes of our country is not less than has been supposed but infinitely greater. The official services of America, national, state, and municipal, in all their branches and departments, except the judiciary, are saturated in corruption, bribery, falsehood, mal-administration; and the judiciary is tainted. The great cities reek with respectable as much as non-respectable robbery and scoundrelism. . . . In business (this all-devouring modern word, business), the one sole object is, by any means, pecuniary gain. . . . [M]oney-making is our sole magician's serpent, remaining today sole master of the field. . . . I say that our New World democracy, however great a success in uplifting the masses out of their sloughs, in materialistic development, products, and in a certain highly deceptive superficial popular intellectuality, is, so far, an almost complete failure in its social aspects, and in really grand religious, moral, literary, and esthetic results."[2] In short, America was adversely affected by the material forces at work.

The differences between the views of Carnegie and Whitman were by no means atypical; Americans have always been ambivalent in their attitudes toward material affluence. While emphasizing the virtues of acquisitiveness, individualism, and competition, they have been unable to throw off the influence of their religious heritage and the sense that the nation as a whole has a mission. At times this dual heritage has created an internal conflict because attempts to harmonize American materialism and idealism have not always succeeded. Some Americans have dealt with this conflict by proclaiming that material well-being is a prerequisite of spiritual and intellectual achievement; others have criticized a system that emphasizes material values at the expense of other values; still others have insisted that America's abundance was proof of its superior moral character.

This ambivalent attitude toward our heritage has exercised a profound impact on the writing of American history. Historians, on the whole, have also displayed divided attitudes when studying the rise of industry and its implications for American society. Nowhere can this dichotomy of thought be better seen than in the changing image of such great entrepreneurs as Rockefeller and Carnegie. To many his-

---

[2]Walt Whitman, "Democratic Vistas," in *Prose Works 1892*, Floyd Stovall, ed., 2 vols. (New York, 1963–1964), 2:370.

torians these captains of industry represented more than the rise of industrialism; they symbolized some of the basic characteristics of modern American culture.

The first attempts to evaluate the achievements of these industrial giants occurred at the beginning of the twentieth century. Many of the early studies took their cue from the writings of Henry Demarest Lloyd. A journalist and a scholar, Lloyd, until his death in 1903, played a significant part in reform movements that developed out of the social and economic unrest of that era. Critical of laissez-faire corporate monopoly he insisted that the American people were confronted with a choice between reform or revolution. Public ownership of monopolies and an increased role for government were absolutely necessary, according to Lloyd, if the American people were to avoid the fratricidal class struggles that had wracked other nations in the Western world.

In 1894 Lloyd spelled out his case in *Wealth Against Commonwealth*, a book that anticipated the writings of later muckrakers and Progressive journalists and also set the stage for much of the controversy among historians over the captains of industry. The book ostensibly was a study of the Standard Oil Company and the techniques used by John D. Rockefeller to gain a virtual monopoly over the petroleum industry. Actually *Wealth Against Commonwealth* was an indictment of the entire capitalistic system as it then existed. Businessmen, wrote Lloyd, paid lip service to the ideal of competition, but their true purpose was to achieve monopoly. If the captains of industry continued to have their way, the result would probably be a violent and bloody class struggle. There was little time to act, declared Lloyd, for the nation was already faced with "misery, plagues, hatreds, [and] national enervation."[3]

While Lloyd's principal purpose was to issue a call for national regeneration, he had drawn an unfavorable yet influential portrait of the typical industrial tycoon to make his point. His stereotype of the American businessman was in many respects similar to the one held by other American reformers, including the Populists, as well as many Progressives. Much of the debate over reform in the years from 1900 to 1917, indeed, centered about the unbridled power and selfishness of the captains of industry—a group, many claimed, who were motivated only by a desire to amass great wealth regardless of the cost to the American people. The specific political issues of the Progressive era— monopolies, trusts, federal regulation—were all based upon the proposition that Americans could no longer afford to permit these autocratic barons to shape the nation's destiny.

---

[3]Henry Demarest Lloyd, *Wealth Against Commonwealth* (New York, 1894), p. 517.

Many of the studies dealing with the American businessman written prior to World War I were done not only by historians, but by social scientists and, to a lesser extent, socialists seeking to prove that the system of capitalism was identified with social and individual selfishness and egoism. Among the social scientists were economists and sociologists such as Thorstein Veblen and E. A. Ross, who implicitly denounced the predatory, profit-seeking, amoral businessman for refusing to recognize the pressing needs of society. In the latter category were Gustavus Myers and Algie Simons, who portrayed businessmen as malefactors of wealth and looked forward to their eventual extinction as the historical process reached its inevitable destiny in the emergence of a socialist utopia.

While the interpretation of the businessman as robber baron was being etched in the public's imagination, historians, under the influence of the New History, were themselves beginning to inquire into the economic realities of capitalism in order to buttress their own predilection for democracy and reform. But not until the 1920s—a decade that was notable for the debunking activities of a small group of intellectuals—did historians turn their full attention to the study of the rise of American industry. With the publication in 1927 of Charles and Mary Beard's *Rise of American Civilization* and the first volume of Vernon L. Parrington's monumental *Main Currents in American Thought*, the scene was set for a radical reevaluation of the role of the businessman in American history.

Although the Beards refrained from any direct or outward condemnation of the industrial tycoon in their panoramic study of American civilization, their description suggested the analogy of a medieval baron—an individual who was despotic and autocratic within his own sphere. The story of American industry, they wrote, is "the story of aggressive men, akin in spirit to military captains of the past, working their way up from the ranks, exploiting natural resources without restraint, waging economic war on one another, entering into combinations, making immense fortunes, and then, like successful feudal chieftains or medieval merchants, branching out as patrons of learning, divinity, and charity. Here is a chronicle of highly irregular and sometimes lawless methods, ruthless competition, menacing intrigues, and pitiless destruction of rivals."[4]

Parrington, on the other hand, was much clearer and far less ambiguous in his description of postwar industrial developments. Writing

---

[4]Charles and Mary Beard, *The Rise of American Civilization*, 2 vols. (New York, 1927), 2:177.

within a Jeffersonian agrarian framework, which stressed individualistic values, he sought to defend his particular vision of liberalism. In Parrington's eyes the predatory and materialistic tycoon of industry represented the greatest threat to those humane and democratic values that had made America great. Businessmen had created the America of the present, with "its standardized life, its machine culture, its mass-psychology—an America to which Jefferson and Jackson and Lincoln would be strangers." These giants of industry, Parrington wrote in colorful and emotion-laden terms, "were primitive souls, ruthless, predatory, capable; single-minded men; rogues and rascals often, but never feeble, never hindered by petty scruple, never given to puling or whining—the raw materials of a race of capitalistic buccaneers."[5]

The debunking atmosphere of the 1920s and depression years of the 1930s provided a favorable climate of opinion for the growing idea of the businessman as a robber baron. For decades the business community had taken great pains to convince the American people that the nation's greatness rested on the achievements of ambitious and energetic entrepreneurs. A. C. Bedford, a tycoon in the oil industry, made this point very clear in 1925. In his eyes work was even of more importance than love, learning, religion, or patriotism. "I have come to the conclusion," he wrote, "that industry is the fundamental basis of civilization. The high office of civilization is to train men to productive efforts."[6] Other business leaders during the 1920s echoed Bedford's observations; if anything they were even more ecstatic in extolling the contributions of business to American civilization. With the exception of a dissenting minority of reformers, many Americans agreed with President Coolidge's dictum that "The business of America is business."

Having taken credit for the apparent prosperity of the 1920s the business community, ironically enough, was forced to accept responsibility for the catastrophic depression of the 1930s. The capitalist free enterprise system, which supposedly accounted for the greatness of America, seemingly failed in 1929. Millions who sought work were unable to find jobs; bankruptcies increased at an astounding rate; and many Americans even faced a real threat of starvation. Indeed, the United States appeared to be on the threshold of disaster. For once the business community found that the time-honored cliché that wealth was the product of ambition, talent, and drive, no longer held true.

---

[5]Vernon L. Parrington, *Main Currents in American Thought*, 3 vols. (New York, 1927–1930), 3:12 and 26.

[6]Quoted in James W. Prothro, *The Dollar Decade: Business Ideas in the 1920's* (Baton Rouge, 1954), p. 67.

Capitalism and free enterprise perhaps had come to the end of the road, many argued, and new approaches were required if the needs of a modern, complex industrial society in America were to be satisfied.

Given these conditions it was not surprising that much of the historical scholarship of the 1930s took an antibusiness turn. Beard and Parrington had anticipated this development; their writings during the late 1920s echoed some of the critical literature of this era. Sinclair Lewis's unforgettable portrait of Babbitt, while not wholly intended to debunk businessmen, contributed to a stereotype already widely held. The massive attack on the image of the American businessman, however, came in the Great Depression. During the 1930s the robber baron idea came to full bloom.

In presenting a highly unfavorable portrait of the industrial tycoon most writers in this tradition were implicitly attacking an economic system that they thought had failed to live up to its promises and expectations. Oddly enough many—though not all—of the critical studies during the 1930s were written by nonacademic figures who were critical of capitalism rather than by academic historians. Thus Lewis Corey, a socialist, in his *The House of Morgan* (1930), detailed the techniques whereby a major banking and investment concern exercised near dictatorial control over corporations having assets well in excess of twenty billion dollars. His lesson was not lost upon his readers. It was Corey's purpose to marshal as much evidence as possible to demonstrate the evil, selfish, and corrupting nature of industrial and finance capitalism. Other historical and literary writers, attracted by Marxian ideas, lent support to the growing body of critical studies of the American economic system.

The book that did the most to fix in American historical scholarship the enduring stereotype of the late nineteenth-century industrialist, however, was Matthew Josephson's brilliantly written *The Robber Barons: The Great American Capitalists 1861–1901*, which appeared in 1934. Fittingly enough, Josephson dedicated his book to Charles and Mary Beard, who themselves had interpreted American history in terms of a struggle between haves and have-nots, debtors and creditors, agrarians and industrialists, workers and capitalists. Josephson set the tone of his work in his introduction. "This book," he began, "attempts the history of a small class of men who arose at the time of our Civil War and suddenly swept into power. . . . These men more or less knowingly played the leading roles in an age of industrial revolution. . . . Under their hands the renovation of our economic life proceeded relentlessly: large-scale production replaced the scattered, decentralized mode of production; industrial enterprises became more concentrated, more 'efficient' technically, and essentially 'cooperative,' where they had been purely individualistic and lamentably wasteful. But all this revolutionizing effort is branded with the motive of private gain on the part of the new captains of industry. To organize and exploit the resources of a nation upon a gigantic scale, to regiment its farmers and workers into harmonious corps of producers, and to do this only in the name of an uncontrolled appetite for private profit— here surely is the great inherent contradiction whence so much disaster, outrage, and misery has flowed." Josephson conceded that the robber barons had many imposing achievements to their credit. On the other hand the debits far outweighed the credits. Ultimately, he concluded, the "extremes of management and stupidity would make themselves felt. . . . The alternations of prosperity and poverty would be more violent and mercurial, speculation and breakdown each more excessive; while the inherent contradictions within the society pressed with increasing intolerable force against the bonds of the old order."[7] The implications of Josephson's ideas were obvious.

The unfavorable portrait of the American businessman persisted as a theme in American historical writing. In the first selection in this chapter John Tipple notes that a relatively small number of late-nineteenth-century entrepreneurs used the corporate form of organization to amass great wealth, and in so doing contributed to the decline of individualistic institutions and values. Critics of businessmen, he suggests, were generally correct in their assessment of the negative consequences that followed the rise to dominance of such figures as John D. Rockefeller and Andrew Carnegie. Special privilege and the corporation went hand in hand; the result was the transfer of power to a relatively small economic elite.

At the same time the robber baron concept was reaching maturity another school of thought was emerging. Although it is difficult to give this school a particular name, the designation "business history" is not wholly inaccurate. The foundation of business history had already been laid by the 1930s. As a result of the work of Norman S. B. Gras and others at the Harvard Graduate School of Business Administration as well as the publication of a number of sympathetic biographies of individual business leaders, some historians and economists began to depart from the unfavorable stereotype of the American industrialist. Business history, however, was not merely a reevaluation of the contributions of industrialists; it represented a radically new approach to the study of American economic history. Indeed, business historians by the 1950s—because of their differences with other academic his-

---

[7]Matthew Josephson, *The Robber Barons: The Great American Capitalists 1861–1901* (New York, 1934), pp. vii–viii and 453. For a discussion of the robber baron theme, see Hal Bridges, "The Robber Baron Concept in American History," *Business History Review* 32 (Spring 1958):1–13.

torians—had created their own professional organization, developed a new vocabulary and research techniques, published their own journal, and in some cases had even founded new departments within the university separate from regular history departments.

Generally speaking business historians insisted that the careers of industrial leaders were far more complex than earlier scholars had realized. Business leaders were not predatory money seekers. Indeed, in many cases they were talented individuals whose creative contributions to the economy—and to American society as a whole—were very great. Allan Nevins, who published a major revisionist biography of John D. Rockefeller in 1940, argued that much of the blame heaped on this man was unwarranted. It was true, Nevins conceded, that Rockefeller used methods that were of dubious moral character. On the other hand the kind of monopoly control attained by Standard Oil was a natural response to the anarchical cutthroat competition of the period and reflected the trend in all industrial nations toward consolidation. To Nevins Rockefeller was not a robber baron; he was a great innovator who imposed upon American industry "a more rational and efficient pattern." Rockefeller's objective was not merely the accumulation of wealth; he and others like him were motivated by "competitive achievement, self-expression, and the imposition of their wills on a given environment."[8]

Thirteen years later Nevins pushed this thesis even further when he published a second biography of Rockefeller. He was, Nevins forcefully argued, an "innovator, thinker, planner, bold entrepreneur." Taking a confused and disorganized industry, Rockefeller organized it with completeness, efficiency, and constructive talent; in his philanthropy he set a model for all to follow. Had it not been for men like him—men who helped to create within a brief span of time great and powerful industrial units in steel, oil, textiles, chemicals, electricity, and automotive vehicles—"the free world might have lost the First World War and most certainly would have lost the Second."[9]

The points that Nevins made about Rockefeller were not fundamentally different from those made by other students of business history. The great nineteenth-century entrepreneurs, business historians emphasized, actually played a vital role in making the United States

---

[8]Allan Nevins, *John D. Rockefeller: The Heroic Age of American Enterprise*, 2 vols. (New York, 1940), 2:707–714.

[9]Allan Nevins, *Study in Power: John D. Rockefeller, Industrialist and Philanthropist*, 2 vols. (New York, 1953), 1:viii–ix; 2:436. For a direct confrontation of views see the enlightening article, "Should American History Be Rewritten? A Debate Between Allan Nevins and Matthew Josephson," *Saturday Review* 37 (February 6, 1954):7–10 and 44–49.

the greatest industrial power in the world and giving its people the highest standard of living. Far from being immoral, unethical, or evil individuals—although sometimes their methods involved questionable tactics—these industrial statesmen stepped into a disorganized, unstructured, anarchic economy, restored order and rationality, created giant organizations that were in a position to exploit fully the great natural resources of the nation, and took full advantage of the potentialities of the American economy.

Like students in the robber tradition of American historiography, business historians began with certain underlying assumptions that undoubtedly influenced the way in which they approached their subject. It is quite clear that they rejected the hostile critique of Progressive historians who believed that the social and economic costs of late-nineteenth-century industrialization could have been far lower and less painful and degrading to the great mass of Americans, and that the result need not have been a dangerous centralization of economic power that ostensibly threatened freedom and democracy. On the contrary business historians tended to eulogize rather than to disparage the American economic system. Did not the growth and development of the large corporation, they maintained, give the American people the highest standard of living in the world and make possible the victory against totalitarianism? Was not America's industrial capacity responsible for the strength of a large part of the free world in the struggle with communism? To put it another way these historians concluded that the large corporation, despite its monopolistic and oligopolistic position, was far more of an asset than a liability. Unlike Progressive historians who defined the problem in terms of a tension between democracy and the menace of the concentration of economic power in the hands of a few, business historians minimized the threat of such dangers and opposed efforts to employ historical analysis as an ideological anticorporation weapon.

Perhaps the most sophisticated example of recent developments in business history is the work of Alfred D. Chandler, Jr. Unlike Nevins, Chandler was essentially disinterested in the biographical approach that sought to vindicate the career of an individual against his detractors. He was more concerned in the process whereby new forms, methods, and structures came into being in the late nineteenth and twentieth centuries. In a major work issued in 1962 Chandler identified four stages in the development of large industrial enterprise. First came a period of expansion and the accumulation of resources. During the second period these resources were "rationalized." In the third phase the organization expanded its operations to include new products in order to ensure the most efficient use of existing resources. In the fourth and final phase new structures were created to promote effective use of resources in order to meet immediate and long-range demands. Borrowing heavily from work in the social sciences Chandler saw large corporations as complex economic, political, and social systems with common administrative problems. He insisted, moreover, that most large firms went through similar stages of development. "Strategic growth," he noted, "resulted from an awareness of the opportunities and needs—created by changing population, income, and technology— to employ existing or expanding resources more profitably. A new strategy required a new or at least refashioned structure if the enlarged enterprise was to be operated efficiently."[10] The result was the large, decentralized, multidivisional corporation.

Less interested in the moral dimensions of industrial entrepreneurship, Chandler attempted to analyze the forces that led businessmen to develop new products, new markets, and new sources of raw materials. By 1900, he pointed out, these industrial leaders had created the modern corporation, which integrated the functions of purchasing, manufacturing, marketing, and finance. Each of the major processes was managed by a separate department, and all were coordinated and controlled by a central office. Such a complex organization was a response to the emergence of the urban market that followed the creation of a national transportation system. Minimizing the role of technological innovation Chandler concluded that entrepreneurs like Rockefeller and others were successful because they accurately analyzed the economic situation and responded in a creative manner. Their contributions, he suggested, played an important role in the dramatic growth of the economy and the creation of an affluent society.[11] The second selection in this chapter is an article by Chandler on the role of business in American society.

In a subsequent Pulitzer Prize–winning book, *The Visible Hand*, Chandler analyzed the manner in which the development of large-scale vertically organized corporations altered the American economy between the Civil War and the depression of the 1930s. He once again reiterated the crucial role of management and business executives in guiding these changes, and suggested that Adam Smith's concept of the market as the decisive element in the economy was no longer applicable to the present. Nevertheless *The Visible Hand* also paid tribute to the crucial role of technology. Indeed, Chandler argued that modern business first appeared, grew, and flourished in industries char-

---

[10]Alfred D. Chandler, Jr., *Strategy and Structure: Chapters in the History of the Industrial Enterprise* (Cambridge, Mass., 1962), p. 15.

[11]Alfred D. Chandler, Jr., "The Beginnings of 'Big Business' in American Industry," *Business History Review* 33 (Spring 1959):1–31.

acterized by new and advancing technology and by expanding markets.[12]

Business historians have also dealt with the role of individuals in modern economic development. Harold C. Livesay, for example, noted that the rise of bureaucratic structures did not stifle the creative and innovative processes that are the hallmark of capitalism and free enterprise. Bureaucracy, he concluded, did not necessarily obliterate the entrepreneurial spirit nor did it blur (as Joseph Schumpeter suggested) the differences between mature capitalist and socialist systems. Some individuals make institutions; in this sense human beings are not helpless captives of impersonal social and economic systems and structures.[13]

Business historians tended to see the large corporation as essentially an economic organization. Other scholars, however, were less concerned with understanding the corporation in structural and functional terms; they were more concerned with the political aspects of business and the threat to democratic institutions posed by such huge conglomerations. This concern took two different forms in the 1950s and 1960s. The first was a sophisticated body of scholarship that examined business in a critical vein, though not with a view that sought the end of capitalism and the establishment of a socialist society. Typical of this approach was the work of Carl Kaysen, an economist who also served for a time as the director of the Institute for Advanced Study in Princeton, New Jersey. Kaysen noted the overwhelmingly disproportionate importance of large corporations in the economy. Because of their size these large units were less influenced by changes in economic activity and exercised considerable power over their smaller suppliers and customers. Their investment decisions and research activities, moreover, had important implications for society. The bigger market power that absolute and relative size gave to the large corporation also resulted in political and social as well as economic power. Kaysen noted that American society possessed three alternate ways of controlling business power: the promotion of competitive markets, control by agencies external to business, and institutionalization within the firm of responsibility for the exercise of power. Traditionally the United States relied on the first in the form of antitrust activities, although far more could have been done along this line. Kaysen's

---

[12]Alfred D. Chandler, Jr., *The Visible Hand: The Managerial Revolution in American Business* (Cambridge, Mass., 1977). For a brief and clear summary of the findings of business historians see Glenn Porter, *The Rise of Big Business, 1860–1910* (New York, 1973).

[13]Harold C. Livesay, "Entrepreneurial Persistence Through the Bureaucratic Age," *Business History Review* 51 (Winter 1977):415–443.

conclusions were equivocal, for he felt that effective control of business power remained an unfinished task.[14]

Scholars like Kaysen were essentially in a reform tradition; they sought to eliminate imperfections in American society rather than overthrow it. By the early 1960s, however, a small but growing number of scholars in a variety of disciplines were coming to the conclusion that American society was fundamentally immoral and that a radical change in its structure was required. This point of view was best expressed by historians associated with the New Left. War, poverty, racism, they argued, were direct outgrowths of American capitalism. If this were so then only the abolition of capitalism could make possible the establishment of a just and peaceful society. This belief, of course, led to a rejection of those scholars who had defended business as well as those who were critical of it but did not seek its destruction.

One of the first monographs embodying a New Left approach was Gabriel Kolko's *The Triumph of Conservatism: A Reinterpretation of American History, 1900-1916,* which appeared in 1963. Kolko argued that the distinctive feature of American society—what he designated as political capitalism—dated only from the first two decades of the twentieth century. Rejecting the belief that large-scale business enterprise was inevitable, Kolko maintained that competition was actually increasing at the turn of the century. Even the merger movement and the capitalization of new combinations on an unprecedented scale failed to stem the tide of competitive growth. Corporate leaders, therefore, turned to government to control competition and to prevent the possibility of a formal political democracy that might lead to a redistribution of wealth. The result was a synthesis of business and government, with the former emerging as the dominant element. In contrast to Chandler Kolko believed that large-scale units turned to government regulation precisely because of their inefficiency. The lack of a viable alternative to political capitalism at that time made its victory a certainty, for neither the Populists nor the socialists (who themselves accepted the necessity of centralization) understood that the Progressive movement—far from being antibusiness—was actually a movement that defined the general welfare in terms of the well-being of business.[15]

Kolko's controversial thesis did not persuade other scholars, many of whom rejected his radical ideological assumptions and questioned

---

[14]Carl Kaysen, "The Corporation: How Much Power? What Scope?," in *The Corporation in Modern Society,* Edward S. Mason, ed. (Cambridge, Mass., 1959), Chapter 5.

[15]In addition to *The Triumph of Conservation: A Reinterpretation of American History, 1900-1916* (New York, 1963), see Kolko's *Railroads and Regulation 1877-1916* Princeton, 1965) for an illustrative case study of his interpretation.

his conclusions. Shortly after Kolko published his study of railroad regulation in 1965, Edward A. Purcell, Jr., criticized his thesis that businessmen favored government regulation because they feared competition and desired to forge a government-business coalition in which they would be the dominant partner. In an examination of the attitudes of businessmen during the passage of the Interstate Commerce Act of 1887 Purcell came to a quite different conclusion. Rejecting the idea that the actions of businessmen grew out of a particular ideology, he insisted that entrepreneurs and managers were more interested in solving particular problems than they were in adhering to any coherent body of thought. Hence some favored regulation while others opposed it. In general, Purcell concluded, diverse economic groups who felt threatened by the new national economy and rate discrimination turned to the federal government in the hope of protecting their interests. Political control of the economy was not their ultimate goal; they simply wanted to protect their own interests.[16]

More recently the history of American business and the history of technology have drawn closer, if only because of the intimate relationship between industrial growth and technology. Even Alfred D. Chandler—whose work dealt largely with the origins and development of business organizations—gave technology a more important place. In focusing on technology historians have raised new and difficult issues. What is responsible for technological innovation? How has technology shaped or been shaped by the social and economic organization of modern society?

Business historians, of course, tended to see technology as a positive force in its own right.[17] Others have come to very different conclusions. David F. Noble, for example, argued that machines and technology are never by themselves "the decisive forces of production." At every point technology was mediated by "social power and domination, by institutional fantasies of progress, and by the contradictions rooted in the technological projects themselves and the social relations of production." In *America by Design* Noble attempted to demonstrate

---

[16]Edward A. Purcell, Jr., "Ideas and Interests: Businessmen and the Interstate Commerce Act," *Journal of American History* 54 (December 1967):561–578. See also Albro Martin, "The Troubled Subject of Railroad Regulation in the Gilded Age—A Reappraisal," ibid. 61 (September 1974):339–371; and *Enterprise Denied: Origins of the Decline of American Railroads 1897–1917* (New York, 1971); and Thomas K. McGraw, "Regulation in America: A Review Article," *Business History Review*, 49 (Summer 1975):159–183; and Thomas K. McGraw, ed., *Regulation in Perspective: Historical Essays* (Cambridge, Mass., 1981).

[17]For a discussion of this point see Louis Galombos, "Technology, Political Economy, and Professionalization: Central Themes of the Organizational Synthesis," *Business History Review* 57 (Winter 1983):472–478.

how engineering failed to develop an independent point of view, and thus came to serve the needs of corporate capitalism. In a subsequent work he specifically rejected the allegation that technology was an independent variable. Implicit in his work was a political point: that the social relations of production rather than technological determinism were crucial, and only a movement from below could liberate the mass of workers from an economic system that degraded rather than enhanced their lives. Noble's work is a recent restatement of an older antibusiness tradition from the perspective of the modern political left.[18]

In assessing businessmen and corporations since the late nineteenth century it is important to understand that differing interpretations often reflect diverging viewpoints regarding the nature of economic development and the impact of technological innovation. Ironically enough adherents of the robber baron and New Left school implicitly (and sometimes explicitly) extol the virtues of a competitive economy when they criticize the monopolistic objectives of most entrepreneurial and financial leaders. Business historians, on the other hand, tend to argue that the movement toward consolidation arose out of a cutthroat and disorganized economy whose productive potential could never have been achieved without the large, decentralized, multidivisional corporation. Still others see the problem within a far more complex framework; decisions made by individuals often gave rise to results that were not anticipated.

Which of these viewpoints is correct? Was consolidation a necessary prerequisite for the emergence of a complex industrial economy? Is bigness synonymous with efficiency? Was technology a beneficent or a destructive force? On all these issues opposing schools of thought give very different answers. The upholders of the robber baron and New Left approach insist that the monopolistic control that often accompanies large productive units frequently reflects the inability of those units to meet the challenges of smaller competitors who do not have high overhead and fixed costs. Thus consolidation actually reflects inefficiency rather than efficiency. Some of these historians, moreover, argue that the movement toward consolidation was the result of bureaucratic business reorganizations rather than an effort to increase efficiency. Similarly a specific use of technology ensured the dominance of capitalism. Most business historians, on the other hand, reject

---

[18]David F. Noble, *America by Design: Science, Technology, and the Rise of Corporate Capitalism* (New York, 1977); "Social Choice in Machine Design: The Case of Automatically Controlled Machine Tools, and a Challenge for Labor," *Politics & Society* 8, Nos. 3–4 (1978):313–347; and *Forces of Production: A Social History of Industrial Automation* (New York, 1984).

this interpretation. They tend to correlate consolidation with order and efficiency: great entrepreneurs are perceived as creative individuals interested not in profit alone but in productive efficiency as well. Technology, which is both shaped by and shapes the economic environment, is generally considered a positive force by most business historians.

In the final analysis any interpretation of the careers and accomplishments of American industrialists and the role of the large corporation will depend in large measure on the starting assumptions and values of the scholars making a particular judgment. Despite claims of objectivity it is difficult, if not impossible, for historians to divest themselves of beliefs and standards that influence their analysis of this problem. In some ways an evaluation of business and businessmen is even more controversial than other problems in American history. For underlying such an evaluation is the larger problem of the quality and meaning of the American experience. To some historians the significance of America is directly related to its productive capacity. America, they maintain, has demonstrated to the world that an affluent society is possible to achieve within a democratic capitalist framework. Thus the American economy—a creation of industrial pioneers and bold entrepreneurs—should be given more credit than many have admitted. Similarly technology, although not without risks, has been a positive force. Other historians, however, argue along different lines. The social costs of industrialism, they maintain, could have been far lower had it not been for the greed and quest for power by businessmen. By placing a premium on acquisitive and amoral values, by creating a system of great inequality of wealth, they insist, these entrepreneurs and their large corporations contributed to the narrowness and materialism of American life. Political capitalism, moreover, was responsible for the wars, racism, and poverty that characterized much of the twentieth century. The use of technology for business purposes tended to dehumanize rather than enrich the lives of millions of Americans. Any judgment on this historical problem, then, often becomes a judgment on the nature and quality of American civilization itself.

John Tipple

JOHN TIPPLE (1916–   ) is professor of history at California State University in Los Angeles. He has compiled *The Capitalist Revolution: A History of American Social Thought 1899–1919* (1970) and *Crisis of the American Dream: A History of American Social Thought, 1920–1940* (1968).

It is more than coincidence that the beginning of the robber baron legend, the portrayal of the big businessman as a warlike brigand cheating and plundering his way to millions, was contemporaneous with the inauguration of the corporation as the major instrument of business control in the United States. After the Civil War, the large corporation began to dominate the American economic scene. In those same years, Charles Francis Adams, Jr., launched his first assault against the "Erie robbers," and his brother, Henry Adams, warned of the day when great corporations, "swaying power such as has never in the world's history been trusted in the hands of mere private citizens," would be controlled by one man or combinations of men who would use these new leviathans to become masters of the nation.[1]

Such dangerous potentialities were not recognizable prior to the Civil War because the majority of businesses operated as local enterprises, usually as individual proprietorships, partnerships, or as small closed corporations in which ownership and control were almost invariably synonymous.[2] Under most circumstances, the power and influence of the businessmen were limited to the immediate environs of operation and seldom extended beyond state boundaries. Equally important, there existed among most businessmen of prewar days a nearly universal desire and a practical necessity for community esteem. This governed their conduct, kept their ventures well within the limits of individual liability, and tended to restrain irresponsible profiteering. Antebellum criticisms of the businessman therefore were few and spo-

---

From *The Gilded Age*, revised and enlarged edition, edited by H. Wayne Morgan (Syracuse: Syracuse University Press, 1970). Copyright © 1970 by Syracuse University Press. Reprinted by permission.

[1]Charles F. Adams, Jr., and Henry Adams, *Chapters of the Erie and Other Essays* (Boston, 1871), p. 134.

[2]Adolph Berle, Jr., and Gardiner Means, *The Modern Corporation and Private Property* (New York, 1932), pp. 10–17.

radic. Disapproval usually focused on the speculator or stock gambler, and was often inspired by an agrarian distrust of big-city ways.[3]

The bloody struggles of the Civil War helped bring about revolutionary changes in economic and political life. War needs created almost insatiable demands for goods—arms, munitions, clothing—and offered some manufacturers unsurpassed opportunities to make fortunes. Most important, the stimulus of massive military demands alerted entrepreneurs to new concepts of the power and possibilities of large-scale enterprise: "The great operations of war, the handling of large masses of men, the influence of discipline, the lavish expenditure of unprecedented sums of money, the immense financial operations, the possibilities of effective cooperation, were lessons not likely to be lost on men quick to receive and apply all new ideas."[4] Though the war prevented general economic expansion, the new ideas were profitably applied to the peacetime economy.

With the rich resources of the trans-Mississippi West open to private exploitation, the businessman had singular opportunities to become wealthy. Before him spread an immense untapped continent whose riches were his virtually for the taking; new means to turn these resources to profitable account were at hand. A host of new inventions and discoveries, the application of science to industry, and improved methods of transportation and communication were ready to assist the businessman. But all these aids would have been valueless without effective means to put them to work. The practical agency to meet these unprecedented entrepreneurial demands on capital and management proved to be the corporation. The stockholding system provided immense capital beyond the reach of any individual, and the corporate hierarchy presented a feasible solution to the greatly augmented problems of management.

The corporation was no novelty. It had served political as well as economic purposes in seventeenth-century America; as an instrumentality of business its use antedated the discovery of this continent. Seldom before in American history, however, had the corporation been used on such a large scale. From a relatively passive creature of legalistic capitalism, it was transformed by fusion with techniques into a dynamic system spearheading economic expansion.

The impact of the newborn corporation on American society was almost cataclysmic. In the first few decades of its existence the modern

---

[3]Cf. Frederick Jackson. *A Week in Wall Street by One Who Knows* (New York: n.p., 1841); James K. Medbery, *Men and Mysteries of Wall Street* (Boston, 1870).

[4]Adams and Adams, *Chapters of Erie*, p. 135.

corporate system enabled the nation to develop more wealth more rapidly than in any period since the discovery. But it also menaced hallowed economic theories and usages, threatening to ride like a great tidal wave over the traditional democratic social and political beliefs. Its size alone was sufficient to change fundamental social and economic relationships. Of the newly formed United States Steel Corporation an awed commentator wrote at the turn of the century: "It receives and expends more money every year than any but the very greatest of the world's national governments; its debt is larger than that of many of the lesser nations in Europe; it absolutely controls the destinies of a population nearly as large as that of Maryland or Nebraska, and indirectly influences twice that number."[5] Moreover, this concentrated economic power normally gravitated into the hands of a few, raising up a corporate ruling class with great economic authority.[6]

Though the meteoric rise of the so-called robber baron to unheralded positions of power was inseparably bound to the large corporation, there were other factors behind his sudden emergence into popular view as the outstanding phenomenon of nineteenth-century business life. One of the most important of these was a stable government dedicated to the preservation of private property and devoted to an ambiguous concept of laissez-faire. Through political alliances, principally with the Republican party, the big businessman consolidated his economic triumphs. Although in the past the commercial and manufacturing interests of the North had received favors from the federal government in the form of bounties to fisheries and protective tariffs, after the defection of the South they were in the envied position of a pampered only child. With almost incestuous concern, a dotingly partisan Congress bestowed upon them lavish railroad subsidies, new and higher tariffs, and a series of favorable banking acts.

The economic supremacy of the North had been guaranteed by military victory in 1865, but it was doubly insured by the actions of the Radical Republicans during the process of Southern reconstruction. The Fourteenth Amendment, whether intended for such purposes or not, was used by the courts to protect the corporation and to prevent attempts by the states to undermine its position of power.[7] The election of General Grant to the presidency in 1868 and 1872, backed by the leading representatives of the business community, the great financiers, and speculators, politically secured the issue of northern prosperity. Despite the panic of 1873, there were obvious signs that the

---

[5]Ray Stannard Baker, "What the United States Steel Corporation Really Is and How It Works," *McClure's* 18(1901):6.

[6]Berle and Means, *The Modern Corporation*, pp. 2–6.

[7]Charles Wallace Collins, *The Fourteenth Amendment and the States* (Boston, 1912).

business of the country had, as the *Nation* put it, "adapted itself to the situation created for it by Republican legislation."[8]

Within this artificial paradise, private profits were sacred. The inheritance tax had expired in 1870, the income tax was abandoned in 1872, and an attempt to revive it in 1894 was invalidated by the Supreme Court in 1895.[9] Corporate or excess profits taxes did not exist. By 1890, the bulk of government revenue was derived from customs duties and excises on liquor and tobacco, all taxes upon the nation's consumers.[10] Under such conditions, stock market volume attained the million-share mark in December, 1886, and industrial capital almost doubled itself every ten years.[11]

The dedicated businessman could make money on an unprecedented scale. Though John D. Rockefeller never quite became a billionaire, his fortune in 1892 reportedly amounted to $815,647,796.89.[12] Andrew Carnegie did nearly as well. The profits from his industrial empire in the decade 1889 to 1899 averaged about $7,500,000 a year and, in 1900 alone, amounted to $40,000,000.[13] In the following year he sold out his interest for several hundred million dollars.[14] Such fortunes, exceptional even for those days, emphasized the wealth available to the big businessman. In 1892, two New York newspapers engaged in a heated contest to count the number of American millionaires, the *World* uncovering 3,045 and the *Tribune* raising it to 4,047.[15] Regardless of the exact total, millionaires were becoming fairly common. By 1900, for instance, the Senate alone counted twenty-five millionaires among its members, most of them well-paid agents of big business—a notorious fact that led some suspicious folk to dub that august body the "Rich Man's Club" and the "House of Dollars."[16]

---

[8]*The Nation,* September 30, 1880, p. 232.

[9]*Pollock* vs. *Farmer's Loan and Trust Co.,* 157 U.S. 429, 158 U.S., 601.

[10]*Annual Report of the Secretary of the Treasury 1890* (Washington; GPO, 1890), p. xxi.

[11]*Commercial and Financial Chronicle,* December 18, 1886, p. 739; *U.S. Census 1910* (Washington: GPO, 1913), 8, 32–33; Willard Long Thorp, *Business Annals* (New York, 1926), pp. 129–130.

[12]Allan Nevins, *A Study in Power: John D. Rockefeller, Industrialist and Philanthropist,* 2 vols. (New York, 1953), 2:613.

[13]James H. Bridge, *The Inside History of the Carnegie Steel Company* (New York, 1903), p. 295.

[14]*Ibid.,* p. 364.

[15]*Tribune Monthly* 4 (1892):92; Sidney Ratner, ed., *New Light on the History of Great American Fortunes* (New York, 1953), pp. xviii–xxiii; Ida M. Tarbell, *The Nationalizing of Business* (New York, 1936), p. 113.

[16]David Graham Phillips, *The Shame of the Senate,* reprint from *Cosmopolitan,* 2 (1906):94.

This sudden leap of big businessmen into new positions of wealth and power caught the public eye. To Americans accustomed to thinking primarily of individuals, the big businessman stood out as the conspicuous symbol of corporate power—his popular image encompassing not only his personal attributes and failings but combining also the more amorphous and impersonal aspects of the business organization by which he had climbed to fortune. Just as the diminutive Andrew Carnegie came to represent the entire steel-making complex of men and decisions which bore his name, so the lean, ascetic John D. Rockefeller personified Standard Oil, and the prominent nose and rotund figure of J. P. Morgan signified the whole of Wall Street with its thousands of operators, its ethical flaws, and its business virtues.

Big businessmen were usually attacked not for personal failings, though they had them as well as the lion's share of wealth, but as the recognizable heads of large corporations. When Carnegie and Rockefeller gave up business careers and became private citizens, the rancor against them almost ceased. Instead of being censured for past actions, which had been widely and vehemently criticized, they were praised as benefactors and good citizens. Public castigation of the steel trust was shifted from "Little Andy" to the broader shoulders of Charles Schwab. The odium of monopoly which had surrounded his father was inherited by John D. Rockefeller, Jr. Only as the active and directive heads of great corporations, and not as subordinates or members of a business elite, were big businessmen branded "robber barons" and indicted for alleged crimes against society.[17]

If the big businessman was not resented as an individual but as a power symbol wielding the might of the great corporation, the provocative question arises of why there was such resentment against the corporation. The answer is that the large industrial corporation was an anomaly in nineteenth-century America. There was no place for it among existing institutions and no sanction for it in traditional American values.

Institutions and values had been built around the social and political concept of the free individual. Born to the natural rights of life, liberty, and property, he was originally subject only to the law of nature. By being or becoming a member of society, the individual did not renounce his natural rights (because this gift of God could not be alienated) but submitted to certain restraints beyond those imposed by nature for the evident good of the whole community. The basis of this ideology was the presumed constancy of nature in moral as well as physical operations, and the universal efficacy of its laws. By asserting that these inevitable laws of nature constituted truth, and by setting

---

[17]See John Tipple, "Who Were the Robber Barons?" (forthcoming).

out from the will of God or nature, eighteenth-century Americans sought to erect an inviolable system proceeding from natural causes and therefore not subject to human error. Fanciful as they seemed, these were the generally accepted premises of government and society inherited by Americans of the nineteenth century.

In such a closed system there was no ready place for the large industrial corporation which was neither an individual nor a natural manifestation. As an artificial person created by charter and comprising many individuals and their wealth, the corporation was infinitely greater in size and power than the isolated individual about whom American society had been conceived. Unlike the individual, the corporate body was not ordinarily exposed to natural hazards of decay and death, having in effect been guaranteed immortality by the society which fathered it. Where individual accumulation of wealth and power was limited to a lifetime, corporate possibilities were almost limitless. Freed from death, and incidentally from death dues and inheritance taxes, the corporation waxed strong upon the accumulated lifetimes and earnings of many individuals.

A further complication, the hazard of which increased directly in proportion to corporate size and power, was that the corporation as an unnatural creation was born without natural reason—"the common rule and measure God hath given mankind"—and was therefore not intrinsically subject to the governance of nature. In ideological terms, the corporation, since it could not be counted upon to follow the moral precepts of nature, was an outlaw to the society which spawned it.

What was to be done with such a monster? Either the corporation had to be made to conform to American institutions and principles or those institutions and principles had to be changed to accommodate the corporation. This was the dilemma first seriously confronted by Americans during the Gilded Age, and the issue that set off the great movement of introspection and reform which activated the American people for the next fifty years.

Most flagrantly apparent was the destructive effect of the large corporation upon free competition and equal opportunity. According to the accepted theory, which was a projection of the doctrines of liberal democracy into the economic sphere, the ideal economy—the only one, in fact, sanctioned by nature—was made up of freely competing individuals operating in a market unrestricted by man but fairly ruled by the inexorable forces of natural law. The ideal polity was achieved by bargaining among free and equal individuals under the benevolent eye of nature. It was assumed that, in economic affairs, impartial rivalry between individual entrepreneurs and free competition would automatically serve the best interests of society by preventing anyone from getting more than his fair share of the wealth.

In early-nineteenth-century America, this self-regulating mechanism seemed to work. Where businesses and factories were small, prices and output, wages and profits, rose and fell according to supply and demand. Every man appeared to have equal opportunity to compete with every other man. Even after the war, the individual businessman was forced, in the interests of self-preservation, to observe the common rules of competition. Ordinarily his share of the market was too small to permit any attempt at price control unless he joined with others in a pool, a trade association, or another rudimentary price-fixing agreement. The average businessman eschewed trade agreements, not out of theoretical considerations but for the practical reason that such coalitions did not work very well, often suffering from mutual distrust and the pursuit of centrifugal aims.

But what was true in a world of individual proprietors and workers was not necessarily correct for the corporation. It possessed greater unity of control and a larger share of the market and could either dictate prices or combine successfully with other corporations in monopolistic schemes.[18] By bringing to bear superior economic force which to a great extent invalidated the tenets of the free market, the large organization put the big businessman in the favored position of operating in an economy dedicated to the idea of freely competing individuals, yet left him unhampered by the ordinary restrictions. Under such auspicious circumstances, he soon outdistanced unorganized rivals in the race for wealth.

This unfair advantage did not go unchallenged. As the earliest of the large corporations in the United States, the railroads were the first to come under concentrated attack. The immense extension of railways after 1865, and the crucial nature of their operations as common carriers, exposed their activities to public scrutiny and subjected their mistakes or misdeeds to considerable publicity. Popular resentment against the railroads in the early 1870s grew hottest in the farming states of the Midwest, but indignant reports from all over the country accused railroads of using monopoly power against equal opportunity.

A most frequent criticism, common to both East and West, was that railway superintendents and managers showed unreasonable favoritism by discriminating between persons and places, offering rate concessions to large shippers, charging more for short than long hauls, and giving preferential treatment to large corporations in the form of secret rebates and drawbacks. That these preferential rates might sometimes have been forced upon the railroads by pressure from business made little difference. The popular consensus was that this elaborate system of special rates denied the little man equal opportunity

---

[18]*Commercial and Financial Chronicle* 43 (March 27, 1886):393.

with the rich and influential, breaking the connection between individual merit and success. The ultimate effect extended further monopoly by preventing free competition among businesses where railway transportation was an important factor.[19]

The Standard Oil Company seemed to be the outstanding example of a monopoly propagated in this manner, the charge being that the determining factor behind Rockefeller's spectacular conquest of the oil business had been this railway practice of secrecy and favoritism which had aided his company and ruined others. By collecting rebates on their own shipments and drawbacks on those of competitors, Standard had gained virtual control of oil transportation. It then could regulate the prices of crude oil, with the detrimental result, so Henry Demarest Lloyd charged, that by 1881, though the company produced only one-fiftieth of the nation's petroleum, Standard refined nine-tenths of the oil produced in the United States and dictated the price of all of it.[20]

As the whipping boy among trusts, Standard undoubtedly got more than its share of criticism, yet by contemporary standards of competition, the corporation was fairly adjudged a monopoly. Through the testimony of H. H. Rogers, an executive of the company, the Hepburn Committee in 1879 was able to establish that 90 to 95 percent of all the refiners in the country acted in harmony with Standard Oil.[21] In 1886, the monopolistic proclivities of the oil trust were attested to by the Cullom Committee:

> It is well understood in commercial circles that the Standard Oil Company brooks no competition; that its settled policy and firm determination is to crush out all who may be rash enough to enter the field against it; that it hesitates at nothing in the accomplishment of this purpose, in which it has been remarkably successful, and that it fitly represents the acme and perfection of corporate greed in its fullest development.[22]

Similar convictions were expressed by a New York Senate committee before which Rockefeller and other executives testified in 1888.[23] Four years later, in 1892, the Supreme Court of Ohio declared that the object of the Standard Oil Company was "to establish a virtual monopoly of

[19]James F. Hudson, *The Railways and the Republic* (New York, 1886), pp. 25–66; A. B. Stickney, *The Railway Problem* (St. Paul, 1891), pp. 27–35; Frank Parsons, *The Railways, the Trusts, and the People* (Philadelphia, 1906), pp. 25–56.

[20]Henry Demarest Lloyd, *Lords of Industry* (New York, 1916), p. 2; Ida M. Tarbell, *The History of the Standard Oil Company*, 2 vols. (New York, 1904), 2–111.

[21]*Report of the Special Committee on Railroads* (Albany, 1879), pp. 49–50 (*Hepburn Report*).

[22]Senate Reports, 49th Congress, 1st Session, no. 46, p. 199 (*Cullom Report*).

[23]*New York Senate Report*, no. 50 (1888), p. 10.

the business of producing petroleum, and of manufacturing, refining and dealing in it and all its products, throughout the entire country, and by which it might not merely control the production, but the price, at its pleasure."[24]

These findings were reaffirmed by new investigations. In 1902, the United States Industrial Commission reported that Standard, through its control of pipe lines, practically fixed the price of crude oil. In 1907, the commissioner of corporations supported and amplified this conclusion. The company might fall short of an absolute monopoly, the commissioner pointed out, but its intentions were monopolistic.[25] In 1911, the United States Supreme Court confirmed this allegation, observing that "no disinterested mind" could survey the history of the Standard Oil combination from 1870 onward "without being irresistibly driven to the conclusion that the very genius for commercial development and organization . . . soon begot an intent and purpose . . . to drive others from the field and to exclude them from their right to trade and thus accomplish the mastery which was the end in view."[26]

Far from regarding the intricate system of business combination he had developed as a monster to be curbed or destroyed, a big businessman such as Rockefeller looked proudly upon his creation as a marvel of beneficence, an extraordinary and distinctive expression of American genius. And Carnegie contended "not evil, but good" had come from the phenomenal development of the corporation. He and others pointed out that the world obtained goods and commodities of excellent quality at prices which earlier generations would have considered incredibly cheap. The poor enjoyed what the richest could never before have afforded.[27]

The big businessman supported his actions as being entirely in keeping with the business requisites of the day. Rather than engaging in a conscious conspiracy to undermine equal opportunity, he had sought only the immediate and practical rewards of successful enterprise, rationalizing business conduct on the pragmatic level of profit and loss.

Instead of deliberately blocking free competition, big businessmen maintained that their actions were only natural responses to immutable law. Charles E. Perkins, president of the Chicago, Burlington and Quincy Railroad Company, denied deliberate misuses of power in es-

---

[24]*State of Ohio* vs. *Standard Oil Company*, 49 Ohio State, p. 137.

[25]*Report of the Commissioner of Corporations on the Petroleum Industry* (Washington: GPO, 1907), 1:xvi (*Smith Report*).

[26]*Standard Oil Co. of New Jersey et al.* vs. *United States*, 221 U.S., 1.

[27]Andrew Carnegie, "Wealth," *North American Review* 168 (June 1889):657 and 654; *The Gospel of Wealth* (New York, 1900), p. 5.

tablishing rates, and claimed that the price of railroad transportation, like all other prices, adjusted itself. Discriminatory practices were viewed as part of an inevitable conflict between buyer and seller, a necessary result of competition.[28] The payment of rebates and drawbacks was simply one method of meeting the market. In answer to the accusation that the railroads had made "important discriminations" in favor of Standard Oil, an executive of that company replied: "It may be frankly stated at the outset that the Standard Oil Company has at all times within the limits of fairness and with due regard for the law sought to secure the most advantageous freight rates and routes possible."[29] Rockefeller went on record as saying that Standard had received rebates from the railroads prior to 1880, because it was simply the railroads' way of doing business. Each shipper made the best bargain he could, hoping to outdo his competitor.

Furthermore, Rockefeller claimed this traffic was more profitable to the railroads than to the Standard Oil Company, stating that whatever advantage the oil company gained was passed on in lower costs to the consumer. Just as his company later justified certain alleged misdemeanors as being typical of the sharp practices prevailing in the oil fields in the early days, so Rockefeller exonerated the whole system of rebates and drawbacks on the grounds that everybody was doing it, concluding cynically that those who objected on principle did so only because they were not benefiting from it.[30]

Yet despite his public rationalizations, the big businessman's attitude toward competition was ambivalent. He lauded it as economic theory, but denied it in practical actions. Theoretically, there was no such thing as an absolute monopoly; there was always the threat of latent competition. Whenever a trust exacted too much, competitors would automatically appear.[31] Competition as a natural law would survive the trusts. "It is here; we cannot evade it," declaimed Carnegie. "And while the law may be sometimes hard for the individual, it is best for the race, because it insures the survival of the fittest in every department."[32]

In practical matters, however, the big businessman acted as if the law had long since become outmoded, if not extinct. Progressive opin-

[28]*Cullom Report,* appendix, pp. 213–215.

[29]Ralph W. and Muriel E. Hidy, *Pioneering in Big Business 1882–1911* (New York, 1955), pp. 678–679; cf. p. 43.

[30]John D. Rockefeller, *Random Reminiscences of Men and Events* (New York, 1909), p. 112.

[31]John Bates Clark, "The Society of the Future," *Independent* 53 (July 18, 1901):649–651.

[32]Carnegie, "Wealth," *North American Review* 168 (June 1889):655.

ion in the business world heralded the growing monopolistic trend as a sign of economic maturity. Increased concentration in capital and industry was defended as necessary and inevitable.[33] Monopolistic practices in general were upheld in business circles on the grounds that they prevented disastrous competition. In the long run they benefited, rather than plundered, the public by maintaining reasonable rates and prices.[34] "There seems to be a great readiness in the public mind to take alarm at these phenonena of growth, there might rather seem to be reason for public congratulation," announced Professor William Graham Sumner of Yale. "We want to be provided with things abundantly and cheaply; that means that we want increased economic power. All these enterprises are efforts to satisfy that want, and they promise to do it."[35] Many big businessmen believed that, practically at least, the trust proved the superiority of combination over competition.

Though the claim was not always true, the business virtues of economy and efficiency were allegedly the trust's chief advantages. The combination was spared the folly and wastefulness of unrestrained competition, and gained huge savings in cross freight, advertising, sales, and executive expenses. The survival of only the most productive forms of business resulted in greater efficiency and cheapened production which in turn meant higher wages and lower prices.[36] In this respect, Standard Oil was represented as a model trust. According to its supporters, it was formed to curb speculation, waste, and overproduction. As Standard took pains to inform stockholders, the company owed its success not to illegal or reprehensible methods but to efficient organization.[37]

In his account of the birth of America's first great trust, Rockefeller advanced a generalization common to big businessmen, that combination arose in response to economic necessity. It was accurate up to a point, but not universally applicable. Rockefeller's description of the founding of Standard Oil was an interesting description of the genesis of monopoly from the big businessman's viewpoint. In the begin-

---

[33]John Moody, *The Truth About the Trusts* (New York, 1904), p. v.

[34]See appended testimony to *Cullom Report*.

[35]William Graham Sumner, "The Concentration of Wealth: Its Economic Justification," *Essays of William Graham Sumner*, 2 vols. (New Haven, 1934), 2:166.

[36]This view had extensive support in the business world. For a useful compendium see James H. Bridge, *The Trust: Its Book* (New York, 1902). See also Jonathan P. Dolliver, "Facts About Trusts: Arguments for Protection," *American Industries* 2 (May 16, 1904); Franklin Head, ed., *Chicago Conference on Trusts* (Chicago, 1900).

[37]J. C. Welch and J. N. Camden, "The Standard Oil Company," *North American Review* 136 (February 1883):181–200; Hidy and Hidy, *Pioneering in Big Business*, pp. 658, 680.

ning, Rockefeller related, because refining crude petroleum was a simple and easy process and because at first the profits were very large, all sorts of people went into it—"the butcher, the baker and the candlestick maker began to refine oil." The market was soon glutted, and the price fell until the trade was threatened with ruin. At that moment "It seemed absolutely necessary to extend the market for oil . . . and also greatly improve the processes of refining so that oil could be made and sold cheaply, yet with a profit." So, "We proceeded to buy the largest and best refining concerns and centralize the administration of them with a view of securing greater economy and efficiency."[38] Though the birth pangs of Standard Oil obviously have been softened and somewhat simplified in the telling, it was on essentially this same basis that Carnegie explained the genesis of trusts in manufactured articles.[39]

Clearly, the operative point of view that consolidation of capital and industry was indispensable to the successful execution of the tasks which had developed upon modern business was the one embraced by big businessmen. In principle most of them agreed with the blunt statement of America's leading financier: "I like a little competition," J. P. Morgan was quoted as saying, "but I like combination better."[40] The choice was not between competition and monopoly, but between fighting to secure a monopoly by driving out competition in a bitter, destructive war and trying to obtain price control through industrywide agreement.

Many, nevertheless, still paid lip service to the abstraction, though most had already rejected competition in practice.[41] This glaring incongruity between behavior and theory ridiculed the notion that such economic generalizations as free competition were natural "laws" timeless and placeless and entitled to sanctity. Rather than a competent expression of fact, the hedonistic theory of a perfect competitive system had turned out to be simply an expedient of abstract reasoning.

What in earlier and more halcyon days had been attributed to the benign operation of the law of competition was, in most instances, an absence of competition. Before the Civil War, competition was virtually dormant in many parts of the United States largely because of intervening geographical factors. Where it did exist, it usually operated on a local rather than a national scale, cushioning a large portion of

---

[38]Rockefeller, *Reminiscences*, pp. 81–82.

[39]Andrew Carnegie, "The Bugaboo of Trusts," *North American Review* 148 (February 1889):141–142.

[40]*Literary Digest* 45 (December 28, 1912):1213.

[41]Edward C. Kirkland, *Dream and Thought in the Business Community* (Ithaca, 1956), p. 27.

the economy from the hardships of rigorous competition. The limitation of the nation's transportation system often allowed local businessmen a certain amount of monopoly power, and backward communications, particularly a lack of reliable market information, had a similar effect.[42] The trouble in many localities was that there was not always enough competition. These imperfections of competition in the antebellum period, however, tended to be eliminated by tremendous postwar advances in transportation and communication. Business rivalry also was intensified by the application of new technology to industry and nationalized by the substitution of the big interstate corporation for smaller local, individual, and partnership enterprises. The immediate outcome was competition with a vengeance, and the inauguration of a species of commercial warfare of a magnitude and violence unheard of in economic history. In the long run, the brutal realities of this cutthroat struggle were unpalatable to the public and big businessmen alike. But while the latter sought to shield themselves by erecting monopolistic barriers, the American people extolled the virtues of free competition and looked back fancifully to an earlier, more ideal state of economic affairs which, if anything, had been distinguished by a notable lack of competition.

The faith in the mythical virtues of competition prevailed widely. The majority of the American people took it for granted that competition was the normal way of life in business.[43] Henry Demarest Lloyd, an outstanding critic of big business, found it highly paradoxical that the American people who were so unalterably opposed to anarchy in politics advocated it in business. Worse yet, Americans had accepted industrial anarchy as their ideal of economic conduct.[44] Free competition was the shibboleth of practically all reform movements except that of the Socialists. It spurred the Grange, motivated the Single-Taxers and the Populists, and dominated the economic thought of the Progressives. Most of them desired, or thought they desired, free competition. On this matter there existed no clear partisan line. Members of Congress proclaimed "the norm of a free competition too self-evident to be debated, too obvious to be asserted."[45]

The belief in competition was an assertion of economic egalitarianism midway between the Gospel of Wealth and the Social Gospel,

---

[42]Hans B. Thorelli, *The Federal Antitrust Policy* (Baltimore, 1955), p. 66.

[43]*Ibid.*, pp. 500–554.

[44]Henry Demarest Lloyd, *Wealth Against Commonwealth* (New York, 1899), p. 496.

[45]Walton Hamilton and Irene Till, *Antitrust in Action* (Washington: GPO, 1940), p. 6.

adopting neither the doctrine of stewardship by the chosen few nor the sweeping substitution of cooperation for competition.[46] It was a subtle interweaving of the Anglo-Saxon belief that the common law, as well as natural law, always favored competition over monopoly and native American opposition to privilege.[47] Some of the basic attitudes in this complex were clearly derived from classical economic theory. The economists whose works were most widely read were Adam Smith, John Stuart Mill, and David Ricardo; their laissez-faire attitude toward monopoly dominated the teaching of economics. "All our education and our habit of mind make us believe in competition," said the president of Yale. "We have been taught to regard it as a natural if not a necessary condition of all healthful business life. We look with satisfaction on whatever favors it, and with distrust on whatever hinders it."[48] The Darwinian theory of biological evolution was also generally interpreted as supporting popular notions about competition and individual initiative, although this was more apparent than real.[49] This ingrained habit of economic reasoning retarded public understanding of the new financial and industrial order, but the belief proved more important than its actual relevance. Sentiment, not fact, prompted American action against big business.[50]

On the question whether the corporation had to be made to fit American institutions and principles, or those institutions and principles had to be changed to accommodate the corporation, the American people almost unanimously declared for the first. If economic despotism was the outcome of unchecked corporate growth, then the corporate monster must be brought under control. The way out was the way back. The economy must be restored to a former golden time of competitive capitalism when the older individualistic values held sway, and the common man was free from monopolistic pressures.

The way backward, however, was not to be all the way. Completely breaking the trusts was rejected by the more realistic who wanted regulation. Somewhat paradoxically, they proposed to liberate competition by imposing new restrictions in the name of freedom. They were

---

[46]Thorelli, *The Federal Antitrust Policy*, p. 556.

[47]Frederick Pollock, *The Genuis of the Common Law* (New York, 1912), p. 95.

[48]Arthur T. Hadley, *Railroad Transportation: Its History and Its Laws* (New York, 1885), pp. 69–70.

[49]Richard Hofstadter, *Social Darwinism in American Thought, 1860–1915* (Philadelphia, 1945), p. 201.

[50]John Lydenburg, "Pre-Muckraking: A Study of Attitudes Toward Politics as Revealed in American Fiction from 1870 through 1901" (unpublished Ph.D. Dissertation, Harvard University, 1946), p. 59.

not too sure that unrestrained competition was the economic panacea they sought. They justified the theoretical incongruity of their stand on the moral grounds that such restrictions were to be imposed only to prevent unfair competition. Apparently it never occurred to them that to acknowledge the defective working of natural law against corporate immorality was an ingenuous admission that the sacrosanct principle of competition was invalid in the long run. Willfully blind to the logical inconsistencies of this position, the majority clamored for governmental regulation in the interests of equal opportunity: "We must either regulate . . . or destroy."[51]

Responding to popular demand, Congress in 1890 passed the Sherman Act "to protect trade and commerce against unlawful restraints and monopolies," thus converting an economic myth into public policy. According to the ideology behind this law, there existed a direct cause and effect relationship between competition and monopoly. If the monopolistic obstacles in business were removed, the trend would immediately reverse itself; full and free competition would automatically return. Despite the stark realities of the growing trust and combination movement of the late 1880s, the public's confidence in the efficacy of this self-regulating mechanism set the tone of all subsequent federal action, whether for regulation or trust-busting.[52] Facts, however, proved otherwise. The Sherman Act, even when bolstered by later legislation, failed to halt or reverse the combination movement. It made evident the ineptitude of any legislation that regarded competition as a self-perpetuating and natural guarantor of economic justice rather than an intellectual hypothesis without institutional support.

The principal effect of legalizing the myth of competition was to encourage the growth of large combinations by deflecting the attack upon them into purely ideological channels. Since 1890, federal antitrust laws have symbolized the American democratic belief that "the only proper type of society is composed of unorganized competitive individuals." All attempts to curb big business by government action have been a ritual clash between an anachronistic ideal and a modern need, "the answer of a society which unconsciously felt the need of great organizations, and at the same time had to deny them a place in the moral and logical ideology of the social structure."[53]

Though the corporation had seemingly conformed to American institutions and principles under antitrust laws, those institutions and

---

[51]Lloyd, *Wealth Against Commonwealth*, p. 496.

[52]Senate Reports, no. 59, January 10, 1900; B and D, 951.

[53]Thurman W. Arnold, *The Folklore of Capitalism* (New Haven, 1937), p. 211.

principles had really accommodated the corporation. By declaring the corporation to be an individual, with natural rights of life, liberty, and property, the Supreme Court in 1886 had seriously invalidated that basic concept of American society, the free individual.[54] This doctrine could be applied logically only to the individual as proprietor, partner, or even operating owner of a small company, but the jurists ignored the intrinsic conflict between the individualistic myth and the corporate reality, evoking the strained future efforts of the Supreme Court to dress "huge corporations in the clothes of simple farmers and merchants."[55]

In establishing the legal fiction that the corporation was a person before the law, entitled to the rights and privileges of a citizen, the court undermined the ideal of the morally responsible individual by extending the individualistic ethic to the amoral impersonality of the modern corporation, and in the long run it subordinated the ideal to the right of property. To accord a legal robot equal rights with a living person in the holding and protection of property under the Constitution was to exalt corporate property above the individual person and to prevent the traditional faith in individualism into a juridical sophism. As the course of American legal history from 1886 to the 1930s amply disclosed, such was the ultimate effect of the personification of the corporation.

In condemning trusts as "dangerous to Republican institutions" and in branding corporate leaders as robber barons "opposed to free institutions and free commerce between the states as were the feudal barons of the middle ages," aroused Americans of the Gilded Age had clearly seized upon the major issue.[56] They had somehow recognized that American society with its individualistic traditions was engaged in a life-and-death struggle with the organized forces of dissolution.

The once-welcome business and industrial concentration threatened the foundations of the nation. There was more individual power than ever, but those who wielded it were few and formidable. Charles Francis Adams, Jr., denounced these "modern potentates for the autocratic misuse of that power":

> The system of corporate life and corporate power, as applied to industrial development, is yet in its infancy. . . . It is a new power, for which our language contains no name. We know what aristocracy, autocracy, democracy are; but we have no word to express govern-

[54]*Santa Clara Co.* vs. *Southern Pacific Railroad Co.*, 118 U.S., 394.

[55]Arnold, *The Folklore of Capitalism*, p. 189.

[56]See H. S. Commager, ed., *Documents of American History*, 2 vols. in 1 (New York, 1949), 2:78.

ment by monied corporations. . . . It remains to be seen what the
next phase in this process of gradual development will be. History
never quite repeats itself, and . . . the old familiar enemies may even
now confront us, though arrayed in such a modern garb that no sus-
picion is excited. . . . As the Erie ring represents the combination of
the corporation and the hired proletariat of a great city; as Vanderbilt
embodies the autocratic power of Caesarism introduced into cor-
porate life, and neither alone can obtain complete control of the gov-
ernment of the State, it, perhaps, only remains for the coming man
to carry the combination of elements one step in advance, and put
Caesarism at once in control of the corporation and of the proletariat,
to bring out vaunted institutions within the rule of all historic prec-
edent.[57]

Yet the public already sensed that something had gone wrong with
American institutions and values. With less understanding than Adams, they felt that somehow the old rules had been broken. Behind
their growing animosity to the big businessman was the feeling that
in some way he cheated his countrymen. The belief was becoming
fairly common that extreme wealth was incompatible with honesty.
"The great cities," Walt Whitman wrote in 1871, "reek with respectable as much as non-respectable robbery and scoundrelism."[58] There
were undoubtedly moral men of wealth, but many Americans agreed
with Thomas A. Bland, who in *How to Grow Rich* suggested: "In all
history, ancient and modern, the examples of men of honest lives and
generous hearts who have become rich . . . is so rare as to be exceedingly exceptional, and even these have invariably profited largely . . .
by the labor of others."[59]

Very revealing in this regard was the portrayal of the big businessman in contemporary fiction. Socialist writers naturally depicted him
as a "criminal of greed" or an "economic monster" who with other
"business animals" preyed upon the life of the nation. Oddly enough,
however, in an age when the corporation made unprecedented achievements in production and organization to the enrichment of countless
people, when material success was widely favored as a legitimate goal,
scarcely a single major novelist presented the big businessman as a
hero or even in a favorable light. Except at the hands of a few hack
writers, the business or industrial leader was consistently portrayed as
powerful and capable, but nonetheless an enemy of American soci-

---

[57]Adams and Adams, *Chapters of Erie,* pp. 96–99.
[58]Mark Van Doren, ed., *The Portable Walt Whitman* (New York, 1945), p. 400.
[59]See Irvin G. Wyllie, *The Self-Made Man in America* (New Brunswick, 1954), p.
147.

ety.[60] This may have reflected the bias of the aesthetic or creative temperament against the pragmatic money-maker, but the big businessman was in disfavor with most of American society.

In the popular mind, the vices of lying and stealing were legendarily associated with Wall Street. The big businessmen who dominated "the street" were regarded by some as the ethical counterparts of the pirate and buccaneer. By the simple devices of "stock-watering" or the issuance of fictitious securities not backed by capital assets, speculators were generally believed to have stolen millions of dollars from the American people.[61] In the opinion of the more jaundiced, the men of Wall Street had barely escaped prison bars. "If the details of the great reorganization and trustification deals put through since 1885 could be laid bare," contended Thomas W. Lawson, a financier turned critic, "eight out of ten of our most successful stock-jobbing financiers would be in a fair way to get into State or federal prisons."[62]

The iniquity of Wall Street was not merely legendary, but had firm basis in fact. Though not all speculators were swindlers nor all speculation gambling, only a small number of the stock exchange transactions were unquestionably of an investment character. The vast majority were virtually gambling.[63] Many corporations, although offering huge blocks of stock to the public, issued only the vaguest and most ambiguous summary of assets and liabilities. While this was not iniquitous in itself, secrecy too often cloaked fraud.[64]

The men at the top who had used the corporate device to make millions did not see it this way at all. They justified their millions on the ground that they had fairly earned it.[65] Cornelius Vanderbilt, at the age of eighty-one, boasted that he had made a million dollars for every year of his life, but added that it had been worth "three times that to the people of the United States."[66] Others shared his belief. In *The Railroad and the Farmer*, Edward Atkinson made practically the same statement, asserting that the gigantic fortune of the older Vanderbilt

[60]Edward Everett Cassady, "The Business Man in the American Novel: 1856 to 1903" (unpublished Ph.D. Dissertation, University of California, Berkeley, 1939), p. 199.

[61]Medbery, *Men and Mysteries*, p. 282; Fowler, 299.

[62]Thomas W. Lawson, *Frenzied Finance* (New York, 1905), p. 174.

[63]See *Report on Governor Hughes' Committee on Speculation in Securities and Commodities* (Albany, 1909), pp. 4, 15; Alexander D. Noyes, "The Recent Economic History of the United States," *Quarterly Journal of Economics* 19 (June 1905):167–209.

[64]Lloyd, *Lords*, p. 341.

[65]W. A. Croffutt, *The Vanderbilts and the Story of Their Fortune* (Chicago, 1886), p. 129.

[66]Francis A. Walker, "Democracy and Wealth," *Forum* 10 (September 1890):245.

was but a small fraction of what the country gained from the development of the railway system under his genius.[67] The Reverend Julian M. Sturtevant of Illinois College also envisioned the Vanderbilts and Astors of the world as "laborers of gigantic strength, and they must have their reward and compensation for the use of their capital."[68] Carnegie maintained that great riches were no crime. "Under our present conditions the millionaire who toils on is the cheapest article which the community secures at the price it pays for him, namely, his shelter, clothing, and food."[69]

Most Americans, however, did not so readily accept his evaluation. Some recognized that the big businessman in pursuing private ends had served national prosperity—the majority felt that he had taken extravagant profits entirely out of proportion to the economic services he had rendered. Rockefeller's millions were thought to be typical of the fortunes made by the robber barons, representing "the relentless, aggressive, irresistible seizure of a particular opportunity, the magnitude of which . . . was due simply to the magnitude of the country and the immensity of the stream of its prosperous industrial life."[70] The feeling was general that the great fortunes of all the big business magnates—Vanderbilt, Gould, Harriman, Stanford, Carnegie, Morgan, and the rest—represented special privilege which had enabled them to turn the abundant natural resources and multitudinous advantages offered by a growing nation into a private preserve for their own profit.

The public at large was not clearly aware of it, but the chief instrument of special privilege was the corporation. Though public franchises and political favoritism played a large part in the aggrandizement of the robber barons, in the money-making world of late-nineteenth-century America special privilege invariably meant corporate privilege. The corporation enabled Vanderbilt to unify his railroads while making large speculative profits on the side. The same device made it possible for men like Rockefeller to create and combine private enterprises embodying new technological and financial techniques while diverting enormous profits to themselves. The corporation was the constructive power behind the building of the cross-country railroads, but it was also the destructive instrument used by Jay Gould, Tom Scott, Collis P. Huntington, and others to convert them

---

[67]Joseph Dorfman, *The Economic Mind in American Civilization*, 5 vols. (New York, Viking, 1946–1959), 3:73.

[68]Andrew Carnegie, *The Empire of Business* (New York, 1902), p. 140.

[69]Henry George, *Progress and Poverty* (New York, 1880), pp. 174–175; Lyman Abbott, "Industrial Democracy," *Review of Reviews* 4 (June 1890):662.

[70]Burton J. Hendrick, "The Vanderbilt Fortune," *McClure's* 19 (November 1908):46–62.

into quick money-making machines with no regard for their obligations as public carriers.[71]

The problem remained of establishing the relationship of big businessmen to the corporation. Judging by their conduct, they were not
fully cognizant of the tremendous power placed in their hands by the
corporation with single men controlling "thousands of men, tens of
millions of revenue, and hundreds of millions of capital." Or they willfully exerted this prodigious force for private benefit regardless of consequences to the nation or ideals. Unhappily, most of those labeled
robber baron by their contemporaries fell into the latter category.[72]
Cornelius Vanderbilt held the law in contempt. Except where his own
interests were involved, he had little regard for the consequences of
his actions, manipulating and watering every corporate property he
captured. One year after he took over the New York Central Railroad,
he increased the capitalization by $23 million, almost every cent of
which represented inside profits for himself and friends. When ad-
monished that some of his transactions were forbidden by law, he supposedly roared, "Law! What do I care about the law? Hain't I got the
power?"[73] He confirmed this attitude in testimony before the committee on railroads of the New York State Assembly in 1869.[74] But
Vanderbilt's methods were in no way exceptional. Most of the biggest
businessmen made their millions in similar fashion. Twenty-four who
because of notoriety and conspicuous power might be regarded as "typical" robber barons combined the role of promoter with that of entrepreneur. Stock manipulation along with corporate consolidation was
probably the easiest way to wealth that ever existed in the United
States. The exuberance with which promoters threw themselves into
it proved that they were well aware of its golden possibilities.

As a consequence of these reckless corporate maneuverings, however, public opinion turned against the big businessman. While from
a corporate point of view the conduct of the money-makers was often
legal, although ethically dubious, the public often felt cheated. Puzzled
and disenchanted by the way things had turned out, they questioned
the way every millionaire got his money, and were quite ready to believe that a crime was behind every great fortune. While its exact nature escaped them, they felt they had been robbed. The classic state-

---

[71]New York State, *Assembly Documents*, 1867, no. 19, pp. 205–210.

[72]See John Tipple, "The Anatomy of Prejudice: The Critical Foundations of the Robber Baron Legend" (unpublished Ph.D. Dissertation, Stanford University, 1958), pp. 15–
17.

[73]Frederick A. Cleveland and Fred W. Powell, *Railroad Promotion and Capitalization in the United States* (New York, 1909), p. 141.

[74]New York State, *Assembly Documents*, op. cit.

ment of this feeling of outrage appeared in the Populist platform of
1892: "The fruits of the toil of millions are boldly stolen to build up
colossal fortunes for a few, unprecedented in the history of mankind;
and the possessors of these, in turn, despise the Republic and endanger
liberty."[75]

The inchoate charges were basically accurate: too much wealth
was being selfishly appropriated by a few. By the irresponsible use of
the corporation, essentially a supralegal abstraction above the traditional laws of the land, they were undermining individualistic institutions and values. Big businessmen like John D. Rockefeller were attacked as robber barons because they were correctly identified as
destroyers, the insurgent vanguard of the corporate revolution.

---

[75]See Edward Stanwood, *A History of Presidential Elections* (Boston, 1892), pp. 474–
478.

Alfred D. Chandler

ALFRED D. CHANDLER (1918–   ) is Straus Professor of Business History at the Harvard Graduate School of Business Administration. He is the author of a number of books in American business history, including *Henry Varnum Poor* (1956), *Strategy and Structure* (1969), and the Pulitzer Prize-winning *The Visible Hand* (1977).

For a paper on the historical role of business in America to provide a solid foundation for discussions of the present and future, it must examine a number of questions: Who were the American businessmen? How did they come to go into business? How were they trained? How broad was their outlook? And, of even more importance, what did they do? How did they carry out the basic economic functions of production, distribution, transportation, and finance? How was the work of these businessmen coordinated so that the American economic system operated as an integrated whole? Finally, how did these men and the system within which they worked adapt to fundamental changes in population, to the opening of new lands, resources, and markets, and to technological developments that transformed markets, sources of supply, and means of production and distribution? The answers to these questions, as limited as they may be, should help to make more understandable the present activities and future capabilities of American business.

The Colonial Merchant

The merchant dominated the simple rural economy of the colonial period. By the eighteenth century he considered himself and was considered by others to be a businessman. His economic functions differentiated him from the farmers who produced crops and the artisans who made goods. Although the farmers and artisans occasionally carried on business transactions, they spent most of their time working on the land or in the shop. The merchant, on the other hand, spent nearly all his time in handling transactions involved in carrying goods

Alfred D. Chandler, "The Role of Business in the United States: A Historical Survey," *Daedalus* 98 (Winter 1969):23–40. Reprinted by permission of *Daedalus*, Journal of the American Academy of Arts and Science, Boston, Mass.

through the process of production and distribution, including their transportation and finance.

The colonial merchant was an all-purpose, non-specialized man of business. He was a wholesaler and a retailer, an importer and an exporter. In association with other merchants he built and owned the ships that carried goods to and from his town. He financed and insured the transportation and distribution of these goods. At the same time, he provided the funds needed by the planter and the artisan to finance the production of crops and goods. The merchant, operating on local, inter-regional, and international levels, adapted the economy to the relatively small population and technological changes of the day and to shifts in supply and demand resulting from international tensions.

These men of business tended to recruit their successors from their own family and kinship group. Family loyalties were important, indeed essential, in carrying on business in distant areas during a period when communication between ports was so slow and uncertain. Able young clerks or sea captains might be brought into the family firm, but sons and sons-in-law were preferred. Trading internationally as well as locally, the merchants acquired broader horizons than the farmer, artisan, and day laborer. Only a few of the great landowners and leading lawyers knew the larger world. It was the colonial merchants who, allied with lawyers from the seaport towns and with the Virginia planters, encouraged the Revolution, brought about the ratification of the Constitution, and then set up the new government in the last decade of the eighteenth century.

The Rise of the Wholesaler, 1800–1850

During the first half of the nineteenth century, although the American economy remained primarily agrarian and commercial, it grew vigorously. The scope of the economy expanded as the nation moved westward into the rich Mississippi Valley, and as increasing migration from Europe still further enlarged its population. Even more important to American economic expansion were the technological innovations that occurred in manufacturing in Great Britain. Without the new machines of the Industrial Revolution, the westward movement in the United States and the migration to its shores would have been slower. These innovations reshaped the British textile industry, creating a new demand for cotton from the United States. Before the invention of the water frame, the spinning jenny, the mule, and then the power loom, cotton had never been grown commercially in the United States, but by 1800 it had become the country's major export. The new plantations in turn provided markets for food grown on the smaller farms in both the Northwest and Southwest. The growth of eastern commercial cities and the development of the textile industry in New England and the middle states enlarged that market still further. The titanic struggle between Great Britain and Napoleon obscured the significance of these economic developments, but shortly after 1815 the economy's new orientation became clear.

The merchants who continued to act as economic integrators had the largest hand in building this new high-volume, regionally specialized, agrarian-commercial system. The merchants of Philadelphia, Baltimore, and New York took over the task of exporting cotton, lumber, and foodstuffs and of importing textiles, hardware, drugs, and other goods from Great Britain and the Continent. Those in the southern coastal and river ports played the same role in exporting cotton and importing finished goods to and from the eastern entrepôts; those in the growing western towns sent out local crops and brought in manufactured goods in a similar way. At first the western trade went via rivers of the Mississippi Valley and New Orleans. Later it began to be transported east and west through the Erie Canal and along the Great Lakes. To meet the needs of the expanding trade, the merchants, particularly those of the larger eastern cities, developed new forms of commercial banking to finance the movement of crops, set up packet lines on "the Atlantic Shuttle" between New York and Liverpool to speed the movement of news and imports, founded specialized insurance companies, and helped to organize and finance the new canals and turnpikes that improved transportation between them and their customers.

These innovations enabled the merchants to handle still more business, and the high-volume trade in turn forced the merchants to alter their functions and, indeed, their whole way of life. They began to specialize, becoming primarily wholesalers or retailers, importers or exporters. They came to concentrate on a single line of goods—dry goods, wet goods, hardware, iron, drugs, groceries or cotton, wheat or produce. Some became specialists in banking and insurance and spent their time acting as managers for these new financial corporations.

Of the new specialists, the wholesalers played the most influential role, taking the place of the colonial merchants as the primary integrators and adaptors of the economy. More than the farmers or the retailers, the wholesalers were responsible for directing the flow of cotton, corn, wheat, and lumber from the West to the East and to Europe. More than the manufacturers, they handled the marketing of finished goods that went from eastern and European industrial centers to the southern and western states.

Moreover, the wholesalers financed the long-term growth of the economy. Enthusiastic promoters of canals, turnpikes, and then railroads, they provided most of the local capital for these undertakings. They pressured the state and municipal legislatures and councils (on which they or their legally trained associates often sat) to issue bonds or to guarantee bonds of private corporations building transportation enterprises. At times they even persuaded the state to build and operate transport facilities.

The wholesalers also encouraged the adoption of the new technology in manufacturing. In Boston, the Appletons, the Jacksons, and the Cabots financed the new textile mills of Lowell and Lawrence. In New York, the Phelps and the Dodges started the brass industry in the Connecticut Valley, while in Philadelphia and Baltimore wholesalers like Nathan Trotter and Enoch Pratt financed the growing Pennsylvania iron industry. They not only raised the funds for plants and machinery, but also supplied a large amount of the cash and credit that the new manufacturers needed as working capital to pay for supplies and labor.

Although the wholesalers made important contributions to early-nineteenth-century economic life, they played a less dominant role in the economy than had the colonial merchant of the eighteenth century. The economic system had become too complex—involving too many units of production, distribution, transportation, and finance—for one group to supervise local, inter-regional, and international flows. Nonetheless, the wholesalers had more influence in setting prices, managing the flow of goods, and determining the amount and direction of investment than had other groups—the farmers, manufacturers, retailers, and bankers.

As the economy expanded, the recruitment of businessmen became more open than it had been in the colonial period. At the same time, the outlook of even the most broad-gauged businessmen grew narrower. Family and family ties became less essential, although they could still be a useful source of capital. Businessmen began to place more value on personal qualities, such as aggressiveness, drive, and self-reliance. Nor did one need any lengthy training or education to set up a shop as a wholesaler. Because of their increasing functional specialization, this new breed of wholesalers rarely had the international outlook of the colonial merchants. Not surprisingly, they and the lawyers and politicians who represented them saw their needs in sectional rather than national terms—as did so many Americans in the years immediately prior to the Civil War.

The Rise of the Manufacturer Before 1900

By mid-century the American agrarian and commercial economy had begun to be transformed into the most productive industrial system in the world. The migration of Americans into cities became more significant in this transformation than the final settling of the western frontier. Immigration from Europe reached new heights, with most of the new arrivals staying in the cities of the East and the old Northwest. By 1900, therefore, the rate of growth of the rural areas had leveled off. From then on, the nation's population growth would come almost wholly in its cities.

The second half of the nineteenth century was a time of great technological change—the age of steam and iron, the factory and the railroad. The steam railroad and the steamship came quickly to dominate transportation. In 1849 the United States had only six thousand miles of railroad and even fewer miles of canals, but by 1884 its railroad corporations operated 202,000 miles of track, or 43 per cent of the total mileage in the world. In 1850 the factory—with its power-driven machinery and its permanent working force—was a rarity outside the textile and iron industries, but by 1880 the Bureau of the Census reported that 80 per cent of the three million workers in mechanized industry labored in factories. And nearly all these new plants were powered by steam rather than by water.

America's factories made a vital contribution to the nation's economic growth. By 1894 the value of the output of American industry equalled that of the combined output of the United Kingdom, France, and Germany. In the next twenty years American production tripled, and by the outbreak of World War I the United States was producing more than a third of the world's industrial goods.

As manufacturing expanded, the wholesaler continued for many years to play a significant role in the economy. The period up to 1873 was one of increasing demand and rising prices. The manufacturers, concentrating on building or expanding their new factories, were more than happy to have the wholesalers supply them with their raw and semifinished materials and to market their finished goods. In addition, wholesalers continued to provide manufacturers with capital for building plants, purchasing equipment and supplies, and paying wages.

After the recession of 1873, however, the manufacturers began to replace the wholesaler as the man who had the most to say about coordinating the flow of goods through the economy and about adapting the economy to population and technological changes. The shift came for three reasons. First, the existing wholesale network of hundreds of thousands of small firms had difficulty in handling efficiently the growing output of the factories. Secondly, the manufacturer no longer needed the wholesaler as a source of capital. After a generation of production, he was able to finance plant and equipment out of retained profits. Moreover, until 1850 the commercial banking system had been almost wholly involved in financing the movement of agricultural products, but about mid-century it began to provide working capital for the industrialist. Commercial banks also began to provide funds for plant and equipment, particularly to new manufacturing enterprises.

The third and most pervasive reason why the manufacturer came to a position of dominance resulted from the nature of factory production itself. This much more efficient form of manufacturing so swiftly increased the output of goods that supply soon outran demand. From the mid-1870's to the mid-1890's, prices fell sharply. Moreover, the large investment required to build a factory made it costly to shut down and even more expensive to move into other forms of business activity. As prices fell, the manufacturers organized to control prices and the flow of goods within their industries. If the wholesalers would and could help them in achieving such control, the manufacturers welcomed their cooperation. If not, they did it themselves. In most cases, the industrialist came to play a larger role than the wholesalers in integrating the economy.

The wholesaler was pushed aside in transportation before he was in manufacturing. Railroad construction costs were high, and after 1849 when railroad expansion began on a large scale, the local merchants simply could not supply the necessary capital. Modern Wall Street came into being during the 1850's to meet the need for funds. By 1860 the investment banker had replaced the wholesaler as the primary supplier of funds to American railroads.

In the 1850's and 1860's the railroads also captured many of the merchant's functions. They took over freight forwarding in large towns and eliminated the merchant by handling through traffic in many commercial centers along the main routes west and south. Indeed, during the 1860's the railroads had absorbed most of the fast freight and express companies developed earlier by the wholesalers in order to use the new rail transportation. By the 1870's the coordination of the flow of most inter-regional transportation in the United States had come under the direction of the traffic departments of a few large railroads.

The first manufacturers to move into the wholesalers' domain were those who found that the wholesaler could not meet their special needs. These were of two types. The makers of new technologically complex and relatively expensive durable products quickly realized that wholesalers were unable to handle the initial demonstration to the consumer, provide consumer credit, or ensure the repair and servicing of the products sold. Thus manufacturers of agricultural implements, sewing machines, typewriters, cash registers, carriages, bicycles, or, most important of all, electrical machinery and equipment created national and even international marketing organizations well before the turn of the century. So did the second type, the processors of perishable goods requiring refrigeration, quick transportation, and careful storage for their distribution—fresh meat, beer, bananas, and cigarettes.

Once the pioneers of both types of enterprises—the McCormicks, the Remingtons, George Westinghouse and Charles Coffin, the Swifts and Armours, the Pabsts and Schlitzes, Andrew Preston and James B. Duke—had created their widespread distribution networks, they began again to eliminate the wholesaler by doing their own purchasing. They could not run the risk of stopping complex fabricating or assembling processes because they lacked critical parts or materials. Some integrated backwards even further, doing their own purchasing by building or buying factories to manufacture parts, controlling their own iron, steel, or lumber, or obtaining their own refrigerated cars and ships.

The manufacturers who produced standard commodities that might be distributed easily through the existing wholesaler network were slower to move into wholesaling. Even though the pioneering firms were demonstrating the economies resulting from a combination of mass production and mass distribution, most manufacturers had to be pushed rather than enticed into a strategy of vertical integration. They did so only after they failed to meet the oppressive pressure of falling prices by the more obvious methods of price control through trade associations, cartels, and other loose combinations.

The railroads pioneered in developing ways to control prices in the face of excess capacity and heavy fixed costs. During the 1870's, the railroads formed regional associations, of which the Eastern Trunk Line Association was the most powerful. By the 1880's, however, the railroad presidents and traffic managers admitted defeat. The associations could only be effective if their rulings were enforced in courts of law, but their pleas for legalized pooling went unheard. Indeed, the Interstate Commerce Act of 1887 specifically declared pooling illegal. As a result, the American railroad network became consolidated into large "self-sustaining," centrally managed regional systems. By 1900 most of American land transportation was handled by about twenty-five great systems informally allied in six groupings.

Where the railroads had hoped for legalized pooling, the manufacturers sought other ways of obtaining firmer legal control over the factories in their industries. They began personally to purchase stock in one another's companies. After 1882 when the Standard Oil Company devised the trust as a way of acquiring legal control of an industry, companies began to adopt that device. The holding company quickly superseded the trust as a more effective and inexpensive way of controlling price and production after 1889, when New Jersey passed a general incorporation law that permitted one company to hold stock in many others. The Supreme Court's interpretations of the Sherman Antitrust Act (1890) encouraged further consolidation in manufacturing. Court decisions discouraged loose combinations of manufacturers (or railroads) in any form, but (at least until 1911) appeared to permit consolidation of competing firms through a holding company if that company came to administer its activities under a single centralized management.

In many cases these new consolidations embarked on a strategy of vertical integration. Where the railroads formed "self-sustaining" systems to assure control of traffic over primary commercial routes, the manufacturers attempted to assure the uninterrupted flow of goods into and out of their production and processing plants. John D. Rockefeller and his associates at Standard Oil were the first of the combinations to adopt this strategy. The Standard Oil Trust had been formed after associations in the petroleum industry had proven to be, in Rockefeller's words, "ropes of sand." Legal control of the industry was followed by administrative consolidation of its refineries under a single centralized management. In the mid-1880's, the trust began to build its own distribution network of tank farms and wholesaling offices. Finally, after enlarging its buying organization, it moved in the late-1880's into the taking of crude oil out of the ground.

The examples of Standard Oil, the Swifts, the McCormicks, and others who had by-passed the wholesaler, the rulings of the Supreme Court, the memories of twenty years of declining prices resulted between 1898 and 1902 in the greatest merger movement in American history. Combinations, usually in the form of holding companies, occurred in nearly all major American industries. Holding companies then were often transformed into operating companies. After manufacturing facilities were centralized under a single management, the new consolidated enterprise integrated forwards and backwards.

At the same time, retailers who began to appreciate the potential of mass markets and economies of scale also moved to eliminate the wholesalers—although they did so in a more restricted way than the manufacturers. The mail order houses (Sears, Roebuck and Montgomery Ward), which turned to the rural markets, and the department and chain stores, which looked to the growing cities, began to buy directly from the manufacturers. By the turn of the century, some large retailers had even bought into manufacturing firms. As a result, wholesalers' decisions were of less significance to the operation of the economy than they had been fifty years earlier. Far more important were the decisions of the manufacturers who had combined, consolidated, and integrated their operations and the few giant retailers who had adopted somewhat the same strategy.

As manufacturers replaced wholesalers as key coordinators in the national economy, they became the popular symbol of American business enterprise. The industrialists and the railroad leaders were indeed the reality as well as the symbol of business power in the Gilded Age. The recruitment of this new dominant business group remained open, at least for a generation. As had been true earlier for the wholesaler, aggressiveness, drive, and access to capital or credit were prerequisites for success. Lineage or specialized learning were less important, but some technological knowledge was an advantage. Although the manufacturers' horizons were more national and less regional than the wholesalers', they came to view the national scene from the perspective of their particular industry. They and their representatives in Washington tended to take positions on the major issues of the day— tariff, currency, immigration, and the regulation of business—from an industrial rather than a sectional or regional viewpoint.

It was not long, however, before the needs of the manufacturers and their response to these needs altered the recruitment and training of the nation's most powerful businessmen. The increasingly high investment required for large-scale production made the entry of new men and firms more difficult. The emergence of the vertically integrated enterprise limited opportunities still further. By 1900 it was becoming easier to rise to positions of business influence by moving through the new centralized managements than by starting a business enterprise of one's own. This pattern was already clear in the railroads, the nation's first modern business bureaucracies.

The Dominance of the Manager Since 1900

Although the twentieth century was to become the age of the manager, the growing significance of the manager's role in the operation of the American economy was not immediately apparent. Until the 1920's manufacturers and their assistants concentrated on rounding out their integrated enterprises, creating the internal structures and methods necessary to operate these business empires, and employing the managers necessary to staff them.

At first, external conditions did not seriously challenge the new enterprises. Population trends continued, and heavy migration from abroad sustained urban growth until the outbreak of World War I. During the war, migration from the rural areas to the cities increased. At the same time, impressive technological innovations, particularly those involved with the generating of power by electricity and the internal combustion engine created new industries and helped transform older ones. The continuing growth of the city, the expansion of the whole electrical sector, and the coming of the automobile and auxiliary industries made the first decades of the twentieth century ones of increasing demand and rapid economic growth.

The initial task of the men who fashioned the first integrated giants at the beginning of this century was to build internal organizational structures that would assure the efficient coordination of the flow of goods through their enterprises and permit the rational allocation of the financial, human, and technological resources at their command. First came the formation of functional departments—sales, production, purchasing, finance, engineering, and research and development. At the same time, central offices were organized, usually in the form of an executive committee consisting of the heads of the functional departments. These offices supervised, appraised, and coordinated the work of the departments and planned long-term expenditures.

By the late-1920's the pioneer organization-builders at du Pont, General Motors, General Electric, Standard Oil of New Jersey, and Sears, Roebuck had developed new and sophisticated techniques to perform the vital coordinating and adaptive activities. They based both long- and short-term coordination and planning on a forecast of market conditions. On the basis of annual forecasts, revised monthly and adjusted every ten days, the companies set production schedules, purchases of supplies and semifinished products, employment and wage rolls, working capital requirements, and prices. Prices were determined by costs, which in turn closely reflected estimated volume of output. The annual forecasts took into consideration estimates of national income, the business cycle, seasonal fluctuations, and the company's normal share of the market. Long-term allocations were based on still broader estimates of demand. After 1920, the managers of many large corporations began to include in these allocations the funds and personnel needed to develop new products and processes through technological innovation. From that time on, the integrated firm began to diversify. The Depression and World War II helped to spread these methods, so that by mid-century most of the key industries in the United States were dominated by a few giant firms administered in much the same way.

Their managers considered themselves leaders in the business community and were so considered by others. Yet they differed greatly from the older types of dominant businessmen—the merchants, the wholesalers, and the manufacturers. They were not owners; they held only a tiny portion of their company's stock; they neither founded the enterprise nor were born into it; and most of them had worked their way up the new bureaucratic ladders.

Even to get on a ladder they were expected to have attended college. Studies of business executives in large corporations show that by 1950 the large majority had been to college—an advantage that was shared by few Americans of their age group. Like most of those who did receive higher education, these managers came primarily from white Anglo-Saxon Protestant stock. Once the college man with his WASP background started up the managerial ladder, he usually remained in one industry and more often than not in a single company. That company became his career, his way of life.

As he rose up the ranks, his horizon broadened to national and international levels. Where his firm diversified, his interests and concerns spread over several industries. Indeed, in some ways his perspectives were wider in the 1950's than those of most Americans; nevertheless, because of his specialized training, he had little opportunity to become aware of the values, ideas, ambitions, and goals of other groups of Americans. He had even fewer direct contacts with farmers, workers, and other types of businessmen than had the wholesaler and the manufacturer.

The dominance of the large integrated enterprise did not, of course, mean the disappearance of the older types of businessmen. Small business remained a basic and essential part of the American economy. The small non-integrated manufacturer, the wholesaler, and retailer have all continued to be active throughout the twentieth century. The number of small businesses has continued to grow with the rapid expansion of the service industries (such as laundries and dry cleaners, service and repair shops not directly tied to the large firm); with the spread of real-estate dealers, insurance agencies, and stock brokerage firms; and with the continuing expansion of the building and construction industries. Throughout the century small businessmen have greatly outnumbered the managers of big business. The former were, therefore, often more politically powerful, particularly in the local politics, than the latter. Economically, however, the managers of the large integrated and often diversified enterprises remained the dominant decision-makers in the urban, industrial, and technologically sophisticated economy of the twentieth century. Their critically significant position has been repeatedly and properly pointed out by economists ever since Adolph A. Berle and Gardner C. Means wrote the first analysis of the role and functions of the modern corporation in 1932.

In many ways, the managers were more of an elite than the earlier businessmen had been. Even though this elite was based on performance rather than birth and played a critically constructive role in building and operating the world's most productive economy, its existence seemed to violate basic American democratic values. At the same time, its control of the central sector of the American economy challenged powerful economic concepts about the efficacy of a free market. After 1930, the managers came to share some of their economic power with others, particularly the federal government. Nevertheless, they were forced to do so *not* because of ideological reasons, but because they failed by themselves to assure the coordination and growth of the economy, the basic activities they had undertaken after 1900.

Until the Depression, the government had played a minimal part in the management of the American economy. The merchants had used the government to assist in financing internal improvements that they found too costly or risky to undertake themselves, and the manufacturers had called upon the government to protect them from foreign competition. Small businessmen—wholesalers and retailers—had joined farmers and workers to use the government to regulate the large corporation, but such regulation did not deter the growth of big business nor significantly alter the activities of the managers. Before the Depression, the government had developed few means to influence consciously the over-all performance of the American economy, the major exception being the creation of a central banking system in 1913.

The Depression clearly demonstrated that the corporation managers alone were unable to provide the coordination and adaptation necessary to sustain a complex, highly differentiated, mass-production, mass-distribution economy. The coming of the Depression itself reflected population and technological developments. Legislation in the 1920's cut immigration from abroad to a tiny flow. After World War I, migration from country to city slowed. Meanwhile, new industries, particularly the electric and automobile industries, reached the limit of demand for their output permitted by the existing size and distribution of the national income. At the same time, improved machinery as well as the more efficient management of production and distribution meant that in still other industries potential supply was becoming greater than existing demand. By the mid-1920's prices had begun to decline. Only the existence of credit helped maintain the economy's momentum until 1929.

Corporate giants, like General Motors, General Electric, and du Pont, fully realized that the demand was leveling off in the 1920's, but they could do little more than maintain production at the existing rate or even cut back a bit. When the 1929 crash dried up credit and reduced demand, they could only roll with the punch. As demand fell, they cut production, laid off men, and canceled orders for supplies and materials. Such actions further reduced purchasing power and demand and led to more cuts in production and more layoffs. The downward pressure continued relentlessly. In less than four years, the national income was slashed in half. The forecasts at General Motors and General Electric for 1932 indicated that, at best, the firms would operate at about 25 per cent capacity.

The only institution capable of stopping this economic descent appeared to be the federal government. During the 1930's it undertook this role, but with great reluctance. Until the recession of 1937, Franklin D. Roosevelt and his Secretary of the Treasury still expected to balance the budget and to bring the end to government intervention in the economy. Roosevelt and his Cabinet considered large-scale government spending and employment only temporary. When Roosevelt decided in 1936 that the Depression was over despite high unemployment, he sharply reduced government expenditures. National income, production, and demand immediately plummeted in 1937. The nation then began to understand more clearly the relationship between government spending and the level of economic activity, although acceptance of the government's role in maintaining economic growth and stability was a decade away.

World War II taught other lessons. The government spent far more than the most enthusiastic New Dealer had ever proposed. Most of the output of these expenditures was destroyed or left on the battlefields of Europe and Asia. But the resulting increased demand sent the nation into a period of prosperity the like of which had never before been seen. Moreover, the supplying of huge armies and navies fighting the most massive war of all time required a tight, centralized control of the national economy. This effort brought corporate managers to Washington to carry out one of the most complex pieces of economic planning in history. That experience lessened the ideological fears over the government's role in stabilizing the economy. This new attitude, embodied in legislation by the Employment Act of 1946, continued to be endorsed by Eisenhower's Republican Administration in the 1950's.

The federal government is now committed to ensuring the revival of investment and demand if, and only if, private enterprise is unable to maintain full employment. In 1949 and again in 1953, 1957, and 1960, the government carried out this role by adjusting its monetary and fiscal policies, building roads, and shifting defense contracts. The continuing Cold War made the task relatively easy by assuring the government ample funds. The new role has been defined so that it meets the needs of the corporate managers. The federal government takes action only if the managers are unable to maintain a high level of aggregate demand; it has not replaced the managers as the major coordinators in the economy, but acts only as a coordinator of last resort.

The Depression helped bring the federal government into the economy in another way. During the late-nineteenth and twentieth centuries, workers, farmers, and (to some extent) retailers, wholesalers, and other small businessmen had formed organizations to help them share in making the economic decisions that most intimately affected their well-being. During the 1930's, when the managers were having difficulties in maintaining economic stability, these numerically larger and more politically influential groups were able to get the federal and state governments to support their claims. Through government intervention many workers acquired a say in determining policies in wages, hours, working rules, promotions, and layoffs; farmers gained control over the prices of several basic commodities; and retailers and wholesalers increased their voice in the pricing of certain goods they sold. Nevertheless, the Wagner Act, the Agricultural Adjustment Acts, the Robinson-Patman Act, and the "fair trading" laws did not seriously infringe on the manager's ability to determine current output and to allocate resources for present and future economic activities.

The growth of organized labor during the twentieth century indicates much about the economic power of the large corporation, for this politically powerful group has been able to impress its will on the decisions of corporate managers only in a limited way. Until the Depression, labor unions had little success in organizing key industries dominated by large, managerially operated enterprises. Even during its first major period of growth at the turn of the century, the American Federation of Labor was not successful in the manufacturing industries. From the start, organized labor's strength lay in mining, transportation, and the building and construction trades. In the manufacturing sector, the Federation's gains came not in factory but small-shop industries, such as cigar, garment, hat, and stove-making and ship-building. During the first quarter of the twentieth century, organized labor acquired its members in those industries where skilled workers achieved their goals by bargaining with many small employers. (The railroads were the exception.) The geographically oriented operating structure developed by the American Federation of Labor unions was admirably suited to this purpose.

Precisely because the craft union had grown up in industries where the factory and the large integrated enterprise had never been dominant, the American Federation of Labor found itself in the 1930's unable to organize, even with strong government support, the mass-production, mass-distribution industries so basic to the operation of the modern economy. To unionize these industries required the creation of a structure to parallel the structure of the large integrated enterprise and a program that appealed to semiskilled rather than skilled workers. The AF of L failed to meet this challenge. Only after "a civil war" within the ranks of labor and the creation of a new national labor organization, the CIO, did the automobile, iron and steel, nonferrous metal, rubber, electrical machinery, and other key industries become fully unionized.

During the great organizing drives of the late-1930's and immediately after World War II, union leaders rarely, if ever, sought to gain more than a voice in the determination of wages and hours, working rules, and hiring as well as promotion and layoff policies. Even when they asked (unsuccessfully) for an opportunity "to look at the company's books," union spokesmen did so primarily with the hope of assuring themselves that they were obtaining what they considered a fair share of the income generated by the firm. The critical issue over which management and labor fought in the years immediately following World War II was whether the managers or the union would control the hiring of workers. The unions almost never asked to take part in decisions about output, pricing, or resources allocation. With the passage of the Taft-Hartley Act of 1947, the managers obtained a control over hiring which has never been seriously challenged. Nor have any further inroads into "management's prerogatives" been seriously proposed.

Since 1950, business managers have continued to make the decisions that most vitally affect the coordination of the economy and the pace of its growth. They have also continued to have a major say in how the economy adapts to external forces generated by population movements and technological change.

Population movements in the 1960's present a different challenge than they did before the 1930's. Migration from abroad has remained only a trickle and that from the country to the city has continued to drop. The move to the suburbs, the most significant post-Depression development, has expanded the urban sprawl and undermined the viability of the central city. The resulting problems are, however, more political and social than economic. Whether government officials are better trained than corporate managers to handle these new problems is open to question. If the business managers fail to meet these new challenges, the government will obviously have to do so.

Meanwhile, technological change has maintained a revolutionary pace. Through their concentration on research and development of new products and new methods of production and distribution, corporate managers have been trained to handle the processes and procedures of technological innovation. The large corporation had so "internalized" the process of innovation that this type of change is no longer simply an outside force to which businessmen and others in the economy adjust. Here the expertise of the business manager covers a broader field than that of governmental or military managers. In most of the costly government programs involving a complex technology, the development and production of new products have been turned over to the large corporations through the contracting process. The federal government does, however, supply the largest share of funds for research and development. Thus, even though the business manager continues to play a critical part in adapting the economy to technological change, government officials are in a position to determine the direction and the areas in which research and development will be concentrated.

This brief history of the role of business in the operation of the American economy suggests several tentative conclusions. From the beginning, it seems, businessmen have run the American economy. They can take the credit and the blame for many of its achievements and failures. They, more than [any] other group in the economy, have managed the production, transportation, and distribution of goods and services. No other group—farmers, blue-collar workers, or white-collar workers—has ever had much to do with the over-all coordination of the economic system or its adaptation to basic changes in population and technology.

Over the two centuries, however, the businessman who ran the economy has changed radically. Dominance has passed from the merchant to the wholesaler, from the wholesaler to the manufacturer, and from the manufacturer to the manager. In the last generation, businessmen have had to share their authority with others, largely with the federal government. Even so, the government's peace-time role still remains essentially a supplementary one, as coordinator of last resort and as a supplier of funds for technological innovation.

In the past, businessmen have devoted their energies to economic affairs, giving far less attention to cultural, social, or even political matters. Precisely because they have created an enormously productive economy and the most affluent society in the world, the non-economic challenges are now becoming more critical than the economic ones. There is little in the recruitment, training, and experience of the present business leaders—the corporate managers—to prepare them for handling the difficult new problems, but unless they do learn to cope with this new situation, they may lose their dominant position in the economy. As was not true of the merchant, wholesaler, or manufacturer, the corporate managers could be replaced by men who are not businessmen. To suggest how and in what way the managers will respond to the current challenges is, fortunately, not the task of the historian. Such analyses are properly left to social scientists and businessmen.

☆ 3 ☆

Women in History

MAINSTREAM OR MINORITY?

American women, astonishing as it sounds, have been "invisible" in the historical literature throughout most of American history. To be sure, there were sometimes quick glimpses in the past of a few famous women in the pages of history books—heroines like Amelia Earhart, authors such as Harriet Beecher Stowe, and reformers like Jane Addams. But by and large one was given the impression that American men had given birth to themselves, and were nurtured and raised by their fellow males. "From reading history in textbooks one would think half our population made only a negligible contribution to history," complained Arthur Schlesinger, Sr., the eminent Harvard historian, in 1922. With the rise of the women's liberation movement in the 1960s, however, there came a dramatic change. Women's groups suddenly became visible to the public eye, and when that happened they became visible to scholars. Since the 1960s there has been a veritable explosion in women's studies and books on the role of women in American culture.

One issue has dogged women's studies, however. There has been a kind of identity crisis regarding the subject as a whole. Was the study of women in history part of the mainstream of American history? Or was women's history to be treated as "minority history"—a history separated and unconnected from "men's history"? Should the findings in women's studies be related to trends in traditional American history? Or should women in history be treated as a subgroup—even though they have comprised half of the American population? Was women's history a subfield of social history? Or was the experience of women so different because of their sex that they should be considered in a completely different category?

The tradition of neglecting women in history was a reflection of

79

the way in which historical writing developed down through the ages. For centuries kings and generals provided the main focus for most historians. In the nineteenth century politicians and businessmen, as they advanced to hold more power, came into greater historical prominence. Women, with the exception of a few queens here and there, had traditionally been excluded from the seats of power and were rarely mentioned in history books as a result.

With the development of American social history in the first half of the twentieth century, however, groups previously ignored by historians—working people, racial and ethnic minorities, and women— were scrutinized more carefully by scholars. But the history of women was still restricted to their struggles for suffrage or for more legal rights because that seemed to be the only part of the story worth telling. Only in the past quarter century have scholars begun to give this important subject the attention it deserves. For this reason women's history in America is still in its infancy.

The development of the field of women's history has been hampered, moreover, by two interrelated factors: the lack of any general conceptual scheme to show the direction in which social changes were moving; and the lack of agreement on assumptions regarding the field as a whole. Despite these persistent problems historians have managed to make some scholarly contributions on the subject.

In chronological terms historical writings about women in America may be broken down roughly into four stages. First, there was the formative stage—1607–1900—during which initial steps were taken to write works and to collect materials for a more systematic study of the role of women in society. Second, the Progressive stage of historiography—1900 to the end of World War II—when many but not all of the writings were produced or influenced by Progressive historians. Third, the preparatory period—the mid-1940s to 1960—when a number of fine scholarly works were written, but during which women's studies remained a subfield of American history. Finally, the contemporary period—1960 to the present—when women's studies came into its own as a major field and witnessed an outpouring of books on the subject.

During the formative stage in the seventeenth and eighteenth centuries almost nothing was written about women and women's history. Lacking the right to vote and absent from the seats of power, women were not considered an important force in history. Anne Bradstreet wrote some significant poetry in the seventeenth century, Mercy Otis Warren produced the best contemporary history of the American Revolution, and Abigail Adams penned important letters showing she exercised great political influence over her husband, John. But little or no notice was taken of these women and their contributions. During these first two centuries women remained invisible in history books.

Throughout the nineteenth century this lack of visibility continued despite the efforts of female authors writing about members of their own sex. These writers, like most of their male counterparts, were amateur historians. Their writings were celebratory in nature and they were uncritical in their selection and use of sources.

During the nineteenth century, however, certain feminists showed a keen sense of history by keeping records of activities in which women were engaged. National, regional, and local women's organizations compiled accounts of their doings. Personal correspondence, newspaper clippings, and souvenirs were saved and stored. These sources form the core of the two greatest collections for women's history in America—one at the Elizabeth and Arthur Schlesinger Library at Radcliffe College, and the other the Sophia Smith Collection at Smith College. Such sources provided valuable materials for later generations of historians.

Throughout the nineteenth century most of the writing about women conformed to the "great women" theory of history, just as much of mainstream American history concentrated on "great men." To demonstrate that women were making significant contributions to American life, female authors singled out women leaders and wrote biographies, or else important women produced their autobiographies. Most leaders were involved in public life either as reformers, suffragettes, or authors, and were not representative at all of the great mass of ordinary women. The lives of ordinary women remained untold in the American histories being published for the most part.

Elizabeth Cady Stanton wrote what was surely the most famous women's document of the nineteenth century when she framed the Declaration of Sentiments for the women's rights convention held in Seneca Falls, New York, in 1848. She deliberately shaped the document to echo the language in the Declaration of Independence—though within a different context. "We held these truths to be self-evident: that all men and women are created equal," she wrote. In a brilliant paraphrase she suggested that the male sex dominated women in the same way George III had oppressed the colonists. It was a masterful propaganda stroke and fired the imagination of those present. Stanton, along with Susan B. Anthony, a colleague in the woman's suffrage movement, helped to compile the first three volumes of the *History of Woman Suffrage* and published them from 1881 to 1886. Two years later Stanton produced her memoirs, *Eighty Years or More*, which defined her particular brand of feminism and proclaimed it to be the dominant one for her era.

Susan B. Anthony, Stanton's close friend and collaborator, was equally anxious to spread her ideas through her writings. She not only contributed a fourth volume to the *History of Woman Suffrage,* but used her personal funds to buy up most of the first edition and presented the volumes to colleges and universities. In 1908 a three-volume work entitled *Life and Work of Susan B. Anthony* was produced by Ida Husted Harper, an editor who had worked on the women's suffrage series.

Stanton and Anthony identified themselves with a particular brand of feminism, one that was shaped by a special set of circumstances and carried with it certain assumptions. By background they were both middle class, educated, and white. They may be seen as the first generation of equal-rights feminists—women who came to their sweeping assessment of the subordination of women through their participation in the reform movements for abolitionism and temperance. Their demand for equality sprang from their frustration in seeking moral reforms that could not be realized without legislative and judicial change. Their inability to bring about such change led them to search for a constituency or group that might support such reforms—the first such constituency being black, the second the working-class movement, and the final one middle-class women who were interested mainly in gaining the right to vote.

While groping their way to this final constituency both women were radicalized by a series of events. First, by the rejection of the women's cause by black men and by fellow white male reformers. Second, by their hostile encounters with members of the trade union movement. And finally, by their contacts and brief alignment with Victoria Woodhull—an American editor who supported such controversial issues as women's suffrage, free love, and socialism. These developments led Stanton and Anthony to adopt a conspiracy theory in their account of the women's suffrage movement. They attributed the delays in securing the vote to two groups: male politicians, who were fearful of the women's vote; and to the liquor interest, which worried lest enfranchised women might impose prohibition.[1]

A different brand of feminism was espoused by Frances Willard, showing that the Stanton-Anthony conspiracy theory was not necessarily sound. Willard's attitudes were shaped by a different set of circumstances. Coming from a poor family and an isolated rural background in New York State, Willard differed from most nineteenth-century reformers who were drawn from the middle class and hailed from urban areas. She discovered her constituency with relative ease

---

[1]The foregoing analysis was drawn largely from Jill K. Conway's excellent bibliography, *The Female Experience in Eighteenth- and Nineteenth-Century America* (New York, 1982), p. 199.

among Methodist women in the West. Willard, who had a genius for
organization, helped to mobilize these women around a movement for
temperance reform. Her own experiences and those of other leaders in
the Women's Christian Temperance Union were described in two
books—her autobiography, *Glimpses of Fifty Years*, published in 1889,
and her *Portraits and Biographies of Prominent American Women*,
written with a colleague and issued twelve years later.

Willard's writings showed that her attitudes and those of her compatriots were at some variance with the ideas of Stanton and Anthony,
the equal-rights feminists. Willard's interests extended to a number of
different reforms including suffrage, women's dress, and labor reform—though her main focus remained on temperance. She stressed
the religious roots and motivation of her movement and its effect in
preserving the woman's sphere in the home. Willard's brand of feminism, therefore, was interested less in raising women to an equal status with men and more in simply enhancing the authority of women.

The writings by and on these nineteenth-century women were representative of an entire genre that dealt with other important female
figures. Some were eulogistic biographies of women involved in reform
movements: Dorothea Dix, who was interested in the care of the insane; Lucretia Mott, the Quaker abolitionist; and the Grimke sisters,
who were involved in both abolitionism and the women's rights movement. Others dealt with leading literary figures, such as Harriet Beecher
Stowe and Margaret Fuller. Catharine Beecher, on the other hand, made
her national reputation by writing a housekeeping manual in which
she portrayed domestic life as the very foundation of a stable democracy.[2]

There was relatively little writing or attention paid, however, to
working-class women. Lucy Larcom, a factory textile worker in Lowell, Massachusetts, left a classic autobiography, *A New England Girl-
hood*, published in 1889, telling of her experiences. In her book Larcom
described firsthand the boardinghouse system, the attempts to organize mill workers, and the creation of a local female culture. Daniel D.
Addison five years later wrote the story of Larcom's life and published
a collection of her letters.[3]

Carroll Wright, the first United States Commissioner of Labor,

---

[2]Francis Tiffany, *Life of Dorothea Lynde Dix* (Boston, 1892); Anna Hallowell, ed.,
James and Lucretia Mott (Boston, 1884); Catherine H. Birney, *The Grimke Sisters* (Boston, 1885); Theodore Weld, *In Memory: Angelina Grimke Weld* (Boston, 1880); Charles
E. Stowe, *Harriet Beecher Stowe* (Boston, 1890); Annie Fields, *Life and Letters of Harriet
Beecher Stowe* (Boston, 1898); Thomas W. Higginson, *Margaret Fuller Ossoli* (Boston,
1884); Julia Ward Howe, *Margaret Fuller* (Boston, 1890); and Catharine Beecher, *A Trea-
tise on Domestic Economy* (Boston, 1841).

[3]Daniel D. Addison, *Lucy Larcom* (Boston, 1894).

meanwhile, was compiling invaluable information on the conditions of women's employment in his *Industrial Evolution of the United States,* issued in 1895. Although there were great masses of ordinary women in the society undergoing different experiences—immigrant women; women from different ethnic, racial, and religious groups; and women suffering the rigors of the frontier—for the most part, they escaped the attention of historians until 1900.

During the second stage of writing on women's history—1900 to the mid-1940s—much but not all of the writing reflected the work or influence of four major Progressive historians—Mary R. Beard, Charles A. Beard, Arthur M. Schlesinger, Sr., and Frederick Jackson Turner. The Progressive historians, generally speaking, dominated the field of American history from the turn of the century down to the end of World War II. Stressing class and sectional conflict as major interpretive themes they rewrote the outlines of American history as a whole. When it came to writing women's history they stressed these same themes, and emphasized social and economic factors as the most important forces operating in history. The Progressive historians tended also to take a more materialistic approach in explaining the workings of history. Besides such attitudes these scholars were professionally trained historians and introduced a more scholarly and conceptual approach in the writing of women's history.

During the first four and a half decades of the twentieth century, moreover, conditions changed the climate of opinion regarding the status of women. Writers in the seventeenth and eighteenth centuries had viewed the women's sphere as being confined to domestic affairs and being divinely ordained. Throughout most of the nineteenth century writers felt that the woman's place was in the home. But in the first half of the twentieth century a different spirit was abroad in the land. In economic terms women entered industry in massive numbers—especially during World War I and World War II. Politically women received the vote in 1920 and became a force to be reckoned with at the polls. Socially, in these decades, a more liberated woman emerged in the form of the flapper—an archetype who became a symbol for greater sexual and social freedom. These changes helped to set the stage for a different approach in the writing of women's history.

Mary R. Beard, for example, developed an important theory of women's history in her *Woman as Force in History,* a remarkable, wide-ranging book. Written at the very end of the Progressive stage of historiography—in 1946—this work advanced a broad conceptual approach for giving women a more prominent place in history. Mary Beard's main argument was that the endless subjugation women had had to endure throughout world history had caused them to misunderstand their strength in the past. Women had internalized this myth of secondary status and had built this analysis into their view of themselves. By stressing only the obstacles to their fulfillment as persons rather than their strengths, women had been prevented from understanding the potential power they had held down through the ages.

Mary Beard went on to propose an outline of world history—one that would describe the contributions women had made to world civilization in their roles as rulers, queens, teachers, abbesses, and builders of institutions. She was concerned primarily with the role and effect of women operating in the public world rather than in the domestic sphere. Because she believed in the inevitability of democratic progress she conceptualized the reconstruction of women's history in which their role as a civilizing force would be stressed. She had great faith, moreover, that the women of her day were about to cast off their chains and to emerge as leaders in the progress of civilization.[4]

During the Great Depression of the 1930s Mary Beard wrote two books that laid the groundwork for her major work of the following decade. In 1931 she published *On Understanding Women*. In 1933 she wrote *America through Women's Eyes* to show how differently American history looked when seen from a female point of view.

Mary Beard also coauthored a two-volume work with Charles Beard, *The Rise of American Civilization*, in 1927—one of the most influential college textbooks of its time. The Beards insisted upon the importance of public life, in part because of their focus on power as a major motivating force in history. For this reason they viewed women's roles as crucial and presented a whole range of women's contributions in the field of politics, economics, and religion. Through their efforts the Beards succeeded in moving women's history somewhat closer to the mainstream of American history.

Arthur Schlesinger, Sr., another Progressive historian, was also a prime mover in the attempts to bring women's studies nearer to the mainstream. In his *New Viewpoints of American History*, published in 1922, Schlesinger protested that most standard textbooks left women out of their treatment of American history. They therefore gave the impression that women had not made any worthwhile contributions to American history. "Before accepting the truth of this assumption," Schlesinger went on, "the facts of our history need to be raked over from a new point of view." Schlesinger then added, "It should not be forgotten that all great historians have been men and were likely therefore to be more influenced by a sex interpretation of history all the

---

[4]Ann D. Gordon, Mari Jo Buhle, and Nancy Schrom, "Women in Society," *Radical America* 5 (1971):4–5.

more potent because [it was] unconscious."[5] In *The Rise of the American City*, published in 1933, Schlesinger devoted an entire chapter to women's history. He sought to place women's history in the mainstream rather than have it treated as a kind of minority history. Despite his challenge and the example he set Schlesinger's call went largely unheeded by his academic colleagues.

Although Frederick Jackson Turner did not deal directly with women's studies his influence could be seen in several major books published during the Progressive stage. One was Arthur W. Calhoun's *Social History of the American Family*, a three-volume work published from 1917 to 1919. For decades this work remained the classic study of the American family. Calhoun's discussion of courting customs, marriage, and the family within the various sections of the country was clearly derived from Turner. Although Calhoun's statistics about early marriages in colonial times, fertility rates, and family size were found by present-day historians to be inaccurate, it was a pioneering work in its time in terms of the questions it raised.

Turner's influence was also evident in the work of Richard B. Morris whose *Studies in the History of American Law*, published in 1930, employed a Turnerian approach to demonstrate how frontier conditions in the colonies brought about changes in British law. Morris showed how American courts stretched the letter and spirit of British law to allow women greater latitude in marriage contracts, property holding, and property settlements. In his *Government and Labor in Early America*, published in 1946, Morris also integrated valuable information regarding the status of women in colonial times.

Throughout the Progressive stage there were a number of important works by other historians showing the significant contributions that women made to economic and social life in colonial days. Elizabeth Dexter in *Colonial Women of Affairs*, published in 1924, ransacked newspapers and business directories to reconstruct the working lives of women in colonial times, and revealed a wide range of female skills and occupations. In *Women in Eighteenth-Century America*, issued in 1935, Mary Benson contributed a pioneering work on the subject. Julia Cherry Spruill's *Women's Life and Work in the Southern Colonies*, which appeared in 1938, was another scholarly work covering women during the colonial period.

One of the major works to appear stressing the influence of ideas in marriage and the family in colonial New England was Edmund Morgan's *Puritan Family*, published in 1944. Morgan's book provided a sensitive portrait of how Puritanism defined a woman's rights within mar-

---

[5] Arthur M. Schlesinger, Sr., *New Viewpoints in American History* (New York, 1922), p. 126.

riage as well as her relations with her husband. His work was a superb synthesis and demonstrated how intellectual history, religious history, and women's history could be integrated.

As America matured and women began moving out of the home and into the factory other scholars focused on the impact of industrialization on women's lives. The work of Helen Sumner was of the utmost importance in this regard. She edited, along with John Commons and others, the fifth and sixth volumes of *Documentary History of American Industrial Society*, an eleven-volume work issued in 1910. Sumner also produced a major study entitled "Women in Industry in the United States," which was later incorporated into the nineteen-volume *Report on the Condition of Women and Child Wage Earners in the United States*, issued in 1910.

In another important economic study, *Women in Industry*, which also appeared in 1910, Edith Abbott surveyed the working conditions of women in certain industries—textiles, printing, and cigar-making. The position of women in these businesses, Abbott concluded, was undermined by the steady process of mechanization. Abbott pointed out, moreover, the increasing disparity that took place between men's and women's wages in jobs within these industries.

From the turn of the century to the end of World War II—the period labeled the Progressive stage of historiography—women's history had made considerable progress. Some outstanding scholars had contributed important works and had begun promoting the cause of women's history. Despite the advances made, however, the field still lay outside the accepted confines of the discipline as a whole. Women were still "invisible" whenever scholars discussed the most important forces or groups shaping American history.

The preparatory period from the mid-1940s to 1960 witnessed the appearance of two works, one in France and the other in the United States, which set the stage for the contemporary period to come. Simone de Beauvoir's *The Second Sex*, written by France's outstanding philosopher intellectual, was a wide-ranging work of stunning brilliance. De Beauvoir postulated a grand synthesis of all previous feminist arguments, and described women's subordinate position and status in all known societies in Western culture. Although Beauvoir's monumental book failed to exercise a decisive influence on feminist thinkers when it first appeared in America in translation in 1953, it had a great impact in subsequent years.

De Beauvoir argued that in every known society persons were assigned specific roles and indoctrinated to perform to certain expectations established within their respective societies. For women this process invariably meant socialization to a value system that imposed upon them greater restrictions regarding their range of choices than those imposed upon men. This meant that women had been socialized to fit into institutions created, shaped, and controlled by men. The definitions of selfhood and fulfillment by women as a result always remained subordinate to patriarchal concepts. In this sense women everywhere have always been "the second sex," and relegated to a position comparable to that of racial minorities. De Beauvoir's book helped to radicalize the thought of many American feminist theorists of the 1960s.

The most important book written in America during the preparatory period was Eleanor Flexner's *Century of Struggle,* published in 1959. Her work covered the women's rights movement from 1820 to 1920, when the fight for the right to vote was finally successful. Flexner's book was no narrow history of the women's rights movement. It provided a synthesis of women's history by setting the subject within the broad context of the labor movement and other reform movements. The questions Flexner raised, her meticulous research, and her carefully couched conclusion that after a century of agitation for their rights women had made only relatively modest gains, prepared the way for the next generation of historians of women.

The impact of Flexner's pioneering effort was not immediately apparent, however. At the start of the contemporary period beginning in the 1960s David Potter, the distinguished American historian, was still calling attention to the invisibility of women in American history. He challenged the generally held assumption that historical events in America applied equally to both men and women. Pointing to the Turner thesis Potter commented that in almost all the accounts that thesis was shown to apply to men alone. The city, not the countryside, was the "frontier" that provided the greatest opportunities for women, Potter argued.[6]

The contemporary period of women's studies began under a different set of circumstances. Developments during the early 1960s on both the international and domestic fronts created new conditions outside of the scholar's study that affected the writing of history. Changes inside the scholar's study—within the historical profession itself—also brought about new assumptions, approaches, and techniques within the discipline.

On the international front the high point had been reached in America's confidence as a world leader. The assumption kept growing that the American model was the path along which all modern soci-

---

[6]David Potter, "National Character," in *American History and Social Science,* Edward Saveth, ed. (New York, 1964), p. 427.

eties would probably develop until they had reached the relatively perfected democracy found within the United States. This view of America as world leader created a more sympathetic environment for the
emergence of the women's liberation movement that burst upon the
American scene in the late 1960s. American women were seen as making gains not only for themselves but for women throughout the world.

On the domestic front a series of changes by the mid-1960s also
signaled that the day of a new feminism was at hand. A government
commission appointed by President Kennedy published a report in 1963
documenting the widespread discrimination against women when
seeking employment, educational opportunities, or political advancement. In that same year the publication of Betty Friedan's best-selling
The Feminine Mystique gave evidence that modern feminism had
emerged as an important topic in the public mind. In 1964 Congress
added the word *sex* in the Civil Rights Act, thereby prohibiting discrimination against women in employment. The founding of the National Organization for Women (NOW) under the presidency of Betty
Friedan in 1966, proclaimed the appearance of a new mass movement
for the civil rights of women. This newfound public interest in wom-
en's issues had the effect of raising the consciousness of historians in
writing about women's history in a more serious and scholarly vein.

At the same time changes taking place within the historical profession itself also affected the writing of women's history. The women's
liberation movement and the rise of the "new social historians" occurred more or less simultaneously. Many of the influences affecting
the "new social historians"—the *Annales* school of French historians
with its emphasis on demographic and multidisciplinary methods, the
renewed interest in the findings of the social and behavioral sciences,
and the resort to new computer and quantification techniques—affected women's studies as well. Thus the writing of women's history
followed the methodological innovations generally affecting the field
of American history as a whole.

The sheer quantity of writing on women's history in the 1960s,
1970s, and 1980s has been so great that it is impossible in so short a
space to discuss meaningfully the many scholarly works produced. The
most useful way, perhaps, of surveying the work that was done is to
deal with several of the major themes set forth.

One major theme concerned the changes in the status of women
in American society over time. Betty Friedan's *The Feminine Mystique*
led the way with a forceful statement of the situation as she saw it
during the 1950s on the eve of the women's liberation movement. The
legal fiction of equal political rights for women, she wrote, masked a
culture that still assigned women to a separate sphere of domestic life.
Thus those women who pursued a career, sought an education, or tried

for political office were somehow made to feel guilty and unfeminine. There existed a mystique of feminine fulfillment in America, she said, a mystique about how women were supposed to act and feel when they were sexually defined as women. Friedan then analyzed the life-style of educated middle-class housewives who were pursuing this so-called feminine mystique with its emphasis on domesticity, conformity, and consumerism. Most of them found their lives to be empty, boring, and unsatisfying, she concluded. Her book raised the consciousness of millions of women, and in so doing helped to launch the women's liberation movement.[7]

Academics soon picked up the subject of the status of women and set it within a historical context. Gerda Lerner, a leading scholar, wrote a series of articles and books tracing the status of women throughout the whole course of American history. Among other things Lerner focused on the age of Jackson in the 1830s as a critical turning point in women's status because of the advent of industrialization. Newly built textile factories in New England required great numbers of workers, she noted. For the first time thousands of young farm girls left their homes and moved to milltowns to live and work in what became a predominantly female labor force. In the course of her exploration of another subject—female reformers—Lerner observed that women involved in one reform quite often became interested in other movements. It was their participation in the antislavery movement, she pointed out, that ultimately led the Grimke sisters of South Carolina to become involved in feminist reforms. To further encourage the study and teaching of women's history Lerner also wrote a number of historiographical works, thereby helping to introduce this important subject into the college curriculum.[8]

The issue of women's status soon gave rise to a major historiographical controversy as to whether women were better off in the colonial period than either their descendants in nineteenth-century America or their contemporaries in England. Older works had claimed that conditions for women were more favorable in earlier times for several reasons. The number of women was small during the early days of settlement, and work by all hands, male and female, was desperately needed simply for survival. Distinctions between sex roles could not be tolerated under such circumstances, the argument ran. Women engaged in whatever occupations they wished, and encountered few legal

[7]Betty Friedan, *The Feminine Mystique* (New York, 1963).

[8]Gerda Lener, "The Lady and the Mill-Girl: Changes in the Status of Women in the Age of Jackson," *Mid-Continent American Studies Journal* 10 (1969):5–15; *The Grimke Sisters from South Carolina* (Boston, 1967); *The Female Experience*, (Indianapolis, 1977); and *The Majority Finds Its Past* (New York, 1979).

or social restraints if they sought work outside the home. Moreover, the high sex ratio of men over women—especially in the Southern colonies—presumably gave women a better bargaining position in the marriage market. Children at the time were viewed as assets because they became part of the labor force on family farms. As a result women and their work were highly prized by men and by society at large. Colonial women, it was argued, were also better off than their English counterparts. English common law, which restricted women's independence, was never fully enforced in the American colonies, or else it was circumvented.[9]

This theory of a "golden age" for women in colonial times was fully developed by the mid-1940s and was later incorporated into the scholarship on women's studies in the 1960s and 1970s. The interpretation was often used to contrast the condition of women in the nineteenth century and to demonstrate that a loss of status had taken place. In short, the "golden age" hypothesis held that the position of women had declined between the seventeenth and nineteenth centuries. What was at issue were two questions: What periodization should be employed in any analysis of women's studies? And what changes had the position of women undergone—had it improved, declined, or remained unchanged? By implication the "golden age" theory placed women somewhat closer to the mainstream of American history by assuming that the distinctions between men and women in the colonial period were relatively negligible.

Mary Beth Norton, in an important article published in 1984, took issue with this older interpretation. She suggested a three-stage periodization to reflect more precisely women's experiences in the past. First came the initial period of settlement—from the 1620s to about 1660—when the American patterns of family and community were being laid down, and during which time women in the colonies were more dependent on the family than their counterparts in England. The second stage—1660 to 1750—was a period of transition, an era when American patterns were reinforced and reshaped. Finally there was the third period—1750 to 1815—when other changes occurred in women's lives and altered the definition of their role in society.

Norton concluded that there was no such "golden age" in the colonial period, and that during the revolutionary era, in particular,

---

[9]The following works presented the golden age interpretation: Elizabeth Dexter, *Colonial Women of Affairs* (Boston, 1924); Richard B. Morris, *Studies in the History of American Law* (New York, 1930); Herbert Moller, "Sex Composition and Correlated Culture Patterns of Colonial America," *William and Mary Quarterly*, 3d ser. 2 (1945):113–153; Mary R. Beard, *Woman as Force in History* (New York, 1946); and Roger Thompson, *Stuart England and America* (London, 1974).

changes took place that increased the autonomy of women. The changes in women's roles in society occurred without conscious intent, and were caused by trends taking place within the society as a whole. These changes were so great, Norton claimed, that the country embarked upon a public dialogue on the subject of women and what their proper role in society should be. Norton's provocative thesis tended to view women more as a minority group within American society, and sparked a major controversy regarding women's changing status in the post-revolutionary period.[10]

The main disagreement over women's status after the Revolution was between Norton and Linda Kerber, whose book *Women in the Republic* was published in 1980. Kerber contended that changes in the postwar period decreased rather than increased women's autonomy. In the post-revolutionary era it was believed that a successful republic had to be based on virtuous families. Such families obviously could be created only by virtuous mothers. The model of a republican mother, according to Kerber, tended therefore to retard changes in the post-revolutionary period. This conclusion obviously placed her in direct opposition to Norton's hypothesis of change.[11]

A further hypothesis, called "the cult of domesticity," emerged both in women's studies and in the new and developing discipline of family history. This concept dealt with the status of women from the 1830s and beyond. The "cult of domesticity" constituted a cluster of social attitudes that confined the role of women to the domestic sphere within the home. This sphere was in sharp contrast to the man's sphere, which lay outside in the business world. The sharp difference between the two spheres made the distinction between the respective sex roles more rigid. Within the domestic ideology—an ideology identified mainly with white middle-class women—the traditional family was seen as consisting of the mother, father, and children grouped together within a private household. The family's influence reached outward, affecting the status of the church and state in the society, and inward, helping to shape the character of the individuals involved.

---

[10]Mary Beth Norton, "The Evolution of White Women's Experience in Early America," *American Historical Review* 89 (1984):593–619. For a regional breakdown of a discussion of women's roles, see: Laurel Ulrich, *Good Wives* (New York, 1982), which covers roughly Norton's second stage; Lois Green Carr and Lorena Walsh, "The Planter's Wife: Experiences of White Women in Seventeenth-Century Maryland," *William and Mary Quarterly*, 3d ser. 34 (1977):542–571; and Michael Zuckerman, ed., *Friends and Neighbors* (Philadelphia, 1982).

[11]See Mary Beth Norton's article and her book, *Liberty's Daughters* (Boston, 1980), and Linda Kerber, *Women of the Republic* (Chapel Hill, 1980). See also Joan Hoff-Wilson, "The Illusion of Change: Women and the Revolution," in *The American Revolution*, Alfred Young, ed. (DeKalb, Ill., 1976).

Within the "cult of domesticity" great importance was placed upon woman's role as wife, mother, and manager of the household. The ideology both observed and prescribed accepted behavior for women in domestic life; it glorified the home and the woman's role within it.

But while this idealization placed women on a pedestal, the "cult of domesticity" gave women a limited role to play: it confined them to the home and relegated them to a sex-specific role. Women were to be subordinate to men both in marriage and within society at large. They were also at a profound disadvantage in schools, churches, and in the workplace. When it came to politics they were virtually impotent. Once they were married women had almost no legal existence separate from their husbands. They could not sue, write contracts, or even execute wills on their own. Their persons, estates, and wages were considered to be those of their husbands. Divorce was theoretically possible, but given the social constraints of the time relatively rare. Although women did not have the right to vote they were subject to all the laws of the land.[12]

But as Nancy Cott pointed out in her superb book *Bonds of Womanhood,* published in 1977, the decade of the 1830s presented a paradox. At the same time women were being held down the period proved to be an important turning point in terms of their economic involvement, public participation, and social visibility. During the 1830s women entered the industrial labor force in large numbers for the first time. Middle-class women took up their one political weapon—the petition—to demand legislation to enable wives to retain rights over their property and earnings. Moreover they entered into a variety of reform movements to pursue goals in their own self-interest (women's rights) as well as to improve society at large (antislavery).

These historiographical controversies in women's studies made it clear that the business of measuring women's "status" at any given time was a complex matter. It was obvious, too, that the story of women's status could not be written in linear terms. Neither a history that postulated a straight-line decline nor a progressive development that showed women's status improving in an onward and upward direction would prove satisfactory.[13] Thus the lack of a general conceptual

---

[12]The concept of a "cult of domesticity" grew out of the article by Barbara Welter, "The Cult of True Womanhood, 1820–1860," *American Quarterly* 18 (1966):151–174; Aileen Kraditor introduced the phrase in her readings book, *Up the Pedestal* (Chicago, 1968). See also Nancy Cott, *The Bonds of Womanhood* (New Haven, 1977), from which most of the foregoing account is drawn, as well as Cott's edited work, *Root of Bitterness* (New York, 1972), which brings together fifty documents covering the social history of women from the colonial period to the twentieth century.

[13]Suzanne Lebsock's *Free Women of Petersburg* (New York, 1984) provides a good discussion of this problem.

scheme within which developments in women's history could be placed continued to cause problems.

The status of women was obviously conditioned by their role as wives and mothers, and as a result the subfield of family history made its appearance. As part of the "new social history" family history concerned itself with the role of women in marriage, the family, and as parents. Many scholars in this field suggested that there had been an increased emphasis on love as a prerequisite to marriage beginning in the period after the 1750s. Prior to that time, it was said, marriages were more in the nature of property settlements or economic alliances arranged mainly by parents. After the 1750s there seemed to be a greater emphasis on the notion of marriage as a romantic union. For both men and women the goal of marriage appeared to be the pursuit of happiness rather than the pursuit of property. Family historians consequently focused on those factors that shaped the family: courtship customs, fertility rates, childbearing practices, demographic patterns that indicated the sex ratio between men and women in a given area, the social organization within the household, and the concept of the family cycle.

The work of family historians in America was shaped to a large degree by the studies of foreign scholars—the *Annales* school in France and the work of Phillipe Aries in particular; the findings of Peter Laslett in England; and the research of an English-born scholar, Lawrence Stone, who came to America. *Centuries of Childhood*, Aries's pathbreaking work published in 1962, profoundly changed the view of the family in past times. In it he advanced the hypothesis that the modern concept of childhood in European culture began as late as the seventeenth century. The notion of childhood as a separate stage of development, therefore, appears to have been a relatively recent phenomenon. Laslett's work made a crucial distinction between household and family, showing that in preindustrial England people living under one roof were not always members of a family. Stone, on the other hand, dealt with English attitudes about family, sex, and marriage from the 1500s to the 1800s. He thereby provided a context for subsequent American developments in his *The Family, Sex, and Marriage in England, 1500 to 1800*, published in 1977.

Philip Greven led the way in America with his intensive analysis of colonial families living within a single community—Andover, Massachusetts. In his *Four Generations*, which appeared in 1970, Greven introduced the concept of a family life cycle. Greven found that there was a distinct relationship between landholding patterns and demographic trends in Andover. Landholding patterns often led to the development of what he termed a "modified extended family." His findings revised the idea of a nuclear family in colonial America pictured in an earlier work by Bernard Bailyn—*Education in the Forming of an American Society*. Bailyn has postulated a rapid erosion of parental authority within the presumed nuclear family in colonial America because the frontier and other economic opportunities pulled children away from the home. Greven discovered instead that in the modified extended family, family members although not gathered in a single household, often lived in close proximity to one another. This situation developed because fathers in the first generation, while still living, refused to relinquish their lands to their sons and thereby maintained parental control. Only in the third and fourth generations when the local lands were taken up did sons begin to move away from Andover and beyond parental authority. Greven pointed out, moreover, that it was important to build the picture of the family with systematic comparisons drawn from one generation to the next. Then, and only then, could one see the life cycles through which the family moved over time.[14]

The concept of family life cycle was broadened by Tamara Hareven who undertook studies of individual families over time as opposed to scholars who assumed that a single point in time revealed by a particular census or tax record would supply researchers with an accurate picture of family patterns. Working with nineteenth-century records Hareven showed that the same families exhibited quite different household patterns over time. Boarders and lodgers, for example, were present at some stages in a family cycle of those residing in nineteenth-century industrial cities and absent in others. Thus the patterns of family life cycle were not simple expressions of biological time affecting such matters as fertility and aging. They were also expressions of social patterns that varied according to an internal logic of their own. Historians of the individual life cycle, such as Erik Erikson, had shown that life stages such as childhood and adolescence were socially as well as biologically defined. Hareven suggested that the same might be true for the family life cycle.[15]

Demographic studies also changed the picture of the attitudes and knowledge we have of the American family. We now know that there was a steady decline in fertility rates from 7.04 births in 1800 to 3.56 births in 1900. The growth of population for the country as a whole,

---

[14]See also Philip Greven, *The Protestant Temperament* (New York, 1977), in which the author resorted to an intellectual history approach to produce a major reinterpretation of child-rearing practices in early America. His paradigm was based on three distinct personality types or temperaments—the evangelical, moderate, and the genteel—all derived from child-rearing practices within Protestant families.

[15]John Modell and Tamara K. Hareven, "Urbanization and the Malleable Household: Boarding and Lodging in Nineteenth-Century Families," *Journal of Marriage and the Family* 35 (August 1973):467–479.

therefore, was the result of immigration and not from high birth rates among the native-born. From this demographic data historians inferred certain assumptions regarding sexual behavior in the nineteenth century. There is clear evidence that the native-born were limiting family size by some means. According to Daniel Scott Smith, a historical demographer, women influenced the decision to control fertility in the nineteenth century by insisting upon abstinence from intercourse in marriage.[16]

Family history was affected not only by analytical tools like the concept of family life cycle, but also by major factors that influenced the course of American history as a whole—race, ethnicity, considerations of class, urbanization, and regionalism. In terms of race black families obviously had different experiences than white families, especially when living under slavery. In *Black Family in Slavery and Freedom, 1750–1925* Herbert Gutman examined the role of black women and men and concluded that Afro-Americans managed to create a stable and successful family structure even under slave conditions. The black family not only survived the transition to freedom but continued in the northern urban ghetto—at least until 1925 when Gutman's study ended. Black family patterns were also discussed in Eugene Genovese's *The World the Slaveholders Made*, published in 1969, and his *Roll, Jordan, Roll*, published in 1974.[17] Other groups undoubtedly had different experiences from those of white middle-class families upon whom historians focused primarily, and scholars have only recently begun to investigate this area.

Ethnicity was equally important in studying family history because immigrant families arriving in America invariably underwent different experiences from those of "native stock" families. Immigration was an ongoing phenomenon, and the acculturation of foreign-born families was a continuous process throughout American history. Family patterns obviously differed from one ethnic group to another: in some the women ventured out of their homes to work, and in others they did not; in some a high premium was placed on marriage within the ethnic group, and in others the insistence on such a union disap-

---

[16]Daniel Scott Smith, "Family Limitation, Sexual Control, and Domestic Feminism in Victorian America," in *Clio's Consciousness Raised*, Mary Hartman and Lois Banner, eds. (New York, 1974), pp. 119–136.

[17]Gerda Lerner brought together documents bearing on black women in *Black Women in White America* (New York, 1972). Franklin E. Frazier's older study, *The Negro Family in the United States* (Chicago, 1939), which postulated a black matriarchy theory, occasioned considerable controversy. For a brilliant analysis of white men's attitudes toward the presumed heightened sexuality of black women, see Winthrop Jordan, *White Over Black* (Chapel Hill, 1968).

peared rather quickly; in some childbearing practices lingered for generations, while in others such practices were Americanized in short
order.

There is as yet no comprehensive history of immigrant women in
America, and information on ethnic families is rather scattered and
scant. Besides older works such as Calhoun's *A Social History of the
American Family* and Sophonisba Breckinridge's *The Family and the
State*, published in 1934, the single most useful study was Charles H.
Bindel and Robert W. Habenstein, eds., *Ethnic Families in America*,
which appeared in 1976. This work described sex roles, childbearing
practices, fertility, and intergenerational changes in fifteen different
ethnic groups. The "new ethnicity" and women's liberation movements of the 1960s and 1970s sparked a number of specialized studies
about various ethnic family groups, and this field no doubt will become a fertile one for study in the future.

Class was as significant a variable as ethnicity in studying family
history. With the emphasis that the "new social historians" were placing on the heretofore inarticulate groups in American society, scholars
began paying more attention to working-class family life. One book
that successfully combined a number of variables—class, ethnicity, sex,
age, and generational change—to analyze the relationship between
family life and industrialized labor was Tamara Hareven's *Family Time
and Industrial Time*, published in 1982.

Hareven's work was revisionist in nature and sought to demolish
the myth that industrialization destroyed traditional family ties. Studying the relationships between a textile company and its employees in
a single New England community during the half-century prior to the
1930s, Hareven concluded that the family as a cooperative unit did not
decline. Despite the rise of specialization and the advent of new machinery families continued to perform useful functions in a cooperative way. Families recruited their kinfolk, instructed them in work routines, and allowed workers to cover for one another when breaks from
industrial routines were needed. French Canadians were the dominant
ethnic group in the company, and Canadian-born women were more
likely to work than married women from Eastern Europe. Women's
work usually stopped not so much because of marriage but at a stage
of motherhood, so there was, indeed, some correlation between family
time and factory time. Family patterns changed over generations, but
immigrant households tended to rely to a greater extent on the income
of working children than native-born workers who were better off. Hareven discovered, moreover, that there was a developing sense of working-
class consciousness in this labor force. Worker reactions on a collective
basis were not uncommon, and showed that later generations of in-

dustrial workers were less submissive than the first wave of workers from preindustrial regions.[18]

Family history presented yet another problem: the existence of several differing regional traditions of family. According to William Taylor's *Cavalier and Yankee*, published in 1961, there were contrasting attitudes about family life and women in the North and South during the antebellum period. These separate traditions arose from the emerging sense of regional and cultural differences between the two sections. In the popular imagination a woman in the North—especially in Yankee New England—presented an image as a bourgeois, hardworking, and utilitarian individual. The role of the lady in the South, on the other hand, was seen as being one of aristocratic leisure, decorative in function, and projecting a sense of utter helplessness. Although these two images changed over time and suggested differing concepts of domesticity, female roles within the two regions appeared to differ quite markedly.[19]

The foregoing discussion of family history as a subfield of the "new social history" shows that scholars were becoming increasingly aware of one thing: women could hardly be studied in complete isolation from men. Because women are a separate sex they are often most closely tied to members of the male sex by marriage, physical association, kinship connections, and common interests in raising children than they are to members of their own sex. There was, to be sure, a long-established history of female bonding, affinity, and close association with other women, but this tradition has had to contend with the other stronger structural ties women have to men.

One of the most important studies to appear during the contemporary period was Carl Degler's *At Odds*, published in 1980. Its aim was to integrate the two historical fields—women's studies and family history. The thesis of Degler's book was summed up in his title: women and the family were "at odds" with one another because the family acted as an inhibitor to women's personal plans. The modern family that arose in the 1830s and continued to the present day, according to Degler, created a newfound status for women within society. At the same time this newfound status, combined with declining fertility in the nineteenth century, led to an opening of more opportunities for women outside the family in careers, education, and other activities. The emergence of the modern family made it possible for women not

---

[18]There is still relatively little written on the history of working-class women, but see Alice Kessler Harris, *Women Have Always Worked* (Old Westbury, N.Y., 1981).

[19]For the image of Southern white middle- and upper-class women from 1830 to 1930, see Ann Firor Scott, *The Southern Lady* (Chicago, 1970).

only to think of themselves as individuals, but to pursue individualistic activities separate from their family life. Degler suggested, then,
that women, in creating the modern family, had built both a prison
and a path to freedom for themselves.

Degler claimed that with the coming of the modern family women
achieved a higher status: first as wives, because their husbands loved
and depended upon them; and then as mothers, because American culture began to view children and child-rearing in a more positive light.
But at the same time women were brought into conflict with the family because the family depended for its very existence upon women's
subordination. When women began demanding more autonomy
through feminist causes like suffrage, their drive for individual rights
ran up against the demands imposed upon them by their families.

The national women's organizations that developed in the nineteenth century, said Degler, gained their effectiveness precisely because of the widely accepted view of women's purity. Since women
were considered the moral guardians of both home and society, for example, they could work with impunity on a reform to destroy "demon
rum." Suffrage, on the other hand, was a truly radical demand because
the right to vote was a right based on women's individuality rather
than on their family status. For this and other reasons suffrage took a
long time to achieve, simply because it challenged women's subordination within the family.

Like other scholars Degler dealt with domesticity and feminism
within the same context. He successfully challenged the older view
that the Victorians had been responsible for surrounding sex with a
conspiracy of silence. He showed that Victorian sexual attitudes were
the creation, at least in part, of women themselves. One aspect of this
growing female autonomy was the desire of women for fewer children.
Women influenced the decision to control fertility, and Degler provided extensive evidence that married middle-class white women probably used contraception, abortion, as well as abstinence from sex to do
so. Thus Degler suggested that women were not necessarily victims
of the transformation of family life; they themselves had played a central role in bringing about the changes that took place.

Bringing his study up to the present, Degler looked at the historical
pattern of women's work. Despite changes in the number of working
wives and despite the lifting of discriminatory employment practices,
he argued, women, for the most part, still hold low-paying dead-end
jobs. Women continued to do so, Degler concluded, because they
thought of themselves as secondary workers and oriented their jobs
around their family life. Men, on the other hand, did not think along
such lines to the same degree.

Degler succeeded in integrating the two fields of women's studies and family history, even though some scholars insisted the two should be viewed separately. Although his synthesis was confined mainly to married middle-class white women, it constituted a major breakthrough. Degler's study will set the stage, no doubt, for future works along similar lines.

The theme of feminism that Degler stressed was a subject taken up by other historians in a variety of ways. One book—a study of popular culture—suggested that the culture of nineteenth-century America was conditioned and dominated by two groups: women and the clergy. As Ann Douglas argued in her *Feminization of American Culture,* published in 1977, the popular literature to which this culture gave birth fostered a sentimentalized society. It also marked the beginning of America's mass culture. Douglas claimed that the exclusion of women from the economic and political realities of the pre–Civil War era produced a false consciousness. This condition, concluded Douglas, prevented women from arriving at any clear analysis of the existing contradictions within American society.

Female sexuality was often a subject taken up by scholars with an interest in feminism. In her book of essays entitled *Disorderly Conduct,* published in 1985, Carroll Smith-Rosenberg discussed this difficult subject from several different perspectives. In one article she presented the views of nineteenth-century male doctors on women's sexuality from puberty to menopause. Smith-Rosenberg analyzed the use of these medical views and interpreted them as being one way in which society recognized the importance of women's sexuality, and, at the same time, tried to restrict it solely to the reproductive function. In a second article she examined certain tensions arising from women's roles in the nineteenth century and showed how such conflicts often found expression in the form of hysteria. Hysteria, according to Smith-Rosenberg, was often a form of individual expression or protest against the conditions of frustration and repression arising from the feminine role. In a third article Smith-Rosenberg drew attention to the close female bonding of young women that often took place in the nineteenth century. Such intense female friendships, she noted, often had to contend and compete with the romantic ties with men. Finally, in a fourth article, she dealt with the way in which emerging social pressures placed the responsibility for sexual attractiveness upon the female during the decade of the 1830s. This response, as Smith-Rosenberg saw it, was related to the unrecognized tensions that arose from stressful social changes taking place in the Jacksonian era.[20]

---

[20]Carroll Smith-Rosenberg, *Disorderly Conduct* (New York, 1985). See also her book, *Religion and the Rise of the American City, 1812–1870* (Ithaca, 1971), which links the assignment of benevolent activity to women in the early republic with the development of a consciousness of women's social position, thus setting the stage for the subsequent feminist movement of the 1840s.

Two articles dealing with women's sexuality in the nineteenth century—one by Nancy Cott and the other by Carl Degler—constitute the readings for this chapter.

Several historians writing in the 1960s and 1970s about the women's movement were extremely critical of its shortcomings. They focused upon the apparent failure of the movement for equal rights in the nineteenth century, as well as the seeming emptiness of the victory finally won by the suffragettes in 1920. Robert Riegel, in his *American Feminists*, published in 1963, concentrated on the difficulties of personal adjustment by leaders of the women's movement during the nineteenth century. Their ambiguity regarding their own sexuality and their inability to understand the problem of sexuality, he implied, rendered the leaders incapable of proposing any strategies that might lead to psychological or political equality. William O'Neill, on the other hand, in *Everyone Was Brave*, published in 1969, analyzed the reasons why women failed to make adequate use of those political rights for which they had fought so vigorously. He attributed the decline of most feminist organizations in the 1920s to the style of leadership and to the self-defeating terms on which the women's vote had been sought. William Chafe pushed the story still further by analyzing, among other things, the patterns of women's votes from the 1920s to 1970. In his *The American Woman*, published in 1972, Chafe argued also that the prosperity of the post–World War II era represented a major precondition to the modern woman's movement that arose in the 1960s.[21]

Besides these specialized studies published in the contemporary period, a number of individual and collective biographies were written about outstanding women leaders. The individual biographical studies were far superior to the filiopietistic works written in the nineteenth century. A multivolume biographical dictionary of notable American women who lived between the years 1607 to 1950 was also published in the 1970s and 1980s. This work provided an invaluable reference source for students seeking to identify specific women or to inquire into their backgrounds.[22]

---

[21]For an important article that analyzes the interaction and relationship between women's political activities from 1780 to 1920 and the changing political scene during these same years, see Paula Baker, "The Domestication of Politics: Women and American Political Society, 1780–1920," *American Historical Review* 80 (June 1984):620–647. The article deals not only with the political activities of women but shows they in turn were shaped and affected by American government and politics.

[22]For three fine recent biographies of women leaders see Kathryn Kish Sklar, *Catharine Beecher* (New Haven, 1973); Mary Hill, *Charlotte Perkins Gilman* (Philadelphia, 1980); and Lois Banner, *Elizabeth Cady Stanton* (Boston, 1980). For the biographical dictionary see Edward James et al., eds. *Notable American Women*, 3 vols. (Cambridge, Mass., 1970), and Barbara Sicherman and Carol Hurd Green, eds., *Notable American Women, The Modern Period*, vol. 4 (Cambridge, Mass., 1980).

This historiographical survey touches only on certain major themes presented in the voluminous literature on women's history—one of the most vital and rapidly developing fields in all of American history. But it has failed to answer the question posed at the beginning of this chapter: Was women's history part of the mainstream of traditional American history? Or was it a kind of "minority history"? Women were more visible in American history, to be sure, and that development represented a considerable and long-awaited advance. But had the female experience been incorporated into the writings of historians so that women's activities and their views of the past had become an integral part of American history? Had the field of women's history been established long enough and the female past recovered sufficiently so that women's world view with its female values could be incorporated into the synthesis of traditional American history? One thing is certain: until scholars incorporate women's history and women's views of the past into American history, this field will continue to be seen and treated as a kind of "minority history."

Nancy F. Cott

NANCY F. COTT (1945–   ) is associate professor of American studies at Yale University. She is the author of *The Bonds of Womanhood:
"Woman's Sphere" in New England 1780–1835* (1977).

In 1903 Havelock Ellis announced that the notion of women's sexual "anaesthesia," as he called it, was a nineteenth-century creation.
He had researched literary and medical sources from ancient Greece
to early modern Europe and discovered, to his own amazement, that
women had generally been thought to desire and enjoy sexual relations
more than men. Ellis and his contemporaries initially sought the source
of the idea that women lacked sexual passion in the generations immediately preceding their own. The late nineteenth century was an
era of contention over female sexuality, physiology, health, dress, and
exercise, and one in which medical opinion had become an authoritative sector of public opinion. Since investigators have found rich documentation on these controversies, particularly in medical sources,
they have been little induced to look beyond them. Until quite recently, historians tended not only to follow Ellis's chronological bias
but, like him, to associate the idea that women lacked sexual passion
with social repression and dysfunction. Now that attitude has been
challenged by the possibility that nineteenth-century sexual ideology
held some definite advantages for women, and by the claim that ideology reflected or influenced behavior far less than had been thought.
     A full appraisal of the idea that women lacked sexual passion re-
quires an investigation of its origins. My purpose is to offer a hypothesis, if not a proven case, regarding the initiation and reception of that
central tenet of Victorian sexual ideology which I call "passionlessness." I use the term to convey the view that women lacked sexual
aggressiveness, that their sexual appetites contributed a very minor
part (if any at all) to their motivations, that lustfulness was simply
uncharacteristic. The concept of passionlessness represented a cluster
of ideas about the comparative weight of woman's carnal nature and
her moral nature; it indicated more about drives and temperament than
about actions and is to be understood more metaphorically than literally.

Nancy F. Cott, "Passionlessness: An Interpretation of Victorian Sexual Ideology, 1790–
1850," *Signs*, 4 (Winter 1978):219–236. Reprinted by permission of the author and of the
University of Chicago Press. © 1978 by The University of Chicago.

Obviously, a single conception of women's sexuality never wholly prevails. Western civilization up to the eighteenth century, as Ellis discovered, accentuated women's concupiscence: a fifteenth-century witch-hunters' guide warned, for instance, that "carnal lust . . . in women is insatiable." But the Christian belief system that called unsanctified earthly women the devil's agents allowed, on the other hand, that women who embodied God's grace were more spiritual, hence less susceptible to carnal passion, than men. Nineteenth-century views of female sexuality were also double edged: notions of women's inherent licentiousness persisted, to be wielded against women manifesting any form of deviance under the reign of passionlessness. Acknowledging that notions of women's sexuality are never monolithic, I would nonetheless emphasize that there was a traditionally dominant Anglo-American definition of women as *especially* sexual which was reversed and transformed between the seventeenth and the nineteenth centuries into the view that women (although still primarily identified by their female gender) were *less* carnal and lustful than men.

The following pages focus on early appearances of the idea of female passionlessness, discuss its social context, and analyze if and why it was acceptable, especially to women. The documents in this test case are limited to New England; to apply the interpretive paradigm to literate, Protestant, middle-class women elsewhere would require further testing. I have looked to women's public and private writings in order to put the women involved in the forefront and prevent viewing them as passive recipients of changing ideas. My other sources are largely didactic and popular works, especially religious ones, which influenced women. Most of what is known about sexual ideology before the twentieth century comes from "prescriptive" sources—those manuals, essays, and books that tried to establish norms of behavior. Although religious views, expressed in sermons and tracts, were the most direct and commanding "prescriptions" from the seventeenth through the early nineteenth centuries, they have not been so finely combed for evidence of sexual norms as has been medical advice, a comparable source of "prescriptions" for the later nineteenth century. Religious opinion is particularly relevant to this inquiry because of the churches' hold on the female population. Women became a majority in the Protestant churches of America in the mid-seventeenth century and continued to increase their numerical predominance until, by the mid-nineteenth century, "Christian" values and virtues and "female" values and virtues were almost identical. In my view, the ideology of passionlessness was tied to the rise of evangelical religion between the 1790s and the 1830s. Physicians' adoption of passionlessness was a second wave, so to speak, beginning at mid-century. By the time that physicians took up the question of passionlessness and attempted to reduce the concept to "scientific" and somatic quantities the idea had been diffused through the spiritual realm and had already engendered its own opposition.

Early American prescriptive and legal documents suggest that the New England colonists expected women's sexual appetites to be comparable with men's, if not greater. Calvinists assumed that men and women in their "fallen" state were equally licentious, that sexual drives were natural and God-given in both sexes, and had their proper outlet in marriage. If anything, the daughters of Eve were considered more prone to excess of passion because their rational control was seen as weaker. And yet it was objectionable for women to exercise the sexual initiative; regardless of women's sexual drives, the religious and social context required female subordination. Puritan theology weakened but did not destroy the double standard of sexual morality. In colonial law, for example, fornication was punished equally in either sex, but adultery was defined by the participation of a married woman. A married man did not commit adultery but fornication—unless he took up with another man's wife. In Massachusetts until the Revolutionary period, a wife's adultery was always cause for her husband to divorce her, but wives had little success in freeing themselves from unfaithful husbands. Men also won suits to recover "damages" from their wives' lovers. As Keith Thomas has put it, such suits reflected the underlying tenet of the double standard: "the view that men have property in women and that the value of this property is immeasurably diminished if the woman at any time has sexual relations with anyone other than her husband." There was vast potential for sexual exploitation in a society in which women's sexual nature was considered primary and their social autonomy was slight. The physical and biological consequences of sexual adventure also burdened women more heavily than men in an era lacking effective means to prevent conception or infection.

In the second century of colonial settlement one finds many more numerous prescriptions for the role of women. The reasons for this increase are diverse: new class concern for standards of distinction and taste, the spread of literacy, the growth of printing and journalism, and "enlightened" interest in reformulating social systems and personal relations in "natural," "rational," rather than scriptural, terms. Britain led in discussions of female character and place, setting sex-role conventions for the literate audience. Since British social ideals became more influential in the mid-eighteenth century with the decline in Puritanism, the diffusion of Protestant energies, and the growth of an affluent urban class in the colonies, British "prescriptions" must be taken into consideration. At least three phases of British opinion contributed to the development of the idea of passionlessness. In the beginning of the century when spokesmen for the new professional and commercial middle class began explicitly to oppose aristocratic pretension, vanity, and libertinism, reforming writers such as Daniel Defoe, Jeremy Collier, Richard Steele, and Samuel Richardson portrayed sexual promiscuity as one of those aristocratic excesses that threatened middle-class virtue and domestic security. Their kind of propriety led to an ideal of sexual self-control, verbal prudery, and opposition to the double standard of sexual morality (for the sake of purity for men rather than justice for women). Due to their influence, in part, "the eighteenth century witnessed a redefinition of virtue in primarily sexual terms," Ian Watt has pointed out. By elevating sexual control highest among human virtues the middle-class moralists made female chastity the archetype for human morality.

Out of the upper class came a different prescriptive genre, the etiquette manual. The ones most available to middle-class women in America, such as George Savile's *A Lady's New Year's Gift* or John Gregory's *A Father's Legacy to His Daughters*, consistently held that woman was made for man's pleasure and service; woman was strong only insofar as she could use her own weakness to manipulate the opposite sex (within the bounds of social propriety). These authors advised a great deal of restraint and affectation (not to mention deception) in women's behavior. At the same time, modesty and demureness took center stage among the female virtues enshrined. According to Keith Thomas, the idea of passionlessness emerged in this context as an extension of the ideal of chastity needed to protect men's property rights in women; it was a reification in "nature" of the double standard. Yet it must be objected that in the nineteenth century women who believed in passionlessness usually rejected the double standard of sexual morality. Modesty was the quintessential female virtue in works such as Gregory's, but, amid the manipulative and affected tactics advised, it connoted only demure behavior—a good act—not, necessarily, passionlessness. Indeed, the underlying theme that women had to appeal to men turned modesty into a sexual ploy, emphasizing women's sex objectification. John Gregory did hint that sexual desire was weaker in women, with their "superior delicacy," than in men. He was sure that nature had assigned to wives rather than husbands the "reserve" which would prevent "satiety and disgust" in marital relations. But not until a third phase at the close of the century did emphasis move implacably from modesty to passionlessness, under the Evangelical aegis.

The British Evangelicals were conservative reformers horrified at the French Revolution and its "godlessness"; they worked to regenerate Protestantism in order to secure social and political order. Like earlier middle-class moralists, the Evangelicals opposed aristocratic blasphemies and profligacy, cherished family life, and advocated chastity and prudence in both sexes. Because they observed women's greater piety, and hoped that women would influence men and the next generation, they focused much of their proselytizing zeal on women. In contrast to earlier eighteenth-century didacts, they harped on the theme that women were made for God's purposes, not man's. Thomas Gisborne, for example, clearly considered women moral beings responsible for themselves and to society. His call for self-conscious moral integrity on women's part directly opposed Gregory's insinuations about the shaping of women's behavior to men's tastes; he objected that such behavior was "not discretion, but art. It is dissimulation, it is deliberate imposition." Evangelical works of the 1790s argued that aristocratic models of vanity, artifice, and irreligion had undermined and corrupted women's valuable potential. They claimed that female piety and sincerity would bring "effectual reformation . . . in every department of society," because "all virtues, all vices, and all characters are intimately connected with the manners, principles, and dispositions of our women." The Evangelicals transformed the truism of etiquette books, that individual women influenced individual men's manners, into the proposition that the collective influence of women was an agency of moral reform.

More to the point, the Evangelicals linked moral agency to female character with a supporting link to passionlessness. Their insistence on sincerity or "simplicity," accompanying their emphasis on women's moral potential, caused them to imply that women were virtuous by nature. Continuing to stress the female virtue of modesty, Evangelicals could not (in contrast to Gregory) allow that modesty was a behavior assumed to suit society's conventions and men's preferences. If women were to act modest and sexually passive, and also act without affectation, then, logically, they must be passionless. Gisborne said women had "quicker feelings of native delicacy, and a stronger sense of shame" than men. The anonymous author of *Female Tuition* claimed the female sex was "naturally attached to purity."

Hannah More's work perfected the transformation of woman's image from sexual to moral being. Her *Strictures on the Modern System of Female Education* called for the rescue of religion and morality and located her constituency among her own sex. She detailed further than any predecessor the power that women could command, first making clear that this was power derived from their moral and spiritual endowment, not from their winning or endearing (sexual) ways. "It is humbling to reflect," More began her *Strictures*, "that in those countries in which fondness for the mere persons of women is carried to the highest excess, *they are slaves;* and that their moral and intellectual degradation increases in direct proportion to the adoration which is paid to mere external charms." More offered a resounding alternative to the idea that women were made for men's pleasure—but at the price of a new level of self-control. Since she believed that human nature was corrupt, her educational program consisted of repression as much as enhancement. Her outlook revealed to women a source of power (in moral influence) and an independence of men (through reliance on God) in a female world view that inspired and compelled women throughout the nineteenth century. In her refusal to see women as childish and affectedly weak beings, designed only "to gratify the appetite of man, or to be the upper servant," she agreed with her contemporary, Mary Wollstonecraft. Despite the spectrum of difference between More and Wollstonecraft in politics and personal behavior, they both abhorred "libertine notions of beauty" and "weak elegancy of mind" in women, wished to emphasize women's moral and intellectual powers rather than their "mere animal" capacities, and expected reformed women to reform the world. Their two critiques rose from shared indignation that women were degraded by their sexual characterization.

The new focus on moral rather than sexual determinants of female character in didactic works at the end of the eighteenth century required a reversal in Protestant views of women. In Puritan ideology, earthly women were the inheritors of Eve's legacy of moral danger. By the mid-eighteenth century, however, New England ministers had discarded similes to Eve, probably in deference to their predominantly female congregations, and portrayed women as more sensitive to the call of religion than men. Nineteenth-century Protestantism relied on women for its prime exemplars and symbols. Between 1790 and 1820 particularly, as an evangelical united front spread across the United States and Britain, the clergy intensified their emphasis on women as crucial advocates of religion. Evangelical Protestants constantly reiterated the theme that Christianity had raised women from slaves in status to moral and intellectual beings. The tacit condition for that elevation was the suppression of female sexuality. Christian women were "exalted above human nature, raised to that of angels"; proper understanding of the gospel enabled women to dismiss the earthly pride or sensuality that subjected them to men's whims. The clergy thus renewed and generalized the idea that women under God's grace were more pure than men, and they expected not merely the souls but the bodies of women to corroborate that claim.

The pastors had a double purpose in training their eyes on the moral rather than the sexual aspect of woman's being. It enabled them to welcome women as worthy allies and agents of Protestantism, which seemed more and more essential as men's religious commitment dissipated. Second, a world view in which woman's sexual nature was shadowed behind her moral and spiritual endowment eclipsed her primitive and original power over men, the power of her sexuality. The evangelical view, by concentrating on women's spiritual nature, simultaneously elevated women as moral and intellectual beings and disarmed them of their sexual power. Passionlessness was on the other side of the coin which paid, so to speak, for women's admission to moral equality.

The correlation between passionlessness and a distinctly improved view of women's character and social purpose begins to suggest the appeal of the concept to women. By replacing sexual with moral motives and determinants, the ideology of passionlessness favored women's power and self-respect. It reversed the tradition of Christian mistrust based on women's sexual treacherousness. It elevated women above the weakness of animal nature, stressing instead that they were "formed for exalted purity, felicity, and glory." It postulated that woman's influence was not ensnaring but disinterested. It routed women out of the cul-de-sac of education for attractiveness, thus allowing more intellectual breadth. To women who wanted means of self-preservation and self-control, this view of female nature may well have appealed, as Hannah More's views appealed. . . .

Only a handful of New England women at this time questioned the political inequities of their situation, but sexual and marital subjection—unequal sexual prerogatives—seem to have rankled a much larger population. As *The Female Advocate* pointed out, women had to conform to male tastes and wait to be chosen but resist seduction or suffer ostracism for capitulating; men, meanwhile, were free to take the first step, practice flattery, and escape the consequences of illicit sexual relations. In sexual encounters women had more than an even chance to lose, whether by censure under the double standard, unwanted pregnancy and health problems, or ill-fated marriage. In this perspective, women might hail passionlessness as a way to assert control in the sexual arena—even if that "control" consisted in denial. Some scholars have claimed that women adhered to the ideology of passionlessness to bolster their position in a disadvantageous marriage market, that is, to play "hard to get" with conviction. More essentially, passionlessness served women's larger interests by downplaying altogether their sexual characterization, which was the cause of their exclusion from significant "human" (i.e., male) pursuits. The positive contribution of passionlessness was to replace that sexual/carnal characterization of women with a spiritual/moral one, allowing women to develop their human faculties and their self-esteem. The belief that women lacked carnal motivation was the cornerstone of the argument for women's moral superiority, used to enhance women's status and widen their opportunities in the nineteenth century. Furthermore, acceptance of the idea of passionlessness created sexual solidarity among women; it allowed women to consider their love relationships with one another of higher character than heterosexual relationships because they excluded (male) carnal passion. "I do not believe that men can ever feel so pure an enthusiasm for women as we can feel for one another," Catherine Sedgwick recorded in her diary of 1834, upon meeting Fanny Kemble, "—ours is nearest to the love of angels." "Love is spiritual, only passion is sexual," Mary Grew wrote at the end of the century to vindicate her intense and enduring friendship with Margaret Burleigh. That sense of the angelic or spiritual aspect of female love ennobled the experience of sisterhood which was central to the lives of nineteenth-century women and to the early woman's rights movement. Women considered passionlessness an important shared trait which distinguished them favorably from men.

It must not be assumed that women who internalized the concept of passionlessness necessarily shunned marriage. The pervasive ideology of romantic love, and also the evangelical conflation of the qualities of earthly and spiritual love, bridged the gap and refuted the ostensible contradiction between passionlessness and marriage. On a practical level, belief in female passionlessness could aid a woman to limit sexual intercourse within marriage and thus limit family size. Daniel Scott Smith has postulated a direct relation between women's exertion of that sort of power within the family, which he calls "domestic feminism," and the decline of the birth rate during the nineteenth century. The conviction and the demand that it was woman's right to control reproduction, advocated by health reformers in the 1850s and promulgated in the movement for "voluntary motherhood" in subsequent decades, depended on the ideology of female passionlessness. Linda Gordon has shown the feminist basis of the argument for voluntary motherhood in the claim that women had the right to refuse their husbands' sexual demands, despite the legal and customary requirements of submission to marital "duty."

The degree to which a woman might incorporate the idea of passionlessness is revealed in an 1845 letter of Harriet Beecher Stowe to her husband. Responding to his revelations about "licentiousness" on the part of certain clergymen, she wrote: "What terrible temptations lie in the way of your sex—till now I never realized it—for tho I did love you with an almost insane love before I married you I never knew yet or felt the pulsation which showed me that I could be tempted in that way—there never was a moment when I felt anything by which you could have drawn me astray—for I loved you as I now love God. . . . " Angelina Grimke's passionless attitude was a feminist affirmation of woman's dignity in revulsion from male sexual domination. To the man who would become her husband she revealed her judgment "that men in general, the vast majority, believe most seriously that women were made to gratify their animal appetites, *expressly* to minister to their pleasure—yea Christian men too." She continued: "My soul abhors such a base letting down of the high dignity of my nature as a woman. How I have feared the possibility of ever being married to one who regarded *this* as the *end*—the great design of marriage. In truth I may say that I never was reconciled to the compound [relat]ions of marriage until I read Combe on the Constitution of man this winter."

Yet a belief so at odds with the traditional appreciation of female sexuality, and one which seems to mid-twentieth-century sensibilities so patently counterproductive, so symbolic of the repression and subordination of women, cannot be interpreted simply. Historians' frequent assumption that men devised the ideology of female passionlessness to serve their own interests—"to help gentlemen cope with the problem of controlling their own sexuality"—is partial (in both senses of the word) but not illogical. An ideal of male continence, of virtuous and willed repression of existing carnal desires (as distinct from passionlessness, which implied absence of carnal motivation), figures in nineteenth-century directions for men's respectability and achievement in the bustling new world of industrial capitalism. In one aspect, female passionlessness was a keystone in men's construction of their own self-control. But Howard Gadlin has underlined the paradox of the ideology, as well as reason for its diffusion and rootedness, in his remark that "the nineteenth-century double standard was the vehicle for a desexualization desired by both men and women for opposing purposes. Men wanted to desexualize relationships to maintain their domination; women wanted to desexualize relationships to limit male domination."

Both women's participation in the creation of Victorian sexual standards and the place of passionlessness in the vanguard of feminist thought deserve more recognition. The serviceability of passionlessness to women in gaining social and familial power should be acknowledged as a primary reason that the ideology was quickly and widely accepted. Yet feminists were the first to question and oppose the ideology once it was entrenched. When prudery became confused with passionlessness, it undermined women physically and psychologically by restricting their knowledge of their own sexual functioning. From the first, women health reformers and moral reformers rejected this injurious implication while fostering the positive meanings of passionlessness. Feminist opposition arose when the medical establishment adopted passionlessness and moved the grounds for judging the concept from the spiritual to the somatic. When female passionlessness came to be insisted upon literally, more than one woman reacted as Rebecca Harding Davis did: "In these rough and tumble days, we'd better give [women] their places as flesh and blood, with exactly the same wants and passions as men." Mary Gove Nichols claimed: "A healthy and loving woman is impelled to material union as surely, often as strongly, as man. . . . The apathy of the sexual instinct is caused by the enslaved and unhealthy condition in which she lives." Several woman's rights activists of the later part of the century, including Isabella Beecher Hooker, Alice Stockham, and Elizabeth Cady Stanton, discussed among themselves their belief in the existence and legitimacy of female sexual drives, even while the movement of which they were part banked on women's superior morality and maternal instinct as chief supports. Consistent with the general conflicts and contradictions in sexual ideology after 1860, feminists perceived oppression in prudery while clinging to the promises that passionlessness held out.

The ideology of passionlessness, conceived as self-preservation and social advancement for women, created its own contradictions: on the one hand, by exaggerating sexual propriety so far as to immobilize women and, on the other, by allowing claims of women's moral influence to obfuscate the need for other sources of power. The assertion of moral integrity within passionlessness had allowed women to retrieve their identity from a trough of sexual vulnerability and dependence. The concept could not assure women full autonomy—but what transformation in sexual ideology alone could have done so?

Carl N. Degler

CARL N. DEGLER (1921–   ) is professor of history at Stanford University. He has written many books in American social history, including *Neither Black nor White: Slavery and Race Relations in Brazil and the United States* (1971), *The Other South: Southern Dissenters in the Nineteenth Century* (1974), and *At Odds: Women and the Family in America from the Revolution to the Present* (1980).

As every schoolgirl knows, the nineteenth century was afraid of sex, particularly when it manifested itself in women. Captain Marryat, in his travels in the United States, told of some American women so refined that they objected to the word "leg," preferring instead the more decorous "limb." Marryat also reported seeing this delicacy carried to extremes in a girls' school where a school mistress, in the interest of protecting the modesty of her charges, had dressed all four "limbs" of the piano "in modest little trousers with frills at the bottom of them!" Women's alleged lack of passion was epitomized, too, in the story of the English mother who was asked by her daughter before her marriage how she ought to behave on her wedding night. "Lie still and think of the Empire," the mother advised.

This view of Victorian attitudes toward sexuality is captured in more than stories. Steven Marcus, writing about the attitudes of English Victorians toward sexuality, and Nathan Hale, Jr., summarizing the attitudes of Americans on the same subject, both quote at length from Dr. William Acton's *Functions and Disorders of the Reproductive Organs*, which went through several editions in England and the United States during the middle years of the nineteenth century. Acton's book was undoubtedly one of the most widely quoted sexual-advice books in the English-speaking world. The book summed up the medical literature on women's sexuality by saying that "the majority of women (happily for them) are not very much troubled with sexual feelings of any kind. What men are habitually, women are only exceptionally." Theophilus Parvin, an American doctor, told his medical class in 1883, "I do not believe one bride in a hundred, of delicate, educated, sensitive women, accepts matrimony from any desire for

Carl N. Degler, "What Ought to Be and What Was: Women's Sexuality in the Nineteenth Century," *American Historical Review* 79 (December 1974):1467–1490. Reprinted with the permission of Carl N. Degler.

113

sexual gratification; when she thinks of this at all, it is with shrinking, or even with horror, rather than with desire."

Modern writers on the sexual life of women in the nineteenth century have echoed these contemporary descriptions. "For the sexual act was associated by many wives only with a duty," writes Walter Houghton, "and by most husbands with a necessary if pleasurable yielding to one's baser nature; by few, therefore, with any innocent and joyful experience." Writing about late-nineteenth-century America, David Kennedy quotes approvingly from Viola Klein when she writes that "in the whole Western world during the nineteenth century and at the beginning of the twentieth century it would have been not only scandalous to admit the existence of a strong sex urge in women, but it would have been contrary to all observation." Nathan Hale, Jr., sums up his review of the sexual-advice literature at the turn of the century with a similar conclusion: "Many women came to regard marriage as little better than legalized prostitution. Sexual passion became associated almost exclusively with the male, with prostitutes, and women of the lower classes." Most recently Ben Barker-Benfield has argued that male doctors were so convinced that women had no sexual interest that when it manifested itself drastic measures were taken to subdue it, including excision of the sexual organs. "Defining the absence of sexual desire in women as normal, doctors came to see its presence as disease. . . . Sexual appetite was a male quality (to be properly channelled of course). If a woman showed it, she resembled a man."

Despite the apparent agreement between the nineteenth-century medical writers and modern students of the period, it is far from clear that there was in the nineteenth century a consensus on the subject of women's sexuality or that women were in fact inhibited from acknowledging their sexual feelings. In examining these two issues I shall be concerned with an admittedly limited yet significant population, namely, women of the urban middle class in the United States. This was the class to which the popular medical-advice books, of which William Acton's volume was a prime example, were directed. It is principally the women of this class upon whom historians' generalizations about women's lives in the nineteenth century are based. And though these women were not a numerical majority of the sex, they undoubtedly set the tone and provided the models for most women. The sources drawn upon are principally the popular and professional medical literature concerned with women and a hitherto undiscovered survey of married women's sexual attitudes and practices that was begun in the 1890s by Dr. Clelia D. Mosher.

Let me begin with the first question or issue. Was William Acton representative of medical writers when he contended that women were essentially without sexual passion? Rather serious doubts arise as soon as one looks into the medical literature, popular as well as professional, where it was recognized that the sex drive was so strong in woman that to deny it might well compromise her health. Dr. Charles Taylor, writing in 1882, said, "It is not a matter of indifference whether a women live [sic] a single or a married life. . . . I do not for one moment wish to be understood as believing that an unmarried woman cannot exist in perfect health for I know she can. But the point is, that *she must take pains for it.*" For if the generative organs are not used, then "some other demand for the unemployed functions, must be established. Accumulated force must find an outlet, or disturbance first and weakness ultimately results." His recommendation was muscular exercise and education for usefulness. He also described cases of women who had denied their sexuality and even experienced orgasms without knowing it. Some women, he added, ended up, as a result, with impairment of movement or other physical symptoms.

Other writers on medical matters were even more direct in testifying to the presence of sexual feelings in women. "Passion absolutely necessary in woman," wrote Orson S. Fowler, the phrenologist, in 1870. "Amativeness is created in the female head as universally as in the male. . . . That female passion exists, is as obvious as that the sun shines," he wrote. Without woman's passion, he contended, a fulfilled love could not occur. Both sexes enjoy the sexual embrace, asserted Henry Chevasse, another popular medical writer, in 1871, but among human beings, as among the animals in general, he continued, "the male is more ardent and fierce, and . . . the desires of the female never reach that hight [sic] as to impel her to the commission of crime." Woman's pleasure, though it may be "less acute," is longer lasting than man's, Chevasse said. R. T. Trall, also a popular medical writer, counseled in a similar vein. "Whatever may be the object of sexual intercourse," he wrote, "whether intended as a love embrace merely, or as a generative act, it is very clear that it should be as pleasurable as possible to *both parties.*"

If one can judge the popularity of a guide for women by the number of its editions, then Dr. George Napheys's *The Physical Life of Woman: Advice to the Maiden, Wife, and Mother* (1869) must have been one of the leaders. Within two weeks of publication it went into a second printing, and within two years 60,000 copies were in print. Napheys was a well-known Philadelphia physician. Women, he wrote, quoting an unnamed "distinguished medical writer," are divided into three classes. The first consists of those who have no sexual feelings, and it is the smallest group. The second is larger and is comprised of those who have "strong passion." The third is made up of "the vast majority of women, in whom the sexual appetite is as moderate as all other appetites." He went on to make his point quite clear. "It is a false

notion and contrary to nature that this passion in a woman is a de-
rogation to her sex. The science of physiology indicates most clearly
its propriety and dignity." He then proceeded to denounce those wives
who "plume themselves on their repugnance or their distaste for their
conjugal obligations." Napheys also contended that authorities agree
that "conception is more assured when the two individuals who cooperate in it participate at the same time in the transports of which it
is the fruit." Napheys probably had no sound reason for this point, but
the accuracy of his statement is immaterial. What is of moment is that
as an adviser to women he was clearly convinced that women possessed sexual feelings, which ought to be cultivated rather than suppressed. Concerning sexual relations during pregnancy he wrote,
"There is no reason why passions should not be gratified in moderation
and with caution during the whole period of pregnancy." And since his
book is directed to women, there is no question that the passion he is
talking about here is that of women.

In 1878 Dr. Ely Van de Warker of Syracuse, a fellow of the American Gynecological Society, described sexual passion in women as "the
analogue of the subjective copulative sensations of man, and that the
acme of the sexual orgasm in woman is the sensory equivalent of emis-
sions in man, observing the distinction necessarily implied between
the sexes—that in woman it is psychic and subjective, and that in man
it has also a physical element and is objective," that is, it is accompanied by seminal emission. The principal purpose of Van de Warker's
article was to deplore the fact that some women lacked sexual feeling,
a state which he called "female impotency." What is striking about his
article is that he obviously considered such lack of feeling in women
abnormal and worthy of medical attention, just as impotency in a man
would cause medical concern.

Van de Warker's remarks, as well as his use of the word, make it
evident that physicians were well aware that normal women experienced orgasms. Lest there be any doubt that their meaning of the word
was the same as ours today, let me quote from a physician in 1883 who
described in some detail woman's sexual response. He began by describing the preparatory stage, which, he said,

> may be reached by any means, bodily or mental, which, in the op-
> posite sex, cause erection. Following upon this, then, is a stage of
> pleasurable excitement, gradually increasing and culminating in an
> acme of excitement, which may be called the stage of consumma-
> tion, and the analogue of which in the male is emission. This is fol-
> lowed in both sexes by a degree of nervous prostration, less marked,
> however, in the female, and . . . by a relief to the general congestion
> of all the genital organs which has existed, and perhaps increased,
> from the beginning of the preparatory stage.

All of this evidence, it seems to me, shows that there was a significant body of opinion and information quite different from that advanced on women's sexuality by William Acton and others of his outlook. Now it might be asked how widespread was this counter-Acton point of view? Was it not confined primarily to physicians writing for other physicians? Not at all. Napheys, Chevasse, and Fowler, to name three, were all writing their books for the large lay public that was interested in sexual matters. As we have seen, many of these marriage manuals, particularly Napheys's and Fowler's, were printed in several large editions.

Yet, in the end, there is a certain undeniable inconclusiveness in simply raising up one collection of writers against another, even if their existence does make the issue an open one, rather than the closed one that so many secondary writers have made it. It suggests, at the very least, that there was a sharp difference of medical opinion, rather than a consensus, on the nature of women's sexual feelings and needs. In fact there is some reason to believe, as we shall see, that the so-called Victorian conception of women's sexuality was more that of an ideology seeking to be established than the prevalent view or practice of even middle-class women, especially as there is a substantial amount of nineteenth-century writing about women that assumes the existence of strong sexual feelings in women. One of the historian's recognized difficulties in showing, through quotations from writers who assert a particular outlook, that a social attitude prevailed in the past is that one always wonders how representative and how self-serving the examples or quotations are. This is especially true in this case where medical opinion can be found on both sides of the question. When writers, however, assume the attitude in question to be prevalent while they are intent upon writing about something else, then one is not so dependent upon the tyranny of numbers in quoting from sources. For behind the assumption of prevalence lie many examples, so to speak. Such testimony, moreover, is unintended and therefore not self-serving. This kind of evidence, furthermore, helps us to answer the second question—to what extent were women in the nineteenth century inhibited from expressing their sexual feelings? For in assuming that women had sexual feelings, these writers are offering clear, if unintended, testimony to women's sexuality. . . .

In the light of the foregoing it is difficult to accept the view that women were generally seen in the nineteenth century as without sexual feelings or drives. The question then arises as to how this widely accepted historical interpretation got established? Part of the reason, undoubtedly, is the result of the general reticence of the nineteenth century in regard to sex. The excessive gentility of the middle class has been read by historians as a sign of hostility toward sexuality, particularly in women. The whole cult of the home and women's allegedly exalted place in it was easily translated by some historians into an antisexual attitude. But a good part of the explanation must also be attributable to the simple failure on the part of historians to survey fully the extant sources. The kind of statements quoted from medical writers in this article, for example, was either overlooked or ignored. Another important part of the explanation is that the sources that were surveyed and quoted were taken to be descriptive of the sexual ideology of the time when in fact they were part of an effort by some other medical writers to establish an ideology, not to delineate an already accepted one. In other words, the medical literature that was emphasized by Steven Marcus, Oscar Handlin, or Nathan Hale, Jr., was really normative or prescriptive rather than descriptive.

This misinterpretation was easy enough to make since much nineteenth-century medical literature was often descriptive in form even though in fact it was seeking to set a new standard of sexual behavior. Sometimes, however, the normative concerns and purposes showed through the ostensible description. A close reading, for example, of William Acton's second edition of *The Functions and Disorders of the Reproductive Organs* reveals in several places his desire to establish a new and presumably "higher" standard of sexual attitude and behavior. After pointing out that publicists strongly condemn sexual relations outside marriage, he asks, "But should we stop there? I think not. The audience should be informed that, in the present state of society, the sexual appetites must not be fostered; and experience teaches those who have had the largest means of information on the matter, that self-control must be exercised." So far, he continues, no one has "dared publicly to advocate . . . this necessary regulation of the sexual feelings or training to continence." Or later, when he discusses women in particular, it is evident that he is arguing for a special attitude, not merely describing common practice. "The *best* mothers, wives, and managers of households know little or nothing of sexual indulgence. Love of home, children, and domestic duties are the only passions they feel," he writes.

American writers of the time who followed the lead of Acton as well as quoting him display a similar mixture of prescription and description. Take Dr. John Kellogg's *Plain Facts for Old and Young*, which sold over 300,000 copies by 1910 and went through five editions. Kellogg, like Acton, made it clear that he thought sex was too dominant in the thoughts of people. As we look around us today, he wrote, "it would appear that the opportunity for sensual gratification has come to be, in the world at large, the chief attraction between the sexes. If to these observations," he continued, "we add the filthy disclosures constantly made in police court and scandal suits, we have a powerful confirmation of the opinion." It was this excess that he warns against, drawing upon quotations from Acton to support his arguments. He is at pains to show, too, that continence, especially in men, is not deleterious to health, as some contended. He admits that the medical profession is not in agreement on the amount of sexual indulgence permitted in marriage. "A very few hold that the sexual act should never be indulged except for the purpose of reproduction, and then only at periods when reproduction will be possible. Others, while equally opposed to the excesses . . . limit indulgence to the number of months in the year." Human beings, he advised, should take their cue from animals, who have intercourse only for procreation and then at widely spaced intervals. Instead of heeding this counsel, he writes, loosely quoting from Acton, "the lengths to which married people carry excesses is perfectly astonishing." . . .

It would be a mistake, in short, to accept the prescriptive or normative literature, like that of Acton, Kellogg, and others, as revealing very much about sexual behavior in the Victorian era. It may be possible to derive a sexual ideology from such writers, but it is a mistake to assume that the ideology thus delineated is either characteristic of the society or reflective of behavior. On the contrary, it is the argument of this article that the attitudes and behavior of middle-class women were only peripherally affected by that ideology. Not only did many medical writers, as we have seen, encourage women to express their sexuality, but there is a further, even more persuasive reason for believing that the prescriptive literature is not a reliable guide to either the sexual behavior or the attitudes of middle-class women. It is the testimony of women themselves.

Any systematic knowledge of the sexual habits of women is a relatively recent historical acquisition, confined to the surveys of women made in the 1920s and 1930s and culminating in the well-known Kinsey report. Until recently no even slightly comparable body of evidence for nineteenth-century women was known to exist. In the Stanford University Archives, however, are questionnaires completed by a group of women testifying to their sexual habits. The questionnaires are part of the papers of Dr. Clelia Duel Mosher (1863–1940), a physician at Stanford University and a pioneer in the study of women's sexuality. Mosher began her work on the sexual habits of married women when she was a student at the University of Wisconsin prior to 1892. That year she transferred for her senior year to Stanford, where she received an A.B. degree in 1893 and an M.A. in 1894. In 1900 she earned an M.D. degree from Johns Hopkins University. After a decade of private practice she joined the Stanford faculty as a member of the department of hygiene and medical adviser to women students. Her published work dealt with the physical capabilities of women; she was a well-known advocate of physical exercise for women. Mosher's questionnaires are carefully arranged and bound in volume 10 of her unpublished work, "Hygiene and Physiology of Women." Mosher, however, apparently never drew more than a few impressionistic conclusions from the highly revealing questionnaires. She did not even publish the fact of their existence, and so far as can be ascertained no use has heretofore been made of this manuscript source. Yet the amount and kind of information on sexual habits and attitudes of married women in the late nineteenth century contained in these questionnaires are unique.

The project, which spanned some twenty years, was begun at the University of Wisconsin when Mosher was a student of biology in the early 1890s. She designed the questionnaire when asked to address the Mother's Club at the university on the subject of marriage. In later years she added to her cases and used the information when giving advice to women about sexual and hygienic matters. This initiative, as well as the kind of questions she asked, reveals that Mosher was far ahead of her time. She amassed information on women's sexuality that none of the many nineteenth-century writers on the subject studied in any systematic way at all.

The questionnaire itself is quite lengthy, comprising twenty-five questions, each one of which is divided into several parts. Much of the questionnaire, it is true, is taken up with ascertaining facts about the parents and even the grandparents of the respondents, but over half of the questions deal directly with women's sexual behavior and attitudes. The information contained in the questionnaires not only supports the interpretation of women's sexuality that already has been drawn from the published literature, both lay and medical, but it also provides us with a means of measuring the degree to which the prescriptive marriage literature affected women's sexual behavior.

Since the evidence in this questionnaire, which I call the Mosher Survey, has never been used before, it is first worthwhile to examine the social background of the women who answered the questionnaires. All told there are forty-six useable questionnaires, but since two of the questionnaires seem to have been filled out by the same woman at an interval of twenty-three years, the number of women actually surveyed is forty-five. In the aggregates that follow I have counted only forty-five questionnaires. The questionnaires, it ought to be said, were not administered at the same time, but at three different periods at least; moreover the date of administration of nine questionnaires cannot be ascertained. Of those that do provide that information, seventeen were completed before 1900, fourteen were filled out between 1913 and 1917, and five were answered in 1920.

More important than the date of administration of the questionnaires are the birth dates of the respondents. All but one of the forty-four, women who provided their dates of birth were born before 1890. In fact thirty-three, or seventy per cent of the whole group, were born before 1870. And of these, seventeen, or slightly over half, were born before the Civil War. For comparative purposes it might be noted that in Alfred Kinsey's survey of women's sexuality the earliest cohort of respondents was only born in the 1890s. In short, the attitudes and practices to which the great majority of the women in the Mosher Survey testify were those of women who grew up and married within the nineteenth century, regardless of when they may have completed the questionnaires.

An important consideration in evaluating the responses, of course, is the social origins of the women. From what class did they come, and from what sections of the country? The questionnaire, fortunately, provides some information here, but not with as much precision as one might like. Since the great majority of the respondents attended college or a normal school (thirty-four out of forty-five, with the education of three unknown), it is evident that the group is not representative of the population of the United States as a whole. The remainder of the group attended secondary school, either public or private, a pattern that is again not representative of a general population in which only a tiny minority of young people attented secondary school. But for purposes of evaluating the impact of the prescriptive or marital-advice literature upon American women this group is quite appropriate. For inasmuch as their educational background identifies them as middle- or upper-class women, it can be said that they were precisely those persons to whom that advisory literature was directed and upon whom its effects ought to be most evident.

In geographical origin the respondents to the Mosher Survey seem to be somewhat more representative, if the location of parents, birth-places, and colleges attended can be taken as a measure, albeit impressionistic, of geographical distribution. Unfortunately there is no other systematic or more reliable information on this subject. The colleges attended, for example, are located in the Northeast (Cornell [6], Smith, Wellesley, and Vassar [2]), in the Middle West (Ripon, Iowa State University, and Indiana), and in the Far West (Stanford [9], the University of California, and the University of the Pacific). The South is not represented at all among the colleges attended.

Although the emphasis upon prestigious colleges might make one think that these were women of the upper or even leisure class, rather than simply middle class, a further piece of information suggests that in fact they were not. One of the questions asked concerned working experience prior to marriage. Although seven of the respondents provided no data at all on this point, and eight reported that they had married immediately after completing their education, thirty of the women reported that they had worked prior to marriage. As a side light on the opportunities available to highly educated women in the late nineteenth century, it is worth adding that twenty-seven of the thirty worked as teachers. On the basis of their working experience it seems reasonable to conclude that the respondents were principally middle- or upper-middle-class women rather than members of a leisure class.

Despite the high level of education of these women, they confessed to having a pretty poor knowledge, by modern standards, of sexual physiology before marriage. Only eleven said that they had much knowledge on that subject, obtained from female relatives, books, or courses in college, while another thirteen said that they had some knowledge. The remainder—slightly over half—reported that they had very little or no knowledge. No guidelines were given in the question-naire for estimating the amount of knowledge. The looseness of the definition is shown by the fact that three of the respondents who said that they had no knowledge at all named books on women's physiol-ogy that they had read. From other titles mentioned in passing it is clear that a number of these women had direct acquaintance with the prescriptive and advisory literature of the time. How did it affect their behavior? Did they repress their sexual impulses or deny them, as some of the prescriptive literature advised? Were they in fact without sexual desire? Or were they motivated toward personal sexual satisfaction as the medical literature quoted in this article advised?

The Mosher Survey provides a considerable amount of evidence to answer these and other questions. To begin with, thirty-five of the forty-five women testified that they felt desire for sexual intercourse inde-pendent of their husband's interest, while nine said they never or rarely felt any such desire. What is more striking, however, is the number who testified to orgasmic experience. According to the standard view of women's sexuality in the nineteenth century, women were not ex-pected to feel desire and certainly not to experience an orgasm. Yet it is striking that in constructing the questionnaire Dr. Mosher asked not only whether the respondents experienced an orgasm during inter-course but whether "you *always* have a venereal orgasm?" (my italics). Although that form of the question makes quite clear Mosher's own assumption that female orgasms were to be expected, it unfortunately confuses the meaning of the responses. (Incidentally, only two of the forty-five respondents failed to answer this question.) Five of the women, for instance, responded "no" without further comment. Given the wording of the question, however, that negative could have meant "not always, but almost always" as well as "never" or any response in between these extremes. The ambiguity is further heightened when it is recognized that in answer to another question, three of the five negatives said that they had felt sexual desire, while a fourth said "sometimes but not often," and the fifth said sex was "usually a nuisance." Luckily, however, most of the women who responded to the question concerning orgasm made more precise answers. The great majority of them said that they had experienced orgasms. . . .

This examination of the literature, the popular advice books, and particularly the Mosher Survey makes clear that historians are ill-advised to rely upon the marital-advice books as descriptions either of the sexual behavior of women or of general attitudes toward women's sexuality. It is true that a literature as admittedly popular as much of the prescriptive or normative literature was could be expected to have some effect upon behavior as well as attitudes. But those effects were severely limited. Most people apparently did not follow the prescriptions laid down by the marriage and advice manuals. Indeed some undoubtedly found that advice wrong or misleading when measured against experience. Through some error or accident the same woman was apparently interviewed twice in the Mosher Survey, twenty-three years apart. As a result we can compare her attitudes at the beginning of her marriage in 1896 and her attitude in 1920. After one year of marriage she thought that sexual relations ought to be confined to reproduction only, but when asked the same question in 1920, she said that intercourse ought not to be confined to reproduction, though she thought it should be indulged in only when not pressed with work and when there was time for pleasure. Another woman in the Mosher Survey changed her mind about sexual relations even earlier in her sexual life. She said,

> My ideas as to the reason for [intercourse] have changed materially from what they were before marriage. I then thought reproduction was the only object and that once brought about, intercourse should cease. But in my experience the habitual bodily expression of love has a deep psychological effect in making possible complete mental sympathy, and perfecting the spiritual union that must be the lasting "marriage" after the passion of love has passed away with years.

These remarks were made in 1897 by a woman of thirty after one year of marriage.

Her comments make clear once again that historians need to recognize that the attitudes of ordinary people are quite capable of resisting efforts to reshape or alter them. That there was an effort to deny women's sexual feelings and to deny them legitimate expression cannot be doubted in the light of the books written then and later about the Victorian conception of sexuality. But the many writings by medical men who spoke in a contrary vein and the Mosher Survey should make us doubt that the ideology was actually put into practice by most men or women of the nineteenth century, even among the middle class, though it was to this class in particular that the admonitions and ideology were directed. The women who responded to Dr. Mosher's questions were certainly middle- and upper-middle-class women, but they were, as a group, neither sexless nor hostile to sexual feelings. The great majority of them, after all, experienced orgasm as well as sexual desire. Their behavior in the face of the antisexual ideology pressed upon them at the time offers testimony to the truth of Alex Comfort's comment that "the astounding resilience of human commonsense against the anxiety makers is one of the really cheering aspects of history."

☆ 4 ☆

Black History Since 1865

REPRESENTATIVE OR RACIST?

Historical writings by scholars dealing with black history from the Civil War to the present—the era of the freed blacks—reflect a distinct ambiguity. Most writings were by white historians who claimed to represent the entire profession and said they were treating these subjects with scholarly objectivity, honesty, and fairness. On the other hand one could see in some of these same writings evidence of racial bias either in the positions taken, attitudes adopted, or subjects addressed. White historians for a long time simply assumed that black writers could not be objective about subjects like black Reconstruction or on most matters dealing with race. Such biases reflect the racial prejudice that has existed in America as a whole; American society, its claims and laws to the contrary notwithstanding, remains a race-conscious society.

As long as the United States continues to be race-conscious this prejudice will continue to influence historical writings about blacks. One historian in the late 1950s, for example, described the historiography of the Reconstruction era as "dark and bloody." As Afro-Americans receive more attention in historical writings in the future, that ground will probably be seen as even darker and bloodier.[1]

This persistence in racial bias among American scholars during the past century and a quarter has warped our understanding of the Civil War and Reconstruction eras for one thing. Two illustrations leap to mind which reveal the racial bias of white scholars—a bias often unconscious in its manifestations. First, they have done relatively little research on the careers and accomplishments of those black politicians

---

[1]Bernard Weisberger, "The Dark and Bloody Ground of Reconstruction Historiography," *Journal of Southern History* 25 (1959):427–447.

and black officials who served with distinction during the Reconstruction era, 1865 to 1877. Second, for a long time those phases of black Reconstruction taken up by scholars were treated unfairly because the historians were either prejudiced white Southerners or outright white supremacists.

Despite the fact that both black and white historians have been writing about post–Civil War black history for the past century and a quarter, the field is still in its infancy. This generalization holds true because almost every phase of black history has been shrouded in myths and misconceptions. One of the most persistent and pernicious of these myths was that the blacks were a passive people. Blacks were often cast in the role of victims; they were always acted upon and incapable of acting for themselves. They were viewed, moreover, as a people and a race whose fate was determined solely by their relationship with the white race. Such an approach led inevitably to a number of studies on white attitudes and actions toward blacks.

It has only been in recent years that scholars have finally begun to delve into the historical records for independent ideas and activities by the blacks. Only with the introduction of the "new social history," moreover, have scholars resisted the temptation to present black history as nothing more than a series of biographical sketches to black leaders—of such men as Booker T. Washington, W. E. B. Du Bois, Marcus Garvey, and Martin Luther King, Jr. The shift to writing about black history in different terms—in terms of a changing black social structure, sister institutions separate from those of whites, and values of the black community as a whole—is a relatively recent phenomenon and barely a quarter of a century old.

There were other reasons why scholars were slow to write meaningfully on black history. Black history was invariably viewed in tragic terms; it went contrary to the optimistic outlook usually adopted by most scholars writing before the end of World War II. When writing immigrant history, for example, historians typically traced the arrival of some ethnic group to the New World, depicted its struggles for existence, and then showed how the group was ultimately assimilated into American society to become virtually indistinguishable from earlier immigrant groups. Black history hardly fitted such a pattern. The circumstances of immigration were different: the movement to America was involuntary not voluntary; there was continuing conflict between the two races; and black history did not end on a theme of assimilation. Black history was tragic in its outlook because blacks have yet to be fully accepted into American life; their status in American society remains uncertain.

Black history also did not fit the pattern of most American history written before World War II, which was oriented around success as a theme. Most past scholars emphasized success; they tended to neglect those groups in American history who had failed in some lost cause, such as the Loyalists or the Antifederalists. Even where certain social movements failed to achieve their goals—the Populists, for example—historians often ended on a triumphant note anyway. They usually concluded their discussion with the observation that Populist principles eventually had been incorporated into the Democratic and Republican party platforms. But black history presented a problem: it was difficult to fit its tragic outcome within this typical pattern of progress and success. Because black history could neither be ignored nor readily incorporated into the mainstream, it has been presented in ways that ranged through a whole spectrum of thought—from blatant racism at one end to rather objective representation at the other.

With these distinctions in mind it is possible to break down the writing of black history since 1865 into roughly four different periods. First there was the period of paternalism—1865 to the late 1920s—when many of the standard authorities were patronizing or patently racist in their writings. The second was the period of transition—1920s to 1950s—when the attitude of scholars toward blacks began to change and racist writings were no longer the generally accepted mode. The third was the period of maturation—the 1950s and 1960s—when liberal white scholars first began writing black history on a large scale and became more acutely aware of the racist attitudes of the earlier eras. The fourth was the period of accommodation—the 1970s to the present—during which scholars have become more sensitive about the existence of a separate black subculture—a subculture with its own values, institutions, and attitudes. This did not mean that scholars had reached a millennium; it meant only that historians were writing with fewer myths and misconceptions in mind.

Around 1900 two major works in the period of paternalism set forth a point of view on Reconstruction that persisted for more than two decades. James Ford Rhodes, a Northern businessman who lacked professional training but had a great love of history, published his multivolume *History of the United States from the Compromise of 1850* covering the years between 1865 and 1877. John W. Burgess, a college professor in the field of political science, ex-Confederate, and former slaveholder, released his *Reconstruction and the Constitution* in 1902. These two interpretations laid the groundwork for what came to be called the Dunning school of Reconstruction historiography.

Professor William A. Dunning, who taught at Columbia University, published his rigorous study, *Reconstruction, Political and Economic*, in 1907. Dunning's graduate students proceeded to flesh out his interpretation with a series of state studies. Reconstruction, according to Dunning, was the lowest point in the South's long history. A coalition of carpetbaggers (opportunistic Northerners who moved to the South) and scalawags (turncoat white Southern Republicans) supported by federal troops presided over the prostrate South. Under their rule the most corrupt, expensive, and inefficient state governments in the history of the South held sway. Taxes and public debts soared and fraud was rampant. The real villains of the period were the recently freed blacks, concluded Dunning. Ignorant and uneducated, unprepared for freedom, the former slaves wrought havoc on the region. They refused to work, stole from the public coffers, insulted their former masters, and abused white women. The South, unrepresented in Congress and occupied by Northern military troops, was exploited in every way by rapacious Yankees and Republicans who gave the illiterate blacks free rein.

Popular historians spiced up the Dunning school interpretation with insulting racist remarks. One of the best-selling books on the subject was by Claude Bowers, entitled *The Tragic Era*, which came out in 1929. Bowers, who later served as ambassador to Spain for Franklin D. Roosevelt, described black politicians as "the type seldom seen outside the Congo." "Little above the intellectual level of the mules they drove," Bowers went on, they ran South Carolina with "chuckles and guffaws, the noisy crackling of peanuts and raucous voices. . . . " "Asleep in their chairs, eating peanuts and soaked in whiskey, quarreling, fighting, pursuing one another with murderous intent," they turned Louisiana's Senate into a "monkey-house" and proposed amendments "too obscene to print." Bowers concluded that "the Southern people literally were put to the torture. . . . "[2]

The documentation Bowers employed points up some of the methodological problems that plagued the writing of black history at the time. One of Bowers's most enthusiastically-cited sources was James S. Pike's *The Prostrate State: South Carolina under Negro Government*, published in 1874. Pike, according to his biographer, had a "pronounced racial antipathy toward the Negro." Another Bowers source was *Reconstruction in South Carolina* by John S. Reynolds, issued in 1905. According to W. E. B. Du Bois, the great black scholar, the works of Pike and Reynolds were "openly and blatantly propaganda," and that Bowers's book itself "was absolutely devoid of historical judgment or sociological knowledge."[3]

Many of the other standard secondary sources on the period were similarly paternalistic or racist. The primary sources available at that

---

[2]Claude Bowers, *The Tragic Era* (New York, 1929), pp. vi, 353, 358, 362, and 364.
[3]Robert F. Durden, *James Shepherd Pike* (Durham, N.C., 1957), p. viii; and W. E. B. Du Bois, *Black Reconstruction* (New York, 1935), pp. 720–721.

time often contributed to this racial bias. Since slaves had been forbidden to read or write records of their early years of freedom were sparse. White men often became self-appointed spokesmen for both races, thereby obscuring the viewpoint of the blacks completely. Records of black officials were sometimes deliberately destroyed. The archives of the black Florida superintendent of education who helped to establish the public school system in that state, for example, disappeared once his white successors took office. The state of Alabama tried to obliterate the printed records of black Reconstruction altogether. Libraries and public archives meanwhile were reluctant to gather any documents that were related to the black history of the Reconstruction era.

The Dunning interpretation remained dominant for over two decades. It was openly racist, and any hope of reaching a balanced and more objective point of view was out of the question. Despite the protests of W. E. B. Du Bois and a handful of white historians, the Dunning position prevailed throughout the profession.

The Progressive school of historians who dealt with the whole span of American history and not simply with the Reconstruction era did little to help the cause of black history. This school, while not explicitly racist, served to minimize the significance of blacks in American history. Because of its focus on the impersonal forces operating in history—economic in the case of Beard and environmental in the case of Turner—the Progressive school de-emphasized the role of individuals both black and white. Beard made capitalism and the triumph of Northern industrialism over the South's cotton kingdom the thesis in the two-volume 1927 work entitled *The Rise of American Civilization.* He argued that Northern financiers and industrialists had maneuvered the country into the war, and the South out of and back into the Union, in a successful attempt to wrest control of the national economy from the cotton planters. This interpretation had the effect of reducing black abolitionists, black soldiers, and black politicians (as well as whites for that matter) to mere pawns operating within the context of a gigantic capitalist conspiracy. Frederick Jackson Turner, in his famous essay on "The Significance of the Frontier," written in 1893, concluded that once American history was viewed in the correct light slavery would be seen merely as an "incident" and not an important institution with tragic consequences.

What the Progressives did was to shift the focus of attention away from the blacks. Since the turn of the century the majority of scholars—racists and nonracists alike—had assumed that the blacks had been a crucial factor in the coming of the Civil War and the shaping of Reconstruction. Most historians had accepted the notion that Afro-Americans, both acting and acted upon, had largely dominated the national scene from 1861 to 1877. Progressives like Beard and Turner, however, shifted the perspective away from the blacks. Beard claimed that slavery was in no real sense the central issue of the Civil War. By diminishing the role played by individuals and their ideas—both blacks and whites—and emphasizing instead other deterministic elements which shaped history, the Progressives make blacks less visible.

From the late 1920s to the 1950s—the period of transition—scholars began to view the developments during the Reconstruction era and the role of blacks differently from the Dunning school. The so-called revisionists—an anti-Dunning school—restudied the Reconstruction era and concluded it was not as bad as previously pictured. Influenced in part by the Progressive school they challenged certain findings of the Dunningites. The revisionists refused to view Reconstruction as a kind of morality play—one that depicted the history of the period as a struggle between the forces of good and evil, whites and blacks, Democrats and Radical Republicans.[4]

Although the revisionists accepted many of the findings of the Dunning school, they started from different premises and assumptions. Consequently they arrived at different conclusions. Quite often revisionists did so after examining the very same data the Dunningites had used. The revisionists, for one thing, viewed the blacks and their role during Reconstruction in a much more favorable light. They denied that the worst features of Reconstruction had arisen from black domination of Southern political offices. In no single state in the South had the blacks controlled both houses of the legislature, the revisionists pointed out. There were no black governors elected and only one black state supreme court justice was appointed. On the national level only two blacks were elected to the Senate, and barely fifteen to the House of Representatives. On the basis of such findings the charge of the Dunningites that blacks were responsible for the presumed excesses of Reconstruction governments could hardly be substantiated. The so-called black Reconstruction, it appeared, was not so "black" after all.

The accusation that blacks had been inefficient and unintelligent in government administration in the states where they played a most active political role was also shown to be false. Vernon L. Wharton, in a path-breaking study of the Mississippi state government during the postwar period, *The Negro in Mississippi, 1865–1890*, published in 1947, found little difference on the county level within certain agen-

---

[4]Gerald N. Grob, "Reconstruction: An American Morality Play," in *American History: Retrospect and Prospect*, George Athan Billias and Gerald N. Grob, eds. (New York, 1971), pp. 191–231.

cies when either blacks or whites were in office. As state governments went, that of Mississippi between 1870 and 1876, when a coalition of black and white Republicans was in control, was not a bad one, Wharton concluded.

Finally the revisionists disagreed with the idea that the Radical governments had been unusually expensive or corrupt. Although expenses went up sharply in the postwar period, it was not always the result of inefficiency or theft, they said. Wartime destruction required the use of public funds to rebuild cities and devastated areas. Even more important was the fact that the South was forced for the first time to provide certain public services for its black slaves–turned–citizens. Schools were erected, hospitals built, and mental institutions established. Such facilities had not existed before the Civil War, and the rise in spending during the Reconstruction era could be accounted for, in large part, by these new social services.

The revisionists revealed as well a greater sensitivity and awareness of the racist attitudes and prejudices of past historians. Francis Simkins, a Southern scholar and leading exponent of the revisionist school, commented on this point in an important article written in 1939. Earlier historians had given a distorted picture of Reconstruction, Simkins said, because they began with the basic premise that blacks were racially inferior. Their approach, as a result, was based on ignorance, and their conclusions were warped by their prejudices. Only by abandoning these biases, Simkins concluded, could scholars hope to arrive at a more accurate understanding of the past.[5]

Black scholars made the same point. W. E. B. Du Bois, a Harvard-trained historian and sociologist, thorough-going professional, and the outstanding black scholar of his day, took issue with the writings of the Dunning school. Proud of his race Du Bois presented an impressive defense of the activities of blacks during Reconstruction in his massive 1935 study entitled *Black Reconstruction*. Du Bois, who had become a Marxist by this time, advanced the rather dubious thesis that the freed blacks had shown considerable class-consciousness during the Reconstruction years.

Carter Woodson, another pioneering black historian, was also sharply critical of the Dunning school. An influential scholar and propagandist for the study of the black past, Woodson founded the *Journal of Negro History*. In the fourth edition of his important book, *The Negro in Our History*, published in 1927, Woodson took racist white historians to task for their prejudices.

---

[5]Francis B. Simkins, "New Viewpoints of Southern Reconstruction," *Journal of Southern History* 5 (1939):49–61. See also the classic article by Howard K. Beale, "On Rewriting Reconstruction History," *American Historical Review* 45 (1939–1940):807–27.

Throughout the period of transition the search for primary sources of black history also grew more intense. During the depression of the 1930s the W.P.A. and other federal agencies made a more concentrated effort to compile and research records for such materials. These steps were taken with the knowledge that better black history could be written if primary sources written by Afro-Americans themselves were available.

Between the 1920s and 1950 the single most significant event that improved the status of blacks within American society was World War II. Confronted with the blatant racism of Nazi Germany toward the Jews, Americans finally were brought face-to-face with the racism against blacks in their own society. How could scholars in a society fighting Nazi racism support overt racism against blacks at home? World War II, then, proved to be a most important turning point for American historians in making them aware of the detrimental effects of racism on scholarly inquiry. This change in the climate of opinion was reflected by a marked shift away from a racist perspective during the period of transition.

A second development in this same period was the work of anthropologists and psychologists who undermined the intellectual respectability of racist ideas. Anthropologist Franz Boas showed that physical types within the human species were not fixed and unalterable. Social psychologists looked again at the evidence on the distribution of high and low levels of intelligence and rejected the notion that some races were superior and others inferior.

The intellectual underpinnings for this more liberal outlook could be seen in the writings of Swedish scholar Gunnar Myrdal, who was commissioned to write a work on American race relations. Myrdal produced a classic on the conditions of blacks in America entitled *An American Dilemma*, which appeared in 1944. He based his study on an explicitly liberal premise. Myrdal assumed that the problem of race relations presented a moral dilemma to most Americans. They deeply believed, on the one hand, in the American moral creed of liberty and justice for all. On the other hand most Americans were painfully aware that they and their society had fallen far short of such ideals. Hence most white Americans were forced to live with the enduring moral dilemma that there was a great gap between their stated ideals and their day-to-day existence.

Despite the move toward a less racist stance among historians during and after World War II, there was by no means unanimity within the profession. As late as 1947—at the very end of the period of transition—E. Merton Coulter, a distinguished Southern scholar, published a patently racist study entitled *The South During Reconstruction*. The work appeared, moreover, in the "History of the South" series—a series whose aim was to present the latest and best scholarship written about the region.

The climate of opinion about blacks changed even more dramatically during the period of maturation—the decades of the 1950s and 1960s. With the 1954 Supreme Court decision of *Brown et al.* v. *Board of Education in Topeka* the segregation of black and white children in public schools was ruled illegal. This ruling, calling for equal and integrated schools for blacks, helped to set off the greatest civil rights movement in American history. Liberal white public opinion in the North began to move slowly toward a more racially egalitarian viewpoint. Martin Luther King, Jr., and other black leaders, meanwhile, were demonstrating that nonviolent direct action could succeed in bringing about change in parts of the South.

The dynamics of international power politics likewise contributed to the domestic changes already in progress. Soviet propaganda about racism in America was part of the intellectual offensive in the Cold War; it embarrassed Americans and caused many of them to reassess their position on this issue. The rise of newly emerging African nations in the 1950s and 1960s, moreover, gave some American blacks a more confident self-image at home. Pan-Africanism provided a newfound sense of pride.

All these developments gave rise to what was called a "black revolution in expectations." Blacks no longer felt they had to put up with the humiliation of second-class citizenship—segregated schools, disenfranchisement, and discrimination in employment practices. Such humiliations, though not as great as in the past, seemed more intolerable than ever before. This increasing impatience and dissatisfaction led to a mounting crescendo of nonviolent direct action in the late 1950s in the form of student sit-ins and massive protest marches. In the mid-1960s, however, the tension exploded in mass race riots in many major American cities. There were a series of such race riots after Martin Luther King, Jr., the revered black leader, was assassinated in 1968. These changes in the world outside the scholar's study spurred white historians to take up the study of black history more than ever before.

At the same time changes within the historical profession itself caused scholars to look at black history anew. There was a profound change in perspective among historians, and a shift toward analyzing the totality of human social experience. Influenced in part by the French *Annales* school, in part by the populist-oriented concerns of the 1960s, and in part by the impact of emerging behavioral science methodologies—such as computer quantification techniques—scholars began writing the "new social history." Scholars realized that the discipline of history had to encompass more than a compilation of facts about the lives, thoughts, and perceptions of political and intellectual leaders—the elites in American society. To comprehend more fully the total sum of human experience many "new social historians" felt compelled to study the lives, habits, customs, and practices of all persons, the common and everyday folk as well as the learned and the great. It was within this context that more white scholars proceeded to take up the study of black history.

One other change affected the writing of history in the 1950s and 1960s, and that was the political activism of some younger scholars. Certain young historians, such as the New Left, either became participants in or were close observers of the civil rights movement during these two decades. The failure of American society to allow significant changes in the lives of most blacks—especially those living in Northern urban ghettoes and the black belt regions of the lower South—demonstrated to these scholars how deeply racism was entrenched in American society. Some historians were radicalized as a result. They regarded racism not as some anomaly—as was implied when slavery was termed the "peculiar institution"—but rather as a phenomenon functional in American society from its very start. Such radical historians did not perceive American society as a pluralistic "melting pot" and the blacks as simply another immigrant group: the blacks had been brought unwillingly to the New World, they pointed out, and for most blacks the melting pot never melted.[6]

Such developments gave rise to a new school of Reconstruction historiography in the 1950s called the "neorevisionists." These scholars tended to stress moral rather than economic considerations in their interpretation of the Reconstruction era. The differences between the revisionists and the neorevisionists were often slight; the neorevisionists, in fact, frequently relied on the findings of the revisionists to reach their conclusions. For this reason it is difficult to distinguish or label clearly certain historians as belonging to one group or another. The major difference between the two groups was this: the neorevisionists rejected the revisionist approach which interpreted the Reconstruction era basically from an economic point of view.

Another major distinction between the two groups was that the neorevisionists placed a heavy emphasis on race as a moral issue. Kenneth Stampp, a major neorevisionist, published, in 1965, *The Era of Reconstruction*—a work that stressed such a moral perspective. Stampp

---

[6]During the period of maturation there were also some Marxist historians writing on blacks in the Reconstruction era. See Herbert Aptheker, ed., *Documentary History of the Negro People in the United States* (New York, 1951), which has many documents on the activities of black leaders during the 1860s; and Philip S. Foner, *The Life and Writings of Frederick Douglass*, 4 vols. (New York, 1950–1955), especially volumes 3 and 4.

argued there was one central question during the Reconstruction period: What was to be the place of the recently freed slaves within American society as a whole and especially within Southern society? President Andrew Johnson and his followers believed in the innate inferiority of blacks on racial grounds. They were opposed, therefore, to any program based upon egalitarian assumptions. The Radical Republicans, on the other hand, took seriously the ideals of equality, natural rights, and democracy. Many of the Radical Republicans, in fact, had been associated with the abolitionist movement before the war, and carried over their ideas and attitudes to the Reconstruction era. Stampp recognized that many Radical Republicans also had some self-interest in supporting blacks: they hoped that the freed blacks would join the Republican party out of gratitude for what it had done for them. But to claim that the Radicals had solely selfish motives, Stampp said, was to do them an injustice and to present a distorted picture of the postwar era.

The Radical Republicans, according to Stampp, failed to achieve their aims. Most Americans at the time harbored racial prejudices—either consciously or unconsciously—and were unwilling to accept blacks as equals. By the 1870s the North was weary and anxious to abandon the blacks and their fate to Southern whites for three reasons. First, there was a deep desire to return to normal relations between the two regions. Second, Northern industrialists were eager to invest in Southern plants. And third, there was a growing conviction that the cause of the blacks was no longer worth the trouble it was creating within the country.

But the heroic struggle of the Radicals was not in vain, Stampp said. The Radical state governments passed certain laws that protected the rights of blacks. More important, on the national level, the Radicals succeeded in framing the Fourteenth and Fifteenth amendments. "[I]t was worth a few years of radical reconstruction to give the American Negro the ultimate promise of equal civil and political rights," Stampp concluded.[7]

The single most important scholar writing during the period of maturation was the liberal white historian C. Vann Woodward. In his *Strange Career of Jim Crow*, published in 1955, Woodward argued that the system of segregation established by the infamous Jim Crow laws did not commence right after the Civil War. Instead these laws were primarily the result of the intensified hostility aroused among Southern whites druing the late nineteenth and early twentieth centuries.

The Civil Rights Act of 1875 and similar legislation had had an effect, Woodward claimed, and the period from the end of Reconstruc-

---

[7]Kenneth Stampp, *The Era of Reconstruction, 1865–1877* (New York, 1966), p. 215.

tion in 1877 to the 1890s was marked by a rough equality in law and practice between the races. Woodward concluded that segregation though in evidence was not so harsh and rigid during this interim period. The Jim Crow laws really resulted from the politics of the 1890s. When the Populist threat of a new coalition between black and white farmers under the leadership of white agrarian radicals arose, Southern white conservatives reacted violently. They feared possible racial amalgamation or the renewal of another era of black rule. To put down this Populist threat, blacks were terrorized by lynchings, disenfranchised at the polls, and segregated socially in public life in the 1890s and thereafter. Woodward's study constituted a historiographical landmark, and its appearance was timely because national attention was being focused on the civil rights movement following the Supreme Court decision of 1954.

Woodward's work soon became the center of a historiographical controversy. Other scholars had located the genesis of the Jim Crow system elsewhere in terms of space and time. Leon Litwack's 1961 study, *North of Slavery*, provided examples of widespread racial discrimination in the antebellum North, showing that racism was a national and not simply a Southern problem. Richard Wade in his *Slavery in the Cities*, published in 1964, found that Jim Crow practices had originated in Southern cities before the Civil War in response to the growing urban black population. Joel Williamson's *After Slavery*, which appeared in 1965, dated the origins of Jim Crow within a specific time period. Williamson furnished evidence that in South Carolina whites tried to expand the system of segregation only after slavery had been destroyed. When Woodward published a revised third edition of his *Strange Career of Jim Crow* in 1974, he acknowledged the validity of the arguments of Wade and Williamson, but held nevertheless quite closely to his original thesis.[8]

Black scholars meanwhile were also busy making major contributions to black history during the 1950s and 1960s. Prior to this time black history had been largely the domain of black scholars from black colleges and universities who published in such learned periodicals as the *Journal of Negro History*. A survey of the articles in this journal

------

[8]C. Vann Woodward, *Strange Career of Jim Crow* (New York, 1974), Chapter 1; August Meier and Elliott Rudwick, in "A Strange Chapter in the Career of Jim Crow," in *The Making of Black America*, Meier and Rudwick, eds. (New York, 1969), II:14–19, believe there is some validity to all three positions of Woodward, Wade, and Williamson.

Woodward, resorting to the use of such ideas as "social distance" and "physical distance" derived from the fields of sociology and comparative history, stressed that such concepts should be applied in any future study of race relations and Jim Crow laws in America; see his chapter in *American Counterpoint* (Boston, 1971), pp. 234–260.

prior to the period of maturation reveals the surprising degree to which black scholars had anticipated the work done later by white scholars. The work of black scholars on matters dealing with race was generally confined to this journal because they encountered obstacles when they attempted to publish their findings in the standard historical periodicals.

John Hope Franklin, the most distinguished black scholar writing during this period, made several important contributions at this time and subsequently. Many of Franklin's writings dealt with the era before 1865: these included *The Militant South*, issued in 1956; *The Emancipation Proclamation*, which appeared in 1963; and parts of his textbook, *From Slavery to Freedom*, first published in 1947 and revised periodically over the next three decades. But Franklin's *Reconstruction: After the Civil War*, which came out in 1961, took up the time period covered in this chapter. Franklin's book not only revised the Dunning interpretation, but also undertook to make some overall generalizations regarding the Reconstruction era. He presented conclusive evidence that Radical Reconstruction was neither overwhelmingly "black" nor wholly inept. Although Franklin agreed that some black legislators were corrupt, he argued corruption was a nationwide problem and not confined to the South alone. Franklin ended his volume with a harsh indictment of the failure by the country to carry through its wartime promises of racial justice for blacks.

Benjamin Quarles, another black historian, in his *Negro in the Civil War*, published in 1953, revised sharply the role of blacks during that conflict. He demonstrated and documented the contributions blacks had made to the Union cause. His *Lincoln and the Negro*, in 1962, covered that important subject. Quarles's *Black Abolitionists*, which appeared in 1969, however, dealt with the prewar as well as postwar periods. This book revealed that the tensions that arose between black and white abolitionists before the war resulted from the race prejudices of the whites. White abolitionists had a totally unrealistic view of what the rights of freed blacks ought to be. In the Reconstruction era these enduring tensions caused a split between the two groups, driving the black abolitionists to resort to their own devices and to pursue their own goals.

Charles Wesley, another black historian, reflected in an article published in 1964 the major problem facing many black historians at that time. In his piece Wesley argued for the instrumentalist use of history—that is, to use black history not to inquire but to instruct. Using Jewish history as his example Wesley claimed that the knowledge and awareness of their past triumphs had enabled Jews to achieve great things in the face of hopeless odds, and to instill group pride in the current generation. Blacks, Wesley argued, should employ their past in the same way: to use black history as a tool for building black pride rather than to inquire after the truth in an objective way.[9]

The problem became a pressing one for scholars—both black and white—in the 1950s and 1960s as the civil rights movement burst upon the scene. There was a tendency among some historians to apply a compensatory principle and to applaud the achievements of blacks in history in an uncritical way. Sometimes such scholars were overreacting to the neglect black history had suffered in the past. They sought to make amends, therefore, by blowing out of proportion the historical importance of black leaders, black groups, and the black people as a whole. At other times such scholars were white historians motivated by a sense of guilt about race prejudice in America; they wrote in a mood of contrition as though they might expatiate their guilt. In some ways this approach resembled the kind of celebratory history written earlier about certain immigrant groups, which had stressed their achievements in an overly laudatory manner. Scholars writing in this vein about blacks presented black history as though it were a succession of individuals like Benjamin Banneker, the brilliant mathematician and astronomer; George Washington Carver, the chemist; Jackie Robinson, the baseball player; and Martin Luther King, Jr.

This approach so troubled C. Vann Woodward, a liberal with profound sympathy for blacks, that he wrote an article in 1969 and protested that this tendency was unprofessional. Black history written by whites in the past, he noted, had been characterized by two approaches: the "invisible man solution," and the "moral-neutrality approach." The "invisible man solution" portrayed American history without any blacks because they failed to fit the image of America as a country of ideal democratic fulfillment. The "moral-neutrality approach" was characterized by Beard and Turner. They recognized the existence of blacks but then ignored the moral problems raised by their presence or else diminished such problems by writing about them with morally neutral explanations in mind. Neither approach was satisfactory any more, said Woodward. Nor for that matter was the myth-making and filiopietism in which black and white scholars had indulged when motivated by the impulse for compensatory exaggeration.

Woodward called for a revision of black history—one that would on one hand honestly credit the achievements of blacks when warranted, and, on the other, recount the painful and tragic relations between the two races. One possible solution, Woodward suggested, was to deal with black history in terms of irony and humor. "Anything so

---

[9]Charles H. Wesley, "Creating and Maintaining an Historical Tradition," *Journal of Negro History* 49 (1964):13–33.

full of tears as the black experience, and anything so full of the absurd as the relations between the races in America, cannot be wholly devoid of existential humor," he observed.[10] The Woodward article is the first selection for this chapter.

During the 1960s as well, there were writings on black history by blacks who were not scholars, strictly speaking, but who reflected nevertheless the wide spectrum of black thought of the day. Martin Luther King, Jr., the brilliant black leader, expressed his credo in *Strength to Love*, published in 1963. King believed in the idea of non-violence both as a tactic and a philosophy—as a means and an end. As a tactic nonviolence could so stir the conscience of an opponent, he believed, that reconciliation could finally become a reality. Adopting the course of nonviolent resistance implied that the resister had to love his enemy. On a philosophical level King declared that nonviolent resistance was the key to building a new world. Down through history man had met violence with violence and hate with hate. King believed that only nonviolence and love could break this vicious cycle of revenge and retaliation. His hope was that blacks, through the use of nonviolent resistance, could help bring about a new day. Before King could finish his work he was tragically assassinated.[11]

By the mid-1960s the civil rights movement had hit its peak and black people were being attracted to black leaders other than King. One of the most dynamic was Malcolm X, whose *Autobiography of Malcolm X* appeared in 1966. His book provided some important and realistic insights into twentieth-century black America. Although born Malcolm Little he identified himself as Malcolm X to symbolize with his number that he had been robbed of his name and heritage by whites. His ancestors had been taken forceably from Africa by whites, he noted, making it impossible for him to locate his roots or to trace his history. Coming from the ghetto, Malcolm X could appeal to ghetto residents in a way that King, whose origins were middle class, could not. Joining the Black Muslim movement—an antiwhite separatist group dedicated to the Islamic religion—Malcolm X emerged as a charismatic leader. In 1964 he broke with the Black Muslims, however, and after a trip to Africa planned to start a secular black nationalist movement of his own. Toward the end of his life Malcolm X qualified his black racism as a result of his travels in Africa. Formerly his hatred toward whites was such that he had referred to them as "devils." But after his visit to Africa, he began to preach reconciliation between the two races. In

---

[10]C. Vann Woodward, "Clio with Soul," *Journal of American History* 56 (1969):19.

[11]The tactic of nonviolent resistance among American blacks was first used in the summer of 1942 by members of CORE (the Congress of Racial Equality). See August Meier and Elliott Rudwick, *CORE* (New York, 1973), pp. 1–23.

1965 he was gunned down before he had an opportunity to formulate his new philosophy.

In the summer of 1966 the slogan "Black Power" burst upon the public consciousness and reverberated across the country. Stokely Carmichael, a young black leader, employed this motto to question the worth of nonviolence as a tactic and the value of integration as a goal. Carmichael attacked the idea of building a coalition between a group that was economically secure—middle-class white liberals—and one that was insecure—poor blacks. Carmichael also challenged the concept of integration, claiming that it would result in the continuance of white supremacy. Both societies—black and white—should build the kind of communities they wanted, he said, and integration instead of being a one-way street should be reciprocal. In *Black Power: The Politics of Liberation,* written with Charles Hamilton in 1968, Carmichael stressed that America's existing political structure would have to be changed if racism was to be overcome.

The thinking of other blacks, both in the past and present, became a focus of major concern for historians during the 1960s. The ideas of contemporary blacks during the period of racial violence were expressed in H. Rap Brown's *Die, Nigger, Die,* published in 1969; Eldridge Cleaver's *Soul on Ice,* in 1968; and Claude Brown's autobiography *Manchild in the Promised Land,* which came out in 1965. But there were also more scholarly books published. Harold Cruse's provocative *Crisis of the Negro Intellectual,* in 1967, was critical of most leading black figures of the twentieth century. August Meier, on the other hand, produced *Negro Thought in America, 1880–1915* in 1963—an outstanding analysis of black thought and life during those years.

This all-too-brief account of books on black history written in the period of maturation hardly touches the mountain of literature on the subject that appeared during these two decades. Historiographical controversies raged over numerous topics in the field—the extent to which Southern blacks had participated in the Populist party and the degree of their equality in this political involvement; the contrast between the leadership of Booker T. Washington and W. E. B. Du Bois; the attitude of the labor movement toward blacks in different periods; Marcus Garvey's back-to-Africa movement; the New Deal and its policies toward blacks; the participation of blacks in World War II; the civil rights movement and the conflicting ideas of its leaders; and the precise role of the black power movement. This explosion of articles, monographs, and books demonstrated that the subject of black history had become at last a matter of vital concern to scholars.

But as millennial expectations waned in the late 1960s many black scholars objected to what was going on in the field of black history. They protested that by segregating so-called black topics from the rest of American history the historical profession was, in effect, indulging in racism under a different guise. This charge that black history still reflected elements of racism showed that black scholars were not yet prepared to accept the works produced as unprejudiced and unbiased.

The proliferation of works on black history during the period of accommodation since 1970 was even more impressive than in the past. The reason for this advance was two-fold. First, black history was accepted by now as a legitimate field of study. Second, the "new social historians" writing on the subject became more aware of the existence of a separate black community with a set of values all its own. To describe the workings of this community and its value system, scholars sometimes resorted to the concept of a black subculture.

During the 1970s, the "new social historians" interested in demography began to study the migration of blacks from the rural South to the urban North in the first three decades of the twentieth century. This mass movement was, without doubt, the most momentous event in the history of American blacks between their emancipation and the World War I era. Pushed by poverty and the destruction wrought by the boll weevil, and pulled by the bright promise of a living wage and a better life, blacks by the thousands trekked to the North's great industrial cities. George Groh's *Black Migration* and Robert Grant's *Black Man Comes to the City*, both published in the early 1970s, presented statistics on this mass movement that ranks as one of the greatest internal migrations of peoples in American history. Florette Henri in her *Black Migration*, published in 1976, showed that this move during the years 1900 to 1920 eventually opened up a newfound sense of black identity in two ways. One was a literal separatist path epitomized by Marcus Garvey and his back-to-Africa movement in the 1920s. The other way was metaphorical: the return to pride in African culture and heritage through an artistic movement called the "Harlem Renaissance."

Other "new social historians," such as Stephan Thernstrom, analyzed the workings of black communities. In his *The Other Bostonians*, published in 1973, Thernstrom devoted one chapter to Boston blacks among the other groups he investigated. Thernstrom viewed the blacks from two perspectives: the effect that the Boston community had upon them; and the effect they had had upon Boston. Boston, to be sure, was not a typical Northern metropolis; it had attracted less than its share of blacks during the era of the great migration. Thernstrom, nevertheless, was able to present some interesting findings.

Like incoming immigrants arriving from southern and eastern Europe during the first three decades of the twentieth century, Thernstrom found that Boston blacks tended to cluster in ghettoes. But he argued against the "last-of-the-immigrants" theory advanced by other scholars—writers who compared the experiences of blacks with the arriving European newcomers. There was some upward social mobility experienced in the labor force by first- and second-generation immigrants, he noted, especially after they had resided in Boston for some time. But for first- and second-generation blacks arriving from the South a lengthy stay in the city made little difference in their social mobility: they stayed stuck in low-paying, low-skilled jobs. His conclusion was obvious: racism had prevented blacks from making much progress. Thernstrom's study proved to be a welcome addition to two earlier studies in the 1960s on the rise of black ghettoes—Gilbert Osofsky's *Harlem: The Making of a Ghetto, Negro New York, 1890–1930,* and Allan Spear's *Black Chicago: The Making of a Negro Ghetto, 1890– 1920.*[12]

The migration to the urban North stirred black intellectuals to a new sense of self-confidence and black consciousness. In the 1920s many of them—poets, novelists, sculptors, historians, and sociologists—became involved in a movement called the Harlem Renaissance. Some black artists took great pride in their African ancestry and deliberately cultivated a form of Pan-African cultural nationalism. An impressive number of works were produced revealing the cultural and intellectual achievements of Afro-Americans. These works gained the respect of the New York community at large and at the same time strengthened the cultural hopes and traditions of the black community itself. In producing such works black artists confronted two dangers. First, they ran the risk of appealing, either consciously or unconsciously, to the conventional concepts of excellence as defined by the white middle class. Second, some artists in their works tended to reinforce or to refer to certain white stereotyped notions of black life. Nathan I. Huggins, in his *Harlem Renaissance,* published in 1971, presented the fullest scholarly treatment of this fascinating movement.

The migration northward also plunged some blacks into the midst of an industrial world for which they were ill-prepared because of their Southern rural background. Manufacturers faced a labor shortage during World War I when the supply of cheap immigrant labor was cut off, and this situation opened opportunities for American blacks. However, the numbers accepted in factories were few because of racial discrimination. But it was the white workers more than the employers who raised objections to hiring blacks. The record of the organized labor movement in this regard was largely negative up to the depression

---

[12]For a work on Pittsburgh from 1900 to 1960, which takes issue with certain of Thernstrom's findings about Boston blacks, see John Bodnar, Roger Simon, and Michael Weber, *Lives of Their Own* (Urbana, Ill., 1982).

of the 1930s. Scholars were slow to write about the black worker—as they were about so many areas of black life—and the works on this subject in the decades from the 1920s to the 1950s had been few and far between.

But in the 1970s the "new social historians" took a renewed interest in labor history in general and in the black worker in particular. Two scholars made noteworthy contributions in this regard. Milton Cantor published a book of collected essays by various scholars, entitled *Black Labor in America*, in 1970. The work was mostly by younger scholars, many of whom considered themselves to be "new labor historians." Herbert Gutman, whose main interest was in the black family, produced a number of stimulating pieces in the 1960s and 1970s that presented a series of case studies of black workers in different places at different periods of time.[13]

The subject of the black family likewise came under close scrutiny in the 1970s. Herbert Gutman's *The Black Family in Slavery and Freedom, 1750–1925*, published in 1976, emerged as the most insightful work on the subject. Gutman was stirred to write in reaction to the 1965 report entitled *The Case for National Action on the Negro Family* prepared by Daniel Patrick Moynihan, then assistant secretary of labor. Moynihan had pointed with alarm to the dangerous "pathology" of the black family in the urban ghettoes, and underscored the widespread illegitimacy and high number of female-headed households that he claimed existed. Embracing the current literature Moynihan endorsed the idea that the decline of the black family could be traced back to the slave experience. Many slave owners had neither fostered Christian marriages among their slave couples nor had hesitated to separate couples at slave auctions. The result was that marriage had meant little to the slaves, according to Moynihan. The slave household developed into a female-headed family in which no father was present. This pattern had persisted into the twentiety century, Moynihan suggested, and was the major cause for the numerous welfare cases in black ghettoes.

Gutman, using the analytical tools of demography developed by the "new social historians," discovered an altogether different pattern. He concluded on the basis of case studies of certain plantations that Afro-Americans managed to establish remarkably stable and long-lived

---

[13]Herbert Gutman, "Reconstruction in Ohio: Negroes in the Hocking Valley Coal Mines in 1873 and 1874," *Labor History* 3 (1962):243–264; "The Negro in the United Mine Workers," in *The Negro and the American Labor Movement*, Julius Jacobson, ed., (New York, 1968), pp. 49–127; and comments on blacks in the articles in *Work, Culture and Society in Industrializing America* (New York, 1976). See also Theodore Purcell and Gerald Cavanagh, *Blacks in the Industrial World* (New York, 1972), for blacks and their participation especially in the electrical industry.

marriages despite the debilitating slave system. Strong family ties existed, black fathers were present, and they helped to raise and discipline the children. So strong was this family tradition among blacks, Gutman declared, that this pattern survived the migration from the rural South to the urban North. Elizabeth Pleck's *Black Migration and Poverty, Boston, 1865–1900*—a case study of the black movement to Boston that was published in 1979—reinforced Gutman's findings.

Since 1970 historians have resorted to a different methodology—comparative history—in their efforts to view slavery, racism, and segregation within a much broader context. The classic work that set slavery within the widest possible perspective was David Brion Davis's *The Problem of Slavery in Western Culture*, published in 1966. His brilliant book analyzed the attitudes toward slavery throughout the Western world from ancient times to the era of the early American abolitionists in the mid-nineteenth century. In 1975 Davis carried his comparative history approach further by contrasting the views of Americans toward slavery with other peoples in the Western world during the years 1770 to 1823 in *The Problem of Slavery in the Age of Revolution*.

George Frederickson took a different tack in employing the comparative history approach. He used South African racism as a yardstick by which to measure the nature, extent, and evolution of American racism in his *White Supremacy*, which appeared in 1981.

One year later John Cell resorted to comparative history in his *The Highest Stage of White Supremacy*. Having lived in the South for forty years, and being a scholar of British imperialism, Cell was eminently qualified to undertake this difficult methodology. He compared the origins of segregation, which he labeled the highest stage of white supremacy, in South Africa and the American South. Cell demonstrated how the pattern of race relations in the two societies were destined to diverge in the twentieth century—one leading to apartheid and the other to greater civil rights. Difficult though the comparative history method might be, it yielded rewarding results, shook American scholars loose from their provincial perspective, and no doubt will be employed more frequently in the future.

Black scholars continued to be active in the period of accommodation as they had been all along. John Hope Franklin, generally acknowledged as the foremost black historian of his generation, wrote *Racial Equality* in 1976. Published in the year of the bicentennial the three lectures in his book traced the course of race relations in the United States and focused on three epochs: the American Revolution, the Reconstruction era, and the twentieth century. In the revolutionary era the founding fathers were not really committed to equality as was generally believed because they failed to change the status of blacks within the new nation. Franklin's picture of Reconstruction was equally gloomy. Congress was no better prepared to extend equality to blacks, Franklin concluded, than it was to guarantee their freedom. The Reconstruction era was marked by some half-hearted steps taken to introduce only a semblance of racial equality.[14]

In the twentieth century, Franklin conceded, the concept of equality became more important to the American people. But, he claimed, the prime concern of policymakers was to create distinctions between those who were regarded as equals and those who were not, i.e., blacks. He acknowledged that whites had played a significant role in the civil rights movement, and that the government had assumed responsibility for promoting equality. But at the same time, Franklin said, there was no real American heritage of liberalism upon which blacks could rely. Although past generations had promoted racial justice, American society as a whole had yet to extend equality of treatment and opportunity to blacks. Franklin's bleak view that racism was still entrenched in America provided a strong argument against those scholars who claimed that their writings were representative and not race-conscious, and that the recent advances made by blacks were evidence that America's liberal tradition had triumphed after all.

Franklin was elected president of the American Historical Association in 1980 and used his presidential address to protest the shortcomings of the profession in dealing with certain aspects of black history. He pointed out that one of the more popular college textbooks written in the 1960s and still in use in 1980—Thomas Bailey's *The American Pageant*—contained racist remarks. Franklin complained, moreover, that few major studies tried to synthesize or to generalize about the history of freedom from emancipation to the present day, to say nothing about the Reconstruction era. Noting that scholars tended to focus more on the period of slavery than the subsequent era of freedom, Franklin complained, "Whatever the reason [for this emphasis], the result has been to leave the major thrust of the Reconstruction story not nearly far enough from where it was in 1929 when Claude Bowers published *The Tragic Era*."[15] The second selection in this chapter is from John Hope Franklin's presidential address.

Thus the most distinguished black scholar in America was implying that vestiges of racism still lingered in the profession, and that the writings of American scholars were not truly representative of the de-

---

[14]For two recent works written on Reconstruction in the period of accommodation since 1970, see William Gillette, *Retreat from Reconstruction 1869–1879* (Baton Rouge, 1979), and Otto H. Olsen, ed., *Reconstruction and Redemption in the South* (Baton Rouge, 1980).

[15]John Hope Franklin, "Mirror for Americans: A Century of Reconstruction History," *American Historical Review* 85 (1980):12.

velopments in black history as he viewed them.[16] Students of history, therefore, were left to ponder the following questions: Does black history written by American scholars, both white and black, represent a true picture of the events that took place? Or is there an inherent racial bias in these writings in terms of the periods studied, the emphases given, and the values stressed? Is black history an essential part of American history, and, of necessity, should it be included in the American story as told by scholars? Or is it a subject that should be segregated and treated as a subfield? Is it possible for white historians to write black history, as Woodward claimed? Or are the attitudes, values, and mind sets of whites and blacks so different that such an assignment is impossible? One thing is certain: given the remarks of John Hope Franklin, the question of whether black history since 1865 is representative or racist remains a live issue in the mid-1980s.

---

[16]For the range of disagreement among black scholars, see William Julius Wilson, *The Declining Significance of Race* (Chicago, 1978), and Alphonso Pinkney, *The Myth of Black Progress* (New York, 1984).

C. Vann Woodward

C. VANN WOODWARD (1908–   ) is Sterling Professor of History
Emeritus at Yale University. He is the author of many works on the history
of the South, including *Tom Watson, Agrarian Rebel* (1938), *The Battle for
Leyte Gulf* (1947), *Origins of the New South 1877–1913* (1951), *Reunion
and Reaction* (1951), *The Burden of Southern History* (1960), *American
Counterpoint* (1971), and *The Strange Career of Jim Crow* (3rd ed., 1974).

In spite of the warning admonitions of Herbert Butterfield and others about the moral interpretation of history, Negro history seems destined to remain the moral storm center of American historiography. It
is hard to see how it could very well be otherwise, at least for some
time to come. Slavery was, after all, the basic moral paradox of American history. It was what Dr. Samuel Johnson had in mind when he
asked: "How is it that we hear the loudest *yelps* for liberty among the
drivers of Negroes?" But the paradox is older and deeper than the temporary embarrassments of 1776, of slaveholders yelping for liberty,
writing the Declaration of Independence, and fighting for the natural
rights of man. Back of that were the European dreamers of America as
an idyllic Arcadia, the New Jerusalem, the Promised Land, the world's
new hope of rebirth, fulfillment, and redemption. Before the dreamers
came the discoverer of America, who returned from one of his voyages
with a cargo of Indian slaves. After him came the explorers and colo-
nizers who competed in the lucrative African slave trade and brought
millions of slaves to the New World. It is, in fact, difficult to see how
Europeans could have colonized America and exploited its resources
otherwise. David B. Davis has phrased the paradox perfectly: "How
was one to reconcile the brute fact that slavery was an intrinsic part
of the American experience with the image of the New World as un-
corrupted nature, as a source of redemption from the burdens of history, as a paradise which promised fulfillment of man's highest aspirations?"

One way of dealing with the problem was that of J. Hector St. John
de Crèvecoeur, who wrote the classic statement of the American idyll
of democratic fulfillment. "What then is the American, this new man?"
was his famous question. And his answer was: "He is either an Eu-

---

C. Vann Woodward, "Clio With Soul," *Journal of American History* 56 (June 1969):5–
20. Reprinted by permission of the *Journal of American History* and C. Vann Woodward.

ropean, or the descendent of an European. . . . " Crèvecoeur simply defined the Negro out of American identity. It is significant that the tacit exclusion went unnoticed for nearly two centuries. Arthur M. Schlesinger, Sr., took the title and text of his presidential address to the American Historical Association in 1942 from this passage of Crèvecoeur without referring to its racial exclusion. Crèvecoeur's precedent was widely followed in the writing of American history. It might be called the "invisible man" solution.

Another way of dealing with Davis' problem of brute fact and idyllic image was that of Beard and Turner. They recognized the Negro's existence all right, but they either ignored moral conflicts and paradoxes in moral values forced by his existence and status, or they attempted to reduce them to other and morally neutral categories of explanation. Referring to Beard, W. E. B. Du Bois remarked that one has the "comfortable feeling that nothing right or wrong is involved." Beard and Turner are merely two conspicuous examples of the numerous practitioners of what might be called the moral-neutrality approach.

Neither the invisible-man solution nor the moral-neutrality approach is any longer acceptable. Moral engagement ranging upward to total commitment now predominates. This approach divides into overlapping though distinguishable categories. One is embraced in the general class of paternalistic historiography, but divides broadly into northern and southern schools. Northern-type paternalism is usually the more self-conscious. One representative of this school assures the Brother in Black that "Negroes are, after all, only white men with black skins, nothing more, nothing less," endowed natively with all the putative white attributes of courage, manhood, rebelliousness, and love of liberty. Another concedes the deplorable reality of the "Sambo personality," but attributes it to potency of the plantation master as white father image and to other misfortunes. Others console the Negro for not producing more Nat Turners and slave rebellions by offering ingenious theories to explain his accommodation to slavery. Still others assure him that he would have been better advised to have chosen men of Iberian and Catholic background rather than those of English and Protestant heritage as masters of the plantation school.

The modern Southern paternalist, falling back on his regional heritage, takes to the role more naturally and with less self-consciousness. He disavows the Phillipsian concept of the benevolent plantation school for Africans, but proceeds as if the school actually worked admirably, with some exceptions, and turned out graduates fully prepared for freedom and equality. Any shortcomings or failings on the part of the blacks are attributed to delinquencies of the "responsible" whites, the paternalists. These assumptions result in a charitable picture of the freedmen during emancipation and Reconstruction and the era following. Instead of a "white man with a black skin," the Negro is elected an honorary southerner by paternalists below the Potomac.

Moral preoccupations and problems shape the character of much that is written about the Negro and race relations by modern white historians, but they are predominately the preoccupations and moral problems of the white man. His conscience burdened with guilt over his own people's record of injustice and brutality toward the black man, the white historian often writes in a mood of contrition and remorse as if in expiation of racial guilt or flagellation of the guilty. In this connection it is well to recall Butterfield's observation that "since moral indignation corrupts the agent who possesses it and is not calculated to reform the man who is the object of it, the demand for it—in the politician and in the historian for example—is really a demand for an illegitimate form of power." It is "a tactical weapon," says Butterfield, valued for its power "to rouse irrational fervour and extraordinary malevolence against some enemy." It is a weapon that is especially useful in polemics—polemics of region against region, party against party, and class against class.

This is not to deny to the historian the role of moral critic or to dismiss what has been written out of deep concern for moral values. The history of the Negro people and race relations has profited more from the insights and challenges of this type of writing in the last two decades than from the scholarship of the preceding and much longer era of moral neutrality and obtuseness. Nor is it to deny the value of what white historians have contributed to the understanding of Negro history. For better or for worse, the great majority of scholars working in this field have been and will continue to be white. Without their contribution, Negro history would be far more impoverished and neglected than it now is.

Granting the value of the part white historians have played in this field, the Negro still has understandable causes for dissatisfaction. For however sympathetic they may be, white historians with few exceptions are primarily concerned with the moral, social, political, and economic problems of white men and their past. They are prone to present to the Negro as *his* history the record of what the white man believed, thought, legislated, did and did not do *about* the Negro. The Negro is a passive element, the man to whom things happen. He is the object rather than the subject of this kind of history. It is filled with the infamies and the philanthropies, the brutalities and the charities, the laws, customs, prejudices, policies, politics, crusades, and wars of whites *about* blacks. "Racial attitudes" or "American attitudes" in a title mean white attitudes. "The Negro Image" means the image in white minds. In this type of history, abolitionists, Radical Republicans, and carpetbaggers are all of the same pale pigmentation. A famous history of the Underground Railroad virtually omitted reference to the blacks, who incurred most of the risks, did most of the work, and suffered nearly all the casualties. The largest and most comprehensive book on the antislavery movement could spare only nine pages for the black abolitionists. Not until the civil rights workers of the 1960s do the prime movers and shakers of Negro history take on a darker hue in the history books, and not in all of them at that.

Negro history in this tradition—and many Negro historians themselves followed the tradition, virtually the only one available in university seminars—was an enclave, a cause or a result, a commentary on or an elaboration of white history. Black history *was* white history. Denied a past of his own, the Negro was given to understand that whatever history and culture he possessed was supplied by his association with the dominant race in the New World and its European background. Thoroughly Europo-centric in outlook, American whites subscribed completely to the myth that European culture, *their* culture, was so overwhelmingly superior that no other could survive under exposure to it. They also shared the European stereotypes, built up by three centuries of slave traders and elaborated by nineteenth- and twentieth-century European imperialists, of an Africa of darkness, savagery, bestiality, and degradation. Not only was the African stripped of this degrading heritage on American shores and left cultureless, a Black Adam in a new garden, but also he was viewed as doubly fortunate in being rescued from naked barbarism and simultaneously clothed with a superior culture. The "myth of the Negro past" was that he had no past.

So compelling was this myth, so lacking any persuasive evidence to the contrary, so universally prevalent the stereotypes of Africans in their American world that until very recently Negroes adopted it unquestioningly themselves. Carter Woodson remarked in 1937 that "Negroes themselves accept as a compliment the theory of a complete break with Africa, for above all things they do not care to be known as resembling in any way these 'terrible Africans.'" And Du Bois wrote that NAACP members had a "fierce repugnance toward anything African. . . . Beyond this they felt themselves Americans, not Africans. They resented and feared any coupling with Africa." White friends of the Negro defended him against any slurs associating him with Africa as if against insults. And Negroes commonly used the words "African" and "black" as epithets of an opprobrious sort. They were *Americans* with nothing to do with Africa or its blackness, nakedness, and savagery. Africa, like slavery, was something to be forgotten, denied, suppressed. With an older American pedigree and a far better claim than first- and second-generation immigrants of other ethnic groups, Negroes could protest the remoteness of their foreign origins and the exclusiveness of their American identity. . . . Until very recently these were the received opinions, the prevailing attitudes of most Negro Americans.

A few years ago a French writer used the word *"décôlonisation"* in the title of a book on the contemporary movement for Negro rights in America. While the analogy that this word suggests is misleading in important respects, it does call attention to the wider environment of the national experience. The dismantling of white supremacy since World War II has been a worldwide phenomenon. The adjustment of European powers to this revolution has appropriately been called decolonization, since this is the political effect it has had on their many possessions in Asia, Africa, and the Caribbean Sea. The outward trappings, the political symbols, the pomp and ceremony of decolonization doubtless contained a considerable amount of collective ego gratification for the ethnic groups concerned. These included the lowering of old flags and the raising of new ones, the drawing of national boundaries, the establishment of new armies, navies, and air forces with new uniforms, foreign embassies, and seats in the United Nations—the full protocol of national sovereignty in the European tradition. The result has been the appearance of thirty-two new black nations, seventeen of them in the year 1960 in Africa alone, and many tiny ones in the Caribbean. But even more gratifying perhaps was the physical as well as symbolic withdrawal of the dominant whites, together with the debasement of their authority and the destruction of the hated paraphernalia of exclusiveness and discrimination. . . .

The dismantling of white supremacy was simultaneously taking place in the United States, but the process was accompanied by no such pomp and circumstance and no such debasement of white authority and power. What did take place in America was far less dramatic. It came in the form of judicial decisions, legislative acts, and executive orders by duly constituted authority that remained unshaken in the possession of power. It came with "all deliberate speed," a speed so deliberate as to appear glacial or illusory. The outward manifestations were the gradual disappearance of the little signs, "White" and "Colored," and the gradual appearance of token black faces in clubs, schools, universities, and boards of directors. Some of the tokens were more impressive: a cabinet portfolio, a Supreme Court appointment, a seat in the Senate, the office of mayor. By comparison with the immediately preceding era in America, these developments were striking indeed. But by contrast with the rituals and symbols of decolonization in Africa and the Caribbean, they took on a much paler cast. And while the outcome abroad was separation and independence for black people, the outcome for black people at home was desegregation and integration—or rather the renewal of unfulfilled promises of them.

While Africa was being transformed from degraded European colonies to aggressively independent nations with famous heroes of liberation and a conspicuous visibility on the world scene, American Negro attitudes toward the ancestral homeland changed profoundly. The traditional indifference or repugnance for things African, the shame and abhorrence of association with Africa, gave way to fascinated interest, pride, and a sense of identification. . . .

We are destined to hear a great deal more about Africa from Afro-Americans as time goes on. This will find its way into historical writing, and some manifestations may seem rather bizarre. Before we assume a posture of outrage or ridicule, it might be well to put this phenomenon into historical perspective. We might recall, for example, that the "scientific" school at the end of the last century placed great emphasis on "Teutonic" and "Anglo-Saxon" tribal customs and institutions and that in doing so it was dipping several centuries deeper into the past for primitive origins than the Afro-Americans are now. . . .

The assimilation of European ethnic groups in America throughout the history of immigration has not only been a story of deculturation and acculturation—the shedding of foreign ways and the adoption of new values. It has also been a story of fierce struggles to assert and maintain ethnic interests and identity. One key element in that struggle has been the group's sense of its past. Each immigrant group of any size established its historical societies and journals in which filiopietism has free rein. . . . These assertions of group pride in a common past, mythic or real, have accompanied a strong urge for assimilation and integration in American society. In the opinion of the anthropologist Melville J. Herskovits, "the extent to which the past of a people is regarded as praiseworthy, their own self-esteem will be high and the opinion of others will be favorable."

The priests who taught the children of the Irish slums that St. Brendan, Bishop of Clonfert, discovered America in the sixth century, or the rabbis who taught their charges in the Jewish slums that the Indians were the lost tribes of Israel, or the Bohemians and Poles and Swedes and Italians who assured the children that it was *their* countrymen who saved the day at Bunker Hill or Bull Run or the Bloody Angle were not advancing the cause of history. But they *were* providing defenses against the WASP myths of the schoolbooks and some sense of group identity and pride and self-esteem to slum dwellers who were, in their turn, regarded by the Best People as the scum of the earth.

Denied a praiseworthy past or for that matter a past of any sort that is peculiarly their own, Negro Americans have consequently been denied such defenses and self-esteem as these resources have provided other and less vulnerable American groups. Now that they are seeking to build defenses of their own and a past of their own, they are likely to repeat many of the ventures in mythmaking and filiopietism in which other minorities, including the WASPs, have indulged.

One of their temptations will be to follow the exciting example of their brothers in Africa who are now in search of national identity for brand-new nation-states. Nationalists have always invoked history in their cause and abused it for their purposes. No nations have been so prone to this use of history as new nations. Unable to rely on habituation of custom by which old states claim legitimacy and the loyalty of their citizens, newborn nations (our own for example) invoke history to justify their revolutions and the legitimacy of new rulers. Like their American kin, the Africans had also been denied a past of their own, for European historians of the imperialist countries held that the continent, at least the sub-Saharan part, had no history before the coming of the white man. Historians of the new African states have not been backward in laying counterclaims and asserting the antiquity of their history and its importance, even its centrality in the human adventure. . . . How much of this overwrought nationalism of the emergent African states will take root in American soil remains to be seen. . . .

It seems possible that the new pride in Africa's achievements, identification with its people and their history, and the discovery of ancestral roots in its culture could contribute richly to the self-discovery and positive group identity of a great American minority. What had been suppressed or regarded with shame in this American subculture could now be openly expressed with confidence and pride. The extent of African survivals in Negro-American culture has been debated for a generation by anthropologists. No doubt such survivals have been exaggerated and admittedly there are fewer in the United States than in Latin America and the West Indies. But the acknowledged or imagined African survivals in religious and marital practices, in motor habits, in speaking, walking, burden carrying, and dancing, however the anthropologists may assess them, have gained new sanction and a swinging momentum.

It seems to me that the reclaimed African heritage could give a third dimension to the tragically two-dimensional man of the Du Bois metaphor. "One ever feels his two-ness," he wrote, "—an American, a Negro; two souls, two thoughts, two unreconciled strivings; two warring ideals in one dark body. . . . " Du Bois thought that, "The history of the American Negro is the history of this strife . . . " and that "this double-consciousness, this sense of always looking at one's self through the eyes of others" was his tragedy. The recovery of an African past and a third dimension of identity might have a healing effect on the schizoid "two-ness," the "two-soul" cleavage of the Negro mind.

There are, unhappily, less desirable consequences conceivable for the preoccupation with Africa as a clue to racial identity. For in the hands of nationalist cults, it can readily become a mystique of skin color and exclusiveness, of alienation and withdrawal. It can foster a new separatism, and inverted segregation, a black apartheid. It can seek group solidarity and identity by the rejection of the White Devil and all his works simply because of white association. This is part of what Erik Erikson meant by "negative identity," the affirmation of identity by what one is not. With reference to that concept, he remarked on "the unpleasant fact that our god-given identities often live off the degradation of others." The most profound insight to be gained from Winthrop D. Jordan's study of American attitudes toward the Negro from English origins to the early nineteenth century is precisely the "negative identity" use that Europeans and white Americans made of Africans. To achieve their own group identity and unity, they systematically debased the Negro to a symbol of the barbarism and licentiousness to which they feared life in the wilderness might reduce Europeans themselves. The Negro thus became, as Jordan says, "a counter image for the European, a vivid reminder of the dangers facing transplanted Europeans, the living embodiment of what they must never allow themselves to become." American society and identity were thus based on white supremacy. It would be one of the most appalling ironies of American history if the victims of this system of human debasement should in their own quest for identity become its imitators.

One manifestation of black nationalism in academic life is the cry that only blacks are truly qualified to write or to interpret or to teach the black experience. In the special sense that, other things being equal, those who have undergone an experience are best qualified to understand it, there is some truth in this claim. George A. Myers, the Negro friend and faithful correspondent of James Ford Rhodes, pleaded with the historian to do justice to the Negro, but doubted his capacity to do so. "You cannot fully appreciate this," he wrote, "because you have never been discriminated against." Since white historians have written most of American history, including the part assigned the Negroes, it was inevitable that they should have determined the concepts, priorities, values, and interpretations of American historiography and that the values of the white man should have generally prevailed over those of the black man. This situation calls for correction and represents a present challenge to Negro historians.

American history, the white man's version, could profit from an infusion of "soul." It could be an essential corrective in line with the tradition of countervailing forces in American historiography. It was in that tradition that new immigrant historians revised first-family and old-stock history, that Jewish scholars challenged WASP interpretations, that western challengers confronted New England complacencies. . . . Negro historians have an opportunity and a duty in the same tradition.

An obligation to be a corrective influence is one thing, but a mandate for the exclusive preemption of a subject by reason of racial qualification is quite another. They cannot have it both ways. Either black history is an essential part of American history and must be included by all American historians, or it is unessential and can be segregated and left to black historians. But Negro history is too important to be left entirely to Negro historians. To disqualify historians from writing Negro history on the grounds of race is to subscribe to an extreme brand of racism. It is to ignore not only the substantial corrective and revisionary contributions to Negro history made by white Americans but also those of foreign white scholars. To export this idea of racial qualifications for writing history to Latin America is to expose its narrow parochialism. The United States is unique, so far as I know, in drawing an arbitrary line that classifies everyone as either black or white and calls all people with any apparent African intermixture "Negroes" or "blacks." In Latin America and the Caribbean, the gradations of color, hair, and features—often very fine gradations—are all important. Some Americans who present themselves as qualified by color to write "black" history would mystify many Latin Americans, since by their standards such people are not black at all, and deem themselves so only by unconsciously adopting white racist myths peculiar to the United States.

The fact is that there are few countries left in the New World that are not multiracial in population. In many of them racial intermixture and intermarriage are prevalent. To impose the rule of racial qualification for historians of such multiracial societies as those of Trinidad, Cuba, Jamaica, Brazil, or Hawaii would be to leave them without a history. What passes for racial history is often the history of the relations between races—master and slave, imperialist and colonist, exploiter and exploited, and all the political, economic, sexual, and cultural relations, and their infinitely varied intermixtures. To leave all this history of these relations in the hands of the masters, the imperialists, or the exploiters would result in biased history. But to segregate historical subjects along racial lines and pair them with racially qualified historians would result in fantastically abstract history. This is all the more true since it is the relations, attitudes, and interactions between races that are the most controversial and perhaps the most significant aspects of racial history.

Some would maintain that the essential qualification is not racial but cultural and that membership in the Afro-American subculture is essential to the understanding and interpretation of the subtleties of speech, cuisine, song, dance, folklore, and music composing it. There may be truth in this. I am not about to suggest that the Caucasian is a black man with a white skin, for he is something less and something more than that. I am prepared to maintain, however, that, so far as their culture is concerned, all Americans are part Negro. Some are more so than others, of course, but the essential qualification is not color or race. When I said "all Americans," unlike Crèvecoeur, I included Afro-Americans. They are part Negro, too, but only part. So far as their culture is concerned they are more American than Afro and far more alien in Africa than they are at home, as virtually all pilgrims to Africa have discovered.

Many old black families of Philadelphia and Boston are less African in culture than many whites of the South. The southern white "acculturation" began long ago and may be traced in the lamentations of planters that their children talked like Negroes, sang Negro songs, preferred Negro music at their dances, and danced like Negroes. . . . But as Herskovits says, "Whether Negroes borrowed from whites or whites from Negroes, in this or any other aspect of culture, it must always be remembered that the borrowing was never achieved without resultant change in whatever was borrowed." If there was a "black experience" and a "white experience," there was also a "gray experience."

Whether the revision of Negro history is undertaken by black historians or white historians, or preferably by both, they will be mindful of the need for correcting ancient indignities, ethnocentric slights, and paternalistic patronizing, not to mention calculated insults, callous indifference, and blind ignorance. They will want to see full justice done at long last to Negro achievements and contributions, to black leaders and heroes, black slaves and freedmen, black poets and preachers.

As for white historians, I doubt that their contribution to this revision would best be guided by impulses of compensatory exaggeration. The genuine achievements of Negro Americans throughout our history are substantial enough in view of the terrible handicaps under which they labored. They should receive the credit that they have been denied. But during the greater part of the struggle for power and place and fame that make up so much of history, black men were kept in chains and illiteracy and subject thereafter to crippling debasement and deprivation. The number of landmarks and monuments they were able to leave on the history of their country was necessarily limited. It is a misguided form of white philanthropy and paternalism that would attempt to compensate by exaggerating or by celebrating ever more obscure and deservedly neglected figures of the past. Equally misguided are impulses of self-flagellation and guilt that encourage the deprecation of all things European or white in our civilization and turn its history into a chorus of *mea culpas*. The demagoguery, the cant, and the charlatanry of historians in the service of a fashionable cause can at times rival that of politicians. Also suspect is the standard assumption, supported by a long New England tradition, that this subject can be properly discussed only with an attitude of humorless solemnity. Anything so full of tears as the black experience, and anything so full of the absurd as the relations between the races in America, cannot be wholly devoid of existential laughter. . . .

The Negro historian under present circumstances labors under a special set of pressures and temptations. One that will require moral fiber to resist is the temptation to gratify the white liberal's masochistic cravings, his servile yearnings to be punished. This is indeed a tempting market, but historians would do well to leave it to the theater of the absurd. Another temptation, given present license and indulgence, is to give uninhibited voice to such sentiments as Du Bois expressed in his declaration: "I believe in the Negro race, in the beauty of its genius, the sweetness of its soul. . . . " A sincere sentiment, no doubt. But before releasing such pronouncements for publication it might be advisable to substitute the word "white" for the word "Negro" and play it back for sound: "I believe in the *white* race, in the beauty of its genius, the sweetness of its soul. . . . " At present, the celebratory impulse runs powerfully through the historiography of this field. Now is the time to praise famous men. Now is the time to do honor to heroes, justice to the obscure, and to demonstrate beyond doubt that the downtrodden seethed constantly with resistance to oppression and hostility to their oppressors. The demand for such history is understandable. But the historian will keep in mind that the stage of history was never peopled exclusively by heroes, villains, and oppressed innocents, that scamps and timeservers and anti-heroes have always played their parts. . . .

It is to be hoped that white as well as black historians will reserve some place for irony as well as for humor. If so, they will risk the charge of heresy by pointing out in passing that Haiti, the first Negro republic of modern history, though born of a slave rebellion, promptly established and for a long time maintained an oppressive system of forced labor remarkably similar to state slavery; that Liberia, the second Negro republic, named for liberty, dedicated to freedom, and ruled by former slaves from the United States, established a flourishing African

slave trade; and that Kwame Nkrumah, dictator of Ghana, with a misguided instinct for symbolism, selected as his official residence at Ac-
cra the Christiansborg Castle, one time barracoon from which his
ancestors had sold their kinsmen into slavery.

These instances are not adduced to alleviate the guilt of the white
man, who rightfully bears the greater burden. I would subscribe in general to the admonition of Barrington Moore, Jr., that, "For all students
of human society, sympathy with the victims of historical processes
and skepticism about the victors' claims provide essential safeguards
against being taken in by the dominant mythology." In all the annals
of Africa there could scarcely be a more ironic myth of history than
that of the New World republic which reconciled human slavery with
natural rights and equality, and on the backs of black slaves set up the
New Jerusalem, the world's best hope for freedom. The mythic African
counterparts look pale beside the American example. They do serve,
however, as reminders that the victims as well as the victors of the
historical process are caught in the human predicament.

John Hope Franklin

JOHN HOPE FRANKLIN (1915–   ) is James Duke Professor Emeritus of History at Duke University. He has written widely in Afro-American history, and his books include *The Free Negro in North Carolina 1790–1860* (1943), *The Militant South 1800–1861* (1956), *Reconstruction After the Civil War* (1961), *The Emancipation Proclamation* (1963), and *From Slavery to Freedom* (5th ed., 1980).

Perhaps no human experience is more searing or more likely to have a long-range adverse effect on the participants than violent conflict among peoples of the same national, racial, or ethnic group. During the conflict itself the stresses and strains brought on by confrontations ranging from name-calling to pitched battles move people to the brink of mutual destruction. The resulting human casualties as well as the physical destruction serve to exacerbate the situation to such a degree that reconciliation becomes virtually impossible. The warring participants, meanwhile, have done irreparable damage to their common heritage and to their shared government and territory through excessive claims and counterclaims designed to make their opponents' position appear both untenable and ludicrous.

Situations such as these have occurred throughout history; they are merely the most extreme and most tragic of numerous kinds of conflicts that beset mankind. As civil conflicts—among brothers, compatriots, coreligionists, and the like—they present a special problem not only in the prosecution of the conflict itself but in the peculiar problems related to reconciliation once the conflict has been resolved. One can well imagine, for example, the utter bitterness and sense of alienation that both sides felt in the conflict that marked the struggle for power between the death in 1493 of Sonni Ali, the ruler of the Songhay empire, and the succession of Askia Muhammad some months later. The struggle was not only between the legitimate heir and an army commander but also between the traditional religion and the relatively new, aggressive religion of Islam, a struggle in which the military man and his new religion emerged victorious.

Historians have learned a great deal about these events, although

John Hope Franklin, "Mirror for Americans: A Century of Reconstruction History," *American Historical Review* 85 (February 1980):1–14. Reprinted with the permission of the American Historical Association and John Hope Franklin.

they are wrapped in the obscurity and, indeed, the evasive strategies of the late Middle Ages. Despite the bitterness of the participants in the struggle and the dissipating competition of scholars in the field, we have learned much more about the internal conflicts of the Songhay empire of West Africa and about the details of Askia Muhammad's program of reconstruction than we could possibly have anticipated—either because the keepers of the records were under his influence or because any uncomplimentary accounts simply did not survive. Interestingly enough, however, the accounts by travelers of the energetic and long-range programs of reconstruction coincide with those that the royal scribes provided.

Another example of tragic internal conflict is the English Civil War of the seventeenth century. The struggle between Charles I and those who supported a radical Puritan oligarchy led not only to a bloody conflict that culminated in the execution of the king but also to bizarre manifestations of acrimony that ranged from denouncing royalism in principle to defacing icons in the churches. Not until the death of Oliver Cromwell and the collapse of the Protectorate were peace and order finally achieved under Charles II, whose principal policies were doubtless motivated by his desire to survive. The king's role in the reconstruction of England was limited; indeed, the philosophical debates concerning, as well as the programs for, the new society projected by the Protectorate had a more significant impact on England's future than the restoration of the Stuarts had.

Thanks to every generation of scholars that has worked on the English Civil War and its aftermath, we have had a succession of illuminations without an inordinate amount of heat. Granted, efforts to understand the conflict have not always been characterized by cool objectivity and generous concessions. But, because historians have been more concerned with understanding the sources than with prejudging the events with or without the sources, we are in their debt for a closer approximation to the truth than would otherwise have been the case.

I daresay that both the Africanists concerned with Songhay and the students of the English Civil War will scoff at these general statements, which they may regard as a simplistic view of the struggles that they have studied so intensely. I am in no position to argue with them. The point remains that, whether one views the internal conflicts of the people of Songhay in the fifteenth century, the English in the seventeenth century, or the Americans in the nineteenth century, the conflict itself was marked by incomparable bitterness and extensive bloodshed. The aftermath, moreover, was marked by continuous disputation over the merits of the respective cases initially as well as over the conduct of the two sides in the ensuing years. These continuing disputations, it should be added, tell as much about the times in which they occurred as about the period with which they are concerned. And, before I do violence either to the facts themselves or to the views of those who have studied these events, I shall seek to establish my claim in the more familiar environment of the aftermath of the Civil War in the United States.

In terms of the trauma and the sheer chaos of the time, the aftermath of the American Civil War has few equals in history. After four years of conflict the burden of attempting to achieve a semblance of calm and equanimity was almost unbearable. The revolution in the status of four million slaves involved an incredible readjustment not only for them *and* their former owners but also for all others who had some understanding of the far-reaching implications of emancipation. The crisis in leadership occasioned by the assassination of the president added nothing but more confusion to a political situation that was already thoroughly confused. And, as in all similar conflicts, the end of hostilities did not confer a monopoly of moral rectitude on one side or the other. The ensuing years were characterized by a continuing dispute over whose side was right as well as over how the victors should treat the vanquished. In the post-Reconstruction years a continuing argument raged, not merely over how the victors did treat the vanquished but over what actually happened during that tragic era.

If every generation rewrites its history, as various observers have often claimed, then it may be said that every generation since 1870 has written the history of the Reconstruction era. And what historians have written tells as much about their own generation as about the Reconstruction period itself. Even before the era was over, would-be historians, taking advantage of their own observations or those of their contemporaries, began to speak with authority about the period.

James S. Pike, the Maine journalist, wrote an account of misrule in South Carolina, appropriately called *The Prostrate State*, and painted a lurid picture of the conduct of Negro legislators and the general lack of decorum in the management of public affairs. Written so close to the period and first published as a series of newspaper pieces, *The Prostrate State* should perhaps not be classified as history at all. But for many years the book was regarded as authoritative—contemporary history at its best. Thanks to Robert Franklin Durden, we now know that Pike did not really attempt to tell what he saw or even what happened in South Carolina during Reconstruction. By picking and choosing from his notes those events and incidents that supported his argument, he sought to place responsibility for the failure of Reconstruction on the Grant administration and on the freedmen, whom he despised with equal passion.

A generation later historians such as William Archibald Dunning and those who studied with him began to dominate the field. Dunning was faithfully described by one of his students as "the first to make scientific and scholarly investigation of the period of Reconstruction." Despite this evaluation, he was as unequivocal as the most rabid opponent of Reconstruction in placing upon Scalawags, Negroes, and Northern radicals the responsibility for making the unworthy and unsuccessful attempt to reorder society and politics in the South. His "scientific and scholarly" investigations led him to conclude that at the close of Reconstruction the planters were ruined and the freedmen were living from hand to mouth—whites on the poor lands and "thriftless blacks on the fertile lands." No economic, geographic, or demographic data were offered to support this sweeping generalization.

Dunning's students were more ardent than he, if such were possible, in pressing their case against Radical Republicans and their black and white colleagues. Negroes and Scalawags, they claimed, had set the South on a course of social degradation, misgovernment, and corruption. This tragic state of affairs could be changed only by the intervention of gallant men who would put principle above everything else and who, by economic pressure, social intimidation, and downright violence, would deliver the South from Negro rule. Between 1900 and 1914 these students produced state studies and institutional monographs that gave more information than one would want about the complexion, appearance, and wearing apparel of the participants and much less than one would need about problems of postwar adjustment, social legislation, or institutional development.

Perhaps the most important impact of such writings was the influence they wielded on authors of textbooks, popular histories, and fiction. James Ford Rhodes, whose general history of the United States was widely read by contemporaries, was as pointed as any of Dunning's students in his strictures on Reconstruction: "The scheme of Reconstruction," he said, "pandered to ignorant negroes, the knavish white natives, and the vulturous adventurers who flocked from the North. . . . " Thomas Dixon, a contemporary writer of fiction, took the findings of Rhodes's and Dunning's students and made the most of them in his trilogy on Civil War and Reconstruction. In *The Clansman*, published in 1905, he sensationalized and vulgarized the worst aspects of the Reconstruction story, thus beginning a lore about the period that was dramatized in *Birth of a Nation*, the 1915 film based on the trilogy, and popularized in 1929 by Claude Bowers in *The Tragic Era*.

Toward the end of its most productive period the Dunning school no longer held a monopoly on the treatment of the Reconstruction era. In 1910 W. E. B. Du Bois published an essay in the *American Historical Review* entitled, significantly, "Reconstruction and Its Benefits." Du Bois dissented from the prevailing view by suggesting that something good came out of Reconstruction, such as educational opportunities for freedmen, the constitutional protection of the rights of all citizens, and the beginning of political activity on the part of the freedmen. In an article published at the turn of the century, he had already hinted "that Reconstruction had a beneficial side," but the later article was a clear and unequivocal presentation of his case.

Du Bois was not the only dissenter to what had already become the traditional view of Reconstruction. In 1913 a Mississippi Negro, John R. Lynch, former speaker of the Mississippi House of Representatives and former member of Congress, published a work on Reconstruction that differed significantly from the version that Mississippi whites had accepted. Some years later he argued that a great deal of what Rhodes had written about Reconstruction was "absolutely groundless." He further insisted that Rhodes's account of Reconstruction was not only inaccurate and unreliable but was "the most one-sided, biased, partisan, and prejudiced historical work" that he had ever read. A few years later Alrutheus A. Taylor published studies of the Negro in South Carolina, Virginia, and Tennessee, setting forth the general position that blacks during Reconstruction were not the ignorant dupes of unprincipled white men, that they were certainly not the corrupt crowd they had been made out to be, and that their political influence was quite limited.

The most extensive and, indeed, the most angry expression of dissent from the well-established view of Reconstruction was made in 1935 by W. E. B. Du Bois in his *Black Reconstruction*. "The treatment of the period of Reconstruction reflects," he noted, "small credit upon American historians as scientists." Then he recalled for his readers the statement on Reconstruction that he wrote in an article that the *Encyclopaedia Britannica* had refused to print. In that article he had said, "White historians have ascribed the faults and failures of Reconstruction to Negro ignorance and corruption. But the Negro insists that it was Negro loyalty and the Negro vote alone that restored the South to the Union, established the new democracy, both for white and black, and instituted the public schools." The *American Historical Review* did no better than the *Encyclopaedia Britannica*, since no review of *Black Reconstruction*, the first major scholarly work on Reconstruction since World War I, appeared in the pages of the *Review*. The work was based largely on printed public documents and secondary literature because, the author admitted, he lacked the resources to engage in a full-scale examination of the primary materials and because Du Bois thought of his task as the exposure of the logic, argument, and conclusions of those whose histories of Reconstruction had become a part of the period's orthodoxy. For this task he did not need to delve deeply into the original sources.

From that point on, works on Reconstruction represented a wide spectrum of interpretation. Paul Herman Buck's *Road to Reunion* shifted the emphasis to reconciliation, while works by Horace Mann Bond and Vernon L. Wharton began the program of fundamental and drastic revision. No sooner was revisionism launched, however, than E. Merton Coulter insisted that "no amount of revision can write away the grievous mistakes made in this abnormal period of American history." He then declared that he had not attempted to do so, and with that he subscribed to virtually all of the views that had been set forth by the students of Dunning. And he added a few observations of his own, such as "education soon lost its novelty for most of the Negroes"; they would "spend their last piece of money for a drink of whisky"; and, being "by nature highly emotional and excitable . . . , they carried their religious exercises to extreme lengths."

By mid-century, then, there was a remarkable mixture of views of Reconstruction by historians of similar training but of differing backgrounds, interests, and commitments. Some were unwilling to challenge the traditional views of Reconstruction. And, although their language was generally polite and professional, their assumptions regarding the roles of blacks, the nature of the Reconstruction governments in the South, and the need for quick—even violent—counteraction were fairly transparent. The remarkable influence of the traditional view of Reconstruction is nowhere more evident than in a work published in 1962 under the title *Texas under the Carpetbaggers.* The author did not identify the carpetbaggers, except to point out that the governor during the period was born in Florida and migrated to Texas in 1848 and that the person elected to the United States Senate had been born in Alabama and had been in Texas since 1830. If Texas was ever under the carpetbaggers, the reader is left to speculate about who the carpetbaggers were! Meanwhile, in the 1960s one of the most widely used college textbooks regaled its readers about the "simple-minded" freedmen who "insolently jostled the whites off the sidewalks into the gutter"; the enfranchisement of the former slaves set the stage for "stark tragedy," the historian continued, and this was soon followed by "enthroned ignorance," which led inevitably to "a carnival of corruption and misrule." Such descriptions reveal more about the author's talent for colorful writing than about his commitment to sobriety and accuracy.

Yet an increasing number of historians began to reject the traditional view and to argue the other side or, at least, to insist that there was another side. Some took another look at the states and rewrote their Reconstruction history. In the new version of Reconstruction in Louisiana the author pointed out that "the extravagance and corruption for which Louisiana Reconstruction is noted did not begin in 1868," for the convention of 1864 "was not too different from conventions and legislatures which came later." Others looked at the condition of the former slaves during the early days of emancipation and discovered that blacks faced freedom much more responsibly and successfully than had hitherto been described. Indeed, one student of the problem asserted that "Reconstruction was for the Negroes of South Carolina a period of unequaled progress." Still others examined institutions ranging from the family to the Freedmen's Savings Bank and reached conclusions that were new or partly new to our understanding of Reconstruction history. Finally, there were the syntheses that undertook, unfortunately all too briefly, to make some overall revisionist generalizations about Reconstruction.

Up to this point my observations have served merely as a reminder of what has been happening to Reconstruction history over the last century. I have not intended to provide an exhaustive review of the literature. There have already been extensive treatments of the subject, and there will doubtless be more. Reconstruction history has been argued over and fought over since the period itself ended. Historians have constantly disagreed not only about what significance to attach to certain events and how to interpret them but also (and almost as much) about the actual events themselves. Some events are as obscure and some facts are apparently as unverifiable as if they dated from several millennia ago. Several factors have contributed to this state of affairs. One factor, of course, is the legacy of bitterness left behind by the internal conflict. This has caused the adversaries—and their descendants—to attempt to place the blame on each other (an understandable consequence of a struggle of this nature). Another factor is that the issues have been delineated in such a way that the merits in the case have tended to be all on one side. A final factor has been the natural inclination of historians to pay attention only to those phases or aspects of the period that give weight to the argument presented. This inclination may involve the omission of any consideration of the first two years of Reconstruction in order to make a strong case against, for example, the Radicals. Perhaps such an approach has merit in a court of law or in some other forum, but as an approach to historical study its validity is open to the most serious question.

Perhaps an even more important explanation for the difficulty in getting a true picture of Reconstruction is that those who have worked in the field have been greatly influenced by the events and problems of the period in which they were writing. That first generation of students to study the postbellum years "scientifically" conducted its research and did its writing in an atmosphere that made the conclusions regarding Reconstruction foregone. Different conclusions were inconceivable. Writing in 1905 Walter L. Fleming referred to James T. Rapier, a Negro member of the Alabama constitutional convention of 1867, as "Rapier of Canada." He then quoted Rapier as saying that the manner in which "colored gentlemen and ladies were treated in America was beyond his comprehension."

Born in Alabama in 1837, Rapier, like many of his white contemporaries, went North for an education. The difference was that instead of stopping in the northern part of the United States, as, for example, William L. Yancey did, Rapier went on to Canada. Rapier's contemporaries did not regard him as a Canadian; and, if some were not precisely clear about where he was born (as was the *Alabama State Journal,* which referred to his birthplace as Montgomery rather than Florence), they did not misplace him altogether. In 1905 Fleming made Rapier a Canadian because it suited his purposes to have a bold, aggressive, "impertinent" Negro in Alabama Reconstruction come from some non-Southern, contaminating environment like Canada. But it did not suit his purposes to call Yancey, who was a graduate of Williams College, a "Massachusetts Man." Fleming described Yancey as, simply, the "leader of the States Rights men."

Aside from his Columbia professors, Fleming's assistance came largely from Alabamians: Thomas M. Owen of the Department of Archives and History, G. W. Duncan of Auburn, W. W. Screws of the Montgomery *Advertiser,* and John W. Du Bose, Yancey's biographer and author of *Alabama's Tragic Decade.* At the time that Fleming sought their advice regarding his Reconstruction story, these men were reaping the first fruits of disfranchisement, which had occurred in Alabama in 1901. Screws's *Advertiser* had been a vigorous advocate of disfranchisement, while Du Bose's *Yancey,* published a decade earlier, could well have been a campaign document to make permanent the redemption of Alabama from "Negro-carpetbagger-Scalawag rule." It is inconceivable that such men would have assisted a young scholar who had any plans except to write an account of the Reconstruction era that would support their views. In any case they could not have been more pleased had they written Fleming's work for him.

But the "scientific" historians might well have been less pleased if they had not been caught up in the same pressures of the contemporary scene that beset Fleming. They, like Fleming, should have been able to see that some of the people that Fleming called "carpetbaggers" had lived in Alabama for years and were, therefore, entitled to at least as much presumption of assimilation in moving from some other state to Alabama decades before the war as the Irish were in moving from their native land to some community in the United States. Gustavus Horton, a Massachusetts "carpetbagger" and chairman of the constitutional convention's Committee on Education in 1867, was a cotton broker in Mobile and had lived there since 1835. Elisha Wolsey Peck, the convention's candidate for chief justice in 1867, moved to Alabama from New York in 1825. A few months' sojourn in Illinois in 1867 convinced Peck that the only real home he could ever want was Alabama. Charles Mayes Cabot, a member of the constitutional convention of 1865 as well as of the one of 1867, had come to Alabama from his native Vermont as a young man. He prospected in the West in 1849 but was back in Wetumka in the merchandising business by 1852. Whether they had lived in Alabama for decades before the Civil War or had settled there after the war, these "carpetbaggers" were apparently not to be regarded as models for Northern investors or settlers in the early years of the twentieth century. Twentieth-century investors from the North were welcome provided they accepted the established arrangements in race relations and the like. Fleming served his Alabama friends well by ridiculing carpetbaggers, even if in the process he had to distort and misrepresent.

In his study of North Carolina Reconstruction published in 1914, Joseph G. de Roulhac Hamilton came as close as any of his fellow historians to reflecting the interests and concerns of his own time. After openly bewailing the enfranchisement of the freedmen, the sinister work of the "mongrel" convention and legislatures, and the abundance of corruption, Hamilton concluded that Reconstruction was a crime that is "to-day generally recognized by all who care to look the facts squarely in the face." But for Reconstruction, he insisted, "the State would to-day, so far as one can estimate human probabilities, be solidly Republican. This was clearly evident in 1865, when the attempted restoration of President Johnson put public affairs in the hands of former Whigs who then had no thought of joining in politics their old opponents, the Democrats." Hamilton argued that in his own time some men who regularly voted the Democratic ticket would not call themselves "Democrats." In an effort to appeal to a solid Negro vote, the Republicans had lost the opportunity to bring into their fold large numbers of former Whigs and some disaffected Democrats. In the long run the Republicans gained little, for the Negroes, who largely proved to be "lacking in political capacity and knowledge, were driven, intimidated, bought, and sold, the playthings of politicians, until finally their so-called right to vote became the sore spot of the body politic." In his account of Reconstruction, which placed the blame on the Republican-Negro coalition for destroying the two-party system in North Carolina, Hamilton gave a warning to his white contemporaries to steer clear of any connection with blacks whose votes could be bought and sold if the franchise were again extended to them.

And the matter was not only theoretical. In 1914, while Hamilton was writing about North Carolina Reconstruction, Negro Americans were challenging the several methods by which whites had disfranchised them, and the Hamilton was sensitive to the implications of the challenge. He reminded his readers that, after the constitutional amendment of 1900 restricting the suffrage by an educational quali- fication and a "grandfather clause," the Democrats elected their state ticket. His eye was focused to a remarkable degree on the current po- litical and social scene. "The negro has largely ceased to be a political question," he commented, "and there is in the State to-day as a con- sequence more political freedom than at any time since Reconstruc- tion." The lesson was painfully clear to him, as he hoped it would be to his readers: the successful resistance to the challenges that Negroes were making to undo the arrangements by which they had been dis- franchised would remove any fears that whites might have of a repe- tition of the "crime" of Reconstruction. Segregation statutes, the white Democratic primary, discrimination in educational opportunities, and, if necessary, violence were additional assurances that there would be no return to Reconstruction.

Unfortunately, the persistence of the dispute over what actually happened during Reconstruction and the use of Reconstruction fact and fiction to serve the needs of writers and their contemporaries have made getting at the truth about the so-called Tragic Era virtually im- possible. Not only has this situation deprived the last three genera- tions of an accurate assessment of the period but it has also unhappily strengthened the hand of those who argue that scientific history can be as subjective, as partisan, and as lacking in discrimination as any other kind of history. A century after the close of Reconstruction, we are utterly uninformed about numerous aspects of the period. Almost forty years ago Howard K. Beale, writing in the *American Historical Review*, called for a treatment of the Reconstruction era that would not be marred by bitter sectional feelings, personal vendettas, or racial animosities. In the four decades since that piece was written, there have been some historians who have heeded Beale's call. It would, in- deed, be quite remarkable if historians of today were not sensitive to some of the strictures Beale made against those who kept alive the hoary myths about Reconstruction and if scholars of today's genera- tion did not attempt to look at the period without the restricting in- fluences of sectional or racial bias. And yet, since the publication of Beale's piece, several major works have appeared that are aggressively hostile to any new view of Reconstruction. Nor has Beale's call been heeded to the extent that it should have been.

If histories do indeed reflect the problems and concerns of their authors' own times, numerous major works on Reconstruction should have appeared in recent years. After all, since the close of World War II this nation has been caught up in a reassessment of the place of Negroes in American society, and some have even called this period the "Second Reconstruction." Central to the reassessment has been a continuing discussion of the right of blacks to participate in the political process, to enjoy equal protection of the laws, and to be free of discrimination in education, employment, housing, and the like. Yet among the recent writing on Reconstruction few major works seek to synthesize and to generalize over the whole range of the freedmen's experience, to say nothing of the problem of Reconstruction as a whole. Only a limited number of monographic works deal with, for example, Reconstruction in the states, the regional experiences of freedmen, the freedmen confronting their new status, aspects of educational, religious, or institutional development, or phases of economic adjustment.

In recent years historians have focused much more on the period of slavery than on the period of freedom. Some historians have been most enthusiastic about the capacity of slaves to establish and maintain institutions while in bondage, to function effectively in an economic system as a kind of upwardly mobile group of junior partners, and to make the transition to freedom with a minimum of trauma. One may wonder why, at this particular juncture in the nation's history, slavery has attracted so much interest and why, in all of the recent and current discussions of racial equality, Reconstruction has attracted so little. Not even the litigation of *Brown* v. *The Board of Education*, which touched off a full-dress discussion of one of the three Reconstruction Amendments a full year before the decision was handed down in 1954, stimulated any considerable production of Reconstruction scholarship. Does this pattern suggest that historians have thought that the key to understanding the place of Afro-Americans in American life is to be found in the slave experience and not in the struggles for adjustment in the early years of freedom? Or does it merely mean that historians find the study of slavery more exotic or more tragic and therefore more attractive than the later period of freedom? Whatever the reason, the result has been to leave the major thrust of the Reconstruction story not nearly far enough from where it was 1929, when Claude Bowers published *The Tragic Era*.

That result is all the more unfortunate in view of what we already know and what is gradually and painfully becoming known about the period following the Civil War. With all of the exhortations by Howard Beale, Bernard Weisberger, and others about the need for more Reconstruction studies, the major works with a grand sweep and a bold interpretation have yet to be written. Recent works by Michael Perman and Leon F. Litwack, which provide a fresh view respectively of political problems in the entire South and of the emergence of the freedman throughout the South, are indications of what can and should be done in the field. And, even if the battle for revision is being won among the professionals writing the monographs (if not among the profes-

sionals writing the textbooks), it is important to make certain that the
zeal for revision does not become a substitute for truth and accuracy
and does not result in the production of works that are closer to political tracts than to histories.

Although it is not possible to speak with certainty about the extent
to which the Reconstruction history written in our time reveals the
urgent matters with which we are regularly concerned, we must take
care not to permit those matters to influence or shape our view of an
earlier period. That is what entrapped earlier generations of Reconstruction historians who used the period they studied to shape attitudes toward problems they confronted. As we look at the opportunities for new syntheses and new interpretations, we would do well to
follow Thomas J. Pressly's admonition not to seek confirmation of our
views of Reconstruction in the events of our own day. This caveat is
not to deny the possibility of a usable past, for to do so would go against
our heritage and cut ourselves off from human experience. At the same
time it proscribes the validity of reading into the past the experiences
of the historian in order to shape the past as he or she wishes it to be
shaped.

The desire of some historians to use the Reconstruction era to bolster their case in their own political arena or on some other ground
important to their own well-being is a major reason for our not having
a better general account of what actually occurred during Reconstruction. To illustrate this point, we are still without a satisfactory history
of the role of the Republican Party in the South during Reconstruction.
If we had such a history, we would, perhaps, modify our view of that
party's role in the postbellum South. We already know, for example,
that the factional fights within the party were quite divisive. The bitter
fight between two factions of Republicans in South Carolina in 1872
is merely one case in point. On that occasion the nominating convention split in two and each faction proceeded to nominate its own slate
of officers. Only the absence of any opposition party assured a Republican victory in the autumn elections. In some instances blacks and
whites competed for the party's nomination to public office, thus indicating quite clearly the task facing a Negro Republican who aspired
to public office. That is the task that John R. Lynch faced when he ran
for Congress in 1872 and defeated the white incumbent, L. W. Pearce,
who was regarded even by Lynch as "a creditable and satisfactory representative." And it was not out of the question for white Republicans to work for and vote for white Democrats in order to make certain
that Negro Republican candidates for office would be defeated. So little
is known of the history of the Republican Party in the South because
the presumption has generally been that Lincoln's party was, on its
very face, hostile to Southern mores generally and anxious to have Ne-

groes embarrass white Southerners. Indeed, had historians been inclined to examine with greater care the history of the Republican Party
in the South, they would have discovered even more grist for the Democratic Party mill.

Thus, studying works on Reconstruction that have been written
over the last century can provide a fairly clear notion of the problems
confronting the periods in which the historians lived but not always
as clear a picture of Reconstruction itself. The state of historical studies and the level of sophistication in the methods of research are much
too advanced for us to be content with anything less than the high
level of performance found in works on other periods of United States
history. There is no reason why the facts of Reconstruction should be
the subject of greater dispute than those arising out of Askia Muhammad's rule in Songhay or Cromwell's rule in Britain. But we are still
doing the spade-work; we are still writing narrowly focused monographs on the history of Reconstruction. We need to know more about
education than Henry L. Swint, Horace Mann Bond, and Robert Morris
have told us. Surely there is more to economic development than we
can learn from the works by Irwin Unger, George R. Woolfolk, Robert
P. Sharkey, and Carl Osthaus. And race, looming large in the Reconstruction era, as is usually the case in other periods of American history, is so pervasive and so critical that the matter should not be left
to Herbert G. Gutman, Howard Rabinowitz, John H. and La Wanda
Cox, Thomas Holt, and a few others.

Recent scholarship on the Reconstruction era leaves the impression that we may be reaching the point, after a century of effort, where
we can handle the problems inherent in writing about an internal
struggle without losing ourselves in the fire and brimstone of the Civil
War and its aftermath. Perhaps we have reached the point in coping
with the problems about us when we no longer need to shape Reconstruction history to suit our current needs. If either or both of these
considerations is true, we are fortunate, for each augurs well for the
future of Reconstruction history. It would indeed be a happy day if we
could view the era of Reconstruction without either attempting to use
the events of that era to support some current policy or seeking anal-
ogies that are at best strained and provide little in the way of an understanding of that era or our own.

"Not since Reconstruction" is a phrase that is frequently seen and
heard. Its principal purpose is to draw an analogy or a contrast. Since
it usually neither defines Reconstruction nor makes clear whether it
is a signpost of progress or retrogression, searching for some other way
of relating that period to our own may be wise, if not necessary. In the
search for the real meaning of Reconstruction, phrases like "not since
Reconstruction" provide no clue to understanding the period. Worse

still, they becloud the relationship between that day and this. To guard against the alluring pitfalls of such phrases and to assure ourselves and others that we are serious about the postbellum South, we would do well to cease using Reconstruction as a mirror of ourselves and begin studying it because it very much needs studying. In such a process Reconstruction will doubtless have much to teach all of us.

☆ 5 ☆

American Imperialism

ALTRUISM OR AGGRESSION?

During the last quarter of the nineteenth century, the United States emerged as a world power. Its industrial and agricultural productivity, large size, growing population, and modern navy gave it a prominence that could not be ignored. The acquisition of an overseas empire added to America's stature. In 1898 and 1899 the United States suddenly acquired the Hawaiian Islands and gained control over Puerto Rico, the Philippines, and part of the Samoan archipelago. Within a year and a half America had become a dominant power in both the Caribbean and the Pacific.

Curiously enough many Americans were ambivalent about their country's new role. Some feared that America's democratic institutions were incompatible with an overseas empire and the large military establishment that would be required to sustain it. Others rejected the concept of empire because they opposed bringing under the American flag groups they regarded as racial or social inferiors. Some Americans, on the other hand, favored the entry of the United States into world affairs either because of a crusading zeal to spread American institutions or a desire to find new economic markets. Although the United States entered the twentieth century as a world power, its people remained divided over the wisdom or desirability of pursuing their new destiny.

These divisions among the public over foreign policy had their counterpart among diplomatic historians. Just as Americans debated the wisdom of particular policies, so historians disagreed about interpretations of past events. The historical debate, in reality, was not confined simply to an analysis of the past; implicit in many interpretations of diplomatic history was a vision of what America ought to be. To argue that the United States traditionally was a champion of freedom and democracy was to take a position on certain contemporary policies toward the nondemocratic world. Similarly the argument that America was an imperialistic nation bent on imposing its economic and military power on the rest of the world had implications for contemporary foreign and domestic policy issues.

The historical literature dealing with the decade of the 1890s, which culminated in the Spanish-American War, is a case in point. Charles and Mary Beard, whose *Rise of American Civilization* symbolized the Progressive school of American historiography, implied that economic issues led President William McKinley to ask for a declaration of war. The Spanish government, after all, had practically acceded to his demands. McKinley, the Beards insisted, revised Cleveland's policy of neutrality, presumably because of the threat to American investments in and trade with Cuba. In the final analysis war grew out of a desire to protect America's economic interests in that region. The ensuing acquisition of overseas territory provided further proof of the Beards' charge that the nation's business community played an important role in determining the country's foreign policy. Although the Beardian thesis was presented in somewhat qualified form, it clearly implied the primacy of economic forces.[1]

Relatively few scholars, however, followed the Beards' interpretation. To Samuel Flagg Bemis, whose synthesis of American diplomatic history appeared in 1936, the acquisition of an overseas empire represented a "great aberration." Before the war, Bemis noted, "there had not been the slightest demand for the acquisition of the Philippine Islands." A military victory, however, fanned imperialist sentiment. McKinley proved unable to resist jingoist sentiment, and he instructed his peace commission to demand the Philippine Islands, a demand that demonstrated "adolescent irresponsibility." McKinley's decision, concluded Bemis, was largely unplanned, and was not in accord with the traditional American aversion to imperialism.[2]

At the same time Bemis's influential textbook appeared Julius W. Pratt published his *Expansionists of 1898*. Also rejecting an economic interpretation of war causation, Pratt suggested instead that intellectual and emotional factors were responsible for the new expansionism. The emergence of social Darwinism, with its emphasis on competition and survival of the fittest, provided some people with an intellectual justification for expanding America's sphere of influence. Many argued

---

[1]Charles A. Beard and Mary R. Beard, *The Rise of American Civilization*, 2 vols. (New York, 1927), 2:369–382.

[2]Samuel Flagg Bemis, *A Diplomatic History of the United States* (4th ed., New York, 1955), pp. 463–475.

that nations, like individuals, were engaged in a remorseless test of their fitness to survive. The criterion of success was dominion over others; failure to expand, on the other hand, meant stagnation and decline. Other expansionist-minded individuals were affected by religious and humanitarian concerns; they wished to bring American civilization and morality to less advanced peoples. Still others accepted the doctrines developed by Captain Alfred Thayer Mahan, who saw growing American sea power as the key to the nation's greatness. Sea power, however, required overseas naval bases. Pratt, interestingly enough, noted that the business community, which was still recovering from the depression that began in 1893, opposed intervention in Cuba for fear that it might block the road to economic recovery. With Admiral Dewey's dramatic victory in the Philippines, American businessmen became converted to the expansionist cause by the alluring prospect of dominating the potentially large Chinese market. These same businessmen now found it easy to apply the same rationale in the Caribbean and supported expansion in that area. The reasons why the United States went to war, therefore, were quite different from the reasons that led its government to acquire an overseas empire. Indeed, Pratt concluded, American imperialism consisted of a blend of religious, humanitarian, and economic components.[3]

These early historians agreed, at least in part, that foreign policy was to a significant extent determined by domestic considerations. There were significant differences, nevertheless, between their approaches. To the Beards the business community, with its emphasis on profits, pushed the nation into war. Bemis, on the other hand, saw the results of war as a repudiation of the traditional antiimperialist sentiment of Americans. To Pratt a variety of influences—domestic and foreign—came into play, although no one in particular exercised the decisive role. In general two approaches ultimately came to dominate the writing of American diplomatic history. Those in the Beard tradition would interpret America's foreign policy primarily in terms of domestic considerations. A second tradition would emphasize, in addition, the importance of actions taken by foreign governments. Although the two approaches would on occasion come together in the work of an individual scholar, more often than not they would remain separate and distinct.

After the publication of Pratt's work in 1936 scholarly interest in American imperialism and the Spanish-American War tended to flag.

---

[3]Julius W. Pratt, *Expansionists of 1898* (Baltimore, 1936), and *America's Colonial Experiment: How the United States Gained, Governed, and in Part Gave Away a Colonial Empire* (New York, 1950).

Between the 1930s and 1950s diplomatic historians were primarily interested in illuminating the causes and consequences of the First and Second World Wars. But in 1959 William Appleman Williams published his influential book *The Tragedy of American Diplomacy*, which had a profound impact on the writing of all diplomatic history. This book, indeed, became the starting point for the work of many revisionist and New Left historians, who believed that America's foreign policies were dominated by the narrow economic interests of a small elite.

The Williams thesis, briefly stated, rested on the premise that foreign policy was a function of the structure and organization of American society. During the depression of the 1880s and 1890s the business community had concluded that foreign markets were indispensable for America's well-being. These markets would help to avoid any internal problems that might arise from economic stagnation resulting from America's tendency to produce more goods than its people consumed. The result was a fundamental shift in the nation's foreign policy. Policymakers adopted what became known as the Open Door policy—an open door "through which America's preponderant economic strength would enter and dominate all underdeveloped areas of the world. . . . [T]he Open Door Policy was in fact a brilliant strategic stroke which led to the gradual extension of American economic and political power throughout the world."[4] Indeed, most of American diplomacy in the twentieth century, Williams insisted, was directed toward the goal of assuring the nation's economic supremacy on a global scale. Pursuit of this goal led to involvement in two world wars, the Korean and Vietnam conflicts, and the Cold War that pitted the Soviet Union and the United States against each other. In other words Williams posited a continuity in American foreign policy from the late nineteenth century to the present.

The origins of modern American foreign policy, Williams argued, could be traced back to the economic crisis of the 1890s. During that decade a new national consensus was reached. Americans no longer debated whether or not an expansionist policy should be pursued but rather what form expansion should take. This expansionist policy was based on the conviction that American diplomacy and prosperity went hand in hand and required access to world markets. Any restrictions on the flow of American goods and capital would lead to a depression and social unrest. Support for economic expansion, therefore, played a

[4]William Appleman Williams, *The Tragedy of American Diplomacy* (2d rev. and enl. ed., New York, 1972), pp. 45–46. See also Williams's *The Roots of the Modern American Empire* (New York, 1969).

crucial role in precipitating the Spanish-American War and in the subsequent debate over the desirability of acquiring overseas possessions.

In 1963 Walter LaFeber published a prize-winning volume on
American expansionism from 1860 to 1898 that lent strong support to
the Williams thesis. The Civil War, LaFeber noted, marked an important dividing line in America's expansionist policies. Before 1860 expansionism was confined to the American continent; it reflected the
desire of an agrarian society to find new and fertile lands. Post–Civil
War expansionism, on the other hand, was motivated by the belief that
foreign markets were vital to America's well-being. By the 1890s the
American business community and policymakers had concluded that
additional foreign markets "would solve the economic, social, and political problems created by the industrial revolution." Given Europe's
imperialist penetration in many regions of the world Americans also
concluded that their country needed strategic bases if they were to
compete successfully. The diplomacy of the 1890s and the Spanish-
American War grew out of these concerns. Indeed, LaFeber insisted that
the debate between the imperialists and antiimperialists during this
decade was a limited one; they differed over the tactical means that
the United States should use in order to attain its objectives. "By 1899,"
concluded LaFeber, "the United States had forged a new empire. American policy makers and businessmen had created it amid much debate
and with conscious purpose. The empire progressed from a continental
base in 1861 to assured pre-eminence in the Western Hemisphere in
1895. Three years later it was rescued from a growing economic and
political dilemma by the declaration of war against Spain. During and
after this conflict the empire moved past Hawaii into the Philippines,
and, with the issuance of the Open-Door Notes, enunciated its principles in Asia."[5]

Since the 1960s many scholars have continued to follow the Williams interpretation of American diplomatic history. In 1967 Thomas
McCormick published a book that traced the growing interest of Americans in the 1890s in the potentially large China market. Four years
later Milton Plesur analyzed the origins of the "large policy" of the
1890s, which he located in the years between 1865 and 1890. The new
diplomacy, he concluded, "was rationalized on the basis of racial and
moral superiority, a sense of national mission, strategic considerations,
enhancement of national prestige, and aversion to a worldwide imperialism from which we were excluded economically. Though originally

---

[5]Walter LaFeber, *The New Empire: An Interpretation of American Expansionism
1860–1898* (Ithaca, 1963), pp. 412–417.

not seeking territory for ourselves, we could not allow other powers to jeopardize what we thought were our legitimate interests." In a similar vein Ernest N. Paolino emphasized the degree to which William H. Seward had laid the foundations for an expansionist policy during the 1860s.[6]

The Williams-LaFeber interpretation of the origins of modern America's foreign policy had a powerful appeal during the 1960s and 1970s, particularly as disillusionment with American society grew during the Vietnam conflict. The argument that the nation's diplomacy was based less on altruism, idealism, and antiimperialism and more on a desire to safeguard an international order that made possible America's economic supremacy, of course, had important implications for contemporary concerns. The Cold War, for example, rather than resting on a moral foundation that pitted freedom against communism, was seen as a product of America's continued insistence on structuring a world order along lines that preserved its liberal capitalist hegemony. Thus American foreign policy, which grew out of domestic institutions and developments, was allegedly responsible in large measure for initiating and perpetuating the Cold War and causing the Vietnam conflict.[7] Williams's work spawned a whole school of historians who proceeded to write revisionist accounts of the history of American foreign policy.

Walter LaFeber—undoubtedly the most articulate scholar associated with the Williams school—continued to emphasize the imperialist basis of American diplomacy. In 1983 he authored a history of United States relations with Central America since the nineteenth century. Almost from the beginning of the American republic, policymakers had been motivated by a desire to strengthen capitalist interests in this region and thus had forged a diplomatic policy aimed at dominating and exploiting Central Americans. The result, according to LaFeber, was the degradation of the indigenous masses in this region and the maintenance in power of right-wing dictatorial regimes. The turbulence of this region in the 1980s, he concluded, was directly at-

---

[6]Thomas McCormick, *China Market: America's Quest for Informal Empire 1893–1901* (Chicago, 1967); Milton Plesur, *America's Outward Thrust: Approaches to Foreign Affairs, 1865–1890* (DeKalb, Ill., 1971), pp. 235–236; Ernest N. Paolino, *The Foundations of American Empire: William Henry Seward and U.S. Foreign Policy* (Ithaca, 1973). See also Charles S. Campbell, *The Transformation of American Foreign Relations 1865–1900* (New York, 1976).

[7]See Walter LaFeber, *America, Russia, and the Cold War 1945–1966* (New York, 1967); Lloyd C. Gardner, "American Foreign Policy 1900–1921: A Second Look at the Realist Critique of American Diplomacy," in *Towards a New Past: Dissenting Essays in American History*, Barton J. Bernstein, ed. (New York, 1968), pp. 202–231; David Healy, *U.S. Expansionism: The Imperialist Urge in the 1890s* (Madison, Wis., 1970).

tributable to the desire of Americans to create an informal imperialist empire.[8]

The Williams thesis, however, did not gain universal acceptance in historical circles. Not all scholars, for example, agreed with this portrait of American society. Others were critical of a viewpoint that emphasized the importance of domestic factors in the determination of foreign policy and belittled or ignored actions by other nations. In their eyes diplomatic policies were also influenced by the external actions and reactions of foreign governments. A more balanced approach, they argued, called for an understanding of the behavior of other governments, which, in turn, implied a multinational approach to diplomacy and multiarchival research. Rejecting the idea of American omnipotence in world affairs they stressed other than economic factors and attempted to demonstrate that the purposefulness attributed to American policymakers was not justified by a critical examination of the sources.

Typical of this approach was Ernest R. May's *Imperial Democracy: The Emergence of America as a Great Power*, published in 1961. May argued that in the 1890s the United States had not sought to play a new role in world affairs. On the contrary diplomatic problems concerning Hawaii, China, Venezuela, and Cuba had almost intruded upon the domestic issues in which most statesmen and political leaders were primarily interested. "Some nations," May observed, "achieve greatness; the United States had greatness thrust upon it."

President McKinley, for example, rather than being the harbinger of imperialism, was portrayed as a leader who was trying to keep his nation out of war and at the same time to resolve the Cuban dilemma that had inflamed public opinion. His initiatives were ultimately doomed to failure, for Spain would neither grant Cuba autonomy nor suppress the rebellion. McKinley then gave Spain an ultimatum, which included American mediation in the event Spain and the Cubans could not reach some arrangement (a mediation that in all likelihood would have meant Cuban independence). To the Spanish government such an ultimatum was unacceptable. McKinley then faced a crucial choice. He could embark upon a war that he did not want or could defy public opinion and accept some compromise. The latter course might have led to the unseating of the Republican party if not the overthrow of constitutional government. "When public opinion reached the point of hysteria, he succumbed," said May.

Did McKinley accept the decision for war because of a need for

---

[8]Walter LaFeber, *Inevitable Revolutions: The United States in Central America* (New York, 1983).

foreign markets and strategic bases as Williams argued? Most assuredly not, insisted May. "Neither the President nor the public had
any aim beyond war itself. The nation was in a state of upset. Until
recently its people had been largely Protestant and English; its economy predominantly rural and agricultural. . . . Now, however, the
country was industrialized and urbanized. Catholics were numerous
and increasing. People of older stock found themselves no longer economically or even socially superior to members of immigrant groups
or to others. . . . The panic of 1893 made this new condition even more
visible by depressing agricultural prices, rents, investment income,
professional fees, and white-collar salaries. . . . In some irrational way,
all these influences and anxieties translated themselves into concern
for suffering Cuba. For the people as for the government, war with monarchical Catholic, Latin Spain had no purpose except to relieve emotion."[9]

In a certain sense May's thesis was anticipated a decade earlier by
Richard Hofstadter. In 1952 Hofstadter published an article that rejected an economic explanation of American diplomacy in the 1890s
and suggested instead that the hysteria and jingoism of this decade
grew out of the anxieties occasioned by social and economic change.
Indeed, shortly thereafter Hofstadter proposed a comparable explanation of the roots of McCarthyism. Although sympathetic to liberalism
Hofstadter's work in the 1940s and 1950s contributed to the emerging
rejection of the basic tenets of the Progressive school of American historiography. In his eyes modern American liberalism reflected less a
concern for the welfare of the masses of Americans and more the inner
feelings of select middle-class groups alienated from their society because of economic and technological change and a consequent decline
in their social status. Foreign policy, implied Hofstadter, mirrored these
irrational and noneconomic influences.[10]

In 1969 May published a second work in which he used concepts
drawn from the social sciences in order to present a fuller portrait of
the diplomacy of those years. In that work May examined the structure
and role of public opinion in order to illuminate how the United States
briefly became imperialistic in outlook and then even more quickly
turned away from overseas expansion. After analyzing public opinion
in terms of various categories involving elites with different interests
and concerns, May argued that the anticolonialist consensus was

---

[9]Ernest R. May, *Imperial Democracy: The Emergence of America as a Great Power*
(New York, 1961), pp. 268–270.

[10]Richard Hofstadter, "Manifest Destiny and the Philippines," in *America in Crisis:
Fourteen Crucial Episodes in American History,* Daniel Aaron, ed. (New York, 1952),
pp. 173–200.

briefly broken in 1898 and 1899, which resulted in the transfer of leadership to a wider circle. The outcome was a new consensus that accepted the desirability of acquiring foreign possessions and owed much of its inspiration to European, and especially British, opinion. Shortly thereafter the more traditional anticolonial view prevailed, especially after the difficulties faced by the British during the Boer War in South Africa and the growth of an antiimperialist movement in Britain. May concluded by insisting that the imperialist-antiimperialist debate could not be understood solely in terms of what Americans said or did, for they were members of a much broader Atlantic civilization.[11]

Another attack on the Williams school came from James A. Field, Jr. Much of the literature on American imperialism, Field charged, was a version of the Whig theory of history. Beginning with perceptions of American immorality in the twentieth century Williams and his followers had interpreted the past with "the same perceptions of false continuities and imputations of sin." The historical literature dealing with the 1890s suffered from a number of failings: the adoption of a strictly rational explanation of events and a rejection of chance; the use of overly broad terms to describe complex situations; a treatment of diplomacy that was excessively ethnocentric; and a discussion that ignored "time, distance, costs, or technological feasibility."

Rejecting explanations of American imperialism based on the application of Darwinian theory, the psychic crisis of imperialism, the new navy, and the importance of the Pacific highway to Asia, Field proposed a new hypothesis. The new American navy that came into existence in the late nineteenth century was a defensive answer to European developments; "its deployment reflected a shrunken perimeter." The search for bases was a response to the strategic problems of the proposed canal linking the Atlantic and Pacific oceans. The ideologists of that period, moreover, were of negligible importance. "What Americans, whether travellers or missionaries or businessmen, wanted of the outer world was the freedom to pursue happiness, to do their thing, to operate insofar as possible unhindered by arbitrary power or obsolete ideas. Proud of their own self-determined independence, they were sympathetic to similar desires on the part of Samoan chiefs, Korean kings, Egyptian khedives, Armenian Christians, Brazilians, Venezuelans, and Chinese. Most of all, because they were nearest and most visible and noisiest, it was the Cubans who engaged this sympathy." Indeed, Field suggested that the rapid deployment of the American navy headed by Admiral Dewey in the Pacific was largely a result of the

[11]Ernest R. May, "American Imperialism: A Reinterpretation," *Perspectives in American History* 1 (1967):123–283; also published as *American Imperialism: A Speculative Essay* (New York, 1968).

rapidity of communication made possible by new cables linking nations and continents. Dewey's victory in turn focused public attention on the Far East; only then did an avalanche of publicity descend upon the American people. "Imperialism," according to Field, "was the product of Dewey's victory." Field's criticisms drew a sharp rejoinder from both LaFeber and Robert Beisner (another diplomatic historian and author of several works on late-nineteenth century American foreign policy). The debate between these three scholars appears as the selection for this chapter.[12]

The discussion over the origins and nature of American "imperialism," of course, involved an evaluation of its consequences as well. To historians critical of the role of America in world affairs in the twentieth century these consequences were largely negative. Williams, for example, argued that American foreign policy to a considerable degree rested on "a posture of moral and ideological superiority." Its leaders believed that underdeveloped nations had to be changed in order for the United States to harvest the fruits of expansionism. The goals of foreign policy (as compared with changing tactics) were to maintain markets for industrial exports, to control access to raw materials, and the right to take part in the economic life of other nations by establishing factories and other enterprises. Economic imperialism, in turn, led to efforts to establish political hegemony. Cuba, Williams noted, was a case in point. The United States "dominated the economic life of the island by controlling, directly or indirectly, the sugar industry, and by overtly and covertly preventing any dynamic modification of the island's one-crop economy. It defined clear and narrow limits on the island's political system. It tolerated the use of torture and terror, of fraud and farce, by Cuba's rulers. But it intervened with economic and diplomatic pressure and with force of arms when Cubans threatened to transgress the economic and political restrictions established by American leaders."[13]

In many respects the Williams-LaFeber approach implies a more general interpretation of the nature of American society. As a matter of fact Thomas J. McCormick, a historian whose sympathies lie with both, has advanced a series of propositions that in his eyes deserve testing. American capitalism, McCormick suggests, has always been concerned with expanding production. Given its bias against income distribution it has turned to marketplace expansionism overseas. Given

---

[12]For a somewhat different rejection of the Williams school, see Richard E. Welch, Jr., *Response to Imperialism: The United States and the Philippine-American War, 1899–1902* (Chapel Hill, 1979).

[13]Williams, *Tragedy of American Diplomacy*, pp. 2 and 59.

the corporatist nature of American society it followed naturally that elite leaders of corporatist syndicates were also the prime makers of foreign policy. Eventually organized labor and the farm bloc were brought in as junior partners. The result was the rationalization of corporate capitalism on the domestic scene, and the expansion of efforts to create a greater global corporatism in the more recent period.[14]

Just as the Williams-LaFeber interpretation of the origins of the Spanish-American War came under criticism, so, too, did their view of twentieth-century American imperialism. Paul A. Varg, for example, argued that a careful examination of the specific actions of the United States in world affairs precluded any simple or facile generalizations about imperialism or America's world power status. China was *not* of major importance to American policy officials. Even the dominant role of the United States in the Caribbean was never pursued solely for economic considerations; strong opposition to any American intervention in that area arose during each crisis. In Varg's view few American leaders pursued foreign policy concerns out of a conviction that the nation's welfare was dependent upon developments in other parts of the world. Although the United States did become a world power it was not because of any master plan designed to control the destiny of other nations.[15]

The claim that American imperialism necessarily had a harmful impact on foreign nations was also challenged indirectly by Stanley Lebergott. Lebergott pointed to the relative insignificance of American foreign investment in Latin America from 1890 to 1929, and denied as well that it worked to the detriment of either workers or landowners in the nations that were affected. Indeed, American foreign investments increased the income of workers and peasants by expanding the need for labor; land values in many Latin American nations increased in value because of the opening of American markets to native products. Lebergott conceded that American business enterprise sometimes destroyed the vested interests of native business groups and their monopoly profits, and also created new entrepreneurial groups. The heart of the ensuing antiimperialist contest, he concluded, was not be-

---

[14]Thomas J. McCormick, "Drift or Mastery? A Corporate Synthesis for American Diplomatic History," *Reviews in American History* 4 (December 1982):318–330.

[15]Paul A. Varg, "The United States as a World Power, 1900–1917: Myth or Reality?," in *Twentieth-Century American Foreign Policy*, John Braeman, Robert H. Bremner, and David Brody, eds. (Columbus, Ohio, 1971), and *The Making of a Myth: The United States and China, 1897–1912* (East Lansing, Mich., 1968). For other examples of work in this tradition see Howard K. Beale, *Theodore Roosevelt and the Rise of America to World Power* (Baltimore, 1956), and Raymond A. Esthus, *Theodore Roosevelt and the International Rivalries* (Waltham, Mass. 1970).

tween America and Latin America, but between two capitalist groups, one native and the other foreign, each fighting over the spoils of progress.[16]

The debate among historians about the nature of late-nineteenth- and early-twentieth-century American diplomacy in part reflected visions not only of what American society was, but what it ought to have been. Charles A. Beard, writing within the Progressive school tradition, tended to emphasize the role of economic factors. In the late 1940s he spelled out more precisely his belief that domestic reform and involvement in world rivalries were incompatible and benefited relatively small groups of affluent elites. Samual Flagg Bemis, on the other hand, wrote within an older patriotic tradition that emphasized the antiimperialist nature of the American people and their desire to avoid foreign adventures; hence he characterized the Spanish-American War as a "great aberration" and a war productive of no good. William Appleman Williams, a critic of American capitalism whose views became influential during the 1960s and 1970s, saw diplomacy as an extension of the need of American capitalism to dominate the world in an economic sense. The two world wars, the Korean and Vietnam conflicts, and the Cold War, he and his followers charged, were all products of internal flaws in American society; only by radical change could these flaws be eradicated. Recent critiques of the Williams approach were in part a reaction to his harsh criticisms of American society and in part a denial of American omnipotence. Events in other nations, as Ernest R. May noted, played a role in shaping American foreign policy, and a knowledge of the domestic determinants of policy, although indispensable, was insufficient by itself.

As long as Americans continue to discuss and fight over the proper role of their nation in world affairs, the events of the 1890s and early part of the twentieth century will continue to hold the interest of historians. In studying the origins and consequences of the Spanish-American War scholars in all probability will continue to raise many of the same questions asked by their predecessors for nearly half a century. Did the United States go to war to resolve basic contradictions within its economic and social systems? Was the acquisition of an overseas empire a cause or a consequence of war? To what degree did moral, religious, and humanitarian sentiments play a role in the diplomacy of the 1890s? To what extent was American foreign policy a response to the diplomacy of other nations and events beyond its control? Did the United States in fact abandon its interests in empire after 1900, or did it create a new form of colonialism through the use of its

---

[16]Stanley Lebergott, "The Returns to U.S. Imperialism, 1890–1929," *Journal of Economic History* 40 (June 1980):229–249.

economic power? Above all, did the United States become a world power because its leaders consciously recognized the importance of other regions to the nation's well-being, or did it simply stumble into its new status without a clear grasp of the underlying issues? Americans will struggle with these and other questions as long as they continue to debate foreign policy issues and the role America has and should play as a world power.

James A. Field, Jr.

JAMES A. FIELD, JR. (1916–   ) is professor of history at Swarthmore
College. He has written a number of works in diplomatic history, including
Japanese at Leyte Gulf (1947) and *America and the Mediterranean World
1776–1882* (1969).

A few months ago the mail brought a copy of a new textbook on
American diplomatic history. Feeling some obligation to the publisher,
I gave it the standard check and read through the chapter on the 1880s
and 1890s—"The New American Spirit." Like so many such chapters,
it failed the test. Disappointed again, I crossed the hall to ask a learned
colleague what he thought was predictably the worst chapter in any
general history of American foreign relations. "The worst?" he asked,
and then answered without a pause, "The one on the end of the nineteenth century."

This "worst chapter" may be summarized somewhat as follows:
The publication of Charles Darwin's *Origin of Species*
gave rise to some new American mutations called John
Fiske, Josiah Strong, Alfred T. Mahan, and Brooks Adams. Unlike their ancestors, they were all racists and
wanted battleships and naval bases. At the same time
the American churches, desirous of saving souls, demanded political control of "native peoples." In the
closing years of the century American farmers began
to ship more wheat and cattle to "Europe and other
places." Standard Oil and other companies were in-
vesting overseas. An "avalanche" of books, articles, editorials, and speeches consequently descended upon the
American people, sending it into the "psychic crisis"
of the 1890s and turning the country to "populism and
jingoism." The result of all of this was the arrival of a
Samoan chief in search of a treaty, a riot in a Valparaiso

James A. Field, Jr., "American Imperialism: The Worst Chapter in Almost Any Book,"
with comments by Walter LaFeber and Robert L. Beisner, *American Historical Review*
83 (June 1978):644–683. (The original footnotes have been reduced in number and magnitude with the permission of the author.) Reprinted by permission of James A. Field,
Jr., Walter LaFeber, and Robert L. Beisner.

saloon, a revolution in Hawaii, and a naval development program that bore fruit in a new secret weapon,
a twenty-inch gun, which was test-fired in the direction of Whitehall in 1895. The "logical outcome" of
this new spirit (described in the next chapter) was "The
War with Spain" and the annexation of the Philippines
as part of a policy of "insular imperialism" aimed at
the markets of China.

This curious narrative, which in mildly variant forms appears to
have gained wide acceptance, represents the product of some fifty years
of historical construction by a number of architects and builders. Surprisingly, the foundations still reflect the handiwork of Julius W. Pratt
(although John A. Hobson and Charles A. Beard have crept back into
the cellar); the eclectic superstructure derives from the efforts of,
among others, Richard Hofstadter, William A. Williams, Walter La-
Feber, and Thomas J. McCormick. Although the mansion was originally designed to house the 1880s and 1890s, the carpenters in recent
years have added wings that extend backward in time to provide lodging for William H. Seward and forward to house Vietnam. The result
of this architectural agglomeration is an inverted Whig interpretation
of history, differing from its predecessor primarily in that now the children of darkness triumph over the children of light. But there remains
the same insistence on seeing the past through the prism of the present, the same perceptions of false continuities and imputations of sin,
and the same tendentious impact on generalization and abridgment.
Works of this genre have a certain utility, no doubt, for classroom discussion of how and how not to write history, but they also raise serious
questions. How should we grapple with this segment of our past? How
escape the conventional formulations so uncritically and tediously
passed from article to article, book to book, and text to text?

Much of the literature on the 1890s suffers from a number of common failings. First, the approach is too rational. Chance (or the unexpected), which plays so important a part in the life of the individual,
seems unacceptable in the life of the nation: these authors simply will
not remember the *Maine*. Events must have their antecedent philosophers and strategists and must also, apparently, flow logically from
previous intentions. Since the United States did entangle itself in Asia
in 1898, these requirements have led to a backward approach to history
and to the transformation of a record of almost total lack of accomplishment—in the search for naval bases, in Hawaiian annexation, in
the construction of Chinese railroads, and in reviving the merchant
marine, reforming the consular service, or revising the tariff—into evidence of an overwhelming wave of imperialism. Second the picture is

too unitary. The use of such terms as "America," "American," and "United States" to describe both public and private doings imposes a deceptive solidity upon a very mixed bag of phenomena, confuses the governmental and private sectors, underplays the many overseas Americans who showed small interest in government support and none in territorial expansion, and obscures regional variation. Mapping late-nineteenth-century American activity abroad produces a whole variety of overlays—economic, strategic, cultural, philanthropic, entrepreneurial—that are by no means geographically coincident. Third, the treatment is excessively ethnocentric. Everything that happens is attributed to the purposeful action of the United States, and the philosophers and strategists must all be American. But while the America of the 1890s possessed a large and influential package of skills and resources, both its strengths and its aims were limited. Indeed, with the recent history of the big influence of small allies available to reinforce that of the Cuban junta and the Hawaiian Annexation Club, it could perhaps be argued that the United States has been as much or more the used as it has the user, and that much of its involvement in the outer world has come in response to Macedonian cries.[1] Fourth, the discussion takes small account of time, distance, costs, or technological feasibility. Words do duty for things and presumed intentions for actual capabilities. Finally, the wrong questions are often asked. In the case of Hawaii, for example, the interesting problem is surely not why it was annexed in 1898, but rather why so "natural" a development was so long delayed. The answer is that ruling circles in the United States did not much want to annex Hawaii, unless, perhaps, to pre-empt annexation by others; contrariwise, influential folk in the islands ardently desired to annex the United States but, with only a small and feeble country at their disposal, had to wait for special circumstances before they could manage it.

Moving from the general to the particular, a brief look at various aspects of the treatments of "American imperialism"—ideological, bureaucratic, semantic, geographical, and technological—may help to separate what is useful from what is not. The presumed necessity for events to follow logically from what preceded, the importance scholars give to words, and the happy fact that quotations to support almost any argument can be rummaged out of the grabbag of the past have led many historians to fall in love with ideology. Hence, the chapters on

---

[1] Acts 16:9–24. The modern reader of this text, observing how Paul became aware of the cry out of Macedonia and what befell him when he answered it, will sense ambiguities which seem to have eluded our missionary-minded forefathers.

"The New American Spirit" and, hence, the emphasis on Darwin and on something called "Social Darwinism." From the *Origin of Species,* it is suggested, came a mental climate that spawned oppressive capitalists at home and promoters of oppressive imperialism abroad. But there are problems here. The kind of activist government required for imperial ventures appears to have had small appeal for capitalists, and few seem to have busied themselves in the cause. The standard ideologists who are alleged to have infected the American people with the disease of Darwinist expansionism were few in number and of doubtful leverage, and the standard quotations from their works are selective and unrepresentative. One should not, it would seem, quote Fiske, Strong, Mahan, Adams, and the rest without having read their works.

Strong's main concerns in the 1880s, for instance, were clearly focused on the country's internal problems. As a high-minded Social Gospeller he worried mightily about Mormonism, Catholicism, drink, and tobacco; and his single chapter on the outer world appears to have been designed to emphasize what was at stake at home. There was, in any case, nothing new in 1885 about his ideas on the triumph of Anglo-Saxondom, Christianity, and civil liberty that would postulate "a new American spirit"; similar sentiments had been voiced in the 1840s by Hollis Read, another missionary author.[2] Fiske's general attitude was strongly antimilitary, and his recipe for the world's future, far from being one of conquest, was essentially that of world federalism, another old American idea with roots reaching back to the eighteenth century.[3]

With Mahan the case is somewhat different: invariably invoked, he is seldom quoted, doubtless because his thought was focused on hemispheric defense—"America is our sphere"—and helpful quota-

[2] Josiah Strong, *Our Country,* Jurgen Herbst ed. (Cambridge, Mass., 1963); Dorothea R. Muller, "Josiah Strong and American Nationalism," *JAH,* 53 (1968):487–503; Frederick Merk, *Manifest Destiny and Mission in American History* (New York, 1963), pp. 239–246; and Hollis Read, *The Hand of God in History* (Hartford, 1849). Strong's much-quoted vision of the Anglo-Saxons of North America pressing down upon the southern continent appears to have been merely the conventional wisdom of the day: projecting the historic growth rates of the English- and Spanish-speaking populations of the New World into the twentieth century, the *Britannica* had recently foreseen for the latter a future confined to the hill country, like the Welsh. *Encyclopaedia Britannica,* 9th ed., 1:716–717.

[3] John Fiske, *American Political Ideas Viewed from the Standpoint of Universal History* (New York, 1885), pp. 101–152; Merk, *Manifest Destiny,* p. 239; and Milton Berman, *John Fiske: The Evolution of a Popularizer* (Cambridge, Mass., 1961), 138–140. For some early expressions of the federal idea, see the sources cited in James A. Field, Jr., *America and the Mediterranean World* (Princeton, 1969), pp. 13–15 and 23–24.

tions about transpacific expansion are hard to find.[4] It may, indeed, be time for a collective rereading of Mahan's pre-1898 writings, although how many will wish to work at length through what Admiral Castex described as a style "particulièrement abstraite et soporifique" is open to question. But such an exercise would find little "imperialism." The feeling that the United States should begin to look outward, "right-eously but not with feeble scrupulosity," is matched by the finding that it was disinclined to do so: if, in fact, imperialism was spreading "like wildfire," Mahan did not know it. There is little stress on the expansion of the merchant marine and no concern for projection of power outside the hemisphere. Sea control, it is clearly stated, will never again be as important as during the eighteenth-century wars for empire. Emphasis is given the "aggressive restlessness" of the Euro-peans, as evidenced in overseas competition, and its implications for the Monroe Doctrine; the danger of possible collision with Britain, Spain, or Germany is raised; some concern is evinced about the awak-ening Orient. If there is a focus, it is on the strategic importance of the isthmus, and on the consequent need for protective offshore bases and a smallish but efficient navy, competent to defend against the detach-ments a European power might send against the United States. But the general effect is cloudy, and certainly no clear "imperialistic" plan emerges: reviewing *The Interest of America in Sea Power*, the British army officer George Sydenham Clarke, a great admirer of *The Influ-*

---

[4]Robert Seager II and Doris D. Maguire, eds., *Letters and Papers of Alfred Thayer Mahan* (hereafter Mahan, *Letters and Papers*), 3 vols. (Annapolis, 1975), 2:443, *passim;* and Alfred T. Mahan, *The Interest of America in Sea Power* (Boston, 1897), pp. 261, and 265, and *The Problem of Asia* (Boston, 1900), pp. 7–8. This hemispheric emphasis was lasting: Mahan's war college lectures of the late 1880s, only slightly revised for later publication, focus on isthmus and Caribbean, and consider the Hawaiian Islands in ref-erence to the West Coast. Mahan, *Naval Strategy* (Boston, 1911), *passim.* But historians have not scrupled to invent what they have failed to discover, and one may marvel at the words that have been put into the captain's mouth. Philip S. Foner has stated that in an article in *Harper's Monthly* in October 1897, Mahan called for "expansion of Amer-ican economic activity in Latin America and Asia," urged aggressive moves into the markets of the Far East, and saw "a clear connection between the Caribbean and the vast market of China . . . , the coaling and cable station system in the Ladrones and Samoa, the Philippines . . . "; "Why the United States Went to War with Spain in 1898," *Science and Society* 32 (1968):57–58. This simply is not true. Mahan's article, "Strategic Features of the Gulf of Mexico and the Caribbean Sea," discussed what the title promised and nothing more; reprinted in Mahan, *Interest of America in Sea Power*, pp. 271–314. For perhaps the best extended discussion of Mahan's influence, see William E. Livezey, *Mahan on Sea Power* (Norman, Okla., 1947). But see, *per contra*, Peter Karsten, "The Nature of 'Influence': Roosevelt, Mahan, and the Concept of Sea Power," *American Quarterly* 23 (1971):585–600. And, for negative evidence, see John D. Long, *The New American Navy* (New York, 1903), and Harry Thurston Peck, *Twenty Years of the Re-public, 1885–1905* (New York, 1906).

ence of Sea Power upon History, found it "extremely difficult to extract a definite meaning from his pages."[5]

It seems possible that one reason for the perdurability of these authors in treatments of this period is their use of the terms "Anglo-Saxon" and "race," in the context of what the twentieth century has done to words like these. But in 1885 there was nothing either very novel or very naughty in this usage. The term "Anglo-Saxon" as an umbrella word for British and Americans was some forty years old. The word "race," as any dictionary will show, can be used in either a biological or a cultural sense, and few contemporaries would have thought that references to the "French race," the "Spanish race," or the "Anglo-Saxon" or "English-speaking" race had anything to do with the vexed question of whether the biological races of mankind numbered five as suggested by Johann Blumenbach, eleven as argued by Charles Pickering, or four as proposed by Thomas Huxley. If talk of the achievements of the "Anglo-Saxon race" seems nowadays a little out of style, they could hardly have been overlooked in the 1880s. In extent of imperial sway no country equalled Great Britain, and in territorial growth none the United States. The Industrial Revolution, commenced in England, had leapt the Atlantic to produce a still greater economic expansion. On the scales of civil liberty and representative democracy none could match the British and Americans. Nor had any other societies deployed so many missionaries and mechanics to carry the gift of salvation, whether by conversion or modernization, to those who dwelt in darkness.

On the question of the "Anglo-Saxon race," these authors—though often confusing in their usage—were anything but racist in the anthropological sense. "I use the term," Strong wrote, "somewhat broadly to include all English-speaking peoples." In his approval of the "commingling of races" that was taking place in America, he was at one with the American editor of the *Riverside Natural History* who, in this same *annus mirabilis* of 1885, argued the superiority of mixed stocks, with Darwin and with Mahan (who was very clear on the mixed origins of both British and Americans and who came to include the Japanese within the "European family"). Even Brooks Adams, who fussed a good deal about the international Jewish banking community, thought the

---

[5]Mahan, *Influence of Sea Power, passim, Interest of America in Sea Power, passim,* and *Letters and Papers, passim;* James A. Field, Jr., "Alfred Thayer Mahan Speaks for Himself," *Naval War College Review* 29 (1976):47–60; and George Sydenham Clarke, "Captain Mahan's Counsels to the United States," *Nineteenth Century* 43 (1898):292–300.

survival of civilizations dependent upon the infusion of "barbarian blood."[6]

Since contemporaries, like later historians, may well have read selectively, one should perhaps test the assertions that these authors were influential. Josiah Strong's *Our Country* sold a good many copies over the years, but the book got short shrift from the establishment press and no one has yet named a policymaker influenced by Strong's ideas. John Fiske's histories decorated everyone's library shelves, but *American Political Ideas*, which contained his piece on " 'Manifest Destiny,' " was not one of his fastest sellers, and the allegation that he delivered this chapter as a speech to a receptive president and cabinet rests on a misreading of the evidence. Brooks Adams published nothing on American foreign policy until the summer of 1898.[7] Captain Mahan no doubt deserves some credit for the increased popularity of navies and the arguments for battleships, but his principal effort to influence policy misfired badly: throughout his life he remained convinced that his annexationist article on Hawaii had brought about his transfer by the Cleveland administration from writing and lecturing at the Naval War College to a greatly undesired tour of sea duty.

If the claimed impact of the so-called "imperialist" tracts on either the American people or important figures in government tends to dissolve on inspection, one would still presume that the publicists themselves, if they were in fact concerned with empire, would have turned excitedly to work as the Cuban crisis deepened. Alas, the picture is far

---

[6]Strong, *Our Country*, pp. xxi, 202, and 210–211; John S. Kingsley, ed., *The Riverside Natural History* (Boston, 1885), 6:471–472; Charles Darwin, *The Descent of Man* (New York, 1888), p. 142; Mahan, *Problem of Asia*, pp. 147–148 and 193; Brooks Adams, *The Law of Civilization and Decay* (New York, 1898), pp. xi, 362–365, and 383; and Arthur Beringause, *Brooks Adams* (New York, 1955), pp. 119, 122, 141–142, and 178–179. Howard Mumford Jones has some sensible comments on nineteenth-century Anglo-Saxonism (as does Mr. Dooley, whom he quotes); Jones, *The Age of Energy* (New York, 1973), pp. 200–211. On the "racism" of Theodore Roosevelt, see Howard K. Beale, *Theodore Roosevelt and the Rise of America to World Power* (Baltimore, 1956), pp. 26–34. The rhetoric of Fiske and Strong is not our rhetoric, no doubt, but toploftiness is not imperialism. Given the world of the 1880s, there seems nothing very tendentious in their formulations. The basic idea, indeed, would shortly prove persuasive to Frenchmen; see Edmond Demolins, *A quoi tient la superiorité des Anglo-Saxons* (Paris, 1897).

[7]For a list of his writings, see Thornton Anderson, *Brooks Adams, Conscientious Conservative* (Ithaca, 1951), pp. 229–231. Foner has stated that Adams's *Law of Civilization and Decay* argued the health of imperialism and "advocated American control of the Western hemisphere and economic dominance of Asia"; "Why the United States Went to War," p. 45. It does not. The book starts with the ancient world and ends with nineteenth-century Britain; its subject is "the origin, rise and despotism of the gold-bug"; the United States is barely mentioned. See, in default of the work itself, Anderson, *Brooks Adams*, pp. 50–72; Beringause, *Brooks Adams*, 117–128; and Ernest Samuels, *Henry Adams, The Major Phase* (Cambridge, Mass., 1964), pp. 127–130.

otherwise. In the spring of 1898 John Fiske, preoccupied with the preparation of lectures on science and religion, was distressed by the possibility of war.[8] Josiah Strong, like the good reformer he was, was busy
founding the League for Social Service. Brooks Adams left Washington
for his home in Quincy in August 1897, sailed for Europe in September,
and did not return until spring; early in 1898, as war seemed imminent,
he wrote his brother Henry, "I am in despair to have this silly business
forced on us, where we can gain neither glory nor profit."[9] Ten weeks
after the navy had begun a precautionary redeployment, six weeks after
the publication of the De Lôme letter, five weeks after the sinking of
the *Maine,* and four weeks after the *Oregon* had been started east, the
secretary of the navy appointed Captain Mahan the United States representative at a Florentine celebration in honor of Vespucci and Toscanelli, and on March 26, 1898, America's best-known strategic thinker
sailed for Naples. Theodore Roosevelt's old racist teacher, John W. Burgess, prostrated by the events of 1898, turned out to be antiwar, antiimperialist, and anti-Roosevelt. The greatest of the Social Darwinists,
William Graham Sumner, thought the upshot of the war disastrous—
The Conquest of the United States by Spain.

Yet, whatever the facts about these much-quoted intellectuals, it
might still be possible that the 1890s were years of burgeoning senti-

---

[8]Clarke, *John Fiske,* 2:472–473; and Berman, *Fiske,* pp. 251–252. In December 1897
Fiske wrote an historical introduction for a book by his son-in-law on the Cuban insurrection. Although Anglo-Saxon attitudes pervaded the discussion of the "absolute despotism" of the Spanish Empire and the "Satanic" Inquisition, a strong sympathy for the
Cuban cause led to the argument that "for the sake of Cuba's best interests, it is to be
hoped that she will win her independence without receiving from any quarter, and especially from the United States, any such favors as might hereafter put her in a position
of tutelage. . . . " Grover Flint, *Marching with Gomez* (Boston, 1898), pp. xv and xxvii.

[9]Beringause, *Brooks Adams,* pp. 161–162; and Frederic Cople Jaher, *Doubters and
Dissenters* (New York, 1964), p. 173. In these circumstances the elevation of Brooks
Adams, whose expansionist efforts were unknown to the generation of Julius W. Pratt,
to the rank of principal pre-1898 imperialist, is surely one of the most remarkable developments in recent historical writing. William A. Williams has described him as
"something of the chairman of an informal policy-planning staff for the executive department in the years from 1896 to 1908," and Walter LaFeber has stated that Adams,
along with Mahan, "exerted more direct influence on policymakers than did any of the
other intellectuals," and that "throughout 1897 and early 1898 Adams" saw great opportunities in the coming war with Spain, entertained such important people as Cushman Davis, Lodge, and Mahan at dinners in Washington, and was hailed as a prophet
by leading figures of the McKinley adminstration. Williams, "The Frontier Thesis and
American Foreign Policy," *Pacific Historical Review* 24 (1955):387; Williams, *America
in a Changing World* (New York, 1978), p. 38; and LaFeber, *The New Empire,* pp. 80 and
84–85. Foner has added that Henry Adams "worked actively in Washington in favor of
intervention in Cuba"; "Why the United States Went to War," p. 45. But Henry was
abroad from April 1897 to November 1898 and learned of the loss of the *Maine* while
boating on the Nile; Samuels, *Henry Adams,* pp. 185 and 589.

ment for imperialism and concern for the China market. If so, one would suppose this could be documented by a bureaucratic analysis and by lists of people who really mattered—presidents, secretaries of state or navy, senior military officers, Wall Street giants—who were energetic in the cause. The task has not been easy, notwithstanding the recent boom for Benjamin Harrison and his secretary of the navy, Benjamin F. Tracy, and their very ineffective efforts to gain a naval base on Hispaniola.[10] Faced with a foot-dragging Senate, and lacking both suitable movers and shakers and evidence in party platforms and presidential messages, the convention has been to fall back on Fiske and Strong, on the Omaha *Bee*, on the social thought of Harry Thurston Peck, and on the improbable (or at least highly irrational) desire of farmers for a China market to absorb the surplus. In place of identifiably influential persons or pressure groups, there has developed a usage which suggests the virtue of semantic analysis. Persuasion is attempted by incantation: by the use of reiterated statements that "the imperialists" did this and "the imperialists" did that, that "imperialism spread like wildfire," and that under the prodding of the remarkably faceless "imperialists" the American people went island-grabbing.[11] What generally escapes notice is that, when the anti-imperialists come on stage, there is no problem at all in producing a formidable roster of distinguished citizens—Carl Schurz, E. L. Godkin, William Vaughan Moody, David Starr Jordan, Andrew Carnegie (who briefly thought of personally purchasing and liberating the Philippines but who, regrettably for the exceptionalism of American history, failed

[10]Walter R. Herrick, *The American Naval Revolution* (Baton Rouge, 1966), and B. F. Cooling, *Benjamin Franklin Tracy: Father of the Modern American Fighting Navy* (Hamden, Conn., 1973). For a useful list of influential individuals who did not want war in 1898, see Wayne S. Cole, *An Interpretive History of American Foreign Relations* (Homewood, Ill., 1968), pp. 268–269.

[11]See, for example, Herrick, *Naval Revolution*, pp. 24, 60, 69, 84–87, 90, 103–107, 196, and 220. On the "imperialism" of one of the few identified "imperialists," Henry Cabot Lodge, see John A. S. Grenville and George B. Young, *Politics, Strategy, and American Diplomacy* (New Haven, 1966), pp. 201–238. In general this literature appears to depend heavily upon code-words ("imperialism," "new empire," "commercial empire," "hegemony," "commercial hegemony of the world," etc.) whose effects seem more emotive than heuristic. For an attractively written example, see Ernest N. Paolino, *The Foundations of American Empire: William Henry Seward and U.S. Foreign Policy* (Ithaca, 1973). Paolino has argued that plans for the rationalization of the world's coinage and the stringing of the international telegraph were intended to bring about (but how?) American "world commercial hegemony"; see, in particular, pages 6, 14, and 25. LaFeber's extensive repetition of the title phrase—*New Empire*—appears to have persuaded many that the concept existed in its own right long before Brooks Adams published his own book with that title in 1902.

to act on this impulse), Mark Twain, William Jennings Bryan—the list goes on and on.[12]

With semantic analysis, in addition to the question of the unidentified "imperialists," other problems appear. It may be proper to speak figuratively of a unitary "American people" after the sinking of the *Maine*, but, given the politics of 1892 and 1896, earlier unqualified use of the phrase seems questionable. A similar problem of precision arises in relation to that naughty minority of "Americans in Hawaii" who were busily conspiring for annexation. For one thing not all were: the most strongly nativist prime minister of the latter years of the Hawaiian kingdom, Walter M. Gibson, had grown up in New York and New Jersey, and the biggest sugar grower, Claus Spreckels, came to oppose annexation. For another, some of these "Americans" had been born and raised in the islands. Is nationality inalienable? Was Albert Gallatin always a Swiss and Andrew Carnegie always a Scot? Was Spreckels a German or an American or a Hawaiian? Despite the obvious goodheartedness of those who inveigh against the Hawaiian annexationists as against the apostles of Anglo-Saxonism, their own usage seems curiously racist.

Another context in which it is useful to remember that words are not things, and to look through the word to the phenomenon for which it stands, is in discussion of navies and naval bases. The creation of the new American navy in the last two decades of the century was an event of undoubted importance, which might, at first glance, seem to provide bureaucratic evidence for an expansionist policy. But navies can be designed for various purposes: there is no necessary connection between naval building and commercial expansion or colonization, and battleships do not equate with empire.[13] The military characteristics of a naval force—the capabilities designed into it—should give some indication of its intended missions; and the reiterated statements of the secretaries to the effect that the New Navy was purely defensive,

---

[12]For a representative treatment, see the chapter on "Empire Beyond the Seas" in John M. Blum *et al.*, *The National Experience* (3d ed, New York, 1973), pp. 491–506. The terms "imperialist," "imperialists, and "imperialism" appear twenty-one times and eight pre-1898 "imperialists" are named (Strong, Burgess, Fiske, and Mahan constitute half of the contingent); the corresponding terms "anti-imperialist," "anti-imperialists," and "anti-imperialism" are used four times and nineteen individuals are identified.

[13]Leaving aside the European great powers, eight nations (Argentina, Brazil, Chile, China, Denmark, Greece, Spain, Turkey) had acquired battleships by 1893, while the United States still had none. At least on paper China and Spain were clearly superior in cruiser strength as well. None of these countries showed much sign of expansionist or imperialist policy. *Report of the Secretary of the Navy, 1893.*

intended only "as a police force for the preservation of order and never for aggression," are substantiated by the instrument that they created.

Given the limitations of American industry, reinforced as they were by American naval tradition, the first phase of naval revival perforce involved the construction of that "fleet of swift cruisers to prey on the enemy's commerce" desired by Mahan. Here the remoteness of the United States from important European trade routes and from such centers of interest as the River Plate, Valparaiso, and Honolulu strongly affected ship characteristics and by 1890 had brought about the design of cruisers of remarkable coal capacity and endurance. Such ships would seem to have been ideally suited for distant ventures; but, once domestic sources of armor and of castings for gun barrels became available, the emphasis switched to the completion of heavily armed monitors for harbor defense and to construction of "sea-going coastline battleships," restricted in range by congressional enactment and in draft by the hydrography of gulf ports, to contest the control of North American waters. Still further expression of these defensive concerns developed during the 1890s in the authorization of a score of short-range torpedo boats and in the recommendation of 1897—based on the argument that "the traditional policy of our Navy has been a defensive one"—that future units of this type be designed to use the new oil fuel available only at home.[14]

In the early years of the building program the emphasis on commerce raiding and defense of home waters had left the ancient mission of maintaining a presence on such distant stations as the China coast and the River Plate to the wooden ships of the Old Navy. But, as these decayed beyond repair or were washed or blown ashore, replacements became necessary. Over a period of ten years, beginning in 1885, authorization was secured for a number of new gunboats for this service; and, since coaling stations in these far-off regions existed neither in fact nor in contemplation, the specifications for four of the class of 1895 called for "full sail power." Finally, it may be noted, the New Navy was not, as seems sometimes assumed, the product of a presum-

---

[14]On commerce raiders, see Mahan, *Letters and Papers*, 1:593. Mahan emphasized the importance of defense against blockade and bombardment; *Influence of Sea Power*, pp. 83–87. So did Theodore Roosevelt in his review of the book; *Atlantic*, October 1890. Shortly after completion of his term as secretary, Hilary A. Herbert noted that battleship design had been predicated on the assumption of employment close to home, pressed the need for torpedo boats, emphasized the vulnerability of coastal cities and coastal shipping, and pointed to the possibility of collision with Great Britain, with Spain over Cuba, or with Japan over the Hawaiian Islands; "A Plea for the Navy," *Forum* 24 (1897):1–15.

ably expansionist Republican Party: by 1896 the two Cleveland administrations had gained authorization for half again as much tonnage as
had those of Arthur and Harrison.[15]

Related to the naval building question is "the search for bases."
Unquestionably, the coming of steam raised serious problems of range
and endurance for the world's navies, but solutions to the coal problem
varied as widely as the intended employment of the forces to be coaled.
A rented site for a coal pile at Yokohama, Honolulu, or Pago Pago was
one thing; a defended position like Gibraltar, Aden, or Hong Kong was
quite another. When considering the meaning of such terms as "base"
and "coaling station," it is well to be as precise as possible, and precision in chronology is also desirable. One should not, for example,
use the "magnificent naval base at Pearl Harbor" as evidence of vigorous transpacific expansionism twenty years before anyone dredged
the mouth of the Pearl River.[16] And, if the search for bases is to be
taken as an index of outward-looking aspiration, it may be well to recognize that the real proliferation of overseas naval facilities came in
the 1840s and 1850s, in the period of maritime greatness, when the
United States had resident navy agents or naval storekeepers in London, Marseilles, Spezia, Porto Praya, Buenos Aires, St. Thomas, Rio de
Janeiro, Lima, Valparaiso, Honolulu, Macao, and Shanghai.[17] Once
again, perhaps, the wrong questions are at issue. Is not more to be
learned about established national policy by asking not what proposals
were made for the acquisition of coaling stations in the Caribbean or
elsewhere, but rather why so little came of them? Why were the pos-

---

[15]*Report of the Secretary of the Navy, 1891, 1895, 1896.* For a convenient listing of
naval units with dimensions, armament, coal capacity, and dates of authorization and
commissioning, see the *Report* for 1897. It seems hardly necessary to debate the proposition that so costly, continuing, and bipartisan a creation as the New Navy was the
product of the status anxiety of junior officers; see Lloyd C. Gardner, Walter F. LaFeber,
and Thomas J. McCormick, *Creation of the American Empire* (Chicago, 1973), pp. 206–
207.

[16]LaFeber, *The New Empire,* p. 141, *passim.* Herrick has American ships (and even
Captain Togo in HIJMS *Naniwa*) entering Pearl Harbor in the years before the War with
Spain; *American Naval Revolution,* pp. 105, 168, 199–200, and 221. But the limiting
depth at the mouth of the Pearl River was two fathoms, the House rejected an appro-
priation for dredging in 1897, funds did not become available until 1908, and the first
major ship entered only in 1911. See Willis E. Snowbarger, "The Development of Pearl
Harbor" (Ph.D. dissertation, University of California, Berkeley, 1950).

[17]Equally, one should not automatically equate the "New Navy" of the 1890s with
a big navy: the total personnel strength of 1897 (11,985) was only 7 percent greater than
that of 1845 (11,189), although the U.S. population had more than tripled. Bureau of the
Census, *Historical Statistics of the United States, Colonial Times to 1957* (Washington,
1960), pp. 7 and 736–737.

sibilities dangled at various times by Portuguese, Danes, Liberians, Peruvians, and Koreans not accepted? Why was so little done before the War with Spain to turn such available sites as Pearl Harbor and Pago Pago to strategic advantage? Why, indeed, was Pacific base development so slow after 1898?

Allied to the semantic question is the cartographic one: just as words are not things, a map is not the country it represents. In the late nineteenth century, the map was the same color from sea to shining sea, but the United States was, as it had always been, an Atlantic nation: on a Mercator world it belonged functionally at the left and not in the center. The frontier may have shaped the American character, but, whatever the history of the West Coast fur trade and of the California clippers, the United States remained an eastward-facing country. Despite the recorded aspirations of Pacific railway promoters and the later assertions of historians, the Far East was not a farther West. Aspiration was less substantial than geographic and economic reality.

For this assertion some evidence may be adduced. The *Empress of China* and a number of other American merchantmen had reached Canton by way of the Cape of Good Hope before Robert Gray arrived in the *Columbia* from the West Coast. American naval ships operated in the Indian Ocean long before the first one entered the Pacific. The sequence of commercial treaty negotiations with nonwestern societies proceeded eastward, from the Barbary powers to Turkey and thence to Muscat and Siam. Edmund Roberts went out by way of the Cape of Good Hope, and so did Caleb Cushing and Matthew C. Perry and Robert W. Shufeldt. The missionary effort indubitably had profound impact in Hawaii, but its first target had been India and its greatest efforts, until late in the century, were devoted to India and the Near East.[18] The big export-import trade was Atlantic in orientation, the product of the eastern concentration of population, wealth, and industry and of the receptivity of European markets to the torrent of agricultural exports that developed in the 1880s. Tenuously connected by rail with the eastern metropolis, the mountain and Pacific states contained in 1890 less than 5 percent of the nation's population. Of the 5 percent of total exports that emanated from the Pacific coast, a considerable portion consisted of grain bound eastward to Europe. Strategically, the same was true: Europe, the traditional enemy, lay to the eastward, and European island bases watched the eastern seaboard; in the 1880s, with memories of the French in Mexico still green, the sub-

---

[18]James A. Field, Jr., "Near East Notes and Far East Queries," in *The Missionary Enterprise in China and America*, John K. Fairbank, ed., (Cambridge, Mass., 1974), pp. 25–26 and 31–38.

division of Africa drew fresh attention to European capabilities, while
the British occupation of Egypt and the presence of Ferdinand De Les-
seps in Panama emphasized what attractive nuisances isthmuses could
become. The existence of a perceived threat to the Atlantic coastline
was evident in the Endicott Board's report on fortifications, the design
and deployment of the New Navy, and to concern for Caribbean base
facilities.[19]

In the Pacific and eastern Asia, by contrast, the position of the
United States was marginal. Captain David Porter's early inspired admission of the inhabitants of Nukahiva to the "great American family" had been permitted to lapse, as had Perry's initiatives regarding
Port Lloyd and Formosa. Against the annexation of archipelagos commenced by the French in 1842, the British in 1874, the Japanese in
1876, and the Germans in 1884, the United States could show only
uninhabited and undredged Midway, some claims to guano islands, paper base rights at an unusable Pearl Harbor, and a share in the tripartite
administration of Samoa. In China, it is true, the 1880s saw the missionary movement enter a period of remarkable growth, but in commercial matters the American position was weakening. China trade as
a percentage of total foreign commerce had been declining since the
1840s, as trade with Europe grew and as Forbeses and Delanos, reacting
to the lack of Asiatic investment opportunity, shifted their assets and
energies from the treaty ports to western railroads. In commercial and
political geography, moreover, the United States had suffered a considerable setback with the opening of the Suez Canal. Prior to 1869, when
the route to the Far East was by way of the Cape of Good Hope, New
York and Liverpool had been roughly equidistant from China, but now
the Europeans were closer by the length of the Atlantic crossing. Although this situation provided southern textile exporters and their representatives in Congress with strong arguments for an isthmian canal,
such a facility would be long in coming. For the balance of the nineteenth century European pressures on the Far East grew steadily, but
until the Battle of Manila Bay American pressures did not.

The Atlantic orientation of the United States was quite naturally
reflected in the distribution of American-owned merchant shipping,
whether of domestic or foreign registry. Of the former there was of

---

[19]For concern about European economic and political ambitions in the Western
Hemisphere, see David M. Pletcher, *The Awkward Years: American Foreign Relations
under Garfield and Arthur* (Columbia, Mo., 1962), pp. 129–134, *passim*. As early as 1880
Mahan had predicted that the prospect of an isthmian canal would require "a very large
Navy . . . [or] we may as well shut up about the Monroe doctrine at once"; *Letters and
Papers*, 1:482. Ten years later he pinned his hopes for "the motive, if any there be, which
will give the United States a navy" upon the isthmus; *Influence of Sea Power*, p. 88.

course not much, and the postwar failure to restore the country's maritime greatness went far to justify Mahan's pessimism about "The United States Looking Outward," and his original choice of title for his article of 1890s, "The United States Asleep." In the Atlantic, nevertheless, efforts at subsidized shipping lines had brought modest results in the establishment of continuous scheduled services with gulf and Caribbean ports and intermittent service with Brazil. "Whitewashed" iron and steel steamship tonnage—American-owned but under foreign registry—was also concentrated in the Atlantic. On the West Coast success was more limited. There, in 1865, the Pacific Mail Steamship Line had been granted a subsidy for monthly service to the Far East. The company's ships, which originally sailed via Hawaii, were soon shifted to the shorter and more economical northern route, with the result that in 1867 the North Pacific Transportation Company received a subsidy for a one-ship service between San Francisco and Honolulu. Such exiguous connections with the islands and the Orient seemed all the traffic would justify. Both lines found greater profit and employed more ships on coastal runs between Panama, Mazatlan, San Francisco, and Puget Sound.[20]

If, indeed, an expanding merchant marine is seen as an index of imperialistic tendencies, these were far less evident in the United States than elsewhere in the Pacific basin. In the Hawaiian Kingdom, of such small interest to American shipping interests, a period of insular expansionism brought the founding in 1881 of J.D. Spreckels's Oceanic Line, connecting Honolulu with San Francisco and reaching southwest to the Antipodes. The completion of the Canadian Pacific Railroad in 1885 was quickly followed by the establishment of subsidized steamship service between Vancouver and Hong Kong. But the truly important developments in Pacific shipping were those of the "insular imperialists" of Japan. In 1890 the 94,000-ton total of Japanese steam tonnage was less than half that which the United States employed in international trade, but with the commencement of state subsidies in that year the Japanese merchant marine entered a period of explosive growth. By 1896 service had been established with China, the East Indies, Australia, San Francisco, and Seattle, and by 1900 the 543,000 tons of Japanese-flag steam tonnage totalled more than half again that of the United States. The contrast between this achieve-

---

[20]The superior attractions of the North Atlantic were strikingly demonstrated, even after the War with Spain had brought presumed Pacific opportunity, in the creation by J. P. Morgan of the International Mercantile Marine Co., the world's largest privately owned fleet, which in 1902 controlled 136 ships totalling more than a million gross tons, all in the Atlantic.

ment and the difficulties that beset the McKinley administration in finding ships to carry troops to the Philippines (as indeed the contrast in end-of-the-century transpacific population movements) may serve as an indication of which Pacific power was outward-looking.

The United States Navy in the 1890s was equally an East Coast Atlantic-oriented institution. In the outward-looking antebellum days, when American merchant shipping covered the globe, the navy had maintained six overseas cruising stations—Mediterranean, Pacific, West Indies, South Atlantic, East Indies, and African—to which the bulk of its active units was assigned. With the end of the Civil War this traditional practice was resumed, "irreflectively," as Mahan later wrote, and by 1872 the Asiatic Squadron, successor to the old East Indies Squadron, had been brought up to a strength of eleven ships, more than a quarter of the total deployed on distant stations. But this return to the ancient ways—also reflected in the concern of Secretary of State William M. Evarts and Secretary of the Navy Richard W. Thompson for foreign markets, in naval interest in the Amazon and Congo basins, Zanzibar, and Korea, and in Secretary of the Navy William E. Chandler's call of 1883 for coaling stations everywhere—ended with the 1880s. The last years of the century witnessed an initial compartmentalization of the world in terms of naval power as the rivalries of the industrialized nations, the range limitations that accompanied the shift to steam, and the logistical and material requirements of modern warships brought a retirement of the world's navies upon their home bases.

This development, most strikingly epitomized in the Royal Navy's redeployment of 1904–05, had become apparent in the distribution of the United States fleet well before the War with Spain. With the shift to coal and the focus on the European threat, talk of markets and bases gave way in the reports of the secretaries to emphasis on foreign building programs and concern for the safety of the hemisphere. Since the coming of steam had given a new predictability to the movements of ships and squadrons, there also followed the first efforts at rational war planning. At the infant Naval War College the focus was on "what is necessary for a state of war," and early sessions concentrated on the study of Atlantic trade routes in preparation for efficient commerce raiding. In 1890 Captain Mahan was called to Washington to draw up contingency plans for hostilities with Great Britain or Spain; the possibility of a German takeover of Dutch possessions in the Western Hemisphere also excited concern. Starting in 1894, as the new battleships began to come into commission, the war college's annual problems focused on the defense of the Atlantic Coast, its lectures and war games emphasized the strategic geography of gulf and Caribbean, and its studies of international law dealt with such matters as the defense of the Hawaiian Kingdom against foreign aggression and the maintenance of the neutrality of an isthmian canal.[21]

Together with the new technology, these concerns governed the deployment of the New Navy. Despite the continuing problems of the China coast, the west coast of Latin America, the Bering Sea seal fisheries, Samoa, and Hawaii, the new steel ships were assigned in the first instance to the North Atlantic Squadron. The first modern warship to serve on the West Coast, the small cruiser *Charleston,* joined the Pacific Squadron only in 1890s, and the show of force that followed the Chilean crisis was provided by units drawn from the Atlantic. Not until 1892, by which time eight protected cruisers had been commissioned, did the first new ship, the 900-ton gunboat *Petrel,* join the Asiatic Squadron. By 1897 the North Atlantic Squadron contained by far the largest concentration of available force. Compared with four first- and second-rates in the eastern Pacific and two in the Asiatic Squadron, the North Atlantic had ten; and, since these included five of the six battleships and both armored cruisers, the disproportion in fighting strength was far greater than the mere number of ships suggests.

The limited forces assigned to the Pacific and Asiatic Squadrons hardly seem indicative of a forward policy. Such a policy, in any event, would not have been easy. The coming of steam had made the geography of coal and of coaling stations a question of prime strategic interest. The developed coal mines of the United States were in the East, and hopes of Alaskan coal deposits to ease the West Coast naval problem had not been fulfilled. Indeed, throughout the Pacific basin the supply of coal was effectively a British monopoly. The needs of the Hawaiian islands had traditionally been filled by sailing ships from England, and the important new regional sources, Vancouver Island and

---

[21]The *Reports of the Secretary of the Navy* in the years from 1877 to 1887 stressed trade expansion, overseas bases, and the problem of the merchant marine; after 1889 the emphasis shifted to the defense of coastal cities. Mahan, *Letters and Papers,* 1:444; for his 1890 "Contingency Plan of Operations in Case of War with Great Britain" and his comments on a plan of 1895 (after the first battleships had been commissioned), see *ibid.,* 3:559–576, 2:425–428; and for his assessment of the German threat, see *ibid.,* 2:27, 37–38, and *Interest of America in Sea Power,* pp. 15 and 294–295. For visual evidence of the central strategic concerns, see the painting by Rufus Zogbaum, which shows the war college class of 1894 gaming the defense of an East Coast harbor (apparently Narragansett Bay) before a large wall chart of the Gulf and Caribbean; *Harper's Weekly,* 39 (1895):149.

New South Wales, were also British. American base facilities to mitigate the magnificent distances of the Pacific were lacking, and few
seemed to care. The capabilities of West Coast navy yards were limited; the Hawaiian request for annexation had been rejected; and Pearl
Harbor and Pago Pago remained undeveloped. The Asiatic Squadron
was, in fact, an eastward projection of an Atlantic-facing country, and
one greatly attenuated by distance. For materiel it depended on the
New York Navy Yard, and its units traditionally proceeded to their
duty stations by way of the Mediterranean and Suez, a passage extraordinarily vulnerable to European interference. With the German seizure
of Tsingtao in 1897, the Asiatic Squadron became the only naval force
in the Far East without a local base of its own. The consequences of
being so far out at the end of the line can be seen in Dewey's coal and
ammunition problems and in the fact that when war came he not only
had to destroy a fleet but also had to capture a harbor. These problems
had been visible long before the war; they were reflected in the limited
nature of the force that was maintained in Asiatic waters for the protection of American interests. In 1898 the Asiatic Squadron was out-
gunned by British, Russian, German, and Japanese forces in the area.
Against a dozen major Japanese units, the United States boasted two—
hardly an armament with which to go adventuring so far from home.

But where does all this leave us? If we rule out the conventional
wisdom about Darwin, the psychic crisis of imperialism, the New
Navy, and the Pacific highway to Asia, what remains? What was, in
fact, the nature of American relations with the outer would between
the end of Reconstruction and the War with Spain?

Generally, it may be said, these relations were far more individual
than governmental. As the wounds of war healed, an extraordinarily
energetic society deployed its representatives abroad in a wide variety
of roles: explorers, tourists, art collectors, philanthropists, missionaries, synarchists, railroad promoters, and mining engineers. Although
much of this activity was sufficiently traditional, its scale and impact
were increasing as a result of the remarkable economic development
of these years, itself evidenced externally in three important and in-
terconnected ways: the growth of North Atlantic trade and the progressive integration of the North Atlantic economic community; the
spillover of American enterprise into Canada, Mexico, and the Caribbean; and the beginnings of direct investment abroad. From these developments, Asia (especially China) was largely excluded: except for
the skills of synarchists—half-missionary and half-mercenary in motivation—and the export of Christian truth, it was primarily a source of

imports, not a market, and only the missionary effort grew significantly in the years before 1898.[22]

But, it may be objected, there were all those naval and diplomatic incidents of the 1880s and 1890s. Did these not constitute the preseason warm-up for imperialism and the projection of national power? Here two points may be noted. First, most of these incidents, like the greater part of the naval modernization program, took place in the administrations of the anti-imperialistic Cleveland, the same president who resisted the treaty provision for base rights at Pearl Harbor, refused to participate in the Berlin agreement on the Congo, withdrew the Hawaiian treaty of annexation, and declined to intervene in China or in Turkey on behalf of the Armenians. The Harrison administration did, it is true, conclude the Samoan treaty of 1889, mount an unsuccessful search for Caribbean bases, and support Hawaiian efforts at annexation; but its liveliest accomplishment was to preside over the consequences of the riot in the True Blue Saloon, and few have suggested that the United States contemplated the annexation of Chile. By contrast, the first Cleveland administration handled the first years of the Samoan fuss and carried out the Panama landings of 1885; the second managed the Brazilian intervention, the Corinto business, and the Venezuela boundary affair. Second, since most American naval interventions occurred in the Western Hemisphere and involved a real or presumed European presence, it would seem reasonable to see them as reflecting the same Monroeist (and Mahanist) strategy that governed the design and deployment of the New Navy. The importance of the Brazil trade, which greatly exceeded that with China, may be conceded, but Valparaiso, Corinto, and Caracas were hardly regions of any very impressive "new empire" economic interest at the time.

All this having been said, it is nevertheless still possible to find a persuasive linkage among economic activity, accelerating diplomacy, and naval demonstrations. To do this one must move again beyond economics and ideology to the generally neglected area of technological capabilities and consider, along with the consequences of steam propulsion, the revolution in communications that occurred with the

---

[22]For useful information on overseas activities in the 1880s, see Milton Plesur, *America's Outward Thrust* (DeKalb, Ill., 1971). Also see Merle Curti and Kendall Birr, *Prelude to Point Four* (Madison, Wis., 1954); and Mira Wilkins, *The Emergence of Multinational Enterprise* (Cambridge, Mass., 1970). For a valuable and much neglected regional treatment, see J. Fred Rippy, *Latin America and the Industrial Age* (New York, 1944). On synarchy, see John K. Fairbank, "Synarchy under the Treaties," in his *Chinese Thought and Institutions* (Chicago 1957), pp. 204–231; and James A. Field, Jr., "Transnationalism and the New Tribe," *International Organization* 25 (1971):353–372. On the growth of missions, see Field, "Near East Notes," pp. 34–38.

coming of ocean cables. As these progressively joined together the already existing regional telegraph nets, those in the Western world who possessed the requisite skills and inclinations found it possible to administer modernity, public or private, at previously unheard-of distances. Without this development, it seems proper to suggest, the world would not have witnessed the late-nineteenth-century growth of multinational enterprise, the particular kind of reactive and competitive European imperialism that marked the 1880s and 1890s, or the rash of international crises of the closing years of the century.

Despite the traditional prominence of the name of Cyrus Field, this wiring of the world was, like so much of nineteenth-century history, primarily a British accomplishment. The principal inventions were British, gutta percha for cable insulation was a British imperial monopoly, in techniques of cable manufacture the British were far in the lead, and only in Britain was investment capital available on the required scale. Logically enough, then, the progress of long-range communications reflected the image of the world held by those looking outward from London. The Dover-Calais cable of 1851 was soon followed by other links to Europe. The Crimean War brought the extension of the overland telegraph, first to Balaclava and then to Constantinople. In 1865 Bombay and the Indian telegraph system was connected with that of Europe. In 1866 the Atlantic cable joined the European and North American telegraph nets. In 1870 an all-British cable route to India was opened, and in the next year Japan and the China coast were tied in, both by landline across Siberia and by cable via India, Singapore, and Saigon.

By the early 1870s, then, much of the world had been linked. When everything was working well, a telegram could be sent (albeit by way of London and at great expense) from San Francisco to Tokyo. But there were as yet no connections with interior China, with Africa south of Egypt, or with Latin America south of the Caribbean; and no cable yet spanned the Pacific. Not unnaturally, given their predominance in communications technology and international trade, it was the British who took the first great steps to link up the southern continents, with cables from Portugal to Brazil in 1874, and down the East African coast to Durban in 1879. But, while the British were progressively tying together what seemed important to them, one American looking outward from New York was connecting up the Western Hemisphere. So now, if we need an "imperialist," or at least an individual who worked purposefully and effectively with Wall Street backing to increase his countrymen's capabilities abroad, we can have one. He is curiously absent from books on the "new empire," but he did exist. His name was James A. Scrymser.

Scrymser, in 1865, organized the International Ocean Telegraph
Company. Two years later, armed with franchises from Congress and
Spain and with support from Secretary of State William H. Seward, he
entered the Caribbean with a line from Florida to Havana. But further
accomplishments in this area were frustrated by British competition
and corporate infighting and there followed a change in aim. In 1878–
79 Scrymser established, with financial backing from J. P. Morgan and
other leaders of the New York financial community, the Mexican Telegraph Company and the Central and South American Telegraph Company and directed his efforts southward toward the west coast of South
America. Mexico City was linked with Galveston in March 1881; by
October 1882, the line had reached Lima with stops at various Central
American way stations; in 1883 a Brazilian connection was established; in 1890 the cable was extended to Valparaiso, and in the next
year the purchase of a trans-Andean telegraph line gave access to Argentina. The result of Scrymser's work was to make possible rapid
communication between the United States and South America without having to route messages through London and Lisbon and with
consequent greater speed, greater security, and diminished cost.[23]

Since the British were a nation of shopkeepers and the business of
America was business, the purpose of the international cable net was
to facilitate the work of the world and its geography reflected existing
economic interest. But, as duplicate cables were laid on major routes,
word-saving business codes were developed, and costs went down, the
new technology took on its own creative role. With their lines eastward to Hong Kong and Shanghai, and across the South Atlantic to
Brazil, the British enhanced their regional economic positions. In the
Western Hemisphere the pattern of the American economic spillover
largely replicated that of the telecommunications network. Increasingly, the successors of William Wheelwright and Henry Meiggs found
themselves under the control of the home office—as was soon shown
by the transfer of control of the Grace enterprises from Lima to New
York in the 1880s and the appearance of two Grace brothers as members of Scrymser's board of directors. In the transatlantic context, where
earlier attempts by American manufacturers to establish plants in
Great Britain had failed, the years after 1866 brought routine success;
as London became more and more the hub of world cable communications, firms such as Singer and Eastman Kodak increasingly en-

---

[23]The attractiveness of Scrymser's venture, as compared to contemporary Chinese
promotional schemes, may be seen in the ease with which he gained financial backing
and in his weighty board of directors, which included, in addition to J. P. Morgan, such
worthies as John E. Alexandre (steamships), William R. and Michael P. Grace (South
American trade and finance), Henry L. Higginson (banking), Charles Lanier (banking
railroads), and Richard W. Thompson (secretary of the navy, French Panama Canal Company).

trusted the administration of Eastern Hemisphere business to their British branches.

In the Pacific the story was very different: there another history of nonaccomplishment further emphasized the marginal nature of American interest. The Collins overland telegraph project had been killed off by the Atlantic cable. In 1870 Admiral David D. Porter urged a Pacific cable, a recommendation repeated by the Congress in 1873 and subsequently by Presidents Grant, Hayes, Cleveland, and Harrison, but to no avail. In Australia interest began to be evident in 1877 and in Canada soon after; in 1894 British imperial concern brought an abortive attempt to annex Necker Island in the Hawaiian chain as a relay station for a cable between Vancouver and the Antipodes. But, despite these signs of British interest and though the Hawaiians granted franchises in 1891 and 1895, though the navy made a hydrographic survey for a Hawaiian cable in 1891–92, though the Hawaiian commissioners urged action in 1893, and though Scrymser organized a Pacific Cable Company in 1896, nothing was done. By 1898 there were twelve active North Atlantic cables, nine of them duplex, and Scrymser had doubled up his South American lines five years before, but no action had yet been taken to span the Pacific.

Although economic interests had shaped the ocean cable network, the blessings of rapid communications transcended the economic sphere. Capabilities are often as determining as intentions—as Mahan once observed, " 'Can,' as well as 'will,' plays a large part in the decisions of life"—and the capability that now existed could be employed in various ways. The new speed of communication, combined with technological advances in printing and papermaking, gave rise to a revolution in journalism and ushered in the great age of the war correspondent, a profession in which such Americans as Januarius Aloysius MacGahan and Richard Harding Davis early attained high place. In countries afflicted with high literacy rates there developed an attentive audience for latter nineteenth-century theatrics—the Crimea, the Nile quest, the Bulgarian Horrors, the Armenian massacres, the sinking of the *Maine*—whose response in times of crisis constituted a new burden for their governments. Compared to the consequences of modern technology and universal education, the contributions of Charles Darwin to jingoism appear small.

There were also more direct consequences for the foreign offices of the world. When information previously transmitted in intermittent chunks could move in a steady flow, and when dispatches that once took weeks or months in transit could now arrive in hours, a wholly new tempo of diplomatic activity developed. The apparent virtue of the quick response, as a means of increasing pressure on the French to withdraw from Mexico, led Seward to run up an enormous cable bill. In the *Virginius* affair of 1873, Scrymser's line to Havana and the pre-existing connections by way of London with Madrid and Mediterranean ports gave Hamilton Fish the country's first experience in "crisis management" and permitted the speedy recall of the European Squadron. From this time on the lives of secretaries of state would never be quite the same, and March 7, 1867, the date of appointment of the department's first telegrapher, may perhaps be taken as the date of origin of the "new paradigm" of diplomacy that developed as the century wore on.[24]

A final important consequence of the extension of ocean cables was the increased speed of naval movements. The revolution in propulsion that had imposed upon navies new base requirements and new limitations of range had also enabled them to steam upwind and in calm. Now, as consuls and ministers could cable for help and governments could cable orders, a wholly new speed of response developed. In 1861 the European Squadron did not reach New York until two and a half months after the firing on Fort Sumter. When summoned back in 1873 at the time of the *Virginius* crisis, it was home in five weeks; and from this time to the Boxer Rebellion a series of unprecedentedly quick arrivals of outside military forces hastened the course of history. The strategic significance of the submarine telegraph was early appreciated: by the late 1870s the Admiralty had cable communication with all important British overseas naval stations; in 1890, in his contingency plan for war with Britain, Captain Mahan called for an immediate cutting of the Halifax-Bermuda cable.[25] The importance of Scrymser's contribution to American capabilities in these matters can be seen in a comparison of the dilatory course of surface-mail diplomacy and the freedom of local initiative that marked the Samoan and Hawaiian questions with the rapid reaction to events in Panama, Chile, Brazil, and Nicaragua and the degree of central control maintained over these demonstrations.

---

[24]Compared to same or next-day delivery by cable, late-nineteenth-century surface mail transit time for State Department dispatches was on the order of ten days to three weeks for Western Europe, three to four weeks for Russia, a month to six weeks for Argentina, Brazil, and Chile, and upwards of six weeks for East Asia. Department of State, Instructions and Despatches, *passim*. Seward's dispatch of November 23, 1866, which cost $13,000 and took two days to decipher, was the wonder of the Parisian diplomatic corps. Fish had made brief use of the cable in the Cuban incident of 1869; in the *Virginius* affair its employment was central.

[25]Field, *Mediterranean World*, pp. 305 and 333–334; and Arthur Hezlet, *The Electron and Seapower* (London, 1975), p. 9. The first instance of continuous governmental control of a distant operation was the bombardment of Alexandria in 1882, when a British cable ship grappled the line from Malta and set up in business offshore. Even more than the fuel question, the problems of communications technology tend to be slighted by naval historians: the anatomists of sea power concentrate on bone and muscle to the neglect of the alimentary and nervous systems.

The responses of the United States government to these events in Latin America were, one may say, defensive in nature, comporting with the fears expressed by Secretary of the Navy Tracy of "the aggressive policy of foreign nations" and of the political threat posed by "the establishment of complete commercial supremacy by a European power in any state in the Western Hemisphere." They were part of intended American policy in a way in which the island conquests of 1898 were not. But when events in Cuba wrenched American policy into a new path, the new technology proved of governing importance in the conduct of what an accomplished army officer subsequently described as a war of "coal and cables." Starting in January 1898, cabled despatches were employed to accomplish a preliminary redeployment of the navy. Cable connections with the Far East (by way of London) carried the orders to Dewey to concentrate his force, keep full of coal, and proceed against the Philippines. A new cable from Hong Kong to Manila forewarned Admiral Montojo and permitted him to gather his ships in shoal water, but no cable yet reached Guam, where the garrison was taken by surprise.[26]

Energetically carrying out his orders, Dewey dispensed with the Spanish squadron and captured the harbor he had to have. In the American press the cabled reports of the battle produced a victory so famous that the politicians could hardly disown it, while the fact, made possible by these same cables' annihilation of distance, that Manila Bay preceded the Cuban landings by six weeks and the Battle of Santiago by two months, worked powerfully to focus public attention on the Far East. Now, at last, an "avalanche" of speeches, editorials, articles, and books did descend upon the American people. "Imperialism," we may say, was the product of Dewey's victory.[27]

It should be emphasized, however, that results had little to do with intentions. Faced with the problem of how to employ the Asiatic Squadron in the event of war with Spain, the naval planners had given no automatic priority to the Philippines. Among the possibilities considered in the year before the outbreak of hostilities was the withdrawal of these units westward to join in an attack on the Canaries.

---

[26]George O. Squier, "The Influence of Submarine Cables upon Military and Naval Supremacy," *U.S. Naval Institute Proceedings* 26 (1900):599; French E. Chadwick, *The Relations of the United States and Spain: The Spanish-American War*, 2 vols. (New York, 1911), 1:3–5. Tribolet, *Electrical Communications*, pp. 155 and 245.

[27]Richard W. Leopold, *The Growth of American Foreign Policy* (New York, 1962), pp. 150–152 and 180–183; and Walter Millis, *The Martial Spirit* (Boston, 1931), pp. 174–177 and 195–199. Since naval officers are often grouped with the "imperialists," it may be worth noting that Dewey never recommended retention of the Philippines. A practical man, he wondered why, if colonies were indeed desired, the United States did not look to such handy locations as Mexico or Central America.

Even after Manila became the settled objective, the aim was merely to gain leverage to pry Spain out of Cuba and to acquire security for the payment of an indemnity. The role reversal that found the Spanish giving up the islands and the United States doing the paying had occurred to none: in the words of the distinguished naval officer who wrote the history of the war, "Perhaps none were more surprised to find a great archipelago at their command than were the gentlemen composing the administration in Washington."[28]

Lamenting the "Great Aberration," Samuel Flagg Bemis once echoed McKinley's observation that, if only "old Dewey" had sailed along home after the battle, it would have saved much subsequent complication. It is in many ways an appealing thought, but to have done so would have been to abandon a war that had barely begun and to forego that "inducement" to Spain to leave Cuba that had been the object of the move against the Philippines. Yet, while departure was unthinkable, to remain was impossible without support from home. As Dewey swung around the anchor in Manila Bay, his ammunition depleted, his communications dependent upon British goodwill, and with an hourly diminishing coal supply, McKinley ordered forth a collier, a cruiser, two monitors, and some army troops.[29] This effort at

---

[28]Grenville and Young, *Politics, Strategy, and Diplomacy,* pp. 267–296; Chadwick, *Spanish-American War,* 1:90–91, 154, 208; 2:472–473. Mahan later wrote that the aim of the war had been "to enforce the departure" of Spain from Cuba, commented on the surprising fact that trouble in Cuba had led onward to Asia, noted that the expanisonist vision had never reached beyond Hawaii, observed that the Philippines had never previously risen above his "mental horizon," and attributed the outcome to the will of God. "The War on the Sea and Its Lessons, I: How the Motive of the War Gave Direction to its Earlier Movements." *McClure's Magazine* 12 (1898):110–118, *Problem of Asia,* pp. 7 and 11, and *Letters and Papers,* 2:566, 579–580, 619. To the financial writer Charles A. Conant it seemed that traditional issues had suddenly been "tinged with a strange, new light by the flash of Dewey's guns in the Bay of Manila"; *The United States in the Orient* (Boston, 1900), p. 226.

[29]Dewey's victory gave rise to novel and difficult problems in the areas of coal and communications. Since the Spanish refused him use of the Manila-Hong Kong cable, his telegraphic dispatches to Washington had first to travel by ship to Hong Kong. The need to fuel *McCulloch* for the round trip (since coal for warlike use was contraband and only on condition of immediately heading homeward could any of his ships have coaled in neutral ports) was in part responsible for the delayed transmission of his action report. Prior to 1898 the British had worried about the vulnerability of their worldwide cable system; since transmission by a neutral of belligerent dispatches raised serious problems of international law, the Americans (and doubtless others) had worried about British control of the world cable network. Learning of Dewey's isolation, Scrymser at once offered to lay a new cable between Hong Kong and Manila with financing by J. P. Morgan, but the proposal was refused by London. The British at Hong Kong did, however, accept Dewey's dispatches under the fiction that the traffic was nonmilitary; it is interesting to speculate on his position had they refused to bend the rules. The five-day minimum reply time imposed by the need to communicate by ship with the Asiatic mainland complicated dealings with Aguinaldo and von Diederichs and made the situation in Manila Bay (as in Samoa and Hawaii) one where central control was diminished and events tended to take charge.

reinforcement underlined once again the marginal American position in the Pacific. The eastward transfer of army forces for the campaign in Cuba had reduced the strength of the Department of California to 25 officers and 418 men and had stripped the Pacific Coast of arms and ammunition. The *Oregon* had been sent east and the cruiser *Charleston*, laid up at Mare Island, had yet to be reactivated. To obtain the twenty merchant ships required for the summer's troop movements, it proved necessary to threaten seizure of some and to transfer others from the Atlantic and from foreign flags. The logistics of the transpacific effort depended upon the enthusiastic unneutrality of the Hawaiian Republic. But, once the troops did reach the Philippines, they stayed; and the problems of administering so distant a dependency brought forth the single preplanned insular annexation of the period, as Wake Island was taken as a landing station for the now-imperative American Pacific cable.

Returning finally to the "worst chapter," we may conclude that much of it is wrong and most of it irrelevant to "imperialism" and the events of 1898.[30] The New Navy was a defensive answer to European developments; its deployment reflected a shrunken rather than an enlarged strategic perimeter. The "search for bases" was a response to the strategic problems of isthmus, Caribbean, and eastern Pacific. Neither missionary work nor burgeoning exports nor the beginnings of

---

[30]It sometimes seems as difficult to discover the "very heart of contemporary revisionism" as it is to elucidate the message of Mahan. If it is that after 1898 American policymakers sought to preserve a "long-term option" in China, one can hardly argue: that is what sensible policymakers try to do. But if, regarding the War with Spain, the "central question" turns on the contention that the acquisition of the Philippines was "the product of a conscious, pragmatic effort to provide . . . integrated, protectible trade routes across the Pacific," the policy seems irrational, the argument dubious, and the evidence lacking. Thomas J. McCormick, "American Expansion in China," *AHR* 75 (1970):1394–1396. What is an "integrated" trade route? Why across the Pacific? The American import-export community was in the East, and the China trade was an Atlantic trade. The route westward from New York was shorter, and faster for passengers (like Commodore Dewey, going out to his new command) and mail. But for freight it involved 3,000 miles of high-cost railroad carriage followed by the transit of an ocean where shipping was scarce and coal much more expensive than on the Atlantic-Suez route. As to whether this route was "protectible," the question is, against whom? Nobody ever solved the problem of the defense of the Philippines. In the early years they seemed vulnerable to German attack; as late as 1911 Mahan conceded to Japan the capability of bagging the Philippines, Guam, and Hawaii and landing on the West Coast before the battle fleet could reach the scene of action. For an interesting visual aid, which may have encouraged latter-day geopolitical misconception, see the schematic map of "Geography and American Sea Power, 1898–1922," In Harold and Margaret Sprout, *Toward a New Order of Sea Power* (Princeton, 1940), p. 22 (reprinted in E. M. Earle, ed., *Makers of Modern Strategy* [Princeton, 1943], p. 428). "Sea Power" appears in the form of enormous arrows projecting from the East and West Coasts, from the isthmus, and from the Hawaiian Islands, with those in the Pacific much the largest. Yet for most of the period in question the entrance to Pearl Harbor was not dredged, the Panama Canal was not completed, and the battle fleet was in the Atlantic.

foreign investment called for the extension of political control. The ideologists, so selectively quoted by posterity, were of negligible importance. What Americans, whether travellers or missionaries or businessmen, wanted of the outer world was the freedom to pursue happiness, to do their thing, to operate insofar as possible unhindered by arbitrary power or obsolete ideas. Proud of their own self-determined independence, they were sympathetic to similar desires on the part of Samoan chiefs, Korean kings, Egyptian khedives, Armenian Christians, Brazilians, Venezuelans, and Chinese. Most of all, because they were nearest and most visible and noisiest, it was the Cubans who engaged this sympathy.

Such traditional aims and attitudes had little to do with any "new American spirit," or with Asiatic markets, or with "insular imperialism." The western Pacific acquisitions, which opened a new era of American history, were in one sense the product of the new technological developments; in another, they can be seen as historical "accidents." If the British had kept the Philippines after the Seven Years' War, the War with Spain would have been confined to the Atlantic. If the Filipinos had been happy under Spanish rule (or if the Asiatic Squadron had been sent against the Canaries), this rule might well have continued. If Spain had either pacified or given up Cuba, there would have been no war; perhaps, indeed, war might have been averted had the *Maine* not been sent to Havana.[31] If this was indeed the case (and unless a conspiracy theory is at once developed on the basis of Lodge's prediction of "an explosion any day in Cuba"), the identity of the ship sent is perhaps the ultimate historical accident. A sunken *Texas*, say, would have contributed little to the torchlight parades of chanting patriots.

If there had been no war, the process of the "Americanization of the world," which so commended itself to the British reformer and journalist W. T. Stead (and which so exasperated other Englishmen), would no doubt have continued.[32] American heiresses would have continued to marry British milords; missionaries and student volunteers would have persisted in their work for China; engineers, promoters, and salesmen would have pressed on with their activities; multinational corporations would have continued to expand; Carnegie libraries would have gone on proliferating throughout the English-speaking world. But in political terms the outward thrust would, in all proba-

---

[31]"Apparently as the result of an accident in Havana Harbor, the path of destiny has been opened for use in the East"; Conant, *United States in the Orient*, p. 63.

[32]W. T. Stead, *The Americanization of the World; or, The Trend of the Twentieth Century* (New York, 1902).

bility, have conformed to the relaxed anticipations of "Jingo Jim" Blaine, the strategic parameters of the "imperialistic" Mahan, and the proposals of the Republican platform of 1896: a suitable measure of control over the impending isthmian canal, over protective Caribbean naval bases, and over the Hawaiian islands. In the circumstances of the time, such a defensive policy seems quite reasonable.

Walter LaFeber

WALTER LAFEBER (1933–   ) is professor of history at Cornell University. He is the author of a number of books dealing with American diplomatic history, including *The New Empire: An Interpretation of American Expansionism 1860–1898* (1963), *America, Russia, and the Cold War 1945–1966* (4th ed., 1980), and *Inevitable Revolutions: The United States in Central America* (1983).

The 1890s—the decade that inaugurated modern America and particularly modern American foreign policy—continues to fascinate many American historians. James A. Field, Jr., however, believes these years to be the "worst chapter" in American diplomatic historiography. He ascribes the problem in part to historians who cling to certain conventional wisdom which, upon examination, should no longer be either conventional or considered wise. The long misplaced emphasis on Social Darwinism is certainly an example of such mistaken conventional wisdom. Thomas McCormick, Paul Holbo, and, in unpublished work, Robert Dawidoff pointed out long ago that Social Darwinism was more a rationale for, than a cause of, American expansionism. Other historians have also previously argued Field's point that, when Josiah Strong discussed foreign policy, he wanted to stress "what was at stake at home." Indeed, these historians have argued that almost *every* American policymaker or public spokesman who discusses foreign policy emphasizes what is at stake at home.

Although the correction of such details is important, Field dismisses the more critical issue of how men and women of the 1890s conceptualized problems in foreign policy and developed (if they were lucky) solutions. In the process Field even attacks many recent historians who have tried to place the 1890s in this broader framework. In important respects, the first section of this essay is misleading, for the later emphasis on cable communication, while adding an important dimension to our knowledge of late-nineteenth-century expansionism, builds on the work and the approaches of, among others, Ernest Paolino, Charles Vevier, Harold Schonberger, and David Pletcher. This is all to the good. The story of how this communication network developed complements much of what we already know and makes it that much easier for us to think in broad terms about the importance of the 1890s.

The essay, however, ultimately fails to reconceptualize the foreign policies of the 1890s. One reason, the less important, is specific: at the critical point—1898—Field is forced to drop his thesis and instead emphasize "accidents" in history. This escape hatch is familiar. In Samuel Flagg Bemis's seminal text on American diplomatic history, written forty years ago, the grand story of American expansion rolls along until the narrative encounters 1898. Bemis could handle the next thirteen years only by calling them an "aberration." Such an explanation does not suffice, for it neither explains the particular events nor develops a framework that allows us to understand the era's importance in the totality of American history. The "aberration" is not dealt with adequately because any attempt to claim that the explosion that sank the *Maine* in February 1898 propelled the United States into war and that the explosion was one of those "accidents" of history begs the central question of why the *Maine* was in Havana harbor in the first place. The answer lies in President McKinley's decision to send it there to protect American lives and property after riots in mid-January indicated that Spanish reforms were not cooling the Cuban revolution and that Spain was losing control. Sending the *Maine* can thus be understood as making an important change in the president's previous policy of watchful waiting, and it anticipates his demands in the final ultimatum that Spain accept an American presence to mediate an end to the revolution. The February explosion may have been accidental, not Spanish-inspired, but there was nothing accidental about the causes or the consequences of the *Maine*'s visit.

This particular problem is part of the larger problem, confronted by most historians of the era. How do the events before 1898 relate to events after 1898? Field sees little relationship. He argues, for example, that United States officials must not have been concerned about Asia before 1898 since so few warships were stationed in the Pacific. When they did consider the area, the officials viewed it as an eastern rather than a western problem. With few exceptions, however, the essay's examples of Americans traveling east to reach Asia are chosen from the years before 1846, that is, before the United States controlled the West Coast. By the 1890s, Seward had talked of traveling to Asia via the Aleutians, Grover Cleveland had called Hawaii (not the Cape of Good Hope) the stepping-stone to Asia, and Theodore Roosevelt was about to proclaim the "Pacific era" of American history.

The question is not how many warships, or cables, were in the Pacific. Neither naval officers nor cable owners made basic foreign policy decisions between 1890 and 1901—or after. (Field notes that James A. Scrymser is "curiously absent from books on the 'New Empire.'" There is nothing curious about it. A number of people are absent from my own account of the "new empire," most of them more important than Scrymser. In weak moments I fear such people may even number in the tens.) The absence of warships did not mean that political figures and business groups were not interested in the Pacific. From the mid-1890s until at least 1906, Alfred Thayer Mahan, for example, increasingly viewed the Pacific as an arena of great importance to the United States. He included Hawaii in this arena, since it is in the Pacific and several thousand miles from the West Coast. In his biography of Mahan, William E. Livezey has suggested that the officer's "program of action" can be summarized as "dominance in the Caribbean, equality and cooperation in the Pacific," and "interested abstention" from strictly European rivalries on the Continent. By 1910, however, Livezey has noted that Japan's rise forced Mahan to plot a retreat from the Pacific. Field emphasizes the later withdrawal but not the advance between the 1890s and 1906. Brooks Adams remains important for the same reasons. As Arthur F. Beringause has pointed out, Adams, Roosevelt, and Henry Cabot Lodge met in Henry Adams's house to plot strategy in 1897, and by the end of that year they reached a consensus on policy. And Thomas J. McCormick has argued that Roosevelt carried that consensus to McKinley.

To restate, the question is not how many battleships or cables were in the Pacific before 1898, but why McKinley and his advisers were able to move so rapidly into the Pacific after Dewey's victory at Manila Bay. Historians have now proven beyond doubt that the policymakers in 1898, like President Cleveland and Secretary of State Bayard before them, understood not only that American interests were developing in Asia but also that they were responsible for defending those interests. Such an argument hardly means that Latin America was unimportant; it was indeed primary in Washington's foreign policy priorities. Field's emphasis on South and Central America thus fits in well with the work of many historians who have noted the significance of the Venezuelan and Cuban crises during the 1890s. Those historians, however, have not argued that Washington officials were incapable of thinking about Latin America and Asia at the same time.

Since the term "new empire" did not appear until 1902, Field cannot understand how my own work has "persuaded many that the concept existed in its own right" before 1902. That puzzlement pinpoints the central problem in the essay. If, the essay asks, the cable system and battleship deployment indicated little interest in Pacific affairs before 1898, why did the United States control a "new empire" by 1900?

The result was no more accidental than McKinley sending the *Maine* to Havana. The course of an earlier empire provides a helpful analogy. By 450 B.C. the Athenians, who had once belonged to a "league," had slowly developed and expanded their own control until they transformed that alliance into their own empire. The result was not termed an empire until after 450 B.C., but the concept and the methods of empire preceded that date. As Russell Meiggs has written, even while Athens and its allies called their relationship a league or alliance, "the tools of empire had already been forged." In the same respect, the term "new empire" was perhaps not known until 1902, but the tools of empire were forged throughout the 1890s. The cable system was one of those tools, but it was hardly the entire toolbox. Others have also identified those tools, and it is inexcusable to say of their work that "much of it is wrong and most of it irrelevant to 'imperialism' and the events of 1898," especially since Field builds on the work of these historians but cannot explain some of the events these historians have succeeded in explaining.

The essay helps to paint our composite picture of the 1890s, but it is unable to finish the job, for in the end it cannot explain the policies of 1898 to 1901. It confuses cables with messages. An explanation of the foreign policies of the 1890s lies less with the communications network than with what officials were saying over the network, and this problem is not considered in the essay. In the 1890s, the media was not yet the message.

Field thus tells us why McKinley should not have annexed the Philippines and made the United States a major Pacific power, but to discover why the president did accomplish those objectives we must return to the work of McCormick, Charles S. Campbell, Jr., William Appleman Williams, Sylvester K. Stevens (who explains the importance if not "magnificence" of Pearl Harbor by the late 1880s), Paul Varg, Ernest May, H. Wayne Morgan, Marilyn Blatt Young, and others. For they have told us how the "tools of empire" that were forged in the 1890s constructed the new foreign policy edifice of 1898 and after. And few, if any of them, have to resort to Social Darwinism as an explanation. Whether or not we agree with their individual interpretations, their work forces us to conceptualize the era as a whole and to reconsider its roots and its significance for our time.

If the 1890s is the "worst chapter" in American diplomatic historiography, and I do not believe it is, the fault does not belong to those who have replaced "aberration" and "accident" with more useful, coherent, and defensible approaches to understanding the decade. Nor did those scholars believe it necessary to build an eye-catching structure on the historical landscape by attempting to reduce the already existing structures to rubble.

Robert L. Beisner

ROBERT L. BEISNER (1936–   ) is professor of history at the American University. He has written several books in American diplomatic history, including *Twelve Against Empire* (1968) and *From the Old Diplomacy to the New 1865–1900* (1975).

James A. Field, Jr.'s effort to restructure the long-standing debate about "American imperialism" especially interests me because of my own recent attempt at the same task. As we all know, scholarly disputes often end in impasse. One scholar argues that unicorns are handsome; another contends that they are ugly; their disciples elaborate the cases pro and con without, however, either changing the terms of argument or resolving the dispute. What we usually need at such times are new questions and an alteration in the terms of debate—perhaps suggested by someone who does not care whether unicorns are handsome or ugly, but who is instead fascinated by their relationship to griffins. Some kind of radical perspective is essential to shoving an old debate in a new direction. Otherwise, the ancient dispute is likely to persist tediously, fueled by students trying to make their mark with a conspicuous entrance into the established debate, by scholars focusing on "false dichotomous questions," or by historians simply miring themselves in the deadening sludge of old questions.

Something of this sort has occurred in the study of late-nineteenth-century American imperialism. The debate about its chronology and its underlying impulses and motives has persisted at least since the publication of Julius W. Pratt's *Expansionists of 1898* in 1936. It took on new but not *different* life with the publication of William A. Williams's *The Tragedy of American Diplomacy* (1959) and Walter LaFeber's *The New Empire: An Interpretation of American Expansion, 1860–1898* (1963). In all the years since Pratt's work, historians have been wrangling over such false dichotomous question as

1898: Aberration or Culmination?

The Spanish-American War: Popular Crusade or Drive for Markets?

McKinley: Chocolate Eclair or Clever Statesman?

Specifically, the debate, which actually encompasses some disparate and distinct interpretative problems, has been dominated by five main issues: (1) the "continuity" issue—that is, whether the events of the late 1890s represented an abrupt departure from the past or the logical product of earlier developments and trends; (2) the "realism" issue—that is, whether the United States sallied off to war in 1898 for emotional and idealistic reasons or fought to achieve "realistic" objectives; (3) the "economic" issue—that is, whether American imperialism was the result of a drive to expand foreign export markets or the consequence of ideological, security, and other motives; (4) the "semantic" issue—that is, whether the phenomena of the 1890s should be called "imperialism," "expansionism," or something else; and (5) the "deliberateness" issue—that is, whether the key events by which we define American imperialism were the result of bungling, emotionalism, and "accident" or the consequences of forethought and deliberate calculation. The current state of the traditional debate is codified, so to speak, in Charles S. Campbell's *The Transformation of American Foreign Relations, 1865–1900* (1976), which is a thorough and excellent book but one that in no way tries to transform the terms of debate.

Clearly, the time has come for a new departure in the study of American imperialism, and it is in this light that I have approached James Field's essay, particularly since his title suggests that his purpose is to rewrite "The Worst Chapter in Almost Any Book." Has he merely offered new fuel to the old debate? Or has he redefined the debate itself? Has he produced a provocative new argument for the beauty of the unicorn? Or has he introduced us to a fabulous new field grazed also by griffins? Field states his first general criticisms of past interpretations with an élan that suggests we are to witness new ground being broken. I heartily concur the presentism, moralism, and a proclivity to see false continuities have had a "tendentious" impact on general views of U.S. foreign relations from 1865 to 1898, though I boggle at the casualness with which he suggests that historians, through an act of will, can avoid "seeing the past through the prism of the present. . . . " I also agree that most interpretations of American imperialism are too "rational," too "unitary," too "ethnocentric," too oblivious of the "environment," and too dependent on asking the wrong questions. Most of the critical parts of his essay—most notably his devastating assault on those attributing great influence to Social Darwinists and other intellectuals—are persuasive. But they do not take us anywhere new. His criticisms of past work in themselves neither define nor clearly point the way toward a novel conception of the historical problem of "American imperialism."

Field's contribution is not, then, his critique but his own new descriptive material. Briefly recapitulated, Field says that

1. The advent of steam propulsion bound modern navies to coal deposits and stations and impelled the United States Navy to abandon far-flung patrols for the security of its own home bases. Thus,

the "New Navy" of the 1890s, however enlarged and modernized, was tied even closer to home and to defensive positions than it had been in the 1880s.

2. Instead of feeling a constant tug westward toward Asia, American exporters, shippers, diplomatic policymakers, and navalists were actually eastward-oriented throughout the era of the "new empire." When Americans "looked outward" for personal contacts or for economic opportunities abroad and when they hunted for potential threats to national security, they looked across the Atlantic, as they always had.

3. The rapid development of a vast network of telegraphic cables had linked Washington and New York to the rest of the world by 1898 but not yet by a direct route across the Pacific to Asia. The cable network can be seen reflected in America's Atlantic orientation and emphasis on hemispheric defense. The cables stimulated business activity abroad, accelerated the pace of diplomacy, shaped maritime strategy, and were eventually crucial in abruptly entangling the United States in the politics of East Asia in 1898.

Still, Field's general purpose is not clear. Is this new material the foundation for a "best chapter" on American imperialism? It may be, but this is certainly not self-evident. Reduced to its essentials—however persuasive and however fascinating—it does not *explain* the historical phenomenon of American imperialism. Instead, by marshalling mostly new evidence, Field has simply produced a set of unfamiliar inferences (descriptive statements) we can make about the past. Thus, just as his spirited destruction of the old saw that intellectuals somehow brought about American imperialism boils down in part to the descriptive statement that "intellectuals neither advocated imperialist policies nor had access to foreign policymakers as much as former historians have maintained," so his new material finally comes down to the following historical inferences:

1. Naval developments in the 1890s betoken a defensive and hemispheric rather than an offensive and imperialist stance.

2. The United States looked eastward rather than westward, and its activities conformed with this point of view.

3. Although generally ignored by historians, the development of an international network of telegraphic cables, which did not include a link across the Pacific between the United States and East Asia, was quite important in this period.

What can bring these new descriptions of the past together into a new explanation of American imperialism or, at least, an argument that would alter the old terms of debate? Though at times Field comes tantalizingly close, he nonetheless fails to propose a general theory that can connect his new knowledge about diplomacy with an explanation of why things happened as they did. Implicitly, at least, he seems to favor some kind of materialistic theory of history. Underlying all of his novel "theses" are the development of two new technologies—steam propulsion and international cables—and new patterns of maritime and diplomatic traffic. Some of his direct statements seem to echo a hidden theoretical commitment: other historians have "words do duty for things and presumed intentions for actual capabilities"; "just as words are not things, a map is not the country it represents"; "aspiration was less substantial than geographic and economic reality"; "capabilities are often as determining as intentions"; "the anatomists of sea power concentrate on bone and muscle to the neglect of the alimentary and nervous systems"; and "results had little to do with intentions." One should especially note his remark that we "must move . . . beyond economics and ideology to the . . . area of technological capabilities. . . ."

Is Field suggesting a materialist (or perhaps behavioralist or environmentalist) theory of history to explain American imperialism? Unfortunately, we do not know, because Field never closes with the issue. And that reluctance to come to grips with theory mars other parts of his essay, especially considering its ambitious objectives. In the absence of an explicit theory discounting the relevance of ideas, sentiments, and rhetoric, for instance, I find his treatment of them wholly unsatisfactory. I am not referring here to his contention that certain intellectuals either did not think what has been attributed to them or did not possess the influence attributed to them (a contention I believe Field convincingly supports). I have in mind, rather, his almost total neglect of ideas. Yes, it would certainly appear that the development of cables was quite important in the acceleration of diplomacy. But which men chose to use those cables, to what purpose, and why? Cables alone cannot dictate the goals of diplomacy any more than computers can determine the policies of industry. Certainly, the availability of a new technological capability might influence the decisions of those responsible for making policy. But how are we going to understand why they chose to do one thing rather than another with the technology unless we determine what they thought, believed, and were concerned about? The U.S. government could choose or not choose to build modern steam-propelled warships. It could send Dewey's squadron to East Asia or somewhere else. Technology cannot account for the decisions that were made, only that certain kinds of decisions could be made.

Field's analysis seems based on what Lionel Trilling has described as the "liberal" sense of reality, which is seen as "hard, resistant, unformed, impenetrable, and unpleasant." Such a perspective caused historians like Charles A. Beard to assume that they could not "really" explain what motivated the Founding Fathers unless they could point to something concrete like land deeds or stock certificates. Given his criticism of the economic approach to American diplomatic history, one would think that Field might apply Trilling's observation to those who find export statistics at the bottom of American imperialism. Nonetheless, his own essay relies exclusively on such "hard" data as steam boilers, coal bins, shipping routes, and telegraphic cables. But we do not know whether he really believes in such a materialist sense of reality because Field has chosen not to grapple with theory directly. This becomes painfully obvious at the end of his essay when, alarmingly, he suddenly states that Americans wanted "the freedom to do their thing, to operate insofar as possible unhindered by arbitrary power or obsolete ideas," that they were "proud of their own self-determined independence," and "sympathetic to similar desires" elsewhere. What is this if not a purely intellectual explanation and, as well, unitary, ethnocentric, and undocumented?

This disinclination to deal directly with the theoretical bases of his arguments and assumptions also partially accounts for some of the highly dubious causal statements in the essay. Can historians of American imperialism rest content with the statement that Commodore Dewey "had to" destroy the Spanish fleet and seize Manila harbor as "a consequence" of "being so far out at the end of the [eastward-directed coal and ammunition] line"? Did new communications technology combined with literate publics leads to an "attentive audience" for war correspondents and thus to emotion-induced "times of crisis"? Why was the audience interested in war correspondents rather than architectural news? Was the U.S. government really so helplessly impressionable? " 'Imperialism,' we may say," Field concludes, "was the product of Dewey's victory." Even allowing for hyperbole or deliberate oversimplification, this statement represents a crude definition of imperialism, a nonchalant dismissal of abundant evidence suggesting other conclusions, as well as a simplistic notion of causality. Even worse are the "arguments" about the "accidental" character of American imperialism that riddle Field's next-to-last paragraph, arguments that do violence to the subtle philosophical and theoretical problems involved in the concept of "historical accident." One could equally well argue that the American Revolution was an accident in that it would not have occurred "if the [colonists] had been happy under [British] rule" or that there would have been no Cold War if Stalin had been converted to capitalism.

Field asks, "But where does all this leave us?" About where we were before, I'm afraid. Some of the old debaters should be out hunting for a white flag to wave, perhaps, and much of Field's new material is suggestive. But its importance depends on what is made of it. It might be possible to argue, for instance, that accelerated diplomacy, in part a product of telegraphic cables, in turn helped to persuade American policymakers in the 1890s that they were performing in a new and more dangerous era than before. The Atlantic-orientation thesis—which needs to be supplemented with social and cultural evidence to become fully convincing—does not necessarily entail Field's conclusion that the American drive toward Asia was weak. I would argue instead that America's preoccupation with Hawaii, China, the Philippines, and Korea, despite the nation's traditional and still-intact Atlantic orientation, graphically demonstrates the strength of the "new paradigm" in American diplomacy that arose in the 1890s. Policymakers' decisions do not depend alone on the circumstances of the so-called real world (for example, cables and ships cross the Atlantic but not the Pacific) nor on what retrospective commentators think they should have done (for example, the general consensus today that the United States greatly exaggerated the importance of East Asia eighty years ago). They also depend on the lenses through which those policymakers "see" the real world, lenses tinted by altering circumstances and shifting perspectives. And the evidence remains convincing that American statesmen at the end of the nineteenth century believed profoundly that the international stakes in Asia were high. It was to Asia, not to Europe, that the United States sent warships and occupation troops; it was in Asia where the United States adamantly retained control of territory, even in the face of armed insurrection; and it was in Asia where the United States joined other great powers in discipling the Chinese Boxers. How extraordinary, considering that the cables, dollars, and freighters were all spanning the Atlantic instead of the Pacific!

Thus, Field's essay has neither given us a persuasive new explanation of "American imperialism" nor substantially altered the terms of the now-wearisome debate. Although he is clearly uncomfortable with the present terms of debate, he does not manage to redefine them. An overriding ambiguity permeates his essay. It is never clear whether his purpose is to argue that American imperialism was an accident or that America was not imperialist at all (it was never a unicorn at all, but a griffin). He nudges the debate in a new direction, to be sure, but he does not succeed in shoving the debate aside. It appears that, when the mail next brings "a copy of a new textbook on American diplomatic history," there, smack on the first page of its "worst chapter," will be that same old picture of a unicorn, a little more elaborately depicted, but the same creature we all know. Is the hope for a new debate a mere chimera?

Reply
by James A. Field, Jr.

Rarely, I am sure, has so argumentative an essay been so politely received by critics who hold other views. And if what is not disputed can be assumed to be conceded (a perhaps somewhat optimistic assumption, given the commentators' limitations of space), I can hardly feel disappointed. But since there seems as yet no complete marriage of minds and since some of the arguments appear to slide past each other (as often in such exchanges), we should perhaps continue the discussion a little longer.

We may perhaps begin with specifics. I think that some of the authors on whom Walter LaFeber suggests I build might better be cited as representatives of the "on to China for economic hegemony" school of which he is so distinguished an exemplar. I quite agree that the dispatch of the *Maine* to Havana marked an escalation of pressure in the Cuban question; but since she presumably was neither sent to be sunk nor dispatched as a first step toward the Philippines, I do not see that her sailing made the Asiatic "New Empire" any the more probable. I thought the early examples of eastward-sailing Americans worth noting in view of prevalent assumptions that the term " 'Far East' . . . hinders the understanding of American expansion [since] the United States has more often considered this area as the Far West" and that the *Empress of China* and Commodore Perry somehow support this conclusion. The Athenian analogy seems to me more curious than enlightening: can it really be said that in 1897 American influence in Hawaii, the Philippines, and China (or, indeed, in Latin America) approximated Athenian control of Ionia in the decade before 450 B.C., that the Americans had already made off with the Delian treasury, or that the United States possessed "instruments of empire" like those described by Russell Meiggs? On the other hand, the underlying argument that facts are more important than labels seems to me central: as Robert Beisner has elsewhere observed, "Behavior, not occasional rhetoric, is the crucial test."

At this point I think I should confess my sneaking admiration for the "new empire" school's concern with the interests and influence of nongovernmental groups, assuming it can be properly articulated and focused. But if we employ it without preconceptions, I doubt we will find pre-1898 pressures for transpacific expansion, or even much pressure for the annexation of Hawaii. Theodore Roosevelt, at least, feared in the spring of 1898 that McKinley was incapable of dealing at once with Cuba and Hawaii, and that the president would let the islands slip away. Writing in 1900, Mahan noted of the expansionists that "their vision reached not past Hawaii, which also, as touching the United States, they regarded from the point of view of defense rather than as a stepping-stone." Thomas A. Bailey concluded that with no war there would have been no annexation, in which view he echoed Mahan: "To Dewey's victory, apparently, is due that we annexed Hawaii."

LaFeber refers twice to the "tools of empire" forged in the 1890s, to which I feel constrained to reply, what tools were these? Not the navy in the Pacific, certainly, and not Pacific merchant shipping (unless the words of Seward and Cleveland are still expected to do duty for real tonnage), and surely not a well-run consular service or a group of lively and energetic business men in hot pursuit of the China market. He observes that historians have "proven beyond doubt" that it was because McKinley and his advisers (which advisers?), like their predecessors (Cleveland?), understood the problem of Asia so well that they could "move so rapidly into the Pacific." The argument is hardly supported by the Philippine reinforcement, an exercise in improvisation if ever there was one, in which the first troops did not sail until three and a half weeks and the monitors (not, perhaps, the best type of ship for this assignment) until six and a half and eight and a half weeks after Manila Bay. If Camara had gone the route, the race promised to be a very tight one, and the slowness of this movement "into the Pacific" was the one thing Mahan later thought culpable in the work of the Naval War Board. Problems such as these seem to me illustrative of the kind of cement that is employed to hold the "worst chapter" together: mutually supporting references ("beyond doubt") and a usage of assertion and verbal prestidigitation which imposes false geographic unities (interest in the eastern Pacific becomes interest in "the Pacific," a far larger area) and confuses words with things ("tools of empire" with ships, prompt orders with delayed ship movements).

This question of "new empire" behavior as against "new empire" rhetoric leads us back to James A. Scrymser. I said "books" and did not mean to single out LaFeber, and of course we all leave some things out. But the surprising fact is that *everybody* leaves Scrymser out, along with his energetic fellow-laborers in southern vineyards. Given all the talk of the American China Development Company, it is instructive to compare the sketches in the *Dictionary of American Biography* of Scrymser, Henry Meiggs (a great-uncle, by the way, of Russell Meiggs, who thus enjoys both inherited and acquired qualifications as an historian of informal empire), Charles J. Harrah, William R. Grace, and

Minor W. Keith, with the notice given them in *The New Empire*, or in Milton Plesur's *America's Outward Thrust* (1971), or indeed in almost any book that comes to mind. This same problem of geographical displacement applies to missionary as well as business enterprise: we still get works that suggest that China was the only American mission field, yet as late as 1900 the four major missionary boards were spending half again as much money and supporting about half again as many workers in India, Burma, and Ceylon (hardly areas of American "imperial" activity) as they were in China.

It also applies within major regions: Beisner affirms America's "preoccupation" with Hawaii, China, the Philippines, and Korea (but at what dates?), yet makes no mention of Japan. But from 1895 to 1898 trade with Japan exceeded that with China, in 1898 in a proportion of three to two; the Japanese were buying such modern commodities as fertilizer and locomotives and electrical equipment; American missionaries in Japan were busy doing good and founding schools and colleges; and throughout the latter part of the century numerous individuals (in addition to the curious LeGendre) like Raphael Pumpelly, Horace Capron and William S. Clark, Ernest Fenollosa, David Murray, and Henry W. Grinnell were (I am sorry to have to say it again) in and out of Japan doing their things. This neglect of Japan is widespread in the literature. Why this geographical discrimination among outward thrusters? Or why the functional discrimination that concentrates on Denby and Wilson in China to the neglect of W. A. P. Martin, Philo McGiffin, and W. Pethick?

I am puzzled as to how to answer accusations of materialism and "almost total neglect of ideas," the more so, as I am simultaneously reproached for the use of "purely intellectual explanation." Certainly, I believe capabilities to be important. My critics are, of course, quite right in observing that the message on the cable is what starts things moving. Equally, however, if there is no cable to carry the message, Dewey will not get underway, and, if he has no coal, he cannot. I must confess to a slightly bruised *amour propre* in that Beisner did not find, in the continuous information flow made possible by cable communications, the explanation of the shift from "incidents" to "policy" in the "new paradigm" diplomacy which he propounded but never accounted for. In any case, I do not see how material matters and ideas can be divorced. Artifacts embody previous thought. Cables do not lay themselves, nor do freighters choose their own destinations, and the location of cables and shipping lines surely reflected contemporary views of what was important and what profitable.

On the question of accident in history, I can only feel that Beisner fails to understand me. Of course there are subtle and complex problems here, but in a one-paragraph treatment I would not think it necessary to explore them at length (any more than I would think it necessary at this date to heap up evidence to show America's social and cultural orientation toward Europe). The problem, it appears to me, is to get our minds out of the traditional boxes and to let them consider alternative possibilities (as those who were then running things surely had to do). So let me make one more attempt. As things were at the time, it was surely not too far-fetched to have hoped (as Cleveland and McKinley apparently did) that Spain might somehow manage to resolve the Cuban question on its own. If that had happened, would Beisner think we would have seen American troops fighting their way up to Peking in 1900? Or to take a fresh example: what if on that moonless night Dewey's navigator had piled the squadron up on the rocks while attempting to enter Manila Bay? Here, at last, we can profitably employ the Athenian analogy: if the commodore and his crews had suffered the fate of Nicias, what would the next decade have brought with regard to American policy in China?

To LaFeber's feeling that none should attack those who try to place the 1890s in a larger framework, and that it is "inexcusable" to say that much of their work is wrong or irrelevant, I would merely observe that I do not attack either the individuals or the effort, but merely the conclusions, and that criticism is one of the conventions of the profession. Beisner chides me for not having reformulated the entire argument and provided the entire answer. I think he asks too much of a single article. In any case he asks more than I undertook to do, which was to question some things that seemed to me wrong—although widely accepted—and to suggest some new ideas for consideration. The best chapter, like the "worst chapter" (if it is, in fact, the "worst chapter"), will surely turn out to be the product of collaborative effort.

It must be clear by now that much of my concern is with the monochromatic straight-line interpretation of the history of American foreign relations, which implies (in its most vulgarized textbook versions) that when Daniel Boone headed for Kentucky and Huck Finn lit out for the territory they were merely the advance guard of a relentless westward advance that, in due course, would cross the Pacific to end in the Cambodian incursion; and with the one-size-fits-all interpretation, which suggests that if only we repeat, like John Randolph's whippoorwill, "empire, empire, empire," everything from Jefferson to Nixon will be explained. The past is surely more interesting and diverse than this. So in conclusion I may perhaps be permitted to suggest "what is to be done," or at least a few things that I would like to see done, or not done.

It is true that I do not define "American imperialism" (nor do most writers on the period) nor, indeed, so far as I am aware does Beisner, although he uses the term liberally in both his critique and his book.

In fact, I tried very hard not to use the word outside of quotation marks or paraphrase. I think it undesirable to begin with an assumption of an undefined "American imperialism": better describe the attitudes, the aims, the capabilities, and the events, and then see what they add up to. The question of "influence" is both important and difficult, but I doubt that snippets from the writings of historians and clergymen should be claimed as influential if they cannot be shown to be; here Karsten's observations on the influence of Mahan seem to me susceptible of wider application. As to Brooks Adams, I have to confess feelings of despair: I thought he was dead, but clearly he will not lie down, and it may turn out that he is immortal. Nevertheless, I must report that I find no evidence in the pages in Arthur Beringause's biography cited by LaFeber of Adams plotting strategy with Roosevelt and Lodge, nor have I been able to discover in Thomas McCormick's study of the China Market any reference to Roosevelt's carrying the good word from Adams to McKinley. In this context it may be worth noting that Roosevelt's prewar correspondence provides unflattering judgments on the quality of Adams's thought.

I think more attention should be given to negative evidence of the sort that Holmes understood but that the unimaginative Inspector Gregory did not ("Silver Blaze"): if the dog does not bark in the night, if presidents will not urge, if the senate will not consent, if congress will not dredge, if capitalists will not invest, if the navy will not deploy, the facts seem to me at least as important for an understanding of "American policy" as the pleas of enthusiasts. I think chronology important: what happens second can hardly cause what happens first (even though it may help to explicate it), and the current literature is far too rich in the use of post-Manila Bay quotations to define prewar aspirations. My critics speak of Mahan's views "from the mid-1890s until at least 1906," of the "decade of the 1890s," and of the "whole decade." Such chronological conflation seems particularly dangerous in periods like this. One may no doubt generalize about the years before 1898, and again regarding some period beginning in the summer of that year. But it appears to me that there is an important intervening break in which (to conflate Conant and Mahan) an accident at Havana and the flash of Dewey's guns first brought the Philippines above the mental horizon. I may not be able to persuade everybody, but I remain myself persuaded that unanticipated events can bring unanticipated results and that the *Maine* and Manila Bay (like Fort Sumter and Pearl Harbor) led to attitudes and consequences that could hardly have been foreseen.

One last thought on periodization as opposed to the straight-line view of history. Is it not possible that Seward's spread-eagle oratory, the "irreflective" re-establishment of the antebellum squadrons, the commercial concerns of Shufeldt and Evarts, and Chandler's call for lots of naval bases represent less a first step toward the Asian involvement of 1898 than the last manifestations of attitudes formed during the great age of sail and of the world-wide merchant marine and commerce-protecting navy? And that beginning in the late 1880s the new age of steam and of the navies of industrialism was finding its appropriate expression in concern for the defense of East Coast and Caribbean, in Mahan's emphasis on battleships and concentration of force, and in his growing realization that, although sea power may originally have derived from commerce, the missions of some modern navies (like the Russian and American) were primarily political?

My hope in this article has been to raise some questions and arguments, substantive and procedural, for consideration by the trade. If my colleagues (or at least those who are interested) will read it, and decide what they think persuasive and what not, then perhaps we can get back to the drawing boards and try to find out what the years preceding 1898 were all about, leaving the labeling until later. If this can be done the rubble question will solve itself: to the extent that they were founded upon rock, the pre-existing structures will presumably survive any winds that I or anyone else can blow against them; to the extent that they were build on sand, they may not, and perhaps should not.

☆ 6 ☆

The Progressive Movement

LIBERAL OR CONSERVATIVE?

The rise of American industry in the decades following the Civil War was a development whose impact can hardly be exaggerated. It involved more than a shift from a commercial and agrarian economy to an urban and industrial one; indeed, it effected fundamental changes in the nature and quality of American society. The far-reaching technological and industrial innovations forced Americans to reexamine their traditional values and beliefs, many of which seemed obsolete, if not irrelevant, to the problems of a new age.

Traditionally Americans were accustomed to think in terms of individualistic values. The rise of industry itself was often rationalized in the ideology of the self-made man who claimed he attained success by virtue of his own talents, drive, and ambition. By the end of the nineteenth century, however, it was becoming more difficult to conceive of industrial progress solely in terms of the achievements of a few creative individuals. The growth of a national transportation and communications system, which led to the rise of a national market, had stimulated the formation of large industrial units. This organizational revolution, to use Kenneth Boulding's convenient phrase,[1] was to have profound implications. Americans at the turn of the twentieth century found that their nation was being increasingly dominated by large corporations whose establishment resulted in the partial curtailment, if not abolition, of competition—a development that collided sharply with the ideology of individualism and freedom.

---

[1] Kenneth E. Boulding, *The Organizational Revolution: A Study in the Ethics of Economic Organization* (New York, 1953).

229

The position of the individual within the nation's increasingly industrialized society became a major source of concern for many Americans. If America's greatness was related to individual achievement, what would happen as freedom and social mobility were more and more circumscribed by giant corporations with their impersonal and machinelike qualities? Did not the emphasis of corporations on efficient production and material objectives distort the human qualities that had been responsible for America's rise to greatness? Was not the growing disparity between rich corporations and poor workingmen creating a situation akin to that existing in many European countries where there was open class strife? These and similar questions led many Americans to advocate reforms that would restore dignity to the individual and give meaning to his life.

The forces of reform gradually gathered momentum in the last quarter of the nineteenth century. Although critics of American society could not agree upon a specific diagnosis, let alone remedial measures, they were united in a common conviction that some changes would have to be made if the United States was to survive with its historic values intact. The solutions presented were often diffuse. Many were all-embracing panaceas that called for the preservation of a competitive and individualistic society, but, at the same time, did not sacrifice the affluence associated with technological progress. Henry George, for example, gained international fame by presenting his single tax scheme in 1879 in his book *Progress and Poverty*, while Edward Bellamy, in his utopian novel *Looking Backward* (1886), argued that only the nationalization of all the means of production and distribution would solve most of America's major problems. In a similar vein, many Protestant clergymen who were disturbed by the cleavages in American society offered their own answers in what came to be known as the Social Gospel. These religious critics argued that an immoral society was incompatible with the ideals of moral men. Society, therefore, would have to be remade in the form of a Christian socialist commonwealth, thereby offering individuals an opportunity to lead moral lives. Others, including the Populists, socialists, advocates of civil service reform, and academic critics also contributed to the swelling chorus of reform.

Between 1900 and 1917 these uncoordinated efforts at reform were institutionalized in what came to be known as the Progressive movement. Pluralistic rather than unitary, the Progressive movement was actually a series of movements operating at the local, state, and national levels of government and society. The movement consisted of a loose coalition of reformers who sought a variety of goals: political reforms such as the initiative, referendum, recall, and the destruction of urban political machines and corruption; economic reforms such as the regulation of public utilities and the curtailment of corporate power; and social reforms such as the Americanization of the immigrant, the amelioration of the lot of the urban poor, and regulation of child and woman labor as well as many others. Among the symbolic leaders of the movement were two presidents, Theodore Roosevelt and Woodrow Wilson. These two men not only revived the moral authority and leadership-potential inherent in the presidency, but they supported the enactment of a series of laws embodying major social reforms.

Until the period after World War II there was relatively little controversy among historians about the nature and character of the Progressive movement. Most American historians were writing within the tradition of the Progressive school. Consequently they interpreted these reform movements and reformers within a liberal framework. In their eyes the reformers in the movement had been challenging the dominant position of the business and privileged classes. The reformers' goals had been clear and simple: to restore government to the people; to abolish special privilege and ensure equal opportunity for all; and to enact a series of laws embodying principles of social justice. These reformers, Progressive historians emphasized, were not anticapitalist; they had not advocated the abolition of private property nor sought the establishment of a socialist society. On the contrary they had taken seriously the American dream; their fundamental goal had been a democratic and humane society based on egalitarian ideals and social compassion. The real enemies of society were the businessmen, dishonest politicians, and "special interests," all of whom posed a serious threat to the realization of American democracy.

Such an approach put progressivism squarely within the American liberal tradition and on the side of the "people" as opposed to the forces of wealth, self-interest, and special privilege. Vernon L. Parrington, one of the best-known Progressive historians, saw progressivism as a "democratic renaissance"—a movement of the masses against a "plutocracy" that had been corrupting the very fabric of American society since the Civil War. Thus the movement concerned itself not only with political democracy but with economic democracy as well. To Parrington progressivism was a broad-based movement that included members of the middle class, journalists, and scholars—men, in other words, whose consciences had been aroused by the "cesspools that were poisoning the national household," and who had set for themselves the task of reawakening the American people.[2]

Implicit in this point of view was the conviction that the course of American history had been characterized by a continuous struggle

---

[2]Vernon L. Parrington, *Main Currents in American Thought*, 3 vols. (New York, 1927–1930), 3:406.

between liberalism and conservatism, democracy and aristocracy, and equal opportunity and special privilege. Most historians writing in the Progressive tradition believed that reformers, regardless of their specific goals or the eras in which they appeared, were cast in the same mold because they invariably supported the "people" against their enemies. Such was the position of John D. Hicks, an outstanding American historian whose textbooks in American history were used by tens of thousands of high school and college students between the 1930s and 1960s. Hicks in 1931 published *The Populist Revolt*, the first major account of populism based on wide research in the original sources. To Hicks the Populists carried the banner of reform in the 1890s and represented the first organized protest of the masses against the encroachments of a monopolistic plutocracy. Although the Populist movement ultimately failed, it was victorious in the long run, Hicks held, because much of its program was taken over by later reformers and enacted into law during the first two decades of the twentieth century. To a large extent his thesis rested on the assumption that American reform efforts drew much of their inspiration from the Jeffersonian agrarian tradition which had survived intact among the nation's farmers and rural population.[3]

Not all historians were as friendly and well-disposed toward populism and progressivism as was Hicks. Those historians writing within a socialist and Marxian tradition, for example, were highly critical of progressivism because of its superficial nature and its refusal to adopt more radical solutions to meet the basic needs of American society. To John Chamberlain, a young Marxist who in 1932 published a devastating critique of American reform, the Progressive movement was an abysmal failure. Its adherents, claimed Chamberlain, were motivated by an escapist desire to return to a golden past where honesty and virtue had dominated over egoism and evil.[4]

Oddly enough many of the detractors of the achievements of the reform movement from 1890 to 1917 were, like Chamberlain, within the Progressive school of history in that they accepted the idea that class conflict had been the major determinant of progress and social change in America. Many of them, particularly during the depression of the 1930s, condemned the Progressive reforms as being piecemeal and superficial in nature. The failure of the Progressive generation, these critics emphasized, had led to the reaction of the 1920s, which in turn had resulted in the disastrous depression of the 1930s. Disil-

---

[3]John D. Hicks, *The Populist Revolt: A History of the Farmers' Alliance and the People's Party* (Minneapolis, 1931).

[4]John Chamberlain, *Farewell to Reform* (New York, 1932).

lusionment with the Progressive movement, however, did not necessarily imply disillusion with the efficacy of reform or with the aspirations and ideals of the liberal tradition in America. Even those
intellectuals who flirted with Marxism during the depression did so
out of their conviction that America could still be redeemed from the
hands of its enemies.

Beginning in the 1940s and continuing in the 1950s and 1960s the
mood of American historians began to change. The increasing homo-
geneity of American society began to dissolve the sectional, class, and
ethnic groupings that had been employed by the Progressive school of
history. No longer did historians have to vindicate the claims of the
West against the East, the South against the rest of the nation, or to
establish conclusively the contributions of the Puritans, the immigrants, the working class, or the businessmen. Such narrow loyalties
appeared parochial in a milieu where national similarities seemed to
be more significant than group differences.

The change in mood, however, was due to far more fundamental
factors than a mere shift in the class and ethnic backgrounds of historians. Much more basic was the change in attitude and outlook that
accompanied the revolutionary changes in the world since the 1940s.
To scholars writing after 1940 the Progressive ideology appeared much
too facile and simplified. Like many philosophers and theologians they
began to criticize Progressive historians for underestimating man's
propensities for evil and for overestimating his capacity for good. In
brief, these critics argued that the interpretation of the Progressive
school of history rested on an unrealistic evaluation of human nature.
The result, they concluded, was that Americans had been unprepared
for the dilemmas and challenges that they faced in the Great Depression of the 1930s and the worldwide conflict of the 1940s because of
their tendency to view history in terms of a simple morality play where
good always triumphed over evil.

The challenge to democracy by communism since World War II
gave rise to a new group of scholars—the neoconservative historians—
who have been critical of the Progressive school and who embarked
upon their own reevaluation of America's past. Writing from a conservative point of view these historians stressed the basic goodness of
American society and the consensus that has characterized the American people throughout most of their history. Thus these scholars insisted that American history could not be written in terms of a struggle
between democracy and aristocracy or the people against the special
interests. On the contrary they tended to stress the unity and homo-
geneity of America's past, the stability of basic institutions, and the
existence of a monistic national character. While they did not deny
that conflicts and struggles between sections, classes, and special in-

terest groups have occurred, the neoconservative historians insisted that such struggles were always fought within a liberal framework and that the protagonists were never really in disagreement over fundamentals. Moreover, these scholars were also much less certain about the value of desirability of social change. Having witnessed the effects of revolutionary movements in other parts of the world the neoconservatives questioned whether conflict and change would necessarily lead to a better society.

The result of this changed outlook was a sharp shift in the way historians interpreted the Progressive movement. The Progressive school of history had looked upon the Progressive era as but one phase in the continuing struggle against special privilege and business. The newer neoconservative school, in rejecting the older view, now began to ask new and different questions. If progressivism was not in the Jeffersonian liberal tradition, in what tradition could it be placed? If Progressives were not necessarily moral individuals fighting on behalf of the masses, who were they and what did they stand for? If they did not democratize and reform America by their efforts, just what did they accomplish? Such were the questions raised by historians who rejected the older Progressive view.

The attack on the Progressive school interpretation was led by Richard Hofstadter, the distinguished Columbia University historian. Oddly enough Hofstadter was writing within the Progressive tradition and as a liberal partisan. Yet he could not find very many constructive achievements to attribute to the American liberal tradition. Indeed, he found the liberal ideology to be narrow and deficient in many respects. In a number of brilliant books Hofstadter attempted to expose, by historical analysis, the shortcomings, inadequacies, and failures of American liberalism.

In 1948 Hofstadter published *The American Political Tradition and the Men Who Made It.* In this book he attempted to delineate the basic characteristics of the American political tradition by studying the careers of nearly a dozen presidents and political leaders, including Andrew Jackson, John C. Calhoun, Abraham Lincoln, Theodore Roosevelt, Woodrow Wilson, and Franklin Delano Roosevelt. Hofstadter's thesis was that the liberal tradition had failed because it was based upon the idea of a return to an ideology that emphasized acquisitive and individualistic values. Thus the Populists and Progressives had similar deficiencies; neither had faced up to the fundamental problems of an industrialized and corporate America. Even Franklin Delano Roosevelt, who did not share the nostalgia common to the Progressive tradition, was a pragmatist whose attraction lay in the force of his personality rather than in any consistent ideology or philosophy.

Seven years later Hofstadter spelled out his case in even greater detail in *The Age of Reform: From Bryan to F.D.R.* The Populists, he argued, were unsophisticated and simplistic reformers. Rather than approaching the farm problem within a broad national and international context they placed the blame for their difficulties upon elements of American society which were alien to them—Easterners, Wall Street bankers, Jews, and foreigners. Associated with populism, therefore, was a combination of attitudes made up of a curious blend of racism, nativism, and provincialism—attitudes that helped to explain the fears of agricultural and rural America that later manifested themselves in national paranoic scares. "The Populists," Hofstadter emphasized, "looked backward with longing to the lost agrarian Eden, to the republican America of the early years of the nineteenth century in which there were few millionaires and, as they saw it, no beggars, when the laborer had excellent prospects and the farmer had abundance, when statesmen still responded to the mood of the people and there was no such thing as the money power. What they meant—though they did not express themselves in such terms—was that they would like to restore the conditions prevailing before the development of industrialism and the commercialization of agriculture."[5]

Nor were the Progressives, according to Hofstadter, very much more sophisticated. Traditionally progressivism had been viewed by historians as a liberal reform movement aimed at readjusting American institutions to the imperatives of a new industrial age. To Hofstadter, on the other hand, progressivism was something quite different. Borrowing heavily from the work of behavioral scientists he argued that progressivism was related to other influences, notably status anxiety. Playing down the role of economic factors in individual and group motivation, Hofstadter maintained that to a large extent American political conflicts reflected the drive of different ethnic and religious groups for a secure status in society. By the latter third of the nineteenth century a number of groups—clergymen, lawyers, professors, older Anglo-Saxon Protestant families—were finding themselves displaced from the seats of power and their traditional positions of leadership by a dangerous plutocracy and new political machines under the control of alien elements. The response of this displaced elite was a moral crusade to restore older Protestant and individualistic values—the Progressive movement. This crusade was based on the simple idea that only men of character—the "right sort of people"—should rule.

---

[5]Richard Hofstadter, *The Age of Reform: From Bryan to F.D.R.* (New York, 1955), p. 62.

Few Progressive leaders, including Theodore Roosevelt and Woodrow Wilson, were realistic in their appraisals of and solutions to America's problems. "In the attempts of the Populists and Progressives to hold on to some of the values of agrarian life, to save personal entrepreneurship and individual opportunity and the character type they engendered, and to maintain a homogeneous Yankee civilization," Hofstadter wrote, "I have found much that was retrograde and delusive, a little that was vicious, and a good deal that was comic."[6] Blinded by their moral absolutism and their righteous convictions, the Progressives were unable to foresee that much of their ideology was narrow and undemocratic and would prepare the groundwork for a later reaction that would threaten the very fabric of American liberty.

The implications of Hofstadter's interpretation were indeed striking. In brief, his line of thought led to the conclusion that American liberalism was not a liberal movement, but a movement by fairly well-to-do middle-class groups alienated from their society because of technological and industrial changes. There is no doubt that Hofstadter himself was writing from the left of the political spectrum, but it is clear also that he felt strongly that the United States never had had a viable and constructive liberal tradition. Implicit in his views, therefore, was the assumption that American history occurred within an illiberal or conservative mold, that a genuine struggle between classes—as portrayed by the Progressive historians—had never taken place.

Hofstadter's general interpretation of progressivism rested to a large degree upon the research of others, particularly the work of George E. Mowry. Author of a number of important books on Theodore Roosevelt and the Progressive movement, Mowry was one of the first historians to see progressivism as a movement by a particular class aimed at reasserting its declining position of leadership. Motivated by an intense faith in individualistic values these groups opposed the rapid concentration of power in the hands of large corporate entities and the consequent emergence of an impersonal society. The Progressives, Mowry concluded, sought to recapture and reaffirm the older individualistic values, but they attempted to do so without undertaking any fundamental economic reforms or altering to any great extent the structure of American society.[7]

While the specific formulations of the Mowry-Hofstadter thesis

---

[6]*Ibid.*, p. 11.

[7]George E. Mowry, "The California Progressive and His Rationale: A Study in Middle Class Politics," *Mississippi Valley Historical Review* 36 (September 1949):239–250.

have not been universally accepted,[8] most recent historians seem to agree that the older interpretation of progressivism as a struggle between the people and special interests is oversimplified, if not erroneous. Thus Louis Hartz, in his fascinating book *The Liberal Tradition in America: An Interpretation of American Political Thought Since the Revolution* (1955), argued that because America never had a feudal tradition it did not experience the struggles between conservatives, reactionaries, liberals, and Marxians that characterized the history of most European countries. On the contrary the United States had a three-century-long tradition of consensus, wherein all Americans subscribed to the Lockean tenets of individualism, private property, natural rights, and popular sovereignty. The differences between Americans, Hartz maintained, have been over means rather than ends. Thus Americans never had a conservative tradition in the European and Burkean sense of the term because American liberalism, by virtue of its continuity, was a conservative tradition. To view American history in terms of class struggle, said Hartz, was to misunderstand the basic agreements that united all Americans.

As a result of the rise of the neoconservative school of historians the Progressive movement had begun to be interpreted in a new and different light. Some of these scholars, for example, neatly reversed the Progressive school approach. Instead of seeing early-twentieth-century progressivism as a liberal movement, they argued that it was essentially conservative in nature—a characteristic that was a source of strength rather than of weakness. Thus the historical stature of Theodore Roosevelt rose as historians such as John M. Blum saw him as a conservative though responsible president who was flexible enough to deal with the major issues of the day in a constructive yet practical manner. Conversely the reputation of Woodrow Wilson among some historians tended to decline because of his righteous moralism. Wilson's New Freedom, they wrote, was unrealistic because of its worship of a bygone age where all individuals had equal opportunity in the economic sphere. His foreign policies also turned out to be dismal failures

---

[8]A number of historians have pointed to what they regard as a methodological flaw in the Mowry-Hofstadter analysis. To argue—as Mowry and Hofstadter have done—that the Progressives were a cohesive group requires that they show that the anti-Progressives represented a quite different social and economic group. One recent historian who did a study of the anti-Progressives in one state found that their social and economic and ideological characteristics were almost identical with those of the Progressives. See Richard B. Sherman, "The Status Revolution and Massachusetts Progressive Leadership," *Political Science Quarterly* 78 (March 1963):59–65; and Jerome M. Clubb and Howard W. Allen, "Collective Biography and the Progressive Movement: The 'Status Revolution' Revisited," *Social Science History* 4 (1977):518–534.

because they rested on an exclusively moral foundation that omitted any appreciation of the national interest or the realities of international affairs.[9]

Conversely the reputation of many American reformers suffered as a result of the writings of neoconservative historians. Rather than writing about their contributions and achievements historians have shown the shortcomings and failures of various reform leaders. They have exposed the personal and selfish factors that supposedly motivated the behavior of reformers and implicitly determined their unrealistic approach to contemporary problems. Above all, such historians scored the reformers for accepting an optimistic moralism based on their faith in progress. According to neoconservative scholars Progressive reformers tragically misunderstood man's propensity for evil. As a result they failed to prepare Americans for the inevitable reaction that followed their failure to establish a democratic utopia at home and a peaceful international community of nations abroad in the first two decades of the twentieth century.

At the same time that neoconservative scholars were attempting to undermine the Progressive school emphasis on reform and class conflict, other historians were in the process of developing an entirely new synthesis to explain American history since the late nineteenth century. Influenced by work in the social and behavioral sciences they began to apply organizational theory to historical study. Building on the impressive contributions of Max Weber and others, organizational historians saw American society as being increasingly dominated by hierarchical and bureaucratic structures, which were accompanied by a sharp acceleration in the process of professionalization. Associated with these developments was a corresponding shift in the nation's value system. Through the mid-nineteenth century individualistic values remained dominant; after that time they were replaced by an orientation that stressed ideals of efficiency, order, rationality, and systematic control.[10]

The organizational model—as we have already seen—had been employed by business historians such as Alfred D. Chandler, Jr., to explain the emergence of large corporations. But such a model was also capable of being applied in a far more inclusive manner. A number of histori-

---

[9]John M. Blum, *The Republican Roosevelt* (Cambridge, Mass., 1954). For a critical, but by no means unsympathetic, interpretation of Wilson see Arthur S. Link, *Woodrow Wilson and the Progressive Era 1910–1917* (New York, 1954).

[10]For a penetrating discussion of this problem see Louis Galambos, "The Emerging Organizational Synthesis in Modern American History," *Business History Review* 44 (Autumn 1970):279–290, as well as his follow-up analysis, "Technology, Political Economy, and Professionalism: Central Themes of the Organizational Synthesis," *ibid.* 57 (Winter 1983):471–493.

ans, for example, advanced the thesis that progressivism represented largely an attempt to govern society in accordance with the new ideals of scientific management and efficiency. The conservation movement, to take one concrete illustration, was not—as historians of the Progressive school had maintained—a struggle by the American people and their champions against special interests and large corporate enterprises bent on depriving the nation of its natural resources and despoiling the landscape. On the contrary the conservation movement, according to Samuel P. Hays, was a movement of scientists and planners interested in "rational planning to promote efficient development and use of all natural resources." Frequently large corporations—which were profoundly influenced by the ideals of scientific management—were ardent supporters of conservationist policies because of their interest in long-range resource planning. Conversely small farmers, small cattlemen, homesteaders, and other groups that Progressive historians equated with the democratic masses often opposed conservation because it conflicted with their hopes of becoming rich quickly. "The broader significance of the conservation movement," Hays concluded, "stemmed from the role it played in the transformation of a decentralized, nontechnical, loosely organized society, where waste and inefficiency ran rampant, into a highly organized, technical, and centrally planned and directed social organization which could meet a complex world with efficiency and purpose."[11] Implicit in this approach was the assumption that conservation had little or nothing to do with the liberal-conservative categories of the Progressive school of historiography.

In a similar vein Hays argued that support for reform in municipal government came from business and professional groups. These groups felt that the welfare of the city could best be served if decision-making were centralized in their hands. In this way city governments would be run in a rational and businesslike manner. Hays's article appears as the first selection in this chapter.

In stressing the role of the "expert" and the ideals of scientific management as basic to an understanding of the Progressive era, organizational historians also reinterpreted other aspects of early-twentieth-century American history. Many of the Progressive reforms, they stressed, were directed not at making the government more democratic and responsive to the wishes of the American people, but to making it and the economy more efficient. The movement for federal regulation of business was not, as the Progressive school of historians

---

[11] Samuel P. Hays, *Conservation and the Gospel of Efficiency: The Progressive Conservation Movement, 1890–1920* (Cambridge, Mass., 1959), pp. 2 and 265. See also *American Political History as Social Analysis: Essays by Samuel P. Hays* (Knoxville, 1980).

had argued, motivated by fear or hatred of large corporate enterprise. Its goal, according to these newer historians, was the elimination of senseless and destructive competition in the economic system by making business and government partners in the effort to eliminate the ups and downs of the business cycle. Progressivism, therefore, reflected the desire of various professional groups to substitute planning for competition, to raise the "expert" to a position of paramount importance, and to end the inherent defects of democratic government by making government conform to the ideals of efficiency and rational planning.

The decline of the older view of the Progressive era was also evidenced in the changing historical interpretation of business and businessmen. For a good part of the twentieth century the liberal assumptions of most historians led them to portray the business community not only as monolithic in character but as being made up of men who were grasping, selfish, and narrow in their outlook. In recent scholarship, on the other hand, the businessman has been studied within a quite different framework. Business historians found in the careers of great entrepreneurs a creative and constructive leadership that brought into being America's phenomenal industrial capacity. Similarly a number of recent scholars have denied that the business community was necessarily reactionary or that all businessmen shared a common ideology. Instead they attempted to demonstrate that businessmen divided into various groups with conflicting ideas and that many of the Progressive reforms of the early twentieth century were actually introduced, supported, and endorsed by businessmen. In a study of the relationship between businessmen and the Progressive movement, for example, Robert H. Wiebe found a complex situation. Businessmen, he noted, rarely tried to improve the lot of low-income groups; they fought against unions and social insurance legislation; and while desiring to purify democracy they opposed its extension. Economic regulation, on the other hand, aroused a quite different response, for "at least one segment of the business community supported each major program for federal control. In this area businessmen exercised their greatest influence on reform and laid their claim as progressives."[12]

In *Businessmen and Reform* (1962) Wiebe had referred to the Progressive era as an "age of organization." Businessmen, he averred, turned to organization as a means of survival in an impersonal and changing world. Five years later, in a major work, Wiebe carried his analysis much further and provided one of the first attempts to synthesize American history around an organizational core. For much of

---

[12]Robert H. Wiebe, *Businessmen and Reform: A Study of the Progressive Movement* (Cambridge, Mass., 1962), p. 212.

the nineteenth century American society was composed of autono-
mous and semiautonomous "island communities." The United States
was a nation more in name than in fact, for most individuals resided
in relatively small, personal centers, each of which managed its affairs
independently of other communities. By the 1880s, however, these
communities no longer functioned in their traditional manner, for
technological and economic forces had undermined their cohesiveness
and caused "dislocation and bewilderment." The result, according to
Wiebe, was a "search for order." Some attempted to restore the local
community to a position of significance; others turned to agrarian reform; still others joined moral crusades in the belief that a return to
traditional values would solve many problems. Ultimately most Progressives turned to organization to bring a new order and equilibrium
to American society. In such diverse fields as law, medicine, economics, administration, social work, architecture, business, labor, and agriculture—to cite only a few examples—a new middle class appeared,
tied together by their conviction that their expertise and occupational
cohesiveness provided the means of ordering a fragmented society.
"The heart of progressivism," wrote Wiebe, "was the ambition of the
new middle class to fulfill its destiny through bureaucratic means."[13]
Slowly but surely America was brought "to the edge of something as
yet indefinable. In a general sense the nation had found its direction
early in the twentieth century. The society that so many in the ni-
neties had thought would either disintegrate or polarize had emerged
tough and plural; and by 1920 the realignments, the reorientations of
the Progressive era, had been translated into a complex of arrangements nothing short of a revolution could destroy."[14]

Curiously enough neoconservative, consensus, and organizational
interpretations of the Progressive movement that grew in influence in
the 1950s and 1960s were also echoed by New Left historians. Disillusioned by the continued existence of war, poverty, and racism, New
Left scholars tended to write about the shortcomings and failures of
American reform, a point of view that grew out of their own belief that
only radical changes in the framework and structure of American society would solve these problems. Consequently the New Left interpretation of early-twentieth-century progressivism was written within
a partial consensus framework (although those individuals writing
within this radical tradition clearly rejected the consensus on which
this movement was based) and an awareness of the importance of organizations in twentieth-century America.

---

[13]Robert H. Wiebe, *The Search for Order 1877–1920* (New York, 1967), p. 166.
[14]*Ibid.*, pp. 301–302.

To New Left historians the Progressive movement was anything but a reform movement. In one of the most significant studies of early-twentieth-century American history Gabriel Kolko argued that both major political parties shared a common ideology and set of values. This ideology—what Kolko called political capitalism—sought the elimination of a growing competition in the economy. Political capitalism, he noted, "redirected the radical potential of mass grievances and aspirations"; rather than federal regulation *of* business the norm became federal regulation *for* business. Between 1900 and 1916 a unique synthesis of economics and politics occurred. Progressivism, argued Kolko,

> *was initially a movement for the political rationalization of business and industrial conditions, a movement that operated on the assumption that the general welfare of the community could be best served by satisfying the concrete needs of business. But the regulation itself was invariably controlled by leaders of the regulated industry, and directed toward ends they deemed acceptable or desirable. In part this came about because the regulatory movements were usually initiated by the dominant businesses to be regulated, but it also resulted from the nearly universal belief among political leaders in the basic justice of private property relations as they essentially existed, a belief that set the ultimate limits on the leaders' possible actions.*

Since neither populism nor the Socialist party developed a specific diagnosis of existing social dynamics and relationships, Americans had no viable alternatives, for the two major political parties became the means through which business domination was institutionalized. "The Progressive Era," concluded Kolko, "was characterized by a paucity of alternatives to the status quo, a vacuum that permitted political capitalism to direct the growth of industrialism in America, to shape its politics, to determine the ground rules for American civilization in the twentieth century, and to set the stage for what was to follow."[15]

The reaction against the liberal interpretation of the Progressive movement, however, has not been shared by all historians. While admitting that older historians may have been wrong in their emphasis on a class conflict of the people versus the special interests, some scholars continue to see progressivism as an attempt to deal effectively with many social and economic problems that grew out of industrialism and the resulting concentration of power in the hands of a few individuals and groups. J. Joseph Huthmacher, for example, explicitly

---

[15]Gabriel Kolko, *The Triumph of Conservatism: A Reinterpretation of American History, 1900–1916* (New York, 1963), pp. 2–3, 285, and 303. See also James Weinstein, *The Corporate Ideal in the Liberal State, 1900–1918* (Boston, 1968).

rejected the Mowry-Hofstadter idea that progressivism was a middle-class movement dominated by a system of values espoused by rural-Yankee-Protestant groups. On the contrary Huthmacher maintained that progressivism was much more broadly based, and that lower-class groups played an important role in the movement. Implicitly rejecting the neoconservative thesis Huthmacher argued that progressivism was an attempt to cope with the complex dilemmas of an urban-industrial society. Although he clearly rejected the Jeffersonian agrarian interpretation of progressivism his point of view was essentially a modification and elaboration of the Progressive school that saw the reform movement of 1900–1920 as a continuing phase in the perennial struggle of liberalism versus conservatism.[16]

Nor was Huthmacher alone in reasserting a version of the older interpretation of progressivism. John C. Burnham, for example, pointed to the voluntaristic flavor of progressivism and its effort to merge Protestant moral values with the hard facts of scientific and technological change. Indeed, Burnham insisted that moral commitment and immediacy lay at the heart of this movement, which left behind a number of specific achievements. Similarly John D. Buenker pointed to the broad-based nature of progressivism that included middle- and lower-class elements.[17]

Increasingly the Mowry-Hofstadter thesis that status tensions and insecurity were central to the origins of progressivism came under attack as well. Using the state of Wisconsin as a case study David P. Thelen could find no correlation between an individual's social characteristics and his political affiliation and ideology. Rejecting the sociological and psychological interpretation that progressivism was rooted in social tensions, he argued instead that its roots went back into the nineteenth century. The depression of the 1890s was of particular importance for it dramatized the failures of industrialism and gave rise to a search for alternatives. Out of this search came a broad consensus on a series of reform programs that cut across class lines. All groups could unite on the urgent necessity for tax reform and the need to control "corporate arrogance." "When the progressive characteristically spoke of reform as a fight of 'the people' or the 'public interest' against the 'selfish interests,' he was speaking quite literally of his political coalition because the important fact about progressiv-

---

[16]J. Joseph Huthmacher, "Urban Liberalism and the Age of Reform," *Mississippi Valley Historical Review* 44 (September 1962):231–241.

[17]John D. Buenker, John C. Burnham, and Robert M. Crunden, *Progressivism* (Cambridge, Mass., 1977). This volume is composed of three separate essays by three historians. Although there are important differences among them the degree of similarity is also striking. See also John D. Buenker, *Urban Liberalism and Progressive Reform* (New York, 1973).

ism, at least in Wisconsin, was the degree of cooperation between previously discrete social groups now united under the banner of the 'public interest.' . . . Both conceptually and empirically it would seem safer
and more productive to view reformers first as reformers and only sec-
ondarily as men who were trying to relieve class and status anxieties."[18]

Most interpretations of progressivism rested on studies of midwestern and eastern states. In a significant analysis of Alabama during
the Progressive era, on the other hand, Sheldon Hackney found that
many of the standard generalizations were open to question. He noted,
for example, that there was little continuity between populism and
progressivism in Alabama; following the demise of their party Populists either voted Republican or else withdrew from politics. Holding a
social philosophy that viewed society in static terms they clearly preferred a minimal rather than an activist government; they were "primitive rebels." Nor were Progressives motivated by status anxiety or
committed to producer values; they saw society in dynamic terms and
insisted that economic opportunity could come about only through
greater economic growth stimulated in part by positive governmental
action. Unlike their forebears, Progressives were earnestly interested
in changing southern society and bringing it into the modern industrial
era. Indeed, Hackney found that Alabama progressivism resembled
more the eastern, urban Roosevelt brand than the western, rural Bryan
variety.

But progressivism, as Hackney observed, also had sharp implications for the status of black Americans in Alabama. During the years
from 1890 to 1910 the pattern of race relations in that state was highly
fluid; inconsistency was its primary characteristic. One manifestation
of this uncertainty was the high frequency of lynchings. Stability came
to Alabama only when the Constitutional Convention of 1901 in effect
eliminated black citizens from political participation. Curiously
enough the movement for disfranchisement was led by opponents of
reform. Their success helped Progressives create a new coalition from
the purged electorate that owed little to Populist antecedents. Progressivism in Alabama, therefore, rested on the institutionalization of
legal and political inequality. Hackney's book raised significant questions about the nature of progressivism and gave little support to either
liberal, conservative, or radical schools of historical interpretation.[19]

Oddly enough virtually all historians, whether they are in the older

---

[18]David P. Thelen, "Social Tensions and the Origins of Progressivism," *Journal of
American History* 56 (September 1969):323–341, and *The New Citizenship: Origins of
Progressivism in Wisconsin, 1885–1900* (Columbia, Mo., 1972).

[19]Sheldon Hackney, *Populism to Progressivism in Alabama* (Princeton, 1969).

Progressive or the newer neoconservative, organizational, or New Left traditions, seem to be in agreement on at least one major point; namely, that progressivism was an urban rather than a rural-centered movement. Once again historians seem to have been reflecting their milieu. In the past many of the major historians had come out of an environment dominated by rural and agrarian values; their attitude toward cities was partly conditioned by the prevailing view that American democracy was the creation of a rural agrarian society. Within the past two or three decades, however, the majority of historians have tended to come from a society and regions of the country much more concerned with the problems of urban life. They do not share the antiurban attitudes held by many of their predecessors. As a result these historians have written about the contributions to American history of cities and growing urban areas.

More recently historians interested in progressivism once again turned their attention to the analysis of politics and political parties at the turn of the century. Most scholars had accepted the view that progressivism was a pluralistic, not a unitary, movement. No historian, however, had provided a persuasive explanation as to why so many groups committed to social, economic, and political changes appeared simultaneously on both the state and national level. It was precisely on this point that the work of Walter Dean Burnham, a political scientist, became relevant to historians. Burnham had identified a major shift in American politics at this time: namely, a weakening of party loyalty accompanied by a massive decline in voting. The decline of party, in turn, magnified the significance of pressure groups of all kinds.[20]

The problem for historians was to explain why the pull of parties had declined and what significance this development had upon American society. In dealing with this problem the stage was set for a shift in the interpretations of progressivism. In his book on New York State politics in the Progressive era Richard L. McCormick had shown how the hold of party bosses had been undermined by the attacks of reformers and antiparty crusaders, and how new issues had arisen that were incapable of being resolved by the traditional party technique of distributing favors as widely as possible. In a subsequent article McCormick pointed to the remarkable transformation that occurred between 1904 and 1908. The regulatory authority of government at this time increased in precisely the same period that voter turnout declined, ticket-splitting increased, and organized pressure groups gained

---

[20]Walter Dean Burnham, "The Changing Shape of the American Political Universe," *American Political Science Review* 59 (March 1965):7–28, and *Critical Elections and the Mainsprings of American Politics* (New York, 1970), *passim*.

power at the expense of party. In discovering that business corrupted politics during this era Americans created a demand for the regulatory and administrative state, thus facilitating the activities of organizationally minded individuals from business and the professions determined to complete a political transformation. Although not in fundamental disagreement with organizational historians such as Hays, McCormick insisted on the relevancy of ideas and perceptions that often shaped the outcome of events in unpredictable ways.[21] McCormick's article on the discovery that business corrupted politics appears as the second selection in this chapter.

As Daniel Rodgers has recently observed, historians no longer attempt to describe the Progressive era within a static ideological framework. Indeed, the roots of the Progressive distrust of arbitrary and unregulated power had diverse and even conflicting sources. But if Progressives lacked a systematic and coherent intellectual system they did possess tools that were sufficiently powerful to make an impact. In Rodgers's eyes, therefore, progressivism can only be understood in terms of dynamic and changing social and political structures. "To acknowledge that these are the questions that matter and to abandon the hunt for the *essence* of the noise and tumult of that era may not be . . . to lose the whole," he concluded. "It may be to find it."[22]

As the historiography of the Progressive movement shows it is difficult to evaluate the specific contributions of the movement without dealing with certain moral values that inevitably influence the historical judgments of scholars studying the subject. To the Progressive school of historical scholarship progressivism was one of the first efforts to adjust American values to an urban, industrialized society. The concentration of economic power was thwarting the workings of American democratic institutions as well as corrupting the moral fiber of its citizens. Since they agreed with the goals of reformers who were attempting to ameliorate this situation, the writings of the Progressive school of historians on the movement tended to be a favorable one. More recent scholars, on the other hand, operated within quite a different value structure. Business and other nonconservative historians, precisely because they emphasized the constructive achievements of American business, did not see much good in a movement which they believed was based on superficial knowledge, amateurism, and demagoguery. Because these historians were more complacent, even proud,

---

[21]Richard L. McCormick, *From Realignment to Reform: Political Change in New York State, 1893–1910* (Ithaca, 1981), and "The Discovery that Business Corrupts Politics: A Reappraisal of the Origins of Progressivism," *American Historical Review* 86 (April 1981):247–274.

[22]Daniel T. Rodgers, "In Search of Progressivism," *Reviews in American History* 10 (December 1982):113–132.

of the accomplishments of American society they saw less need for radical reforms in America's past history. Hence they either emphasized the conservative nature of progressivism or else pointed to its lack of realism or its optimistic illusions in order to show why the movement failed. Similarly New Left scholars were equally hostile in their analysis of progressivism; they saw the movement as one dedicated to the control of government by business, giving it a reactionary rather than a reform character. Some historians who identified themselves with the liberal tradition also argued that American liberalism fell far short of enacting truly meaningful reforms during the Progressive era. Thus it was possible for neoconservative, liberal, and radical scholars to be critical of the Progressive movement from their respective viewpoints. And even organizational historians evidenced considerable ambivalence; they were not at all certain that a society based on bureaucratic values and structures was necessarily good.

The problem of evaluating the nature of the Progressive movement, therefore, is by no means easy or simple. Despite considerable research on this important era of American history the divisions among historians are not necessarily disappearing. On the contrary these divisions are in some respects growing sharper because of differences among historians pertaining to the nature and meaning of the American liberal tradition. In the final analysis, when historians are assessing progressivism, they are assessing also the ability of Americans to adapt themselves to new problems in any given era.

Aside from the ideological and philosophical conflicts among historians, there are several major questions and problems that must be dealt with in evaluating the Progressive movement. Was there a relationship between the Progressive movement and earlier as well as later reform movements, including populism and the New Deal? Who were the Progressives and what did they represent? Similarly what groups opposed progressivism and why did they do so? Were the reforms that were enacted between 1900 and 1917 constructive? What impact, if any, did they have upon American life? What significance did progressivism have for black Americans and other minority groups? Why did the Progressive movement come to an end as an organized movement, or did it, indeed, come to an end at all?

These are only a few of the questions that historians have dealt with in an effort to understand the development of American society during the first two decades of the twentieth century. It is difficult, if not impossible, to avoid addressing oneself to these issues because of the bearing they have upon the larger question of understanding the nature of the American experience.

Samuel P. Hays

SAMUEL P. HAYS (1921–   ) is professor of history at the University of Pittsburgh. He has written widely in American social and political history; his books include *The Response to Industrialism 1885–1914* (1957), *Conservation and the Gospel of Efficiency* (1959), and *American Political History as Social Analysis* (1980).

In order to achieve a more complete understanding of social change in the Progressive Era, historians must now undertake a deeper analysis of the practices of economic, political, and social groups. Political ideology alone is no longer satisfactory evidence to describe social patterns because generalizations based upon it, which tend to divide political groups into the moral and the immoral, the rational and the irrational, the efficient and the inefficient, do not square with political practice. Behind this contemporary rhetoric concerning the nature of reform lay patterns of political behavior which were at variance with it. Since an extensive gap separated ideology and practice, we can no longer take the former as an accurate description of the latter, but must reconstruct social behavior from other types of evidence.

Reform in urban government provides one of the most striking examples of this problem of analysis. The demand for change in municipal affairs, whether in terms of overall reform, such as the commission and city-manager plans, or of more piecemeal modifications, such as the development of citywide school boards, deeply involved reform ideology. Reformers loudly proclaimed a new structure of municipal government as more moral, more rational, and more efficient and, because it was so, self-evidently more desirable. But precisely because of this emphasis, there seemed to be no need to analyze the political forces behind change. Because the goals of reform were good, its causes were obvious; rather than being the product of particular people and particular ideas in particular situations, they were deeply imbedded in the universal impulses and truths of "progress." Consequently, historians have rarely tried to determine precisely who the municipal reformers were or what they did, but instead have relied on reform ideology as an accurate description of reform practice.

Samuel P. Hays, "The Politics of Reform in Municipal Government in the Progressive Era," *Pacific Northwest Quarterly* 55 (October 1964):157–169. Reprinted by permission of the *Pacific Northwest Quarterly*.

The reform ideology which became the basis of historical analysis is well known. It appears in classic form in Lincoln Steffens' *Shame of the Cities.* The urban political struggle of the Progressive Era, so the argument goes, involved a conflict between public impulses for "good government" against a corrupt alliance of "machine politicians" and "special interests."

During the rapid urbanization of the late nineteenth century, the latter had been free to aggrandize themselves, especially through franchise grants, at the expense of the public. Their power lay primarily in their ability to manipulate the political process, by bribery and corruption, for their own ends. Against such arrangements there gradually arose a public protest, a demand by the public for honest government, for officials who would act for the public rather than for themselves. To accomplish their goals, reformers sought basic modifications in the political system, both in the structure of government and in the manner of selecting public officials. These changes, successful in city after city, enabled the "public interest" to triumph.

Recently, George Mowry, Alfred Chandler, Jr., and Richard Hofstadter have modified this analysis by emphasizing the fact that the impulse for reform did not come from the working class. This might have been suspected from the rather strained efforts of National Municipal League writers in the "Era of Reform" to go out of their way to demonstrate working-class support for commission and city-manager governments. We now know that they clutched at straws, and often erroneously, in order to prove to themselves as well as to the public that municipal reform was a mass movement.

The Mowry-Chandler-Hofstadter writings have further modified older views by asserting that reform in general and municipal reform in particular sprang from a distinctively middle-class movement. This has now become the prevailing view. Its popularity is surprising not only because it is based upon faulty logic and extremely limited evidence, but also because it, too, emphasizes the analysis of ideology rather than practice and fails to contribute much to the understanding of who distinctively were involved in reform and why.

Ostensibly, the "middle-class" theory of reform is based upon a new type of behavioral evidence, the collective biography, in studies by Mowry of California Progressive party leaders, by Chandler of a nationwide group of that party's leading figures, and by Hofstadter of four professions—ministers, lawyers, teachers, editors. These studies demonstrate the middle-class nature of reform, but they fail to determine if reformers were distinctively middle-class, specifically if they differed from their opponents. One study of 300 political leaders in the state of Iowa, for example, discovered that Progressive-party, Old Guard, and Cummins Republicans were all substantially alike, the Progressives differing only in that they were slightly younger than the others and had less political experience. If its opponents were also middle-class, then one cannot describe Progressive reform as a phenomenon whose special nature can be explained in terms of middle-class characteristics. One cannot explain the distinctive behavior of people in terms of characteristics which are not distinctive to them.

Hofstadter's evidence concerning professional men fails in yet another way to determine the peculiar characteristics of reformers, for he describes ministers, lawyers, teachers, and editors without determining who within these professions became reformers and who did not. Two analytical distinctions might be made. Ministers involved in municipal reform, it appears, came not from all segments of religion, but peculiarly from upper-class churches. They enjoyed the highest prestige and salaries in the religious community and had no reason to feel a loss of "status," as Hofstadter argues. Their role in reform arose from the class character of their religious organizations rather than from the mere fact of their occupation as ministers. Professional men involved in reform (many of whom—engineers, architects, and doctors—Hofstadter did not examine at all) seem to have come especially from the more advanced segments of their professions, from those who sought to apply their specialized knowledge to a wider range of public affairs. Their role in reform is related not to their attempt to defend earlier patterns of culture, but to the working out of the inner dynamics of professionalization in modern society.

The weakness of the "middle-class" theory of reform stems from the fact that it rests primarily upon ideological evidence, not on a thorough-going description of political practice. Although the studies of Mowry, Chandler, and Hofstadter ostensibly derive from behavioral evidence, they actually derive largely from the extensive expressions of middle-ground ideological position, of the reformers' own descriptions of their contemporary society, and of their expressed fears of both the lower and the upper classes, of the fright of being ground between the millstones of labor and capital.

Such evidence, though it accurately portrays what people thought, does not accurately describe what they did. The great majority of Americans look upon themselves as "middle-class" and subscribe to a middle-ground ideology, even though in practice they belong to a great variety of distinct social classes. Such ideologies are not rationalizations or deliberate attempts to deceive. They are natural phenomena of human behavior. But the historian should be especially sensitive to their role so that he will not take evidence of political ideology as an accurate representation of political practice.

In the following account I will summarize evidence in both secondary and primary works concerning the political practices in which municipal reformers were involved. Such an analysis logically can be broken down into three parts, each one corresponding to a step in the traditional argument. First, what was the source of reform? Did it lie in the general public rather than in particular groups? Was it middle-class, working-class, or perhaps of other composition? Second, what was the reform target of attack? Were reformers primarily interested in ousting the corrupt individual, the political or business leader who made private arrangements at the expense of the public, or were they interested in something else? Third, what political innovations did reformers bring about? Did they seek to expand popular participation in the governmental process?

There is now sufficient evidence to determine the validity of these specific elements of the more general argument. Some of it has been available for several decades; some has appeared more recently; some is presented here for the first time. All of it adds up to the conclusion that reform in municipal government involved a political development far different from what we have assumed in the past.

Available evidence indicates that the source of support for reform in municipal government did not come from the lower or middle classes, but from the upper class. The leading business groups in each city and professional men closely allied with them initiated and dominated municipal movements. Leonard White, in his study of the city manager published in 1927, wrote:

> The opposition to bad government usually comes to a head in the local chamber of commerce. Business men finally acquire the conviction that the growth of their city is being seriously impaired by the failures of city officials to perform their duties efficiently. Looking about for a remedy, they are captivated by the resemblance of the city-manager plan to their corporate form of business organization.

In the 1930s White directed a number of studies of the origin of city-manager government. The resulting reports invariably begin with such statements as, "the Chamber of Commerce spearheaded the movement," or commission government in this city was a "businessmen's government." Of thirty-two cases of city-manager government in Oklahoma examined by Jewell C. Phillips, twenty-nine were initiated either by chambers of commerce or by community committees dominated by businessmen. More recently James Weinstein has presented almost irrefutable evidence that the business community, represented largely by chambers of commerce, was the overwhelming force behind both commission and city-manager movements.

Dominant elements of the business community played a prominent role in another crucial aspect of municipal reform: the Municipal

Research Bureau movement. Especially in the larger cities, where they had less success in shaping the structure of government, reformers established centers to conduct research in municipal affairs as a springboard for influence.

The first such organization, the Bureau of Municipal Research of New York City, was founded in 1906; it was financed largely through the efforts of Andrew Carnegie and John D. Rockefeller. An investment banker provided the crucial support in Philadelphia, where a Bureau was founded in 1908. A group of wealthy Chicagoans in 1910 established the Bureau of Public Efficiency, a research agency. John H. Patterson of the National Cash Register Company, the leading figure in Dayton municipal reform, financed the Dayton Bureau, founded in 1912. And George Eastman was the driving force behind both the Bureau of Municipal Research and city-manager government in Rochester. In smaller cities data about city government were collected by interested individuals in a more informal way or by chambers of commerce, but in larger cities the task required special support, and prominent businessmen supplied it.

The character of municipal reform is demonstrated more precisely by a brief examination of the movements in Des Moines and Pittsburgh. The Des Moines Commercial Club inaugurated and carefully controlled the drive for the commission form of government. In January 1906 the club held a so-called "mass meeting" of business and professional men to secure an enabling act from the state legislature. P. C. Kenyon, president of the club, selected a Committee of 300, composed principally of business and professional men, to draw up a specific proposal. After the legislature approved their plan, the same committee managed the campaign which persuaded the electorate to accept the commission form of government by a narrow margin in June 1907.

In this election the lower-income wards of the city opposed the change, the upper-income wards supported it strongly, and the middle-income wards were more evenly divided. In order to control the new government, the Committee of 300, now expanded to 530, sought to determine the nomination and election of the five new commissioners, and to this end they selected an avowedly businessman's slate. Their plans backfired when the voters swept into office a slate of anticommission candidates who now controlled the new commission government.

Proponents of the commission form of government in Des Moines spoke frequently in the name of "the people." But their more explicit statements emphasized their intent that the new plan be a "business system" of government, run by businessmen. The slate of candidates for commissioner endorsed by advocates of the plan was known as the "businessman's ticket." J. W. Hill, president of the committees of 300 and 530, bluntly declared: "The professional politician must be ousted and in his place capable business men chosen to conduct the affairs of the city." I. M. Earle, general counsel of the Bankers' Life Association and a prominent figure in the movement, put the point more precisely: "When the plan was adopted it was the intention to get businessmen to run it."

Although reformers used the ideology of popular government, they in no sense meant that all segments of society should be involved equally in municipal decision-making. They meant that their concept of the city's welfare would be best achieved if the business community controlled city government. As one businessman told a labor audience, the businessman's slate represented labor "better than you do yourself."

The composition of the municipal reform movement in Pittsburgh demonstrates its upper-class and professional as well as its business sources. Here the two principal reform organizations were the Civic Club and the Voters' League. The 745 members of these two organizations came primarily from the upper class. Sixty-five percent appeared in upper-class directories which contained the names of only 2 percent of the city's families. Furthermore, many who were not listed in these directories lived in upper-class areas. These reformers, it should be stressed, comprised not an old but a new upper class. Few came from earlier industrial and mercantile families. Most of them had risen to social position from wealth created after 1870 in the iron, steel, electrical equipment, and other industries, and they lived in the newer rather than the older fashionable areas.

Almost half (48 percent) of the reformers were professional men: doctors, lawyers, ministers, directors of libraries and museums, engineers, architects, private and public school teachers, and college professors. Some of these belonged to the upper class as well, especially the lawyers, ministers, and private school teachers. But for the most part their interest in reform stemmed from the inherent dynamics of their professions rather than from their class connections. They came from the more advanced segments of their organizations, from those in the forefront of the acquisition and application of knowledge. They were not the older professional men, seeking to preserve the past against change; they were in the vanguard of professional life, actively seeking to apply expertise more widely to public affairs.

Pittsburgh reformers included a large segment of businessmen; 52 percent were bankers and corporation officials or their wives. Among them were the presidents of fourteen large banks and officials of Westinghouse, Pittsburgh Plate Glass, U.S. Steel and its component parts (such as Carnegie Steel, American Bridge, and National Tube), Jones and Laughlin, lesser steel companies (such as Crucible, Pittsburgh, Superior, Lockhart, and H. K. Porter), the H. J. Heinz Company, and the Pittsburgh Coal Company, as well as officials of the Pennsylvania Railroad and the Pittsburgh and Lake Erie. These men were not small businessmen; they directed the most powerful banking and industrial organizations of the city. They represented not the old business community, but industries which had developed and grown primarily within the past fifty years and which had come to dominate the city's economic life.

These business, professional, and upper-class groups who dominated municipal reform movements were all involved in the rationalization and systematization of modern life; they wished a form of government which would be more consistent with the objectives inherent in those developments. The most important single feature of their perspective was the rapid expansion of the geographical scope of affairs which they wished to influence and manipulate, a scope which was no longer limited and narrow, no longer within the confines of pedestrian communities, but was now broad and citywide, covering the whole range of activities of the metropolitan area.

The migration of the upper class from central to outlying areas created a geographical distance between its residential communities and its economic institutions. To protect the latter required involvement both in local ward affairs and in the larger city government as well. Moreover, upper-class cultural institutions, such as museums, libraries, and symphony orchestras, required an active interest in the larger, municipal context from which these institutions drew much of their clientele.

Professional groups, broadening the scope of affairs which they sought to study, measure, or manipulate, also sought to influence the public health, the educational system, or the physical arrangements of the entire city. Their concerns were limitless, not bounded by geography, but as expansive as the professional imagination. Finally, the new industrial community greatly broadened its perspective in governmental affairs because of its new recognition of the way in which factors throughout the city affected business growth. The increasing size and scope of industry, the greater stake in more varied and geographically dispersed facets of city life, the effect of floods on many business concerns, the need to promote traffic flows to and from work for both blue-collar and managerial employees—all contributed to this larger interest. The geographically larger private perspectives of upper-class, professional, and business groups gave rise to a geographically larger public perspective.

These reformers were dissatisfied with existing systems of municipal government. They did not oppose corruption per se—although there was plenty of that. They objected to the structure of government which enabled local and particularistic interests to dominate. Prior to the reforms of the Progressive Era, city government consisted primarily of confederations of local wards, each of which was represented on the city's legislative body. Each ward frequently had its own elementary schools and ward-elected school boards which administered them.

These particularistic interests were the focus of a decentralized political life. City councilmen were local leaders. They spoke for their local areas, the economic interests of their inhabitants, their residential concerns, their educational, recreational, and religious interests— i.e., for those aspects of community life which mattered most to those they represented. They rolled logs in the city council to provide streets, sewers, and other public works for their local areas. They defended the community's cultural practices, its distinctive languages or national customs, its liberal attitude toward liquor, and its saloons and dance halls which served as centers of community life. One observer described this process of representation in Seattle:

> The residents of the hill-tops and the suburbs may not fully appreciate the faithfulness of certain downtown ward councilmen to the interests of their constituents. . . . The people of a state would rise in arms against a senator or representative in Congress who deliberately misrepresented their wishes and imperilled their interests, though he might plead a higher regard for national good. Yet people in other parts of the city seem to forget that under the old system the ward elected councilmen with the idea of procuring service of special benefit to that ward.

In short, pre-reform officials spoke for their constituencies, inevitably their own wards which had elected them, rather than for other sections or groups of the city.

The ward system of government especially gave representation in city affairs to lower- and middle-class groups. Most elected ward officials were from these groups, and they, in turn, constituted the major opposition to reforms in municipal government. In Pittsburgh, for example, immediately prior to the changes in both the city council and the school board in 1911 in which citywide representation replaced ward representation, only 24 percent of the 387 members of those bodies represented the same managerial, professional, and banker occupations which dominated the membership of the Civic Club and the Voters' League. The great majority (67 percent) were small businessmen—grocers, saloonkeepers, livery-stable proprietors, owners of small hotels, druggists—white-collar workers such as clerks and bookkeepers, and skilled and unskilled workmen.

This decentralized system of urban growth and the institutions which arose from its reformers now opposed. Social, professional, and economic life had not only developed in the local wards in a small community context, but had also on a larger scale become highly integrated and organized, giving rise to a superstructure of social organization which lay far above that of ward life and which was sharply divorced from it in both personal contacts and perspective.

By the late nineteenth century, those involved in these larger institutions found that the decentralized system of political life limited their larger objectives. The movement for reform in municipal government, therefore, constituted an attempt by upper-class, advanced professional, and large-business groups to take formal political power from the previously dominant lower- and middle-class elements so that they might advance their own conceptions of desirable public policy. These two groups came from entirely different urban worlds, and the political system fashioned by one was no longer acceptable to the other.

Lower- and middle-class groups not only dominated the pre-reform governments but vigorously opposed reform. It is significant that none of the occupational groups among them, for example, small businessmen or white-collar workers, skilled or unskilled artisans, had important representation in reform organizations thus far examined. The case studies of city-manager government undertaken in the 1930s under the direction of Leonard White detailed in city after city the particular opposition of labor. In their analysis of Jackson, Michigan, the authors of these studies wrote:

> The Square Deal, *oldest Labor paper in the state, has been consistently against manager government, perhaps largely because labor has felt that with a decentralized government elected on a ward basis it was more likely to have some voice to receive its share of privileges.*

In Janesville, Wisconsin, the small shopkeepers and workingmen on the west and south sides, heavily Catholic and often Irish, opposed the commission plan in 1911 and in 1912 and the city-manager plan when adopted in 1923. "In Dallas there is hardly a trace of class consciousness in the Marxian sense," one investigator declared, "yet in city elections the division has been to a great extent along class lines." The commission and city-manager elections were no exceptions. To these authors it seemed a logical reaction, rather than an embarrassing fact that had to be swept away, that workingmen should have opposed municipal reform.

In Des Moines working-class representatives, who in previous years might have been council members, were conspicuously absent from the "businessman's slate." Workingmen acceptable to reformers could not be found. A workingman's slate of candidates, therefore, appeared to challenge the reform slate. Organized labor, and especially the mineworkers, took the lead; one of their number, Wesley Ash, a deputy sheriff and union member, made "an astonishing run" in the primary, coming in second among a field of more than twenty candidates. In fact, the strength of anticommission candidates in the primary so alarmed reformers that they frantically sought to appease labor.

The day before the final election they modified their platform to pledge both an eight-hour day and an "American standard of wages." They attempted to persuade the voters that their slate consisted of men who represented labor because they had "begun at the bottom of the ladder and made a good climb toward success by their own unaided efforts." But their tactics failed. In the election on March 30, 1908, voters swept into office the entire "opposition" slate. The business and professional community had succeeded in changing the form of government, but not in securing its control. A cartoon in the leading reform newspaper illustrated their disappointment; John Q. Public sat dejectedly and muttered, "Aw, What's the Use?"

The most visible opposition to reform and the most readily available target of reform attack was the so-called "machine," for through the "machine" many different ward communities as well as lower- and middle-income groups joined effectively to influence the central city government. Their private occupational and social life did not naturally involve these groups in larger citywide activities in the same way as the upper class was involved; hence they lacked access to privately organized economic and social power on which they could construct political power. The "machine" filled this organizational gap.

Yet it should never be forgotten that the social and economic institutions in the wards themselves provided the "machine's" sustaining support and gave it larger significance. When reformers attacked the "machine" as the most visible institutional element of the ward system, they attacked the entire ward form of political organization and the political power of lower-and middle-income groups which lay behind it.

Reformers often gave the impression that they opposed merely the corrupt politician and his "machine." But in a more fundamental way they looked upon the deficiencies of pre-reform political leaders in terms not of their personal shortcomings, but of the limitations inherent in their occupational, institutional, and class positions. In 1911 the Voters' League of Pittsburgh wrote in its pamphlet analyzing the qualifications of candidates that "a man's occupation ought to give a strong indication of his qualifications for membership on a school board." Certain occupations inherently disqualified a man from serving:

> *Employment as ordinary laborer in the lowest class of mill work*
> *would naturally lead to the conclusion that such men did not have*
> *sufficient education or business training to act as school directors.*
> *. . . Objection might also be made to small shopkeepers, clerks, work-*
> *men at many trades, who by lack of educational advantages and*
> *business training, could not, no matter how honest, be expected to*
> *administer properly the affairs of an educational system, requiring*
> *special knowledge, and where millions are spent each year.*

These, of course, were precisely the groups which did dominate Pittsburgh government prior to reform. The League deplored the fact that
school boards contained only a small number of "men prominent
throughout the city in business life . . . in professional occupations
. . . holding positions as managers, secretaries, auditors, superintendents and foremen" and exhorted these classes to participate more actively as candidates for office.

Reformers, therefore, wished not simply to replace bad men with
good; they proposed to change the occupational and class origins of
decision-makers. Toward this end they sought innovations in the formal machinery of government which would concentrate political
power by sharply centralizing the processes of decision-making rather
than distribute it through more popular participation in public affairs.
According to the liberal view of the Progressive Era, the major political
innovations of reform involved the equalization of political power
through the primary, the direct election of public officials, and the initiative, referendum, and recall. These measures played a large role in
the political ideology of the time and were frequently incorporated into
new municipal charters. But they provided at best only an occasional
and often incidental process of decision-making. Far more important
in continuous, sustained, day-to-day processes of government were
those innovations which centralized decision-making in the hands of
fewer and fewer people.

The systematization of municipal government took place on both
the executive and the legislative levels. The strong-mayor and city-
manager types became the most widely used examples of the former.
In the first decade of the twentieth century, the commission plan had
considerable appeal, but its distribution of administrative responsibility among five people gave rise to a demand for a form with more centralized executive power; consequently, the city-manager or the com-
mission-manager variant often replaced it.

A far more pervasive and significant change, however, lay in the
centralization of the system of representation, the shift from ward to
citywide election of councils and school boards. Governing bodies so
selected, reformers argued, would give less attention to local and particularistic matters and more to affairs of citywide scope. This shift,

an invariable feature of both commission and city-manager plans, was often adopted by itself. In Pittsburgh, for example, the new charter of 1911 provided as the major innovation that a council of twenty-seven, each member elected from a separate ward, be replaced by a council of nine, each elected by the city as a whole.

Cities displayed wide variations in this innovation. Some re-grouped wards into larger units but kept the principle of areas of rep-resentation smaller than the entire city. Some combined a majority of councilmen elected by wards with additional ones elected at large. All such innovations, however, constituted steps toward the centraliza-tion of the system of representation.

Liberal historians have not appreciated the extent to which mu-nicipal reform in the Progressive Era involved a debate over the system of representation. The ward form of representation was universally condemned on the grounds that it gave too much influence to the sep-arate units and not enough attention to the larger problems of the city. Harry A. Toulmin, whose book *The City Manager* was published by the National Municipal League, stated the case:

> *The spirit of sectionalism had dominated the political life of every city. Ward pitted against ward, alderman against alderman, and leg-islation only effected by "log-rolling" extravagant measures into op-eration, mulcting the city, but gratifying the greed of constituents, has too long stung the conscience of decent citizenship. This constant treaty-making of factionalism has been no less than a curse. The city-manager plan proposes the commendable thing of abolishing wards. The plan is not unique in this for it has been common to many forms of commission government. . . .*

Such a system should be supplanted, the argument usually went, with citywide representation in which elected officials could consider the city "as a unit." "The new officers are elected," wrote Toulmin, "each to represent all the people. Their duties are so defined that they must administer the corporate business in its entirety, not as a hodge-podge of associated localities."

Behind the debate over the method of representation, however, lay a debate over who should be represented, over whose views of public policy should prevail. Many reform leaders often explicitly, if not im-plicitly, expressed fear that lower- and middle-income groups had too much influence in decision-making. One Galveston leader, for exam-ple, complained about the movement for initiative, referendum, and recall:

> *We have in our city a very large number of negroes employed on the docks; we also have a very large number of unskilled white laborers; this city also has more barrooms, according to its population, than*

any other city in Texas. Under these circumstances it would be extremely difficult to maintain a satisfactory city government where all ordinances must be submitted back to the voters of the city for their ratification and approval.

At the National Municipal League convention of 1907, Rear Admiral F. E. Chadwick (USN Ret.), a leader in the Newport, Rhode Island, movement for municipal reform, spoke to this question even more directly:

Our present system has excluded in large degree the representation of those who have the city's well-being most at heart. It has brought, in municipalities . . . a government established by the least educated, the least interested class of citizens.

It stands to reason that a man paying $5,000 taxes in a town is more interested in the well-being and development of his town than the man who pays no taxes. . . . It equally stands to reason that the man of the $5,000 tax should be assured a representation in the committee which lays the tax and spends the money which he contributes. . . . Shall we be truly democratic and give the property owner a fair show or shall we develop a tyranny of ignorance which shall crush him.

Municipal reformers thus debated frequently the question of who should be represented as well as the question of what method of representation should be employed.

That these two questions were intimately connected was revealed in other reform proposals for representation, proposals which were rarely taken seriously. One suggestion was that a class system of representation be substituted for ward representation. For example, in 1908 one of the prominent candidates for commissioner in Des Moines proposed that the city council be composed of representatives of five classes: educational and ministerial organizations, manufacturers and jobbers, public utility corporations, retail merchants including liquor men, and the Des Moines Trades and Labor Assembly. Such a system would have greatly reduced the influence in the council of both middle- and lower-class groups. The proposal revealed the basic problem confronting business and professional leaders: how to reduce the influence in government of the majority of voters among middle- and lower-income groups.

A growing imbalance between population and representation sharpened the desire of reformers to change from ward to citywide elections. Despite shifts in population within most cities, neither ward district lines nor the apportionment of city council and school board seats changed frequently. Consequently, older areas of the city, with wards that were small in geographical size and held declining populations (usually lower- and middle-class in composition), continued to be overrepresented, and newer upper-class areas, where population was growing, became increasingly underrepresented. This intensified the reformers' conviction that the structure of government must be changed to give them the voice they needed to make their views on public policy prevail.

It is not insignificant that in some cities (by no means a majority) municipal reform came about outside of the urban electoral process. The original commission government in Galveston was appointed rather than elected. "The failure of previous attempts to secure an efficient city government through the local electorate made the business men of Galveston willing to put the conduct of the city's affairs in the hands of a commission dominated by state-appointed officials." Only in 1903 did the courts force Galveston to elect the members of the commission, an innovation which one writer described as "an abandonment of the commission idea," and which led to the decline of the influence of the business community in the commission government.

In 1911 Pittsburgh voters were not permitted to approve either the new city charter or the new school board plan, both of which provided for citywide representation; they were a result of state legislative enactment. The governor appointed the first members of the new city council, but thereafter they were elected. The judges of the court of common pleas, however, and not the voters, selected members of the new school board.

The composition of the new city council and new school board in Pittsburgh, both of which were inaugurated in 1911, revealed the degree to which the shift from ward to citywide representation produced a change in group representation. Members of the upper class, the advanced professional men, and the large business groups dominated both. Of the fifteen members of the Pittsburgh Board of Education appointed in 1911 and the nine members of the new city council, none were small businessmen or white-collar workers. Each body contained only one person who could remotely be classified as a blue-collar worker; each of these men filled a position specifically but unofficially designed as reserved for a "representative of labor," and each was an official of the Amalgamated Association of Iron, Steel, and Tin Workers. Six of the nine members of the new city council were prominent businessmen, and all six were listed in upper-class directories. Two others were doctors closely associated with the upper class in both professional and social life. The fifteen members of the Board of Education included ten businessmen with citywide interests, one doctor associated with the upper class, and three women previously active in upper-class public welfare.

Lower- and middle-class elements felt that the new city governments did not represent them. The studies carried out under the direction of Leonard White contain numerous expressions of the way in which the change in the structure of government produced not only a change in the geographical scope of representation, but also in the groups represented. "It is not the policies of the manager or the council they oppose," one researcher declared, "as much as the lack of representation for their economic level and social groups." And another wrote:

> There had been nothing unapproachable about the old ward aldermen. Every voter had a neighbor on the common council who was interested in serving him. The new councilmen, however, made an unfavorable impression on the less well-to-do voters. . . . Election at large made a change that, however desirable in other ways, left the voters in the poorer wards with a feeling that they had been deprived of their share of political importance.

The success of the drive for centralization of administration and representation varied with the size of the city. In the smaller cities, business, professional, and elite groups could easily exercise a dominant influence. Their close ties readily enabled them to shape informal political power which they could transform into formal political power. After the mid-1890s the widespread organization of chambers of commerce provided a base for political action to reform municipal government, resulting in a host of small-city commission and city-manager innovations. In the larger, more heterogeneous cities, whose subcommittees were more dispersed, such communitywide action was extremely difficult. Few commission or city-manager proposals materialized here. Mayors became stronger, and steps were taken toward centralization of representation, but the ward system or some modified version usually persisted. Reformers in large cities often had to rest content with their Municipal Research Bureaus, through which they could exert political influence from outside the municipal government.

A central element in the analysis of municipal reform in the Progressive Era is governmental corruption. Should it be understood in moral or political terms? Was it a product of evil men or of particular sociopolitical circumstances? Reform historians have adopted the former view. Selfish and evil men arose to take advantage of a political arrangement whereby unsystematic government offered many opportunities for personal gain at public expense. The system thrived until the "better elements," "men of intelligence and civic responsibility," or "right-thinking people" ousted the culprits and fashioned a political force which produced decisions in the "public interest." In this scheme of things, corruption in public affairs grew out of individual personal failings and a deficient governmental structure which could not hold those predispositions in check, rather than from the peculiar nature of social forces. The contestants involved were morally defined: evil men who must be driven from power, and good men who must be activated politically to secure control of municipal affairs.

Public corruption, however, involves political even more than moral considerations. It arises more out of the particular distribution of political power than of personal morality. For corruption is a device to exercise control and influence outside the legal channels of decision-making when those channels are not readily responsive. Most generally, corruption stems from an inconsistency between control of the instruments of formal governmental power and the exercise of informal influence in the community. If powerful groups are denied access to formal power in legitimate ways, they seek access through procedures which the community considers illegitimate. Corrupt government, therefore, does not reflect the genius of evil men, but rather the lack of acceptable means for those who exercise power in the private community to wield the same influence in governmental affairs. It can be understood in the Progressive Era not simply by the preponderance of evil men over good, but by the peculiar nature of the distribution of political power.

The political corruption of the "Era of Reform" arose from the inaccessibility of municipal government to those who were rising in power and influence. Municipal government in the United States developed in the nineteenth century within a context of universal manhood suffrage which decentralized political control. Because all men, whatever their economic, social, or cultural conditions, could vote, leaders who reflected a wide variety of community interests and who represented the views of people of every circumstance arose to guide and direct municipal affairs. Since the majority of urban voters were workingmen or immigrants, the views of those groups carried great and often decisive weight in governmental affairs. Thus, as Herbert Gutman has shown, during strikes in the 1870s city officials were usually friendly to workingmen and refused to use police power to protect strikebreakers.

Ward representation on city councils was an integral part of grassroots influence, for it enabled diverse urban communities, invariably identified with particular geographical areas of the city, to express their views more clearly through councilmen peculiarly receptive to their concerns. There was a direct, reciprocal flow of power between wards and the center of city affairs in which voters felt a relatively close connection with public matters and city leaders gave special attention to their needs.

Within this political system the community's business leaders grew in influence and power as industrialism advanced, only to find that their economic position did not readily admit them to the formal machinery of government. Thus, during strikes, they had to rely on either their own private police, Pinkertons, or the state militia to enforce their use of strikebreakers. They frequently found that city officials did not accept their views of what was best for the city and what direction municipal policies should take. They had developed a common outlook, closely related to their economic activities, that the city's economic expansion should become the prime concern of municipal government, and yet they found that this view had to compete with even more influential views of public policy. They found that political tendencies which arose from universal manhood suffrage and ward representation were not always friendly to their political conceptions and goals and had produced a political system over which they had little control, despite the fact that their economic ventures were the core of the city's prosperity and the hope for future urban growth.

Under such circumstances, businessmen sought other methods of influencing municipal affairs. They did not restrict themselves to the channels of popular election and representation, but frequently applied direct influence—if not verbal persuasion, then bribery and corruption. Thereby arose the graft which Lincoln Steffens recounted in his *Shame of the Cities*. Utilities were only the largest of those business groups and individuals who requested special favors, and the franchises they sought were only the most sensational of the prizes, which included such items as favorable tax assessments and rates, the vacating of streets wanted for factory expansion, or permission to operate amid anti-liquor and other laws regulating personal behavior. The relationships between business and formal government became a maze of accommodations, a set of political arrangements which grew up because effective power had few legitimate means of accomplishing its ends.

Steffens and subsequent liberal historians, however, misread the significance of these arrangements, emphasizing their personal rather than their more fundamental institutional elements. To them corruption involved personal arrangements between powerful business leaders and powerful "machine" politicians. Just as they did not fully appreciate the significance of the search for political influence by the rising business community as a whole, so they did not see fully the role of the "ward politician." They stressed the argument that the political leader manipulated voters to his own personal ends, that he used constituents rather than reflected their views.

A different approach is now taking root, namely, that the urban political organization was an integral part of community life, expressing its needs and its goals. As Oscar Handlin has said, for example, the "machine" not only fulfilled specific wants, but provided one of the few avenues to success and public recognition available to the immigrant. The political leader's arrangements with businessmen, therefore, were not simply personal agreements between conniving individuals; they were far-reaching accommodations between powerful sets of institutions in industrial America.

These accommodations, however, proved to be burdensome and unsatisfactory to the business community and to the upper third of socioeconomic groups in general. They were expensive; they were wasteful; they were uncertain. Toward the end of the nineteenth century, therefore, business and professional men sought more direct control over municipal government in order to exercise political influence more effectively. They realized their goals in the early twentieth century in the new commission and city-manager forms of government and in the shift from ward to citywide representation.

These innovations did not always accomplish the objectives that the business community desired because other forces could and often did adjust to the change in governmental structure and reestablish their influence. But businessmen hoped that reform would enable them to increase their political power, and most frequently it did. In most cases the innovations which were introduced between 1901, when Galveston adopted a commission form of government, and the Great Depression, and especially the city-manager form which reached a height of popularity in the mid-1920s, served as vehicles whereby business and professional leaders moved directly into the inner circles of government, brought into one political system their own power and the formal machinery of government, and dominated municipal affairs for two decades.

Municipal reform in the early twentieth century involves a paradox: the ideology of an extension of political control and the practice of its concentration. While reformers maintained that their movement rested on a wave of popular demands, called their gatherings of business and professional leaders "mass meetings," described their reforms as "part of a worldwide trend toward popular government," and proclaimed an ideology of a popular upheaval against a selfish few, they were in practice shaping the structure of municipal government so that political power would no longer be broadly distributed, but would in fact be more centralized in the hands of a relatively small segment of the population. The paradox became even sharper when new city charters included provisions for the initiative, referendum, and recall. How does the historian cope with this paradox? Does it represent deliberate deception or simply political strategy? Or does it reflect a phenomenon which should be understood rather than explained away?

The expansion of popular involvement in decision-making was frequently a political tactic, not a political system to be established permanently, but a device to secure immediate political victory. The prohibitionist advocacy of the referendum, one of the most extensive sources of support for such a measure, came from the belief that the referendum would provide the opportunity to outlaw liquor more rapidly. The Anti-Saloon League, therefore, urged local option. But the League was not consistent. Towns which were wet, when faced with a countrywide local-option decision to outlaw liquor, demanded town or township local option to reinstate it. The League objected to this as not the proper application of the referendum idea.

Again, "Progressive" reformers often espoused the direct primary when fighting for nominations for their candidates within the party, but once in control they often became cool to it because it might result in their own defeat. By the same token, many municipal reformers attached the initiative, referendum, and recall to municipal charters often as a device to appease voters who opposed the centralization of representation and executive authority. But, by requiring a high percentage of voters to sign petitions—often 25 to 30 percent—these innovations could be (and were) rendered relatively harmless.

More fundamentally, however, the distinction between ideology and practice in municipal reform arose from the different roles which each played. The ideology of democratization of decision-making was negative rather than positive; it served as an instrument of attack against the existing political system rather than as a guide to alternative action. Those who wished to destroy the "machine" and to eliminate party competition in local government widely utilized the theory that these political instruments thwarted public impulses, and thereby shaped the tone of their attack.

But there is little evidence that the ideology represented a faith in a purely democratic system of decision-making or that reformers actually wished, in practice, to substitute direct democracy as a continuing system of sustained decision-making in place of the old. It was used to destroy the political institutions of the lower and middle classes and the political power which those institutions gave rise to, rather than to provide a clear-cut guide for alternative action.

The guide to alternative action lay in the model of the business enterprise. In describing new conditions which they wished to create, reformers drew on the analogy of the "efficient business enterprise," criticizing current practices with the argument that "no business could conduct its affairs that way and remain in business," and calling upon business practices as the guides to improvement. As one student remarked:

*The folklore of the business elite came by gradual transition to be
the symbols of governmental reformers. Efficiency, system, orderli-
ness, budgets, economy, saving, were all injected into the efforts of
reformers who sought to remodel municipal government in terms of
the great impersonality of corporate enterprise.*

Clinton Rodgers Woodruff of the National Municipal League explained
that the commission form was "a simple, direct, businesslike way of
administering the business affairs of the city . . . an application to city
administration of that type of business organization which has been
so common and so successful in the field of commerce and industry."
The centralization of decision-making which developed in the business corporation was now applied in municipal reform.

The model of the efficient business enterprise, then, rather than
the New England town meeting, provided the positive inspiration for
the municipal reformer. In giving concrete shape to this model in the
strong-mayor, commission, and city-manager plans, reformers engaged
in the elaboration of the processes of rationalization and systematization inherent in modern science and technology. For in many areas
of society, industrialization brought a gradual shift upward in the location of decision-making and the geographical extension of the scope
of the area affected by decisions.

Experts in business, in government, and in the professions measured, studied, analyzed, and manipulated ever wider realms of human
life, and devices which they used to control such affairs constituted
the most fundamental and far-reaching innovations in decision-
making in modern America, whether in formal government or in the
informal exercise of power in private life. Reformers in the Progressive
Era played a major role in shaping this new system. While they expressed an ideology of restoring a previous order, they in fact helped
to bring forth a system drastically new.

The drama of reform lay in the competition for supremacy between two systems of decision-making. One system, based upon ward
representation and growing out of the practices and ideas of representative government, involved wide latitude for the expression of
grass-roots impulses and their involvement in the political process. The
other grew out of the rationalization of life which came with science
and technology, in which decisions arose from expert analysis and
flowed from fewer and smaller centers outward to the rest of society.
Those who espoused the former looked with fear upon the loss of influence which the latter involved, and those who espoused the latter
looked only with disdain upon the wastefulness and inefficiency of the
former.

The Progressive Era witnessed rapid strides toward a more centralized system and a relative decline for a more decentralized system. This development constituted an accommodation of forces outside the business community to the political trends within business and professional life rather than vice versa. It involved a tendency for the decision-making processes inherent in science and technology to prevail over those inherent in representative government.

Reformers in the Progressive Era and liberal historians since then misread the nature of the movement to change municipal government because they concentrated upon dramatic and sensational episodes and ignored the analysis of more fundamental political structure, of the persistent relationships of influence and power which grew out of the community's social, ideological, economic, and cultural activities. The reconstruction of these patterns of human relationships and of the changes in them is the historian's most crucial task, for they constitute the central context of historical development. History consists not of erratic and spasmodic fluctuations, of a series of random thoughts and actions, but of patterns of activity and change in which people hold thoughts and actions in common and in which there are close connections between sequences of events. These contexts give rise to a structure of human relationships which pervade all areas of life; for the political historian the most important of these is the structure of the distribution of power and influence.

The structure of political relationships, however, cannot be adequately understood if we concentrate on evidence concerning ideology rather than practice. For it is becoming increasingly clear that ideological evidence is no safe guide to the understanding of practice, that what people thought and said about their society is not necessarily an accurate representation of what they did. The current task of the historian of the Progressive Era is to stop taking the reformers' own description of political practice at its face value and to utilize a wide variety of new types of evidence to reconstruct political practice in its own terms. This is not to argue that ideology is either important or unimportant. It is merely to state that ideological evidence is not appropriate to the discovery of the nature of political practice.

Only by maintaining this clear distinction can the historian successfully investigate the structure of political life in the Progressive Era. And only then can he begin to cope with the most fundamental problem of all: the relationship between political ideology and political practice. For each of these facets of political life must be understood in its own terms, through its own historical record. Each involves a distinct set of historical phenomena. The relationship between them for the Progressive Era is not now clear; it has not been investigated.

But it cannot be explored until the conceptual distinction is made clear and evidence tapped which is pertinent to each. Because the nature of political practice has so long been distorted by the use of ideological evidence, the most pressing task is its investigation through new types of evidence appropriate to it. The reconstruction of the movement for municipal reform can constitute a major step toward that goal.

Richard L. McCormick

RICHARD L. McCORMICK (1947–   ) is professor of history at Rutgers University. He has written about American politics in the nineteenth and twentieth centuries, and his books include *From Realignment to Reform: Political Change in New York State, 1893–1910* (1981) and *The Party Period and Public Policy: American Politics from the Age of Jackson to the Progressive Era* (1986).

Shortly after 1900, American politics and government experienced a decisive and rather rapid transformation that affected both the patterns of popular political involvement and the nature and functions of government itself. To be sure, the changes were not revolutionary, but, considering how relatively undevelopmental the political system of the United States has been, they are of considerable historical importance. The basic features of this political transformation can be easily described, but its causes and significance are somewhat more difficult to grasp.

One important category of change involved the manner and methods of popular participation in politics. For most of the nineteenth century, high rates of partisan voting—based on complex sectional, cultural, and communal influences—formed the American people's main means of political expression and involvement. Only in exceptional circumstances did most individuals or groups rely on nonelectoral methods of influencing the government. Indeed, almost no such means existed within the normal bounds of politics. After 1900, this structure of political participation changed. Voter turnout fell, and even among those electors who remained active, pure and simple partisanship became less pervasive. At approximately the same time, interest-group organizations of all sorts successfully forged permanent, nonelectoral means of influencing the government and its agencies. Only recently have historians begun to explore with care what caused these changes in the patterns of political participation and to delineate the redistribution of power that they entailed.

American governance, too, went through a fundamental transition

Richard L. McCormick, "The Discovery that Business Corrupts Politics: A Reappraisal of the Origins of Progressivism," *American Historical Review* 86 (April 1981):247–274. Reprinted with the permission of Richard L. McCormick.

in the early 1900s. Wiebe has accurately described it as the emergence of "a government broadly and continuously involved in society's operations." Both the institutions of government and the content of policy reflected the change. Where the legislature had been the dominant branch of government at every level, lawmakers now saw their power curtailed by an enlarged executive and, even more, by the creation of an essentially new branch of government composed of administrative boards and agencies. Where nineteenth-century policy had generally focused on distinct groups and locales (most characteristically through the distribution of resources and privileges to enterprising individuals and corporations), the government now began to take explicit account of clashing interests and to assume the responsibility for mitigating their conflicts through regulation, administration, and planning. In 1900, government did very little in the way of recognizing and adjusting group differences. Fifteen years later, innumerable policies committed officials to that formal purpose and provided the bureaucratic structures for achieving it.

Most political historians consider these changes to be the products of long-term social and economic developments. Accordingly, they have devoted much of their attention to tracing the interconnecting paths leading from industrialization, urbanization, and immigration to the political and governmental responses. Some of the general trends have been firmly documented in scholarship: the organization of functional groups whose needs the established political parties could not meet; the creation of new demands for government policies to make life bearable in crowded cities, where huge industries were located; and the determination of certain cultural and economic groups to curtail the political power of people they considered threatening. All of these developments, along with others, occurred over a period of decades— now speeded, now slowed by depression, migration, prosperity, fortune, and the talents of individual men and women.

Yet, given the long-term forces involved, it is notable how suddenly the main elements of the new political order went into place. The first fifteen years of the twentieth century witnessed most of the changes; more precisely, the brief period from 1904 to 1908 saw a remarkably compressed political transformation. During these years the regulatory revolution peaked; new and powerful agencies of government came into being everywhere. At the same time, voter turnout declined, ticket-splitting increased, and organized social, economic, and reform-minded groups began to exercise power more systematically than ever before. An understanding of how the new polity crystalized so rapidly can be obtained by exploring, first, the latent threat to the old system represented by fears of "corruption"; then, the pressures for political change that had built up by about 1904; and, finally, the way in which the old fears abruptly took on new meaning and inspired a resolution of the crisis. . . .

The evidence concerning these disclosures is familiar to students of progressivism, but its meaning has not been fully explored. The period 1904–08 comprised the muckraking years, not only in national magazines but also in local newspapers and legislative halls across the country. During 1905 and 1906 in particular, a remarkable number of cities and states experienced wrenching moments of discovery that led directly to significant political changes. Usually, a scandal, an investigation, an intraparty battle, or a particularly divisive election campaign exposed an illicit alliance of politics and business and made corruption apparent to the community, affecting party rhetoric, popular expectations, electoral behavior, and government policies.

Just before it exploded in city and state affairs, business corruption of politics had already emerged as a leading theme of the new magazine journalism created by the muckrakers. Their primary contribution was to give a national audience the first systematic accounts of how modern American society operated. In so doing, journalists like Steffens, Baker, Russell, and Phillips created insights and pioneered ways of describing social and political relationships that crucially affected how people saw things in their home towns and states. Since so many of the muckrakers' articles identified the widespread tendency for privilege-seeking businessmen to bribe legislators, conspire with party leaders, and control nominations, an awareness of such corruption soon entered local politics. Indeed, many of the muckraking articles concerned particular locales—including Steffens's early series on the cities (1902–03); his subsequent exposures of Missouri, Illinois, Wisconsin, Rhode Island, New Jersey, and Ohio (1904–05); Rudolph Blankenburg's articles on Pennsylvania (1905); and C. P. Connolly's treatment of Montana (1906). All of these accounts featured descriptions of politico-business corruption, as did many of the contemporaneous exposures of individual industries, such as oil, railroads, and meat-packing. Almost immediately after this literature began to flourish, citizens across the country discovered local examples of the same corrupt behavior that Steffens and the others had described elsewhere.

In New York, the occasion was the 1905 legislative investigation of the life insurance industry. One by one, insurance executives and Republican politicians took the witness stand and were compelled to bare the details of their corrupt relations. The companies received legislative protection, and the Republicans got bribes and campaign funds. In California, the graft trials of San Francisco city officials, beginning in 1906, threw light on the illicit cooperation between businessmen and public officials. Boss Abraham Ruef had delivered special privileges to public utility corporations in return for fees, of which he kept some and used the rest to bribe members of the city's Board of Supervisors. San Francisco's awakening revitalized reform elsewhere in California, and the next year insurgent Republicans formally organized to combat their party's alliance with the Southern Pacific Railroad. In Vermont, the railroad commissioners charged the 1906 legislature with yielding "supinely to the unfortunate influence of railroad representatives." Then the legislature investigated and found that the commissioners themselves were corrupt!

Other states, in all parts of the country, experienced their own versions of these events during 1905 and 1906. In South Dakota, as in a number of Midwestern states, hostility to railroad influence in politics—by means of free passes and a statewide network of paid henchmen—was the issue around which insurgent Republicans coalesced against the regular machine. Some of those who joined the opposition did so purely from expediency; but their charges of corruption excited the popular imagination, and they captured the state in 1906 with pledges of electoral reform and business regulation. Farther west Denver's major utilities, including the Denver Tramway Company and the Denver Gas and Electric Company, applied for new franchises in 1906, and these applications went before the voters at the spring elections. When the franchises all narrowly carried, opponents of the companies produced evidence that the Democratic and Republican Parties had obtained fraudulent votes for the utilities. The case made its way through the courts during the next several months, and, although they ultimately lost, Colorado's nascent progressives derived an immense boost from the well-publicized judicial battle. As a result, the focus of reform shifted to the state. Dissidents in the Republican Party organized to demand direct primary nominations and a judiciary untainted by corporate influence. These questions dominated Colorado's three-way gubernatorial election that fall.

To the south, in Alabama, Georgia, and Mississippi, similar accusations of politico-business corruption were heard that same year, only in a different regional accent. In Alabama, Braxton Bragg Comer rode the issue from his position on the state's railroad commission to the governorship. His "main theme," according to Sheldon Hackney, "was that the railroads had for years deprived the people of Alabama of their right to rule their own state and that the time had come to free the people from alien and arbitrary rule." Mississippi voters heard similar rhetoric from Governor James K. Vardaman in his unsuccessful campaign against John Sharp Williams for a seat in the U.S. Senate. Georgia's Tom Watson conjured up some inane but effective imagery to illustrate how Vardaman's opponent would serve the business interests: "If the Hon. John Sharp Williams should win out in the fight

with Governor Vardaman, the corporations would have just one more doodle-bug in the United States Senate. Every time that a Railroad lobbyist stopped over the hole and called 'Doodle, Doodle, Doodle'—soft and slow—the sand at the little end of the funnel would be seen to stir, and then the little head of J. Sharp would pop up." In Watson's own state, Hoke Smith trumpeted the issue, too, in 1905 and 1906.
. . .

State party platforms provide further evidence of the awakening to politico-business corruption. In Iowa, to take a Midwestern state, charges of corporation influence in politics were almost entirely confined to the minor parties during the years from 1900 to 1904. Prohibitionists believed that the liquor industry brought political corruption, while socialists felt that the powers of government belonged to the capitalists. For their part, the Democrats and Republicans saw little of this—until 1906, when both major parties gushed in opposition to what the Republicans now called "the domination of corporate influences in public affairs." The Democrats agreed: "We favor the complete elimination of railway and other public service corporations from the politics of the state." In Missouri, a different but parallel pattern emerges from the platforms. There, what had been a subordinate theme of the Democratic Party (and minor parties) in 1900 and 1902 became of central importance to both parties in 1904 and 1906. The Democrats now called "the eradication of bribery" the "paramount issue" in the state and declared opposition to campaign contributions "by great corporations and by those interested in special industries enjoying special privileges under the law." In New Hampshire, where nothing had been said of politico-business corruption in 1900 and 1904, both major parties wrote platforms in 1906 that attacked the issuance of free transportation passes and the prevalence of corrupt legislative lobbies. Party platforms in other states also suggest how suddenly major-party politicians discovered that business corrupted politics.

The annual messages of the state governors from 1902 to 1908 point to the same pattern. In the first three years, the chief executives almost never mentioned the influence of business in politics. Albert Cummins of Iowa was exceptional; as early as 1902 he declared, "Corporations have, and ought to have, many privileges, but among them is not the privilege to sit in political conventions or occupy seats in legislative chambers." Then in 1905, governors across the Midwest suddenly let loose denunciations of corporate bribery, lobbying, campaign contributions, and free passes. Nebraska's John H. Mickey was typical in attacking "the onslaught of private and corporation lobbyists who seek to accomplish pernicious ends by the exercise of undue influence." Missouri's Joseph W. Folk advised that "all franchises, rights and privileges secured by bribery should be declared null and void." By

1906, 1907, and 1908, such observations and recommendations were common to the governors of every region. In 1907 alone, no less than nineteen state executives called for the regulation of lobbying, while a similar number advised the abolition of free passes.

What is the meaning of this awakening to something that Americans had, in a sense, known all along? Should we accept the originality of the "discovery" that monied interests endangered free government or lay stress instead on the familiar elements the charge contained? It had, after all, been a part of American political thought since the eighteenth century and had been powerfully repeated, in one form or another, by major and minor figures throughout the nineteenth century. According to Richard Hofstadter, "there was nothing new in the awareness of these things." In fact, however, there was much that was new. First, many of the details of politico-business corruption had never been publicly revealed before. No one had ever probed the subject as thoroughly as journalists and legislative investigators were now doing, and, moreover, some of the practices they uncovered had only recently come into being. Large-scale corporation campaign contributions, for instance, were a product of the 1880s and 1890s. Highly organized legislative lobbying operations by competing interest groups represented an even more recent development. In his systematic study of American legislative practices, published in 1907, Paul S. Reinsch devoted a lengthy chapter to describing how business interests had developed a new and "far more efficient system of dealing with legislatures than [the old methods of] haphazard corruption."

Even more startling than the new practices themselves was the fresh meaning they acquired from the nationwide character of the patterns that were now disclosed. The point is not simply that more people than ever before became aware of politico-business corruption but that the perception of such a national pattern itself created new political understandings. Lincoln Steffens's autobiography is brilliant on this point. As Steffens acknowledged, much of the corruption he observed in his series on the "shame" of the cities had already come to light locally before he reported it to a national audience. What he did was take the facts in city after city, apply imagination to their transcription, and form a new truth by showing the same process at work everywhere. Here was a solution to the problem the Adams brothers had encountered in writing *Chapters of Erie:* how to report shocking corruption without making it seem too astounding to be representative. The solution was breadth of coverage. Instead of looking at only two businessmen, study dozens; explore city after city and state after state and report the facts to a people who were vaguely aware of corruption in their own home towns but had never before seen that a single process was at work across the country. This concept of a "process" of corruption was central to the new understanding. Uncovered through systematic journalistic research and probing legislative investigations, corruption was now seen to be the result of concrete historical developments. It could not just be dismissed as the product of misbehavior by "bad" men (although that kind of rhetoric continued too) but had to be regarded as an outcome of identifiable economic and political forces. In particular, corruption resulted from an outmoded policy of indiscriminate distribution, which could not safely withstand an onslaught of demands from private corporations that were larger than the government itself.

Thus in its systematic character, as well as in its particular details, the corruption that Americans discovered in 1905 and 1906 was different from the kind their eighteenth- and nineteenth-century forebears had known. Compared to the eighteenth-century republican understanding, the progressive concept of corruption regarded the monied interests not as tools of a designing administration but as independent agents. If any branch of government was in alliance with them, it was probably the legislature. In a curious way, however, the old republican view that commerce inherently threatened the people's virtue still persisted, now informed by a new understanding of the actual process at work. Compared to Andrew Jackson, the progressives saw big corporations not as monsters but as products of social and industrial development. And their activist remedies differed entirely from his negativistic ones. But, like Jackson, those who now discovered corruption grasped that private interests could conflict with the public interest and that government benefits for some groups often hurt others. The recognition of these two things—both painfully at odds with the nineteenth century's conventional wisdom—had been at the root of the floundering over principles of political economy in the 1890s and early 1900s. Now, rather suddenly, the discovery that business corrupts politics suggested concrete answers to a people who were ready for new policies but had been uncertain how to get them or what exactly they should be.

Enacted in a burst of legislative activity immediately following the awakening of 1905 and 1906, the new policies brought to an end the paralysis that had gripped the polity and constituted a decisive break with nineteenth-century patterns of governance. Many states passed laws explicitly designed to curtail illicit business influence in politics. These included measures regulating legislative lobbying, prohibiting corporate campaign contributions, and outlawing the acceptance of free transportation passes by public officials. In 1903 and 1904, there had been almost no legislation on these three subjects; during 1905 and 1906, several states acted on each question; and, by 1907 and 1908, ten states passed lobbying laws, nineteen took steps to prevent corporate contributions, and fourteen acted on the question of passes (see Table 1). If these laws failed to wipe out corporation influence in politics, they at least curtailed important means through which businesses had exercised political power in the late nineteenth and early twentieth centuries. To be sure, other means were soon found, but the flood of state lawmaking on these subjects, together with the corresponding attention they received from the federal government in these same years, shows how prevalent was the determination to abolish existing forms of politico-business corruption.

Closely associated with these three measures were two more important categories of legislation, often considered to represent the essence of progressivism in the states: mandatory direct primary laws and measures establishing or strengthening the regulation of utility and transportation corporations by commission. These types of legislation, too, reached a peak in the years just after 1905–06, when so many states had experienced a crisis disclosing the extent of politico-business corruption. Like the laws concerning lobbying, contributions, and passes, primary and regulatory measures were brought forth amidst intense public concern with business influence in politics and were presented by their advocates as remedies for that problem. Both types of laws had been talked about for years, but the disclosures of 1905–06 provided the catalyst for their enactment.

TABLE 1

Selected Categories of State Legislation, 1903–08

Type of Legislation	1903–04	1905–06	1907–08	1903–08
Regulation of Lobbying	0	2	10	12
Prohibition of Corporate Campaign Contributions	0	3	19	22
Regulation or Prohibition of Free Railroad Passes for Public Officials	4	6	14	24
Mandatory Direct Primary	4	9	18	31
Regulation of Railroad Corporations by Commission	5	8	28	41
Totals	13	28	89	130

Note: Figures represent the number of states that passed legislation in the given category during the specified years.

Even before 1905, the direct primary had already been adopted in some states. In Wisconsin, where it was approved in 1904, Robert M. La Follette had campaigned for direct nominations since the late 1890s on the grounds that they would "emancipate the legislature from all subserviency to the corporations." In his well-known speech, "The Menace of the Machine" (1897), La Follette explicitly offered the direct primary as "the remedy" for corporate control of politics. Now, after the awakening of 1905–06, that same argument inspired many states that had failed to act before to adopt mandatory direct primary laws (see Table 1). In New York, Charles Evans Hughes, who was elected governor in 1906 because of his role as chief counsel in the previous year's life insurance investigation, argued that the direct primary would curtail the power of the special interests. "Those interests," he declared, "are ever at work stealthily and persistently endeavoring to pervert the government to the service of their own ends. All that is worst in our public life finds its readiest means of access to power through the control of the nominating machinery of parties." In other states, too, in the years after 1905–06, the direct primary was urged and approved for the same reasons that La Follette and Hughes advanced it.

The creation of effective regulatory boards—progressivism's most distinctive governmental achievement—also followed upon the discovery of politico-business corruption. From 1905 to 1907 alone, fifteen new state railroad commissions were established, and at least as many existing boards were strengthened. Most of the new commissions were "strong" ones, having rate-setting powers and a wide range of administrative authority to supervise service, safety, and finance. In the years to come, many of them extended their jurisdiction to other public utilities, including gas, electricity, telephones, and telegraphs. Direct legislative supervision of business corporations was also significantly expanded in these years. Life insurance companies—whose corruption of the New York State government Hughes had dramatically disclosed—provide one example. "In 1907," as a result of Hughes's investigation and several others conducted in imitation of it, Morton Keller has reported, "forty-two state legislatures met; thirty considered life insurance legislation; twenty-nine passed laws. . . . By 1908 . . . [the basic] lines of twentieth century life insurance supervision were set, and thereafter only minor adjustments occurred." The federal regulatory machinery, too, was greatly strengthened at this time, most notably by the railroad, meat inspection, and food and drug acts of 1906.

The adoption of these measures marked the moment of transition from a structure of economic policy based largely on the allocation of resources and benefits to one in which regulation and administration played permanent and significant roles. Not confined for long to the transportation, utility, and insurance companies that formed its most immediate objects, regulatory policies soon were extended to other industries as well. Sometimes the legislative branch took responsibility for the ongoing tasks of supervision and administration, but more commonly they became the duty of independent boards and commissioners, staffed by experts and entrusted with significant powers of oversight and enforcement. Certainly, regulation was not previously unknown, nor did promoting commerce and industry now cease to be a governmental purpose. But the middle years of the first decade of the twentieth century unmistakably mark a turning point—that point when the direction shifted, when the weight of opinion changed, when the forces of localism and opposition to governmental authority that had sustained the distribution of privileges but opposed regulation and administration now lost the upper hand to the forces of centralization, bureaucratization, and government actions to recognize and adjust group differences. Besides economic regulation, other governmental policy areas, including health, education, taxation, correction, and the control of natural resources, increasingly came under the jurisdiction of independent boards and commissions. The establishment of these agencies and the expansion of their duties meant that American governance in the twentieth century was significantly different from what it had been in the nineteenth.

The developments of 1905–08 also changed the nature of political participation in the United States. Parties emerged from the years of turmoil altered and, on balance, less important vehicles of popular expression than they had been. The disclosures of politico-business wrongdoing disgraced the regular party organizations, and many voters showed their loss of faith by staying at home on election day or by casting split tickets. These trends had been in progress before 1905–06—encouraged by new election laws as well as by the crisis of confidence in traditional politics and government—but in several ways the discovery of corruption strengthened them. Some reigning party organizations were toppled by the disclosures, and the insurgents who came to power lacked the old bosses' experience and inclination when it came to rallying the electorate. And the legal prohibition of corporate campaign contributions now meant, moreover, that less money was available for pre-election entertainment, transportation to the polls, and bribes.

While the party organizations were thus weakened, they were also more firmly embedded in the legal machinery of elections than ever before. In many states the direct primary completed a series of new election laws (beginning with the Australian ballot in the late 1880s and early 1890s) that gave the parties official status as nominating bodies, regulated their practices, and converted them into durable, official bureaucracies. Less popular now but also more respectable, the party organizations surrendered to state regulation and relinquished much of their ability to express community opinion in return for legal guarantees that they alone would be permanently certified to place nominees on the official ballot.

Interest organizations took over much of the parties' old job of articulating popular demands and pressing them upon the government. More exclusive and single-minded than parties, the new organizations became regular elements of the polity. Their right to represent their members before the government's new boards and agencies received implicit recognition, and, indeed, the commissions in some cases became captives of the groups that were supposed to regulate. The result was a fairly drastic transformation of the rules of political participation: who could compete, the kinds of resources required, and the rewards of participation all changed. These developments were not brand new in the first years of the twentieth century, but, like the contemporaneous changes in government policy, they derived impressive, decisive confirmation from the political upheaval that occurred between 1905 and 1908.

Political and governmental changes thus followed upon the discovery that business corrupts politics. And Americans of the day explicitly linked the two developments: the reforms adopted in 1907–08 were to remedy the ills uncovered in 1905–06. But these chronological and rhetorical connections between discovery and reform do not fully explain the relationship between them. Why, having paid relatively little heed to similar charges before, did people now take such strong actions in response to the disclosures? Why, moreover, did the perception of wrongdoing precipitate the particular pattern of responses that it did—namely, the triumph of bureaucracy and organization? Of most importance, what distinctive effects did the discovery of corruption have upon the final outcome of the crisis?

By 1905 a political explosion of some sort was likely, due to the accumulated frustrations people felt about the government's failure to deal with the problems of industrialization. So combustible were the elements present that another spark besides the discovery of politico-business corruption might well have ignited them. But the recognition of such corruption was an especially effective torch. Upon close analysis, its ignition of the volatile political mass is unsurprising. The accusations made in 1905–06 were serious, widespread, and full of damaging information; they explained the actual corrupt process behind a danger that Americans had historically worried about, if not always responded to with vigor; they linked in dark scandal the two main villains—party bosses and big businessmen—already on the American scene; they inherently discredited the existing structure of economic policy based on the distribution of privileges; and they dramatically suggested the necessity for new kinds of politics and government. That businessmen systematically corrupted politics was incendiary knowledge; given the circumstances of 1905, it could hardly have failed to set off an explosion.

The organizational results that followed, however, seem less inevitable. There were, after all, several other known ways of curtailing corruption besides expert regulation and administration. For one, there was the continued reliance on direct legislative action against the corruption of politics by businessmen. The lobbying, anti–free pass, and campaign-contribution measures of 1907–08 exemplified this approach. So did the extension of legislative controls over the offending corporations. Such measures were familiar, but obviously they were considered inadequate to the crisis at hand. A second approach, favored by Edward Alsworth Ross and later by Woodrow Wilson, was to hold business leaders personally responsible for their "sins" and to punish them accordingly. There were a few attempts to bring individuals to justice, but, because of the inadequacy of the criminal statutes, the skill of high-priced lawyers, and the public's lack of appetite for personal vendettas, few sinners were jailed. Finally, there were proposals for large structural solutions changing the political and economic environment so that the old corrupt practices became impossible. Some men, like Frederic C. Howe, still advocated the single tax and the abolition of all privileges granted by government. Many more believed in the municipal ownership of public utilities. Hundreds of thousands (to judge from election returns) favored socialist solutions, but most Americans did not. In their response to politico-business corruption, they went beyond existing legislative remedies and avoided the temptation to personalize all the blame, but they fell short of wanting socialism, short even of accepting the single tax.

Regulation and administration represented a fourth available approach. Well before the discoveries of 1905–06, groups who stood to benefit from governmental control of utility and transportation corporations had placed strong regulatory proposals on the political agendas of the states and the nation. In other policy areas, the proponents of an administrative approach had not advanced that far prior to 1905–06, but theirs was a large and growing movement, supported—as recent historians have shown—by many different groups for varied, often contradictory, reasons. The popular awakening to corruption increased the opportunity of these groups to obtain enactment of their measures. Where their proposals met the particular political needs of 1905–08, they succeeded most quickly. Regulation by commissions seemed to be an effective way to halt corruption by transferring the responsibility for business-government relations from party bosses and legislators to impartial experts. That approach also possessed the additional political advantages of appearing sane and moderate, of meeting consumer demands for government protection, and, above all, of being sufficiently malleable that a diversity of groups could be induced to anticipate favorable results from the new policies.

In consequence, the passions of 1905–06 added support to an existing movement toward regulation and administration, enormously speeded it up, shaped the timing and form of its victory, and probably made the organizational revolution more complete—certainly more sudden—than it otherwise would have been. These accomplishments alone must make the discovery of corruption pivotal in any adequate interpretation of progressivism. But the awakening did more than hurry along a movement that already possessed formidable political strength and would probably have triumphed eventually even without the events of 1905–06. By pushing the political process toward so quick a resolution of the long-standing crisis over industrialism, the passions of those years caused the outcome to be more conservative than it otherwise might have been. This is the ultimate irony of the discovery that business corrupts politics.

Muckraking accounts of politico-business evils suggest one reason for the discovery's conservative impact. Full of facts and revelations, these writings were also dangerously devoid of effective solutions. Charles E. Russell's *Lawless Wealth* (1908)—the title itself epitomizes the perceptions of 1905–06—illustrates the flaw. Published originally in *Everybody's Magazine* under the accusatory title, "Where Did You Get It, Gentlemen?," the book recounts numerous instances of riches obtained through the corruption of politics but, in its closing pages, merely suggests that citizens recognize the evils and be determined to stop them. This reliance on trying to change how people felt (to "shame" them, in Steffens's phrase) was characteristic of muckraking and of the exposures of 1905–06. One can admire the muckrakers' reporting, can even accept David P. Thelen's judgment that their writing "contained at least as deep a moral revulsion toward capitalism and profit as did more orthodox forms of Marxism," yet can still feel that their proposed remedy was superficial. Because the perception of politico-business corruption carried no far-reaching solutions of its own or genuine economic grievances, but only a desire to clean up politics and government, the passions of 1905–06 were easily diverted to the support of other people's remedies, especially administrative answers. Had the muckrakers and their local imitators penetrated more deeply into the way that business operated and its real relationship to government, popular emotions might not have been so readily mobilized in support of regulatory and administrative agencies that business interests could often dominate. At the very least, there might have been

a more determined effort to prevent the supervised corporations themselves from shaping the details of regulatory legislation. Thus, for all
of their radical implications, the passions of 1905–06 dulled the capacity of ordinary people to get reforms in their own interest.

The circumstances in which the discovery of corruption became a
political force also assist in explaining its conservatism. The passions
of 1905–06 were primarily expressed in state, rather than local or national, politics. Indeed, those passions often served to shift the focus
of reform from the cities to the state capitals. There—in Albany, or
Madison, or Sacramento—the remedies were worked out in relative
isolation from the local, insurgent forces that had in many cases originally called attention to the evils. Usually the policy consequences
were more favorable to large business interests than local solutions
would have been. State utility boards, for example, which had always
been considered more conservative in their policies than comparable
local commissions, now took the regulatory power away from cities
and foreclosed experimentation with such alternatives as municipal
ownership or popularly chosen regulatory boards. In gaining a statewide hearing for reform, the accusations of politico-business corruption actually increased the likelihood that conservative solutions
would be adopted.

Considering the intensity of the feelings aroused in 1905 and 1906
("the wrath of thousands of private citizens . . . is at white heat over
the disclosures," declared a Rochester newspaper) and the catalytic political role they played, the awakened opposition to corruption was
surprisingly short-lived. As early as 1907 and 1908, the years of the
most significant state legislative responses to the discovery, the messages of the governors began to exhibit a more stylized, less passionate
way of describing politico-business wrongdoing. Now the governors
emphasized remedies rather than abuses, and most seemed confident
that the remedies would work. Criticism of business influence in government continued to be a staple of political rhetoric throughout the
Progressive era, but it ceased to have the intensity it did in 1905–06.
In place of the burning attack on corruption, politicians offered advanced progressive programs, including further regulation and elec-
tion-law reforms. The deep concern with business corruption of politics and government thus waned. It has stirred people to consciousness
of wrongdoing, crystalized their discontent with existing policies, and
pointed toward concrete solutions for the ills of industrialism. But it
had not sustained the more radical, antibusiness possibilities suggested by the discoveries of 1905–06.

Indeed, the passions of those years probably weakened the insurgent, democratic qualities of the ensuing political transformation and
strengthened its bureaucratic aspects. This result was ironical, but its

causes were not conspiratorial. They lay instead in the tendency—shared by the muckrakers and their audience—to accept remedies unequal to the problems at hand and in political circumstances that isolated insurgents from decision-making. Once the changes in policy were under way after 1906, those organized groups whose interests were most directly affected entered the fray, jockeyed for position, and heavily shaped the outcomes. We do not yet know enough about how this happened, but studies such as Stanley P. Caine's examination of railroad regulation in Wisconsin suggest how difficult it was to translate popular concern on an "issue" into the details of a law. It is hardly surprising that, as regulation and administration became accepted public functions, the affected interests exerted much more influence on policy than did those who cared most passionately about restoring clean government.

But the failure to pursue antibusiness policies does not mean the outcry against corruption was either insincere or irrelevant. Quite the contrary. It was sufficiently genuine and widespread to dominate the nation's public life in 1905 and 1906 and to play a decisive part in bringing about the transformation of American politics and government. Political changes do not, of course, embrace everything that is meant by progressivism. Nor was the discovery that business corrupts politics the only catalytic agent at work; certainly the rise of consumer discontent with utility and transportation corporations and the vigorous impetus toward new policies given by Theodore Roosevelt during his second term as president played complementary roles. But the awakening to corruption—as it was newly understood—provided an essential dynamic, pushing the states and the nation toward what many of its leading men and women considered progressive reform.

The organizational thesis sheds much light on the values and methods of those who succeeded in dominating the new types of politics and government but very little on the political circumstances in which they came forward. Robert H. Wiebe, in particular, has downplayed key aspects of the political context, including the outcry against corruption. Local uprisings against the alliance of bosses and businessmen, Wiebe has stated, "lay outside the mainstream of progressivism"; measures instituting the direct primary and curtailing the political influence of business were "old-fashioned reform." Yet those local crusades, by spreading the dynamic perception that business corrupts politics, created a popular demand for the regulatory and administrative measures that Wiebe has claimed are characteristic of true progressivism; and those "old-fashioned" laws were enacted amidst the same political furor that produced the stunningly rapid bureaucratic triumph whose significance for twentieth-century America Wiebe has explained so convincingly. What the organizational thesis mainly lacks is the sense that political action is open-ended and unpredictable. Consequences are often unexpected, outcomes surprising when matched against origins. While it is misleading, as Samuel P. Hays has said, to interpret progressivism solely on the basis of its antibusiness ideology, it is equally misleading to fail to appreciate that reform gained decisive initial strength from ideas and feelings that were not able to sustain the movement in the end. The farsighted organizers from business and the professions thus gained the opportunity to complete a political transformation that had been begun by people who were momentarily shocked into action but who stopped far short of pursuing the full implications of their discovery.

☆ 7 ☆

The New Deal

REVOLUTIONARY OR
CONSERVATIVE?

Franklin Delano Roosevelt was perhaps the most controversial president ever to occupy the White House. For over twelve years he led the American people, first through the worst depression in their history and then through a war that encompassed virtually the entire globe. To his admirers he was an individual of heroic stature, a leader who firmly believed that it was possible to preserve free and democratic institutions by internal reforms without adopting authoritarian or totalitarian methods and overturning the basic structure of American society. To his enemies he was a misguided, even immoral, individual who mistakenly believed that he could save American democracy by taking the people down the road to the welfare state—a road that would eventually end in socialism and therefore the negation of individual freedom. Unlike some other presidents Roosevelt had the uncanny ability to arouse strong passions. He was a person who was either loved or hated; few remained neutral toward him or reacted blandly to his personality or accomplishments.

Why did Roosevelt arouse such strong passions? The answer to this ostensibly simple question is anything but simple. Certainly there was little in his background or his accomplishments prior to 1933 that would explain the controversial nature of his presidential tenure. Even those friends and associates who worked closely with Roosevelt during his dozen years in the White House were not always able to grasp his many-sided personality or understand why he acted as he did. Frances Perkins, his longtime secretary of labor, described him as "the most complicated human being I ever knew," a comment that was echoed by others such as Henry Morgenthau and Robert E. Sherwood.

The controversy that surrounded Roosevelt's years in the White House has almost been matched by the quantity and quality of books written about him by friends, associates, and enemies. Unlike other presidents whose careers were not chronicled until decades after their death, Roosevelt has already been the subject of literally hundreds of books and articles. Part of the reason for this situation undoubtedly lies in the fact that much of the source material left by Roosevelt[1] and his associates was opened up to scholars within a surprisingly short time after his death in 1945. But part of the reason surely lies in the fascination with the New Deal and the changes that American society underwent during the years from 1933 to 1945. However the Roosevelt years are interpreted it is difficult to avoid the conclusion that the United States was a very different nation in 1945 as compared with 1933.

It was the sheer magnitude of the New Deal innovations early in his presidential career that caused Roosevelt to become such a highly controversial figure. Although his victory in 1932 was relatively broad-based he soon alienated many businessmen as well as other powerful interest groups. As a result he came under increasingly harsh attacks as the 1930s progressed. Some accused him of subverting traditional American ideals of individualism and liberty by moving toward a welfare state that could end only in socialism and an omnipotent state. Such a staunch Democrat as Al Smith, for example, hotly argued during the presidential campaign of 1936 that Roosevelt was indeed taking the American people down the road to socialism. "It is all right with me if they [the Roosevelt administration] want to disguise themselves as Norman Thomas or Karl Marx, or Lenin, or any of the rest of that bunch," Smith shouted, "but what I won't stand for is allowing them to march under the banner of Jefferson, Jackson and Cleveland."[2]

The attack on Roosevelt's New Deal from the right was echoed also by the critics of the left. There were many who felt that the traditional American attachment to individualistic values had been rendered obsolete by the nation's industrial and technological advances. Rexford G. Tugwell, a professor of economics and one of the early New Deal "brain trusters," was one such critic. He was convinced that America's competitive economy had never worked well; to attempt to reform it with minor changes would prove hopelessly inadequate. What

---

[1] It has been estimated that Roosevelt's personal papers occupy more than 9,000 cubic feet at the Hyde Park Library; this figure does not include the papers of other important New Deal officials.

[2] Quoted in William E. Leuchtenburg, *Franklin D. Roosevelt and the New Deal 1932–1940* (New York, 1963), p. 178.

was required, Tugwell concluded, was thorough and effective governmental planning for all aspects of the economic system; only in this way could the economy be stabilized and future depressions avoided. Much to his disappointment the New Deal seemed too pragmatic. Roosevelt, he finally concluded, was either unwilling or unable to plan in a rational and systematic manner. To the left of men like Tugwell stood the socialist and Communist groups in America. Their criticism was that the New Deal was too conservative; the only proper approach to the depression was a complete overhaul of America's social and economic system and the establishment of a socialist state.

Thus during the depression years the New Deal was attacked from many points of view. To some it was too radical; to others it was too conservative or reactionary. Still others viewed Roosevelt's policies as a series of pragmatic and expedient moves in response to specific events and deplored the fact that the president never seemed to give much thought to the overall dimensions of the crisis facing the American people. To be sure, many of these critics were reflecting to a large extent the passions and emotions of the age in which they were living. Faced with the problem of coming to grips with the greatest depression the country had ever known, they did not have the perspective nor the dispassionate attitude required to view the issues at stake in a detached or objective manner. Their criticisms, nevertheless, helped to establish the framework of reference with which later writers were to approach the New Deal. In brief, the question usually raised by contemporary commentators and later historians revolved around the role of the New Deal in American life. Was the New Deal simply an extension of the Progressive tradition or did it involve a radical departure from the mainstream of American history?

For historians reared in the tradition of the Progressive school there was little doubt about the basic nature of the New Deal. Viewing America's past in terms of a conflict between liberalism and conservatism and the people versus the vested interests, they saw the New Deal as simply another phase in the struggle against monopoly, privilege, and special interests. To them the New Deal was related to earlier reform movements, including Jeffersonian and Jacksonian Democracy, populism, and progressivism, all of which had represented the people in their continuing struggle to achieve a greater measure of political, economic, and social equality. While they often referred to the revolutionary character of the New Deal, their use of the term "revolutionary" did not necessarily imply a sharp break with the past. Louis Hacker, although not squarely in the Progressive tradition, referred to the New Deal as the "Third American Revolution" in the mid-1940s. His description of the New Deal, however, was anything but revolutionary. Some of its policies, he wrote, were improvisations; some were descended from populism and progressivism; but always "there existed the thought that the responsibility of public authority for the welfare of the people was clear and that the intervention of the state was justifiable."[3] Hacker's last point, while by no means acceptable to all Americans, was hardly novel; reformers and intellectuals had been urging government-sponsored reforms since the mid-nineteenth century.

To Henry Steele Commager, one of America's most distinguished historians, the relationship between the New Deal and earlier reform movements was obvious. Writing at the time of Roosevelt's death Commager explicitly denied the revolutionary character of the New Deal. What was simply a new deal of old cards appeared radical for two reasons: the rapidity with which the New Deal program was enacted into law; and the fact that the movement contrasted so sharply with the do-nothing attitude of the Harding-Coolidge-Hoover administrations. If the New Deal was compared with the Progressive era rather than the 1920s, Commager maintained, "the contrast would have been less striking than the similarities. . . . [For] precedent for the major part of New Deal legislation was to be found in these earlier periods." The achievements of Roosevelt—the restoration of self-confidence, the reassertion of faith in democracy, and the rehabilitation of the nation's human and natural resources—all demonstrated the affinity of the New Deal to the earlier reform movements in American history.[4]

Perhaps the fullest and most eloquent argument favoring the idea that the New Deal was a continuation and extension of America's liberal past was advanced by the outstanding historian writing in the Progressive tradition, Arthur M. Schlesinger, Jr. A former professor at Harvard University, Schlesinger has been the most persuasive and brilliant historian writing within and in defense of America's liberal tradition. He was, of course, much more than a historian. A leading intellectual, important member of the Kennedy administration, and shrewd commentator on current affairs, Schlesinger has been an activist as well as a scholar. As a historian Schlesinger since the close of World War II has championed a modified brand of American liberalism whose roots, he believed, go far back into the nation's history. Thus his Pulitzer Prize-winning study, *The Age of Jackson* (1945), argued that Jacksonian Democracy was a liberal political movement based on a coalition of urban workers and other democratic groups in American society. Schlesinger attempted also to rebuild the intellectual foundations of

---

[3]Louis M. Hacker, *The Shaping of the American Tradition* (New York, 1947), pp. 1125–1126.

[4]Henry Steele Commager, "Twelve Years of Roosevelt," *American Mercury* 40 (April 1945):391–401.

the liberal ideology in his writings. In *The Vital Center* (1948) he incorporated Niebuhrian theology into the corpus of American liberalism so as to give the latter a more realistic and viable character. Taking cognizance of the reaction against liberal ideas since the 1940s, Schlesinger borrowed Reinhold Niebuhr's emphasis on original sin and reinterpreted the liberal ideology in order to purge that ideology of the charge that its utopian optimism had been unrealistic and its adherents had been incapable of meeting the challenge of totalitarianism since the 1930s.

All of American history, according to Schlesinger, was characterized by a cyclical movement which saw periods of liberal reform followed by alternate periods of conservative consolidation. In his eyes Jacksonian Democracy followed the decline of Jeffersonian Democracy, the Progressive era followed the age of the robber barons, and the New Deal came after the sterile conservatism of the 1920s. Indeed, Schlesinger argued, the New Frontier of John F. Kennedy and the Great Society of Lyndon B. Johnson were themselves reactions to the inaction of the Eisenhower years. The generative force behind this cycle was social conflict—conflict which arose from a constant accumulation of disquietude and discontent within American society. Schlesinger spelled out his thesis in a series of books and articles, one of which was *The Age of Roosevelt,* a multivolume study of the New Deal.[5]

In the first selection in this chapter, Schlesinger discusses the origins of the New Deal. To him the New Deal represented much more than a mere response to the depression. On the contrary, the New Deal was an integral part of the history of American liberalism; it was another phase of the liberal-conservative cycle in American history. By the 1920s, Schlesinger claimed, the nation had tired of the Progressive crusade. National disinterest in politics meant that power gravitated inevitably toward powerful economic interests, and government increasingly came under the control and influence of the business community. As a result of this shift in power there was a progressive alienation of various groups from American society, including the farmers, workers, minority ethnic groups, and disenchanted intellectuals. Even without a depression, Schlesinger suggested, the New Deal was bound to have happened in one form or another. What the depression did was to give the New Deal its particular character—a political movement responding to the immediate problem of an impending eco-

---

[5]Schlesinger has to date published three volumes of this study: *The Crisis of the Old Order, 1919–1933* (Boston, 1957), *The Coming of the New Deal* (Boston, 1958), and *The Politics of Upheaval* (Boston, 1960).

nomic collapse. The New Deal, he concluded, rejected the dogmatic absolutes and the simplistic dichotomies posed in contemporary ideologies such as communism and fascism. To Schlesinger the New Deal was a practical, energetic, and pragmatic movement based on the assumption that a "managed and modified capitalist order achieved by piecemeal experiment could combine personal freedom and economic growth."

Schlesinger's approach to the New Deal was echoed by other historians. Frank Freidel, author of what appears to be the most definitive multivolume biography of Roosevelt, wrote in much the same historiographical tradition as that of Schlesinger. Freidel, however, posed the discussion in quite different terms. To him the New Deal was basically the work of a number of persons who had grown to maturity during the Progressive era and who still shared the moral fervor of that period. Like Roosevelt they were conservative men whose primary goal was to save rather than to destroy the free enterprise system. These humanitarian reformers were willing to use the machinery and authority of government to improve the lot of the common man. Taken as a whole the New Deal was based on "American objectives and experience in the Progressive Era and during the first World War."[6] To put it another way Roosevelt's program was squarely within the American tradition; his goals were essentially to conserve the existing economic and social system by eliminating obvious defects rather than changing it by radical programs.

Historians such as Commager, Schlesinger, and Freidel were all favorably disposed to the New Deal because they identified themselves with the American liberal or Progressive tradition. This is not to imply that they were uncritical toward Roosevelt and the New Deal; in many instances they found much that was inadequate, wrong, or misleading about the goals, program, and administration of many New Deal experiments. Generally speaking, however, they wrote with approval of Roosevelt's pragmatism, his faith in American democracy, and his obvious distaste for totalitarian methods. The alternative to the New

---

[6]Frank Freidel, *The New Deal in Historical Perspective* (2 ed., Washington, D.C., 1965), p. 6. To date Freidel has published four volumes of his study of Roosevelt: *Franklin D. Roosevelt: The Apprenticeship* (Boston, 1952), *The Ordeal* (Boston, 1954), *The Triumph* (Boston, 1956), and *Launching the New Deal* (Boston, 1973).

In a recent study of Hoover, Roosevelt, the "Brain trust," and the origins of the New Deal, Elliot A. Rosen argued that Roosevelt's domestic and diplomatic objectives were shaped in 1932 by a small group of advisers who gave the domestic economy priority. "A better distribution of income, achievement of the social minima, and federal intervention where necessary for social and economic purposes became part of our permanent past. This has remained the legacy of Roosevelt and the Brains Trust." Elliot A. Rosen, *Hoover, Roosevelt, and the Brain Trust: From Depression to New Deal* (New York, 1977), p. 380.

Deal, they hinted, might very well have been a dictatorship of the right or left if the nation had continued to drift along as it had under Hoover.

While such historians who identified themselves in the Progressive tradition were interpreting the New Deal in a favorable light, others, particularly those adhering to a conservative ideology, were writing in quite a different vein. Conceiving of individual freedom and competition in almost absolutist terms, they saw the New Deal as a violent departure from traditional American values. To them the New Deal was anything but a continuation of America's political tradition; it represented rather an outright rejection of everything that was good and desirable within that tradition. During the decade of the thirties, many critics, especially spokesmen of conservative social groups and businessmen, took this position on the New Deal. Former President Hoover, for example, sounded a note of warning in 1934 when he condemned the expansion of the federal government's role and the subsequent regimentation of American life. "It is a vast shift," he wrote, "from the American concept of human rights which even the government may not infringe to those social philosophies where men are wholly subjective to the state. It is a vast casualty to Liberty if it shall be continued."[7]

Hoover's hostility was matched by other writers like John T. Flynn, a former liberal who had become progressively disillusioned by America's liberal tradition. The author of several books on Roosevelt Flynn's antagonism against the New Deal reached a peak in his *The Roosevelt Myth.* Specifically denying the achievements that liberal historians had credited to the New Deal, he argued that Roosevelt had substituted for the free enterprise system one that operated upon "permanent crises and an armament economy." In the process of implementing New Deal programs the vigor of state governments had been sapped, the authority of Congress had been eroded, and unprecedented power had been concentrated in the hands of the president. One result of Roosevelt's New Deal policies was the appearance of a staggering federal debt; "a debt that can never be paid and which can be taken off our shoulders only by a great and devastating inflation."[8]

The charge by conservative writers that the New Deal represented a break with the past, interestingly enough, was echoed by some Progressive historians. One of these was Richard Hofstadter who, although writing within a liberal framework, was among the severest critics of America's liberal tradition. American liberalism, Hofstadter argued, had failed because of its moralizing tendencies and its inability

---

[7]Herbert Hoover, *The Challenge to Liberty* (New York, 1934), p. 103.

[8]John T. Flynn, *The Roosevelt Myth* (rev. ed.; New York, 1956), pp. 414 and 445.

to come to grips with the fundamental issues of the day. In *The Age of Reform: From Bryan to F.D.R.*, he insisted that the New Deal could not under any circumstances be interpreted as a continuation of the liberal-Progressive tradition. The section in his book devoted to the New Deal was appropriately entitled "The New Departure."

To Hofstadter the New Deal was markedly different from any other indigenous American political movement. Past reform movements, Hofstadter noted, had generally operated under the assumption that their purpose was to clear the way for new enterprises and new men— to smash established privilege and monopoly and to provide all Americans with an equal opportunity in life. Within this context the national government was considered to be either negative in its nature or an obstacle in the way of success. Earlier reform movements had taken it for granted that American society was essentially healthy but one that needed further democratization to reach its full potential.

The New Deal, according to Hofstadter, was based on entirely different premises. Instead of viewing American society as healthy New Deal reformers saw it as a sick society in need of changes that could only be instituted through federal action. Thus the New Deal accepted the idea of federal responsibility for the relief of the unemployed, supported legislation for social security, unemployment insurance, wages and hours, and public housing, and did not fear massive expenditures that resulted in deficit spending. Many of the traditional aims of past reform movements—to restore government to the people and to destroy big business and monopolies—were simply bypassed or ignored by Roosevelt. Considering the nature and magnitude of New Deal programs, Hofstadter concluded, the movement had to be considered a new departure in American life. "The New Deal, and the thinking it engendered," wrote Hofstadter, "represented the triumph of economic emergency and human needs over inherited notions and inhibitions. . . . At the core of the New Deal, then, was not a philosophy (F.D.R. could identify himself philosophically only as a Christian and democrat), but an attitude, suitable for practical politicians, administrators, and technicians, but uncongenial to the moralism that the Progressives had for the most part shared with their opponents."[9]

The New Deal, Hofstadter pointed out with an ironic touch, represented a change of the usual ideological roles of American conservatives and reformers. The conservatives had traditionally prided themselves on their sense of realism, their distrust of abstract plans for remaking society, and their belief in the necessity for institutional con-

---

[9] Richard Hofstadter, *The Age of Reform: From Bryan to F.D.R.* (New York, 1955), pp. 314 and 323.

tinuity. Reformers, on the other hand, had invariably appealed to moral sentiments, denounced existing injustices, and aroused the indignation of the community. By the 1930s, however, the traditional roles of the two had become reversed. Reformers appealed not to moral abstractions, but to concrete grievances of specific groups—farmers without markets, unemployed men without bread, laborers seeking to organize in unions of their own choosing, and to those groups concerned with the soundness of banks, investment markets, and manufacturing enterprises. Conservatives were now in the position of moral critics— they denounced the New Deal precisely because of its violation of traditional rules, its abandonment of the nation's moral heritage, its departure from sound principles, and its imposition of a federal tyranny upon the American people.

Oddly enough Hofstadter was unhappy with the efforts of both conservatives and reformers. The reformers from the New Deal on, according to him, had refused to think in terms of rational planning and remained content to respond in a pragmatic way to individual pressures and situations as they arose. The criticisms of the conservatives, on the other hand, were "hollow and cliché-ridden," the complaints of a class increasingly cut off from the world of reality. But all that Hofstadter could do—at least in his role as historian and contemporary critic—was to hope that a better understanding of America's past political tradition might help future politicians to formulate a more realistic philosophy.

A similar criticism was voiced by Rexford G. Tugwell, a Columbia University professor who had joined Roosevelt's administration in the early 1930s as a strong advocate of governmental economic planning. The old faith in a self-regulating market, he maintained, had never been justified; it was part of the American mythology of a free enterprise system. Distrustful of business and businessmen Tugwell felt that only the federal government was in a position to control the economy in such a way as to make it run smoothly and efficiently.

After leaving government service to return to the academic world, Tugwell set out to write a biography of Roosevelt, which was finally published in 1957, although parts had appeared in a series of long articles somewhat earlier. The picture Tugwell drew of Roosevelt and the New Deal was a friendly one, but one also marked with a sense of disappointment. According to Tugwell the productive capacity of the American economy by the late 1920s had far outrun purchasing power, thus giving rise to a fundamental maladjustment which resulted in the depression. The Republicans under Hoover initially denied that the economic situation was serious. Later they adopted halfway measures and encouraged private rather than public relief. When Roosevelt came to power he was faced with a grave emergency but one which gave him an unprecedented opportunity such as no other president had had. Although he was a master improviser and politician, Roosevelt never conceived of New Deal measures in terms of rational planning. Many of the New Deal innovations, indeed, resulted from careful balancing between the claims of various competing pressure groups. Roosevelt, Tugwell concluded, was a political pragmatist with a progressive bent. Despite his essential greatness he was unable or unwilling to seize the opportunity and institute far-reaching reform measures. Whether future historians would continue to look upon the New Deal in this manner, Tugwell admitted, was an open question.[10]

Both Hofstadter and Tugwell were critical of Roosevelt because of his political opportunism and his pragmatic approach to serious problems. Implicit in their writings was the belief that the New Deal could not be interpreted as a part of America's liberal tradition. Oddly enough they were in agreement with recent neoconservative historians who had also rejected the thesis that American history could be understood in terms of class and ideological conflict. In the eyes of these more recent historians American history had been marked not by conflict and divisions, but by stability and unity. Domestic struggles in the United States, they maintained, were over means, never over ends. To look upon the politics of the 1930s as an expression of fundamental divisions among the American people, they concluded, was a mistake.

But if the New Deal did not reflect fundamental class and ideological divisions, what did it reflect? To Heinz Eulau, a political scientist at Stanford University writing in essentially a neoconservative vein, the New Deal defied ideological classification. It is true, he admitted, that many individuals associated with Roosevelt had their own particular blueprints for the reconstruction of American society. Taken as a whole, however, the New Deal had many sides, and for this reason was not the product of a cohesive and rational ideology. Nor did the New Deal articulate a faith in a better tomorrow; it did not call upon people to join a crusade to remake their society or to experiment with new and untried schemes. But if the New Deal was not an ideology, a faith, a crusade, an experiment, a revolt, or a utopia, what was it? To Eulau the answer to this question was clear. The New Deal, he suggested, was "both a symbol and evidence of the nation's political maturity"; it represented an effort to solve problems "through politics rather than through ideology or violence." In Eulau's eyes a mature politics involves adjustment, compromise, and integration. By this

---

[10]Rexford G. Tugwell, "The New Deal in Retrospect," *Western Political Quarterly* 1 (December 1948):373–385. See also Tugwell's full length study of Roosevelt, *The Democratic Roosevelt* (New York, 1957).

standard the New Deal symbolized a mature politics because it was seeking solutions to problems rather than imposing preconceived solutions on problems.[11]

By implication Eulau was agreeing with those neoconservative historians who rejected class and ideological interpretations of American history in favor of an approach that emphasized the stability of American institutions and the pragmatism of American culture. The distinguishing characteristic of American history, therefore, was a rejection of the unrealistic intellectual and ideological characteristics of European thought and the substitution in their place of common sense. To writers like Eulau the New Deal must be understood as part of the basic commonsense approach of most Americans and their rejection of the world of ideology. In this sense the New Deal was not comparable to earlier liberal movements; the New Deal was simply an attempt to cope with unique problems in a simple and sensible manner.

During the 1960s the stature of Franklin D. Roosevelt and the New Deal again began to change as younger scholars asked some searching questions. If the New Deal had modified and humanized American society, why did poverty and racism continue to exist? If the New Deal had truly reformed an unbridled capitalism and made it more responsive to the needs of people, why were so many different groups—blacks, Puerto Ricans, Mexican Americans, and middle-class youths—alienated from their society? If the New Deal had led to a change for the better in terms of America's role in world affairs, how had the nation become involved first in the Korean War and then in the Vietnam conflict? Given the tensions and crises of the 1960s it was perhaps inevitable that the historical image of the New Deal would once again change.

Perhaps the sharpest critique—though by no means the only one—came from the pens of historians identified with the New Left. Many of these scholars were committed to radical changes in the structure of American society and they saw history as a discipline that would illuminate the present by a searching examination of the past. We have "sought explicitly," wrote the editor of a book of essays representing in part New Left scholarship, "to make the past speak to the present, to ask questions that have a deep-rooted moral and political relevance. In moving occasionally beyond description and causal analysis to judge significance, we have, by necessity, moved beyond objective history in the realm of values."[12]

---

[11]Heinz Eulau, "Neither Ideology Nor Utopia: The New Deal in Retrospect," *Antioch Review* 19 (Winter 1959–1960):523–537.

[12]Barton J. Bernstein, ed., *Towards a New Past: Dissenting Essays in American History* (New York, 1968), p. xiii.

Given their own values and commitment to social change it was natural that radical historians would see the New Deal in an unfavorable light. In an essay discussing the place of the New Deal in American history, for example, Barton J. Bernstein argued that the liberal reforms of the 1930s had not transformed the American system; rather they conserved and protected corporate capitalism. Nor had the New Deal significantly redistributed power in any way, or granted any meaningful recognition to unorganized peoples. Even its bolder programs had not extended the beneficence of government beyond affluent groups or used the wealth of the few for the needs of the many. The New Deal followed essentially conservative goals, for it was intended to maintain the American system intact. "The New Deal," Bernstein concluded, "failed to solve the problem of depression, it failed to raise the impoverished, it failed to redistribute income, it failed to extend equality and generally countenanced racial discrimination and segregation. It failed generally to make business more responsible to the social welfare or to threaten business's pre-eminent political power. . . . In acting to protect the institution of private property and in advancing the interests of corporate capitalism, the New Deal assisted the middle and upper sectors of society. It protected them, sometimes, even at the cost of injuring the lower sectors. Seldom did it bestow much of substance upon the lower classes."[13]

From the vantage point of the political left, therefore, the New Deal was a failure. Committed to capitalism it could not offer the lower classes anything but rhetoric and psychological comfort. So wrote even Paul K. Conkin in a penetrating analysis of Roosevelt and the New Deal. Judging the New Deal more from the perspective of a social democrat rather than a partisan of the New Left, he expressed considerable admiration for Roosevelt's political astuteness and charismatic qualities. Yet Conkin denied that Roosevelt was even a pragmatist, for his thought was too shallow and superficial and concerned largely with immediate issues. "For the historian," noted Conkin in his critical but compassionate summation, "every judgment, every evaluation of the past has to be tinged with a pinch of compassion, a sense of the beauty and nobility present when honest hopes and humane ideals are frustrated. He sees that the thirties could have brought so much more, but also so much worse, than the New Deal. The limiting context has to be understood—the safeguards and impediments of our political system, Roosevelt's intellectual limitations, and most of all the appalling economic ignorance and philosophic immaturity of the American electorate. . . . The New Deal solved a few problems, ameliorated a few

---

[13]Barton J. Bernstein, "The New Deal: The Conservative Achievements of Liberal Reform," in *ibid.*, pp. 264 and 281–282.

more, obscured many, and created new ones. This is about all our political system can generate, even in crisis."[14]

Much of the historiography of the New Deal, therefore, reflected to some degree personal ideological commitments. To Progressive scholars Roosevelt was a hero; to conservatives he was too radical; and to radicals he was too conservative, if not reactionary. Each group, of course, judged Roosevelt in terms of the direction they felt America *should* have taken.

In a major study of New Deal economic policy, however, Ellis W. Hawley approached the problem quite differently. Americans, he noted, shared a commitment to two value systems that were not wholly compatible. On the one hand they cherished liberty and freedom, which implied a competitive economic and social order. On the other hand they valued order, rationality, and collective organization, and associated large business units and economic organizations generally with abundance, progress, and a rising standard of living. Yet the latter value posed a potential threat to the former; monopoly negated, at least in theory, freedom and competition. Much of twentieth-century American history, Hawley observed, revolved around the search for a solution "that would preserve the industrial order, necessarily based upon a high degree of collective organization, and yet would preserve America's democratic heritage at the same time." New Deal economic policy mirrored this basic ambivalence; it vacillated between rational planning and antimonopoly, neither of which was completely compatible. Hawley's conclusion offered little support to any of the competing ideologies that underlay many of the historical interpretations of Roosevelt and the New Deal. "If the experiences of the nineteen thirties have any relevance at all," he wrote, "it is in illustrating the limitations of logical analysis, the pitfalls inherent in broad theoretical approaches, the difficulty of agreeing on policy goals, and the necessity of making due allowances for the intellectual heritage, current trends of opinion, and the realities of pressure-group politics."[15]

In the second selection in this chapter, Hawley analyzes the nature of business-government relationships in the New Deal era. Rejecting either the glorification or denigration of the mixed economy created during the 1930s Hawley emphasizes instead the tensions between organizational capitalism and the liberal-democratic ethos, as well as Franklin Delano Roosevelt's tendency to resist ideological systems. Nor does he accept the claim that business groups dominated policymaking during the depression. What emerged from the New Deal, he

---

[14]Paul K. Conkin, *The New Deal* (New York, 1967).

[15]Ellis W. Hawley, *The New Deal and the Problem of Monopoly: A Study in Economic Ambivalence* (Princeton, 1966), p. 493.

concludes, "was the creation not of an omnipotent corporate elite but of a complex interaction between conflicting interest groups, resurgent liberal ideals, and the champions of competing reform models, all of which, after all, contemplated the salvation and stabilizing of corporate capitalism as well as the democratizing of it."

In recent years historians have begun to occupy a middle ground as the political passions of the 1930s faded. In his political analysis, for example, Albert U. Romasco argued that Roosevelt wanted to cooperate with the business community, thereby stimulating investment and productivity. If Roosevelt was hostile to business he nevertheless confronted the business community with a little stick and a big carrot. Similarly Nancy Weiss has exploded the myth that Roosevelt was overly concerned with the plight of black Americans during the Great Depression. On racial issues the New Deal offered little; Roosevelt was reluctant to support antilynching legislation for fear of alienating Southern Democrats. Insofar as economic issues were concerned blacks benefited only because they were not excluded from those broad New Deal programs designed to assist the poor and the unemployed as a whole. Consequently blacks embraced the Democratic party and abandoned the Republican party even though Roosevelt did not directly woo black support.[16]

Considering, then, the many ways historians have written about the New Deal, is it possible to come to any sort of definitive conclusions about its essential nature? Can Roosevelt and the New Deal be positioned precisely in terms of their place within the American political tradition? In dealing with this question it should be emphasized that many of the apparent differences among students writing about the New Deal are partly semantical in nature. When describing the operation of specific New Deal programs, for example, the differences of opinion between historians tend to narrow sharply. Thus what the WPA, NRA, and other federal agencies *did* is often not a subject of dispute. The issue that invariably leads to conflict is the *intent* of the participants involved. The controversy involves not the relief activities of the 1930s, to cite one instance, but whether or not the concept of federal relief undermined the cherished American ideals of individualism and liberty.

The semantic difficulty may be seen in the various ways historians have used the word *pragmatic*. When Roosevelt was described as a "pragmatic leader," what did this mean? Actually the term was used in at least three different ways. Edgar E. Robinson, for example, has

---

[16]Albert U. Romasco, *The Politics of Recovery: Roosevelt's New Deal* (New York, 1983), and Nancy J. Weiss, *Farewell to the Party of Lincoln: Black Politics in the Age of FDR* (Princeton, 1983).

described Roosevelt's personal leadership as "pragmatic—an individual playing by ear." What Robinson meant by his characterization was that Roosevelt, in order to gain an immediate political advantage, never considered the long-range effects of his policies. "Roosevelt's failure," Robinson concluded, "lay in his unsuccessful attempt to justify the means or establish the ends he had in view." Underlying Robinson's thesis was the criticism that the New Deal resulted in an almost fatal concentration of power in the hands of the executive—a "power that could destroy the world or build it in the image of an entirely new scientific perspective."[17]

A second use of the term "pragmatic," as we have already seen in Tugwell's case, involved the criticism that Roosevelt never even understood the need for long-range economic planning. Roosevelt limited himself to immediate problems and tended to neglect more fundamental issues. Consequently he never took advantage of the unparalleled opportunity for reform that arose out of the greatest single economic crisis that the American people had ever faced. While New Deal measures were important in giving status and material benefits to groups in American society that had been hitherto neglected, relatively speaking, these reforms fell short of their real potential. This view of Roosevelt, which has been echoed by many writers, is based on the underlying assumption that New Deal pragmatism and rational governmental planning were incompatible.

The term "pragmatic" has been used in a third way to describe a mental attitude and frame of mind that rejected the dogmatic thinking of the 1930s and remained open and receptive to new ideas. William E. Leuchtenburg, a Columbia University historian, has argued that the pragmatism of the New Deal seemed striking only because the period as a whole was characterized by rigid ideological thinking. The New Deal was pragmatic, Leuchtenburg maintained, "only in contrast to the rigidity of Hoover and of the Left." Moreover the movement was pragmatic in the sense that reformers themselves remained skeptical about final utopias and ultimate solutions and were always open to experimentation. To Leuchtenburg the New Deal was more than a movement to experiment or to improvise; it was a movement led by men who were committed to the proposition that it was possible to make human life more tolerable, that depressions were by no means inevitable events, and that human affairs were not necessarily guided by inexorable deterministic laws.[18]

---

[17]Edgar Eugene Robinson, *The Roosevelt Leadership 1933–1945* (Philadelphia, 1955), pp. 383, 397, and 408.

[18]William E. Leuchtenburg, *Franklin D. Roosevelt and the New Deal 1932–1940* (New York, 1963), pp. 344–345.

Because of the preoccupation with the New Deal as a national phenomenon historians have generally not dealt with its actual impact on the lives of individuals. In a recent study of Boston during the 1930s, Charles H. Trout observed that the "New Deal's manifestations were treated piecemeal and were perceived by individuals and groups according to their particular needs." Indeed, many federal programs involving social and economic change were resisted by Bostonians precisely because of the weight of tradition and history; the concept "of a national or even a municipal communality of interest was seldom grasped."[19] From a local perspective, therefore, the accomplishments of the New Deal were limited and more remote.

The problem of understanding and assessing the achievements of the New Deal and its place in American history, therefore, is one whose answer will largely be determined by a series of prior assumptions about the nature of the American past and the nation's ideals in both the present and future. To those historians whose view is that America is founded upon an atomistic philosophy—that the nation's greatness arose from the achievements of talented and ambitious individuals and was not always related to the activities of government—the New Deal will always appear as a movement alien and hostile to traditional values. In this context the New Deal represents a new departure in American history that will end perhaps in a collectivistic and authoritarian government. On the other hand, to those scholars who adhere to a corporate philosophy—that society is more than a mere aggregate of private individuals and that a modern complex industrial economy requires a certain amount of public regulation as well as government-sponsored reform—the New Deal becomes a political movement inspired by proper ideals. Instead of being an aberration in terms of the American political tradition the New Deal was a movement consonant with previous struggles for justice and equality. Finally, to those historians who maintain that only a radical restructuring of American society could eliminate poverty, racism, war, and inequality, the New Deal appears as a palliative or sham designed to gloss over fundamental defects.

The problem of judging the nature and accomplishments of the New Deal is, then, a difficult one, for it involves the entire fabric of the American past. Indeed, to avoid any broad judgments is in effect to render a judgment, albeit on an unconscious level. In the final analysis, therefore, historians will continue to grapple with the place of the New Deal in American life. Was the New Deal a continuation of America's liberal tradition or was it a repudiation of that tradition?

---

[19]Charles H. Trout, *Boston, The Great Depression, and the New Deal* (New York, 1977), pp. 321–322.

Did the New Deal reflect an attempt by corporate capitalism to maintain its power intact by forging a partnership with the federal government, with the latter in a subordinate position? Or did the New Deal give a significant voice to minority groups that in the past had been powerless? Can the New Deal even be understood in ideological terms or should it be viewed as a political movement characterized by an underlying pragmatism? Or were the alleged inconsistencies of the New Deal a reflection of the underlying commitment of Americans to the values of order and freedom, which in turn gave rise to ambivalent policies? These are only some of the broad questions that must be answered in order to assess the nature and significance of the New Deal.[20]

[20]For a penetrating analysis of the historical literature on the New Deal, see Alfred B. Rollins, Jr., "Was There Really a Man Named Roosevelt?," in *American History: Retrospect and Prospect*, George A. Billias and Gerald N. Grob, eds. (New York, 1971), pp. 232–270.

Arthur M. Schlesinger, Jr.

ARTHUR M. SCHLESINGER, JR. (1917–   ) is Albert Schweitzer Professor of the Humanities at the City University of New York. He was also a special assistant to President John F. Kennedy. Among his many published works are *The Age of Jackson* (1945), *The Age of Roosevelt*, 3 vols. (1957–1960), *A Thousand Days: John F. Kennedy in the White House* (1965), and *Robert Kennedy and His Times* (1978).

In the background of any historical episode lies all previous history. The strands which a historian may select as vital to an understanding of the particular episode will vary widely according to his interest, his temperament, his faith and his time. Each man must unravel the seamless web in his own way. I do not propose here any definitive assessment of the sources of the New Deal. I doubt whether a final assessment is possible. I want rather to call attention to certain possible sources which may not have figured extensively in the conventional accounts, including my own—to the relation of the New Deal to the ebb and flow of American national politics and then its relation to the international dilemma of free society in this century.

Such relationships are speculative; nonetheless, an attempt to see them may perhaps cast light on some of the less discussed impulses behind the New Deal itself. To begin—and in order to make a sharp issue—let me ask this question: Would there have been a New Deal if there had been no depression? Without a depression, would we have had nothing but a placid continuation, so long as prosperity itself continued, of the New Era of the twenties?

I would answer that there would very likely have been some sort of New Deal in the thirties even without the depression. I think perhaps our contemporary thinking has come too unreflectively to assume depression as the necessary preliminary for any era of reform. Students of American history know better. The fight against depression was, to be sure, the heart of the New Deal, but it has not been the central issue of traditional American reform: it was not the heart of Jeffersonian Democracy nor of Jacksonian Democracy nor of the antislavery movement nor of the Progressive movement.

What preceded these other epochs of reform was an accumulation

---

of disquietudes and discontents in American society, often noneconomic in character, and producing a general susceptibility to appeals for change—this and the existence within society of able men or groups who felt themselves cramped by the status quo and who were capable of exploiting mounting dissatisfaction to advance policies and purposes of their own. This combination of outsiders striving for status and power and a people wearying of the existing leadership and the existing ideals has been the real archetype of American reform.

The official order in the twenties presented perhaps the nearest we ever came in our history to the identification of the national interest with the interests, values, and goals of a specific class—in this case, of course, the American business community. During the generation before Harding, the political leaders who had commanded the loyalties and the energies of the American people—Theodore Roosevelt and Woodrow Wilson—expressed strains in American life distinct from and often opposed to the dominant values of business. They represented a fusion of patrician and intellectual attitudes which saw in public policy an outlet for creative energy—in Lippmann's phrase, they stood for mastery as against drift. In the service of this conception, they led the people into great national efforts of various sorts, culminating in the convulsive and terrible experience of war. Two decades of this—two decades under the glittering eyes of such leaders as [Theodore] Roosevelt and Wilson, Bryan and La Follette—left the nation in a state of exhaustion.

By 1920 the nation was tired of public crisis. It was tired of discipline and sacrifice. It was tired of abstract and intangible objectives. It could gird itself no longer for heroic moral or intellectual effort. Its instinct for idealism was spent. "It is only once in a generation," Wilson himself had said, "that a people can be lifted above material things. That is why conservative government is in the saddle two-thirds of the time." And the junior official to whom he made this remark, the young Assistant Secretary of the Navy, also noted soon after his unsuccessful try for the vice-presidency in 1920, "Every war brings after it a period of materialism and conservatism; people tire quickly of ideals and we are now repeating history." John W. Davis, the Democratic candidate in 1924, said a few years later: "The people usually know what they want at a particular time. . . . In 1924 when I was a candidate what they wanted was repose."

A nation fatigued with ideals and longing for repose was ready for "normalcy." As popular attention receded from public policy, as values and aspirations became private again, people stopped caring about politics, which meant that political power inevitably gravitated to society's powerful economic interests—the government of the exhausted nation quite naturally fell to the businessmen. And for nearly a decade the business government reigned over a prosperous and expanding country.

Yet, for all the material contentment of the twenties, the decade was also marked by mounting spiritual and psychological discontent. One could detect abundant and multiplying symptoms of what Josiah Royce, after Hegel, used to call a self-estranged social order. The official creed began to encounter growing skepticism, and even opposition and ridicule, in the community at large. Able and ambitious groups, denied what they considered fitting recognition or opportunity, began to turn against the Establishment.

If the economic crash of 1929 astonished the experts, a spiritual crash was diagnosed well in advance. "By 1927," reported Scott Fitzgerald, "a widespread neurosis began to be evident, faintly signaled, like a nervous beating of the feet, by the popularity of crossword puzzles." In the same year Walter Lippmann pointed more soberly to the growing discrepancy between the nominal political issues of the day and the actual emotions of the people. If politics took up these real issues, Lippmann said, it would revolutionize the existing party system. "It is not surprising, then, that our political leaders are greatly occupied in dampening down interest, in obscuring issues, and in attempting to distract attention from the realities of American life."

What was wrong with the New Era was not (as yet) evidence of incompetence or stupidity in public policy. Rather, there was a profound discontent with the monopoly of power and prestige by a single class and the resulting indifference of the national government to deeper tensions. Those excluded from the magic circle suffered boredom, resentment, irritation and eventually indignation over what seemed the intolerable pretensions and irrelevances of their masters. Now it is the gravest error to underrate the power of boredom as a factor in social change. Our political scientists have pointed out convincingly how the human tendency toward inertia sets limits on liberalism; I wish they would spend equal time showing how the human capacity for boredom sets limits on conservatism. The dominant official society—the Establishment—of the twenties was an exceedingly boring one, neither bright nor witty nor picturesque nor even handsome, and this prodded the human impulse to redress the balance by kicking up heels in back streets.

All this encouraged the defection of specific groups from a social order which ignored their needs and snubbed their ambitions. Within the business community itself there were dissident individuals, especially in the underdeveloped areas of the country, who considered that opportunities for local growth were unduly restrained by Wall Street's control of the money market. The farmers felt themselves shut out from the prevailing prosperity. Elements in the labor movement re-

sented their evident second-class citizenship. Members of foreign nationality groups, especially the newer immigration and its children,
chafed under the prevalent assumption that the real America was
Anglo-Saxon, Protestant, middle class, and white. In time some of the
younger people of the nation began to grow restless before the ideals
held out to them; while others, in accepting these ideals, acquired a
smug mediocrity which even depressed some of their elders.

Gravest among the symptoms was the defection of the intellectuals: writers, educators, newspapermen, editors—those who manned
the machinery of opinion and who transmitted ideas. The fact of their
particular estrangement and discontent guaranteed the articulation,
and thus, to a degree, the coordination of the larger unrest. The intellectuals put the ruling class in its place by substituting for its own ad-
miring picture of itself a set of disrecpectful images, which an increasing number of people found delightful and persuasive; the insiders, who
had before been seen in the reverent terms of Bruce Barton and the
American Magazine, were now to be seen less reverently through the
eyes of H. L. Mencken and Sinclair Lewis. Satire liberated people from
the illusion of business infallibility and opened their minds to other
visions of American possibility. The next function of the intellectuals
was precisely to explore and substantiate those other visions. They did
so with zest and ingenuity; and the result was that, beneath the official
crust, the twenties billowed with agitation, criticism and hope. Dewey
affirmed man's capability for social intervention and management; Beard
argued that intelligent national planning was the irresistible next phase
in history; Parrington insisted that Jeffersonian idealism had a sound
basis in the American past, and indeed, expressed a truer Americanism
than did materialism. Together the satirists and the prophets drew a
new portrait of America—both of the American present and of the
American promise—and the increasingly visible discrepancy between
what was and what might be in America armed the spreading discontent.

The well of idealism was rising again; energies were being replen-
ished, batteries recharged. Outsiders were preparing to hammer on the
gates of the citadel. The 1928 election, in which an Irish Catholic challenged Yankee Protestant supremacy, illustrated the gathering revolt
against the Establishment. And, though Hoover won the election, Samuel Lubell has pointed out that "Smith split not only the Solid South,
but the Republican North as well." Smith carried counties which had
long been traditionally Republican; he smashed the Republican hold
on the cities; he mobilized the new immigrants. In losing, he polled
nearly as many votes as Calvin Coolidge had polled in winning four
years before. He stood for the vital new tendencies of politics; and it
is likely that the prolongation of these tendencies would have assured
a national Democratic victory, without a depression, in 1932 or cer-

tainly by 1936. And such a Democratic victory would surely have meant the discharge into public life of able and ambitious people denied preference under a business administration—much the same sort of people, indeed, who eventually came to power with the New Deal; and it would have meant new opportunities for groups that had seen the door slammed in their faces in the Twenties—labor, the farmers, the ethnic minorities, the intellectuals.

The suspicion that a political overturn was due even without a depression is fortified, I think, by the calculations of my father in his essay of some years back "The Tides of National Politics." In this essay he proposed that liberal and conservative periods in our national life succeeded themselves at intervals of about fifteen or sixteen years; this alternation takes place, he wrote, without any apparent correlation with economic circumstances or, indeed, with anything else, except the ebb and flow of national political psychology. By this argument, a liberal epoch was due in America around 1934 or 1935, depression or no.

In short, the New Deal was, among other things, an expression of what would seem—to use a currently unfashionable concept—an inherent cyclical rhythm in American politics. The depression did not cause the cycle: What the depression did was to increase its intensity and deepen its impact by superimposing on the normal cycle the peculiar and unprecedented urgencies arising from economic despair. One might even argue—though I do not think I would—that the depression coming at another stage in the cycle would not necessarily have produced a New Deal. It is certainly true, as I said, that depressions did not induce epochs of reform in 1873 or in 1893. I think myself, however, that the magnitude of the shock made a political recoil almost certain after 1929. Still, the fact that this recoil took a liberal rather than a reactionary turn may well be due to the accident that the economic shock coincided with a liberal turn inthe political cycle.

In any event, the fact remains that the historical New Deal, whether or not something like it might have come along anyway, was after all brought into being by the depression. It assumed its particular character as it sought to respond to the challenge of economic collapse. And, in confronting this challenge, it was confronting a good deal more than merely an American problem. Mass unemployment touched the very roots of free institutions everywhere. "This problem of unemployment," as Winston Churchill said in England in 1930, "is the most torturing that can be presented to civilized society." The problem was more than torturing; it was something civilized society had to solve if it were to survive. And the issue presented with particular urgency was whether representative democracy could ever deal effectively with it.

Churchill, in the same Romanes lecture at Oxford in 1930, questioned whether it could: Democratic governments, he said, drifted along the lines of least resistance, took short views, smoothed their path with platitudes, and paid their way with sops and doles. Parliaments, he suggested, could deal with political problems, but not with economic. "One may even be pardoned," Churchill said, "for doubting whether institutions based on adult suffrage could possibly arrive at the right decisions upon the intricate propositions of modern business and finance." These were delicate problems requiring specialist treatment. "You cannot cure cancer by a majority. What is wanted is a remedy."

The drift of discussion in the United States as well as in Britain in the early thirties revealed an increasingly dour sense of existing alternatives; on the one hand, it seemed, was parliamentary democracy with economic chaos; on the other, economic authoritarianism with political tyranny. Even more dour was the sense that history had already made the choice—that the democratic impulse was drained of vitality, that liberalism was spent as a means of organizing human action. Consider a selection of statements from American writers at the time, and their mortuary resonance:

> The rejection of democracy is nowadays regarded as evidence of superior wisdom. (Ralph Barton Perry)
>
> The moral and intellectual bankruptcy of liberalism in our time needs no demonstration. It is as obvious as rain and as taken for granted. (Nathaniel Peffer)
>
> To attempt a defense of democracy these days is a little like defending paganism in 313 or the divine right of kings in 1793. It is taken for granted that democracy is bad and that it is dying. (George Boas)
>
> 'Liberalism is dead.' So many people who seem to agree upon nothing else have agreed to accept these three sweeping words. (Joseph Wood Krutch)
>
> Modern Western civilization is a failure. That theory is now generally accepted. (Louise Maunsell Fields)
>
> Why is it that democracy has fallen so rapidly from the high prestige which it had at the Armistice . . . Why is it that in America itself—in the very temple and citadel of democracy—self-government has been held up to every ridicule, and many observers count it already dead? (Will Durant)

Only the most venerable among us can remember the creeping fear of a quarter of a century ago that the free system itself had run out of energy, that we had reached, in a phrase Reinhold Niebuhr used as a part of the title of a book in 1934, the "end of an era." What this pessimism implied for the realm of public policy was that democracy had exhausted its intellectual and moral resources, its bag of tricks was played out, and salvation now lay in moving over to a system of total control.

In affirming that there was no alternative between laissez-faire and tyranny, the pessimists were endorsing a passionate conviction held both by the proponents of individualism and the proponents of collectivism. Ogden Mills spoke with precision for American conservatives: "We can have a free country or a socialistic one. We cannot have both. Our economic system cannot be half free and half socialistic. . . . There is no middle ground between governing and being governed, between absolute sovereignty and liberty, between tyranny and freedom." Herbert Hoover was equally vehement: "Even partial regimentation cannot be made to work and still maintain live democratic institutions." In such sentiments, Hoover and Mills would have commanded the enthusiastic assent of Stalin and Mussolini. The critical question was whether a middle way was possible—a mixed system which might give the state more power than conservatives would like, enough power, indeed, to assure economic and social security, but still not too much as to create dictatorship. To this question the Hoovers, no less than the Stalins and Mussolinis, had long since returned categorical answers. They all agreed on this, if on nothing else: no.

As I have said, economic planning was not just an American problem. Great Britain, for example, was confronting mass unemployment and economic stagnation; moreover, she had had since 1929 a Labor government. In a sense, it would have been hard to select a better place to test the possibilities of a tranquil advance from laissez-faire capitalism to a managed society. Here was a Labor leadership, sustained by a faith in the "inevitability of gradualness," ruling a nation committed by tradition and instinct to the acceptance of empirical change. How did the British Labor government visualize its problem and opportunity?

The central figures in the Labor government of 1929 were Ramsay MacDonald, now prime minister for the second time, and Philip Snowden, his sharp and dominating chancellor of the exchequer. Both were classic Socialists who saw in the nationalization of basic industry the answer to all economic riddles. Yet in the existing political situation, with a slim Labor majority, nationalization was out of the question. With socialism excluded, MacDonald and Snowden—indeed, nearly all the Labor party leaders—could see no alternative to all-out socialism but nearly all-out laissez-faire. A capitalist order had to be operated on capitalist principles. The economic policy of the Labor government was thus consecrated as faithfully as that of Herbert Hoover's Republican administration in the United States to the balanced budget and the gold standard—and, far more faithfully than American Republicanism, to free trade.

Socialism across the Channel was hardly more resourceful. As the German Social Democrat Fritz Naphtali put it in 1930, "I don't believe that we can do very much, nor anything very decisive, from the point of view of economic policy, to overcome the crisis until it has run its course." In this spirit of impotence, the democratic Socialists of Europe (until Léon Blum came to power some years later) denied the possibility of a middle way and concluded that, short of full socialization, they had no alternative but to accept the logic of laissez-faire.

The assumption that there were two absolutely distinct economic orders, socialism and capitalism, expressed, of course, an unconscious Platonism—a conviction that the true reality lay in the theoretical essences of which any working economy, with its compromises and confusions, could only be an imperfect copy. If in the realm of essences socialism and capitalism were separate phenomena based on separate principles, then they must be kept rigorously apart on earth. Nor was this use of Platonism—this curious belief that the abstraction was somehow more real than the reality, which Whitehead so well called the "fallacy of misplaced concreteness"—confined to doctrinaire capitalists and doctrinaire socialists. The eminent Liberal economist Sir William Beveridge, director of the London School of Economics, braintruster for the Lloyd George welfare reforms before the First World War, spoke for enlightened economic opinion when he identified the "inescapable fatal danger" confronting public policy in the depression as "the danger of mixing freedom and control. We have to decide either to let production be guided by the free play of prices or to plan it socialistically from beginning to end. . . . Control and freedom do not mix." Beveridge, encountering Donald Richberg in Washington in the glowing days of 1933, asked a bit patronizingly whether Richberg really believed that there was "a half-way between Wall Street and Moscow." As for Britain, "there is not much that anyone can do now to help us," Beveridge said. "We must plan to avoid another crisis later. We shall not by conscious effort escape this one."

So dogma denied the possibility of a managed capitalism. But could dogma hold out in Britain against the urgencies of depression? Some Englishmen dissented from the either/or philosophy. In the general election of 1929, for example, John Maynard Keynes and Hubert Henderson had provided the Liberal party with the rudiments of an expansionist policy, based on national spending and public works. As unemployment increased in 1930, so too did the pressure for positive government action. That year Sir Oswald Mosley, a member of the Labor government, proposed to a cabinet committee on unemployment an active program of government spending, accompanied by controls over banking, industry and foreign trade. But he could make no impression on the capitalist orthodoxy of the Socialist leaders; Snowden rejected the Mosley memorandum. Another minister suggested leaving the gold standard; Snowden covered him with scorn. To the party conference of 1930, MacDonald said, "I appeal to you to go back to your Socialist faith. Do not mix that up with pettifogging patching, either of a Poor Law kind or Relief Work kind." In other words, socialism meant all or—in this case—nothing!

As economic pressure increased, more and more had to be sacrificed to the balancing of the budget; and the implacable retrenchment meant more governmental economy, reduction in salaries, reduction in normal public works, until in time, the frenzy for economy threatened the social services and especially the system of unemployment payments on which many British workers relied to keep alive. The summer crisis of 1931, after the failure of *Kreditanstalt*, weakened the pound; and to Snowden and the Labor government nothing now seemed more essential than staying on the gold standard. To keep Britain on gold required American loans; American loans would not be forthcoming unless satisfactory evidence existed of a determination to balance the budget; and the evidence most likely to satisfy J. P. Morgan and Company, which was arranging the American credit, was a cut in unemployment benefits.

In August 1931, MacDonald and Snowden confronted the cabinet with this dismal logic. Arthur Henderson made it clear that the whole cabinet absolutely accepted Snowden's economic theory: "We ought to do everything in our power to balance the Budget." But MacDonald's proposal for a cut in the dole seemed downright wrong; the Labor government fell. MacDonald soon returned to office as head of a National government. The new government, slightly more adventurous than its predecessors, took Britain off gold in a few weeks. Sidney Webb, Labor's senior intellectual, provided the Labor government its obituary: "no one ever told *us* we could do that!"

The Labor government having immobilized itself by its intellectual conviction that there was no room for maneuver, no middle way, now succeeded through its collapse in documenting its major premise. Then the experience of 1931 displayed the Right was too hardboiled ever to acquiesce in even the most gradual democratic change. "The attempt to give a social bias to capitalism, while leaving it master of the house," wrote R. H. Tawney, "appears to have failed."

If piecemeal reforms were beyond the power of the Labor government, as they were beyond the desire of a Tory government, then the only hope lay in the rapid achievement of full socialism; the only way socialism could be achieved seemed to be through ruthlessness on the Left as great as that on the Right. Such reasoning was responsible for the lust for catastrophic change that suffused the British Left and infected a part of the American Left in the early thirties. No one drew

more facile and sweeping conclusions than Harold Laski. The fate of
the MacDonald government, Laski wrote, was "tantamount to an insistence that if socialists wish to secure a state built upon the principles of their faith, they can only do so by revolutionary means."

From this perspective Laski and those like him quite naturally
looked with derision on the advocate of the middle way. In December
1934, for the perhaps somewhat baffled readers of *Redbook* magazine,
Laski debated with Maynard Keynes whether America could spend its
way to recovery. Public spending, Laski said with horror, would lead
to inflation or heavy taxation or waste; it would mean, he solemnly
wrote, "an unbalanced budget with the disturbance of confidence (an
essential condition of recovery) which this implies": it would bequeath
a "bill of staggering dimensions" to future generations. "Government
spending as anything more than a temporary and limited expedient,"
he concluded, "will necessarily do harm in a capitalist society." This
was, of course, not only the argument of Ramsay MacDonald but of
Herbert Hoover; Laski's novelty was to use it to defend, not a balanced
budget and the gold standard, but—socialist revolution.

One way or another, the British Left began to vote against liberal
democracy. Sir Oswald Mosley, who had championed the most constructive economic program considered within the MacDonald government, indicated the new direction when, with John Strachey and
others, he founded the authoritarian-minded New Party in 1931. Mosley's excesses soon led him toward fascism and discredit; but plenty
of others were reaching similar conclusions about the impossibility of
reform under capitalism. Sidney and Beatrice Webb abandoned Fabi-
anism for the mirage of a new civilization in the Soviet Union. All
peaceful roads to progress seemed blocked. After a visit with Roosevelt
in Washington, Cripps wrote, "My whole impression is of an honest
anxious man faced by an impossible task—humanizing capitalism and
making it work." "The one thing that is not inevitable now," said
Cripps, "is gradualness."

Both Right and Left—Hoover and Stalin, John W. Davis and Mussolini, Ogden Mills and Stafford Cripps—thus rejected the notion of a
socially directed and managed capitalism, of a mixed economy, of
something in between classical free enterprise and classical socialism.
And the either/or demonstration commanded considerable respect in
the United States—self-evidently on the American Right; and to some
degree on the American Left. So Laski had made clear in *Democracy
in Crisis* that the American ruling class would be as tough and hopeless as any other:

> *What evidence is there, among the class which controls the destiny
> of America, of a will to make the necessary concessions? Is not the*

execution of Sacco and Vanzetti, the long indefensible imprisonment
of Mooney, the grim history of American strikes, the root of the an-
swer to that question?

In 1932 both Right and Left thus stood with fierce intransigence
on the solid ground of dogma. In so doing, they were challenging an
essential part of the American liberal tradition. When Professor Rexford G. Tugwell of the Columbia University economics department,
on leave in Washington, revisited his campus in 1933, he rashly bragged
of the new Deal's freedom from "blind doctrine," and the *Columbia
Spectator*, then edited by a brilliant young undergraduate named James
Wechsler, seized on this boast as the fatal weakness of Tugwell's argument and of the whole New Deal. "This is the crux of the problem,"
the *Spectator* said; "the blind stumbling in the most chaotic fashion—
experimenting from day to day—without any anchor except a few
idealistic phrases—is worthless. It is merely political pragmatism."

Merely political pragmatism—to ideologists, whether of Right or
of Left, this seemed conclusive evidence of intellectual bankruptcy. As
the conservatives had said that any attempt to modify the capitalist
system must mean socialism, so the radicals now said that any attempt to maintain the capitalist system must mean fascism. "Roosevelt's policies can be welded into a consistent whole," wrote I. F. Stone,
"only on the basis of one hypothesis . . . that Mr. Roosevelt intends to
move toward fascism." "The essential logic of the New Deal," wrote
Max Lerner, "is increasingly the naked fist of the capitalist state."

Convinced of the fragility of the system, the radicals saw themselves as the forerunners of apocalypse. "American commercial agriculture is doomed," wrote Louis Hacker; capitalism was doomed, too,
and the party system, and the traditional American way of life. In 1934
Sidney Hook, James Burnham, Louis Budenz, V. F. Calverton, James
Rorty and others addressed "An Open Letter to American Intellectuals." "We cannot by some clever Rooseveltian trick," the letter
warned,

> *evade the unfolding of basic economic and political developments*
> *under capitalism. . . . Let us not deceive ourselves that we shall not*
> *have to face here also the choice between reaction, on the one hand,*
> *and a truly scientific economy under a genuine workers' democracy*
> *on the other.*

In 1935 the *New Republic* stated with magisterial simplicity the
argument of the radicals against the New Dealers, of New York against
Washington, of the Marxists against the pragmatists.

> *Either the nation must put up with the confusions and miseries of*
> *an essentially unregulated capitalism, or it must prepare to supersede*

capitalism with socialism. There is no longer a feasible middle course.

Both radicalism and conservatism thus ended in the domain of either/or. The contradictions of actuality which so stimulated the pragmatists of Washington, only violated the properties and offended the illusions of the ideologists. While they all saw themselves as hardheaded realists, in fact they were Platonists, preferring essence to existence and considering abstractions the only reality.

The great central source of the New Deal, in my judgment, lay precisely in the instinctive response of practical, energetic and compassionate people to those dogmatic absolutes. This passion to sacrifice reality to doctrine presented a profound challenge to the pragmatic nerve. Many Americans, refusing to be intimidated by abstractions or to be overawed by ideology, responded by doing things. The whole point of the New Deal lay in its belief in activism, its faith in gradualness, its rejection of catastrophism, its indifference to ideology, its conviction that a managed and modified capitalist order achieved by piecemeal experiment could combine personal freedom and economic growth. "In a world in which revolutions just now are coming easily," said Adolf Berle, "the New Deal chose the more difficult course of moderation and rebuilding." "The course that the new Administration did take," said Harold Ickes, "was the hardest course. It conformed to no theory, but it did fit into the American system—a system of taking action step by step, a system of regulation only to meet concrete needs, a system of courageous recognition of change." Tugwell, rejecting laissez-faire and communism, spoke of the "third course."

Roosevelt himself, of course, was the liberal pragmatist *par excellence.* His aim was to steer between the extremes of chaos and tyranny by moving always, in his phrase, "slightly to the left of center." "Unrestrained individualism," he wrote, had proved a failure; yet "any paternalistic system which tries to provide for security for everyone from above only calls for an impossible task and a regimentation utterly uncongenial to the spirit of our people." He constantly repeated Macaulay's injunction to reform if you wished to preserve.

Roosevelt had no illusions about revolution. Mussolini and Stalin seemed to him, in his phrase, "not mere distant relatives" but "blood brothers." When Emil Ludwig asked him about his "political motive," he replied, "My desire is to obviate revolution. . . . I work in a contrary sense to Rome and Moscow." He said during the 1932 campaign:

> *Say that civilization is a tree which, as it grows, continually produces rot and dead wood. The radical says: "Cut it down." the conservative says: "Don't touch it." The liberal compromises: "Let's prune, so that we lose neither the old trunk nor the new branches."*

This campaign is waged to teach the country to march upon its appointed course, the way of change, in an orderly march, avoiding alike the revolution of radicalism and the revolution of conservatism.

I think it would be a mistake to underestimate the extent to which this pragmatic attitude was itself a major source of New Deal vitality. The exaltation of the middle way seems banal and obvious enough today. Yet the tyranny of dogma was such in the early years of the Great Depression that infatuation with ideology blocked and smothered the instinctive efforts of free men to work their own salvation. In a world intoxicated with abstractions, Roosevelt and the New Dealers stood almost alone in a stubborn faith in rational experiment, in trial and error. No one understood this more keenly than the great English critic of absolutes, Keynes, in an open letter to Roosevelt at the end of 1933, stated the hopes generated by the New Deal with precision and eloquence. "You have made yourself," Keynes told Roosevelt,

the trustee for those in every country who seek to mend the evils of our condition by reasoned experiment within the framework of the existing social system. If you fail, rational choice will be gravely prejudiced throughout the world, leaving orthodoxy and revolution to fight it out. But, if you succeed, new and bolder methods will be tried everywhere, and we may date the first chapter of a new economic era from your accession to office.

The question remains: Why did the New Deal itself have the pragmatic commitment? Why, under the impact of depression, was it not overborne by dogma as were most other governments and leaders in the world? The answer to this lies, I suspect, in the point I proposed earlier—in the suggestion that the New Deal represented, not just a response to depression, but also a response to pent-up frustration and needs in American society—frustrations and needs which would have operated had there been no depression at all. The periodic demand for forward motion in American politics, the periodic breakthrough of new leadership—these were already in the works before the depression. Depression, therefore, instead of catching a nation wholly unprepared, merely accelerated tendencies toward change already visible in the national community. The response to depression, in short, was controlled and tempered by the values of traditional American experimentalism, rather than those of rigid ideology. The New Deal was thus able to approach the agony of mass unemployment and depression in the pragmatic spirit, in the spirit which guaranteed the survival rather than the extinction of freedom, in the spirit which in time rekindled hope across the world that free men could manage their own economic destiny.

Ellis W. Hawley

ELLIS W. HAWLEY (1929–   ) is professor of history at the University
of Iowa. He is the author of *The New Deal and the Problem of Monopoly:
A Study in Economic Ambivalence* (1966).

As depicted by most American historians in the 1950s, the "mixed
economy" of the United States was a superlative blend of two worlds,
a system that combined rational direction, organizational security, and
stable growth with a large measure of democratic decision-making, individual liberty, and local and private initiative. While bringing competitive excesses and harmful fluctuations under administrtive control, it had also developed a system of "countervailing powers," a
"corporate conscience," and a vigorous "inter-industry competition,"
all of which had enabled it to retain the dynamism and safeguards associated with free markets and competitive enterprise. And though it
was still far from perfect, its amazing productivity had all but solved
the quantitative problems of production and distribution, thus providing the material base for a new type of qualitative and cultural reform.
Looking back, moreover, these writers credited Franklin D. Roosevelt
and his New Deal with much of the historical development responsible for this happy state of affairs. By modernizing and defending the
American political system, they argued, and by using it to stabilize,
democratize, and humanize an unruly corporate capitalism, the pragmatic New Dealers had provided the basic framework within which
the nation's liberal-democratic ideals could be preserved and realized.

More recently, as views of the economy have changed, this older
image of the New Deal has become somewhat tarnished. The central
development in recent American history, according to a new group of
institutionalist scholars, has been the rise of bureaucratic industrialism, not the further advance of liberal democracy; and the chief impetus to reform, they insist, has come from organizational elites in
search of stability and order, not from liberal democrats seeking equality and social justice. Hence, the New Deal was more the product of
corporate capitalism rather than the shaper of it. In essence, it provided

a threatened managerial elite market behavior, and solved the problems of aggregate demand and developmental capital. And the results,
according to another group of younger and more radical scholars, have
been tragic. Out of the failure of "reform," they contend, came a bas-
tard liberalism, a "corporate" variety, which, in the name of "progress," built illiberal and undemocratic institutions that have, in effect,
perpetuated social injustice and economic tyranny, required constant
involvement abroad, and transformed what should be a free people into
mindless bureaucrats and earnest consumers.

These divergent views, of course, may well tell us more about the
1950s and 1960s than about the 1930s. Yet, they do raise major questions concerning the nature of the political economy that was ham-
mered out during the New Deal years, who it was that did the ham-
mering, and how such conflicting estimates of it could be made. They
also suggest that New Deal activities might be profitably explored
within a broader perspective, one that would see them as part of a continuing but never wholly successful effort to resolve the tensions between bureaucratic industrialism and a liberal-democratic ethos. In the
1930s, as the political arena became a confusing battleground for conflicting industrial groups seeking stability and salvation, rival groups
of reformers seeking to remedy a "defective" and "oppressive" economic structure, and competing models of how one could reconcile a
technocorporate order with America's democratic heritage, the tensions became particularly acute. But the dilemma that underlay them
was not new. Nor would it disappear with the passing of the New Deal.

For business-government relations, in fact, the period of the New
Deal is probably best viewed as a time when one resolution of these
tensions between organizational capitalism and the liberal-democratic
ethos, the resolution that emerged in the 1920s, broke down, lost cre-
dence, and was rejected as being both unworkable and tyrannical. The
result was an intense but confused search for another synthesis, one,
so most agreed, that would necessarily involve a larger role for government. And New Deal policy, as it fluctuated between competing
models and built new bureaucracies, did lay the groundwork for the
point of resolution that was lauded in the 1950s. In this sense, it represented a new departure. Yet it was also tied to the past, both in the
sense that it was trying to cope with a continuing problem, one that
antedated the depression, and in the sense that most of the competing
models offered as solutions derived from past experience, particularly
from conflicting progressive visions, variants of the "planned economy" of World War I, or logical extensions of the cooperative associationalism that had been hailed as the answer during the New Era but
found wanting after 1929. Seen in perspective, the origins, formulation, and effects of New Deal policy fit into a broader framework of
long-standing tensions and repeated efforts at resolution; and it is to

the task of examining them within this framework that the remainder of this essay will be devoted.

In recent years, historians have disagreed sharply about business-government relations during the Progressive era. But from all they have said, two things seem to stand out. One was the rapid rise of an organizational economy, which brought with it large areas of "private government," new bureaucratic-scientific-professional values, and a persistent search for order and stability, primarily through the creation of ever larger associative and hierarchic structures, the infusing of these with a new set of managerial attitudes and group loyalties, and the use of the state, where necessary and expedient, to further the process. The other was an ambivalent cluster of reform efforts, striving in general to resolve the tensions between the new order and the liberal-democratic-village values that it threatened, yet deeply divided over the point at which this should take place, the degree of centralization needed, and the method by which liberty could best be advanced. Not surprisingly, different reform models appeared; and around these, as seekers of order and both "old" and "new" liberals clashed, compromised, and merged into one another, many of the period's debates swirled.

Four models, in particular, were significant. The first, best known as Wilson's New Freedom and best articulated by Louis Brandeis, held that bureaucratic centralism had gone beyond technological needs, that this "new tyranny" rested chiefly on special privilege and "unfair" or "unnatural" behavior, and that the state could best advance freedom by removing these aids to concentration and forging an economy that was not only modern and scientific but competitive, ethical, and decentralized as well. The second model, the New Nationalism of Herbert Croly and Theodore Roosevelt, held just the opposite: that concentration and cooperation did stem from technological needs, and consequently, to liberate and democratize, the state must forge national controls and use them to advance social justice, promote cooperation in the public interest, and provide the material base for a new and higher individualism. The third model, generally labeled the New Competition and associated particularly with the trade association promoter and spokesman for business progressivism Arthur J. Eddy, held that through self-regulating associations, codes of ethics, and schemes of "industrial betterment," the new economy was itself developing an "industrial democracy," a "purer" competition, a "higher individualism." Hence, it needed only encouragement and guidance, not regulation and restructuring. And finally, implicit in much agitation and explicit with a few theorists, was an incipient model of interest-group liberalism, one that would allegedly advance liberty by balancing groups against each other and allowing this to take the place of classical competition. . . .

The shift from Hoover to Roosevelt, then, did bring a new departure in business-government relations. After three years of deepening depression climaxed by a banking crisis, demands for change had become insistent; and under an administration committed to "doing something," the government's role in the economy quickly became a larger one. The novelty of this "new deal," however, has often been exaggerated. The shift was not from laissez-faire to a managed economy, but rather from one attempt at management, that through informal business-government cooperation, to another more formal and coercive attempt. The tensions that had reappeared, although altered somewhat by the economic situation and the relative decline of an older middle class of small capitalists and independent professionals, were essentially the same ones that earlier policy-makers had tried to resolve. And the guiding models for a new order were mostly inherited ones, not alien imports or instant improvisations. They derived from what innovators had envisioned during the Progressive period, from the experience during World War I, from agitation outside the consensus of the 1920s, and from what seemed to be the "lessons" of Hoover's experience or "logical extensions" of his approach.

The new administration, moreover, despite its critics' charges and its own claims of "pragmatism," was committed to change only within a relatively rigid "middle way," one that, to be sure, was broader than Hoover's, but at the same time was clearly limited by fixed ideological boundaries. Ruled out on one side were stabilizing arrangements involving the open avowal of a "closed," "authoritarian," or "monopolistic" system. Ruled out on the other were liberalizing or democratizing reforms that would seriously jeopardize capitalist incentives, constitutional safeguards, modern technology, or recovery prospects. And ruled out, even when they came within these limits, were programs whose implementation would require excessive conflict or some radically new type of politics or administration. The disposition, by and large, was to adjust differences, make accommodations, and build on existing institutions.

Still, within these elements of continuity, there was a commitment to change, or at least to "action." And once the government had changed hands, a variety of different types of activists began pushing their particular visions of what should replace the Hoover approach to business-government relations. Some, ranging from Rexford Tugwell on the left to Hugh Johnson on the right, were either national or business-oriented "planners." Deriving their models from either the New Nationalism, the war experience, or the vision of an associational capitalism, they were ready now to accept an organizational as opposed to a competitive system, restructure it somewhat in the interests of better "balance," and then "manage" it so as to insure sustained expansion and make possible a reflowering of the liberal-democratic heritage. Others, including western "antimonopolists" like William Borah and Wright Patman, Brandeisian-oriented lawyers like Thomas Corcoran and Benjamin Cohen, farm leaders like Edward O'Neal and John Simpson, and spokesmen for urban labor like Robert Wagner, were either decentralizers or balancers. Heirs of the New Freedom or spokesmen for disadvantaged interest groups, they were insistent now that recovery and freedom must come not by centralizing power but by dispersing it, revitalizing the market system, or strengthening a previously exploited group. And still others, men like the agricultural economist George Warren, the Oklahoma inflationist Elmer Thomas, and the Utah banker Marriner Eccles, were "reflationists," concerned not with structural reform but with using monetary-fiscal levers to "reflate" the economy or "compensate" for its defects.

Within each camp, moreover, further divisions existed. Small-business decentralizers of both the populist and Brandeisian types disagreed at times with those pushing consumer, farmer, or labor welfare; permanent spenders clashed with "pump primers," "currency tinkerers," and "budget balancers"; and leftist "planners" differed sharply with those of the center and right. "Planning," as men like Tugwell saw it, must be done by "public men," not by corporate interests, who almost always opted for scarcity profits. But as envisioned by others, particularly by a man like Adolf Berle, a "regenerated" business could be used in the public interest. And for still others, men like Hugh Johnson, George Peek, or Raymond Moley, all of whom seemed to believe that a more powerful "private government" could deliver on the New Era promises, the answer was a "partnership" with federal authority in a supportive role.

On the business side, too, similar divisions existed. Now flirting with corporate statism were substantial numbers of association officials, former war chieftains, spokesmen for "sick" industries, and other leaders of the corporate "enlightenment." Included in their ranks, for example, were trade association lawyers like Benjamin Javits, Gilbert Montague, and David Podell, economists like Edgar Heermance and Philip Cabot, wartime administrators like Bernard Baruch and Howard Coffin, corporate paternalists like Gerard Swope and Henry Dennison, and prominent association officials like Charles Abbott of the Structural Steel Institute, Wilson Compton of the National Lumber Manufacturers Association, and Walker Hines of the Cotton Textile Institute. Yet these people did not, as some revisionists would have it, constitute a united, omnipotent elite moving confidently toward a corporate order. Among themselves they frequently despaired of agreeing on a specific scheme. Unlike assured rulers, they worried constantly about creating an apparatus that might be used against them. And clearly, they did not speak for all businessmen, particularly not for those who tended to cling either to entrepreneurial modes of thought or to the dream of private coordination. Groups like the American Trade Association Executives, under the leadership of Leslie C. Smith, and the National Association of Manufacturers, with its long history of attacks on "big government" and business-labor cooperation, had not endorsed antitrust revision, chiefly for fear it would lead to unfriendly controls or powerful labor unions. Hard-pressed independents, especially in retail fields and the "sick" or chaotic industries, complained bitterly about their "monopolistic" rivals. Most of the talk about planning, as they saw it, amounted to schemes through which "predatory interests" hoped to join with "big government" and "big labor" to crush "independent enterprise." And intermingled with these views was a discordant medley of others, sentiments ranging from such stout defenses of "rugged individualism" and "natural law" as those set forth by the financier Albert Wiggin or the banking economist Benjamin Anderson to the support for "reflationary schemes" that emanated from James Rand's Committee for the Nation and to time-hallowed calls for tax relief, economy, union-busting, and tariff adjustment.

For a leader who valued consistency, such divided counsels might have required either a choice or a delay in the promised action. But for Roosevelt, with his penchant for resisting ideological systems, mixing opposites, and administering by conflict, the answer was to give "something" to everyone, institutionalize the divisions, and avoid, at least for the time being, a definite commitment to any one reform model. Consequently, what most of the recovery-reform program did as it took shape in 1933, was to create new administrative frameworks, give them vague or ambivalent mandates, and leave it to clashing administrators, competing idologies, and conflicting pressure groups to fill in the details. This was true, for example, of the act creating the Tennessee Valley Authority, of the Emergency Transportation Act, of the farm law, and, to some extent, of the financial legislation. But it was true, above all, of the National Industrial Recovery Act. Its formulators, by setting forth vague goals, giving industrial code-makers a virtually blank check, and adding licensing provisions and public works, Section 7a for labor, and a mixture of antitrust exemptions with incantations against "monopoly," had provided an "economic charter" rather than a definite policy, a framework that different sets of administrators could use to build quite different versions of an "industrial democracy." Reform through administration, a route upon which the progressives had embarked, had seemingly come into its own. . . .

In practice, though this brand of business-government cooperation, like Hoover's earlier brand, failed to generate expansion and was therefore quickly charged with being tyrannical and oppressive. . . .

In 1934, then, the gap between promise and performance brought the New Deal's initial approach, that embodied in the NRA codes, under increasing attack, particularly from farm and labor leaders, dissident businessmen, "market restorers," and "national planners." Measures like the Securities Exchange Act, the Air Mail Act, and the new trade law, based as they were on competitive models and ideals, were all indications that this initial approach was in retreat. So were the opening shots in a campaign to dismantle the "power trust." And within the NRA, the shift in sentiment and political pressure was reflected in drives to scrap the price and production provisions, strengthen the labor clauses, and restructure the code authorities. A coherent alternative, however, was slow to emerge. Throughout 1934, the conflicting thrusts—the battles between internationalists, nationalists, and intranationalists in trade policy, between regulators, nationalizers, and decentralizers in the utility and financial fields, and between the "business planners" and their critics in the NRA—tended to cancel each other out and bring stalemate and confusion rather than a new synthesis. The NRA, in particular, became a study in frustration. There the agitation for reform succeeded in hampering formal cartelization, forcing Johnson out, and producing new policy statements, but the agitators were unable to reshape the code structure and use it to implement a new reform model.

During the first half of 1934, for example, those who would restore competition as the regulator did make their influence felt. Picking up support from discontented groups, academic economists, and progressive politicians, from other governmental agencies, and from such inquiries as that conducted by Clarence Darrow's National Recovery Review Board, the "market restorers" within the NRA's technical and advisory divisions were able to block various code provisions from going into effect and eventually to put through Office Memorandum 228 reaffirming faith in competitive goals and renouncing price-fixing and production control. Yet, against the entrenched opposition of the existing code authorities and their supporters, a group whose cooperation the administration seemed anxious to retain, the champions of the new policy found that they could not even revise codes that violated it, much less write new provisions to achieve its goals. The most they could do was to complain vigorously about the gap between policy and practice, thus making administrators reluctant to defend openly or enforce very actively many of the trade practice provisions. For groups needing strong government support to keep "chiselers" in check, the result was renewed competition; but for those needing only tacit cooperation, it was not. Conflicting lines of action, it seemed, although they might provide a sense of movement and involvement, had reduced the effects of government intervention to little more than an equivalent of laissez-faire.

A similar inability to translate policy into practice was also characteristic of those who would build "industrial democracy" by strengthening organized labor, particularly now by preventing the independent unionism desired by a majority of employees from being undercut by company organizations or individual bargaining. Here again, official policy, as set forth by the National Labor Board and its successor, the National Labor Relations Board, did interpret Section 7a as requiring a "majority rule," an arrangement, in other words, under which the labor organization that received a majority of employee votes would be recognized as the bargaining agent for all workers in the bargaining unit. Yet, when confronted with the antagonism of NRA administrators, the desire to avoid legal tests, and the tendency of Roosevelt to split the differences, the champions of this interpretation were unable to swing the NRA's enforcement machinery behind it or to prevent special presidential interventions from exempting key industries. Consequently, they were unable to create much of a countervailing force. Throughout the NRA period, increased unionization came chiefly in fields where strong industrial unions were already active, and employee benefits still tended to approximate those considered necessary by "enlightened" industrialists. The rise of "big labor" as a major force would await the type of law that Senator Robert Wagner would finally secure in 1935.

Even less successful and more frustrating was the experience of those who hoped to turn the NRA into an instrument for collectivist planning, one in which broad policy goals would emerge from restructured code authorities representing all interests, strong technical agencies would provide the data and "plans," and powerful "public men," using the licensing provisions if necessary and exercising control over profits and investment as well as pricing and production, would put the "plans" into effect. Only through such a system, ran the argument of men like Tugwell, Lorwin, and Galloway, could Americans have abundance, efficiency, and democracy, all at the same time, and supporting this general view now were detailed memorandums from such economists as Gardiner Means and Mordecai Ezekiel. Unlike the "market restorers," however, these "collectivists" were regarded by many of their fellow citizens as being either un-American or impractical. They lacked popular or political support; and because Roosevelt was both dubious about their approach and unwilling to antagonize the opponents of it, their influence was minimal. The licensing power expired without being invoked. Agitation for such things as profit controls, quality standards, tripartite code authorities, or systematic "expansion plans" was mostly in vain. And the limiting of code authority powers and functions that did take place seemed to stem mostly from complaints about abuse and discrimination, not from efforts to facilitate central planning.

To this agitation for change in 1934, some of the supporters of "business planning" were willing to accommodate themselves. In some fields, the need for government support was still strong enough to override the reluctance to pay a higher "price," and as some business leaders saw it, reform could still be kept in conservative channels that would promote stability and improve rather than threaten the corporate structure. More typically, however, as resentment against, or fear of, the critics mounted and as their influence with Roosevelt seemed more evident, the reaction was one of outrage, alarm, and bitter resistance. Some, still desirous of antitrust immunity and willing to pay some "price" for it, dug in along the line of the existing code structure. Some, convinced that things had already gone too far in opening the door to "socialism," "anarchy," and "labor monopolies," demanded revisions that would guarantee industrial autonomy and allow the open shop. Some, thoroughly disenchanted with the workings of the NRS or deeply frightened by the directions in which its official policies might take it, joined with those who had opposed it from the start to demand that the whole program be scrapped.

Increasingly, it seemed, as the year 1934 drew to a close, the greatest villain in business circles was becoming not "destructive competition" but "New Deal tyranny," or, for those inclined to personalize matters, "that man in the White House." Those opposed to, or disenchanted with, "business planning," those who believed that it had not been given a fair trial, and those frightened by the attacks on it could all agree that top priority now must be given to limiting or rolling back the power of a threatening, unpredictable, and potentially dangerous state bureaucracy. It was this power and its potential misuse, they decided, that were the real sources of instability, the things that frightened investors and blocked recovery. And in attacking it, they were soon invoking, with varying degrees of sincerity, either the ideals of the New Era or those of entrepreneurial capitalism, classical economics, and Jeffersonian liberalism. Many, to be sure, still felt that excessive competition and chaotic disorder were major problems; but with crisis conditions surmounted, the possibilities of solving them privately seemed greater again. Or, at least, they seemed preferable to relying upon public tools that were not properly delimited or were capable of great "abuse" when wielded by ill-informed, impractical, or hostile bureaucrats.

Such fears and beliefs also led most businessmen to oppose the deficit financing, work relief projects, and social insurance programs that might have solved most of their problems. To later generations, such measures would appear as basically conservative, designed, it seemed, to bring stable prosperity without structural change and to undercut the power bases of the system's critics. But with a few exceptions, corporate leaders in 1934 did not view them as such. Instead, they were seen as burdens upon business, as immoral departures from the "American way," as preludes to crippling taxes, capital levies, and economic disaster, or as devices to elect corrupt politicians and strengthen a menacing and wasteful bureaucracy. Recovery and security, according to numerous business speeches now, must come by shrinking government and insisting upon sound finance, not by expanding it and taking risks with the public credit. And partly in response to such criticism, partly because Roosevelt himself remained basically a "budget balancer," the administration coupled its expansion of social services and subsidies with a fiscal orthodoxy that kept the expansionary power of federal deficits far below what was needed to achieve full employment.

As the year 1935 dawned, then, the New Deal had not yet discovered the arrangements that would allow an effective corporate capitalism to function within a liberal-democratic framework. The form of business-government cooperation adopted in 1933 was under severe attack as being both unworkable and tyrannical. Yet most of its supporters, instead of modifying their model to remedy the defects, seemed bent upon resurrecting the discredited models of the 1920s or 1890s. Their rivals, moreover—the "market restorers," "collectivist planners," and "counterorganizers"—were still too weak to force a trial of their solutions. And as yet, no new philosophy had arisen capable of reconciling the conflicting thrusts into what Americans might accept as a new and superior synthesis. In a sense, to be sure, the maze of contradictory activities, particularly those of the NRA, had brought an institutionalization of conflicting pressures; but the result for most participants was a feeling of stalemate and frustration, not one of having broken through to a desirable and satisfying arrangement. That Roosevelt's optimism and "experimentation" might yet produce one, the critics of "business planning" seemed convinced. But the stalemate that the NRA had become by 1935 had few real friends, and to many the Schechter decision, sweeping away the codes and their appendages, seemed to remove an obstacle rather than block needed reforms. At least, it made possible fresh starts.

As one might expect, however, the program that eventually took shape in 1935 clearly had its seeds in earlier developments, particularly in the efforts of those who would limit or check business power rather than trying to use it in the public interest. It was to these groups that Roosevelt now swung his support, partly, it seems, because the end of the NRA afforded him room to maneuver, partly because business hostility had led him to shift his political base toward farm and labor groups, partly because he wished to prevent antibusiness demagogues from making inroads on his left flank. He was limited, moreover, by the political, legal, and ideological obstructions that now lay in the way of other options. Business planning under government auspices, even if it could be made to pass legal muster, was a discredited approach, not only with the public and most "liberals" but also with the business elements that had been frightened and irritated by their NRA experience. The small group that kept trying to revive such an arrangement found itself unable to develop much support in either business or political circles. And "collectivist planning" was even less feasible. Although a few of its advocates—notably, men like Tugwell, Mordecai Ezekiel, and Jerome Frank—worked out and agitated for an "NRA in reverse," so constructed as to bring about "planned expansion," their chances of implementing such a vision seemed to dwindle rather than grow. Added to their encumbrances now was the argument that any planning program must of necessity follow the pattern of the NRA and be dominated by "selfish monopolists."

What emerged, then, as the "market restorers" and "counterorganizers" moved to the fore, was essentially a mixture of selective "trustbusting," government-backed unionization, limited expansion and nationalization of social services, and continued but disguised cartelization for "exceptional" groups willing to pay the "price" and able to pull the right political and ideological levers. . . .

The other major aspect of the Second New Deal was the expansion and nationalization of social services, exemplified particularly in the Social Security Act, the work relief program, the housing and conservation activities, and the protective labor and rural rehabilitation measures. In one sense now, "welfare capitalism," community-centered welfare, and the patronage-oriented welfare of urban political machines were all giving way to a larger and broader "welfare statism." Yet again, significant as this change was, the patterns adopted worked in some respects to strengthen rather than displace existing institutions. Local communities still remained key units in dispersing welfare; political machines strengthened themselves by investments or were "bribed" into becoming "partners" along the welfare frontier; discontented elements, potentially disruptive, were converted into more conservative citizens; and frequently, despite the humanitarianism involved, groups needing aid and protection the most were the ones exempted. Again, the degree of business opposition seemed disproportionate to the extent and nature of "reform" or "socialization."

Logically, the "enlightened" group of corporate leaders willing to go along with, or join in, most of the social program should have been much larger.

Logically, too, both corporate leaders and Second New Dealers might have moved quickly now from the mixture taking shape in 1937 to the "mixed economy" that seemed so satisfactory to similar groups in the 1950s. The latter synthesis, after all, did contain many of the same elements, particularly the same curious blend of private controls and pressure-group "planning" with antitrust ideals, selective "trust-busting," capitalistic labor unions, and modest measures of semina-tionalized social services. What it contained beyond this was, first of all, a general conviction that such a blend did represent a new and superior synthesis, and second, a more effective set of techniques for promoting and regulating economic growth. Had those shaping policy in 1937 been willing to make the required psychological adjustments, divert somewhat more resources to trade expansion and technological development, and seize the theory of supplementary public invest-ment being advanced by a few New Dealers and Keynesians, it seems possible that the new "American system" might have come in the late 1930s rather than the 1950s.

This development, however, was not to be. Instead, the great ma-jority of corporate leaders and their political allies continued to blame the lack of new investment and the failure to achieve sustained ex-pansion on the New Deal's "shackling," "burdening," and "frighten-ing" of business, whereas various groups of New Dealers continued to see a defective corporate structure in need of income redistribution, "market restoration," or systematic "coordination" and "balancing." By many in both camps, Keynesianism was seen as being either count-erproductive, wasteful, dishonest, or a type of "artificial" solution, de-signed by their opponents to perpetuate "unnatural" structures and controls in need of change. And the result, since nothing done so far had really remedied the system's inability to generate the needed in-vestment and purchasing power, was another breakdown and contrac-tion. In the first half of 1937, as tax increases offset the expansionary effects of the Bonus Act and the administration pursued a deflationary policy, one intended to check a wage-price spiral, curb a speculative inventory boom, strengthen the market for government bonds, and bring the long-sought budget, the stage was set for a new collapse. In the fall, limited recovery and what had seemed to be an emerging equi-librium gave way to the "Roosevelt depression" and to another round of policy conflicts.

As conditions worsened in late 1937, a few business leaders began once more to urge some type of government-backed "business plan-ning." For them, the source of instability had again become "destruc-

tive competition." For the great majority, however, the source was political in nature. It lay particularly in the undistributed profits tax of
1936, the federal labor policy, and unwarranted "attacks upon business." And the way to eliminate it and start the needed flow of new
investment funds, so the argument ran, was to revise taxes, unwind
much of the New Deal, and roll back federal power. Again there were
exceptions, but much of organized business, it seemed, had not yet
come to view the arrangements of the Second New Deal as really being
"stabilizers" and "balance wheels." Nor was it ready yet to adopt the
view that contraction called for larger federal deficits. Although the
tax revision that business groups lobbied through Congress in early
1938 did mean a larger deficit and thus a dose of Keynesianism, this
was not the intention. In the business theory of recovery, subscribed
to by most supporters of the legislation, tax cuts were supposed to be
accompanied by reduced governmental expenditures and a return to
balanced budgets.

Meanwhile, various groups in the government were also analyzing
the breakdown and urging changes in policy, again largely in terms of
what they had been advocating earlier. One group, for example, represented by men like Secretary of Commerce Daniel Roper, RFC Director Jesse Jones, and Secretary of the Treasury Henry Morgenthau,
Jr., seemed willing now to adopt the business formula and try to restore
"confidence" by balancing the budget, revising the tax laws, and declaring a recess on reform. A second, led by Donald Richberg and other
former NRA officials, wanted to check the new outbreak of "destructive competition" by setting up a new program of "business planning"
through industrial codes. A third, consisting of "collectivist planners"
like Ezekiel and congressional "mavericks" like Thomas Amlie, advocated an Industrial Expansion Act, a measure, in other words, that
would create machinery similar to the code structure of the NRA but
this time with proper safeguards and with mechanisms that would insure its use to underwrite full production rather than restricted output.
A fourth, led by men like Harold Ickes, Thomas Corcoran, Leon Henderson, and antitrust chief Robert Jackson, urged that the "market restoration" activities of the Second New Deal be drastically broadened,
primarily to deal with the "monopolistic" groups whose "administered" price increases had brought a new failure of purchasing power
and a subsequent "strike of capital." And finally, an increasingly influential but still small group, spearheaded by men like Lauchlin Cur-
rie and Alvin Hansen, was now ready to pronounce the existing structure acceptable and use planned deficits as a way of stabilizing it.
Armed now with Keynes's *General Theory*, this group had acquired a
new confidence and cohesion; but much of its support in the subsequent debate still came from people who wanted to spend on human-

itarian or social grounds, who saw spending as an aid to other types of reform, or who viewed it as a temporary expedient until something better could be done.

As in 1933, Roosevelt himself seemed reluctant to choose and inclined to give everyone "something." While promising a balanced budget and urging business to take up the slack, he also authorized a resumption of some spending and lending activities, encouraged those who were attacking "concentrations of economic power," discussed the need to "manage" price relationships, and talked about reviving some kind of "business planning." For a time, confusion prevailed. But gradually, some options were ruled out and others limited. "Planning," after all, was still politically unfeasible; "budget-balancing" seemed completely ineffective and would not long remain possible without tax increases; and since few could agree on just what a "decentralization" effort should include, the demands for it were channeled into the protracted studies of a Temporary National Economic Committee. This left a program consisting chiefly of the mixture of 1937 plus two major additions. One was the attempt, under Thurman Arnold's direction, to use the Sherman Act as a weapon of price control. In key areas now, where high prices and costs were felt to constitute economic "bottlenecks," an enlarged Antitrust Division set out to bring them down through highly publicized enforcement "drives" and the negotiation of numerous consent decrees. The other innovation, much more significant for the future, was Roosevelt's acceptance of planned deficits as a way of expanding the economy. Having decided in favor of a new spending program, he proceeded to justify it in Keynesian terms and to claim credit for the upturn that followed it.

As the decade drew to a close, both of these innovations engendered heated debates, and what would have happened to them had there been no World War II is difficult to say. Probably, considering the defeat of the new spending bill in 1939, it would have taken another severe recession or two before Keynesianism became the established way of regulating and stabilizing aggregate demand. And probably, considering Arnold's flair for the dramatic and the initial expansion of his program, it would have taken somewhat longer before corporate planners and other organizational leaders managed to move the antitrust enterprise back into the relatively safe areas of checking marginal abuses and protecting one business group from another. As it turned out, the war hastened both processes. The Arnold program, after coming into sharp conflict with the business-oriented war agencies, was finally shelved and forgotten, at least to the extent that there have been no subsequent efforts to use the antitrust apparatus as a major and continuing tool of price management. And Keynesianism, vindicated by the impact of the war spending, quickly became a part of the "American way," particularly since the war debt, the wartime expansion of the public sector, and the "need" for spending on armaments, technology, and foreign aid all made possible a type of fiscal management that business leaders found more palatable. Instead of being dependent on fluctuating public expenditures that could "subvert" capitalist virtues and create "competition for private enterprise," they could now rely upon a stable core of "desirable" spending and depend upon fluctuations in government revenue to regulate aggregate demand. Corporate capitalism, so "liberal" spenders seemed to think, had finally been "liberalized"; but the reverse effect, a "corporatization" of the "liberals," seemed to be somewhat closer to what had actually happened.

In the 1940s, partly because of their new "partnership" with government during the war, partly because of their subsequent success in scrapping reconversion controls and checking labor power, most corporate leaders also came to accept the other innovations of the New Deal. A mixture of properly limited "welfare statism" with "responsible" labor unions, pressure-group "planning," and devices to maintain "workable" competition, they concluded, did make for a stable environment in which corporate organizations could prosper and grow. And on the other side, deeply impressed by the wartime and postwar performance of the economy, by the changing attitudes of corporate leaders, and by the need to protect a going system from the "mindlessness" of a "radical right," those who had set out to "democratize" and "liberalize" the corporate order came to the conclusion that they had been successful. Admittedly, they noted, much power remained in the hands of a corporate elite. But now, in view of the "corporate conscience," the "workable competition," and the system of "countervailing powers" that reform had created, the power would aid rather than threaten the continued advance of liberty and democracy.

Seemingly, the tensions between corporate values and those of the liberal-democratic creed had been resolved into a new and higher synthesis, that of "democratic pluralism," the "mixed economy," or the "vital center." But the broad belief that such was the case would not endure. Deeply dissatisfied with the type of society that the new "American way" appeared to be creating, a new generation of critics would soon proclaim it to be a "new tyranny" controlled, or at least "manipulated," by an irresponsible "power elite" and a modern set of "feudal fiefdoms." "Reform," so the lament ran, had not only failed to "democratize" the area of "private government"; it had aided the "interests" and the "machine" to take over the public apparatus as well. And though the result had been prosperity for the corporation and its dependents, it had also been an expansion of "imperialism" and "exploitation," an organizational society that left the individual "alienated" and "powerless," and inaction or "repression" in the face of festering social problems. Like New Era associationalism, the pluralistic theories of the 1950s had been merely a smoke screen to hide an undemocratic system of decision-making; and like progressive reform, the New Deal had been another "triumph of conservatism."

That this tarnished image of the New Deal innovations overcompensated for the glowing view of the 1950s seems fairly obvious. The criteria of judgement, after all, were frequently unrealizable ideals or expanded definitions of what constituted "democracy," not the arrangements that preceded the New Deal, the experience of other nations, or the realistic assessment of available alternatives. Roosevelt, it must be conceded, was not the ideal philosopher-politician who might have clarified and resolved the dilemmas of industrial America, but it is hard to conceive of any political figure in the 1930s who could have filled this role. It is also difficult, considering the experience of the Hoover years and of other nations, to argue that rational systematization would have produced better results; and it is doubly difficult, considering the previous pace of reform and what preceded the New Deal innovations, to argue that the period brought a setback rather than a significant advance for democracy. Clearly, the new labor structure, despite its "corporatist" and oligarchic tendencies, was a more democratic arrangement than the company unionism of the New Era. And most believers in democracy, it would seem, would prefer the "new welfare," the expanded federal bureaucracy, and the stabilized, subsidized corporate capitalism that finally emerged, "manipulative," "elitist," and "impersonal" though they might be, to the welfare, governmental, and economic structures that existed in 1932.

The tarnished image, moreover, frequently carried with it an erroneous impression concerning the role of business groups in policymaking. Since they seemed to have benefited most from the innovations of the period, the temptation was strong to conclude that they must have planned it that way and used the New Dealers either as their tools or as camouflage for their operations. In reality, so the evidence at hand indicates, they had neither the power, the unity, nor the vision to do this. They could, to be sure, push an initial program upon the new administration, limit the efforts at structural reform, and secure desired stabilization measures for certain types of industries. But they could not make the initial program work or retain the initiative; and instead of seeing that their long-range interests lay with the pattern taking shape after 1934 and moving quickly to adopt it, most of them spent the next six years fighting a bitter and expensive delaying action. What emerged was the creation not of an omnipotent corporate elite but of a complex interaction between conflicting interest groups, resurgent liberal ideals, and the champions of competing reform models, all of which, after all, contemplated the salvation and stabilizing of corporate capitalism as well as the democratizing of it.

If the revised image overcompensated, however, it did bring into focus some glaring defects in the earlier one, particularly its magnification of the degree of change, its search for continuities only in "reform" rather than in business circles, and its assumptions that the New Deal had solved the problems of power and maldistribution, transformed corporate capitalism into an obedient servant of the people, and found the way to reconcile a technocorporate order with competitive and democratic ideals. The innovations of the 1930s, significant though they were in strengthening the economy and bringing new groups and beneficiaries into the political process, had not altered the fundamental dilemmas confronting earlier reforms. They had merely shifted them into somewhat different settings. And probably, despite the disillusionment of many critics with a "middle way," the conflicting traditions and drives that underlay the dilemmas would persist, producing, along with some "progress," another confused search for a synthesis and new but transitory claims that one had been found. Significantly, the new concern with "abuses of power," with "overorganization," and with subversion of the "public interest" was producing not only fringe rejections of liberalism and technology but also revivals of the Brandeisian model, new dreams of associationalism, and updated notions of "public men" independent of the tug and pull of interest groups. History, of course, did not run in cycles, but surely there were parallels.

☆ 8 ☆

The Coming of World War II

AVOIDABLE OR INEVITABLE?

During the Great Depression of the 1930s the American people and their leaders remained preoccupied for much of the period with a myriad of domestic concerns. Concentrating on solving the problems of unemployment, underproduction, agricultural distress, and an economy that seemed to be on the verge of collapse, most individuals gave relatively little thought to events on the international scene. With a few notable exceptions the aim of Americans was to solve their internal problems; foreign relations were important only to the extent that they threatened to involve the nation in another world holocaust similar to the one that began in 1914 and ended tragically four years later. Indeed, the desire to remain isolated from developments on the international scene was so pervasive that between 1934 and 1937 the Congress enacted and the president signed a series of acts designed precisely to prevent a repetition of the events from 1914 to 1917 that eventually ended in America's participation in World War I.

The outbreak of World War II in Europe in 1939 proved to be an important turning point in the development of American foreign policy. Domestic concerns such as the Great Depression and mass unemployment receded into the background as the fear of war swept over the country. Unlike Woodrow Wilson Roosevelt refused to ask his countrymen to remain neutral in thought as well as action. "This nation," he told the American people in a fireside chat in September 1939, "will remain a neutral nation, but I cannot ask that every American remain neutral in thought as well." From the very beginning of hostilities Roosevelt's hope was to offer as much military aid to the Allies as he could without going to war. Upon presidential urging Congress repealed the arms embargo that was then in effect because the two-year cash-and-carry clause of the Neutrality Act of 1937 had expired. The fall of France in the spring of 1940 intensified Roosevelt's desire to rebuild America's military forces and to give England all aid short of war. In 1941 the program of military aid to the Allied cause was expanded considerably by the Lend-Lease Act that was passed in March. By the summer of that year the United States was involved in an undeclared naval war with Germany as American naval forces assumed the responsibility of protecting shipping in the western half of the North Atlantic. The most dramatic gesture of American sympathy for the British cause came in August of 1941 when Roosevelt and Churchill met off the coast of Newfoundland and agreed to a joint statement on mutual war aims. Known as the Atlantic Charter the document not only spelled out the hopes of the two leaders for a better world, but referred specifically to "the final destruction of the Nazi tyranny" as a war aim.

The situation in Asia was equally explosive. Beginning in 1937 Japan renewed her attack upon the Nationalist regime of Chiang Kai-shek. The United States, having long been committed to the preservation of the territorial integrity and independence of China, found itself facing a diplomatic crisis. Nazi victories in Europe had the effect of stimulating Japanese ambitions even further; after the fall of France Japan occupied northern Indochina and signified its desire to establish a "coprosperity sphere" throughout eastern Asia—a euphemism for Japanese hegemony.

Roosevelt responded slowly to these developments in Asia. First, the American government adopted various forms of economic pressure. After Japan occupied southern Indochina in July of 1941 Roosevelt took the decisive step of imposing all-inclusive economic sanctions. At this point Japan faced the choice of curtailing its ambitions, particularly in China, or breaking the restrictions by resorting to armed conflict. During the remainder of the year Japan and the United States remained on a collision course that finally culminated in the fateful attack on Pearl Harbor on December 7, 1941.

Throughout the course of World War II, few Americans expressed any doubts over the issue of war guilt or their own involvement. Faced by totalitarian regimes in Germany, Italy, and Japan—regimes committed to the goal of regional or world domination—the United States, most felt, had no choice but to defend itself and become the champion of the free world. Roosevelt tried his best to avoid war and the use of American troops overseas, but the march of events seemed to destroy his hopes. The Japanese attack on Pearl Harbor settled the issue of going to war in a conclusive manner. From that point on America committed its industrial and military might against the forces of aggression. Such was the position taken by most contemporary scholars and writers who dealt with American diplomacy from 1937 to 1941.

The first criticisms concerning America's foreign policies in the years prior to 1941 came toward the end of World War II. Not until after the war was over, however, did the revisionists—as those critical of Roosevelt came to be known—spell out their case in great detail. The reaction against Roosevelt's policies after 1945 was not a totally unexpected or surprising development. After each of America's past wars, a debate had taken place over the question of whether the nation ought to have become involved in overt hostilities. More important in explaining the criticisms of Roosevelt's diplomacy, however, was the widespread disillusionment in the United States with the results of World War II. America had gone to war in 1941 to destroy the forces of totalitarianism and then found itself faced with an even greater menace—the Soviet Union. Germany was divided, half of Europe lay under Russian domination, and the United States and the Soviet Union entered upon a period of tense diplomatic relations in the postwar era that quickly became known as the Cold War. When the Soviet Union developed an atomic bomb of its own in 1949, the United States felt its physical security threatened for the first time since 1783. America's wartime allies, Britain and France, could no longer be considered first-rate powers, and the British Commonwealth was facing a severe crisis as a result of the rise of Asian and African nationalism. In the Far East the situation looked equally bleak: the destruction of Japanese power left a vacuum that was quickly filled by the Chinese Communist regime; India, gaining its independence, was weak; and Korea was left divided. At home the coming of the Cold War posed problems of internal security as some persons feared that the nation was being threatened by subversives and Communists. The result was a period of repression in the early 1950s that seriously impaired the civil rights that American citizens had traditionally enjoyed under the Constitution. All of these developments raised some doubts over the wisdom of America's participation in World War II.

Many of the major critics of Roosevelt's foreign policies, interestingly enough, had taken an isolationist position as regards America's foreign policy in the 1930s, and some even had been associated with the school of revisionist writers who opposed America's entry into World War I. Harry Elmer Barnes, the father of World War I revisionism, consistently opposed Roosevelt's diplomatic policies and addressed meetings of the America First Committee—an isolationist organization of the 1930s and early 1940s. Charles A. Beard spoke out against any American entanglements in the 1930s and testified before the Senate Foreign Relations Committee in opposition to the idea of a lend-lease program. And Charles C. Tansill, who published the leading study in the 1930s critical of Wilson's foreign policies between 1914 and 1917, also played a key role in attacking New Deal diplomacy.

One of the first scholarly attempts to discredit Roosevelt's diplomacy came in 1946 and 1948 when Charles A. Beard published *American Foreign Policy, 1932–1940,* and *President Roosevelt and the Coming of the War, 1941,* respectively. Beard's works, receiving a good deal of attention because of the eminent reputation of their author, were quickly followed by a series of other books. Although the positions they took varied markedly, all the revisionists were in basic agreement on certain fundamental points. Moreover, most of them had nothing but contempt for historians who refused to accept their anti-Roosevelt thesis. Harry Elmer Barnes, for example, characterized those who disagreed with him as "court historians," thereby implying that they had sacrificed their scholarly integrity to gain favor in government circles.

The revisionist hypothesis was based on a number of assumptions. First, the revisionists denied that the Axis powers had threatened America's vital interests. Germany had no plans to attack the Western Hemisphere, they claimed, and the Japanese were concerned only about Asia. Roosevelt's charge that the American people were being directly threatened from abroad, therefore, had little or no substance. Second, Roosevelt's foreign policy was one that he knew would inevitably lead to war in Europe and Asia. Indeed, some revisionists went so far as to suggest that Roosevelt deliberately misled the American people by telling them that he was working for peace while, in reality, he was laying the foundation for war. His famous speech in Boston during the presidential campaign of 1940 in which he promised that American boys would not fight on foreign soil was simply one example of his cupidity. Finally, the revisionists emphasized that the long-term results of America's involvement in World War II were largely negative—if not disastrous; the United States, by upsetting the European balance of power and creating a power vacuum, made possible the emergence of the Soviet Union—a nation that presented a far more serious threat to American security than did Nazi Germany.

Many, though not all, of the revisionists looked upon Roosevelt as a leader who deliberately misled and lied to the American people. In his critical study of New Deal diplomacy Charles A. Beard made this point quite explicit. Roosevelt, Beard wrote, kept reassuring the American people that he was doing everything he could to avoid war and maintain a neutral position. Yet every action that he took belied his statements. He gave military aid and assistance to Britain, first through the destroyer-base exchange, then through the lend-lease program, and finally by ordering American naval vessels to escort convoys. All of these steps were undertaken consciously; they were not forced upon a reluctant or unwilling president by events beyond his control. Roosevelt, claimed Beard, acted on the assumption that he was wiser than the American people and consequently did not feel that he had to tell them the truth. The American people, Beard concluded, were faced with the fact "that the President of the United States possesses limitless authority publicly to misrepresent and secretly to control foreign policy, foreign affairs, and the war power."[1] Beard's thesis was echoed by other revisionists. As William Henry Chamberlain put it in 1953, "One is left, therefore, with the inescapable conclusion that the promises to 'keep America out of foreign wars' were a deliberate hoax on the American people, perpetrated for the purpose of insuring Roosevelt's re-election and thereby enabling him to proceed with his plan of gradually edging the United States into war."[2]

Although the revisionists were critical of Roosevelt's European diplomacy they usually reserved their heaviest ammunition for his Far Eastern policy. Indeed, most of the criticism of Roosevelt centered around his dealings with Japan in the period from 1937 to 1941. Reduced to its simplest form the revisionist indictment boiled down to the fact that Roosevelt deliberately provoked the Japanese into attacking Pearl Harbor. At that point the president was able to take the American people into a war that he secretly wanted but had not desired to ask for publicly.

Such a thesis, of course, rested on the assumption that the Japanese leaders wanted peace—but that Roosevelt's maneuverings had forced them into an untenable position that could be resolved only by war. Although not all revisionists argued along precisely the same lines, their general arguments were remarkably similar. They maintained that Japan's desire for peace was sincere and that she wished to end her four-year-old war in China. Facing a crucial shortage of oil and other resources the Japanese hoped to end the conflict on the Asiatic mainland in order to assure themselves continued access to those materials that were indispensable to the economic well-being of the nation. To achieve these objectives the Japanese leaders did everything within their power to arrive at a satisfactory *modus vivendi* with the United States.

President Roosevelt, according to the revisionists, was not interested in peace; he wanted war. Instead of dealing with Japan on the basis of justice and equity he pursued a policy that he knew would ultimately provoke Japanese retaliation. During 1941 the United States

---

[1]Charles A. Beard, *President Roosevelt and the Coming of the War, 1941: A Study in Appearances and Realities* (New Haven, 1948), p. 598.

[2]William Henry Chamberlain, "The Bankruptcy of a Policy," in *Perpetual War for Perpetual Peace*, Harry Elmer Barnes, ed. (Caldwell, Idaho, 1953), p. 491.

increased its economic pressures upon Japan by curtailing the shipments of oil and other raw materials. At the same time the United
States refused to agree to any concessions to Japan regarding China.
By mid-1941 all Japanese assets in the United States had been frozen,
and in August Roosevelt sent a strong warning to Japan to abandon her
expansionist policies. All of these moves, the revisionists claimed, were
deliberately designed to provoke Japan into some form of retaliation.

The final step, said the revisionist writers, was taken in late November 1941 when Secretary of State Cordell Hull submitted a ten-
point proposal to Japan. This document demanded that Japan pull out
of China and Indochina. To the revisionists the document represented
an American "ultimatum" and not one that could serve as the basis
for diplomatic discussions. The perfidy of American leaders became
even clearer in the days preceding the attack on Pearl Harbor. Some-
time earlier the United States had broken Japan's secret code. Roosevelt and his advisers, therefore, knew that Japan really desired peace,
but that she was ready to take military action if the American government persisted in its unyielding course. High American officials, including the president, even knew that a Japanese attack on the military
and naval installations at Pearl Harbor was imminent. According to
the revisionists the desire of the Roosevelt administration for war was
so strong that government officials did not inform the military commanders in Hawaii of the possibility of an attack. In the end, then,
Roosevelt's harsh policies provoked the Japanese into an attack on the
unprepared military at Pearl Harbor, and gave him the declaration of
war that he had so ardently desired. To achieve his goal, some revisionists maintained, Roosevelt knowingly sacrificed American lives as
well as a large part of the American fleet at Pearl Harbor. As Harry
Elmer Barnes wrote in *Perpetual War for Perpetual Peace*—a volume
in which a number of leading revisionists spelled out their case—"The
net result of revisionist scholarship applied to Pearl Harbor boils down
essentially to this: In order to promote Roosevelt's political ambitions
and his mendacious foreign policy some three thousand American boys
were quite needlessly butchered. Of course, they were only a drop in
the bucket compared to those who were ultimately slain in the war
that resulted, which was as needless, in terms of vital American interests, as the surprise attack on Pearl Harbor."[3]

For the most part American historians have rejected this revision-

---

[3]*Ibid.*, p. 651. By far the most detailed revisionist interpretation of the events leading up to Pearl Harbor is Charles C. Tansill, *Back Door to War: Roosevelt Foreign Policy,
1933–1941* (Chicago, 1952). Other revisionist accounts include George Morgenstern, *Pearl
Harbor: The Story of the Secret War* (New York, 1947); William H. Chamberlin, *America's Second Crusade* (Chicago, 1950); and Robert A. Theobald, *The Final Secret of Pearl
Harbor: The Washington Contribution to the Japanese Attack* (New York, 1954).

ist hypothesis. They have done so largely on the grounds that it rests upon a simplistic conspiracy theory of history. Human beings, they claim, are complex creatures who are affected by complex motives. To argue that Franklin Delano Roosevelt knew the precise results of his policies would be to credit him with an omniscience that no human could possibly possess. As a leading nonrevisionist historian pointed out, it is one thing to charge that the Roosevelt administration mis-understood Japan's intentions and underestimated her military strength; it is quite another matter to conclude that the tragic disaster of December 7, 1941, was a matter of calculated diplomatic planning by a scheming American president.[4]

The revisionist argument—at least in a modified version—never-theless offers a historical thesis that cannot be easily dismissed. In the first selection in this chapter Paul W. Schroeder discusses America's policy toward Japan in the crucial months preceding Pearl Harbor. Schroeder raises a number of issues which cast some doubt upon the wisdom of America's diplomatic moves. The major point at stake was whether the United States had been well-advised in taking a "hard" line toward Japan. The issue raised two interesting questions: Should the United States have made the liberation of China a central aim of its policy, thereby requiring the immediate evacuation of Japanese troops; and should Roosevelt have declined the invitation of the Jap-anese premier to a personal meeting between the two leaders to discuss their differences? To Schroeder the answer to both these questions is an emphatic "no." Until mid-1941 American planners had consis-tently sought two reasonable and rather limited objectives: splitting the three Axis powers, and stopping Japan's advance with Asia. With these goals within its reach, the United States then added a third: the liberation of China. The last objective, however, was not a limited one, nor could it be attained short of war. Because of its misguided sym-pathy toward China the American government drove Japan back into the arms of the Axis powers and made inevitable an armed confron-tation between the two nations. American policymakers, Schroeder concluded, were not evil men determined to bring about war; they were instead men who were blinded by a sense of their own moral right-eousness and had abandoned that pragmatism required of all human beings if differences between nations are not always to end in war.

Schroeder's thesis, in many respects, had already been anticipated by other writers on this subject. George F. Kennan, the former ambas-sador to Russia, State Department official, and historian, for example, had argued in 1951 that the United States erred grievously in the twen-

---

[4]Robert H. Ferrell, "Pearl Harbor and the Revisionists," *Historian* 17 (Spring 1955):233.

tieth century when it committed itself to the Open Door and the preservation of the territorial and administrative integrity of China. Although a nation-state, Kennan wrote, China had many attributes which
failed to coincide with the European national state that had evolved
in the eighteenth and nineteenth centuries. Consequently the Open
Door policy was difficult to implement because it rested on the fal-
lacious assumption that China was no different from other states. More
important, Kennan insisted, the United States continuously "hacked
away, year after year, decade after decade, at the positions of the other
powers on the mainland of Asia, and above all the Japanese, in the
unshakable belief that, if our principles were commendable, their consequences could not be other than happy and acceptable. But rarely
could we be lured into a discussion of the real quantities involved: of
such problems as Japan's expanding population, or the weaknesses of
government in China, or the ways in which the ambitions of other
powers could be practicably countered. Remember that this struck a
particularly sensitive nerve in the case of countries whose interests on
the Asiatic mainland were far more important to them than our interests there were to us. . . . There was always a feeling, both among
the Japanese and among the British, that we were inclined to be spend-
thrift with their diplomatic assets in China for the very reason that
our own stake in China meant so much less to us than theirs did to
them."[5] The result, he concluded, was that the United States never
exploited the possibility of arriving at a mutually satisfactory compromise with Japan. Like Schroeder, however, Kennan vehemently denied
that the failure to reach a meaningful compromise was a deliberate
choice of evil and scheming leaders.

The majority of writers dealing with America's diplomacy in the
years prior to Pearl Harbor, however, took an exactly opposite point of
view from the revisionists. The internationalist or interventionist
school—to differentiate it from the revisionist school—based its arguments upon an entirely different set of assumptions. Writers of the
internationalist school began with the proposition that the Axis powers had, in fact, posed a very serious threat to America's security and
national interests. By the summer of 1940 the Nazis had conquered
most of western and central Europe and Britain seemed to be on the
verge of surrender. When Hitler invaded the Soviet Union in June 1941
a German victory appeared to be a certainty. The danger, according to
the internationalist school, was that America might have to face the
victorious Axis powers alone. German and Italian campaigns in North
Africa created a fear that control of that continent might provide a

---

[5]George F. Kennan, *American Diplomacy 1900–1950* (Chicago, 1951), p. 48.

springboard for an attack upon the Western Hemisphere. Axis successes in Europe, meanwhile, had stimulated the Japanese to increase
their aggressive moves in Asia on the theory that the Allies were too
preoccupied in the West to divert any forces to the Far East.

Roosevelt, according to the internationalist school, believed that
Germany represented the greatest threat to America's security. It was
in the national interest, therefore, to follow a policy designed to bring
about a German defeat. Thus Roosevelt embarked upon a program of
extending to England all aid short of war in the belief that such a policy
might prevent a Nazi victory and contribute to the eventual downfall
of Germany. Although renouncing impartial neutrality, Roosevelt
hoped that aid to England would permit his nation to protect its security without committing American troops to a foreign conflict. The
undeclared naval war in the North Atlantic against Germany represented the limit of America's involvement.

Roosevelt's primary interest lay in Europe—the internationalist
interpretation continued—and his Far Eastern policy was designed to
avert any showdown with Japan. The steps that he took in 1940 and
1941 were intended to check Japan by all means short of war. The embargo on oil and other resources, the freezing of Japanese assets in the
United States, the aid to China, and the massing of the American fleet
in the Pacific were aimed at deterring, not provoking, the Japanese.
America's objective was to seek a peaceful settlement with Japan, but
a settlement that would uphold American security and principles, protect China, and honor the British, French, and Dutch interests in the
Far East. Japan's expansionist ambitions, however, proved to be too
great, and Roosevelt came to realize that an armed conflict between
the two nations was inevitable. According to the internationalist
school of writers his policy at this point became one of stalling for time
in order to permit an American military buildup.

Although the internationalist school by no means approved of all
of Roosevelt's diplomatic policies, they believed that the fundamental
causes for America's involvement in the war lay outside the United
States and in the trend of world events over which this country had
little, if any, control. Most of them were convinced that Roosevelt had
sought the goal of peace with great sincerity. In fact, many argued that
his desire for peace led him to overestimate the opposition to his internationalist policies, which he could have pursued even more vigorously than he did.

Almost all of the historians in the internationalist school violently
rejected the revisionist point of view—particularly the insinuation that
Roosevelt had plotted to provoke the Japanese assault on Pearl Harbor.
While many admitted that there might have been some blundering in
both Washington and Hawaii, there was general agreement that the

attack came as a genuine surprise. In Washington neither civilian nor military authorities had interpreted the decoded Japanese messages correctly; virtually everyone assumed that the Japanese were moving to attack British and Dutch installations in the southwest Pacific. Although it was true that the army and navy commanders in Hawaii were not given all of the information gained from breaking the Japanese code, most internationalist historians believed that the military officials on the spot would have interpreted the messages in the same light as their superiors in Washington. Even if they had been able to divine Japanese intentions correctly, there is some doubt as to whether a military disaster could have been avoided; the American fleet was extremely vulnerable to air attack and there were insufficient land-based planes to ward off a Japanese raid. In retrospect, then, the internationalist historians looked upon Pearl Harbor as a tragic disaster that grew out of faulty military and diplomatic planning rather than part of a presidential conspiracy.[6]

The second selection in this chapter is by Dexter Perkins, one of the deans of American diplomatic history, and represents the views of internationalist scholars while vigorously attacking the revisionist school. To Perkins historical revisionism at the close of a military conflict seems to be a common occurrence among Americans. In part this response stems from the letdown or disillusionment that results from a failure to secure all of the goals for which the war was fought; it is related also to the inevitable reaction against the strong executive leadership that characterizes most wartime administrations. Whatever the reasons for its rise, Perkins defines such revisionism as "history by hypothesis"; it suggests that the world would have been a better place had the United States remained aloof from any involvement in World War II. Perkins goes on to argue that a victorious Germany would have been a very serious menace to America. Nor did Roosevelt deceive the American people, according to Perkins. The president was basically in accord with public opinion, for even the Republican party nominated Wendell Willkie in 1940 and took an internationalist position on foreign affairs. Although Roosevelt may have been devious in his public statements from time to time he accurately reflected the mood and thinking of his fellow countrymen. In the final analysis Perkins ends up with a favorable, though by no means uncritical, appraisal of Roosevelt's foreign policy prior to the war.

Other internationalist scholars have also argued strongly against the revisionist thesis that Roosevelt deliberately exposed the Ameri-

---

[6]See especially Roberta Wohlstetter, *Pearl Harbor: Warning and Decision* (Stanford, 1962).

can fleet at Pearl Harbor in order to provoke a Japanese attack. Herbert Feis, for example, insisted that Japan was bent on dominating Asia, thus threatening America's interests in that part of the world. Had the United States not placed an embargo on trade with Japan it would have been in the strange position of having undertaken preparations for war while at the same time strengthening the opponent it might meet in battle. Feis denied that there was conclusive evidence that Prince Konoye's offer to meet with Roosevelt in the autumn of 1941 might have averted a conflict. He rejected also the thesis that Secretary of State Cordell Hull's note of November 26, 1941, was in any sense an ultimatum. The basic cause of the war, concluded Feis, was Japan's insistence on becoming the dominant power in the Far East. Short of a complete surrender on America's part, the chances of avoiding war by means of diplomatic negotiations had always been remote.[7]

It should be emphasized that there are many points of disagreement among individual historians of the internationalist school even though all of them rejected the revisionist hypothesis. The differences between internationalist historians frequently reflected the same divisions that existed among Roosevelt's advisers prior to December 7, 1941. For example, Secretary of State Cordell Hull was generally cautious in his approach; he favored limiting overt action to steps short of war. Secretary of War Henry L. Stimson, on the other hand, believed that the policy of all aid short of war would not result in the defeat of the Axis powers, and that America would have to intervene sooner or later. Indeed, Stimson believed that the American people would have supported Roosevelt in a declaration of war even before Pearl Harbor. Similarly some internationalist historians, including Herbert Feis and Basil Rauch, were sympathetic to Hull and Roosevelt, while others, notably William L. Langer and S. Everett Gleason, argued that Roosevelt overestimated isolationist opposition to his policies and that the president actually lagged behind public opinion on the desirability of taking strong measures against the Axis powers.[8]

Beginning in the late 1950s, however, the internationalist school began to come under sharp attack from scholars who saw a close re-

[7]Herbert Feis, "War Came at Pearl Harbor: Suspicions Considered," *Yale Review* 45 (Spring 1956):378–390.

[8]Herbert Feis, *The Road to Pearl Harbor: The Coming of War Between the United States and Japan* (Princeton, 1950); Basil Rauch, *Roosevelt: From Munich to Pearl Harbor* (New York, 1950); William L. Langer and S. Everett Gleason, *The Challenge to Isolation, 1937–1940* (New York, 1952), and *The Undeclared War, 1940–1941* (New York, 1953). Other internationalist works include Donald F. Drummond, *The Passing of American Neutrality* (Ann Arbor, 1955); Robert A. Divine, *The Reluctant Belligerent: American Entry into World War II* (New York, 1965); and John E. Wiltz, *From Isolation to War, 1931–1941* (New York, 1968).

lationship between foreign and domestic policy, with the former growing out of the latter. These scholars took a quite different approach to the problem of war causation; rather than focusing on the immediate events that led to Pearl Harbor they studied the long-range trends in American foreign policy and provided an alternative framework for understanding our entry into World War II. Perhaps the most influential scholar in this regard was William Appleman Williams, who offered in a series of important books a view of American diplomacy that was sharply at variance with his internationalist contemporaries.

The Williams thesis, in its simplest form, was that American foreign policy since the late nineteenth century reflected a particular ideology known as Open Door imperialism. A reflection of American capitalism, this policy was based on the premise that foreign markets were indispensable for domestic prosperity and tranquility. By the 1890s, therefore, the United States had moved to acquire overseas possessions, strategically situated so as to facilitate trade and provide naval bases but involving few of the usual responsibilities associated with an extensive overseas empire. The Open Door policy, argued Williams, was designed to win victories without wars; "it was derived from the proposition that America's overwhelming economic power would cast the economy and the politics of the poorer, weaker, underdeveloped countries in a pro-American mold."[9] Ultimately the ideology of the Open Door would lead the United States into a more and more militant opposition to any economic system—socialist, Communist, totalitarian—that might diminish its overseas trade.

Williams's thesis led directly to a new interpretation of the diplomacy of the 1930s and the coming of World War II. The New Deal, according to Williams, was intended to define and institutionalize the roles, functions, and responsibilities of three important segments of industrial society—capital, labor, government—and to do so in harmony with the principles of capitalism. In foreign policy the New Deal continued to seek the overseas markets on which American prosperity supposedly rested; even Secretary of State Cordell Hull's reciprocal trade program was intended to control foreign sources of raw materials while simultaneously providing for the selling of American surpluses abroad. The result was a strengthening of free trade imperialism, which in turn led to a rising distrust of the United States by nations increasingly fearful of domination by American capitalism. When Japan began to move south into China in 1937 and Germany became more active in Latin America, Roosevelt and his advisers moved toward an activ-

---

[9]William Appleman Williams, *The Tragedy of American Diplomacy* (rev. ed., New York, 1962), p. 49. See also Williams's *The Roots of the Modern American Empire* (New York, 1969).

istic and interventionist foreign policy because of the threat to our economic interests throughout the world. During World War II America's
economic leaders also became enthusiastic converts to the mission to
reform the world. This crusading zeal, in conjunction with Open Door
imperialism, was in large measure responsible for the advent of the
Cold War and the disastrous course that involved the nation in two
wars in the 1950s and 1960s.[10]

The Williams thesis about the nature of foreign policy proved extraordinarily attractive to individuals and groups committed to fundamental changes in American society in the 1960s. Indeed, Williams
himself concluded that the United States had to adopt a new foreign
policy that rejected the assumptions that an informal empire was necessary for our welfare, that trade was a weapon against those nations
with whom we had disagreements or was necessary in order to pay for
the costs of military security abroad. Moreover the United States had
to stop seeing communism in terms of an absolute evil. "Once freed
from its myopic concentration on the cold war, the United States could
come to grips with the central problem of reordering its own society
so that it functions through such a balanced relationship with the rest
of the world, and so that the labor and leisure of its own citizens are
invested with creative meaning and purpose."[11] While Williams himself was more within a social democratic tradition, other historians—
particularly those associated with the New Left—picked up where Williams had left off. In the eyes of these scholars war, racism, and poverty
were all outgrowths of the evil nature of American capitalism, a system that rested on the exploitation of the many by the few. Only radical changes that involved a sharp redistribution of economic and political power would make it possible for the American people to
confront their problems and develop appropriate solutions.[12]

Curiously enough, relatively few New Left historians have written
about the events that immediately preceded American entry into World
War II. While emphasizing American culpability for the advent of the
Cold War they tended to shy away from dealing with World War II,
perhaps because of the difficulty of ignoring the nature of Nazi Germany. With the exception of Williams's general interpretation of

---

[10]A detailed study of New Deal diplomacy in the Williams tradition is Lloyd C.
Gardner's *Economic Aspects of New Deal Diplomacy* (Madison, Wis., 1964).

[11]Williams, *Tragedy of American Diplomacy*, p. 306. Walter LaFeber's *America,
Russia, and the Cold War 1945–1966* (New York, 1967) and Lloyd C. Gardner's *Architects of Illusion: Men and Ideas in American Foreign Policy 1941–1949* (Chicago, 1970)
are both in the Williams tradition.

[12]See Gabriel Kolko, *The Politics of War: The World and United States Foreign
Policy 1943–1945* (New York, 1968), and *The Roots of American Foreign Policy* (Boston,
1969).

American diplomacy and Lloyd C. Gardner's study of the economic
aspects of New Deal diplomacy, relatively little has been written on
the origins of World War II by those with an affinity for the New Left.

Recently there has been a tendency among historians to avoid extreme interpretations of the events that led to American entry into
World War II. Between 1939 and 1941, according to Robert Dallek, Roosevelt attempted to balance the nation's antiwar sentiment with the
contradictory impulse to assure a Nazi defeat. Initially he attempted
to fuse both by providing the Allies with military aid. Even when Roosevelt concluded in the spring of 1941 that American involvement in
the conflict was all but inevitable, according to Dallek, "he refused to
force an unpalatable choice upon the nation by announcing for war."
Nor did the United States provoke an attack by Japan. Roosevelt's anti-
Fascist commitment made it impossible for him to discriminate between Germany and Japan; "both had to be opposed at the same time."
The attack on Pearl Harbor on December 7, 1941, was an unforeseen
surprise. "Seeing the fleet in Hawaii as a deterrent rather than a target,
lulled by the belief that the Japanese lacked the capability to strike at
Pearl Harbor and by the information or 'noise' . . . indicating that an
attack might come at any one of a number of points," Dallek noted,
"Roosevelt, like the rest of the nation, failed to anticipate the Pearl
Harbor attack. Later contentions to the contrary had less to do with
the actuality of Roosevelt's actions than with the isolationists' efforts
to justify the idea that the country had never in fact been vulnerable
to attack." David Reynolds likewise demonstrated that the relationship between Great Britain and the United States between 1937 and
1941 was not altogether smooth. The British were not always certain
about America's reliability, and feared its economic expansionist tendencies. Americans, on the other hand, were suspicious of their British
brethren and disliked its imperial system. Ultimately a common culture and language, plus fear of Nazi Germany, proved decisive, and in
the end the American hope of remaining neutral was frustrated by the
Japanese attack on Pearl Harbor.[13]

To evaluate in a fair and objective manner the events leading up
to Pearl Harbor, then, is not a simple task for scholars. The complexity
of this historical problem arises from many reasons: the tangled web
of interrelated events in the period before December 1941, which
makes it difficult, if not impossible, to separate causes and to point to
any particular one as "definitive"; the fact that some of the goals for
which America went to war were not achieved by the end of the con-

---

[13]Robert Dallek, *Franklin D. Roosevelt and American Foreign Policy, 1932–1945*
(New York, 1979), pp. 530–532; David Reynolds, *The Creation of the Anglo-American
Alliance 1937–41: A Study in Competitive Cooperation* (Chapel Hill, 1982).

flict; and the problem of ascertaining the precise motives of the national leaders and various interest groups of the period. Historical judgment, furthermore, rests to a considerable degree upon the starting assumptions held by various scholars; different historians approach the problem with a different set of starting assumptions and hence reach conflicting conclusions.

In contrasting the revisionist with the international school of historians, several differences are clearly discernible. First, both deal in a very different way with the issue of whether or not the Axis powers represented an immediate threat to American security. The revisionists maintained that there was no evidence that Hitler hoped to move into the Western Hemisphere. Even if he had the revisionists held that the best policy would have been for America to have waited until Germany and Russia had destroyed each other; such a policy would have avoided the power vacuum that developed in Europe in the postwar period that enabled the Soviet Union to expand without checks. In the Far East America also made a mistake by pushing Japan into the war by an inflexible policy and a refusal to offer any reasonable compromises. The internationalists, on the other hand, believed that a victorious Germany posed a serious threat to American security, especially if one considers the military prowess and scientific potential of the Third Reich. Given Hitler's past behavior there was no reason to assume that his ambitions would have been satisfied after conquering England and the Soviet Union. Insofar as the Far East was concerned the internationalists took the view that Japan's unwillingness to abandon its imperialist policy was the prime cause of the war. Scholars within the Williams tradition tended to see the diplomacy of the 1930s as an outgrowth of American economic expansionism; they paid relatively little attention to the Axis powers and to the question whether or not American security was, in fact, threatened by developments in Europe and the Far East.[14]

A second issue that scholars dealt with was the motivation behind Roosevelt's foreign policy. Did Roosevelt deceive the American people by telling them that his policy would lead to peace when in reality he wanted war? To this question the revisionists answered in the affirmative and the internationalists in the negative. The Williams school as well as those scholars writing within the tradition of the New Left, on the other hand, tended to occupy a middle position, if only because

[14]Cf. Alton Frye, *Nazi Germany and the American Hemisphere, 1933–1941* (New Haven, 1967); James V. Compton, *The Swastika and the Eagle; Hitler, the United States, and the Origins of World War II* (Boston, 1967); Bruce M. Russett, *No Clear and Present Danger: A Skeptical View of the United States Entry into World War II* (New York, 1972); and Thomas A. Bailey and Paul B. Ryan, *Hitler vs. Roosevelt: The Undeclared Naval War* (New York, 1979).

this question was not central to their analysis. All schools had a serious problem on this score, however, because the issue revolved about the motivation and intentions of one man. How can the historian gauge the motives of any individual, particularly when so few human beings ever record their innermost convictions or are completely honest with themselves?

In many respects the most important difference separating the various schools was their judgment concerning the results of the war. To the revisionists the outcome of the war was dramatic evidence of the blundering and evil policy followed by Roosevelt and his advisers. The United States, after all, had gone to war to destroy the menace of totalitarianism. Instead, it was confronted after 1945 with the Soviet Union, a far greater menace than Nazi Germany. On the continent Russia controlled all of eastern and a good part of central Europe; in the Far East the destruction of Japanese power created a situation that ultimately led to a Communist takeover of China. The internationalist school, by way of comparison, readily admitted that the results of the war were anything but desirable, but its adherents also argued that these results did not necessarily make Hitler the lesser of two evils. Moreover, history suggests a tragic view of human destiny; for each problem solved more arise in its place. To expect a final solution to all problems is to be unrealistic. While Roosevelt may have miscalculated in some of his policies he did not do so knowingly or deliberately; his mistakes were due to the limitations that characterize all human beings. The Williams school and New Left historians saw in World War II the origins and beginnings of the Cold War, for during that time America's economic imperialism was fused with a messianic sense; the result was a crusade against any system not modeled after the example of the United States.

In general, then, the differing interpretations of America's entry into World War II reflect the personal faith of the historians in the particular policy they are advocating. The internationalist school believed that the United States, as a world power, could not neglect its responsibilities nor ignore events in other parts of the world. The world is far too small a place for the provincial isolationism that characterized American diplomacy in the early years of the republic. Consequently they believed that Roosevelt was on the right track even though some of his specific moves may not have been correct ones. The revisionists, on the other hand, argued that America's national interest could have been best served by remaining aloof from conflicts that did not immediately threaten the United States. Roosevelt, therefore, made a grievous error when he committed his nation—against the will of its people—to a world conflict. The American people, the revisionists concluded, are still paying the price of that mistake. Those in the tradition of Williams or the New Left argue by way of contrast that only a basic transformation in America's foreign policy (and hence domestic policies) can bring peace and an atmosphere conducive to meaningful social change. Consequently—with some exceptions—they see American diplomacy in the 1930s as a grievous error.

Which of these schools of thought is correct? Were the revisionists justified in their claim that the United States should have stayed out of World War II? Were they right in attributing evil and invidious motives to Roosevelt and his advisers? Or were the internationalist historians right in arguing that World War II involved vital American interests and that Roosevelt was simply trying to safeguard these interests even though it meant that the nation might eventually enter the war? Or were Williams and New Left historians correct in attributing war to Open Door imperialism? These are some of the basic issues confronting the student who is attempting to understand the background and events that led up to Pearl Harbor.

Paul W. Schroeder

PAUL W. SCHROEDER (1927–   ) is professor of history at the University of Illinois. He is the author of several books on diplomatic history; the book from which the present selection is taken was the recipient of the Beveridge Prize of the American Historical Association.

In judging American policy toward Japan in 1941, it might be well to separate what is still controversial from what is not. There is no longer any real doubt that the war came about over China. Even an administration stalwart like Henry L. Stimson and a sympathetic critic like Herbert Feis concur in this. Nor is it necessary to speculate any longer as to what could have induced Japan to launch such an incredible attack upon the United States and Great Britain as occurred at Pearl Harbor and in the South Pacific. One need not, as Winston Churchill did in wartime, characterize it as "an irrational act" incompatible "with prudence or even with sanity." The Japanese were realistic about their position throughout; they did not suddenly go insane. The attack was an act of desperation, not madness. Japan fought only when she had her back to the wall as a result of America's diplomatic and economic offensive.

The main point still at issue is whether the United States was wise in maintaining a "hard" program of diplomatic and economic pressure on Japan from July 1941 on. Along with this issue go two subsidiary questions: the first, whether it was wise to make the liberation of China the central aim of American policy and the immediate evacuation of Japanese troops a requirement for agreement; the second, whether it was wise to decline Premier Konoye's invitation to a meeting of leaders in the Pacific. On all these points, the policy which the United States carried out still has distinguished defenders. The paramount issue between Japan and the United States, they contend, always was the China problem. In her China policy, Japan showed that she was determined to secure domination over a large area of East Asia by force. Apart from the legitimate American commercial interests which would be ruined or excluded by this Japanese action, the United States, for reasons of her own security and of world peace, had sufficient stake in

Reprinted from Paul W. Schroeder, *The Axis Alliance and Japanese-American Relations, 1941*, pp. 200–216. Copyright © 1958 by the American Historical Association. Used by permission of the publisher, Cornell University Press.

Far Eastern questions to oppose such aggression. Finally, after ten years
of Japanese expansion, it was only sensible and prudent for the United
States to demand that it come to an end and that Japan retreat. In order
to meet the Japanese threat, the United States had a perfect right to
use the economic power she possessed in order to compel the Japanese
to evacuate their conquered territory. If Japan chose to make this a
cause for war, the United States could not be held responsible.

A similar defense is offered on the decision to turn down Konoye's
Leaders' Conference. Historians may concede, as do Langer and Gleason, that Konoye was probably sincere in wanting peace and that he
"envisaged making additional concessions to Washington, including
concessions on the crucial issue of the withdrawal of Japanese troops
from China." But, they point out, Konoye could never have carried the
Army with him on any such concession. If the United States was right
in requiring Japan to abandon the co-prosperity sphere, then her leaders
were equally right in declining to meet with a Japanese premier who,
however conciliatory he might have been personally, was bound by his
own promises and the exigencies of Japanese politics to maintain this
national aim. In addition, there was the serious possibility that much
could be lost from such a meeting—the confidence of China, the cohesiveness of the coalition with Great Britain and Russia. In short, there
was not enough prospect of gain to merit taking the chance.

This is a point of view which must be taken seriously. Any judgment on the wisdom or folly of the American policy, in fact, must be
made with caution—there are no grounds for dogmatic certainty. The
opinion here to be developed, nonetheless, is that the American policy
from the end of July to December was a grave mistake. It should not
be necessary to add that this does not make it treason. There is a "back
door to war" theory, espoused in various forms by Charles A. Beard,
George Morgenstern, Charles C. Tansill, and, most recently, Rear Admiral Robert A. Theobald, which holds that the president chose the
Far East as a rear entrance to the war in Europe and to that end deliberately goaded the Japanese into an attack. This theory is quite different and quite incredible. It is as impossible to accept as the idea that
Japan attacked the United States in a spirit of overconfidence or that
Hitler pushed the Japanese into war. Roosevelt's fault, if any, was not
that of deliberately provoking the Japanese to attack, but of allowing
Hull and others to talk him out of impulses and ideas which, had he
pursued them, might have averted the conflict. Moreover, the mistake
(assuming that it was a mistake) of a too hard and rigid policy with
Japan was, as has been pointed out, a mistake shared by the whole
nation, with causes that were deeply organic. Behind it was not sinister
design or warlike intent, but a sincere and uncompromising adherence
to moral principles and liberal doctrines.

This is going ahead too fast, however; one needs first of all to define the mistake with which American policy is charged. Briefly, it was this. In the attempt to gain everything at once, the United States lost her opportunity to secure immediately her essential requirements in the Far East and to continue to work toward her long-range goals. She succeeded instead only in making inevitable an unnecessary and avoidable war—an outcome which constitutes the ultimate failure of diplomacy. Until July 1941, as already demonstrated, the United States consistently sought to attain two limited objectives in the Far East, those of splitting the Axis and of stopping Japan's advance southward. Both aims were in accordance with America's broad strategic interests; both were reasonable, attainable goals. Through a combination of favorable circumstance and forceful American action, the United States reached the position where the achievement of these two goals was within sight. At this very moment, on the verge of a major diplomatic victory, the United States abandoned her original goals and concentrated on a third, the liberation of China. This last aim was not in accord with American strategic interests, was not a limited objective, and, most important, was completely incapable of being achieved by peaceful means and doubtful of attainment even by war. Through her single-minded pursuit of this unattainable goal, the United States forfeited the diplomatic victory which she had already virtually won. The unrelenting application of extreme economic pressure on Japan, instead of compelling the evacuation of China, rendered war inevitable, drove Japan back into the arms of Germany for better or for worse, and precipitated the wholesale plunge by Japan into the South Seas. As it ultimately turned out, the United States succeeded in liberating China only at great cost and when it was too late to do the cause of the Nationalist Chinese much real good.

This is not, of course, a new viewpoint. It is in the main simply that of Ambassador Grew, who has held and defended it since 1941. The arguments he advances seem cogent and sensible in the light of present knowledge. Briefly summarized, they are the following: First is his insistence on the necessity of distinguishing between long-range and immediate goals in foreign policy and on the folly of demanding the immediate realization of both. Second is his contention that governments are brought to abandon aggressive policies not by sudden conversion through moral lectures, but by the gradual recognition that the policy of aggression will not succeed. According to Grew, enough awareness of failure existed in the government of Japan in late 1941 to enable it to make a beginning in the process of reversal of policy— but not nearly enough to force Japan to a wholesale surrender of her conquests and aims. Third was his conviction that what was needed on both sides was time—time in which the United States could grow

stronger and in which the tide of war in Europe could be turned definitely against Germany, time in which the sense of failure could grow
in Japan and in which moderates could gain better control of the situation. A victory in Europe, Grew observed, would either automatically solve the problem of Japan or make that problem, if necessary,
much easier to solve by force. Fourth was his belief that Japan would
fight if backed to the wall (a view vindicated by events) and that a war
at this time with Japan could not possibly serve the interests of the
United States. Even if one considered war as the only final answer to
Japanese militarism, still, Grew would answer, the United States stood
to gain nothing by seeking a decision in 1941. The time factor was
entirely in America's favor. Japan could not hope to gain as much from
a limited relaxation of the embargo as the United States could from
time gained for mobilization; Roosevelt and the military strategists
were in fact anxious to gain time by a *modus vivendi.*

There is one real weakness in Grew's argument upon which his
critics have always seized. This is his contention that Konoye, faced
after July 26 with the two clear alternatives of war or a genuine peace
move, which would of necessity include a settlement with China, had
chosen the latter course and could have carried through a policy of
peace had he been given the time. "We believed," he writes, "that
Prince Konoye was in a position to carry the country with him in a
program of peace" and to make commitments to the United States
which would "eventually, if not immediately" meet the conditions of
Hull's Four Points. The answer of critics is that, even if one credits
Konoye's sincerity and takes his assurances at face value, there is still
no reason to believe that he could have carried even his own cabinet,
much less the whole nation, with him on any program approximating
that of Hull. In particular, as events show, he could not have persuaded
the army to evacuate China.

The objection is well taken; Grew was undoubtedly over-optimistic
about Konoye's capacity to carry through a peaceful policy. This one
objection, however, does not ruin Grew's case. He countered it later
with the argument that a settlement with Japan which allowed Japanese garrisons to remain in China on a temporary basis would not have
been a bad idea. Although far from an ideal solution, it would have
been better, for China as well, than the policy the United States actually followed. It would have brought China what was all-important—
a cessation of fighting—without involving the United States, as many
contended, in either a sacrifice of principle or a betrayal of China. The
United States, Grew points out, had never committed herself to
guaranteeing China's integrity. Further, it would not have been necessary to agree to anything other than temporary garrisons in North
China which, in more favorable times, the United States could work

to have removed. The great mistake was to allow American policy to be guided by a sentimental attitude toward China which in the long run could do neither the United States nor China any good. As Grew puts it:

> *Japan's advance to the south, including her occupation of portions of China, constituted for us a real danger, and it was definitely in our national interest that it be stopped, by peaceful means if possible, by force of arms if necessary. American aid to China should have been regarded, as we believe it was regarded by our Government, as an indirect means to this end, and not from a sentimental viewpoint. The President's letter of January 21, 1941, shows that he then sensed the important issues in the Far East, and that he did not include China, purely for China's sake, among them. . . . The failure of the Washington Administration to seize the opportunity presented in August and September, 1941, to halt the southward advance by peaceful means, together with the paramount importance attached to the China question during the conversations in Washington, gives rise to the belief that not our Government but millions of quite understandably sympathetic but almost totally uninformed American citizens had assumed control of our Far Eastern policy.*

There remains the obvious objection that Grew's solution, however plausible as it may now seem, was politically impracticable in 1941. No American government could then have treated China as expendable, just as no Japanese government could have written off the China Affair as a dead loss. This is in good measure true and goes a long way to explain, if not to justify, the hard American policy. Yet it is not entirely certain that no solution could have been found which would both have averted war and have been accepted by the American people, had a determined effort been made to find one. As F. C. Jones points out, the United States and Japan were not faced in July 1941 with an absolute dilemma of peace or war, of complete settlement or open conflict. Hull believed that they were, of course; but his all-or-nothing attitude constituted one of his major shortcomings as a diplomat. Between the two extremes existed the possibility of a *modus vivendi*, an agreement settling some issues and leaving others in abeyance. Had Roosevelt and Konoye met, Jones argues, they might have been able to agree on a relaxation of the embargo in exchange for satisfactory assurances on the Tripartite Pact and southward expansion, with the China issue laid aside. The United States would not have had to cease aid, nor Japan to remove her troops. The final settlement of the Far Eastern question, Jones concludes,

> *would then have depended upon the issues of the struggle in Europe. If Germany prevailed, then the United States would be in no position to oppose Japanese ambitions in Asia; if Germany were defeated, Ja-*

pan would be in no position to persist in those ambitions in the face
of the United States, the USSR, and the British Commonwealth.

Such an agreement, limited and temporary in nature, would have involved no sacrifice of principle for either nation, yet would have removed the immediate danger of war. As a temporary expedient and as
an alternative to otherwise inevitable and useless conflict, it could have
been sold by determined effort to the public on both sides. Nor would
it have been impossible, in the writer's opinion, to have accompanied
or followed such an agreement with a simple truce or standstill in the
China conflict through American mediation.

This appraisal, to be sure, is one based on realism. Grew's criticism
of Hull's policy and the alternative he offers to it are both characterized
by fundamental attention to what is practical and expedient at a given
time and to limited objectives within the scope of the national interest. In general, the writer agrees with this point of view, believing that,
as William A. Orton points out, it is foolish and disastrous to treat
nations as morally responsible persons, "because their nature falls far
short of personality," and that, as George F. Kennan contends, the right
role for moral considerations in foreign affairs is not to determine policy, but rather to soften and ameliorate actions necessarily based on
the realities of world politics.

From this realistic standpoint, the policy of the State Department
would seem to be open to other criticisms besides those of Grew. The
criticisms, which may be briefly mentioned here, are those of inconsistency, blindness to reality, and futility. A notable example of the
first would be the inconsistency of a strong no-compromise stand
against Japan with the policy of broad accommodation to America's
allies, especially Russia, both before and after the American entrance
into the war. The inconsistency may perhaps best be seen by comparing the American stand in 1941 on such questions as free trade, the
Open Door in China, the territorial and administrative integrity of
China, the maintenance of the prewar status quo in the Far East, and
the sanctity of international agreements with the position taken on
the same questions at the Yalta Conference in 1945.

The blindness to reality may be seen in the apparent inability of
American policymakers to take seriously into account the gravity of
Japan's economic plight or the real exigencies of her military and strategic position, particularly as these factors would affect the United
States over the long run. Equally unrealistic and more fateful was the
lack of appreciation on the part of many influential people and of wide
sections of the public of the almost certain consequences to be expected from the pressure exerted on Japan—namely, American involvement in a war her military strategists considered highly undesirable.

The attitude has been well termed by Robert Osgood, "this blind in-difference toward the military and political consequences of a morally-inspired position."

The charge of futility, finally, could be laid to the practice of in-sisting on a literal subscription to principles which, however noble, had no chance of general acceptance or practical application. The best example is the persistent demand that the Japanese pledge themselves to carrying out nineteenth-century principles of free trade and equal access to raw materials in a twentieth-century world where economic nationalism and autarchy, trade barriers and restrictions were every-where the order of the day, and not the least in the United States under the New Deal. Not one of America's major allies would have sub-scribed wholeheartedly to Hull's free-trade formula; what good it could have done to pin the Japanese down to it is hard to determine.

But these are all criticisms based on a realistic point of view, and to judge the American policy solely from this point of view is to judge it unfairly and by a standard inappropriate to it. The policy of the United States was avowedly not one of realism, but of principle. If then it is to be understood on its own grounds and judged by its own stan-dards the main question will be whether the policy was morally right—that is, in accord with principles of peace and international justice. Here, according to its defenders, the American policy stands vindi-cated. For any other policy, any settlement with Japan at the expense of China, would have meant a betrayal not only of China, but also of vital principles and of America's moral task in the world.

This, as we know, was the position of Hull and his co-workers. It has been stated more recently by Basil Rauch, who writes:

> No one but an absolute pacifist would argue that the danger of war is a greater evil than violation of principle. . . . The isolationist be-lieves that appeasement of Japan without China's consent violated no principle worth a risk of war. The internationalist must believe that the principle did justify a risk of war.

This is not an argument to be dismissed lightly. The contention that the United States had a duty to fulfill in 1941, and that this duty consisted in holding to justice and morality in a world given to inter-national lawlessness and barbarism and in standing on principle against an unprincipled and ruthless aggressor, commands respect. It is not answered by dismissing it as unrealistic or by proscribing all moral considerations in foreign policy. An answer may be found, however, in a closer definition of America's moral duty in 1941. According to Hull, and apparently also Rauch, the task was primarily one of upholding principle. This is not the only possible definition. It may well be con-tended that the moral duty was rather one of doing the most practical good possible in a chaotic world situation and, further, that this was the main task President Roosevelt and the administration had in mind at least till the end of July 1941.

If the moral task of the United States in the Far East was to uphold a principle of absolute moral value, the principle of nonappeasement of aggressors, then the American policy was entirely successful in fulfilling it. The American diplomats proved that the United States was capable of holding to its position in disregard and even in defiance of national interests narrowly conceived. If, however, the task was one of doing concrete good and giving practical help where needed, especially to China, then the American policy falls fatally short. For it can easily be seen not only that the policy followed did not in practice help China, but also that it could not have been expected to. Although it was a pro-China and even a China-first policy in principle, it was not a practical fact designed to give China the kind of help needed.

What China required above all by late 1941 was clearly an end to the fighting, a chance to recoup her strength. Her chaotic financial condition, a disastrous inflation, civil strife with the Communists, severe hunger and privation, and falling morale all enfeebled and endangered her further resistance. Chiang Kai-shek, who knew this, could hope only for an end to the war through the massive intervention of American forces and the consequent liberation of China. It was in this hope that he pleaded so strongly for a hard American policy toward Japan. Chiang's hopes, however, were wholly unrealistic. For though the United States was willing to risk war for China's sake, and finally did incur it over the China issue, the Washington government never intended in case of war to throw America's full weight against Japan in order to liberate China. The American strategy always was to concentrate on Europe first, fighting a defensive naval war in the Far East and aiding China, as before, in order to keep the Japanese bogged down. The possibility was faced and accepted that the Chinese might have to go on fighting for some years before eventual liberation through the defeat of Japan. The vehement Chinese protests over this policy were unavailing, and the bitter disillusionment suffered by the Chinese only helped to bring on in 1942 the virtual collapse of the Chinese war effort during the later years of the war.

As a realistic appraisal of America's military capabilities and of her worldwide strategic interests, the Europe-first policy has a great deal to recommend it. But the combination of this realistic strategy with a moralistic diplomacy led to the noteworthy paradox of a war incurred for the sake of China, which could not then be fought for the sake of China and whose practical value for China at the time was, to say the least, dubious. The plain fact is that the United States in 1941 was not capable of forcing Japan out of China by means short of war and was neither willing nor, under existing circumstances, able to throw the Japanese out by war. The American government could conceivably have told the Chinese this and tried to work out the best possible program of help for China under these limitations. Instead, it yielded to Chinese importunities and followed a policy almost sure to eventuate in war, knowing that if the Japanese did attack, China and her deliverance would have to take a back seat. It is difficult to conceive of such a policy as a program of practical aid to China.

The main, though not the only, reason why this policy was followed is clearly the overwhelming importance of principle in American diplomacy, particularly the principle of nonappeasement of aggressors. Once most leaders in the administration and wide sections of the public became convinced that it was America's prime moral duty to stand hard and fast against aggressors, whatever the consequences, and once this conviction became decisive in the formulation of policy, the end result was almost inevitable: a policy designed to uphold principle and to punish the aggressor, but not to save the victim.

It is this conviction as to America's moral duty, however sincere and understandable, which the writer believes constitutes a fundamental misreading of America's moral task. The policy it gave rise to was bad not simply because it was moralistic but because it was obsessed with the wrong kind of morality—with that abstract "Let justice be done though the heavens fall" kind which is often, when relentlessly pursued, does more harm than good. It would be interesting to investigate the role which this conception of America's moral task played in the formulation of the American war aims in the Far East, with their twin goals of unconditional surrender and the destruction of Japan as a major power, especially after the desire to vindicate American principles and to punish the aggressor was intensified a hundredfold by the attack on Pearl Harbor. To pursue the later implications of this kind of morality in foreign policy, with its attendant legalistic and vindictive overtones, would, however, be a task for another volume.

In contrast, the different kind of policy which Grew advocated and toward which Roosevelt so long inclined need not really be considered immoral or unprincipled, however much it undoubtedly would have been denounced as such. A limited *modus vivendi* agreement would not have required the United States in any way to sanction Japanese aggression or to abandon her stand on Chinese integrity and independence. It would have constituted only a recognition that the American government was not then in a position to enforce its principles, reserving for America full freedom of action at some later, more favorable time. Nor would it have meant the abandonment and betrayal of China. Rather it would have involved the frank recognition that the kind of help the Chinese wanted was impossible for the United States to give at that time. It would in no way have precluded giving China the best kind of help then possible—in the author's opinion, the offer of American mediation for a truce in the war and the grant of fuller economic aid to try to help the Chinese recover—and promising China greater assistance once the crucial European situation was settled. Only that kind of morality which sees every sort of dealing with an aggressor, every instance of accommodation or conciliation, as appeasement and therefore criminal would find the policy immoral.

What the practical results of such a policy, if attempted, would have been is of course a matter for conjecture. It would be rash to claim that it would have saved China, either from her wartime collapse or from the final victory of communism. It may well be that already in 1941 the situation in China was out of control. Nor can one assert with confidence that, had this policy enabled her to keep out of war with Japan, the United States would have been able to bring greater forces to bear in Europe much earlier, thus shortening the war and saving more of Europe from communism. Since the major part of the American armed forces were always concentrated in Europe and since in any case a certain proportion would have had to stand guard in the Pacific, it is possible that the avoidance of war with Japan, however desirable in itself, would not have made a decisive difference in the duration of the European conflict. The writer does, however, permit himself the modest conclusions that the kind of policy advocated by Grew presented real possibilities of success entirely closed to the policy actually followed and that it was by no means so immoral and unprincipled that it could not have been pursued by the United States with decency and honor.

Dexter Perkins

DEXTER PERKINS (1889–1984) was emeritus professor of history at the University of Rochester. He was the author of many books on various phases of American diplomatic history, including three volumes on the Monroe Doctrine.

Revisionism may be defined as an after-the-event interpretation of American participation in war, with the accent on the errors and blunders that provoked the struggle and on the folly of the whole enterprise. If we accept this definition, we shall certainly agree that there has been plenty of revisionism in the course of our history. The War of 1812 has sometimes been judged to have been futile and sometimes described as a war of intended conquest. The Mexican War has come in for harsh treatment as a war of unnecessary aggression. James G. Randall, one of the foremost students of the Civil War period, suggests that a less passionate view of the sectional problem might have made the conflict avoidable. Again and again it has been stated by reputable historians that William McKinley might have prevented the war of 1898 had he stressed in his message to Congress the very large concessions that had been made by Spain. The First World War was brilliantly represented by Walter Millis as the product of a blundering diplomacy and of economic pressures not entirely creditable. And since 1945 we have had a crop of historians, headed by so eminent a member of his historical generation as Charles A. Beard, attempting to show that the maddest folly of all was our entry into the conflict that ended less than a decade ago. Clearly, revisionism is an American habit; though, in saying this, I do not mean to imply that it is unknown in other lands.

The roots of the revisionist tendency are worth speculating about. Such a point of view, I take it, is particularly apt to find expression in a country where peace is highly treasured and where the glorification of war is relatively uncommon. Just as many Americans easily put away the hates and resentment of war at the end of the struggle and display a tendency towards reconciliation with the vanquished, so they tend to forget the passions that animated them and drove them into the conflict, and to view what at the time seemed reasonable and natural as something that with a little more forbearance or wisdom could

---

"Was Roosevelt Wrong?," *Virginia Quarterly Review* 30 (Summer 1954):355–372. Reprinted with permission of the *Virginia Quarterly Review* and Dexter Perkins.

have been avoided. And there are other factors that reinforce this point of view. Wars are apt to end in disillusionment. After the glorious hopes of the years 1917 and 1918 came the clash of national selfishness at Versailles, and a distraught and threatened world. In 1945 the defeat of Hitler and Japan was soon seen to have left grave problems ahead. In the East, the American defense of China and the hopes of a strong democratic nation in the Orient ended in the victory of the Chinese Reds. And in Europe, though the peril from the ambitions of Hitler was exorcized, the United States found itself face to face with a new totalitarianism, far-ranging in its ambitions like the old. In such a situation it was natural to forget the menace that had been defeated, and to ask whether there might not have been a better solution to the problems that ended with the capitulation ceremonies at Rheims and on the deck of the *Missouri*.

After every large-scale war, moreover, there is a reaction against that strong executive leadership which is almost inevitably associated with periods of crisis in the life of the nation. This was true in 1920; and it was true after 1945. During the conflict the personality of Mr. Roosevelt loomed large, and almost immune from attack. But under the surface there was hostility, and this was to take the form of criticism of his war policies. Sometimes this criticism came, as in the case of Frederic R. Sanborn in his "Design for War," from one who had a strong animus against the New Deal, and who approached the record of the administration in the field of foreign policy with this animus. Sometimes, on the other hand, as in the case of Charles A. Beard, it came from one who regarded the Roosevelt diplomacy as jeopardizing and perhaps wrecking far-reaching programs of internal reform. In these two cases, and in virtually every other, strong emotions entered into the account. It has been a satisfaction to the revisionists to tear down the President; and there has always been—and it was inevitable that there should be—a reading public to fall in with this point of view, either from personal dislike of Roosevelt or from partisan feeling.

Revisionism, then, has roots in the very nature of the case. But, if we analyze it coolly, what shall we think of it? This is the question I propose to examine in this essay.

It seems to me fair to say at the outset that it is impossible to avoid the conclusion that revisionism is essentially history by hypothesis. It suggests—indeed in some instances it almost claims—that the world would have been a better place, or that at any rate the present position of the United States would have been happier, if this country had not intervened in the Second World War. Such a proposition can be put forward, but it cannot be established like a theorem in geometry. We cannot go back to 1939 or 1941 and reenact the events of those stirring and tumultuous years. In a sense, we are bound by the past.

Nonetheless, it seems worthwhile, even though we are in the realm of speculation rather than scientific history, to state the revisionist point of view. First, with regard to Germany the point of view is advanced that the United States was in no essential danger from Adolf Hitler, that he demonstrated no very great interest in the American continents, that he desired until almost the day of Pearl Harbor to keep out of trouble with the United States, that there is no reliable evidence that he meditated an assault upon the New World. It is possible for the revisionist to go further. The ambitions of Hitler, it would be maintained, would have been checked and contained within limits by the presence of the great totalitarian state to the East. The two colossi would act each as a restraint on the other. It needed not the intervention of the American government to preserve the safety of the New World. As to Asia, the argument runs somewhat differently. Less emphasis is placed on the question of national security and more on a certain interpretation of national interest. The United States, we are told, had only a meager interest in China; its trade and investments there were insignificant, and were likely to remain so. They were distinctly inferior to our trade and investments in Japan. The shift in the balance of the Far East that might come about through a Japanese victory over Great Britain was no real concern of the United States. As to the Philippines, they might have been left alone had we stayed out of the war, or conversely, they were not worth the sacrifice involved in maintaining our connection with them. Such are the assumptions, implied, if not always expressed, in the revisionist view of the problem of the Orient.

Now some of the assertions in this rationale are unchallengeable. It is true that Hitler desired to avoid a clash with the United States until just before Pearl Harbor. It is true that the economic interests of the United States in China were inferior to our interests in Japan. These are facts, and must be accepted as facts. But there still remain a good many questions about the revisionist assumptions. For example, was there in 1940 and 1941 no danger of the destruction of British naval power, and would that destruction have had no unhappy consequences for the United States? Granted that the documents show great reluctance on the part of the Führer to challenge the United States, would this reluctance have outlasted the fall of Great Britain? Granted that the Kremlin might have exercised a restraining influence on the Germans, is it certain that the two powers might not have come to an understanding as they did in 1939, and had at other periods in the past? Just how comfortable a world would it have been if the psychopathic leader of Germany had emerged from the Second World War astride a large part of the Continent, with the resources of German science at his command? There are questions, too, that can be asked about the

Orient. Did the United States have no responsibility for the Philippines, and would the islands have been safe for long if the Japanese had dominated the Far East? Could the United States divest itself of all concern for China, abandoning a policy of nearly forty years duration and a deep-seated American tradition? Was the destruction of British power in this part of the world a matter of no concern to this country? Could the defeat of Britain in the East be separated from the fate of Britain in the world at large? These are extremely large questions, and it is a bold man who will brush them aside as inconsequential or trivial, or who will reply to them with complete dogmatism. Indeed, it is because they raise so many problems cutting to the root of our feelings, as well as our opinions, that they arouse so much controversy. Nor is there any likelihood that we can ever arrive at a complete consensus with regard to them.

We must, I think, seek a somewhat narrower frame of reference if we are to answer the revisionists with facts, and not with speculations. One of the ways to answer them, and one particularly worth pursuing with regard to the war in Europe, is to analyze the policy of the Roosevelt administration in its relation to public sentiment.

Foreign policy, in the last analysis, depends, not upon some logical formula, but upon the opinion of the nation. No account of American diplomacy in 1940 and 1941 can pretend to authority which does not take into account the tides of sentiment which must always influence, and perhaps control, the course of government. It is not to be maintained that a president has no freedom of action whatsoever; he can, I think, accelerate or retard a popular trend. But he does not act independently of it; the whole history of American diplomacy attests the close relationship between the point of view of the masses and executive action. A peacefully minded president like McKinley was driven to war with Spain; a president who set great store by increasing the physical power of the nation, like Theodore Roosevelt, was limited and confined in his action; and Franklin Roosevelt himself, when, in the quarantine speech of October 1937, he sought to rouse the American people against aggression, was compelled to admit failure, and to trim his sails to the popular breeze. These things are of the essence; to fail to observe them is to fail to interpret the past in the true historical spirit.

Let us apply these conceptions to the period 1939 to 1941. It will hardly be denied that from the very beginning of the war public sentiment was definitely against Germany. Indeed, even before the invasion of Poland, the public opinion polls show a strong partiality for the democratic nations. As early as January 1939, when asked the question [of] whether we should do everything possible to help England and France in case of war, 69 percent of the persons polled answered in the affirmative, and the same question in October produced a percentage of 62 percent on the same side. No doubt this sentiment did not extend to the point of actual participation in the war, but it furnished a firm foundation for the action of the President in calling Congress in special session, and in asking of it the repeal of the arms embargo on shipments of war in the interest of the Allies. The measure to this effect was introduced in the Congress towards the end of September; and it was thoroughly debated. There are several things to be said in connection with its passage. The first is that after its introduction there was a consistent majority of around 60 percent in the polls in favor of passage. The second is that, though there was a strong partisan flavor to the debate, the defections when they came were more numerous on the Republican than on the Democratic side. It is true that, without the leadership of the President, the repeal could not have been enacted. But also it did not fly in the face of public sentiment (so far as that can be measured), but on the contrary reflected it.

With the fall of France there took place a deep and significant development in public opinion. This change the revisionists usually do not mention. They prefer to treat of American policy as if it were formed in a vacuum without regard to the moving forces that have so much to do with the final decisions. Yet the evidences are ample that in June of 1940 the American people were deeply moved. Take, for example, the action of the Republican nominating convention. There were several outstanding professional politicians in the running in 1940, Senator Taft, Senator Vandenberg, Thomas E. Dewey. Each one of these men represented a policy of caution so far as Europe was concerned. Yet what did the convention do? It turned to a relatively unknown figure, to a novice in politics who had, however, more than once declared himself as advocating extensive assistance to the democracies. The choice of Wendell Willkie as the Republican candidate for the presidency is a fact the importance of which cannot be denied. It is worthwhile calling attention to other like phenomena. One of these is the overwhelming majorities by which the Congress appropriated largely increased sums for the armed forces, not only for the navy but for the army and the air force as well. Perhaps the American people, or the representatives of the American people, ought not to have been perturbed at what was happening in Europe. But the fact is that they were perturbed. They were perturbed in a big way. And the votes in the legislative halls demonstrate that fact.

Or take another example. The movement for a conscription law in time of peace developed rapidly after June of 1940. It developed with very little assistance from the White House. It cut across party lines. And it resulted in a legislative enactment which reflected the excitement of the public mind. How can we interpret the measure otherwise? Was there not a substantial body of opinion in the United States that feared a German victory?

Another important factor to be noted is the formation in June of 1940 of the Committee to Defend America by Aiding the Allies. It is highly significant that this movement arose at all. It is doubly significant that it found a leader in a Kansan Republican such as William Allen White. It is trebly significant that, once initiated, it spread like wildfire, and that by September there were more than 650 chapters in the United States. And it is also to be noted that in New York there soon came into being a more advanced group, the so-called Century Group, which advocated war if necessary to check the aggressions of Germany.

And it is further to be observed that out of the Committee to Defend America came an agitation for what was eventually to be the bases-destroyer deal of September 2, 1940. This deal, by the way, was approved by 62 percent of the persons polled on August 17, 1940, two weeks before it was actually consummated.

Let us go further. The next important step forward in American policy was the lend-lease enactment of the winter of 1941. This measure, it would appear from the polls, was based on a very distinct evolution of public sentiment. In July of 1940, 59 percent of the persons polled preferred to keep out rather than to help England at the risk of war, and 36 percent took the contrary view. In October the percentages were exactly reversed: they were 36 to 59. By January of 1941, 68 percent of those interviewed thought it more important to assist Great Britain than to keep out of war. And the lend-lease enactment, when presented to the Congress, passed the Lower House by the impressive vote of 317 to 71 and the Senate by 60 to 31. As in the legislation of 1939, though the vote again had a partisan flavor, there were more defections from the Republicans in favor of the measure than of Democrats against it. And there is something more to be added to the account in this instance. By the winter of 1941 the America Firsters had appeared upon the scene. A counterpropaganda was now being organized against the administration. Yet this new group, despite its vigorous efforts, failed signally to rally majority opinion. And Senator Taft, who represented the most thoughtful opposition to the administration, himself proposed a measure of assistance to Great Britain.

I shall treat a little later of the various measures requiring no legislative sanction which the President took in the course of the year 1941. But it is important to observe that throughout the period there was a strong public sentiment that believed that it was more important to defeat Germany than to keep out of war. This view was held, according to the polls, by 62 percent of those interrogated in May of 1941 and by 68 percent in December of 1941. As early as April 1941, 68 percent of the pollees believed it important to enter the war if British defeat was certain.

We should next examine the legislation of the fall of 1941. By this time the Congress was ready to authorize the arming of American merchant ships, and this by a heavy vote. The measure was passed by 259 to 138 in the House and the Senate amended it and passed it by 50 to 37. Congress was ready, more reluctantly, to repeal those provisions of the neutrality acts which excluded American vessels from the so-called war zones. It was moving in the direction of fuller and fuller engagement against Hitler. We shall never know, of course, what the next step would have been had not that step been taken by Germany. It was the dictator of the Reich who declared war on the United States, not the American national legislature that declared war on the Führer and his minions. But in the period between 1939 and 1941 it seems safe to say that the foreign policy of the Roosevelt administration was in accord with the majority opinion accepted, and pursuing a course of action which majority opinion approved.

This circumstance is naturally either ignored or obscured in the revisionist literature. And what makes it easier to forget is the undeniable fact that Franklin Roosevelt was unhappily sometimes given to equivocation and shifty conversation. Very early, it is true, as early as the quarantine speech of October 1937, he sounded the alarm against the totalitarians. Very often he stated his conviction that their continued progress presented a threat to the United States. On occasion he took his courage in his hands as, when at Charlottesville in June of 1940, in an election year, he came out frankly in favor of aid to the democracies, or in the declaration of unlimited emergency in the address of May 27, 1941. There is little doubt that he deemed the defeat of Hitler more important than the avoidance of war (as did many other Americans, as we have seen). Yet he was often less than frank in his approach, and the emphasis he laid on his devotion to peace was often excessive. He shocked even his ardent admirer, Robert Sherwood, in the election of 1940. His presentation of the case for lend-lease does not at all times suggest candor; indeed, the very phrase seems a bit of cajolery. With regard to the question of convoy, in the spring of 1941, he was clever and, though verbally correct, hardly wholly open in his approach to the problem. In the famous episode of the *Greer* (an attack by a German submarine on a vessel which was reporting its position to a British destroyer), he misrepresented the facts, or spoke without full knowledge of them. All this it is only right to admit. Yet we must not exaggerate the importance of these considerations. The country knew where it was going with regard to Germany. It accepted lend-lease as desirable. Of the patrolling of the ocean lanes which followed, the President spoke candidly in the speech of May 27, 1941. There was nothing clandestine about the occupation of Greenland or Iceland. The pattern in the fall of 1941 would most probably not have been much altered if Roosevelt had been more scrupulous with regard to the *Greer.* In the last analysis we come back to the essential fact that Roosevelt represented and expressed in action the mood of the country with regard to Germany.

The question is, I believe, more difficult when we come to examine American policy towards Japan. We can say with some assurance that the denunciation of the treaty of commerce of 1911, undertaken by the administration in July of 1939 as an indication of American displeasure with Japanese policy, was distinctly well received. Indeed, if the State Department had not acted, the legislature might have. We can also say that in August of 1939 there was an overwhelming feeling against sending war materials to Nippon. When in September of 1940, an embargo on the export of scrap iron was imposed, 59 percent of the persons polled on this issue approved the step that had been taken. And in 1941 the number of persons who believed that some check should be put on Japan even at the risk of war rose from 51 percent to 70 percent between July and September, and stood at 69 percent at the time of Pearl Harbor.

But we have fewer indications of the direction of public sentiment in the action of Congress, and no actual votes on which to base our estimate of how the representatives of the American people felt with regard to the important problem of our course of action in the Orient. We must, I think, speak less confidently on this question of public opinion than in the case of Germany. We must turn rather to an analysis of the policy of the administration, and to revisionist criticism of that policy.

First of all, let us look at some of the uncontroverted facts. We know that there were militarist elements in Japan. We know that as early as 1934 Japan proclaimed its doctrine of a Greater East Asia in the famous Amau statement. We know that in the same year it upset the naval arrangements made at Washington and London. We know that it set up a special régime in North China in 1935. We know that it became involved in a war with China in 1937. This, of course, was only prelude. The outbreak of the European conflict in Europe, and the collapse of France, offered to the sponsors of further aggressive action a great opportunity. The occupation of northern Indochina followed. In the summer of 1940, the impetuous and aggressive Matsuoka came to the Foreign Office. On September 27, 1940, there was signed a tripartite pact with Japan, which bound Nippon to come to the assistance of the Axis powers if they were attacked by a power then at peace with them. In other words, the Tokyo government sought to confine and limit American policy. In April of 1941 came a neutrality pact with Russia which freed the hands of the Japanese militarists for a policy of advance towards the South. In July came the occupation of the rest of Indochina. The occupation of *northern* Indochina made some sense from the point of view of blocking the supply route to the Chinese Nationalists. The occupation of *southern* Indochina made no sense, except as the prelude to further acts of aggression. And in due course the aggression came.

Admittedly, this is only one side of the story. The question to be examined is, did these acts take place partly as a result of American provocation? Was it possible for a wider and more prudent diplomacy to have avoided the rift that occurred in December 1941? Revisionist criticism of our Oriental policy has been expressed in a variety of ways. In its most extreme form, it suggests that the President and his advisers actually plotted war with Japan. In its less extreme form, it directs its shafts at a variety of actions, of which I shall examine the most important. They are the conversations with the British as to the defense of the Far East, the commitments made to China, the severance of commercial relations, the failure to accept the proposals of Prince Konoye for direct conversations with the President, and the breakdown of the *modus vivendi* proposal of November 1941. I shall examine each of these briefly, but let us first turn to the accusation that American policy was directed towards producing and not avoiding an armed conflict in the Orient.

It seems quite impossible to accept this view on the basis of the documentation. During the greater part of 1940 and 1941, it was certainly not the objective of the Roosevelt administration to bring about a clash in the Far East. On the contrary such a clash was regarded as likely to produce the greatest embarrassment in connection with the program of aid to Britain. The military and naval advisers of the President were opposed to it, and said so again and again. Even on the eve of Pearl Harbor this was the case. In addition, Secretary Hull was opposed to it. Ever the apostle of caution, he made his point of view quite clear almost up to the end. And as for the President, it is worth pointing out that on the occasion of the Japanese occupation of southern Indochina he came forward with a proposal for the neutralization of that territory in the interests of peace, and that in August he frankly stated it to be his purpose to "baby the Japanese along." That he feared Japanese aggression is likely, almost certain; that he desired it is something that cannot be proved.

But let us look at the various specific actions which have awakened criticism on the part of the revisionists. In the first place I cannot see that staff conversations with the British were open to any objections whatsoever. If the object of the Roosevelt administration was to limit Japanese aggression in the Far East, then it seems wholly rational to take precautions against such aggression, and surely it could reasonably be expected that such precautions would serve as a deterrent rather than as an incitement to action. It is, in my judgment, rather distorted thinking that regards such action as provocation. This is precisely the point of view of the Kremlin today with regard to the North Atlantic Treaty and the European defense pact, or, to take another example, very like the contention of the Germans when they invaded Belgium in 1914. Because the British had engaged in military conversations with the Belgians looking to the possible violation of the neutrality treaty of 1939, it was claimed by apologists for Germany that the violation of neutrality was defensible. Where is the possible justification for such reasoning?

There is more to be said with regard to the breaking off, by the United States, of commercial and financial relations with Japan on the heels of the Japanese occupation of southern Indochina in the summer of 1941. Undoubtedly this created an extraordinarily difficult situation for the government in Tokyo. Undoubtedly the cutting off of the oil supply from the United States gave great additional force to the arguments of the militarists. Undoubtedly, in the absence of a far-reaching diplomatic arrangement, it presented a strong reason for "bursting out" of the circle, and going to war. If the administration put faith in this measure of economic coercion as a substitute for physical resistance, its faith was to turn out to be groundless. For myself, I have for a long time believed that economic coercion against a strong and determined power is more likely to produce war than to prevent it. But there are circumstances that ought to be mentioned in favor of the action of the administration. It is to be emphasized that the severance of commercial and financial relations resulted not in a breach of the negotiations with Japan but in a resumption of those negotiations. It is to be remembered that Prince Konoye's proposal for a personal conference with the President came after and not before the President's action. American policy by no means put an end to the efforts of those substantial elements in Japan who feared a clash with this country and who were laboring to prevent it. It must be pointed out, also, that the alternative was by no means a pleasant one. At a time when we were deeply engaged in the Atlantic, when we were being more and more deeply committed with regard to the war in Europe, when our domestic supply of oil might have to be substantially curtailed, the continuation of our exports to the Far East to assist Japan in possible projects of aggression was a very difficult policy to follow. It may even be that it would have proven to be totally impracticable from a political point of view.

We come in the third place to the efforts of Premier Konoye to establish direct contact with President Roosevelt. It is well known that

Ambassador Grew believed at that time, and that he has more than once stated since, that a good deal was to be hoped from such a meeting. And it is by no means clear why, if the objective were the postponement of a crisis, the experiment should not have been tried. Secretary Hull brought to this problem, as it seems to me, a rigidity of mind which may properly be criticized. In insisting on a previous definition of the issues before the meeting was held, he was instrumental in preventing it. While we cannot know what the result of such a meeting would have been, we are entitled, I think, to wish that it had been held. All the more is this true since it would appear likely that Prince Konoye was sincere in the effort which he made to avoid war.

But there is another side to the matter. We cannot be absolutely sure of Konoye's good faith. We can be still less sure of the willingness of the Tokyo militarists to support him in the far-reaching concessions that would have been necessary. And in the final analysis we cannot be sure of the ability of the American government to make concessions on its own part.

And here we come, as it seems to me, to the crux of the matter. It was the American policy in China that created an impassable barrier in our negotiations with Japan. It is necessary to examine that policy. From one angle of vision the patience of the American government in dealing with the China incident seems quite remarkable. There was a good deal to complain of from 1935 onward, certainly from 1937 onward, if one were to think in terms of sympathy for an aggressed people and in terms of the traditional policy of the United States with regard to this populous nation. The Roosevelt administration moved very slowly in its opposition to Japan. It made its first loan to Chiang Kai-shek in the fall of 1938. It denounced the commercial treaty of 1911 with Nippon only in the summer of 1939. And it embarked upon a policy of really substantial aid to China only contemporaneously with the signing of the tripartite pact in the fall of 1940. Its increasing assistant to Chiang is intelligible on the ground that to keep the Japanese bogged down in China was one means of checking or preventing their aggressive action elsewhere.

The fact remains, however, that it was the Chinese question which was the great and central stumbling block in the long negotiations that took place in 1941. Though the Japanese had entered into an alliance with the Axis powers, it seems not unlikely that, in 1941, as the issue of peace or war defined itself more clearly, they would have been willing to construe away their obligations under that alliance had they been able to come to terms with the United States on the Chinese problem. But by 1941 the American government was so far committed to the cause of Chiang that it really had very little freedom of maneuver. The various Japanese proposals for a settlement of the China in-

cident would have involved a betrayal of the Chinese Nationalist
leader. The proposal for a coalition government, a government of the
Nationalists and the puppet régime of Wang Ching-wei, could hardly
have been accepted. The proposal that America put pressure on Chiang
to negotiate, and cut off aid to him if he refused, was by this time
equally impracticable. And the question of the withdrawal of the Japanese troops in China presented insuperable difficulties. True it is that
in October of 1941 the idea of a total withdrawal seems to have been
presented to Mr. Welles by Mr. Wakasugi, Admiral Nomura's associate
in the negotiations. But the idea was emphatically rejected by the militarists in Tokyo, and perhaps there was never a time when they would
have agreed to any proposal that at the same time would have been
acceptable to Chungking. The American government had been brought,
by its policy of association with the Chinese Nationalists, to the point
where understanding with Japan was practically impossible.

This fact is dramatically illustrated by the negotiations over the
modus vivendi in November 1941. At this time, as is well known,
proposals were brought forward for the maintenance of the status quo,
and a gradual restoration of more normal relations through the lifting
of the commercial restrictions, and through the withdrawal of the Japanese from southern Indochina. At first it seemed as if there were a
possibility of working out some such proposal. But the Chinese objected most violently, and Secretary Hull dropped the idea. In the face
of Chinese pressure, and of the possible popular indignation which such
a policy of concession might produce, and acting either under the orders or at least with the assent of the President, he backed down. We
must not exaggerate the importance of this. There is no certainty that
the *modus vivendi* would have been acceptable to Tokyo, and, judging
by the Japanese proposals of November 20, there is indeed some reason
to think otherwise. But the fact remains that our close association with
Chiang was a fundamental factor in making the breach with Japan irreparable. And it seems fair to say in addition that our hopes with regard to Nationalist China were at all times, in 1941 as later, very far
removed from political reality.

Let us not, however, jump to absolute conclusions with regard to
questions that, in the nature of the case, ought not to be a matter of
dogmatic judgment. If there was a party in Japan, and a substantial one,
which feared war with the United States and earnestly sought for accommodation, there was also a party which regarded the course of
events in Europe as a heaven-sent opportunity for national self-
aggrandizement. That this party might in any case have prevailed,
whatever the character of American policy, does not seem by any
means unlikely. It is significant that in July of 1941 the fall of Matsuoka brought no change in policy in the Far East, and that the so-

called moderate, Admiral Toyoda, gave the orders for the crucial and revealing occupation of southern Indochina in the summer of 1941.

Let us not forget, either, that after all it was the Japanese who struck. The ruthless act of aggression at Pearl Harbor was no necessary consequence of the breakdown of negotiations with the United States. If new oil supplies were needed, they were, of course, to be secured by an attack on the Dutch East Indies, not by an attack on Hawaii. Though there were strategic arguments for including America in any warlike move, there were strong political reasons for not doing so. No greater miscalculation has perhaps ever been made than that made by the militarists at Tokyo in December 1941. By their own act, they unified American opinion and made their own defeat inevitable. It will always remain doubtful when the decisive involvement would have come for the United States had the bombs not dropped on Pearl Harbor on the seventh of December of 1941.

What, in conclusion, shall we say of revisionist history? There is a sense in which it is stimulating to the historian, and useful to historical science, to have the presuppositions, the conventional presuppositions, of the so-called orthodox interpreters of our foreign policy, subjected to criticism. There is surely some reason to believe that the candid examination of the views of these critics will, in the long run, result in a more accurate and a more objective view of the great events of the prewar years and in a better balanced judgment of President Roosevelt himself.

But there is another side of the question which, of course, must be recognized. It is fair to say that virtually all revisionist history (like some orthodox history) is written with a *parti pris*. It is hardly possible to speak of it as dictated by a pure and disinterested search for truth. It is, on the contrary, shot through with passion and prejudice nonetheless. It also rests upon hypotheses which, in the nature of the case, cannot be demonstrated, and assumptions that will, it is fair to say, never be generally, or perhaps even widely, accepted. As to its practical effects, there are no signs that the isolationism of the present era has important political effects, so far as foreign policy is concerned. Conceivably, it provides some reinforcement for partisan Republicanism. But even here it seems considerably less effective than the unscrupulous campaign of Senator McCarthy and his colleagues to represent the previous administration as one saturated with Communists. The urgency of present issues may make revisionism less of a force in our time than it was two decades ago. As to this, we shall have to see what the future unfolds.

☆ 9 ☆

America
and the Cold War

CONTAINMENT
OR COUNTERREVOLUTION?

After World War II the American people faced a succession of external and internal challenges for which they had few historical precedents. By 1945 the United States had emerged as the strongest nation on earth. Having triumphed over the forces of Nazi and fascist totalitarianism American citizens looked forward with confidence and optimism to the promise of a bright future. Such hopes and expectations were soon dashed. Within two years after the fighting ended the United States found itself confronting the Soviet Union, its former ally. Instead of peace the American people were plunged headlong into an era of "Cold War"—a series of crises that required economic and military mobilization even in the absence of actual hostilities.

Two developments during the war established the context within which the Cold War would be waged. One was the toppling of five major nations from the ranks of first-rate powers. America's enemies—Germany, Japan, and Italy—were defeated. Her friends—Britain and France—spent so much blood and treasure that they found it impossible to regain their prewar military and economic importance. This situation left only two superpowers—the United States and the Soviet Union. The second development was the technological revolution in warfare. With the exploding of the atomic bomb in 1945, and the capability of destroying mankind, diplomacy entered upon a new age. These two considerations led one historian to liken the relations between the United States and Russia to a scorpion and tarantula together in a bottle, each tragically committed to trying to outdo the other.[1]

Most historians, but by no means all, agreed that World War II created the setting for the Soviet-American confrontation. Although ideological differences existed between the two great powers prior to that time the war produced suspicion, distrust, and a gap in understanding that became increasingly difficult to bridge. The Cold War, most scholars and laymen concluded, arose from two seemingly incompatible conceptions of the ideal shape of the postwar world order. The American point of view pictured the Soviet Union as a ruthless power, driven by its Communist ideology, bent upon global revolution and domination, and headed by leaders like Stalin who embarked upon an aggressive policy of expansion with the ultimate aim of destroying the free world. From Russia's perspective, however, America represented the main threat to peace. The Soviet view was that the United States emerged from the war militantly committed to the idea of a capitalist world order. America, as an imperalist power, sought to encircle the Soviet Union with hostile capitalist countries, to isolate Russia from the rest of the world, and to destroy Communist regimes wherever they existed. Thus the free world and Communist camp each viewed the other side as being dedicated to its destruction.

American scholars disagreed, however, when they came to evaluate the causes of the Cold War and to pass judgment on the roles of the two adversaries. Since 1945 American historians, when inquiring into the origins of the Cold War, divided into three schools: the orthodox, or traditional school; the revisionists; and the realists. Although the arguments of each school changed somewhat with the passing of time and appearance of new developments, they established the framework of the important historiographical debate that took place.

The first to appear was the orthodox school, which came into being during the immediate postwar years. At that time most of the American people, and the vast majority of scholars, were inclined to accept the official explanation of events set forth by the Truman administration in justifying its foreign policy. According to the orthodox interpretation Soviet aggression and expansionist desires were primarily responsible for the coming of the Cold War.

The orthodox or traditional interpretation reflected closely the official view of the American and British governments at the time. Winston Churchill, speaking at Fulton, Missouri, in the spring of 1946, set forth the basic outline of this interpretation. An "iron curtain," said Churchill, had been lowered across Eastern Europe by the Soviets. No

---

[1]Louis Halle, *The Cold War as History* (New York, 1967), p. xiii.

one knew for sure what secret plans for expansion were being hatched behind the iron curtain. The British leader viewed not only the Soviet Union, but Communist ideology, Communist parties, and "fifth column" activities as a growing peril to what he called "Christian civilization." President Truman in 1947 echoed similar sentiments when announcing his now-famous Truman Doctrine. Although the United States had made every effort to bring about a peaceful world, he said, the Soviet Union had used "indirect aggression" in Eastern Europe, "extreme pressure" in the Middle East, and had intervened in the internal affairs of many countries through "Communist parties directed from Moscow." Because of the Truman Doctrine many scholars of the traditionalist school held that the Cold War had officially commenced in 1947.

The orthodox interpretation was presented in scholarly books and journals in the late 1940s and early 1950s by historians like Herbert Feis and policymakers such as George F. Kennan. These men, too, held that the Cold War had been brought about mainly because of Soviet actions. Motivated by the traditional desires for greater security, power, and larger spheres of influence, they said, the Soviet Union resorted to an expansionist foreign policy. Coupled with these age-old drives was the new ideological zeal of communism which made the Soviets ambitious to foment revolution and conquest in behalf of their cause. Scholars sometimes disagreed about the primary motivation of the Soviets; some favored the importance of ideology as an explanation, while others believed the main focus should be placed on Russia's traditional policy of imperialism and pursuit of national interest. But they all tended to agree that no matter what the motivation might be, Soviet objectives were expansionist in scope. The orthodox view also argued that the Soviet Union violated its agreements with the Western powers, including the Yalta accords as they concerned the political future of Eastern Europe and, to a lesser extent, the role of China in the postwar world.

America's foreign policy, according to the orthodox interpretation, was in marked contrast to that of the Soviet Union. The United States, at first, held high hopes for a peaceful postwar world. The actions of its leaders were predicated on the principles of collective security, and they looked to the newborn United Nations for the solution to any future conflicts. Faced with Soviet aggressive moves, however, America was reluctantly forced to change its views and foreign policy. To prevent the Soviet Union from spreading its influence over large parts of the world, the United States finally felt compelled to embark upon a policy of "containment." Without this containment policy, argued many, the Soviet Union would probably have become the master of all Europe—instead of dominating only Eastern Europe.

Many of the arguments of the orthodox position were set forth in an article published by George F. Kennan under a pseudonym, "Mr. X," in 1947. Kennan, an American diplomat, provided many of the insights upon which the foreign policy of the Truman administration was based. In his piece Kennan suggested, among other things, an American containment policy to check Russia's expansionist tendencies. Kennan subsequently claimed, however, that he was not thinking primarily in terms of containment along military lines.[2]

The orthodox version, despite challenges, remains the dominant school of thought on the origins of the Cold War. Many of its proponents, however, differ widely in their interpretations. They all place differing emphases upon such crucial matters as the role of ideology, the inevitability of the conflict, the presumed unintentional provocation of the West, and the like. Although it may seem arbitrary to lump them together, they may be identified as "orthodox" because they generally found that responsibility for the Cold War rested to a major degree with the Soviet Union.[3] Even this categorization remains tenuous, however, because men like Kennan and Feis have changed their minds and shifted their views with the passage of time. Moreover, there are significant differences even among orthodox historians. John Lewis Gaddis, for example, insisted that neither the Soviet Union nor the United States was solely responsible for the Cold War. Yet he also noted that major responsibility rested with Stalin, who had greater opportunity to adjust to American foreign policy than Truman to Soviet policy.[4]

The roots of the revisionist interpretation, like that of the orthodox thesis, also originated in the statements from public figures as well as scholars. From the outset of the Cold War the official explanation of events had not gone unchallenged. Henry Wallace, former vice-president, had raised a powerful voice which questioned the soundness of President Truman's analysis of the international situation during the immediate postwar years. Running as a presidential candidate of

---

[2][George F. Kennan], "The Sources of Soviet Conduct," *Foreign Affairs* 25 (July 1947): 566–582.

[3]For a few examples of the orthodox interpretation see Herbert Feis's three books, *The Road to Pearl Harbor* (Princeton, 1950), *The China Tangle* (Princeton, 1953), and *Roosevelt-Churchill-Stalin* (Princeton, 1957); William H. McNeill, *America, Britain, and Russia: Their Cooperation and Conflict, 1941–1946* (London, 1953); Norman Graebner, *Cold War Diplomacy: American Foreign Policy 1945–1960* (Princeton, 1962); and André Fontaine, *History of the Cold War from the October Revolution to the Korean War, 1917–1950*, 2 vols. (New York, 1968).

[4]John Lewis Gaddis, *The United States and the Origins of the Cold War, 1941–1947* (New York, 1972). See also George G. Herring, Jr., *Aid to Russia, 1941–1946: Strategy, Diplomacy, the Origins of the Cold War* (New York, 1973).

a minority party in 1948 Wallace sought to be more sympathetic toward the Russians. But his relatively poor showing revealed how little public support there was for this position.

Walter Lippmann, one of the nation's leading intellectuals and a scholarly journalist, likewise refused to place the blame for international tensions exclusively on the Soviet Union. It was Lippmann who popularized the term "Cold War" by using it in the title of a book he published in 1947.[5] In his work he argued that America's statesmen expended their energies assaulting Russia's vital interests in Eastern Europe. By doing so they had furnished the Soviet Union with the reasons for rationalizing an iron rule behind the iron curtain. They also gave the Russians grounds to suspect what the Soviets had been conditioned to believe: that a capitalist coalition was being organized to destroy them. As a result of Lippmann's writings, in part, revisionist-minded historians began with one underlying assumption contrary to that of the orthodox interpretation: they were skeptical about accepting the claim that the Soviet Union was primarily or solely responsible for precipitating the Cold War.

Over the years the revisionist approach to the origins of the Cold War gradually came to represent not merely a challenge but an antithetical position to the orthodox thesis. Many revisionists came to the conclusion that the United States and its policies—rather than Russia and communism—had brought about the Cold War. The conflict had been precipitated by Western—and especially American—moves which threatened the Soviets and compelled them to react defensively. This the Russians had done by resorting to strict control over those areas that had fallen under their influence during World War II.

It is difficult to generalize about the revisionists because of the diversity of approaches in this school of scholars. Each historian stressed different aspects of the Cold War, offered different arguments, and professed to see different motives behind the acts of the principal protagonists. Most revisionists, nevertheless, tended to agree that Russia was weak, not strong, after 1945 because of the ravages of war. Beginning with this premise they then argued that the Soviet Union was neither willing nor able to pursue an aggressive policy after the war ended. Indeed, some revisionists maintained that while the Russians feared America's technological superiority and military power, they still viewed the United States as the main potential source of assistance to enable them to recover from the disastrous effects of the war. Other revisionists stressed that under Stalin the Soviet Union consis-

---

[5]Walter Lippmann, *The Cold War* (New York, 1947). Lippmann's book was a collection of newspaper articles written to counter Kennan's interpretation of the motivation behind Soviet policy.

tently pursued only cautious, defensive, and limited goals of foreign policy despite the rhetoric of ideological bravado. Thus the worldwide policy of aggression which the traditionalists believed they had detected in Russia's behavior seemed to the revisionists to be entirely out of character and beyond the means of the Soviet leaders.

During the 1950s and 1960s many differing shades of revisionism appeared among American historians. Some scholars approached the problem by attempting to evaluate the degree to which the United States had been responsible for precipitating the Cold War. In tackling this issue these writers sought to explain and justify Soviet actions since the war. Others analyzed American objectives in such a way as to show that these goals had been the basis for the postwar split. Some radical revisionists, especially those associated with the New Left, went even further: they viewed the United States as having been an aggressive power in the world not only during World War II, but throughout the entire twentieth century.

When revisionist-minded historians came to the matter of America's motivation they were likewise in disagreement and offered different explanations. Some claimed that the Western powers in general, and the Truman administration in particular, tried to deny the Soviet Union its due in the matter of the Yalta agreements: the West, they said, had sought to reinterpret the meaning of these accords, and refused to recognize what Roosevelt and Churchill had been compelled by circumstances to concede at Yalta. Other historians argued that the United States—imbued with the missionary zeal of a latent "manifest destiny"—had hoped to reshape the world to suit its exaggerated attachment to the democratic principles of representative government. Still other scholars stressed the theme of economic expansion—postulating that America's postwar foreign policy represented a drive to capture world markets and to establish this country's economic and political influence all over the globe. Certain historians concluded that the United States used its early monopoly of nuclear weapons and economic strength to browbeat other nation-states and to force them to submit to Washington's leadership. As proof of this position they pointed out that the Truman administration had refused major economic assistance to the Soviet Union, and that the Marshall Plan had been designed in such a way as to preclude Soviet participation in it.

Despite the complexities within the revisionist school it is possible to distinguish two main groups in this category—the moderate revisionists and those associated with the New Left, who were more extreme. Although the revisionist scholars disagreed about the degree of responsibility they assigned to the United States in bringing on the Cold War, they all held America, in large part, accountable for the conflict because of her aggressive and menacing policy toward Russia.

One example of the moderate revisionist position was Denna F. Fleming's two-volume study entitled *The Cold War and its Origins, 1917–1960*, published in 1961. Fleming focused upon President Truman as the crucial figure in the coming of the Cold War. Within weeks after Roosevelt died, Fleming wrote, Truman dramatically reversed the course of America's foreign policy. Roosevelt had been dedicated to a Wilsonian "internationalism," and, recognizing that the Soviet Union would be the key to any new league of nations in the postwar period, had done his utmost to maintain good relations with Russia. But Truman adopted a tough policy toward the Russians as soon as he assumed the presidency. In April 1945 he ordered the Soviets to change their policy in Poland or else America would withdraw certain promised economic aid. Contrary to the orthodox version, which generally dated the beginning of the Cold War in 1947 with the Truman Doctrine, Fleming believed it began in 1945.

Fleming's thesis that America provoked the Cold War was amplified by the picture he presented of the postwar era. The United States was invariably portrayed as taking the initiative in relations between the two powers. Russia, on the other hand, was usually depicted as reacting to events in a defensive way. Fleming's interpretation differed greatly from the orthodox version which had pictured the Soviets as the ruthless aggressor, but his findings were suspect because they were not based on solid documentation.[6]

Writing in the same revisionist tradition was Gar Alperovitz. In *Atomic Diplomacy: Hiroshima and Potsdam*, published in the mid-1960s, Alperovitz held that President Truman had helped to start the Cold War in 1945 by dropping the atomic bomb. Alperovitz added a new viewpoint to the debate by arguing that Truman resorted to "atomic diplomacy." With the United States possessing a monopoly of atomic weapons at the time Truman adopted a hard line toward the Soviets—one which was aimed at forcing Soviet Russia's acquiescence in America's postwar plans. In short, Truman fell back upon the modern equivalent of saber-rattling to play power politics and drive Russia out of East Europe by a show of force.

Like most of the moderate revisionists, however, Alperovitz did not heap all the blame for beginning the Cold War on the United States. The Russians by their actions also helped to poison the postwar atmosphere, he said. "The cold war cannot be understood simply as an American response to a Soviet challenge," he wrote, "but rather as an insidious interaction of mutual suspicions, blame for which must be

---

[6]Denna F. Fleming, *The Cold War and Its Origins, 1917–1960*, 2 vols. (New York, 1961).

shared by all." Nevertheless the thrust of Alperovitz's work clearly placed responsibility for the beginnings of the Cold War on American shoulders.[7]

Most New Left historians were bitter in their condemnation of the orthodox interpretation. In large part this was so because of their own ideological commitments; they were highly critical about the very nature of American society as a whole, and hence unsympathetic with the aims of the United States abroad. Moreover, where the more moderate revisionists tended to picture Roosevelt or Truman as men of limited vision who fumbled their way to disaster in the postwar period, some New Left scholars were inclined to view developments against a much broader background. They wrote within a context that stretched far beyond the immediate postwar years: such New Left scholars held that America's foreign policy in the 1940s, 1950s, and 1960s was simply an extension of a trend that had been under way since the Spanish-American War at the turn of the century.

The most significant assault on the orthodox position came from William Appleman Williams in his books *The Tragedy of American Diplomacy* and *The Contours of American History*, published in the late 1950s and 1960s. Although Williams never regarded himself as a member of the New Left his writings were seized upon and extended by other radical historians. What Williams did was to provide a provocative hypothesis to explain America's diplomacy throughout our entire history. America's foreign policy was expansionist from our very beginnings, he declared. Writing from a neo-Beardian point of view Williams went all the way back to the 1760s. He showed that even before gaining its independence America had adopted a course to achieve economic self-sufficiency within the British Empire by applying English mercantilist principles in the New World environment. Once independence had been won the United States was committed to the idea of an independent American empire to enable the growing new nation to have markets for its products. Until the 1890s that empire lay mostly to the west on the American continent, but once the frontier was gone the search for markets led to overseas expansion. Despite the controversy between imperialists and antiimperialists around the turn of the century, both groups agreed that economic expansion overseas was vital to the nation's prosperity and future. The debate was over means rather than ends. Imperialists felt that physical acquisition of traditional colonies was necessary; antiimperialists, on the other hand, believed that America's economic expansion throughout the world could be achieved without the expense of maintaining a colonial empire.

---

[7]Gar Alperovitz, *Atomic Diplomacy: Hiroshima and Potsdam* (New York, 1965).

The Open Door policy, according to Williams, resolved the dilemma and ultimately became the basis for America's future foreign policy. America's Open Door policy represented an effort to achieve all the advantages of economic expansion without the disadvantages of maintaining a colonial empire. It called for an open door for trade with all foreign countries on a most-favored-nation principle—a principle that had a long tradition in American diplomacy stretching back to 1776. Although formulated originally to apply to China the policy was expanded geographically to cover the entire globe and economically to include American investments as well as trade.[8]

Williams, operating from this premise, saw the Cold War within a different context than the orthodox school of historians. To him the postwar period represented nothing more than the extension of the Open Door policy as America, seeking markets for its goods and money, hoped to penetrate into Eastern Europe and other parts of the globe. Thus America was primarily responsible for the Cold War, for in seeking to extend economic influence she took whatever steps were necessary to maintain or put into power governments that would do business with the United States. Counterrevolution to make the world safe for American capitalism, not containment, was the major motive behind the postwar policies of the United States.[9]

One of Williams's followers, Walter LaFeber (who in 1963 had published an important study of the origins of American expansionism in the late nineteenth century), developed and expanded this view in a monograph that appeared in 1967. LaFeber was critical of both the United States and the Soviet Union for failing to maintain peace. Focusing upon the internal reasons behind the formulation of foreign policy in the two countries he concluded that domestic developments played a large part in determining those foreign policies that finally emerged. In the United States domestic events—presidential campaigns, economic recessions, the era of repression identified with Senator Joseph McCarthy of Wisconsin, and the struggle for power by various factions within the government—contributed as much to the making of America's foreign policy as did external events. Within Russia itself the same was true: the machinations of Stalin and Khrushchev, problems with the Soviet economy, and power struggles within the Communist party laid the basis for most foreign policy changes. In terms of economic penetration LaFeber found that the United States and the Soviet Union showed equal interest in exploiting foreign mar-

---

[8]William A. Williams, *The Tragedy of American Diplomacy* (2d ed.; New York, 1962) and *The Contours of American History* (Cleveland, 1961).

[9]Christopher Lasch, "The Cold War, Revisited and Re-Visioned," *New York Times,* January 14, 1968.

kets wherever possible. Both nations, he concluded, created their postwar policies with an eye to maintaining freedom of action in those areas they considered vital to their economic and strategic interests.

Conflicting aims arising from domestic concerns, LaFeber said, led to a continuing rivalry between the two giant powers as they confronted one another over two decades in many parts of the globe. America's foreign policy was based on the assumption that the nation's political, economic, and psychological needs at home dictated those commitments undertaken abroad. During the first phase of the struggle—1945 to 1953—those commitments were Europe-oriented, and even the Korean War was fought, in part, to preserve America's image as the main bulwark in the West against the Communist monolith. But after the mid-1950s both America and Russia shifted their focus from Europe to the newly emerging nations all over the world, and the Cold War entered its second phase. The Vietnam War, according to LaFeber, represented a "failure" in America's foreign policy because it sought to answer the political and economic global changes posed by the newly emerging nations with military solutions. There was continuity in America's policy, concluded LaFeber, because the American people had decided to accept the responsibility of answering challenges of such a global nature as far back as 1947 with the Truman Doctrine. In a similar vein Lloyd C. Gardner, a student of Williams's at the University of Wisconsin, emphasized the commitment of American leaders to a liberal world order based on the Open Door policy. Haunted by fears of depression these leaders strove to create a world economy conducive to American capitalism and prosperity. "Responsibility for the *way* in which the Cold War developed, at least," Gardner concluded, "belongs more to the United States." [10]

Gardner's work in particular influenced a number of revisionist and New Left scholars. Athan Theoharis, for example, accepted Gardner's contention that the United States was largely responsible for the way in which the Cold War developed. Theoharis insisted that a wide variety of options were available to American policymakers in 1945; nothing compelled the adoption of policies that led to the Cold War. During World War II, for example, Roosevelt followed a diplomatic policy that was strikingly vacillating and ambivalent. At Yalta, on the other hand, he pursued a conciliatory path based upon the acceptance of Soviet postwar influence and the need to arrive at an accommodation that would avert disharmony and conflict. His death, however,

---

[10]Walter LaFeber, *America, Russia, and the Cold War, 1945–1966* (New York, 1967), and Lloyd C. Gardner, *Architects of Illusion: Men and Ideas in American Foreign Policy, 1941–1949* (Chicago, 1970). See also Thomas G. Paterson, *Soviet-American Confrontation: Postwar Reconstruction and the Origins of the Cold War* (Baltimore, 1973).

altered the diplomatic setting by introducing an element of uncertainty. More importantly it brought Harry S. Truman to the White House, an individual who was more rigidly anti-Soviet. Truman's accession to the presidency, according to Theoharis, provided the opening wedge for policy advisers whose recommendations were ignored at Yalta. The result was that the opportunities for détente provided at Yalta were effectively subverted under Truman, and the stage was set for years of conflict and confrontation. The first selection in this chapter is an excerpt from an article on the origins of the Cold War by Theoharis.

While neither Williams, LaFeber, nor Gardner necessarily included themselves as members of the New Left, it was clear that their respective studies could easily serve as a point of departure for radical scholars. In 1968 Gabriel Kolko, whose earlier study of the origins of political capitalism from 1900 to 1917 had heralded the advent of the New Left school of historiography, brought out a detailed study of the origins of the Cold War that picked up where Williams and LaFeber had left off. Kolko dealt with America's foreign policy within a much narrower chronological framework; he covered only the years from 1943 to 1945. But Kolko felt that the policies forged in that crucial period were the key to the long-range plans of the United States in the postwar era. His *The Politics of War* represented an attempt to document in detail and to extend the general themes introduced by Williams. Kolko advanced the thesis that the United States had acted not only to win the war in these two years, but to erect the structure for peacetime politics in the postwar world. To Kolko America's objectives were twofold: to use its military power to defeat the enemy, and to employ its political and economic power to gain leverage for extending America's influence throughout the world. Thus Kolko, like Williams, viewed the United States as a counterrevolutionary force bent on restoring the old order in Europe and making the world safe for American capitalism.[11]

Kolko's assumptions regarding America's postwar policies were typical of many of the New Left scholars. He assumed, first of all, that the United States, not Russia, represented the greatest threat to international stability; that America was mainly responsible for bringing on the Cold War. Second, that the United States was dedicated to worldwide counterrevolution: to a policy of employing her military and economic power to extend her influence throughout the world be-

---

[11]Gabriel Kolko, *The Politics of War: The World and United States Foreign Policy, 1943–1945* (New York, 1968). See also Joyce Kolko and Gabriel Kolko, *The Limits of Power: The World and United States Foreign Policy, 1945–1954* (New York, 1972).

cause American capitalism was dependent upon ever-expanding foreign markets for survival. And third, that the origins of the Cold War lay not solely within World War II but stretched back to World War I and beyond.

Significantly the revisionist view of Cold War diplomacy—both moderate an extremist—developed mainly in the 1960s. This decade was a period of deepening disillusionment among American intellectuals over the nation's foreign policy. Disenchanted by America's intervention in Cuba and Santo Domingo and the escalating involvement in Vietnam, many intellectuals had begun to question whether the United States had not taken too seriously the responsibilities of world leadership; it had involved itself unnecessarily in the internal affairs of other nations where it had no business. Moreover they feared that this country was so conditioned to fighting totalitarianism that American leaders tended to see enemies where none existed. It is not too much to suggest that this reaction among intellectuals helped to shape the unsympathetic view that the revisionists had taken toward America's foreign policy.

To some scholars neither the orthodox nor the revisionist explanations were adequate. Joseph R. Starobin, a former Communist who broke with the American Communist party in the 1950s, insisted that historians had ignored a key element in the origins of the Cold War, namely, the contradictions within the Communist movement itself. During and after World War II, the Soviet Union attempted to overcome the diversity within a system of states and parties in which earlier political and ideological premises had become obsolete. For Stalin, therefore, the Cold War was a struggle involving Russia's internal objectives and the subordination of an international movement. Viewed in this light the struggle between the Soviet Union and the United States was brought about by an internal crisis within the former. Starobin's article is presented as the second selection in this chapter.

If the orthodox and revisionist interpretations represented antithetical views about the origins of the Cold War the realist school has become, in some ways, a middle-of-the-road position. The realists, unlike the revisionists who followed them, were less likely to dismiss containment because it represented in their eyes a necessary response to Soviet expansionism. On the other hand they were critical of the orthodox scholars because of the excessive moralism and legalism in the traditional interpretation. The realists were more prone to view foreign relations in terms of *realpolitik* from which the school derived its name, and to place more emphasis upon power politics and conflicting national interests. Historians of the realist school were less concerned with determining the degree of moral responsibility for the

Cold War and focused their attention instead on the pragmatic political problems facing the policymakers.

Like the other two schools of scholars the realists could trace their origins back to the late 1940s and early 1950s. Their writings began as a response, in part, to the strong criticisms of Roosevelt's role in the developing East-West impasse. These criticisms held that America's supposed weakness in the postwar period had resulted either from Roosevelt's misunderstanding of Soviet intentions or from his failure to foresee the incompatibility of Soviet and American goals. In the eyes of his critics Roosevelt was responsible for the subsequent subjugation of Eastern Europe. But the realists argued that Roosevelt, in fact, was faced with a *fait accompli* in Eastern Europe with powerful Russian armies occupying that area, and that the diplomatic options open to him were severely limited as a result.

Generally speaking the realists held that the blame for the Cold War belonged either to both sides or, more accurately, to neither. Indeed, neither the United States nor the Soviet Union had wanted to precipitate a conflict. Both had hoped that cooperation among the allies would continue—but on their own terms, of course. Each country had sought limited objectives but had expected the other to accept them as such. To be specific the Soviet Union was motivated by fear and acted in the interests of its security rather than out of any expansionist ambitions. However, whenever one side made a move in pursuit of its limited objectives the other side perceived the act as a threat to its existence and, in reacting accordingly, triggered a countermeasure which led to increasing escalation. As a result small and otherwise manageable foreign crises had led inevitably to a widening conflict, which gradually assumed global proportions. In short, the realists found that both sides in pursuing their interests had sought limited goals, but the spiraling effect of such measures had inadvertently precipitated the Cold War.

The realist school tended also to view the Cold War as a traditional power conflict rather than a clash of ideologies. To many of these historians the Cold War was comparable to some of the previous struggles that had taken place to prevent a single power from dominating Europe's east-central regions. Other scholars saw the conflict within the context of the age-old battle over the European balance of power.

When viewing the situation in postwar Europe members of the realist school took a hard look at political realities rather than indulging in speculations about diplomatic possibilities. While stressing Soviet determination to create in Eastern Europe satellite states that would enhance Russia's security, the realists also emphasized how vulnerable the countries in that part of Europe were to outside pressures because their own social, political, and economic systems had proven incapable of solving the problems of their people. These societies were ripe for revolution, the realists concluded, and an easy prey to the indigenous Communist movements that existed and were Moscow-directed. The countries of Western Europe, they argued, were not susceptible to the same pressures; their social, economic, and political institutions, though weakened by the war, were still viable. Hence the realists concluded that the fear expressed in the orthodox interpretation—that Soviet influence might extend across Europe to reach the English Channel—was not only exaggerated but revealed a misunderstanding of the nature of the conflict.

The realists usually disagreed with the moderate revisionists who, like Alperovitz, claimed that the United States had used its monopoly of atomic weapons to force other nation-states into submission. On the other hand they accepted the thesis that in employing nuclear weapons against Japan the American government was motivated not only by a desire to conclude the Pacific war, but by the hope of doing so before the Soviet Union could enter that theater of war. America, they wrote, feared that Moscow might attempt to do in the Far East what it appeared to be doing in Eastern Europe. Thus the presence of nuclear weapons in American hands was believed by the realists to have had a psychological effect upon both the atomic "haves" and "have-nots" during the initial phases of the Cold War.

The realists likewise disagreed with those revisionists associated with the New Left. They challenged the assumptions, ideological considerations, and political misconceptions upon which they felt the New Left historians based their arguments. In his review of Kolko's *The Politics of War*, Hans J. Morgenthau (one of the leading realist scholars) charged that Kolko was reflecting the mood of his own generation in attributing blame for the origins of the Cold War. That mood, Morgenthau noted,

> . . . *reacts negatively to the simple and simplistic equation, obligatory during the war and postwar periods, of American interests and policies with democratic virtue and wisdom, and those of their enemies with totalitarian folly and vice. As the orthodox historiography of the Second World War and the Cold War expressed and justified that ideological juxtaposition, so the revisionism of Professor Kolko expresses and justifies the new mood of ideological sobriety. However, given the moralism behind American political thinking regardless of its content, revisionism tends to be as moralistic in its critique of American foreign policy as orthodoxy is in defending it. While the moralistic approach remains, the moral labels have been reversed: what once was right is now wrong, and vice versa. Yet as historic truth may emerge from the dialectic of opposite extremes, qualified and tempered by charity and understanding, so sound political judg-*

ment requires both the recognition of extreme positions as inevitable
and of their possible transcendence through a morality which is as
alien to the moralism of our political folklore as Thucydidean justice
is to the compensatory justice of opposing historical schools.[12]

Morgenthau's own writings represented one of the best examples of the realist point of view. In them he was critical of what he called the legalistic-moralistic tradition which presumably prevented American statesmen from perceiving foreign policy in terms of national power and national interest in the past. His *In Defense of the National Interest: A Critical Examination of American Foreign Policy,* published in 1951, claimed that America's foreign policies since 1776 had been much too utopian in outlook. Only in the years since World War II, he suggested, had Americans become more realistic and formulated their policy on the basis of power politics and national interest.[13] Nevertheless American policymakers had misunderstood Soviet foreign policy; they failed to see the essential continuity in the expansionist objectives sought by the czars and later by the Communists and focused instead on the new goals supposedly arising out of a revolutionary ideology. Thus Morgenthau criticized the orthodox interpretation by suggesting that the United States had contributed to the coming of the Cold War by its long-standing tendency to view its relationship to the rest of the world in rather unrealistic terms.

Another member of the realist school, Louis Halle, took a somewhat different approach. In *The Cold War as History,* published in the mid-1960s, Halle was more interested in stressing the tragic nature of the conflict. He suggested that neither side was really to blame for the Cold War. Misconceptions on both sides had led to the rise of ideological myths—myths which often had little relation to existing social realities. The West, led by the United States, was governed by the myth of a monolithic conspiracy among Communists the world over to drive for global domination, initially under the leadership of the Soviet Union. The Communists, on their part—Lenin and his associates in 1917–1918 and Mao Tse-tung a generation later in 1949–1950—were under the spell of another myth. Their world view pictured a globe divided between capitalist-imperialists on the one hand and exploited peasants and proletariat on the other. Each of these two Communist

---

[12]Hans J. Morgenthau, "Historical Justice and the Cold War," *New York Review of Books,* July 10, 1969.

[13]Hans J. Morgenthau, *In Defense of the National Interest: A Critical Examination of American Foreign Policy* (New York, 1951). In this same regard it should be noted that George Kennan has come much closer to the realist school by arguing in his memoirs that the Truman administration pursued the wrong priorities in Europe by concentrating on a policy of *military* containment. George F. Kennan, *Memoirs, 1925–1950* (Boston, 1967).

leaders in his own time had believed that the historical moment had come when the oppressed lower classes were about to rise up in revolution, to overthrow their upper-class masters, and to establish a utopian society of the brotherhood of man along lines predicted by Karl Marx. It was the belief in such myths which drove the free world and the Communist camp to embark upon what each side considered to be a struggle for survival.

Historical interpretations, of course, often run in cycles. Just as the revisionists challenged their more orthodox predecessors, so too did they come under scrutiny as the disillusionment of the 1960s and early 1970s gave way to new moods. Their implicit acceptance of American hegemony, moreover, seemed less tenable after the Arab-Israeli war of 1973, when an oil embargo and a subsequent quadrupling of oil prices demonstrated the vulnerability of the United States as well as its inability to use power without restraint. Some of the attacks on the revisionists were frontal in nature. In an analysis of the works of seven leading revisionist historians, Robert J. Maddox accused them of distorting facts to prove their thesis. "Stated briefly," he noted in his introduction, "the most striking characteristic of revisionist historiography has been the extent to which New Left authors have revised the evidence itself. And if the component parts of historical interpretations are demonstrably false, what can be said about the interpretations? They may yet be valid, but in the works examined they are often irrelevant to the data used to support them. Until this fact is recognized, there can be no realistic assessment of which elements of revisionism can justifiably be incorporated into new syntheses and which must be disregarded altogether." Similarly Robert W. Tucker insisted that New Left revisionism was based on a simple-minded explanatory mechanism that related all policy decisions to the imperatives of a capitalist economy. Charles S. Maier, on the other hand, was critical of virtually all scholars who had written on the origins of the Cold War. "Spokesmen for each side," he noted in 1970, "present the reader with a total explanatory system that accounts for all phenomena, eliminates the possibility of disproof, and thus transcends the usual process of historical reasoning. More than in most historical controversies, the questions about what happened are transformed into concealed debate about the nature of freedom and duress, exploitation and hegemony. As a result much Cold War historiography has become a confrontation *manqué*—debatable philosophy taught by dismaying example."[14]

---

[14]Robert J. Maddox, *The New Left and the Origins of the Cold War* (Princeton, 1973), pp. 10–11; Robert W. Tucker, *The Radical Left and American Foreign Policy* (Baltimore, 1971); Charles A. Maier, "Revisionism and the Interpretation of Cold War Origins," *Perspectives in American History* 4 (1970):311–347.

More recently there has been a tendency for historians to avoid extremes. In a study of the decision to use the atomic bomb Martin Sherwin explicitly rejected Gar Alperovitz's contention that the use of the bomb was largely directed at influencing Soviet postwar policy. Sherwin insisted that the decision to use the bomb was laid earlier during Franklin Delano Roosevelt's presidency. Although he conceded that the development of the bomb was predicated on the belief that it would be a diplomatic asset in the postwar era, Sherwin nevertheless insisted that Truman used the bomb to win the war against Japan and not to stop the Soviet Union from entering the war in the Far East. On the other hand Truman hoped that Stalin would recognize American power and adopt a more conciliatory policy. Robert L. Messer, by way of contrast, characterized Truman's foreign policy as inconsistent and somewhat confused. The atomic bomb was used primarily to win the war in the Pacific. The weapon, however, had a subsidiary purpose: to pressure the Russians to make the Yalta agreement a reality. When this failed Truman switched tactics by proposing international control of nuclear weapons. The vagaries of American policy, Messer argued, led to a hard Soviet line, and eventually to the American policy of containment.[15]

Even scholars with a revisionist orientation have muted their explanations of the origins of the Cold War. In 1977 Daniel Yergin observed that wartime and postwar American diplomacy reflected two competing perceptions of the Soviet Union. The first, which he named the Riga axioms, was based on an image of the Soviet Union "as a world revolutionary state, denying the possibilities of coexistence, committed to unrelenting ideological warfare, powered by a messianic drive for world mastery." The second, the Yalta axioms, downplayed ideology and instead saw the Soviet Union as "behaving like a traditional Great Power within the international system, rather than trying to overthrow it." The first remained the dominant element in American foreign policy until the Nazi invasion of Russia in 1941, when Roosevelt decided to aid the beleaguered Soviets. During the war the Yalta axioms replaced the Riga axioms. At the end of the conflict the latter regained its predominance and it was within this framework that Truman formulated his hard-line policy toward the Soviet Union. Although conceding the brutality of Stalin's regime Yergin nevertheless insisted that the "U.S.S.R. behaved as a traditional Great Power, intent upon aggrandizing itself along the lines of historic Russian goals," and

---

[15]Martin J. Sherwin, *A World Destroyed: The Atomic Bomb and the Grand Alliance* (New York, 1975); Robert L. Messer, *The End of an Alliance: James F. Byrnes, Roosevelt, Truman, and the Origins of the Cold War* (Chapel Hill, 1982). See also Gregg F. Herken, *The Winning Weapon: The Atomic Bomb in the Cold War* (New York, 1981).

that American leaders who accepted the Riga axioms" misinterpreted both the range and degree of the Soviet challenge and the character of Soviet objectives and so downplayed the possibilities for diplomacy and accommodation."[16]

In reviewing the three schools of thought—the orthodox, revisionist, and realist—students should decide for themselves the fundamental questions raised regarding America's role in world affairs since the 1940s.[17] Did the Cold War commence with World War II, or did it stretch back in time? Did the move of the Soviet Union into Eastern Europe represent the realization of a centuries-old Russian dream of a sphrere of influence in that region? Or was it an effort by the Kremlin to extend the influence of communism in the immediate postwar period? Had the course of American diplomacy since the Spanish-American War been committed to the defense of a global status quo in an attempt to find the ever-expanding foreign markets supposedly necessary for the survival of American capitalism? Or could the roots of the Cold War crisis be traced back to the mid-1940s, when Russian military forces occupied Eastern Europe? Were America's moves dictated by a containment policy aimed at checking what was believed to be a Soviet plan for spreading communism throughout the world? Or was the United States bent upon a conservative counterrevolution that would maintain the world economic and political order in a state conducive to the purposes of American capitalism? In answering such questions students will cope not only with the issue of the Cold War but with the very nature of American society itself.

---

[16]Daniel Yergin, *Shattered Peace: The Origins of the Cold War and the National Security State* (Boston, 1977), pp. 11–12.

[17]See the fascinating debate in Lloyd C. Gardner, Arthur Schlesinger, Jr., and Hans J. Morgenthau, *The Origins of the Cold War* (Waltham, Mass., 1970). In recent years historians have also begun to study the Cold War in Asia. See Robert J. McMahon, *Colonialism and Cold War: The United States and the Struggle for Indonesian Independence* (Ithaca, 1981), and Robert M. Blum, *Drawing the Line: The Origins of the American Containment Policy in East Asia* (New York, 1982).

Athan Theoharis

ATHAN THEOHARIS (1936–   ) is professor of history at Marquette University. He has written a number of articles and books on American history since 1945, including *The Yalta Myths: An Issue in U.S. Politics, 1945–1955* (1970), and *Seeds of Repression: Harry S. Truman and the Origins of McCarthyism* (1971).

Only recently has the question of the origins of the Cold War seriously divided American historians, the emergence of a revisionist school coinciding with intensive research into primary sources. Yet, revisionists do disagree over whether there existed a discontinuity between President Roosevelt's and President Truman's policies; they disagree in their evaluations of the relative influence of economic and political considerations [and] in their estimates of the role of key advisers in shaping the decisions and priorities of the two presidents.

This paper will emphasize the tactics and personalities of Roosevelt and Truman, their specific responses to Soviet policy and influence. Focusing on Yalta, I shall examine the Truman administration's commitment to the agreements concluded at the conference and Roosevelt's and the State Department's responsibilities for the development of the Cold War. Conceding that the trend of the Open Door ideology was inimical to accommodation with the Soviet Union, I, nonetheless, contend that the discretion available to policymakers did not demand the specific policies adopted after April 1945 that led to the Cold War. Put simply, the thesis of this paper is, to quote Lloyd C. Gardner, that "the United States was more responsible for the *way* in which the Cold War developed."

At issue for American diplomats during the 1940s was how to deal with the progress and consequences of World War II. Given the Soviet Union's strategic political and geographic position and its inevitable physical presence in non-Soviet territories after the war, the development of U.S. policy toward Eastern Europe, Germany, and the Far East would influence the climate of Soviet-American relations. Indeed, the diplomacy of the Roosevelt and Truman administrations in the 1941–1946 period was the product, in part, of their conceptions of the Soviet

Athan Theoharis, "Roosevelt and Truman on Yalta: The Origins of the Cold War." Reprinted with permission from the *Political Science Quarterly* 87 (June 1972):210–241. Footnotes omitted.

involvement in the Far Eastern war and its consequences for postwar China and Japan; and of the status of postwar Germany as determined by decisions concerning the level of German reparations payments.

The dominant role of the post-New Deal presidency in the formulation of foreign policy, the consistency of Truman's policies with those of Roosevelt, and the extent to which either president determined policy or followed recommendations of ostensibly subordinate advisers, furthermore, had crucial significance for U.S.-Soviet relations. During the war, and in the postwar years, U.S. policy was made by the president or his advisers, and not simply at the major summit conferences. At best, the role of the public or of Congress had become that of a potential restraint; policymakers did operate on the premise that Congress or the public might seek to counteract policy decisions. Yet, these were possible deterrents; they did not control policy. As one result of the Executive Reorganization Act of 1939, the president had acquired a bureaucratic apparatus that increased his independence and authority. The post–New Deal president, by resorting to public relations and *fait accompli*, had, as a result, greater freedom to create public opinion and structure the policy debate.

Soviet responses, moreover, were based on an appraisal of the policies of the president, and not on the differing priorities of advisers, the Congress, the public, or the press. While, admittedly, the president, especially Roosevelt, might invoke public, congressional, or press opinion during negotiations with Soviet leaders, this bargaining ploy did not lead Stalin or other leaders in the Kremlin to view U.S. policy as determined by domestic considerations. Concessions might be made in the wording of communiqués to make an agreement more palatable to the American public or press, but Soviet policymakers operated on the assumption that they were dealing with the president and that his policy was based upon understood commitments. For this reason, the nature of presidential leadership influenced immediate postwar relations between the United States and the Soviet Union. Most significantly, the Truman administration's attempts to "undo" the Yalta commitments led to the Cold War.

What was involved was not only the enigmatic and ambiguous nature of Roosevelt's policies, substantial as these ambiguities were, but the noncommitment of key personnel in the State Department to the "soft" line that Roosevelt had adopted at Yalta. . . . The rigidity of their position, in contrast to Roosevelt's at Yalta, contained the seeds of possible conflict with the Soviet Union after Truman's accession to the presidency. Truman's limited understanding, of both international affairs and Roosevelt's specific commitments, would enable policy advisers to become policymakers after April 1945 when determining the meaning of the Yalta agreements. . . .

I

During the war years, Roosevelt's policies toward the potential problems concerning the postwar status of Eastern Europe, Germany, and the Far East were strikingly vacillating and ambivalent. The president, like his conservative secretary of state, Cordell Hull, sought to postpone difficult political decisions until after the war. For a time, he refused even to enter serious discussions with the Soviet Union over territorial and other political matters. Roosevelt's stance on German reparations particularly dramatizes this ambiguity of policy and preference for postponement. Thus, although Hull had agreed both to the principle of reparations in kind and not in money at the Moscow foreign ministers conference of October 1943 and to the establishment of a European Advisory Commission to outline Allied policy toward postwar Germany, no efforts were made to determine the level or basis of reparations payments and to develop plans for postwar occupation. In October 1944, indeed, Roosevelt halted any planning for postwar Germany. Significantly, while the debate between Treasury and State was raging over the level of German reparations, Roosevelt wrote to Hull that "I do not think that at this present stage any good purpose would be served by having the State Department or any other Department sound out the British and Russian views on the treatment of German industry. . . . "

Throughout 1943 and 1944, Roosevelt sustained this noncommital course, thus strengthening the resistance of the London Poles to serious negotiations and thereby contributing to the deterioration of Soviet-Polish relations. Following the Soviet incursion into Polish territory in January 1944, Roosevelt offered his good offices to Mikolajczyk, the prime minister of the London Polish government, to mediate but not guarantee a solution of the Polish border difficulty. Roosevelt abandoned this stance of studied ambiguity only on November 17, 1944, and then after Soviet troops had crossed the Curzon Line (July 22) and after Moscow Radio had announced the formation of a Polish Committee on National Liberation (July 22) and the subsequent signing of a military and political agreement between this committee and the Soviet Union. At that time and with the American presidential election over, Roosevelt informed Mikolajczyk that whatever agreement the Poles and the Soviet Union concluded would be acceptable to the United States but that the United States could not guarantee Poland's frontiers.

U.S. policy had not been simply the product of domestic politics; key policy advisers had continually counseled a firm stand against the Soviets and the need to sustain the London Poles. Indeed, within State, John Hickerson, deputy director of the office of European affairs, recommended, on January 8, 1945, that the United States secure the establishment of a Provisional Security Council, in which the United States would have a major voice, to supervise political developments in Eastern Europe. And, on January 18, 1945, Secretary of State Stettinius made the same recommendation to Roosevelt. Significantly, Stettinius's proposal provided not only for a rotating chairmanship, thereby inplying the equality of the powers, but also for establishing the headquarters in Paris. . . .

Throughout, Roosevelt attempted to secure Soviet military involvement in the war against Japan. He continued to operate on the premise that U.S. policy—to make China a great power—was correct and attainable. A Sino-Soviet accord, he believed, would minimize Soviet intervention in China and force the Chinese Communists to come to terms with Chiang Kai-shek. At the same time, Roosevelt never consistently backed General Stilwell's efforts to reform the Chinese Nationalist regime or to alter its military policy. A sense of wishfulness characterized Roosevelt's estimates of the internal strength of the Nationalist regime, of the prospects for resolving the civil conflict between the Nationalists and Communists without civil war, and of the simply military consequences of Soviet involvement in the war against Japan.

II

Roosevelt's decision to go to Yalta constituted, in essence, a change from wishful thinking and postponement. By early 1945, military developments, and prospective military and political developments, ensured that the Soviets would play a dominant role in Eastern Europe, that Soviet unilateral actions in Germany would complicate Allied occupation policy, and that the Soviet role in the Far East possibly could frustrate the attainment of U.S. objectives. To postpone matters to a postwar peace conference might contribute to the establishment of spheres of influence, to the breakdown of Allied unity and cooperation, and to the radicalization of politics throughout Europe and the Far East.

Roosevelt's diplomacy at Yalta, therefore, reflected not so much over-confidence in his ability to placate Stalin through personal diplomacy, though this was a factor, as his recognition of the weakness of the U.S. diplomatic position and the reality—even legitimacy—of Soviet influence in Eastern Europe, the Far East, and Germany. Although the language is vague, the Yalta agreements did confirm this acceptance of Soviet postwar influence and the importance of accommodation to avert disharmony and conflict.

The most troublesome issue confronting the conferees was Poland.

Roosevelt's phrasing of his requests at Yalta clearly conceded the weakness of the Western bargaining position. He emphasized his need to "save face" when pressing for slight territorial concessions to the Poles from the Curzon Line, emphasized the domestic importance of the Polish-American vote when urging Stalin to make other concessions over the status of the Polish government, and requested "some gesture" to satisfy the demand of the six million Polish-Americans that the United States be "in some way involved with the question of freedom of elections." By basing his requests on American domestic political considerations, Roosevelt undermined his effect on the decisions of the conference. The final communiqué could simply be worded to gloss over what in fact had been conceded. In many respects, this was the result of the negotiations on Poland: Stalin merely agreed to a formula for the formation of a Polish provisional government and the holding of free and democratic elections under tripartite supervision that would not contradict Soviet objectives yet would enable Roosevelt and Churchill to appease the public opinion that they had so regularly cited during conference proceedings.

Moreover, Roosevelt's February 6 demand that a new Polish government be established, maintaining that the Lublin government "as now composed" could not be accepted (a statement which Churchill immediately endorsed), was not pressed at the conference. The reference to Lublin "as *now* composed" and the further assurance to Stalin that the United States would never support in any way any Polish government "that would be inimical to your interests," significantly reduced the impact of this demand. Stalin replied that Poland did not involve merely honor or domestic public opinion, but the security of the Soviet Union. Second, indirectly recalling the example of the Italian surrender, Stalin also emphasized the importance for the Red Army of secure supply lines in its advance into Germany that only a stable, nonhostile local administration could provide.

The result, incorporated in the Declaration on Liberated Europe and the agreement dealing with Poland, amounted to face-saving formulas for the West. The Lublin government was not to be scrapped for a wholly new government, but rather enlarged to provide the basis for the new government. Stettinius's proposal for reorganizing the Lublin government—"fully representative Government based on all democratic forces in Poland and abroad"—was amended by Molotov to "wider democratic basis with the inclusion of democratic leaders from Poland and abroad." And, the language of the amended Declaration on Liberated Europe, by providing for unanimity even before consultations could begin, acknowledged Soviet authority and her right to veto her allies' objections. Further, the initial State Department proposal for "appropriate machinery for the carrying out of the joint responsibilities set forth in this declaration" was also amended by Molotov to provide instead that the three governments "will immediately take measures for the carrying out of mutual consultations." Nor was observation of the proposed future elections by the three governments guaranteed, since, "in effect," ambassadors alone would observe and report on elections.

The Eastern European agreements, one-sided and a tacit repudiation of earlier U.S. policy, indirectly served to create the potential for subsequent U.S.-Soviet problems. The vagueness of the language, the seeming lack (at least as existing published papers of the proceedings reveal) of intensive discussion over significant changes that amounted to U.S. acceptance of the Soviet position, as well as the exclusion of State from a central negotiating role and the implicit rejection of its policy recommendations at Yalta meant that implementation of the agreements would be determined by the commitment of U.S. policymakers to accept the reality of Soviet influence and the spirit underlying the conference.

A similar situation occurred in the Yalta discussions on Germany. Most important matters involving Germany were postponed, though even then it was implicitly agreed that the Big Three would jointly determine occupation and reparations policy. The level of German reparations payments did divide the Allies at Yalta. The final agreement, though, provided for the creation of a reparations commission to discuss this question; the commission was instructed, with Roosevelt and Stalin concurring and Churchill dissenting, that during its deliberations the figure of $20 billion with one-half going to the Soviet Union should provide "the basis for discussion."

At Yalta, Roosevelt had no clearly formulated German policy. Supporting simply a harsh peace, but no longer committed to dismemberment and sizable reparations, he nonetheless remained unwilling to force a dispute with Stalin and accepted the postponement of these issues. Roosevelt's agreement to a stated sum as the basis for discussion, however, could be construed as a commitment in principle to a fixed figure if not to that sum. The only merit of Roosevelt's temporizing was in avoiding division and disharmony. By not providing clear guidelines for future discussions, it served to complicate future U.S.-Soviet relations.

The Yalta discussions on the Far East were characterized by the same imprecision of agreement and absence of thorough negotiations. The general terms of Soviet involvement had tacitly been agreed to at Teheran and during discussions between Stalin and Harriman in 1944. Both Roosevelt and Stalin remained interested, nonetheless, in a more specific understanding. At Stalin's insistence, the conditions for Soviet involvement were set forth in writing at Yalta and agreed to by the three powers (though Britain did not participate in the discussions). Specifically, the Soviet Union was to receive South Sakhalin and the Kurile Islands from Japan. In addition, Russia secured "lease" rights to Port Arthur; her "pre-eminent interests" were to be safeguarded in an internationalized port of Dairen and in a "jointly operated" Sino-Soviet commission for the Chinese-Eastern Railroad and the South-Manchurian Railroad; and the status of Outer Mongolia was to be "preserved." Roosevelt admitted not having discussed the matters of Outer Mongolia, the ports, or the railroads with Chiang Kai-shek and conceded that, for the moment, military considerations required continued secrecy. Stalin then informed Roosevelt that Chinese Foreign Minister T. V. Soong was coming to Moscow in April, that it might be appropriate at that time to inform him of this matter. Ultimately, it was decided that Roosevelt would take the initiative to inform the Chinese and would make his move when so directed by Stalin, the determining factor to be military developments in Europe. In return for these concessions, Roosevelt secured two qualified Soviet commitments: to enter the war against Japan two or three months after the termination of the war in Europe and to conclude a pact of "friendship and alliance" with the Nationalist government.

The Far Eastern agreements, however, had not defined the extent of the Soviet role in Manchuria, particularly in the area surrounding the ports and railroads; the reference to the "pre-eminent interests" of the Soviet Union could result in the establishment of a Soviet sphere of influence. Moreover, whether Roosevelt had accepted the German or Italian model as the basis for joint occupation policy in postwar Japan was not clear from the discussions or agreements reached at Yalta. No specific agreement had been made concerning this matter— the outright cession of South Sakhalin and the Kuriles to the Soviet Union did not establish physical occupation of Japanese territory and a right to have an equal voice in occupation policy. Roosevelt's Soviet involvement, however, and the spirit of mutual assistance and cooperation provided justification for Soviet insistence on equal participation in occupation policy.

In sum, at Yalta, Roosevelt adopted a conciliatory policy, accepting the reality of Soviet power and the legitimacy of her postwar involvement in Eastern Europe, Germany, and the Far East. . . .

III

Roosevelt's death significantly changed the diplomatic setting, by introducing, for one thing, an element of uncertainty about future U.S.-Soviet relations. More important, it introduced Harry S. Truman, a man more rigidly anti-Soviet and, given also his noninvolvement in Roosevelt's policy-making, more responsive to the suggestions of policy advisers whose recommendations had been ignored at Yalta. His personal political style would have far-reaching consequences for the Yalta understandings: Truman would not feel compelled to honor the commitments and would seek to exploit the vague language of the agreements to avoid compliance.

In part, the Truman administration in 1945 bore the legacies of Roosevelt's earlier policy of postponing and avoiding clearly defined commitments and the partial continuing of that policy at Yalta. Despite Yalta, doubt remained over Roosevelt's position on, among other things, German reparations and dismemberment, the character of the postwar governments of Eastern Europe, and the nature of the Soviet postwar role in the Far East. More important, in making concessions to the Soviet Union, Roosevelt had acted unilaterally, without securing the understanding or acquiescence of his subordinates. The imprecision of Roosevelt's administrative leadership thereby provided an opportunity for these subordinates to take advantage of the policy vacuum created by Roosevelt's death, and Truman's woeful ignorance of both international politics and the Yalta commitments, to secure the eventful adoption of their recommendations.

In April, Harriman had a conversation with Stalin that, because it coincided with Roosevelt's death, permitted him to affirm Truman's intention to continue the policies of his predecessor. Capitalizing on Stalin's statement of willingness to work with Truman as he had with Roosevelt, Harriman extracted from the premier a pledge to have Molotov, on his way to San Francisco, stop off in Washington to consult with Truman. Such a move, Harriman insisted, would promote collaboration. Stalin acceded. Intended as a friendly gesture, Molotov's trip was initiated to provide the opportunity for an exchange of views and a testing of cooperation.

Harriman's move, though not necessarily intentionally, coincided with an intensive policy reexamination in Washington involving Truman and key advisers who had urged Truman not to compromise to reach accommodation.

Truman, in fact, adopted a less conciliatory approach in April 1945. On April 16, he and Churchill sent a joint note to Stalin outlining their proposal for resolving the Polish impasse. Their note placed the Western-oriented Polish political leaders on the same basis with the Lublin Poles. Understanding that even the vague language of the Yalta agreements did not support his position, Truman, nonetheless, remained confident that a strong stand would not precipitate a break with the Soviet Union.

The same attitude also prevailed at his meeting with Molotov on

April 23. Truman's language at that meeting was blunt and undiplomatic, specifically rejecting the Yugoslav formula (expanding the existing government by adding a new minister for every four already in the cabinet) as the basis for composing the new Polish provisional government. An agreement had been concluded, Truman self-righteously affirmed, and only required Soviet compliance. In response to Molotov's protests, Truman conceded the vagueness of the language of the agreements (the president had earlier been advised by Leahy, among others, that the Soviet position was consistent with the Yalta agreements). Molotov denied that any agreement had been broken and stressed the need for cooperation, to which Truman reiterated his insistence that the U.S. interpretation was the only one possible.

The result of this meeting, if possibly psychologically satisfying to the frustrated Americans, did not lead to diplomatic resolution. Responding to the April 16 note and the April 23 meeting, Stalin emphasized Poland's importance to Soviet security and protested Western efforts to dictate to the Soviet Union. Truman's refusal to accept Lublin as the core of the new government was inconsistent with the Yalta agreements. Soviet actions in Poland were comparable to those of Britain in Belgium and Greece; the Soviet Union had not sought to interfere in these countries or to ascertain whether British actions made possible representative government. The United States and Great Britain were combining against the Soviet Union and the United States was attempting to secure Soviet renunciation of her security interests.

On May 19, in a seeming about-face, Truman consulted Stalin on Harry Hopkins's proposed mission to Moscow for mutual consultations. Significantly, when the Hopkins mission was first considered in early May, Byrnes and the State Department opposed the idea, recognizing that it meant that Truman had decided to make some concessions to the Soviets.

Truman's objectives for the Hopkins mission remain obscure. The trip did not eliminate the tensions that had surfaced in April, though an agreement worked out on the composition of the Polish provisional government did essentially follow the Yugoslav formula, and on July 5, the Truman administration did recognize the reorganized government.

The Eastern European question, however, had not been amicably resolved. At Potsdam, Truman refused to recognize either the Oder-Neisse line as the western boundary of Poland or Soviet primacy in Bulgaria, Hungary, and Romania. In his public report of August 9 on the results of the conference, Truman declared that Bulgaria and Romania were not to be within the sphere of influence of any one power. And earlier on June 1, 12, and 14, the administration had instructed Harriman to propose to Stalin that the United States and Great Britain be accorded veto power over the actions of Soviet commanders in Hungary, Romania, and Bulgaria.

The Truman administration's decision to accept confrontation rather than seek accommodation also underlay its often shifting and confused, but unbending, German policy. Thus, even though, at the time, these decisions did not necessarily reflect a conscious strategy or policy, on May 10, 1945, Truman unilaterally approved Joint Chiefs of Staff (JCS) directive 1067 and replaced Roosevelt's representative to the Moscow Reparations Commission, Isadore Rubin, with Edwin Pauley. The vagueness of JCS 1067 and the unilateral nature of its promulgation, without consultation with the British, Russians, or French, marked a shift toward a softer policy toward Germany. The directive simply provided general discretion to U.S. military zonal authorities to determine the level of German industrial production and, indirectly thereby, German reparations payments.

During the June discussions in Moscow on reparations, Pauley had adopted an uncompromising line on Soviet requests for specific agreement on German reparations levels, thereby effectively averting progress toward any agreement. The Truman delegation adopted the same stance at Potsdam, indirectly avoiding the issue of joint policy. While paying lip service to the Yalta agreement on reparations, Secretary of State Byrnes refused to respond to Soviet efforts to determine the specific reparations sum that the United States would accept. Dismissing the Yalta figure of $10 billion as "impractical," Byrnes supported a policy whereby, in Molotov's words, "each country would have a free hand in their own zone and could act entirely independently of the others." Despite Assistant Secretary of State Clayton's warning that Byrnes's insistence that reparations come from the zone of the occupying power "would be considered by the Russians as a reversal of the Yalta position," Truman did not alter this position. Potsdam, then, contributed to the division of Germany along zonal lines. In addition, Truman's willingness to reject the Yalta formulas, while publicly proclaiming his commitment to them, added the element of distrust to diplomatic relations. The further complication to joint planning provided later by French obstruction heightened this distrust. A high Soviet official told James Warburg in the summer of 1946 that "after six months of French obstruction, we began to suspect that this was a put-up job—that you did not like the bargain you had made at Potsdam and that you are letting the French get you out of it. . . . "

The vague wording of the Far Eastern agreements presented formidable unresolved diplomatic problems for the entering Truman administration. On the surface, the concessions did not seem major. In fact, however, the extent of the postwar Soviet role in either China or Japan had not been clearly defined. Thus, as soon as he became president, Truman was beset by pressure from key advisers in State, the Foreign Service, and his cabinet to reappraise the Far Eastern agreements. At an April 23 cabinet meeting, the president himself raised the issue of reappraisal. Distressed over Soviet actions in Eastern Europe, Truman suggested that the failure of a Yalta signatory to fulfill any of its commitments might free the other signatories from fulfilling theirs. The main opposition to this position came from the military. General George C. Marshall, then chairman of the Joint Chiefs of Staff, argued that the concessions had to stand because the Far Eastern war could not be won without Soviet military assistance.

While no formal decision on the concessions was reached in the cabinet them, the German surrender on May 8 led to further administration reevaluation of Yalta. During a May 11 meeting in Forrestal's office, Harriman, who was about to return to Moscow, contended that "it was time to come to a conclusion about the necessity for the early entrance of Russia into the Japanese war." He reiterated this case at State on May 12, and it was agreed that Harriman's views should be formulated precisely "for discussion with the President. . . . "

The United States' seeming ambivalence throughout this preliminary negotiating period was indicative not of indifference but of the desire to forestall Soviet involvement in the Far East. Since the Soviet Union had declared its unwillingness to enter the war against Japan until a treaty had been concluded with China, by stalling negotiations on that treaty, the administration could avert the inevitable extension of Soviet influence in China and Japan without formally repudiating the terms laid down at Yalta.

By June, the administration's options had increased as the result of the defeat of Germany. Thereafter, the administration operated on the premise that Soviet military involvement against Japan was not imperative. This shift was revealed on June 18 in another change of position by the Joint Chiefs of Staff, who now described Soviet aid as desirable but not indispensable and recommended that the United States not bargain for Soviet involvement.

With all this in mind, Truman and Byrnes discussed the Far East with Stalin and Molotov at the Potsdam Conference on July 17. First the Soviet leaders informed Truman and Byrnes of their willingness to accept Chinese control of Manchuria as well as to recognize the Nationalists as the sole leaders of China. In reply, Byrnes affirmed that the United States held to a strict interpretation of the Yalta terms. Then, feigning ignorance of the recently concluded Soong-Stalin talks, Byrnes sounded out Stalin about the areas of Sino-Soviet disagreement. On the basis of Stalin's reply, Byrnes and Truman concluded that the

differences between the Soviet and Chinese positions were so fundamental that, at least in the immediate future, a Sino-Soviet treaty was
highly unlikely.

The Potsdam discussions between the U.S. and Soviet military
staffs provided further assurances for the administration that a Sino-
Soviet treaty was still a necessary precondition for Russia's entering
the Japanese war. Moreover, at Potsdam, the administration remained
in contact with the Chinese Nationalists. On July 20, Chiang Kai-shek
informed Truman about Soong's mission, arguing that the Chinese had
bargained in good faith and could make no further concessions to secure the treaty. Truman agreed—in fact, he directed Chiang specifically to make no more concessions. Despite this, Truman insisted on
the implementation of the Yalta terms and urged Chiang to have Soong
return to Moscow to continue negotiations.

While the administration continued formally to support the Yalta
commitments, in view of the July 17 meeting with Stalin and Molotov,
Truman's instructions to Chiang—if Soong followed them—would effectively stymie the conclusion of a treaty. Moreover, the successful
testing of the atomic bomb led Marshall to concede to Stimson and
Truman on July 23 that Soviet entry into the war against Japan was
no longer necessary, but Marshall again maintained that the Soviet
Union could enter anyway and obtain "virtually what they wanted in
the surrender terms." Byrnes came away from the discussion hoping
only that the Sino-Soviet discussions might be stalled and thereby "delay Soviet entrance and the Japanese might surrender." Finally, instead
of consulting the Soviets, the administration unilaterally drafted the
formal declaration demanding unconditional Japanese surrender; it also
decided unilaterally to accept the Japanese request of August 10 for
clarification of the surrender terms.

Moreover, once the second phase of the Sino-Soviet discussions began, the United States adopted a more rigid stance, advising the
Chinese to stand firm even if that firmness prevented agreement. On
August 5, Byrnes asked Harriman officially to inform Soong that the
United States opposed concessions beyond those agreed to at Yalta. He
specifically warned the Chinese not to make further concessions over
the status of Dairen or Soviet reparations demands. The essence of this
new administration position was to support the Chinese at the same
time that it opposed concessions needed to conclude the treaty; only
if the Soviet Union reversed its attitude and radically changed its demands would a treaty result prior to Japanese surrender.

Truman's policy failed to forestall the Soviet Union's entrance into
the Japanese war. Although a formal Sino-Soviet treaty had not been
concluded and although the United States finally neither requested nor
encouraged Soviet intervention, the Russians nonetheless declared war

on Japan on August 8 and moved troops into North China and Manchuria. Simultaneously, Stalin warned Soong on August 10 that, should a formal Sino-Soviet agreement not be concluded, Chinese Communist troops would be permitted to move into Manchuria. Fearful of Soviet support of the Chinese Communists, Chiang Kai-shek acceded to the Soviet demands on the unresolved issues. The formal Sino-Soviet treaty was then quickly concluded, and its terms announced on August 14.

The administration's indirect opposition to the Yalta provisions created the potential for U.S.-Soviet division once the war with Japan ended. The rapidity of the Japanese surrender and the last-minute Soviet entry into the war had complicated surrender proceedings. The administration had had little time to devise formal terms indicating to whom Japanese troops should surrender. Indeed, until Soviet entry, there had been no discussion about Soviet rights to direct or control Japan during the period of occupation. Thus, when unilaterally issuing General Order #1, the United States directed Japanese troops to surrender to the Nationalists in all areas of China south of Manchuria and to the Russians in Manchuria, Korea north of the thirty-eighth parallel, and Karafutu. These surrender orders were intended to achieve two purposes: to preclude Japanese surrender to Chinese Communist troops and to minimize the Soviet occupation role in China and Japan.

Immediately, on August 16, the Soviet Union protested that these surrender provisions violated the Yalta agreements. Stalin demanded that the Soviet surrender zone include the Kuriles and Hokkaido (the northern sector of Japan). Unwilling to create the opportunity for Soviet military presence in Japan, Truman on August 18 acceded to the Soviet request for the Kuriles but not for Hokkaido. At the same time he pressed for an American air base on the Kuriles. In a sharp rejoinder on August 22, Stalin reiterated his earlier demand for Hokkaido and opposed Truman's request for the air base.

This was no mere territorial conflict; it involved the more basic question of the Truman administration's policy toward the Soviet occupation of Japan. At issue was whether the administration was formally prepared for confrontation. Truman at the time hesitated to reject the prospect of a negotiated settlement and replied to Stalin's sharp note of August 22 that the United States had not sought air base but only landing rights on the Kuriles. Truman further pointed out that the Kuriles were not Soviet territory. Yalta had only permitted Soviet occupation, he said; their final status would have to be determined at a future peace conference. On August 30, Stalin acceded to the request for landing rights. He denied, however, that the status of the Kuriles was unclear, contending that the cession had been permanent and that future peace talks would merely ratify this fact.

Directly or indirectly, the objective of limiting Soviet influence in the Far East underlay administration policy toward the Yalta agreements. Truman and Byrnes cunningly, but shortsightedly, here too sought to have it both ways: to avert the effect of the agreements without formally repudiating or renegotiating them.

IV

This clearly contradictory policy required the administration to continue to refrain from publishing the Yalta agreements on the Far East. Publication would have bound the administration to fulfilling them and would have established earlier U.S. insistence on Soviet involvement, negating the limited Soviet military contribution to defeating Japan. Therefore, the Truman administration neglected to publish the Far Eastern agreements on three ostensibly favorable occasions: when the Soviet Union declared war on Japan on August 8, when the Sino-Soviet treaty was announced on August 14, or when Soviet troops occupied the Kurile Islands on August 27.

The U.S. troop withdrawal that permitted Soviet occupation of the Kuriles precipitated bitter protests by conservatives in both Congress and the press, who charged that Soviet possession of these "strategic" islands would directly threaten the security of the United States and Japan. In a September 4 press conference, on the eve of his departure for the London Foreign Ministers Conference, Byrnes attempted to allay this protest. The decision leading up to U.S. withdrawal, he informed the press, had resulted from "discussions" (as opposed to "agreements," he implied) conducted at Yalta, not Potsdam. Byrnes, claiming that his attendance at Yalta had provided him with "full' knowledge of these "discussions," attributed the responsibility for them to Roosevelt rather than Truman. He then announced his intention to review them at London; a final agreement on the status of the Kuriles, he concluded, could be made only at a forthcoming peace conference.

Byrnes dissembled in two respects at this press conference: first, in implying that the status of the Kuriles had not yet been defined and, second, in failing to report the existence of the other Far Eastern agreements. His statements were to have serious ramifications for the Truman administration.

Byrnes's secretiveness on the second point stemmed from the administration's desire to prevent the Soviets from assuming a controlling role in China and in the occupation of Japan. This objective necessarily conflicted with Soviet policy and contributed to the atmosphere of distrust that prevailed during the September meetings of the Council of Foreign Ministers in London. Although Molotov then protested the unilateral character of U.S. occupation policy in Japan, demanding the establishment of an Allied control commission, Byrnes equivocated and, in the end, succeeded in postponing any final decision on Japan.

This strategy and the attendant necessity not to publish the Far Eastern agreements—or even, for that matter, admit their existence—would seriously compromise the administration's position. The first public hint of the existence of the agreements occurred in November 1945 during the controversy surrounding the resignation of Hurley as U.S. ambassador to China. In resigning, Hurley charged that U.S. foreign policy had been subverted by "imperialists" and "communists" in both the State Department and the Foreign Service, charges which led to special hearings by the Senate Foreign Relations Committee in December.

The tone of the committee's questioning of Hurley was sharp, at times even hostile. Attempting to defend Hurley, who had repeated his charges of employee disloyalty and insubordination, a sympathetic Senator Styles Bridges asked whether at Yalta—given the absence of Chinese representatives—any agreement concerning China had been concluded. Although he had not attended the conference, Hurley claimed knowledge about the China discussions. He added that Secretary of State Byrnes was a better authority on that subject.

In his prepared statement the next day, Byrnes dismissed Hurley's charges against the personnel of the State Department and the Foreign Service as wholly unfounded. Senator Bridges, however, was much more concerned with the Truman and Roosevelt administrations' China policy. Repeating his question of the day before, he asked Byrnes whether any agreement concerning China was concluded at Yalta in the absence and without the consent of Chiang Kai-shek. Bridges's confident tone, and the possibility that he had secured access to the Yalta text through Hurley or another source in the State Department, complicated Byrnes's reply. To admit that agreements had been concluded at Yalta without advising or consulting Chiang, and had not yet been published, would put the administration on the defensive and possibly expose its earlier dissembling. Faced with this dilemma, Byrnes neither affirmed nor denied that an agreement had been made:

I do not recall the various agreements [of the Yalta Conference]. It is entirely possible that some of the agreements arrived at at Yalta affected China some way or another, and I have told you that I would gladly furnish you the communique and then you could decide whether or not they affected China. If they were made they certainly were made by the heads of government and certainly only the three Governments were represented there.

Bridges then observed that had any agreement on China been concluded, the secretary could not have been unaware of its existence.
Thus, when the administration would publish the Far Eastern agreements, it would have to offer a convincing rationale both for its earlier
failure to publish them and for Byrnes's seeming ignorance of the matter.

This situation came to pass in February 1946. The event precipitating the publication of the Far Eastern agreements was the administration's announcement in January that it had turned over to an international trusteeship certain Pacific islands the United States
captured from Japan during World War II. During a January 22 press
conference, Acting Secretary of State Dean Acheson was asked whether
the Soviet Union would similarly be required to turn over the Kuriles
to an international trusteeship. In answer, Acheson pointed out that
the Yalta agreements had provided only for Soviet occupation of the
Kuriles; the final disposition would have to be determined at a future
peace conference. Acheson conceded, however, that such a conference
might simply affirm Soviet control. On January 26, Moscow Radio
challenged Acheson's remarks, denying that Soviet control of these territories was temporary or that Soviet occupation was related only to
the prosecution of the war against Japan.

At a press conference on January 29, Byrnes announced that the
Kuriles and South Sakhalin had in fact been ceded to the Soviet Union
at Yalta. He further disclosed that agreements concerning Port Arthur
and Dairen had also been concluded. But these agreements would become binding only after the formal conclusion of a peace treaty with
Japan.

The most dramatic aspect of Byrnes's press conference was not the
disclosure of the agreements themselves but his attempts to explain
the Truman administration's earlier failure to release them or indeed
even to admit their existence. What Byrnes did was to tell the press
that although he had been a delegate to Yalta, he had left the conference on the afternoon of February 10, before the concluding session
the next day. He had not learned about the specifics of the Far Eastern
agreements until August 1945, a few days after the Japanese surrender.
In response to further questions, Byrnes said he did not know whether
former Secretary of State Stettinius knew about the agreements or
where, in fact, the text was deposited. It was not, he stated, in the State
Department archives, but it might be in the White House files.

Once again, Byrnes had adroitly covered his tracks. He had shifted
responsibility for both the Yalta agreements and the failure to publish
them to the Roosevelt administration's tactics of secrecy. His statement did, however, raise two important questions: first, had the agreements been privately concluded by Roosevelt without the knowledge

of other White House or State Department personnel and, second, where was the text.

During a January 31 press conference, Truman sought to resolve these questions. The text, he claimed, had always been in the White House files, except when under review either by members of the White House staff or other administration personnel. While he had always known the whereabouts of the text, Truman said, he had not reviewed it until he began to prepare for the Potsdam Conference. Asked when the agreements would in fact be published, Truman answered that it would be necessary first to consult the British and the Russians. Most of the agreements, he added, had already been made public; the others would be disclosed at the "proper" time.

The Truman administration's policy toward the Yalta Far Eastern agreements and other administration tactics strained the already uneasy relations between the United States and the Soviet Union. It was in the area of tactics and personality that the rigidity and moralistic tone of postwar U.S.-Soviet relations derived important substance, and not simply from conflicting ideologies and objectives. In this sense, the Cold War was an avoidable conflict: the "way" it evolved being a product of shortsighted political leadership. The opportunities for détente provided by Yalta were effectively subverted by the Truman administration, and U.S.-Soviet relations suffered until a change in presidents brought an administration less rigidly bound to the self-righteous politics of confrontation. Eisenhower's politics remained conservative; but, with the Geneva summit conference of 1955, his presidency marked a new, less militant phase of the Cold War.

Joseph R. Starobin

JOSEPH R. STAROBIN (1913–1976) was for many years a prominent member of the American Communist Party. He broke with the party in 1954, although never renouncing his commitment to Marxism. In his later career he was professor of political science at the University of Toronto. Among his publications were *Paris to Peking* (1955) and *American Communism in Crisis, 1943–1957* (1972).

It is surely a suggestive irony that just at the point when younger American historians had made serious intellectual headway with their reinterpretation of the Cold War, fixing historical responsibility in terms of the mistakes, delusions, and imperatives of U.S. policy, the Soviet Union astonished friends and foes by overwhelming Czechoslovakia and turning its clock of history backwards. If the Cold War has not revived, small thanks are due the Soviet leaders. Their extraordinary nervousness, their maneuvers to propitiate both the outgoing and incoming American administrations, indicate very plainly how much they have feared political retaliation; this in itself is a comment on where responsibility for the Cold War today should rest. That Prague should have been the vortex in 1968 as it was in 1948 of critical problems within communism is uncanny, but on deeper examination it may not be fortuitous.

After all, the least credible explanation of Moscow's desperate attempt to resolve the crisis within its own system of states and parties is the one which pictures Czechoslovakia as the helpless Pauline at the crossroads of Europe, about to be dishonored by West German *revanchards*, with agents of the CIA grinning in the background, suddenly saved by the stalwart defenders of socialist honor and morality. Today this type of argument is reserved within the Communist world for its most backward members—that is, for the Soviet public and the fringes of the most insignificant and expendable Communist parties. Yet arguments of this kind had wide currency a generation ago. New Left historians would have us believe that Stalin was simply reacting to external challenge. In their view, the Cold War might not have set in if small-minded American politicians had not been determined to

---

Joseph R. Starobin, "Origins of the Cold War: The Communist Dimension," *Foreign Affairs* 47 (July 1969): 681–696. Reprinted by permission from *Foreign Affairs*. Copyright 1969 by Council on Foreign Relations, Inc.

reverse bad bargains, if congenital imperialists had not been mesmer-ized by the monopoly of atomic weapons which statesmen and sci-entists knew to be temporary. Since all this is so plainly a half-truth when juxtaposed to events of today, then clearly the half-truth of yes-teryear will hardly explain the whole of the Cold War.

Sophisticated Communists, both East and West, are asking why Czechoslovakia, which escaped the upheavals in Poland and Hungary of 1956 after a decade of Stalinist pressure, then experienced such a mounting crisis in the subsequent decade of relative détente and peace-ful competition. How is it that twenty years after Communist rule had been secured in February 1948 basic verities are now placed in ques-tion—whether centralized planning may not be counterproductive, whether a one-party régime can really articulate the needs of a polit-ically evolved people, whether the inner relations of such an unequal alliance as that administered by the Soviet Union are not so inherently antagonistic as to become explosive? Indeed, why did the rebirth of Czechoslovak political life in the first half of 1968—viewed with hope and excitement by Western Communists—raise such menacing ghosts from the past and such fearful question marks for the future that sup-posedly sober-minded men in Moscow took fright?

Twice within a dozen years the unmanageability of the Commu-nist world has been revealed. The crisis which shattered the Sino-So-viet alliance after manifesting itself first in Eastern Europe now re-bounds at the supposed strong-point of Czechoslovakia. And it has done so both in conditions of intense external pressure and times of rela-tively peaceful engagement. Perhaps it is here, in the dimension of communism as a contradictory and intractable system, that one may find the missing element in the discussions thus far on the origins of the Cold War.

II

That world history would someday polarize around two great na-tions, America and Russia, was a de Tocquevillean insight with which Communists were familiar a long time ago. Stalin gave it what seemed like a very clear definition back in 1927 during a talk with an Amer-ican labor delegation. He envisaged that a socialist center would arise "binding to itself the countries gravitating toward socialism" and would engage the surviving capitalist center in "a struggle between them for the possession of the world economy." The fate of both would be decided by the outcome of this struggle. What appeared at first glance as a sweeping projection was, however, profoundly ambiguous on close examination. Stalin did not spell out how the countries "gravitating to socialism" would get there. Good Communists believed this could come about only by the formulas of the October Revolution; yet even Lenin, in 1922, had lamented that perhaps a "big mistake" was being made in imposing Russian precepts on foreign Communists. Nor did Stalin elucidate how new nations recruited to socialism would order their relations with Russia as the hub of the socialist center. Presumably "proletarian internationalism" would replace the domination of the weak by the strong which was, in their view, the hallmark of capitalism. Yet even by 1927 the Russification of the international movement had brought catastrophic results—in Germany and China.

Stalin did not, moreover, meet the fundamental intellectual challenge of whether "the struggle for the possession of the world economy" necessarily had to be military in character. On this crucial point, everything could be found in the Leninist grabbag. "Peaceful coexistence" is there, but so is the expectation of "frightful collisions" between the first workers' state and its opponents; the caution that socialism had to be secured in one country first is to be found along with pledges that once socialism was strong enough in Russia, it would raise up revolts in the strongholds of capitalism.

The one possibility which Leninism did not anticipate was a stalemate between rival systems, precluding a "final conflict." The notion was not even entertained that an equilibrium between contending forces might set in, that the subsequent evolution of both contenders under the impact of this equilibrium could alter their distinguishing characteristics and therefore outmode the original Leninist theorems.

Out of such doctrinal ambiguities the Second World War created policy choices affecting most of humanity. The Soviet Union and the international Communist movement found themselves allied with democratic-capitalist states among whom public power had grown drastically in an effort to overcome the Great Depression; the welfare state was expanded by the very demands of warfare while democracy was in fact enhanced. Keynes had made a serious rebuttal to Marx. Would capitalism in the West collapse in a repetition of the crisis of the 1930s after withstanding the test of war? Or had the war itself changed something vital within the workings of capitalism? Moreover, the first global war in history led to the end of colonialism and hence a new relation of metropolitan states to subject peoples. Would the former necessarily collapse because, in Lenin's analysis, they had depended so heavily on colonies? Or might they undergo transformations—short of socialism—to make them viable? Would the countries of the underdeveloped world make socialism the indispensable form of their modernization or might they, dialectically enough, find a new relation with capitalism?

Thus, the war brought on to the world stage a powerful Russia on whose survival a rival system's survival also depended. Simultaneously America came to center stage with a greatly expanded economy no longer limited by laissez-faire economics and inwardly altered by technological change created by the war. America was indispensable to Russia as an ally but formidable as a rival in a sense far deeper than its outward power. This wartime relationship was unexpected, and it challenged ideology and practice on all sides.

Something very particular happened with communism, considered as a most uneven system of a single state and a variety of parties. The fortunes of war, thanks perhaps to Churchill's postponement of the second front, brought the soviet armies beyond their own borders where they had to be welcomed by the West if only because their help was also being solicited on the plains of Manchuria once Hitler was defeated. Yet at the moment of Russia's greatest need and harshest difficulties, the Communist movements *least* helpful to her were those of Eastern Europe; in the one country outside of Russia where a decade before the Communists hd been a real power—namely, in Germany—the party lay shattered. No anti-Hitler force of any practical significance emerged. On the East European landscape there were only two exceptions. In Yugoslavia a handful of veterans of Comintern intrigue and the hard school of the International Brigades in Spain had succeeded in establishing their power—prior to the arrival of Soviet forces in the Danubian basin. In Czechoslovakia, a Communist movement of a very different sort—that is, with a legal and parliamentary tradition—was joined by Slovak guerrillas. Both came to terms with the leadership of the government-in-exile, which both Moscow and the West recognized. A long-term cooperation of diverse social forces was implied.

On the other hand, the Communist movements underwent a spectacular resurrection in a wide arc from Greece through Italy, France, the Low Countries and Scandinavia, while in widely separated corners of Asia they also flourished—in Northwest China, in the peninsula of Indochina, in the Philippines and Malaya. All of them were successful to the degree that they identified with the defense of their nationhood and either subordinated social issues or subsumed them in national ones; where this proved too complicated, as in India, long-term disabilities resulted. But all these movements grew at a distance from the Soviet armies; their postwar fate could not depend on physical contact. Even parties at the periphery of world politics showed striking changes. They entered cabinets in Cuba and Chile, emerged from prewar disasters with great dynamism in Brazil, became legal in Canada and stood a chance of legitimizing their considerable influence in Britain and the United States. In these latter countries, they could hope to achieve "citizenship" only by ceasing to be propagandist groups reflecting Soviet prestige, and only as they grappled with the specific peculiarities of their societies in rapid change.

Yet for all this success, and perhaps because of it, communism faced the gravest problems. The peculiarity of the moment lay in the fact that some definition of Russia's relation with the West was essential to assure the most rapid conclusion of the war in Europe, and this had to precede a common strategy in Asia. Hence Moscow was obliged to define relations with the Communist parties. Simultaneously these movements—of such unequal potential and geographical relation to Russia—had to make a fresh judgment of their strategies in view of those changes within capitalism which challenged their own doctrine. Perhaps the most ambitious attempt to do this came in May 1943 with the dissolution of the Communist International.

Stalin, who had sworn at Lenin's bier to guard this "general staff of the world revolution" like the apple of his eye, was now abandoning it; and in so doing he signaled to Churchill and Roosevelt that he would project the postwar Soviet interest in essentially Russian terms. This decision was consistent with the fact that the Russian Communists had not been able to rely on ideology or internationalism in mobilizing their own peoples for the enormous sacrifices of the war. They had been forced to appeal to the Russian love of soil and the solace of the Orthodox faith. "They are not fighting for us," Stalin had once mused to Ambassador Harriman. "They are fighting for Mother Russia."

All of this would not, of course, make Russia easier to deal with. And in studying the details in the monumental accounts of Herbert Feis or W. H. McNeill, one is struck by Stalin's political opportunism and the enormous part which is played in his calculations by the need to exact material resources from friend and foe. Throughout 1944, Stalin dealt with anyone who would cease fighting, or mobilize men and matériel for the Soviet armies, safeguard their lines and pledge reparations; and everyone was suitable to Moscow in terms of these objectives—agrarians and monarchists in the Axis satellites, veteran Communist haters in Finland, a Social Democratic old-timer in Austria, Dr. Beneš in Prague or Comrade Tito in the Yugoslav mountains. Had the putsch against Hitler succeeded in July 1944, Stalin was prepared, by his committee of Nazi generals rounded up at Stalingrad, to bargain.

His only real complication arose over Poland. Here the Soviets had the tactical advantage that a generation earlier the victors at Versailles had been willing to establish the Curzon Line as Russia's western frontier. Churchill and Roosevelt were now obliged not only to ratify this line but to impose it on the intractable London Poles. Moscow's own dilemma lay in the fact that the pro-Soviet Poles, exiled in the U.S.S.R., had little political substance; they had one thing in common with their counterparts in London—lack of standing inside Poland. The Polish

Communists had been decimated in the great purges and the Polish officer corps had been wiped out in the Katyn murders. Perhaps it was the need to shift the balance in his favor that led Stalin to such extraordinary measures as letting the "Home Army" be wiped out at the banks of the Vistula or continuing to murder Polish Socialists as they came to Moscow as guests. The earlier hope of some prestigious figure who would bridge the gap between Poles and yet be satisfactory to all the great powers had faded with the death in an airplane accident of General Wladislaw Sikorski.

But it is questionable whether this Soviet use of vestigial figures of Comintern experience should be viewed, as of 1944, in terms of "communization." Everything we know of the Kremlin at that time denies this. In the remarkable account by Milovan Djilas in his "Conversations with Stalin," the Kremlin was far from being a citadel of revolution, as this young Montenegrin idealist expected (like so many in Moscow for the first time, before and after him). The Kremlin was really a sort of Muscovite camping-ground such as the great Russian painter Repin might have portrayed. Crafty and boorish men, suspicious of all foreigners and of each other, contemptuous of Communists who were non-Russian but expecting their obedience, were crowded around the maps of Europe as around some Cossack camp fire, calculating how much they could extract from Churchill and Roosevelt, to whom they felt profoundly inferior.

Thus, when Ulbricht and Rakosi, Anna Pauker, and even Dmitroff were being prepared to return to the homelands where they had previously failed, Stalin advised them not to spoil their second chance by their chronic leftism and adventurism.[1] They did not go back as revolutionaries. For all of Moscow's hopes that they root themselves in native soil, they were intended to be the guarantors of control, to stabilize this backyard of Europe and mobilize its resources on Russia's behalf. The troubles with the Yugoslavs began for the very reason that as revolutionaries they would not let themselves be used.

Was Stalin already building a bloc? To be sure he was. But he also knew that the onetime *cordon sanitaire* was a veritable swamp of historic and intractable rivalries and economic backwardness, even though wealthier in immediate resources than the U.S.S.R. itself. Hoping to transform this bloc, Stalin also entertained most seriously the idea of

---

[1] Herbert Feis is the source for the famous and revealing anecdote that when Stalin said farewell to Dr. Beneš, after signing a mutual assistance pact, he urged Beneš to help make Klement Gottwald, the Communist leader now become premier, "more worldly and less provincial"—an amazing piece of arrogance. Having themselves helped emasculate their foreign friends, the Russians now taunted them and hoped that perhaps the bourgeois world might make men of them. *Churchill, Roosevelt, Stalin* (Princeton: Princeton University Press, 1957), p. 569.

a long-term relationship with America and Britain based on some common policy toward Germany that would make its much greater resources available to Russia. Thus, when Churchill came to Moscow in September 1944 to work out a spheres-of-influence agreement, demanding 50:50 and 75:25 ratios in the political control of areas already liberated by the Soviet armies, Stalin agreed by the stroke of a pen. He did so without comment. He contemptuously left it to Churchill to decide whether the piece of paper should be retained by him or destroyed. The cobbler's son from Gori, the onetime seminary student, was giving a descendant of the Marlboroughs a lesson in Realpolitik.

But as he disposed of Greeks and interposed with Yugoslavs (without asking their consent) the Soviet dictator demanded no quid pro quo in Western Europe where the ultimate world balance could be determined, and where Communist movements had powerfully revived, guided by intimates of Stalin—Togliatti and Thorez—whose work he respected. Molotov is on record as inquiring about the disposition of Italian colonies, but not about the operations of the American Military Government in Italy in which Russian participation was passive. At the moment when the French Communists were debating whether to turn in their arms, Moscow recognized the Gaullist régime and invited it to sign a treaty with what de Gaulle was to call "chère et puissante Russie." Churchill's assault on Belgian and Greek Communists was reproved, in private. But no Soviet leverage was employed to help them, and the Greek Communists were advised to strike the best bargain they could to avert civil war. Only much later, when assistance was useless to them, did the Soviets reluctantly help the Greeks, though their hapless plight was useful for Cold War propaganda. Even as late as February 1945, at Yalta, Stalin pledged to renew his pact with Chiang Kai-shek in return for special treaty control of Dairen and the Manchurian railways. Half a year later, the Soviet armies ransacked the industrial installations that were by right Chinese. In central Asia they dickered with warlords, advising them against joining the Chinese Communists. Stalin shied away from the governance of Japan, asking and getting its northern islands instead. All this was accompanied by rather snide references by Molotov to Mao Tse-tung's "margarine Communists." American liberals and roving ambassadors may have been more naïve but they were also less offensive in believing the Chinese Communists to be "agrarian reformers."

III

How then did the Communist parties respond to the Comintern's dissolution? Its final document had some curious and pregnant phrases, alluding to "the fundamental differences in the historical development of the separate countries of the world"—differences, it was now discovered, which had "become apparent even before the war"; Communists were now told most authoritatively that they were "never advocates of the outmoded organizational forms." This suggests that a great watershed had been reached. The implicit self-criticism was bound to encourage those Western Communists for whom the "popular front" of the 1930s and the experience of the Spanish Republic were not defensive deceptions but major experiments in skirting the limits of Leninism. The Chinese Communists, as the specialized literature shows, saw in the disappearance of the Communist International a ratification of their own "New Democracy," in which the peasantry and the "national bourgeoisie" had been credited with revolutionary potentials for which no precedent existed in the Russian experience.

The most interesting instance of how new systems of ideas and new organizational forms were bursting the Leninist integument came in the minor party of a major country—among the American Communists. Their leader, Earl Browder, concluded that peaceful coexistence had become obligatory; he saw such coexistence as a whole historical stage in which the contradictions between antagonistic social systems would have to work themselves out—short of war; it is curious that he ruled out war as too dangerous to both sides *before* the advent of the atomic bomb. To give this very novel view some inner logic, Browder postulated a new type of state power, intermediate between capitalism and socialism, which, he thought, would prevail between the Atlantic and the Oder-Neisse Line. Thus he anticipated the "people's democracy" concept which was to have wide currency in the next few years only to be brusquely rejected by the end of 1948, when the Cold War demanded rationales of another kind.

To what extent Browder had sanction in Moscow, or only *thought* he had, or whether this sanction was even intended to be more than temporary are all fascinating matters; but for our discussion what seems more important is the fact that Browder revealed the incoherence of communism and tried to overcome it. Perhaps America was not as backward as European Communists traditionally assumed. The more advanced country was simply showing a mirror to the less advanced of the problems of their own future, to borrow an image from Marx.

One may put this dilemma in very specific terms. In 1944–1945, a quasi-revolutionary situation prevailed in key areas of Western Europe and East Asia. The Communist parties had become mass movements. They were no longer Leninist vanguards but had significant military experience. The old order had been discredited and few charismatic rivals existed. One of two options could be taken, each of them having its own logic. If the Communists seized power they might be able to hold it, as in Yugoslavia, with great good luck. But as the Greek experience was to show, the success of a prolonged civil war would involve the rupture of the Anglo-Soviet-American coalition; and the war with Hitler was by no means over, while the Pacific war appeared only begun. To pursue this option meant to oblige the Soviet Union to assist revolutions at a distance from its own armies at a moment of its own greatest weakness and when it seriously entertained the possibility of a long-range postwar relationship with the West. Alternatively, the U.S.S.R. would be obliged to disavow its own ideological and political allies in an even more explicit way than the dissolution of the Comintern suggested. Stalin's entire diplomacy warned against revolution now. So did his opinion, in a speech of November 6, 1944, that whatever disagreements existed among the great powers could be overcome; he had said flatly that "no accidental, transitory motive but vitally important long-term interests lie at the basis of the alliance of our country, Great Britain and the United States."

On the other hand, to reject the revolutionary path meant for the Western parties (if not for the Chinese and Vietnamese) forgoing an opportunity that might not return; for a generation this choice caused intense misgivings and internal battles within these parties. To take part in the wholehearted reconstruction of their societies on a less-than-socialist basis would have involved a revision of fundamental Leninist postulates, a fresh look at capitalism, and presumably a redefinition of their relations with the Soviet Union. Having taken such a sharply Russocentric course, could Stalin give his imprimatur to the embryonic polycentrism of that time? The U.S.S.R. was in the paradoxical position of trying to be a great power with a shattered economic base, and of trying to lead a world movement whose interests were quite distinct from those of Russia, both in practice and in ideas. The ambiguities inherent in communism, in Stalin's projections of 1927, had come home to roost.

IV

If one tries, then, to make intellectual sense and order out of the bewildering events between early 1945 and mid-1947, the least satisfactory themes are the ones which have been so popular and have dominated the discussion of the origins of the Cold War. The revisionist historians are so hung up on the notion that a meticulous rediscovery of America will reveal the clues to the Cold War that they ignore the dimensions of communism altogether. They have little experience with communism (and perhaps they are better off for it) but they have yet to show the scholarship required to explore it. To say this is not to deny the value of reappraising American policy, especially since so many of today's follies have roots in the past. Communists, anti-Communists, and ex-Communists have all had troubles with the imperatives of coexistence. But this is quite different from explaining the Cold War on one-sided grounds and succumbing to the elementary fallacy of *post hoc, propter hoc.*

On the other hand, the most sophisticated and persuasive rebuttal to the younger historians—that by Arthur Schlesinger, Jr., in these pages[2]—suffered from the limitations of his own major premise: the assumption that communism was a monolithic movement which disintegrated only as the Cold War was vigorously prosecuted. Certainly the monolith functioned in a pell-mell fashion after 1948, but one wonders whether its explosive decomposition in the late fifties, continuing to the events in Czechoslovakia, can be comprehended without realizing that all the elements of crisis within it were already present in its immediate postwar years. It was the futile attempts by Stalin and the Communists who everywhere followed him (even if hesitantly and in bewilderment) to stifle the nascent polycentrism and to curtail the inchoate attempts to adjust to new realities which constitute communism's own responsibility for the Cold War. Herein also is the key to communism's own disasters.

Thus, the events of 1946 and 1947 were in fact incoherent and contradictory, and for that very reason offer an important clue to the origins of the Cold War. For example, Earl Browder was roundly denounced by the French Communist leader, Jacques Duclos, in an article written early in 1945 (with data that was available only in Moscow), on the grounds that the very concept of peaceful coexistence and Europe's reconstruction on a bourgeois-democratic basis was heresy; yet the curious thing is that most of the Communist parties continued to operate on Browder's assumptions—including the party led by Duclos. Such a state of affairs suggests that the Duclos article was not the tocsin of the Cold War but one of the elements of communism's incoherence. By the close of 1946, only the Yugoslavs—and William Z. Foster, who had ousted Browder in the United States—were convinced that even the "temporary stabilization" of capitalism was unlikely. This concept was of course an echo from the 1920s. "Relative and temporary stabilization" was Stalin's own justification in the late 1920s for "turning inward" and seeking a truce in external affairs. Ruling out this concept in the 1940s, Foster went even further than Tito in raising the alarm

[2]Arthur M. Schlesinger, Jr., "Origins of the Cold War," *Foreign Affairs* 46 (October 1967):22–52.

over an ever-more-imminent danger of an American attack on the Soviet Union. It is not generally known that when Browder's successor
visited Europe in March 1947 he was amazed to find that few Communist leaders agreed with his views, and one of those who disagreed
most sharply was Jacques Duclos.

In studying the French Communists of that period one finds un-
usual emphasis on the need for a policy of "confident collaboration"
with "all of the Allied nations, without exception," and a declaration
by Duclos that "we are not among those who confuse the necessity
and fertility of struggle with the spirit of adventurism. That is why—
mark me well—we ask of a specific historic period what it can give
and only what it can give . . . but we do not ask more, for we want to
push ahead and not end up in abortive and disappointing failures."

In this same year of 1946, it is sometimes forgotten that the
Chinese Communists negotiated seriously for a long-term coalition
with Chiang Kai-shek. They did so under the aegis of General George
Marshall, which suggests that their own antagonism to "American imperialism" had its limits; their view that the United States was necessarily hostile to a unified China with a large Communist component
was a later development. During the recent Great Proletarian Cultural
Revolution, Chinese historians blamed this coalition strategy on the
now-disgraced Liu Shao Chi, alleging that he was under the influence
of "Browder, Tagliatti, Thorez and other renegades to the proletariat."
But the official Chinese Communist documents show that at the time
Mao Tse-tung took credit for it and was himself viewed as a "revisionist"—by the Indian Communists, for example. In those same
months, Ho Chi Minh led a coalition delegation to Paris, trying to work
out the terms for remaining within the French Union; it is a curious
but revealing detail that Ho had the previous winter dissolved his own
creation, the Communist Party of Indochina, in favor of an Association
of Marxist Studies, without, however, receiving a rebuke from Jacques
Duclos.

Throughout 1946, almost every Communist leader in the West
voiced the view that peaceful roads to socialism were not only desirable but were—because of objective changes in the world—now theoretically admissible. If in Eastern Europe this popularity of the "people's democracy" can be explained in terms of Stalin's attempt to
stabilize a chaotic region of direct interest to Russia, in Western Europe it was part of a serious effort to implement the nonrevolutionary
option which the Communists had chosen, and for which they needed
a consistent justification.

Nor were the Soviet leaders immune to what was happening within
communism. Stalin himself can be cited in contradictory assertions
which also stimulated the diversity within the Communist world as

well as baffling some of its members. Early in February 1946 Stalin declared that wars could not be abolished so long as imperialism prevailed; this came in his election campaign speech which is viewed by Sovietologists as another tocsin of the Cold War. Yet throughout 1946 Stalin gave interviews to British and American newsmen, and held a long discussion with Harold Stassen that spring, in which the key theme was the viability of peaceful coexistence. In September 1946 Stalin declared that the ruling circles of both Britain and the United States were *not* in fact oriented toward war—a view which Communists from China to Italy hailed, although it baffled Tito and William Z. Foster. Stalin also told a British Labor delegation headed by Harold Laski that socialism might well come to Britain by parliamentary means, with the monarchy remaining as a genuine institution. Earlier in the year, in a polemic with a certain Professor Razin on the significance of the doctrines of Clausewitz, Stalin is quoted as believing "it is impossible to move forward and advance science without subjecting outdated propositions and the judgments of well-known authorities to critical analysis. This applies . . . also to the classics of Marxism." Significantly, this exchange was published a full year later—in February 1947—on the eve of Cold War decisions which made such thinking heretical throughout the Communist movement.

Yet in 1946 Soviet diplomacy was in fact moving "with all deliberate speed" toward settlements of a partial kind with the West—as regards the peace treaties, the evacuation of northern Persia and other matters. Browder was cordially received in Moscow in May after his expulsion from the American party—a rather unprecedented detail in the annals of communism. The deposed Communist leader was heard out by Molotov, at the latter's request, and was given a post which enabled him to work energetically for the next two years in behalf of the proposition that Stalin wanted an American-Soviet settlement.

All students of this period have paused on the famous Varga controversy. The title of the book which the foremost Soviet economist, Eugen Varga, published in November 1946 (it was completed the year before) in itself suggests what was bothering Russian leaders, namely: *Changes in the Economy of Capitalism Resulting from the Second World War.* Within six months, Varga was under severe attack, which he resisted for the following two years. Major issues lay at the heart of the controversy. When might a crisis of overproduction be expected in the United States? How severe would it be? And to what extent would rearmament or a program for rebuilding Western Europe affect capitalism's inherent propensity for crisis, which was, of course, taken for granted. Another question was whether the new role of governmental power, so greatly enhanced by the war, might not have a bearing both on the onset of the crisis and the terrain of Communist activities. Varga did forecast an early crisis, after a brief postwar boom. In so doing, he surely misled Stalin into one of his most fundamental Cold War miscalculations. But Varga also clung to the view that something important had changed within classical capitalism; he insisted that "the question of greater or smaller participation in the management of the state will be the main content" of the political struggle in the West, and he deduced that people's democracy was in fact a transitional form between the two systems, replacing the "either-or" notions of classical Leninism. There was a plaintive protest in Varga's answer to his critics (one of whom was Vosnessensky, who would shortly disappear because of mysterious heresies of his own). "It is not a matter of enumerating all the facts so that they inevitably lead to the former conclusions of Marxism-Leninism," Varga argued, "but to use the Marxist-Leninist method in studying these facts. The world changes and the content of our work must change also."

V

In what sense, then, did all these crosscurrents determine Stalin's decision for Cold War? It would seem that the matter turned on the incompatibility between immediate Soviet objectives and the real interests of the Communist parties—or more exactly, in the particularly Stalinist answer to these incompatibilities. The Russians, it will be remembered, had set out to achieve rapid and ambitious reconstruction including, of course, the acquisition of nuclear weapons. They were most concerned with reparations. When it became plain that little help would come by loans or trade with the West (they had used up what was still in the pipelines after the abrupt cessation of lend-lease in mid-1945 and were not getting a response to their $6 billion request to Washington), they needed either the resources of Germany beyond what they could extract from their own Eastern Zone, or a desperate milking of their friends and former foes in Eastern Europe. At home, moreover, they could not rely on the ultrachauvinist themes which had served them during the war; rejecting liberalization of Soviet society, they tightened the screws and fell back on the doctrine of the primacy of the Soviet party, the purity of its doctrine and the universal validity of that doctrine. Consistent with these objectives, the Soviet leaders wanted to erase all sympathy for America which until then was widespread in the Soviet Union.[3]

---

[3]This task was assigned to the late Ilya Ehrenburg following his 1947 visit to the States, when he deliberately oversimplified everything American with the crudest methods. The pattern for this had been set late in 1946 by Andrei Zhdanov.

These objectives, taken together, ran counter to all the tendencies among the foreign Communist parties. Both the revolutionary ambitions of the Yugoslavs, their jealous quest for autonomy as well as the emphasis on peaceful non-Soviet roads to socialism—that is, the "revisionist" themes so urgently needed by the parties in the West—could be countenanced by Moscow only if it were prepared to accept diversity within international communism. This very diversity (which they had themselves half entertained) now became an obstacle. The Stalinist premise that what was good for Russia was good for all other Communists (a notion which he himself considered abandoning) was now reaffirmed.

The origins of the Cold War lie deeper, however, than any analysis of Russia's own interest. Nor can they be understood only in terms of an attempt to prevent economic recovery and political stability in Western Europe. The Cold War's origins must be found in a dimension larger than the requirements of Soviet internal mobilization or the thrust of its foreign policy; they lie in the attempt to overcome the incipient diversity within a system of states and parties, among whom the changes produced by the war had outmoded earlier ideological and political premises. The conditions for the transformation of a monolithic movement had matured and ripened. The sources of the Cold War lie in communism's unsuccessful attempt to adjust to this reality, followed by its own abortion of this attempt. For Stalin the Cold War was a vast tug-of-war with the West, whereby not only internal objectives could be realized but the international movement subordinated; its constituent parts went along—bewildered but believing—on the assumption that in doing so, they would survive and prosper. The price of the Stalinist course was to be fearsome indeed; and by 1956 the Soviet leaders were to admit that the Cold War had damaged the U.S.S.R. more than the West, that a stalemate of systems had to be acknowledged, and ineluctable conclusions had to be drawn. Thus, the Cold War arose from the failure of a movement to master its inner difficulties and choose its alternatives.

The analysis could be continued to the turning-point of mid-1947—the Marshall Plan decision and Stalin's riposte, for example, in humiliating his Czechoslovak and Polish partners, who thought in terms of what might be good for them, and indirectly for the Soviet Union. Such an analysis would take us through the near insurrections of late 1947 in France and Italy, adventurist upheavals in Asia, the Berlin blockade and the coup in Prague in 1948. But this involves another subject—how the Cold War was fought. It was indeed fought by both sides. But to say this cannot obscure the crisis within communism, where its origins lie. The record would show how recklessly entire Communist movements were expended and to what a dangerous brink the Soviet Union itself was brought. In 1956, Khrushchev was to lament these miscalculations but he did so with such a *desinvolture* as to leave a memory bank of disasters and skeletons that still rattle in communism's closets. Was the Cold War but a test of strength between systems? Or has it not also been the process whereby communism disclosed such an intellectual and political bankruptcy that a dozen years after Khrushchev's revelations, the issues still agonize—as in Czechoslovakia—all the states and parties involved? A world movement claiming to comprehend history and accepting the responsibility for "making history" still grapples with the alternatives opened by the Second World War. It has yet to face what it has tried to avoid at such a heavy cost to coexistence—namely, understanding itself.

☆ 10 ☆

The Rise of the National Security State

LIBERTY OR SECURITY?

"The price of liberty is eternal vigilance," wrote an American clergyman in the nineteenth century. In one sense this statement could refer to the tension that has always existed within a democratic state between protecting the liberties of the citizen while at the same time allowing the nation-state to take the necessary measures to defend itself. The age-old dilemma of reconciling liberty and security did not hit home with full force in the United States until after 1945. With the development of nuclear weapons that threatened instant annihilation, the appearance of long-range bombers and intercontinental ballistic missiles, and America's rise to the status of a superpower with worldwide responsibilities, what was called the "age of free security" for the United States came to an end. The tension that had traditionally existed between protecting the liberty of the individual on the one hand and ensuring the security of the state on the other entered upon a new era.[1]

To protect the liberty of the individual, institutional mechanisms had been created by the founding fathers to limit the powers of gov-

---

[1]The term "age of free security" was coined by historian C. Vann Woodward in his article entitled "The Age of Reinterpretation," *American Historical Review* 66 (1966):1–19. Woodward essentially divided American history into two periods: the period before 1945 being the "age of free security" when the oceans flanking America and weak neighbors to the north and south on the North American continent protected this country from attack; and the post-1945 period when long-range bombers, intercontinental ballistic missiles, and atomic and nuclear bombs exposed the United States to attack and possible annihilation.

ernment such as the Bill of Rights, constitutional guarantees, and the like. Yet to survive in a modern world that resembled an armed camp the United States had increasingly moved toward a greater concentration of governmental power and in the direction of a national security state. These conflicting aims raised a crucial question: Should the liberty of the individual or the security of the state be given the higher priority?

The rise of the "state within a state"—a national security state within the American government—was part of the price the United States had to pay for its rise to world power. During the eighteenth and nineteenth centuries, when America was less important on the world scene, it had been possible to think in terms of clear-cut periods of war and peace. But with the coming of the twentieth century, the emergence of the United States as a world power, and the loss of geographical security, the lines between war and peace became blurred. Conditions normally associated with war extended into peacetime; security measures exercised in wartime became peacetime preoccupations. The concept of a national security state came into being to place the country on a continual wartime footing. Most scholars today would agree that since the close of World War II the United States has been in a virtual wartime posture compared to the prewar era.

The concept of a national security state consisted of a unified triad of three elements—*attitudes, policies,* and *institutions*—aimed at keeping the country in a condition of permanent war preparedness. The attitudes arose from the two major considerations in America's foreign policy since World War II: the idea of containing communism, and the new doctrine of national security designed for an age of missiles and nuclear weapons. The policies included containment, confrontation, and intervention—the methods used by American leaders to try and make the world safe for the United States. The institutions included government bureaucracies—such as the F.B.I., C.I.A., and National Security Council—that served to keep the country in a constant state of readiness.

The term "national security state" was first used by Daniel Yergin in 1977.[2] But the antecedents for all three elements could be traced back to World War I. With respect to the attitudes the strong anti-Communist stand of the United States had its origins in the sharp American reaction to the Russian Revolution of 1917. America's foreign policy emphasizing more internationalism may be said to date from Woodrow Wilson's motto that World War I was waged to "make the world safe for democracy." Insofar as institutions were concerned the use of the F.B.I. against domestic radicals during World War I and

---

[2]Daniel Yergin, *Shattered Peace* (Boston, 1977), pp. 5–6.

the "red scare" of 1919–1920 marked the beginnings of a national police force within the United States.

Those who disagreed about the relative merits of the national security state—and they included historians, political scientists, scholars of international law as well as policymakers—may be said to fall into two broad groups: "idealists" and "realists."

The idealists were those who placed the greatest emphasis on liberty, both at home and abroad. At home they were interested more in protecting the civil liberties of individual citizens, and believed this goal to be as important a priority as the security of the state. As regards events abroad the idealists were convinced that it was necessary to maintain freedom round the world to secure America's own freedom. Hence they urged that the United States should play an activist role in maintaining a liberal world order.

The realists took an opposite point of view. At home they were concerned more with the security of the state and less with the liberties of the individual. On the international scene they were interested more in maintaining a structure of world peace along American lines. They were even willing, during the times of the Nixon-Kissinger détente, to often undertake a policy of *realpolitik* and to enter into a virtual complicity with the Soviet Union in order to maintain a status quo.

The lines between the two groups were not always clear, however, because each recognized that the position of the other had some validity. Idealists realized that the threats from totalitarian countries were real, not imagined; even the most wild-eyed libertarians recognized that all liberties would be lost if the state could not secure and defend itself. By the same token realists who demanded tight security measures realized the irony involved in attacking at times the very liberties they were hoping to protect. It should be noted, moreover, that some individuals who were idealists in the early days of the Cold War changed their minds at a later date and became realists. Conversely, certain realists reversed themselves and became idealists. Thus scholarly writings on this issue could not easily be confined to strict categories.

The term "idealist" presents other difficulties of definition, for it is impossible to eliminate confusion when using this slippery word. In this chapter the word *idealist* will be used in several ways. First, it will be employed to denote those who have presented an interpretation of diplomatic events that differs from the standard Cold War accounts. Second, the term will be used to categorize those persons who believed it was possible to construct a world order along the lines of liberalism. "Liberalism" in this chapter will be understood to mean a mixture of moderate government and a welfare capitalist economy.

The term "realist" presents a similar problem in definition. In this chapter *realist* will be used within a certain context. It will be employed to identify those who accepted the orthodox Cold War interpretation of diplomatic history. These persons supported the containment policy followed by the United States since World War II, and they adhered, generally speaking, to a hard line against the Soviet Union. In terms of domestic policies the realists tended to agree with security measures taken by various administrations—even when such measures were at the expense of civil liberties.

Daniel Yergin, a historian, represented best the idealist point of view in his *Shattered Peace*. In this work Yergin traced the origins of the national security state to Wilsonianism and the ideology of liberal internationalism that lay at the heart of America's foreign policy. Wilson threw the weight of the United States into the politics of the international system, and into the issue at the center of that system: the balance of power in Europe. What Wilson sought, said Yergin, was to project American values into world politics—the values of a liberal society united in a broad Lockean consensus.

The United States hoped to work within the old international system, but only in order to reform and change it. The Wilsonian program aimed to create a middle way between revolution and reaction. It contained a bundle of policies: support for the idea of representative government; democratic liberties and human rights; nonrecognition of revolutionary change; national self-determination; a league of nations; the end to formal empires; the reduction of armaments; a belief in and use of an enlightened public opinion; and the maintenance of a liberal capitalist world economy. Although economic objectives were an important part of the program they represented only one element of the overall scheme. According to Yergin America saw itself as a disinterested, innocent power—one whose own aims were thought to express the yearnings of all people, and whose responsibilities were bound to become inescapable, inevitable, and worldwide.

The Soviet leaders, on the other hand, shared none of these Wilsonian values, Yergin argued. They were concerned primarily with power as it was traditionally conceived in the international system. During the 1920s and 1930s they began to plan for a sphere of influence in the countries on their European borders. While they were doing so a great debate developed among American policymakers regarding Soviet motives. Was that sphere of influence all that Russia wanted, or was it only the first step on the road to worldwide revolution?

Behind this debate lay two questions that confronted American planners who had to shape policy toward the Soviet Union. What was the connection between Marxist-Leninist ideology and Soviet foreign policy? Marxist-Leninist ideology calls for Marxist-Leninists to be conscious agents of revolution. Were the Soviet leaders fomentors of revolution to make the world over in a Communist image? The second question arose out of the brutal horrors of Stalinism—the campaign of terror inside the Soviet Union during the 1920s and 1930s that took an estimated 20 million lives. Did harsh totalitarian practices at home necessarily bring about a foreign policy that was totalitarian in intent abroad? A foreign policy, in other words, committed to the use of force and one dedicated to endless expansion in the pursuit of world domination?

American policymakers struggled from World War I through the mid-1940s to think through these questions and to arrive at an appropriate foreign policy. Two interpretations competed for primacy in this process, according to Yergin. At the heart of the first interpretation was the image of the Soviet Union as a world revolutionary state—one that denied any possibility of coexistence, was committed to unrelenting ideological warfare, and was powered by a messianic drive for world mastery. The second downplayed the role of ideology and the foreign policy consequences of totalitarian domestic practices. It saw the Soviet Union instead behaving like a traditional great power within the international system, rather than trying to overthrow that system.

In the years following World War II, Yergin concluded, the first interpretation became dominant. It provided a foundation for the anti-Communist consensus that was to prevail. With this view in mind, any serious attempts at diplomacy were unthinkable. American policy planners felt they could not deal diplomatically with a revolutionary, messianic, predatory power like Russia. The only possible course of action was confrontation and eventually a policy of containment.

Thus Yergin suggested that American's foreign policy planners had misinterpreted the Soviet challenge and Soviet objectives. In doing so they downplayed the possibilities for diplomacy or accommodation of any kind. They formulated a new doctrine of national security premised on the belief that Russia posed an immediate threat to America. This doctrine presupposed an interpretation of America's security needs that was expansionist in its purpose in order that the United States might protect itself. The new doctrine, according to Yergin, marked a major redefinition of America's relation to the rest of the world from the end of World War II to the 1970s. It caused American leaders to pursue a global, crusading foreign policy. The first selection for this chapter is from Yergin's book.

Other idealist historians suggested interpretations of the policies that flowed from the attitudes suggested by Yergin. Melvyn Leffler took issue with the realist historians in an article he published in the *American Historical Review* in 1984. Leffler's research differed from that of Yergin in several important respects. He concentrated mainly on the work of military planners instead of civilian policymakers. His sources were different because he had available to him recently declassified Pentagon material. And his focus in terms of time was different: he was interested only in World War II and the postwar period. As a result he came to a number of different conclusions regarding America's policies.

Leffler located the origins of the Cold War at an earlier date than many realist historians. Most realists believed that the overt Cold War began around 1947 with the formulation of the containment policy enunciated in the Truman Doctrine. Leffler pointed out, however, that American military men had already begun developing plans for a defense-in-depth in 1944–1945 involving a series of far-flung overseas bases to protect America's security. Two world wars had taught military planners one important lesson in geopolitics, said Leffler. Any power or combination of powers seeking to dominate the Eurasian land mass was to be regarded as hostile by the United States. Since Russia represented the only major power possessing such a capability, America's policies toward the Soviet Union became unnecessarily provocative, according to Leffler.[3]

Turning to the institutions of the national security state Richard Barnet, an idealist political scientist, discussed the professional elite who helped to devise national defense policies. In *Roots of War*, published in 1971, Barnet postulated the presence of a group within the government that he called "national security managers." Serving as advisers to American presidents these men had come to power as the result of an organizational revolution during World War II. This revolution has raised the entire federal bureaucracy to a new position of authority over American society, and within that bureaucracy national security institutions had emerged as the most dominant.

The national security managers were drawn primarily from law and banking, and Barnet's thesis held that they symbolized the triumph of the military-industrial complex over the government. They placed the country on a permanent war economy, and reshaped the idea of America's national interest. Barnet believed that this national security establishment was strongly influenced in its predilection for expansion by its close connections with the American business community. The national security managers, concluded Barnet, were amoral, ruthless, and had a penchant for violence as well as a fascination with the lethal technology of the day.[4]

The institutions of the national security state in one respect pre-

---

[3]Melvyn Leffler, "The American Conception of National Security and the Beginnings of the Cold War, 1945–1948," and "Comments," *American Historical Review* 89 (1984):346–390.

[4]Another book critical of the professional elite in policy-making was I. M. Destler, Leslie Gelb, and Anthony Lake, *Our Own Worst Enemy* (New York, 1984).

sented scholars with a paradox: to defend freedom and the democratic way of life, institutions such as the F.B.I. and C.I.A. sometimes violated the very liberties they had been created to protect. One characteristic of a classic police state was the formation of independent state bureaucracies such as a secret police. Although the United States was far from a police state, the F.B.I. and C.I.A. frequently violated the First Amendment, search-and-seizure constitutional rights, and other civil liberties in the course of their operations.

Such violations had a history stretching back to World War I, according to Frank Donner, an idealist lawyer-historian. In *Age of Surveillance*, published in 1980, Donner noted that the federalization of domestic intelligence operations took place during World War I and the Russian Revolution. During the war and the famed "red scare" of 1919–1920 that followed, the F.B.I. carried out massive assaults against domestic radicals. In the 1930s the Bureau continued to conduct large-scale illegal investigations against political dissidents—almost invariably against left-wingers.

The creation of the C.I.A. in 1947 expanded this political intelligence network. The mission of the C.I.A. was to gather secret information or intelligence for security purposes throughout the world. In 1950, under memorandum NCS-68, it was recommended that the United States employ the same kind of Cold War intelligence methods that the Soviets were using against this country. This recommendation was applied with a vengeance. The C.I.A., F.B.I., and other security agencies rapidly developed into a national police force—one that was fenced off by tight security and operated with little or no oversight by Congress.

In the years that followed, spying on ordinary citizens by such agencies became a common occurrence, Donner noted. The Watergate crisis of the early 1970s revealed that both the C.I.A. and the F.B.I. had engaged in illegal wiretapping and other clandestine operations that violated civil liberties. The C.I.A. it was discovered had for years violated its charter, which specifically forbade it from carrying on operations within the United States. During the Vietnam War it had regularly conducted illegal operations against antiwar protestors and other groups of political dissidents. At the same time it came to light that the F.B.I. had gathered for over three decades political information on journalists, political opponents of sitting presidents, and critics of national policy and delivered such information to the White House. The issue of how far a democratic country should go in using totalitarian methods to defend itself remained a vital one for many idealists.

The outstanding scholar presenting the realist point of view was Samuel P. Huntington, a political scientist at Harvard University. In *The Soldier and the State*, published in 1957, Huntington discussed the idea of a "garrison state." He derived this concept from Harold Laswell, a political scientist who predicted that in the post–World War II period both the United States and the Soviet Union might evolve into garrison states because of a prolonged Cold War era. The garrison state idea possessed many characteristics of the national security state. Within a garrison state a military oligarchy would take charge, Laswell said, because of the overwhelming need for military security. Democratic institutions would be either abolished or become purely ceremonial, since military institutions and democratic institutions would prove incompatible within such a society. The garrison state differed markedly, moreover, from both a capitalist and a socialist state in an economic sense. In the former the ultimate aim of production and natural resources would be for military purposes, while in a capitalist or socialist state the aim of production was use of goods and services by the citizenry.

Huntington explored the implications of the garrison state idea in his book and concluded that the relations between the military and civilian segments of American society had undergone a profound revolution since World War II. Before the war the main question had been: What pattern of civil-military relations was most compatible with America's liberal democratic values? After the war this question had been succeeded by what Huntington considered a more important issue: What pattern of civil-military relations would best maintain the security of the United States? The threat of the Soviet Union, claimed Huntington, had made security and sheer survival the main objective of American policy. In this new age the soldier, not the civilian, was destined to play the more important role; security not liberty was to be the ultimate aim of American society.

The thesis of Huntington's book was that under these circumstances America had to abandon its traditional attitude of suspicion toward the military. Heretofore legislators who dealt with military affairs had been concerned primarily with protecting America's liberal democratic heritage from creeping militarism. According to Huntington, however, liberalism as a philosophy did not permit the nation to think in realistic terms about war and military institutions. In the new age, when security would be America's primary goal, there had to be a more realistic attitude—one that accepted the military more readily and at the same time reduced the high expectations of liberty by American liberals.

Huntington pursued this theme but broadened his focus in subsequent books. In a work entitled *The Crisis of Democracy,* which he coauthored in 1975, Huntington's essay took up the relationship of the military to the state within the context of a much larger problem. That problem was implicit in the question: "Who governs America?" When providing answers to this question Huntington did so with the new age of the national security state in mind. There were two possible answers. Should elites make public policy and rule America—with "elites" being defined as those men whom Barnet termed "national security managers" as well as members of the private establishment made up of important businessmen, banks, law firms, foundations, and the national media? Or should public policy be made through public opinion, mass democracy, and the rule of the people through their elected officials—the president and the Congress? By asking the question "Who governs?," Huntington, by implication, was raising an even more profound historical question. Had the ideology and institutions spawned by the Cold War changed the character of traditional American democracy? Had the nature of American democracy changed from the "great republic" envisioned by the founding fathers in which the people were sovereign into a remote, impenetrable national security state controlled by elites?[5]

When answering the question "Who governs?," Huntington reviewed in his book some of the dynamic changes that had occurred in the United States during the 1960s and early 1970s. The 1960s, he noted, was "a decade of dramatic surge and the reassertion of democratic egalitarianism." This democratic surge manifested itself in a variety of ways. First, there was the increased political participation in electioneering campaigns. Second, there was greater citizen participation in protest movements, demonstrations, marches, and in organizations devoted to causes such as preserving peace and improving the environment. Finally, there was a markedly higher level of self-consciousness among blacks, Indians, Chicanos, white ethnic groups, college students, and women.[6]

This democratic surge, among other things, had resulted in what Huntington called "an excess of democracy." Al Smith had once remarked that "the only cure for the evils of democracy was more democracy." But Huntington concluded that more democracy would simply create more problems. His prescription for America was less democracy: What the country needed in the new age of national security, said Huntington, was fewer democratic demands. In short, liberty was to be sacrificed in the interests of security.[7]

Huntington pushed the implications of his realist thesis in yet another book, *American Politics: The Politics of Disharmony*, published

---

[5]Michael Crozier, Samuel Huntington, and Joji Watanuki, *The Crisis of Democracy* (New York, 1975), pp. 59–118.

[6]*Ibid.*, 60.

[7]*Ibid.*, 113.

in 1981. In this work Huntington explored the tension between the ideal and the real within the political system. He defined as the ideal an American creed made up of a set of beliefs in liberty, individualism, equality, and distrust of authority. The real was comprised of the actual political institutions with their inevitable restraints on freedom. The tension between the two created a persistent gap between the promise of American ideals and the performance of America's political institutions—between what ought to be and what is. Throughout their history as a nation Americans were united by the American creed, said Huntington. At the same time these ideals were perennially frustrated by those institutions and hierarchies required to carry out the functions of governing a democratic society. The clash between the two-American ideals and institutions—resulted in an enduring tension.

Americans, according to Huntington's analysis, tried to adjust to this tension in four ways: by moralistic reform; by cynicism; by complacency; and by hypocrisy. In *American Politics* Huntington was primarily concerned with moralistic reform. Every sixty to seventy years the American people attempted to close the gap between ideals and institutions with outbursts of reform that Huntington termed periods of "creedal passion." The four major reform periods—the American Revolution, Jacksonian period, Progressive movement, and the political rebellion of the 1960s and early 1970s—reflected in his eyes attempts to make political institutions conform more closely to the American creed. Despite some limited successes each of these periods inevitably resulted in a reversion to complacency, cynicism, and hypocrisy. Huntington's analysis provided a cyclical explanation of why America had experienced both so much consensus and so much conflict throughout its history.

Huntington's writings in his various books were aimed at justifying a society far less liberal than the one Americans had experienced throughout their history. Such a society was necessary, he felt, given the needs of America's security in the post–World War II world. He developed the concept of "objective civilian control" in *The Soldier and the State* to justify setting the military apart from the demands of a liberal society, and suggested the scaling down of traditional civilian safeguards in future civil-military relations.[8] In *American Politics* he criticized as "creedal passion" American actions taken in defense of this country's liberal ideology during the 1960s and early 1970s. Huntington, for example, decried the American "crusades" against the activities of the F.B.I. and C.I.A., excessive defense spending, the use of military force abroad, the military-industrial complex, and the so-called "imperial presidency." Such actions in his view threatened to expose,

---

[8]Samuel Huntington, *The Soldier and the State* (New York, 1957), pp. 80–97.

weaken, dismantle, or abolish the very institutions that provided security for America's liberal society against foreign threats.[9] To sum up, Huntington's works provided the clearest exposition of the realist position on the national security state, and advanced the strongest arguments for placing security ahead of liberty. The second selection in this chapter is drawn from Huntington's *The Soldier and the State.*

Unlike Huntington other realists revealed a greater anxiety about the need for a national security state along with the protection of liberty. Hans Morgenthau, a pronounced realist, was one of America's most distinguished scholars of international relations. Although he did not deal directly with the idea of a national security state in his *The Purpose of American Politics,* published in 1960, many of the issues he took up had a bearing on this matter. Morgenthau in his other books had been critical of America's foreign policy from 1776 to World War II as being too utopian, and he suggested that only since 1945 had Americans become realistic and framed their foreign policy in accordance with international power politics and along the lines of national interest.

In *The Purpose of American Politics* Morgenthau raised the question of whether America had lost its national purpose in the twentieth century. From its beginnings, he said, the United States had sought the establishment of equality in freedom in order to present an example to the rest of the world. The depression of the 1930s had brought reforms and a reaffirmation of that principle at home. Americans then moved outward in a manner consistent with its national purpose by fighting Hitler, and, after 1947, in opposing the spread of communism. But from 1947 to 1960 everything had gone wrong according to Morgenthau. The sense of national purpose declined: America failed to keep China in the American camp and accepted a stalemate in Korea; McCarthyism was embraced in the 1950s; the spread of communism was not checked; government was paralyzed by three developments (executive-legislative divisions, a governance-by-committee approach, and too great a reliance on public opinion polls); private interests outweighed public interests; and objective standards of excellence were replaced by the notion that what the majority wanted should prevail. The only hope, as Morgenthau saw it, was a move to recapture the sense of national purpose through reforms at home and through the export abroad of the American concept of equality-in-freedom. To Morgenthau the restoration of the sense of national purpose was a precondition for America's survival.

To remedy the situation Morgenthau proposed a greater degree of

---

[9]Samuel Huntington, *American Politics: The Promise of Disharmony* (Cambridge, Mass., 1981), p. 238.

authoritarianism. A strong president, he felt, would help lead America back to the correct path. The National Security Council, which formulated public policy on the most momentous matters of state affecting security, he believed, should be influenced less by the "government-by-committee" attitude that prevailed in Washington circles. And from his viewpoint there should be "less abdication of government before the specter of public opinion."[10] Although Morgenthau's argument was sophisticated and subtle he was clearly prepared to check excessive liberties in favor of more security.

George Kennan, the policymaker and diplomat, was close to the realist position but showed even more ambivalence on this issue. Like Morgenthau he had been critical of America's foreign policy in the early twentieth century because it was based too much on moral grounds and not enough on realism. Although he had helped frame America's containment policy, Kennan argued in the first volume of his *Memoirs*, published in 1967, that the Truman administration had pursued the wrong priorities in Europe by concentrating on a policy of military containment rather than one which balanced political and military considerations.

As concerns other features of the national security state, Kennan in his second volume published in 1972 described with distaste the events during the McCarthy era when the civil liberties of his colleagues in the State Department were violated in the presumed interests of national security. The excesses of McCarthyism alarmed Kennan. Although he approved of strong measures for purposes of protecting national security, he recognized the dangers of going too far. The greatest threat to America was, he pointed out:

> ... a danger that something may occur in our minds and souls which will make us no longer like the persons by whose efforts this republic was founded and held together, but rather like the representatives of that very power we are trying to combat: intolerant, secretive, suspicious, cruel and terrified of internal dissension. ... The worst thing the Communists could do to us, and the thing we have most to fear from their activities, is that we should become like them.[11]

The fourth and final scholar who represented the realist position, though with serious qualifications, was John Gaddis, who published *Strategies of Containment* in 1981. Gaddis provided an analysis of how America's policy of containment had unfolded over time. It originated with George Kennan's recommendations in 1947, he said, and then

[10]Hans Morgenthau, *The Purpose of American Politics* (New York, 1960), p. 267.
[11]George F. Kennan, *Memoirs*, 2 vols. (Boston, 1967–1972), II:200. Emphasis added.

was articulated more fully in NCS-68—the secret memorandum framed by the National Security Council in 1950. This memorandum—one of the key documents of the Cold War—viewed the world as being divided between America and Russia. Soviet foreign policy was seen as dedicated to two goals: the preservation of Russia's power and ideology, and the extension of Soviet power by the absorption of new satellite states and the weakening of any other competing system of power in the world. To contain such a threat it was proposed that the United States assume unilaterally the defense of the free world. The argument advanced for this policy was that it was no longer possible to distinguish between America's national security and global security. Gaddis then followed the strategies based on this containment policy through Eisenhower's "New Look," the Kennedy-Johnson "flexible response," the Vietnam War, and the Nixon-Kissinger period of détente.

Gaddis believed, however, that the United States had vacillated between two foreign policies personified by the two men mostly responsible for framing the containment policy. Paul Nitze, an arms control expert, held that the United States should respond to each and every Soviet threat—regardless of the cost. George Kennan, then head of the Policy Planning Staff, suggested instead a strategy of selective responses. His strategy called for making a distinction between tolerable and intolerable threats, America's vital and peripheral interests, and bearable and unbearable costs. Oscillating between these two views resulted in disastrous consequences, according to Gaddis. America failed to achieve a national consensus, to develop a coherent approach to foreign policy, or to enhance its authority throughout the world. Gaddis, by taking a more skeptical view of the orthodox interpretation of the Cold War advanced by other realist scholars, might therefore be more fairly categorized as an idealistic realist on the issue of the national security state.

In evaluating these two interpretations on the rise of the national security state it is important to understand that much more than an abstract historical debate is at stake here. Students should be aware that they are choosing the America in which they wish to live. Should Americans place the highest premium on liberty, realizing that if they do so they may be weakening the security of the United States and possibly exposing the country to foreign threats? Or should Americans make security the paramount goal, even at the expense of limiting certain liberties of citizens? Should Americans support the maintenance of American power to a degree necessary to protect and promote American liberal ideals and institutions throughout the world? Or should they curb American power and recognize that if it remained unrestricted such power might pose dangers to liberal ideals and institutions at home? Should Americans try to reduce the gap pointed out by

Huntington between ideals and institutions, realizing that the imperfections of human nature might mean that this gap can never be eliminated? Or should American liberals periodically mount a reform movement to reinvigorate the liberal ideology in hopes of reducing the gap between American ideals and institutional practices? In answering such questions students will be determining not only the future course of America but their own destiny in the years ahead.

Daniel Yergin

DANIEL YERGIN (1947–   ) has taught at the Kennedy School of Government at Harvard University, and is now president of the Cambridge Energy Research Association. He is the author of *Shattered Peace* (1977).

By 1945 the world had been refashioned by death, destruction, and social upheaval. Germany and Japan, two of the most powerful nations, had been defeated and occupied, and the aging European empires were on the way to distintegration. With the defeat or decline of most of the European states, the old international system collapsed, leaving just two powers dominant, the United States and the Soviet Union. Many basic questions had no clear answers in 1945, and even as Stalin spoke in September of that year, the victor states were already busy assessing each other across the devastated lands and the wreckage of states, anxiously calculating possible gains and losses.

The victors never did find the tie that would hold them together. The Grand Alliance gave way to a global antagonism between two hostile coalitions, one led by the United States and the other by the Soviet Union—those two countries standing opposed to each other as nation-states, as ideologies, and as economic and political systems. After 1945 the two superpowers were able to approximate a state of general mobilization without general war being the consequence.

The confrontation brought about fundamental changes in American life, a permanent military readiness in what passed for peacetime. "We are in a period now I think of the formulation of a mood," Dean Acheson told a group of American policymakers at the end of 1947. "The country is getting serious. It is getting impressed by the fact that the business of dealing with the Russians is a long, long job. People don't say any more why doesn't Mr. Truman get together with Uncle Joe Stalin and fix it up. That used to be a common idea. There is less and less talk even among silly people about dropping bombs on Moscow. They now see it as a long, long pull, and that it can only be done by the United States getting itself together, determining that we cannot maintain a counter-balance to the communistic power without strengthening all those other parts of the world which belong in the system with us. That takes money, imagination, American skill and American technical help and many, many years." Confident that the public was coming to accept this view, Acheson added, "We are going to understand that our functions in the world will require all of the power and all the thought and all the calmness we have at our disposal."

Acheson spoke about the "United States getting itself together." By this, he meant that the country had to become organized for perpetual confrontation and for war. The unified pattern of attitudes, policies, and institutions by which this task was to be effected comprise what I call America's "national security state." It became, in fact, a "state within a state." The attitudes were derived from the two commanding ideas of American postwar foreign policy—anticommunism and a new doctrine of national security. The policies included containment, confrontation, and intervention, the methods by which U.S. leaders have sought to make the world safe for America. The institutions include those government bureaucracies and private organizations that serve in permanent war preparedness. These developments have helped to increase dramatically the power of the Executive branch of the U.S. government, particularly the presidency. For the national security state required, as Charles Bohlen put it in 1948, "a confidence in the Executive where you give human nature in effect a very large blank check."

And so the Second World War was succeeded not by the peace that Yalta had promised, but by a new conflict, the Cold War, an armed truce, precarious and dangerous—and still today, the central and defining fact of international life. . . .

This is not a book for those who want a simple story, a morality play, a confirmation of prejudices, or a rationalization for or against present-day policies. It is my hope that the narrative that follows will enable us to penetrate the myths and the polemics so that we might learn how and why the confrontation between the United States and the Soviet Union came about—not as people have chosen to remember it, but as it really happened.

One of the great diplomatic sports between East and West in the latter part of the 1940s was what might be called "onus-shifting"— each side trying to make a record and place blame on the other for the division of Europe and the Cold War itself. In this sense, much of the subsequent writing about the Cold War, both "orthodox" and "revisionist," has been a continuation of the Cold War by other means. The impulse to apportion blame is understandable simply from the magnitude of the circumstance. But the very name "Cold War" has provided an important additional reason, for historians spend much time tracking responsibilities for the outbreak of wars. The Cold War, how-

ever, was something other than a war. If one imagines that this phenomenon had instead become conventionally known as the "global
antagonism," as it might have, then it becomes instantly clear how
difficult it is to assign guilt in a meaningful way. For how do you blame
a single man—whether Stalin, Churchill, or Truman—for so complicated a phenomenon, involving events in so many different countries
and at so many different levels. Of course, it was hard to resist the
impulse during the years when the antagonism was at its sharpest, but
perhaps the passage of time has liberated us from the need to apportion
blame in the course of explanation.

For the fundamental source of the Cold War, we must turn to the
interests and positions of nation-states, which are the basic unit in
international politics. As the historian F. H. Hinsley has observed, "In
an international system the independent state is unable to abandon its
primary concern with advancing the interests of that society in competition with other states, if also by collaboration with them." This
imperative applies as much to states that draw their inspiration and
legitimacy from Marx as to those based on Locke or divine right. The
four-century-old state system that was centered in Europe, and which
had been weakened in the First World War, collapsed in the course of
the Second. A new system would have to emerge. There was much
uncertainty about the shape it would take, and about the two countries
that were sure to dominate it. One of them, the United States, had
been little involved in the old system; the other, the Union of Soviet
Socialist Republics, had been mostly excluded from it in the years between the two world wars. The U.S.A. and the U.S.S.R. had little in
the way of common traditions, no common political vocabulary, pre-
cious few links. They looked upon themselves as rival models for the
rest of mankind. They shared little except distrust.

In a system of independent states, all nations live rather dangerously. Therefore, the reduction of dangers becomes a nation's objective
in international politics. A country will take actions and pursue policies that it considers defensive, but which appear ominous, if not
threatening, to rivals. And so a dialectic of confrontation develops.

But why did the Cold War confrontation take the shape it did? Here
we must look closely at the diplomacy of the postwar period. For it is
central to my argument that diplomacy *did* matter. There has been too
much of a tendency to assume that all that happened was of a single
piece, foreordained and determined. But how world leaders perceived
their interests and acted on those perceptions counted for a very great
deal.

The Soviet outlook was not the only significant ideological factor
involved in the development of the global antagonism. There was also
the American ideology—the ideas and outlook that U.S. leaders brought

to international affairs, their *world set*. The understanding American leaders had of events and possibilities controlled their own actions and reactions in the dialectic of confrontation.

We shall pay close attention to three key elements in their world set—Wilsonianism, an interpretation of Soviet objectives, and the new doctrine of national security.

Wilsonianism, an ideology of liberal internationalism, has been at the heart of twentieth-century American foreign policy. It is a powerful vision of how the world might be organized, and of America's role in it. Woodrow Wilson was its most articulate proponent in the years 1917–19, when the United States threw its full weight into the politics of the international system and into the issue at the center of that system—the balance of power in Europe. Wilson sought to project American values into world politics, the values of a liberal society united in a broad Lockean consensus.

Wilson, like many other American leaders than and now, thought that the often brutal anarchy of the international system and the balance of power could be superseded by a juridical international community, committed to due process and common values. The United States would work within the old system only in order to reform it. The Wilsonian program, meant to produce a middle way between reaction and revolution, included national self-determination, representative government, a league of nations, an end to formal empires, nonrecognition of revolutionary change, democratic liberties and human rights, reduction of armaments, a belief in an "enlightened public opinion," and an open-door world economy. The economic objectives were an important element, but only part of the picture. The United States saw itself as a disinterested, innocent power, whose own desires and aims were thought to express the yearnings of all people, and whose responsibilities were to become inescapable and worldwide.

But, almost immediately after the First World War, a disillusioned American polity put aside the pursuit of the program, though not its values. Europe slid into political and economic chaos, and then again into war. The men guiding U.S. policy in the 1940s had witnessed events in their own lifetimes that provided a compelling impetus for once again trying to make Woodrow Wilson's enterprise work. They saw the Great Depression as a very close call for their own kind of liberal capitalist society. The rise of the dictatorships and the experience of two world wars made their quest for a different kind of world order even more urgent. They wanted to fulfill the Wilsonian vision so that, as Secretary of State Cordell Hull told Congress in 1943, "there will no longer be a need for spheres of influence, for alliances, for balance of power, or any other of the special arrangements through which, in the unhappy past, the nations strove to safeguard their security or to promote their interests." These men thought the best of all worlds was a world without nazism, communism, and colonialism. This desire was not cynical. They feared that a world laden with reaction or revolution would be a world dangerous for American society, a rapacious world soon to be embroiled again in war. And autocracy of any kind offended their deepest democratic instincts.

The unhappy past was much with Ameircan leaders. "I cannot tell you how much I appreciate your very comforting letter recalling the obstacles of 1919," James Byrnes, who became Secretary of State in 1945, wrote to a friend in December of that year, shortly before flying to Moscow to continue the arid attempts to make a postwar settlement with the Russians. "As I read your letter I recalled the hurdles we had to overcome after World War I. . . . It is remarkable how history repeats itself."

But, as it sought to remove conflict and anarchy from international relations, Wilsonianism was truly seeking to abolish the very substance of world politics—balance of power, spheres of influence, power politics. These are the ineluctable features of an international system composed of sovereign nations. It is paradoxical, but in order to achieve his goals, a Wilsonian must be a renegade Wilsonian, like Franklin Roosevelt, facing the world as it is, not as one would wish it to be, using traditional means to achieve Wilsonian ends.

The Soviet leaders, on the other hand, shared none of the Wilsonian values. Though they spoke in the language of Marxism-Leninism, they were primarily concerned with power as traditionally conceived in the international system. They were carving a sphere of influence, a glacis, out of bordering countries. As they did so, a great debate developed within the American policy elite over how to evaluate Soviet intentions and capabilities. Was that sphere all Russia wanted or was it only a first step on a road to world revolution?

Underlying the debate were two related questions that have always confronted those in the West who have to shape policies toward the Soviet Union. They are the same two questions we face today.

The first was raised by the October 1917 Revolution itself. What is the connection between Marxist-Leninist ideology and Soviet foreign policy? The ideology proclaims that communism will inevitably inherit the entire world from capitalism, and calls upon Marxist-Leninists to be the conscious agents of the revolution. But the men who have ruled the Soviet Union were not and are not merely ideologues with many idle hours to dream about tomorrow's utopia. For the most part, they must concern themselves with today, with governing a powerful state that has pressing interests to protect, dangers to avoid, tasks to accomplish, and problems to solve. "There is no revolutionary movement in the West," said Stalin during the debates over the Brest-

Litovsk treaty in 1918. "There are no facts; there is only a possibility, and with possibilities we cannot reckon."

The second question was brutally posed by the horrors of Stalinism, in particular by collectivization and the Great Terror of the 1930s. Does a totalitarian practice at home necessarily produce a foreign policy that is totalitarian in intent, committed to overturning the international system and to endless expansion in pursuit of world dominance? The policies of Adolf Hitler seemed to confirm that a powerful relationship did exist between such domestic practice and international behavior.

The changes wrought by the Second World War gave urgent and highest priority to these questions. What was the American response to be? Within the ensuring debate, there were two sets of generalizations, two interpretations that competed for hegemony in the American policy elite in the middle 1940s. At the heart of the first set was an image of the Soviet Union as a world revolutionary state, denying the possibilities of coexistence, committed to unrelenting ideological warfare, powered by a messianic drive for world mastery. The second set downplayed the role of ideology and the foreign policy consequences of authoritarian domestic practices, and instead saw the Soviet Union behaving like a traditional Great Power within the international system, rather than trying to overthrow it. The first set I call, for shorthand, the Riga axioms; the second, the Yalta axioms.*

The Riga axioms triumphed in American policy circles in the postwar years and provided a foundation for the anticommunist consensus. Charles Bohlen summarized this outlook when he wrote to former Secretary of State Edward Stettinius in 1949. "I am quite convinced myself, and I think all of those who have been working specifically on the problems of relations with the Soviet Union are in agreement," said Bohlen, "that the reasons for the state of tension that exists in the world today between the Soviet Union and the non-Soviet world are to be found in the character and nature of the Soviet state, the doctrines to which it faithfully adheres, and not in such matters as the shutting off of Lend-Lease and the question of a loan."

With a view of this sort, the effort to make a diplomatic settlement became irrelevant, even dangerous, for the Cold War confrontation was thought to be almost genetically preordained in the revolutionary, messianic, predatory character of the Soviet Union.

Though not so named, the Riga and Yalta axioms still today pro-

---

*To my knowledge no one ever before referred to these two interpretative structures as the Riga and Yalta axioms. My reasons for doing so will become clear as the narrative unfolds.

vide the points of reference for the continuing debate about how to organize U.S. relations with the Soviet Union. The Riga axioms help form the outlook of the Cold War. The Yalta axioms underlie détente.

Neither set of axioms had a monopoly on the truth. Both emphasized some aspects of reality, and obscured others. No decent human being, whatever his political values, can be anything but appalled by the monstrous horrors of the Stalinist regime. As Solzhenitsyn has written, the prison camps stretched across the Soviet Union like a great archipelago. As many as twenty million people may have died because of Stalin's tyranny. So awful is the legacy that the Soviet leadership today, a quarter century after the dictator's death, still cannot acknowledge what Khrushchev called Stalin's "crimes." To do so would be to undermine the very legitimacy of the Soviet system.

The terror merely abated during the time of the Grand Alliance. Of her experiences during the war years, Nadezhda Mandelstam, the widow of the poet Osip Mandelstam, writes: "By this time I had talked with many people who had returned from the camps (and most of them were sent back to them in the second half of the forties)." She asks, "What manner of people were they, those who first decreed and then carried out this mass destruction of their own kind?" There is no good answer. But she pleads, "No one should lightly dismiss our experience, as complacent foreigners do, cherishing the hope that with them—who are so clever and cultured—things will be different."

For my part, I do not want to suggest that Stalin's character, intentions, or methods were, by any means, benign or kindly. But in the international arena, Stalin's politics were not those of a single-minded world revolutionist. The truth is that the Soviet Union's foreign policy was often clumsy and brutal, sometimes confused, but usually cautious and pragmatic. The U.S.S.R. behaved as a traditional Great Power, intent upon aggrandizing itself along the lines of historic Russian goals, favoring spheres of influence, secret treaties, Great Power consortiums, and the other methods and mores from the "old diplomacy." Moreover, if the Soviet Union had harbored ambitions of unlimited expansion, it was hardly in a position to pursue them. Unlike the United States, whose gross national product had actually doubled during the war, it was a ruined, ravaged country in 1945.

American leaders who accepted the Riga axioms misinterpreted both the range and degree of the Soviet challenge and the character of Soviet objectives and so downplayed the possibilities for diplomacy and accommodation. It was the new doctrine of "national security" that led them to believe that the U.S.S.R. presented an *immediate military* threat to the United States. That doctrine, an expansive interpretation of American security needs, represented a major redefinition of America's relation to the rest of the world.

If American interests were in jeopardy everywhere in the world, the exercise of Soviet power anywhere outside Russian borders appeared ominous. Any form of compromise was therefore regarded as appeasement, already once tried and once failed.

The doctrine of national security also permitted America's postwar leaders to harmonize the conflicting demands of Wilsonianism and realpolitik—to be democratic idealists and pragmatic realists at the same time. So emboldened, American leaders pursued a global, often crusading, foreign policy, convinced that it was made urgent by something more earthy than the missionary impulse of Woodrow Wilson.

History is shaped by the time in which it is written. This work was researched and executed during the latter years of the Vietnam War and the period of what might be called tentative détente. Consequently, two separate questions have informed my inquiry. First, I wanted to determine, if I could, the origins of the ideologies, policies, and institutions that played a major role in the U.S. intervention in Indochina. That is, what gave rise to the national security state? Of course, it would be simplistic to say that the ideology, policies, and institutions that are the subject of this book in themselves *caused* the Vietnam War. Nor do I mean to suggest that the United States alone is "guilty" of possessing a national security state or that, somehow, the national security state is a creature of capitalism. As embedded as the national security state may be in our political and economic system, a national security state is even more firmly entrenched in the Soviet Union, beyond the reach of question. Indeed, the U.S.S.R. might be called a "total security state." . . .

And so, equipped with the requisite budgets, the national security state grew as an awesome collage of money, institutions, ideology, interests, commitments, capabilities, and firepower. The 1977 peacetime defense budget of the United States was over $104 billion. The national security state has long since acquired a life of its own. It has helped to create a powerful presidency, and has turned legions of "private" companies into permanent clients of the Defense Department. Of course, the national security state does not exist apart from other realities. It has grown, in part, dialectically with the "total security state" of the Soviet Union.

This book has narrated the rise of America's national security state, and the origins of the Cold War and the postwar international system. Today, more than three decades after its inception, the international order wrought by the Cold War is breaking down. Economic issues have become matters of high politics, cutting across political alignments. The respective unities of the Eastern and Western blocs have been reduced, and new power centers are making their influence felt. In the communist world, the schism with Yugoslavia was followed by the much more significant split with China. A third schism between the Soviet Union and the Western communist parties may be imminent. The monopoly over military force by the two superpowers has also been reduced by the proliferation of conventional weapons and of nuclear capabilities.

The American commitment to Vietnam resulted from the postwar world set of U.S. leaders. The Riga axioms and the doctrine of national security made Indochina appear a crucial arena in what was perceived as a struggle to frustrate the "fundamental design" of communism. The consequences of that intervention have taught us that "fundamental designs" may be illusory and that global implications may be secondary to local issues. The Vietnam experience has thus created new checks on both intervention and the imperial presidency, and has also raised central questions about the entire world view.

The marked weakening of the anticommunist consensus in the United States has, on the American side, helped to make possible a new kind of relationship with the Soviet Union—tentative détente. This does not mean an end to the competition between the two superpowers. But it does mean a somewhat more explicit agreement on the rules of competition; a certain number of cooperative projects, of which arms control, based on the purported acceptance of parity, is the most important; increasing communication and contacts on many levels; and a reduction in the state of permanent alarm on both sides. In practice, it means a return to the Yalta axioms as the basic mode of dealing with the Soviet world, and perhaps a vindication for Franklin Roosevelt and his aims and methods in those fateful negotiations with Stalin and Churchill during the winter of 1945 in the ballroom of the Czar's summer palace. Détente is not possible with a world revolutionary state, but it is with a more conventional imperialistic and somewhat cautious nation, interested as much in protecting what it has as in extending its influence. With a country of this sort, the United States can uneasily coexist.

Make no mistake. A reduction in tension does not mean that the worthy Wilsonian vision of a harmonious international order is at hand. In dealing with the Soviet Union, in trying to analyze its objectives and capabilities, we continue to tread, as George Kennan wrote in his diary in 1950, "in the unfirm substance of the imponderables." The global antagonism between the Soviet Union and the United States does remain the single most important and dangerous element in international politics. The balance of terror is now measured in megatons so large that no human being can comprehend the horrors that an atomic war would bring. It continues to be a balance between the United States and the Soviet Union—each one's missiles remain targeted on the other.

So the Cold War is still very much with us, as are the ever-perplexing questions about the Soviet Union's role in international politics and about the means, meaning, and measure of American security. There are no final answers, only the spectacle of men and women moved by ambitions and opportunities, beset by fears and dangers, struggling to find transient certainties midst the onrush of events. We cannot therefore regard the story of the shattered peace as merely a fascinating and tragic history. It is, in truth, still the story of the origins of our own time.

Samuel P. Huntington

SAMUEL P. HUNTINGTON (1927–   ) is professor of government at Harvard University. He has written a number of books on modernization and civil–military relations, including *The Soldier and the State* (1957), *Political Order in Changing Societies* (1960), *The Common Defense* (1961), and (with Joan Nelson) *No Easy Choice* (1976).

The influence of military professionals in American society between 1946 and 1955 was significantly less than it had been during World War II. Nonetheless, it was still at an unprecedented level in the absence of total war. The extent to which professional military officers assumed nonmilitary roles in government, industry, and politics, and developed affiliations with nonmilitary groups was a new phenomenon in American history. Military officers wielded far greater power in the United States during this period than they did in any other major country. Three of the most significant manifestations of their influence were: (1) the influx of military officers into governmental positions normally occupied by civilians; (2) the close ties which developed between military leaders and business leadership; and (3) the widespread popularity and prestige of individual military figures.

In analyzing these postwar military roles, two issues are of peculiar importance. First, was the increased influence of the military due fundamentally to factors associated with World War II, and, consequently, a temporary phenomenon? Or did it arise from causes associated with the Cold War and, consequently, something which might continue indefinitely into the future? Unquestionably, the increased military imperatives stemming from America's involvement in world politics contributed to a much higher level of military influence than ever existed prior to 1940. Nonetheless, military influence during the first postwar decade was also in many respects an aftermath of World War II, a carryover into peacetime both of the prestige and influence which the military acquired between 1940 and 1945 and of the weakness of civilian institutions and leadership during those years.

Second, was increased military influence accompanied by more widespread acceptance of the professional military viewpoint? In general, the inverse relationship between these two factors which had prevailed earlier in American society continued throughout the 1946–1955 period. A significant gap existed between the rapid and extensive rise of military influence and the considerably less success of military demands and military requirements. Those military elements which acquired the greatest political influence went farthest in abandoning the professional ethic, and their diversified roles made it easier for civilians to reject the postulates of professional military thinking. On issues where there was a clear-cut distinction between the professional military viewpoint and the traditional American civilian attitudes, such as universal military service and the size of the military budget, the latter usually triumphed. Indeed, American military policy throughout these years was in many ways a series of continuing efforts to escape from the professional military conclusion that the best means of achieving military security is through the maintenance of substantial forces in being.

Participation in Civil Government

The penetration of professional officers into governmental positions not requiring solely military skills took two forms: military occupancy of conjoint positions combining military and political functions, and military occupancy of civilian positions with exclusively nonmilitary functions.

The most notable examples of conjoint positions were: (1) the military governorships of occupied territories such as existed in Germany until 1949 and in Japan until 1952; (2) international military commands such as the North Atlantic Treaty Organization's SHAPE and the United Nations Korean Command; and (3) military advisory and training groups in nations receiving American aid. The conjoint positions reflected the failure of governmental organization to adjust rapidly enough to increased functional specialization. They were one area where fusionist theory was manifested in reality. In the absence of appropriate institutional mechanisms for the separate performance of the military and political responsibilities, the occupants of the conjoint positions discharged both duties. The occupation governorships were a temporary phenomenon developing out of World War II. While hostilities were still in progress and immediately after their termination, the separation of political and military functions was virtually impossible. Military government and civil affairs were naturally handled through the military command organization. After the end of the war, however, the military security function in the occupied territory declined in importance; the immediate problems were economic, social, political, and constitutional. Theoretically, military control should at this point have given way to civilian direction, and in the French, British, and Russian zones of Germany, civilian control did replace military control. The national popularity and political support of General MacArthur, however, made it impossible to reduce him to the status of a military subordinate to a civilian occupation governor. In Germany, the reluctance of the State Department to undertake the responsibility for occupation rule prolonged military control until 1949. In the Far East and in Germany large staffs, devoted purely to political and civil affairs, developed to assist the military governor in the discharge of his political responsibilities. In one form or another, these staffs, largely civilian in composition, were subsumed under or attached to the military command organization.

The international military commands were a reaction to military security threats stemming from the Cold War. Consequently, as a type they were a more permanent manifestation of conjoint office. The Commanders in Chief of SHAPE and of the United Nations Command in the Far East both had to devote substantial portions of their time to the discharge of political and diplomatic duties. The more *ad hoc* nature of the UN Command precluded any effort to develop means of segregating political and military responsibilities. In Europe, on the other hand, the initial creation of the SHAPE military organization and the piloting of it through its first tests required a unique combination of military, political, and diplomatic skills. Once the structure was established, however, a degree of segregation of function became possible. The more thoroughly military approaches of Ridgway and Gruenther to their job and the emergence of the civilian organization under Lord Ismay both reflected an effort to disassociate military and civilian activities in NATO. The complete segregation of the two functions, however, required the development of new forms of international political institutions which were probably impractical. Consequently, under a military guise and through military mechanisms, the commanders and staffs of NATO continued to perform political functions which the exigencies of politics did not permit to be performed more openly.

The military advisory groups to nations receiving American military assistance combined diplomatic and military responsibilities. By virtue of their control over the most significant form of American assistance, the advisory group and its chief at times tended to absorb duties and influence which properly belonged to the ambassador and the State Department. While the problem of the organizing of civil and military representation in foreign countries on such a scale was relatively new to the United States, it had in the past been effectively dealt with by other nations. American military assistance and advisory groups will undoubtedly continue as a relatively permanent fixture in the conduct of American foreign affairs, and the eventual delimitation of responsibilities and duties between military and civil missions abroad should not present unsoluble difficulties.

Prior to World War II professional military officers occasionally held civilian positions in the national government. However, the scope of military penetration into the civilian hierarchy after World War II was completely without precedent in American history. In 1948 it was estimated that one hundred and fifty military men occupied important policy-making posts in civilian government. Many of the most significant appointive positions in the government were at one time or another occupied by military officers. The reasons behind this influx of officers into civil posts were complex: some represented factors which had long been present in the American scene; some were the result of World War II; some derived from the new and continuing demands of the Cold War.

(1) Traditional appointments had been continuingly characteristic of American civil-military relations. In some areas of the federal government a tradition of military appointments antedated World War II. Officers were appointed to these positions either upon detached duty from their services or after retirement. The most significant areas of traditional appointments were closely associated with the technical specialties of the two services. Naval officers were frequently selected for federal posts connected with maritime affairs. Between 1937 and 1949, for instance, the United States Maritime Commission always had one to three officers among its five members, and throughout much of its life it was headed by an admiral. From an early period, Army engineering officers had been often appointed to civilian public works positions. In the thirties the New Deal utilized the services of a number of officers in the WPA and similar agencies, and their employment in comparable positions was continued by the Truman and Eisenhower administrations. In another area, the directorship of veterans' affairs to which General Bradley was appointed in 1945 had been occupied by another general since 1923. Although Bradley was succeeded by a civilian, it seems legitimate to conclude that a tradition of military occupancy also inheres in this post. The traditional appointments reflected civilian desire to capitalize upon special types of nonmilitary expertise possessed by certain classes of professional officers. They appeared to be a continuing and relatively constant phenomenon in American government.

(2) Honorific and political appointments were peculiarly characteristic of the years immediately following World War II. After World War II many military appointments were designed primarily to honor

or reward military commanders who had distinguished themselves in the war. The selection of leading generals and admirals to serve on the American Battle Monuments Commission, the appointment of various military figures to *ad hoc* commissions, and some appointments of military men as ambassadors fell into this category. Honorific appointments were more frequent under Truman's administration than under Eisenhower's. Many of the military appointments between 1945 and 1953 also undoubtedly reflected the desire of the Truman Administration to utilize the political popularity of the top World War II commanders to carry the burden of its foreign policies. Probably the most notable instance where this motivation was present was the employment of General Marshall as presidential envoy to China, Secretary of State, and Secretary of Defense. Honorific and political appointments were both temporary phenomena. No subsequent administration was likely to have quite the peculiar need for such political support that the Truman Administration did, and nothing short of total war was likely to produce popular military heroes of sufficient stature to furnish such support or to be eligible for honorary posts.

(3) Administrative appointments reflected the new but continuing demands of the Cold War. The great bulk of the military appointments to civil positions in the postwar decade occurred in the foreign affairs and defense agencies and may be termed "administrative" in nature. They derived from new imperatives likely to remain in existence for an indefinite length of time. Before 1933 the personnel requirements of the federal government were fairly small. The expansion of the domestic agencies during the New Deal period was handled by the movement to Washington of program-oriented professional workers, academicians, lawyers, and others. To perform its wartime activities the government attracted business and professional men through the double appeal of the temporary nature of its employment and the patriotic duty of government service. The staffing of those significant foreign affairs and defense activities which continued after 1945, however, presented a difficult problem. The temporary war employees dispersed homeward; the New Dealers were generally uninterested in foreign affairs; and the businessmen were generally unwilling to work for the Democratic administration. No ready source of civilians with administrative and diplomatic skills was available. Consequently, the military were called upon to fill the vacuum. The officers were willing to serve, used to public employment, accustomed to low salaries, untainted by leftist affiliations, and divorced from ties with special interest groups. While military skills were not prerequisite for the positions to which they were appointed, their military background furnished them with certain types of experience and training not possessed by any significant groups of available citizens. The State De-

partment, in particular among civilian agencies, required experienced, competent personnel in the immediate postwar years and utilized the services of professional officers. The proportion of officers in civilian foreign affairs and defense posts tended to decline after 1946 and 1947, and the Eisenhower Administration to some extent replaced professional officers with recruits from business. The complete elimination of military administrative appointments, however, depended upon the development of a continuing source of high-level civilian administrators with education and experience in this field superior to those of the military.

The influx of military men into civilian posts aroused considerable criticism, particularly in the years from 1946 through 1948. The military appointments were held to be a sign of the militarization of the government, the abandonment of civilian control, and the imminency of the garrison state. Congress refused to approve three of President Truman's military appointments. The selection of General Marshall as Secretary of Defense in 1950 stimulated renewed debate of the issue. Some of the Eisenhower Administration's military appointees met vigorous congressional opposition. Virtually all the criticism of the military influx was couched in terms of abstract constitutional and political principles and generalized dangers to civil government. With a few exceptions, it was impossible to demonstrate that the actions of any particular military officer reflected the inherently dangerous qualities of the military mind. It was all very well to cite the general influx of military men as evidence of a trend toward the garrison state. But, when one got down to the specifics of Bradley as Veterans Administrator or Marshall as Secretary of State, the threat of militarization rapidly evaporated. The professional officers blended into their new civilian milieu, serving nonmilitary ends, motivated by nonmilitary considerations, and performing their jobs little differently from their civilian predecessors and successors. Undoubtedly the officers who moved into the State Department in 1946 and 1947 did contribute to the more conservative outlook which developed in that department during those years. Yet even this was largely an adjustment to the civilian environment, for the new approach to foreign policy which became dominant in the Department in 1947 and 1948 had deep roots in the Department's own professional staff. The general ease with which the officers adjusted to their civilian roles and outlook forced their critics to shift to the argument that, although the particular officers appointed were harmless exceptions to the desirable rule, dangerous precedents were being set for the future. This, too, was unconvincing. The "civilianizing" of the officers was not the exception. It was instead the only rule which American liberalism would permit.

The Military-Business Rapprochement

Few developments more dramatically symbolized the new status of the military in the postwar decade than the close associations which they developed with the business elite of American society. Prior to World War II, the professional officers and the capitalists in spirit and in fact had been poles apart. The American business community had little use for military needs, little appreciation of the military outlook, and little respect for military men. The military reciprocated in kind. After World War II, an abrupt change took place in this relationship. Professional officers and businessmen revealed a new mutual respect. Retired generals and admirals in unprecedented numbers moved into the executive staffs of American corporations; new organizations arose bridging the gap between corporate management and military leadership. For the military officers, business represented the epitome of the American way of life. Association with business was positive proof and assurance that they had abandoned their outcaste status and had become respected members of the American community. Financially and psychologically, the military men who moved from the officers corps to the corporation gained in security, acceptance, and well-being. The business firms, on the other hand, capitalized upon the prestige of well-known commanders, the special skills and expertise of the officers in nonmilitary technical fields, their general administrative and organizing abilities, and their assistance in doing business with the Department of Defense. The ties that bound the two groups together in the postwar decade were apparently many and strong. In actuality, they rested upon two quite different foundations: one broad in scope but temporary in duration; the other more restricted but also more permanent.

The more ephemeral basis of the military-business alliance was the prestige of the military from World War II. Big business was eager to employ famous battle commanders: MacArthur went to Remington Rand, Bedell Smith to American Machine and Foundry, Bradley to Bulova, Halsey to International Standard Electric. This type of appointment was necessarily a temporary phenomenon, the Cold War producing few military figures of sufficient prestige to be of interest to business. The businesses which appointed these officers were usually large manufacturing corporations, holding sizable defense contracts, but so large and diversified as to be in most cases neither exclusively nor even primarily dependent upon government business. The military heroes came in at the top of the corporate structure, assuming posts as president, vice president, board chairman, or director. Although a few had occurred after World War I, prestige appointments on this scale were quite unprecedented in the United States. They were the American equivalent of the British practice of rewarding successful generals with peerages, a commercial society substituting corporation presidencies and board chairmanships for earldoms and viscounties. The military heroes, on the other hand, brought glamour and public attention to the businesses. The corporations were honored and so were the generals. The large industrial concerns which hired the military men, however, had been the principal locus of opposition to a large military establishment. They were the major institutional base of business liberalism and the dominating element in the National Association of Manufacturers, which consistently demanded the reduction of military expenditures. There is little evidence that their employment of the military officers signalized any fundamental change in what Walter H. McLaughlin, Jr., has described as their "indifferent attitude" toward military affairs. Nor, apparently, were the officers able to work any change in the business political outlook. The corporations accepted the officers and utilized their talents and reputations, but they did not accept the professional military viewpoint. Insofar as there was a rapprochement in thinking between the military heroes and their business colleagues, it was the military men who made the concessions, adjusting to their new environment by surrendering their professional outlook.

A more restricted but more lasting tie developed between the military leadership and those businesses supplying goods to the Department of Defense. Prior to 1940, the Army and Navy offered little in the way of markets to American industry. In World War I industry had accepted large defense contracts only to suffer dislocation and hardship when they were abruptly canceled at the end of hostilities. As a result, business was most reluctant to take on military orders again in 1939 and 1940. Once the United States entered the war, of course, industry cooperated wholeheartedly in the production of military goods and equipment, and hundreds of businessmen went to Washington to work in the War and Navy Departments. The rapid demobilization in 1945 and 1946 first seemed to indicate a repetition of the post-World War I pattern. In due course, however, and particularly after the outbreak of the Korean War, it became obvious that the Cold War military demand was going to be substantial and relatively stable. The dollar volume of military orders and the complex technological requirements of the modern armed forces brought a significant permanent defense industry into existence for the first time in the United States. The defense suppliers were composed in part of large general manufacturing corporations, such as those in the automobile industry, which furnished military items while at the same time catering to the civilian market. On the other hand, some industries, such as the aircraft manufacturers and sections of the electronics industry, were almost totally dependent upon military orders.

The economic nexus which joined the defense producers to the military was reflected both in the large numbers of former officers who entered the management of these companies and in the various organizations which developed to cement the military-business tie. The officers hired by the defense producers were not normally well-known public figures, but rather younger men who entered the corporations in operational rather than honorific positions. Most of the officers were technical experts in some specialized scientific field and many had held high positions in the Army's technical services and in the Navy's bureaus. Some of them resigned from the service to pursue their careers in business. The technical specialists employed by defense industries constituted the largest single group of general and flag officers hired by private business in the postwar decade. The aircraft companies and their associated industries alone accounted for a significant portion of them. Unlike the prestige appointments, this type of business-military arrangement appeared to increase rather than decrease during the course of the postwar decade.

The professionalization of the military in the 1880's and 1890's and their withdrawal from society had been reflected in the organization of numerous military associations designed for officers only. The return of the military to society and their close links with the Cold War defense industries were marked by the formation of a different type of organization open both to officers and to civilians and business firms. Probably most significant among these groups was the National Security Industrial Association organized by James Forrestal in 1944 to insure that "American business will remain close to the services." The Association in 1954 was composed of six hundred industrial firms, virtually all of whom had significant defense contracts. Many officers of the Association were former generals or admirals. The Association was principally active in helping its member firms and the Department of Defense resolve problems of production techniques, procurement, and patents. The Armed Forces Chemical Association and the Armed Froces Communications Association came into existence in the immediate postwar years to bridge the gap between the interested segments of the military and of business. The previously existing Quartermaster Association, formed in 1920 as an organization of military officers only, was broadened to admit civilians to active membership and to provide for company membership. The Army Ordnance Association, founded in 1919, was reorganized as the American Ordnance Association, covering all three services. While its staff was composed largely of retired military officers, the thirty-five thousand members of AOA were mostly representatives of ordnance manufacturers. Both

the Aircraft Industries Association and the Air Force Association provided links between the aviation industries and the military.

In general, the defense businesses supported for economic reasons
the same military policies which the officers supported for professional
reasons. Exceptions to this existed, of course, in the case of businesses
interested in producing or continuing to produce weapons or equipment not believed essential by professional judgment. But on the whole
a coincidence of viewpoint existed which permitted the officers an easier association with defense industry than with those businesses which
had more diversified customers. Corporation officials and military officials shared a common interest in technological development, and
the defense industries for the first time in American history furnished
the military program with a significant base of economic support. In
other respects, however, association with the defense industries did
not aid military professionalism. Inevitably, the businesses thought of
themselves first and attracted to their staffs many younger officers who
still had many years of useful service to offer their country. In the middle 1950's over two thousand regular officers each year were leaving
the services for the more lucrative positions in business. In addition,
there was the likelihood that the ability to move from one of the technical branches of the armed forces into a well-paying industry job would
enhance the popularity and attractiveness of the technical staffs as
against the line. A very small proportion of the business appointments
in the postwar decade went to military commanders who were neither
famous public figures nor technical specialists, but simply regular line
officers with backgrounds in military command. The businesses who
hired these officers seemed to assume that any general or flag officer
must necessarily be a good aministrator. Their relatively small numbers, however, were indicative of the gap which still remained between
even defense business and the more strictly professional military elements of the services. A major general whose principal experience was
in commanding regiments and divisions had little to offer the manufacturing corporation.

☆ 11 ☆

Welfare in America

SOCIAL CONTROL OR REFORM?

Between the 1960s and the mid-1980s, Americans engaged in an acrimonious debate on a series of major social policy issues. The dialogue often reflected fundamental ideological and philosophical differences about the nature of American society, the proper role of government, and the behavior of individuals within society. Abstract issues were inevitably recast in political terms as Americans tried to come to grips with certain problems such as racism, sexism, crime, and poverty.

Beneath the rhetoric and passion lay conflicting views about the sources from which these social problems sprang, especially poverty and crime. On one side were those who insisted that poverty was a moral rather than an economic or social condition. Poverty resulted from defective character traits; individuals were poor because they were weak, lazy, or immoral. Indeed, the relationship between poverty, crime, and ignorance was so striking that, rather than being mutually exclusive, these categories often overlapped. To be sure, a distinction was made between the "worthy" and "unworthy" poor. The condition of the "worthy poor" was due to external or accidental causes—death, illness, infirmity, or aging. Individuals in this category merited some form of assistance. The "unworthy poor," on the other hand, deserved to be subjected to a harsh public policy—a policy designed to penalize laziness, enforce independence, and correct moral behavior. To those who held to such an ideology the function of government was to be minimal. Government was to provide assistance only on a selective basis and enforce social order against those who habitually violated accepted norms. The obligation of government, in other words, was simply to ensure equal opportunity for all citizens even though the outcome might result in economic inequality.

On the other side were those who insisted that dependency and poverty were rooted in the very structure of American economic and political life. Moral and character deficiencies had little to do with being poor. Some individuals requiring welfare assistance were casualties of unemployment, underemployment, or the victims of racial, sexual, or ethnic discrimination. Many were aged persons with no means of providing for themselves and who were without a family. Some came from families whose incomes were marginal. Others came from households where death or illness had led to reduced economic circumstances. Still others—because of race, ethnicity, or sex—faced structural barriers that severely limited their opportunities and doomed them to a place at the bottom of the economic ladder. Because dependency, poverty, crime, and illness were all rooted in the structure of society, government had a positive obligation to aid its less fortunate citizens. The goal of public policy should be to provide such individuals with the means of survival and to assist them in overcoming those barriers that inhibited equal opportunity.

Between the Great Depression of the 1930s and the 1970s, the American people and both political parties came to accept the ideology of the modern welfare state (although disagreement on specific details persisted). The concept of the welfare state was based on the premise that responsibility for health, education, and welfare rested with both government and the individual. Americans had a right to be protected against the ravages of illness, aging, unemployment, substandard environmental conditions, racism, and sexism. Beginning with the New Deal and continuing to the 1970s federal activities and expenditures expanded rapidly as the national government attempted to meet its new responsibilities.

The election of Ronald Reagan in 1980 ended the consensus that had been forged during the previous half century. Just as Lyndon B. Johnson's Great Society program in the 1960s reflected a commitment to a welfare state ideology, so Reagan's policies represented an effort to dismantle basic social welfare programs and thus reverse the direction of recent American history. The function of the federal government, Reagan insisted, was to defend the United States against external enemies and conduct foreign relations. With the exception of social security Reagan wanted to diminish, if not eliminate, the social welfare responsibilities of the federal government.

The writing of welfare history, curiously enough, did not parallel the public debate. Most historians concluded that poverty and dependency had structural and environmental roots. Heir to the Progressive school tradition they accepted the legitimacy of the welfare state ideology and rejected the claim that poverty grew out of character deficiencies.

Despite their liberal political views American historians before 1945 generally ignored the history of poverty and dependency. In 1931

Marcus W. Jernegan's pioneering study of laboring and dependent classes in the seventeenth and eighteenth centuries appeared, but this classic work was not followed by others.[1] Historians focused upon more traditional topics in political, diplomatic, and economic history; welfare remained a marginal field.

This is not to imply that welfare history was ignored, for such was not the case. Welfare was a central concern of social workers, and the history of welfare held a prominent position in their training curriculum. During the 1930s Edith Abbott and Sophonisba Breckinridge, the driving forces behind the School of Social Service Administration at the University of Chicago, helped to create the field of welfare history by founding the journal *Social Service Review*. They also trained a generation of social workers in the history of social welfare. Both these scholars, as well as their students, stimulated the publication of other works dealing with the development of social work as a profession and the history of public welfare legislation. Their aim was to assist in the training and socialization of young social workers and of future policy officials involved with social policy toward dependent groups. Hence the field of welfare history, at least in its beginnings, represented the practical concerns and needs of social work educators.

It was only after World War II that historians began to recognize welfare history as a legitimate field of inquiry. In 1956 Robert H. Bremner published a seminal work on poverty in the United States. Using a wide range of records he traced the development of attitudes and policies toward poverty and the poor throughout much of American history. Americans, he noted, first became aware of poverty in their midst in the nineteenth century. At the outset slum dwellers and other lower-class groups were viewed with hostility by more fortunate Americans. Solvent and successful Americans attributed poverty to character deficiencies and immoral behavior on the part of the poor. Slowly but surely, however, Americans began to realize that the industrial and economic causes of misery were more significant than the moral, and that social rather than individual reforms were more appropriate remedies for overcoming poverty. This new social view of poverty set the stage for a fundamental transformation in public policy toward dependency in the twentieth century. Bremner's interpretation, of course, was squarely within the Progressive school tradition of American historiography; he interpreted the activities of social reformers in humanitarian and democratic terms and clearly approved their agenda for beneficent social change.[2]

---

[1]Marcus W. Jernegan, *Laboring and Dependent Classes in America 1607–1789* (Chicago, 1931).

[2]Robert H. Bremner, *From the Depths: The Discovery of Poverty in the United States* (New York, 1956).

At about the same time that Bremner was calling attention to the history of poverty and public policy, Merle Curti, the distinguished historian at the University of Wisconsin, was encouraging his graduate students to undertake the study of philanthropy and charity in America. Some of Curti's students soon made some significant scholarly contributions. One of the first, and in many ways the most influential, was Allen F. Davis's analysis of the settlement house movement during the Progressive era. Settlement house workers, Davis wrote, were idealists who believed that they could solve some of the problems of the sprawling, crowded city. Their vision was broad; they fought for educational change, for better housing, for laws to protect working women and children, and for parks and playgrounds. Above all, they insisted that the social environment, not individual weakness, was the single most significant cause of poverty. They urged, therefore, that private philanthropy and government form a partnership to deal with the social problems of an urban industrial order. Conceding that settlement house workers did not accomplish all of their goals, Davis nevertheless gave them high praise for their vision and activities. Like Bremner, Davis wrote within the Progressive school tradition; settlement house workers in his view were part of the liberal struggle for a more humane and democratic social order.[3]

The growing interest in welfare history was reenforced by the founding of the Social History Welfare Archives in 1963 at the University of Minnesota by Clarke Chambers, author of an influential and pioneering book dealing with social reform in the post–World War I era.[4] The Archives began to collect records of the major social work and welfare associations and agencies, thereby stimulating further research. Welfare history thus acquired legitimacy among historians as well as social work educators.

By the early 1960s historians of welfare had arrived at a general interpretation of the subject. In their view the goal of social reform was to ameliorate the harsh conditions created by the rise of the new urban industrial order and changes in the economic and social living conditions of lower-class and disadvantaged groups. Schools, almshouses, mental hospitals, homes for juveniles, settlement houses, social welfare agencies—the institutional products of the activities of social reformers—were all designed to mitigate the harsher aspects of modern society. Their creation was motivated mainly by humanitarian and benevolent concerns. Social reform thus contributed to the diffu-

[3]Allen F. Davis, *Spearheads for Reform: The Social Settlements and the Progressive Movement 1890–1914* (New York, 1967).

[4]Clarke A. Chambers, *Seedtime of Reform: American Social Service and Social Action, 1918–1933* (Minneapolis, 1963).

sion of the benefits of industrialization to those at the bottom of the social scale.[5]

At the same time that welfare history was emerging as a subject in its own right, the focus of American historians began to shift. The traditional concern with leaders and elite groups was replaced by a new sensitivity toward those "inarticulate" social groups who constituted the majority of the population. The movement for racial, sexual, and economic equality that became so pervasive in the 1960s sensitized many Americans to the fact that they were not only citizens, but belonged to racial, sexual, and ethnic groups as well—to say nothing about a great awareness of their class affiliation. Group awareness, in turn, stimulated research into the history of hitherto ignored social groups—blacks, women, children, ethnic minorities, the aged, and others.

Concern over the plight of the inarticulate, the poor, and the powerless mirrored the prevailing social unrest and radicalism of the 1960s and early 1970s. During this era the civil rights movement helped to focus attention on the pervasive racism and sexism in American society, thus preparing the groundwork for significant changes in the status of blacks and women. To the current of protest was added the opposition to militarism and the Vietnam War. Critics of this conflict charged that the policies of the government supported right-wing dictatorships, sanctioned immoral acts in the name of freedom and anticommunism, and were an indication of the bankruptcy of American foreign policy and institutions. The emergence of a counterculture offered further evidence that many young persons no longer believed that they lived in a just and egalitarian nation; they emphasized instead its imperialist, exploitative, and authoritarian side.

The protest movements of the 1960s and 1970s took a variety of forms. But whatever the specific form the focus was on inequality—social, racial, sexual, and economic. The general current of unrest was mirrored in the writings of younger scholars—especially those associated with the "new social history" and the New Left. The study of the inarticulate masses and dispossessed peoples, they believed, would provide conclusive evidence of the need for a fundamental restructuring of American society. Consequently they often took a hostile attitude toward elite or affluent groups in their writings. Many "new social historians" who launched their careers in the 1960s were committed not merely to the writing of history, but to the use of history as a political and ideological weapon in the struggle to bring about changes in what they regarded as an unjust social order.

---

[5]For a summary view see Blanche D. Coll, *Perspectives in Public Welfare* (Washington, D.C., 1969), and James Leiby, *A History of Social Welfare and Social Work in the United States* (New York, 1978).

"New social historians," however, were too preoccuppied with the inarticulate and poor to pay much attention to the history of private and public welfare. Neveretheless their approach to American history had the effect of moving welfare history closer to the mainstream. Like scholars identified with the Progressive school of American history, the "new social historians" began with the assumption that economic and technological forces had transformed American society. But their interpretation of the significance of these changes differed from that of their Progressive predecessors. The consequences of these economic and social changes, they insisted, was the emergence of a capitalist social order that fostered continuous inequalities and injustice. Tensions and conflicts in turn threatened the hegemony of the dominant elite groups in American society. Concerned with maintaining social cohesion and order, privileged groups developed institutional mechanisms designed to control lower-class behavior and to inculcate those traits that would serve to perpetuate the established capitalist order.

During the 1960s historians of welfare and "new social historians" (especially those associated with contemporary social protest movements) came into conflict over the concept of "social control." The idea of social control was not new; it had come into use at the turn of the century. In 1901 E. A. Ross, the distinguished American sociologist, published an influential book dealing with the subject. In his work Ross emphasized that there had always been a tension between the behavior of individuals and the common interests and general welfare of the society at large. In premodern societies primary groups—family, religious groups, or the local community—had socialized and controlled the behavior of individuals. The breakdown of the authority of primary groups in modern history, however, created a need for new controls to protect members of society. Social control—the term he used to distinguish between premodern and modern societies—was a synonym for social welfare. It implied that there should be a balance between the desire for unregulated individual freedom and the needs of society for order and justice. As late as the 1930s Helen Everett, writing in the famous *Encyclopedia of the Social Sciences,* noted that social control represented conscious social planning and a trend away from extreme individualism or laissez-faire.[6]

In the turbulent 1960s, however, the term "social control" ac-

<hr>

[6]E. A. Ross, *Social Control: A Survey of the Foundations of Social Order* (New York, 1901), and Helen Everett, "Control, Social," *Encyclopedia of the Social Sciences* (New York, 1930–1935), 4:344—both cited in James Leiby, "Social Control and Historical Explanation: Historians View the Piven and Cloward Thesis," in *Social Welfare or Social Control? Some Historical Reflections on Regulating the Poor,* Walter I. Trattner, ed. (Knoxville, 1983), pp. 97–98.

quired an entirely new meaning. The concept now referred to the means employed by elite groups to perpetuate their privileged position and authority. Ironically the meaning of the concept had undergone a complete metamorphosis. In the early twentieth century it was identified with the revolt against unregulated economic individualism; in the 1960s it became synonymous with the self-interest of a privileged elite.

When this new concept of social control was applied to American history the results were striking. Scholars writing about the history of welfare had previously agreed that educational, charitable, and health-related institutions grew out of a humanitarian and democratic ideology. These institutions had been created by nineteenth-century Americans seeking to assist lower-class and minority-ethnic groups to overcome barriers that inhibited social mobility and to mitigate the harsher consequences of economic and technological change. Many "new social historians," on the other hand, took a very different view. They argued that propertied and well-to-do groups were fearful of the social dislocations and disorder that followed the disruption of an organic society by industrial and urban change. Since the family and other primary groups could no longer socialize its members in order to promote unity and cohesion, elites turned to formal and quasi-formal institutions. Thus almshouses, mental hospitals, penitentiaries, juvenile reformatories, and schools for the mentally retarded were concerned less about suffering inmates than with the social control objectives of well-to-do groups. Such institutions had two purposes: to incarcerate deviant and dependent groups, and to alter antisocial behavior. Within a brief period of time, however, the custodial functions of these institutions became more important than rehabilitative goals, and they began to serve as dumping grounds for social undesirables. Michael Katz, one of the most productive of the "new social historians," put the issue most succinctly in a recent study of poverty and public policy. Fearful that the lower classes would launch "a massive assault upon American social institutions," propertied groups developed a social policy based on "repression." Their goal was "to bring as many of the dangerous classes as possible under the immediate authority of social agencies and institutions. In this way social policy was the counterpart of sending in the troops to abort a strike."[7]

The debate over the issue of social control assumed its greatest

---

[7]Michael B. Katz, *Poverty and Policy in American History* (New York, 1983), pp. 180–181. See also David Rothman, *The Discovery of the Asylum: Social Order and Disorder in the New Republic* (Boston, 1971), and *Conscience and Convenience: The Asylum and Its Alternatives in Progressive America* (Boston, 1980); and Anthony Platt, *The Child-Savers: The Invention of Delinquency* (Chicago, 1969).

intensity among scholars who studied the nineteenth and early twentieth centuries.[8] The reason for the focus on this period is obvious. During this era Americans established an extensive network of public and quasi-public institutions to deal with dependent and deviant groups. State governments, and later the federal government, created elaborate bureaucratic structures to implement legislative policies aimed at providing care for these groups. And new professions—psychiatry, clinical psychology, social work—assumed the responsibility for providing care. At the same time the modern industrial working class, composed in part of foreign-born immigrants, came into being. The importance of these developments was obvious to scholars, but in treating them historians often disagreed about whether social control was involved or intended.

Historical debates, of course, rarely confine themselves to the academic arena; they generally spill over into contemporary concerns as well. During the 1960s policies regarding poverty and welfare became major public issues. In the process of doing so they became highly politicized. When this happened three groups became involved in the historical controversy that ensued: political leaders, the general public, and scholars drawn from history as well as the social and behavioral sciences.

The heightened concern with poverty had a complex origin. The burgeoning civil rights movement called attention to the impact of low incomes of and discrimination against blacks and other minorities. Rising welfare costs after World War II also aroused apprehension and concern about causes of poverty. The writings of scholars and social critics on the subject likewise contributed to the debate.

Of all the writers in the 1960s Michael Harrington wrote probably the most influential book on the subject, *The Other America.* "The Other America," he wrote, " . . . is populated by failures, by those driven from the land and bewildered by the city, by old people suddenly confronted with the torments of loneliness and poverty, and by minorities facing a wall of prejudice."[9] Harrington and others believed that the presence of poverty in an affluent society was immoral; the United States possessed the resources necessary to abolish this economic evil once and for all.

Political leaders also contributed to the debate over poverty. When John F. Kennedy assumed the presidency in 1961 he gave no sign that

[8]Paul S. Boyer's *Urban Masses and Moral Order in America, 1820–1920* (Cambridge, Mass., 1978) was probably the most sophisticated and moderate statement of the social control model.

[9]Michael Harrington, *The Other America: Poverty in the United States* (New York, 1962), p. 10.

his administration would be concerned with poverty or changes in public welfare. Committed to policies that would sustain economic growth and relieve unemployment Kennedy and his staff pursued relatively traditional programs intended to diminish unemployment, aid depressed areas, and provide job training. Shortly after succeeding Kennedy in late 1963, Lyndon B. Johnson announced his famous War on Poverty program, which was based on the proposition that broadening economic opportunity would diminish poverty. In 1964 Congress passed legislation establishing the Office of Economic Opportunity, an agency dedicated to the idea that conditions could be improved if poor people themselves would take an active part in urban community programs.

A much more significant change, however, was the explosive, yet essentially unplanned, growth in social welfare programs that began in 1965. Expenditures for Medicaid (medical care for poor and indigent persons), Medicare (health insurance for those age sixty-five and older), public housing, food stamps, and social security had the effect of raising millions of Americans above the poverty line by liberalizing eligibility rules. More importantly, during these years social welfare programs came to be regarded as a right rather than a privilege by those in need.

The debate over public welfare in the turbulent sixties and seventies also underwent a marked charge. That political leaders took part in the process was natural, but the participation of academics was a relatively new phenomenon. It reflected the belief that the social sciences could conceive, plan, and execute social welfare programs based on objective analysis. Hence the line between scholarly detachment and political activism tended to become blurred and sometimes altogether nonexistent.

One of the most notable contributions to the debate over public welfare came not from a historian, but from two individuals from different disciplines who were deeply involved in contemporary affairs. In 1971 Frances Fox Piven and Richard Cloward published their widely read and provocative book entitled *Regulating the Poor: The Functions of Public Welfare*. Neither writer was a historian—Piven was a political scientist and Cloward a sociologist and social worker. Their work was extraordinarily eclectic; they borrowed freely from history, economics, political science, and sociology. *Regulating the Poor* was both an interpretation of the past and a clarion call for change in the present. As a popular work their book appealed to those who believed that only major changes in welfare policy could end poverty.

Aside from their advocacy role Piven and Cloward also developed a different interpretation of the history of American public welfare. In their view traditional histories of welfare were "insular and parochial" because of their preoccupation with social reformers, relief practices, and officials associated with policy and bureaucratic innovations. What was needed was an analysis of relief "within a broader context of economy and polity." They argued that public welfare institutions and programs did not arise out of humanitarian concerns but reflected the need of elites for social order and stability. The causes of poverty, they claimed, grew out of economic changes associated with the rise of capitalism. "Relief arrangements," they wrote, "are initiated or expanded during the occasional outbreaks of civil disorder produced by mass unemployment, and are then abolished or contracted when political stability is restored. Expansive relief policies are designed to mute civil disorder, and restrictive ones to reenforce work norms." They elaborated more fully on their basic theme in a series of books that claimed to demonstrate that public welfare was designed to control and discipline America's work force.[10]

From their understanding of the past Piven and Cloward derived a novel strategy. In the absence of fundamental economic reforms the appropriate strategy was to register as many people as possible on the welfare rolls. This would precipitate a crisis and lead to basic changes in the structure and function of public welfare. The first selection in this chapter is taken from *Regulating the Poor.*

Piven and Cloward stimulated the dialogue among scholars writing about the history of welfare. Yet even those who were sympathetic to the social control hypothesis expressed reservations. Piven and Cloward, some wrote, had little or no data to support their interpretation of welfare before the New Deal, and their claims about the period since the 1930s rested on scanty and incomplete research. Other historians questioned the very use of the term "social control." Gerald N. Grob, for example, conceded that institutions and organizations, by definition, performed social control functions. But was social control "the primary motive" or was it "a necessary by-product or concomitant?" A school, he noted, controlled children's behavior by mandating rules and prohibiting such extraneous activities as fighting and sleeping. That the establishment of schools came out of a desire to institute controls, however, did not logically follow. Similarly James Leiby pointed out that Piven and Cloward were social scientists preoccupied with the idea of creating ideal models because of their desire to predict the future and to engage in social planning. The role of historians, Leiby insisted, was simply to reconstruct past characters and events "as they

---

[10]Piven and Cloward discuss the origins of their interpretation of the history of American welfare in the essay "Humanitarianism in History: A Response to the Critics," in *Social Welfare or Social Control?*, Piven and Cloward, eds., pp. 114–148.

really were, in place of what our ideological and theoretical predilections lead us to recall."[11]

In a certain sense the debate between Piven and Cloward on the one hand and their critics on the other was in part a debate over the role that history itself should play. Was the study of history to be a prelude to effective social action as Piven and Coward implied? Or did history as a discipline have an independence and legitimacy of its own quite apart from such didacticism?

Perhaps the most measured response to the social control hypothesis came from James T. Patterson, author of a major study of the twentieth-century American response to poverty. Patterson's book was clearly within the Progressive school tradition; his sympathies were with the poor and he approved of the growing importance of federal policies to reduce poverty and to expand social welfare. Eschewing monolithic explanations Patterson divided the history of twentieth-century welfare into four distinct chronological periods. Before 1930 the goal of welfare was the prevention of dependency. During the Great Depression of the 1930s the federal government was forced by the massive crisis to move toward the establishment of a rudimentary welfare state. The third stage occurred in the early 1960s when the rediscovery of poverty led to a reformulation of the older theme of prevention. Prevention now meant the creation of programs that would expand opportunity and thus diminish dependency. The fourth and most significant stage came in the late 1960s and early 1970s when the number of Americans receiving public assistance doubled, and public expenditures for welfare and health jumped precipitously.

Surprisingly the revolution in welfare did not come about because of a change in the negative public perception of the poor. Nor did Congress play a major role in hastening social change; indeed, legislators were often frustrated by their inability to stop rising public welfare expenditures. The change, Patterson insisted, lay in a complex combination of factors. Social and economic forces stimulated a major migration of poor people in the postwar decades to the urbanized North where eligibility for assistance was less restrictive. Consequently more eligible families applied for and received aid. The expectations of poor people (which included a significant number of aged individuals) changed; public assistance was now perceived as a right, not a privilege. The growing assertiveness of the poor was implicitly encouraged by federal officials who hoped to maximize benefits and services to less

---

[11]Gerald N. Grob, "Welfare and Poverty in American History," *Reviews in American History* 1 (March 1973):49–50 and James Leiby, "Social Control and Historical Explanation," in *Social Welfare or Social Control?*, Piven and Cloward, eds., pp. 90–113.

fortunate members of society. Above all, wrote Patterson, America in this period developed a new definition of citizenship that included certain basic social and economic rights, including the right to a secure and livable income. In this respect the United States was merely following a pattern characteristic of most Western industrial nations. An excerpt from Patterson's book is reprinted as the second selection in this chapter.

Despite overlapping concerns welfare history and the "new social history" have remained quite separate and distinct. The former has continued to emphasize the study of public institutions and public policies, the latter the lives and culture of inarticulate masses and of common, ordinary people. Yet there is a growing body of historical scholarship that in the near future may alter traditional interpretations of American welfare that emphasize public policy. Social and economic distress, which created a need for assistance, often led to *ad hoc* solutions to important problems. The crises that followed unemployment, underemployment, illness, or death often stimulated intervention by families and relatives or by religious groups rather than public agencies. Most religious groups—especially those whose membership was drawn from ethnic or racial minorities—created their own parallel welfare institutions. To study the many private religious benevolent associations created by Catholics, Protestants, and Jews is to concede that welfare, in part, was a private as well as a public function. Even urban political machines—often maligned and misunderstood—played a vital role in assisting impoverished urban dwellers in their quest for survival. In this sense political machines were part of a pervasive welfare system that was neither wholly public nor private. Nor should the existence of private self-help organizations be overlooked. Such organizations aided alcoholics, former mental hospital patients, and other persons who encountered personal crises. Last, but not least, the poor themselves have been active participants in creating what Michael Katz has imaginatively referred to as "strategies of survival," and in so doing have transformed public policies and institutions in subtle but significant ways.[12] In the near future a merger of public welfare history with the "new social history" may very well reshape the ways in which the problems of welfare are perceived and defined.

The debate among historians over welfare and poverty is not without contemporary relevance. During the 1980s, partly as a result of the election of Ronald Reagan, Americans once again were divided over the degree of their responsibility for those requiring assistance, including the poor, the unemployed, the sick, and the aged. Indeed, Re-

---

[12]Katz, *Poverty and Policy, passim.*

agan used the presidency as a forum to argue that welfare policy had to change. "When you create a government program," he observed in 1983, "it becomes the nearest thing to eternal life you'll ever see on this Earth, because the people whose careers and jobs are now in running these programs, they don't want that program to go away. So, welfare recipients become kind of clients to preserve their jobs. And we've got to look at it a little differently."[13] Disclaimers to the contrary the Reagan administration undertook a campaign to dismantle many of the welfare programs created in previous decades to establish a minimum subsistence level. The budgetary constraints of this era, caused in part by tax cuts, sharp increases in defense expenditures and interest payments to service a rapidly rising federal debt, and mandated increases in entitlement programs, gave added urgency to the struggle over welfare policy.

Perceptions of the past, of course, are not necessarily decisive, but they surely help shape our understanding of the present. In this sense the history of American welfare and poverty occupies an important niche. Did dependency and poverty arise out of individual character deficiencies, or was it an outgrowth of broad environmental forces, including unemployment, underemployment, illness, death, and racial and sexual discrimination? Was public welfare designed to preserve the hegemony of elite groups, or was it intended to meet the needs of dependent groups? How and why did public welfare change over time, and what were its achievements and failures? What was the relationship between private and public welfare, and what was the relative significance of each? As long as Americans debate the need for and form of assistance they will seek to learn lessons about welfare from the experiences of the past. The history of American welfare and poverty will in this sense continue to be a controversial subject for the foreseeable future.

---

[13]*Public Papers of the Presidents of the United States. Ronald Reagan, 1983,* 2 vols. (Washington, D.C., 1984), p. 92.

Frances Fox Piven
and Richard A. Cloward

FRANCES FOX PIVEN (1932–   ) is professor of political science at the Graduate Center of the City University of New York, and RICHARD A CLOWARD (1926–   ) is professor of social work at Columbia University. They have collaborated on several books, including *The Politics of Turmoil* (1974), *Poor People's Movements* (1977), and *The New Class War* (1982).

The key to an understanding of relief-giving is in the functions it serves for the larger economic and political order, for relief is a secondary and supportive institution. Historical evidence suggests that relief arrangements are initiated or expanded during the occasional outbreaks of civil disorder produced by mass unemployment, and are then abolished or contracted when political stability is restored. We shall argue that expansive relief policies are designed to mute civil disorder, and restrictive ones to reinforce work norms. In other words, relief policies are cyclical—liberal or restrictive depending on the problems of regulation in the larger society with which government must contend. Since this view clearly belies the popular supposition that government social policies, including relief policies, are becoming progressively more responsible, humane, and generous, a few words about this popular supposition and its applicability to relief are in order.

There is surely no gainsaying that the role of government has expanded in those domestic matters called "social welfare." One has only to look at the steadily increasing expenditures by local, state, and national governments for programs in housing, health care, education, and the like. These expenditures have been prompted by the repercussions that result when such matters as housing or health care are left entirely to the untrammeled forces of the marketplace. Decisions that are reasonable to the profitmaker are obviously not necessarily reasonable to the various groups that are affected, and they may demand that government intervene to protect them. Moreover, once governmental action is inaugurated, the groups who benefit become a supporting constituency and press for further gains. But most such social welfare activity has not greatly aided the poor, precisely because the poor ordinarily have little influence on government. Indeed, "social welfare" programs designed for other groups frequently ride roughshod over the poor, as when New Deal agricultural subsidies resulted in the displacement of great numbers of tenant farmers and sharecroppers, or when urban renewal schemes deprived blacks of their urban neighborhoods.

However, some social welfare programs *do* benefit those at the bottom of the economic order. The most important examples are old-age pensions and unemployment insurance. As the industrial market system became dominant in Western countries, it was less necessary that everyone work; some people, such as the aged, gradually became economically obsolete and were permitted to drop out of the labor force. Moreover, the vagaries of the market system made it desirable that governments institute a buffer against temporary unemployment, such as unemployment insurance.

Although old-age pension and unemployment insurance schemes in the West have improved over time, and to that extent confirm the popular view that the policies of "welfare capitalism" are becoming more responsive and responsible, access to these benefits has not been unconditional. Generally speaking, eligibility for pensions or unemployment insurance is established through the occupational role, and can actually be obtained only if the individual is certified as unneeded in the labor force, whether because of old age or retrenchment. Moreover, some occupations which draw on unskilled and low-wage workers (e.g., many agricultural workers and domestic servants in the United States) have been denied the benefits of these insurance schemes. These workers are left to get what they can from the relief system. In any case, even those certified as unneeded in the labor force have generally been maintained at such low levels of income as to suggest that social insurance programs are not fully free of the taint of being a form of relief.

As for relief programs themselves, the historical pattern is clearly not one of progressive liberalization; it is rather a record of periodically expanding and contracting relief rolls as the system performs its two main functions: maintaining civil order and enforcing work. . . .

During the 1950's the AFDC rolls rose by only 110,000 families, or 17 percent. But from December 1960 to February 1969, some 800,000 families were added to the rolls, an increase of 107 per cent in just eight years and two months. In the course of the 1960's, then, the nation experienced a "welfare explosion"; for all practical purposes, traditional restrictions collapsed and the relief money poured out. As costs rose, the relief system once again became a major public issue, a source of political controversy and conflict, and thus an object of proposals for "reorganization" and "reform." . . .

We shall argue, as we did in our discussion of the relief explosion during the Great Depression, that the contemporary relief explosion was a response to the civil disorder caused by rapid economic change—in this case, the modernization of Southern agriculture. The impact of modernization on blacks was much greater than on whites: it was they who were the chief victims of the convulsion in Southern agriculture, and it was they who were more likely to encounter barriers to employment once relocated in the cities, a combination of circumstances which led to a substantial weakening of social controls and widespread outbreaks of disorder. For if unemployment and forced migration altered the geography of black poverty, it also created a measure of black power. In the 1960's, the growing mass of black poor in the cities emerged as a political force for the first time, both in the voting booths and in the streets. And the relief system was, we believe, one of the main local institutions to respond to that force, even though the reaction was greatly delayed.

The relationship between increasing black power and the expanding welfare rolls is not altogether obvious. Great masses of poor blacks did not rise up in anger against a welfare system that denied them sustenance (although some did). Nor did the increased flow of public aid result from demands made by black political leaders; quite to the contrary, the expanding welfare rolls have often been as much a source of dismay to black elites as to white elites. Finally, there is a puzzling absence of liberalizing legislation. Legislative enactments in the years between 1960 and 1969 were intended not to put more families on the rolls, but to get them off via rehabilitation services (the passage of AFDC-UP is an exception). Indeed, the puzzle deepens because some legislative enactments—particularly the congressional amendments of 1967—actually made the relief system more restrictive. Still, the rolls more than doubled. The politics of the welfare rise, in short, are anything but self-evident.

In our previous analysis of why relief restrictions collapsed in the Great Depression, we found that the critical factor was the growing volatility of those dislodged from the occupational order. Mass unemployment alone did not lead to the expansion of relief arrangements—not, that is, until unemployment had generated so much unrest as to threaten political stability. In other words, economic convulsions which also produce mass turbulence—whether riots in the streets or upheavals in electoral alignments—are likely to lead to the temporary liberalization of relief provisions.

Although unemployment during the Great Depression rapidly produced a political crisis and impelled the expansion of public aid, two decades passed before the unemployment resulting from moderniza- tion and migration after World War II produced mass disorder, and so the relief rolls did not rise appreciably until after 1964. Agricultural modernization and migration to the cities brought blacks within the sphere of electoral politics, to be sure, but larger voting numbers alone did not produce concessions. It was not until this mass of unintegrated people finally became turbulent that both local government and the federal government began to register and react to their presence.

The welfare explosion occurred during several years of the greatest domestic disorder since the 1930's—perhaps the greatest in our his- tory. It was concurrent with the turmoil produced by the civil rights struggle, with widespread and destructive rioting in the cities, and with the formation of a militant grass-roots movement of the poor dedicated to combatting welfare restrictions. Not least, the welfare rise was also concurrent with the enactment of a series of ghetto-placating fed- eral programs (such as the antipoverty program) which, among other things, hired thousands of poor people, social workers, and lawyers who, it subsequently turned out, greatly stimulated people to apply for relief and helped them to obtain it. And the welfare explosion, al- though an urban phenomenon generally, was greatest in just that hand- ful of large metropolitan counties where the political turmoil of the middle and late 1960's was the most acute.

In other words, we shall argue that the expansion of the welfare rolls was a political response to political disorder. . . . In summary, modernization, migration, urban unemployment, the breakup of fam- ilies, rising grant levels, and other factors contributed to a growing pool of "eligible" families in the 1950's and 1960's. Nevertheless, the relief rolls did not rise until the 1960's. And when they did, it was largely as a result of governmental programs designed to moderate widespread political unrest among the black poor. One consequence of these pro- grams was that the poor were suddenly stimulated to apply for relief in unprecedented numbers (except in the South); another consequence was that welfare officials were suddenly stimulated to approve appli- cations in unprecedented numbers. The result was the relief explosion of the late 1960's. The terms in which that crisis must be explained are economic disruption, large-scale migration, mass volatility, and electoral responses—a sequence of disturbances leading to a precipi- tous expansion of the relief rolls.

We conclude, then, that because the 1960's were a time of profound disorder, both North and South, government responded with measures to ease that disorder. Blacks got a little more from some government agencies and suffered a little less at the hands of others, although, con- sidering the magnitude of the political disturbances, it is remarkable to see how few and how modest these concessions were, and how often they turned out to be merely symbolic. Now that ghetto unrest has subsided (at least as of this writing), the liberalization of relief practices stands out, for without that concession the victims of agricultural modernization and of persisting unemployment in the cities would remain perilously close to starvation—as so many did in the late 1940's and the 1950's. And although the processes by which the relief expansion occurred were sometimes covert and circuitous, the moral seems clear: a placid poor get nothing, but a turbulent poor sometimes get something. . . .

In February 1969, there were 1,545,000 families on the combined AFDC and AFDC-UP rolls; by October 1970, some twenty months later, the caseload had risen to 2,400,000 families, an increase of 55 per cent. For the full decade ending in December 1970, the over-all rise exceeded 225 per cent. And the rolls are still rising. The stimulus for this new upsurge was, we believe, the Nixon Administration's anti-inflation strategy, which sharply increased unemployment.

Under ordinary circumstances, as we have stressed repeatedly in this book, increases in unemployment do not produce comparable increases in the welfare rolls, but the late 1960's were no ordinary time. The onset of recession in 1969 occurred at a unique moment, one in which the welfare system was extremely vulnerable owing to the great weakening of traditional restrictions which had taken place during the preceding few years. Among other things, the proportion of applications being approved stood at the unprecedented level of 70 per cent. Moreover, as a result of years of agitation, litigation, and publicity, people's attitudes toward going on welfare had changed; many had come to believe that they have a "right" to assistance. As the recession deepened, therefore, applications for welfare surged, and with the approval level high, a renewed explosion occurred.

From our perspective, a relief explosion is a reform just because a large number of unemployed or underemployed people obtain aid, for many of them would otherwise be forced to subsist without either jobs or income. But from the perspective of most groups in the society, a great expansion of relief constitutes a "crisis" and pressure mounts to reorganize the system, also in the name of "reform." Similar episodes in the past suggest that such calls for reform signal a shift in emphasis between the major functions of relief arrangements—a shift from regulating civil disorder to regulating labor. For reasons we will explain, we are profoundly suspicious of the work-enforcing features of the reforms now being proposed.

Before commenting on these reforms, however, a word should be said about the rising cost of relief, for that is considered by many people to be the crux of the relief crisis. Actually, relief budgets now absorb only a tiny proportion of our over-all national revenues; the problem—as has been true in most times and in most places—is that relief budgets are at least partly locally controlled and financed. As a result, a great expansion of relief strains local revenue sources, local taxes rise, and funds are diverted from other services (such as education and transit). During the early years of the Great Depression, some cities were even brought to the brink of bankruptcy; and today, many cities are staggering under relief costs.

To deal with fiscal troubles, states and localities usually try to "reform" the relief system by lowering the level of benefits or by cutting back the rolls; such measures are now being taken in some places. But as long as the danger of mass disorder persists, the national government is likely to seek some means of relieving local fiscal strains other than cutting the rolls. During the Depression, emergency funds were channeled to localities; today, the national administration is proposing "revenue-sharing" with state and local governments. And some congressmen are calling upon the federal government to foot the entire relief bill. (At this writing, some form of federal action to lighten the burden at the local level seems likely to be enacted by the Congress, and this is the obvious remedy for the fiscal aspect of the relief crisis.)

However, the much more fundamental problem with which relief reform seeks to cope is the erosion of the work role. When large numbers of people come to subsist on the dole, many of them spurning what little low-wage work may exist, those of the poor and near-poor who continue to work are inevitably affected. From their perspective, the ready availability of relief payments (often at levels only slightly below prevailing wages) undermines their chief claim to social status: namely, that although poor they nevertheless earn their livelihood. If most of them react with anger, others react by asking, "Why work?" The danger thus arises that swelling numbers of the working poor will choose to go on relief.

Moreover, when attachments to the work role deteriorate, so do attachments to the family, especially the attachment of men to their families. For all practical purposes, the relief check becomes a surrogate for the male breadwinner. The resulting family breakdown and loss of control over the young is usually signified by the spread of certain forms of disorder—for example, school failure, crime, and addiction. In other words, the mere giving of relief, while it mutes the more disruptive outbreaks of civil disorder (such as rioting), does little to stem the fragmentation of lower-class life, even while it further undermines the patterns of work by which the lower class is ordinarily regulated. When all of this becomes clear to elites, the stage is set for the restoration of the work-maintaining function of the relief system.

Accordingly, as the rolls rise, so does concern with work. The Congress, as early as 1967, reflected this concern by requiring states to make AFDC mothers report for work or work training. These requirements were not much enforced, partly because of the cumbersome administrative problems that enforcement entailed, but mainly because continuing turbulence in the streets of the cities—which led to the welfare explosion in the first place—made enforcement risky. Now, however, the rolls are even higher, and the concern with work has become correspondingly more acute. Consequently, the plans which are now being proposed to enforce work among those who are already recipients, and to prevent the further erosion of the work role among those who are not, have become more far-reaching in scope.

As we noted [earlier] . . . the method of enforcing work adopted during relief explosion tends to vary depending on the nature of the economic dislocation. During depressions, public-works programs are often initiated to augment the faltering demand for labor. But when a process of modernization leaves many people unable or unwilling to work, relief arrangements are usually reorganized to channel recipients into the private market, overcoming their reluctance to work with coercion, and overcoming their low market value with subsidies. The proposals advanced by the Nixon Administration are of this type. A relief family of four members would be permitted to retain its first $720 of earned income without any reduction in a proposed minimum relief grant of perhaps $1,600; thereafter, it could keep half of all additional earned income until a gross of $3,920 was reached, at which point the relief subsidy would be terminated. With a subsidy of some $1,600, the able-bodied poor would be induced or compelled to take the marginal, seasonal, erratic, and low-paid work which, given present relief arrangements, has lately come to be spurned by many of them. If able-bodied people refused to work despite these incentives, the subsidy of $1,600 would be terminated. (Should the current recession worsen, however, pressure for a program of relief-sponsored public work might well mount.) Whether or not this particular plan is enacted, some type of work-enforcing reform seems imminent.

Books on contemporary problems usually conclude with recommendations for reform. Our view is simple enough to state. In principle, there are two ways of dealing with relief explosions and the underlying economic and social dislocations which they reflect. One is by reforms in economic policy that would lead to full employment at decent wages, and the other is by relief reforms. If jobs were created on a large scale, whether by public or private investments, and if the wages paid were adequate, many AFDC mothers would immediately take jobs. Over the long run, however, basic economic reforms would reduce the rolls by a more fundamental process: that of restoring lower-class occupational, familial, and communal patterns. Since men, for example, would no longer find themselves unemployed or employed at wages insufficient to support women and children, they would be able to resume breadwinner roles. A dramatic impact on the relief system would result, for fewer women would be forced to ask for assistance for lack of adequate male support.

Moreover, reforms leading to full employment at decent wages would make possible more humane relief arrangements for those who cannot or should not work. For if the main propositions of this book are true, relief practices are always determined by the conditions of work among the lower classes. Relief payments are not likely to rise above the lowest wages, and will amost invariably be much lower. Nor are relief recipients likely to be treated well as long as there are workers who are so poorly paid that they must be coerced into staying at their jobs by the spectacle of degraded paupers. But if the economy operates at full employment and if the real wages paid to workers rise, the real value of payments to recipients might then be raised as well. Similarly, if full employment and rising wages lessen the society's reliance on other regulatory devices to keep the lower classes in the labor market, then the degradation of non-workers might be lessened. In short, improving the economic circumstances of the working poor would not only reduce the relief roles, but it would permit a more humane relief system to be created as well.

However, we suspect there is not much reason to expect fundamental reforms in economic policy. Nor, it should be added, is there much reason to expect entirely new forms of public assistance—for example, along the lines of a guaranteed income, or a system of allowances to families and children. These and other proposals for the reform of our income-maintenance system have been prepared and debated at some length, but the debate has taken place mainly among technicians; the public has shown little concern. In other words, while these schemes may be of theoretical interest, they have stirred no political interest. Instead, the options being put before the nation are to continue present relief arrangements (perhaps modified by measures to shift the local fiscal burden to the federal government), or to adopt the age-old approach to relief explosions—namely, the introduction of work-enforcing measures. It is a poor choice, to be sure, but it is the politically real choice nevertheless.

We are opposed to work-enforcing reforms. The basis for our opposition is that when similar reforms were introduced in the past, they presaged the eventual expulsion of large numbers of people from the rolls, leaving them to fend for themselves in a labor market where they was too little work and thus subjecting them once again to severe economic exploitation.

Admittedly, the short-run consequence of a work-enforcing reform may be to inflate the relief rolls, for new groups sometimes become officially eligible for aid: in the Depression, the unemployed became eligible for work on public projects; the current proposals call for including millions of the working poor through a system of work-related subsidies. At first blush, the latter scheme appears laudable. But if the history of comparable reforms is any guide, this scheme is not likely to be sustained over the longer run, and for a reason that is more than a little ironic.

The irony is simply this: that large-scale work relief—unlike direct relief which merely mutes the worst outbursts of discontent—tends to stabilize lower-class occupational, familial, and communal life, and by doing so diminishes the proclivities toward disruptive behavior which give rise to the expansion of relief in the first place. Once order is restored in this far more profound sense, *relief-giving can be virtually abolished*, as it has been so often in the past. And there is always pressure to abolish large-scale work relief, for it strains against the market ethos and interferes with the untrammeled operation of the marketplace. The point is not just that when a relief concession is offered up, peace and order reign; it is, rather, that when peace and order reign, the relief concession is withdrawn.

The restoration of work through the relief system, in other words, makes possible the eventual return to the most restrictive phase in the cycle of relief-giving. What begins as a great expansion of direct relief, and then turns into some form of work relief, ends finally with a sharp contraction of the rolls. As the Depression wore on, direct relief was replaced by work relief, then work relief was abolished, and millions of the poor were rapidly shunted into a labor market where there was insufficient work. It was not for three decades that the poor were to get relief again, despite spreading unemployment in agriculture and in the cities. Meanwhile, the few who were allowed to remain on the rolls under the categorical assistance provisions of the Social Security Act— some of the aged, blind, and orphaned—were once again subjected to the punitive and degrading treatment which has been used to buttress the work ethos since the inception of relief several centuries ago. And why should it have been otherwise? With order restored, there was no force to sustain the concessions made at earlier stages. Relief-giving is never popular, work relief costs billions of dollars, and a placid poor hardly constitutes a political constituency whose interests must be taken seriously. Advocates of relief reform may argue that their reforms will be long-lasting, that the restrictive phase in the cycle will not be reached, but past experience suggests otherwise.

In the absence of fundamental economic reforms, therefore, *we take the position that the explosion of the rolls is the true relief reform*, that it should be defended, and expanded. Even now, hundreds of thousands of impoverished families remain who are eligible for assistance but who receive no aid at all.

James T. Patterson

JAMES T. PATTERSON (1935–   ) is professor of history at Brown University. He has written a number of books on twentieth-century American history, including *Congressional Conservatism and the New Deal* (1967), *New Deal and the States: Federalism in Transition* (1969), and *Mr. Republican: A Biography of Robert A. Taft* (1972).

Two dramatic developments changed the face of American poverty and welfare between the mid-1960s and the early 1970s: a fantastic drop in the number of poor and a stunning enlargement of social welfare programs, especially Social Security. These developments did not occur because of changed popular attitudes toward poverty and welfare. Insofar as these attitudes were measurable, they revealed that most middle-class Americans continued to stereotype the poor disparagingly and to recoil at the thought of expanding welfare. Their social philosophy, in Tawney's term, had not changed. The developments also owed little to careful planning by reformers. On the contrary, these were years of social turbulence, when many experts took stock of the situation. Although some activists continued to plan new and better wars on poverty, others doubted the capacity of government to accomplish much on the domestic front. Far from being planned, these turning points were neither popular nor anticipated.

Underlying these transformations were broad social changes, notably unprecedented economic growth. Demographic changes, especially the aging of the population, together with the inexorable expansion of existing programs worked along with that growth. And well-organized pressure groups provided much of the political thrust for them. The result was a virtual revolution.

Some studies of poverty in the late 1960s and early 1970s scarcely suggested changes of such magnitude. Instead they revealed poverty that continued to select out specially deprived groups for lives of deprivation. As ever, people living in the South were more likely to be poor, although by the mid-1970s economic growth in the Sun Belt, combined with massive migrations of poor southerners to the North, dramatically reduced the numbers of poor people below the Mason-

Dixon line. Indeed, most of the officially defined reduction in poverty between 1959 and 1975—11 million of 13 million—was in the South. But the average southerner was still almost twice as likely to be poor as were people living in other sections. The South in the early 1970s still contained around 12 million poor people, or nearly half the official poverty population of 25 million. Of these, around 70 percent were white. All suffered from an "old" poverty rooted in low wages and underemployment.

This southern poverty was a measure of the continuing problems of rural areas. Not that the rural poor were a majority—around 65 percent of the nation's poor lived in cities in 1970, and the percentage was increasing slowly. But the incidence of poverty among rural Americans was 19 percent in 1966, as opposed to 14 percent for those in the cities. And many of the urban poor had fled the even deeper poverty of the farm.

Nonwhites, as always, were especially hard hit by poverty. Though nearly 70 percent of the nation's poor were white in the late 1960s, the nation as a whole was more than 85 percent white. The incidence of poverty among nonwhites remained staggeringly high—41 percent in 1966, as opposed to 12 percent for whites—and was falling more slowly than the white incidence. In 1959 it had been three times that of whites; by the mid-1970s, it was three and a half times as high. More and more of this nonwhite poverty reflected the newer urban poverty of the North. Despite economic progress, there were more poor blacks in the North and West in the early 1970s than there had been in 1959. The scarcity of decent jobs in the city especially afflicted urban blacks aged sixteen to nineteen, whose unemployment rate approximated 30 percent—two to three times that of young urban whites—by the early 1970s.

Low-paying employment remained a key source of poverty. In 1967, 32 percent of the poor, 8.2 million people, lived in households whose head worked full time. Another 25 percent, or 6.5 million, lived in families whose head worked part-time. These statistics merely echoed the litany sung by structuralists from Hunter on: badly paid work—on the farm, in the factory, and increasingly in the service sectors of a postindustrial economy—continued to swell the poverty population.

The aged, historically susceptible to poverty, dramatically improved their status by 1970. About 25 percent of old people were then poor, as opposed to 40 percent in 1959. Thanks to huge increases in Social Security benefits, only 16 percent were poor by 1974. Still, about one in nine Americans under age sixty-five was then officially poor; for the aged the number was closer to one in six. And the aging of the population meant that increasing numbers of old people might slip into poverty.

People living in female-headed families, on the other hand, stayed poor. Economic progress between 1963 and 1969 pulled 12 million people in male-headed families out of poverty but stranded 11 million in female-headed families, the same number as in 1963. This group made up more than 40 percent of the poverty population. Most of these people were children; in the early 1970s around 40 percent of poor Americans were under sixteen. By 1974, 6 percent of white male-headed and 17 percent of nonwhite male-headed families were poor. By contrast, 27 percent of female-headed white families and 55 percent of female-headed nonwhite families were in poverty.

For all these people, poverty officially meant living below the income line set by the Social Security Administration. Reflecting the rising cost of living, this amount rose from $3,000 for an urban family of four in the early 1960s to around $4,200 in 1972 and to $5,500 in 1976. Farm families were supposed to get along on 85 percent of that, or $3,570 in 1972. Certain advantages of these poverty lines sustained their use by public officials. The income standards were objective, not culturally vague definitions subject to subjective stereotyping. But the official line was low for the 1960s, an affluent age of rising expectations. Originally it allotted people only seventy cents per day for food prepared at home, and it allowed nothing for transportation costs to and from work, for taxes paid, for new furnishings or utensils, or for food eaten out. Well before 1970, many experts called for higher poverty lines, such as those used by the Bureau of Labor Statistics, whose "low" budget for a family of four was $6,960 in 1969, almost twice the official level. Such a line would have shown that 33 percent of the population lived in poverty—not the 12–14 percent estimated by the government.

Other critics complained that the official poverty line measured only absolute poverty and thus presented a falsely bright picture of progress in the late 1960s and early 1970s. The government, they said, ought to calculate relative poverty, the relationship of low to median family incomes. Measured by that standard, the median income in that affluent age rose faster than the poverty line, based on the more slowly increasing cost of living. The poverty line was one-half of median family income in 1959, one-third of it in 1974. This development, hardly progressive at any time, was galling in the age of mass communications and expanded expectations. The poor could not help but know how much they were missing. As Dwight Macdonald expressed it, "Not to be able to afford a movie or a glass of beer is a kind of starvation—if everybody else can."

Macdonald and others stressed that the distribution of income had not changed much in the postwar years, when families in the lowest fifth of income earners got between 4.5 and 5.6 percent of the national income. Indeed, the overall income deficit—defined as the total dollars needed to bring all poor Americans up to the poverty line—seemed to increase slightly in the otherwise affluent late 1960s and early 1970s. Because the total number of poor people declined in those years, the people who remained below the line were not just poor, but on the average even poorer. Clearly, the country's economic growth was highly selective.

The limitations of the official, absolute poverty line were perhaps of more than academic importance. In affecting impressions of the size and character of poverty, the line had the potential to influence policy. Use of the official low line tended to identify as poor those at the very bottom of the heap and to magnify the visibility of nonworking people, including the hard-core unemployed and female heads of household. Casual observers, confronting these "facts," could logically conclude that the government ought to respond by developing jobs, manpower training, or "opportunity." Use of a higher poverty line would have identified many more millions of working poor, and encouraged support for measures, such as wage supplements, guaranteeing better pay. A measurement highlighting relative poverty might have encouraged a few idealistic (and politically unrealistic) planners to stress the redistribution of income.

These grim features—the concentration of poverty among particularly disadvantaged groups, the stringency of budgets set at the official poverty line, the persistence of relative poverty in an age of galloping expectations—understandably worried some experts, although none of the trends was altogether new. Knowledgeable writers had long recognized that poverty afflicted certain groups; social workers for years had bemoaned the budgetary standards used in measuring need; Galbraith and a few others had drawn some attention to the problem of relative deprivation. In part for these reasons, few people paid very much attention to the Cassandras.

Instead, they clapped their hands with pride at what was in truth a phenomenal reduction of absolute poverty. According to the official, absolute definitions, the number of poor Americans decreased from 39 million (22 percent of the population) in 1959, to 32 million (17 percent) in 1965, to 25 million (13 percent) in 1968, to 23 million (11 percent) in 1973. The vast majority of those who climbed over the line were previously poor workers and their families, who profited from the astonishing overall growth of the economy during those years. From this perspective, the fact that higher percentages of the poor were "hard-to-reach," such as members of female-headed families, was cause for gratification not despair. It meant that the economy was coming closer to the goal of wiping out all but the "residual" poverty concentrated among those outside the labor force. These people, it followed, could get welfare.

Optimists also stressed that the official poverty line was set at a level that enabled people to live much better than poor people ever had before. It allowed for far better diets and shelter than had been the case in Hunter's time or in 1929, and it offered more than the measures used by liberals in the 1940s and 1950s. By 1977 the line for an urban family of four was almost $6,600, 23 percent higher in purchasing power, in constant 1977 dollars, than the $2,000 used by the Sparkman committee in the 1950s. This upgrading of the line of course reflected the rising expectations of an affluent society. "As time passed," one observer explained, "society agreed that the minimum should increasingly involve more than filling a belly and obtaining a roof."

Studies that began to appear in the mid-1970s also showed that most people did not stay poor for long. The University of Michigan's investigation of "income dynamics" between 1967 and 1975 concluded that about a third of all those in the study fell below the official poverty line in at least one year out of the nine. That was around 70 million Americans, most of whom were near the margin most of the time. Around 50 percent of the poor in 1975, some 13 million, had been poor more than half the time in those nine years. But the study also showed that only 22 percent of the poverty population, 3 percent of American society, was poor all the time. That was less than 6 million people in 1973. If that number still seemed high to some observers—and it is indeed a stern test of poverty—it was nonetheless far smaller than pictured by some contemporaries who imagined millions wallowing forever in a culture of poverty.

The optimists later showed that poverty statistics in some ways grossly overestimated the number who were officially designated as poor in the early 1970s. They pointed in particular to the vitally helpful role of in-kind benefits, including Medicaid, public housing, and food stamps, that proliferated after 1965 but that did not figure in the official measures of income. Writers noted also that poor people (like many Americans) systematically underreported their varied sources of income and property. If the in-kind benefits and unreported money were added to cash incomes, some experts concluded later, the official percentages of those in absolute poverty would have been as low as 6.5 percent by 1972.

But it was not necessary to talk about in-kind benefits and underreporting to sing "Hallelujah" by 1973. Save for the World War II years that ended the Depression, no comparable period in American history witnessed such progress in diminishing poverty as did the 1960s and early 1970s. The percentage that was poor—whether 6 or 12 percent-was so low as to be virtually unbelievable. Hunter, living at a time when perhaps 40 percent of Americans were poor by a lower standard, would have been amazed that capitalism, sustained by government spending, could do so much in seventy years. By any standard, the progress by 1973 was astonishing.

An overview of social welfare policy during these years reveals many of the flaws that had plagued the jerry-built system since its origins in the 1930s. Harrington, ignoring political realities, maintained that the "welfare state benefits those least who need help most" and that it offered "socialism for the rich and free enterprise for the poor." The head of New York City's welfare department said in 1967, "The welfare system is designed to save money instead of people and tragically ends up doing neither." Another expert concluded in 1970, "The current public assistance system of the United States, particularly AFDC, deserves to go down in history with the British poor laws of the early Industrial Revolution."

The AFDC program, by far the largest welfare plan, seemed most open to criticism. Reformers complained that states and localities still managed to avoid federal regulations aimed at humanizing the application of aid. Until the late 1960s, administrators continued the old practices designed either to humiliate recipients or to keep them off the rolls altogether. Midnight raids to detect men in the home, new twists on supposedly outlawed "suitable home" rules, tough residency requirements—all stigmatized or excluded poor people. Until 1967, any earnings were subtracted from welfare checks, thus eliminating all incentive to work. Patronizing social workers were especially resented. One AFDC mother said, "The worst thing is they just make you feel no good at all. They tell you they want to make you into them, and leave you without a cent of yourself to hang on to. I keep asking myself, why don't they fix the country up, so that people can *work*, instead of patching up with this and that."

The continuing variation from state to state in the size of AFDC payments further enraged reformers. By 1970 these variations had actually increased, mainly because the richer states provided more. Payments for old-age assistance, generally higher per individual, ranged equally widely. So did general assistance, which was usually lower than other forms of relief. Despite federal prohibitions, payments within states even varied, with rural areas generally paying less per recipient than the cities.

The grossest flaw in the categorical assistance programs continued to be the low level of payments. All but six states set their standards for AFDC below the federal definitions of poverty, and all but sixteen states failed to appropriate the money necessary to meet their own low standards. In 1966 the average national payment per recipient of AFDC was $36 per month, so a family of four received $144 per month, or $1,728 per year. The official poverty line in that year for a nonfarm family of four was $3,355.

Some people argued that "individualism" and the "work ethic" accounted for America's stinginess in welfare. Some blamed the decentralized political system, which gave local elites wide discretion. Others claimed that keeping welfare low was above all a way of subjugating blacks. Richard Cloward and Frances Fox Piven insisted that welfare had a functional role within the capitalist system, that except when scared by social unrest, elites deliberately kept welfare payments as low as possible to ensure abundant supplies of cheap labor.

Such broad explanations were as difficult to document as they had been in earlier periods. Individualism and the work ethic were virtually unmeasurable, and similar values appeared to be just as widespread in other Western nations, most of which had more extensive welfare programs. Decentralization certainly played into the hands of local elites and accounted for some of the meanness in application of aid. But decentralization was more an institutional manifestation of such meanness than a cause of it. The racial interpretation relied in part on findings that showed eligibility requirements to be stiffest, and average AFDC payments lowest, in states with large percentages of blacks in the population. But these states, mostly in the South, were also the poorest and least prepared to advocate generous public aid. It was therefore difficult to prove that racial attitudes toward blacks—which grew more liberal in the 1960s—independently accounted for the illiberal nature of public welfare.

To a limited degree, the Cloward-Piven critique appears correct. Low welfare levels were clearly functional, particularly for employers of poorly paid farm labor. In agricultural areas, especially in the South, harsh application of welfare coexisted with low wages. But Cloward and Piven were more successful in showing the coexistence of welfare and low wages than in proving a causal connection. Many forces, including the work ethic, hostile attitudes toward blacks, and historically disparaging views of poor people helped account for the low levels of public aid in the South.

Cloward and Piven's argument tends also to slight perhaps the most reliable predictor of welfare standards: the state's ability to pay. In the 1960s, as throughout the recent American past, per capita income provided as good a guide as any to state-by-state differentials in standards and requirements. Northern states, wealthier per capita, were better able than southern states to take advantage of matching-grant provisions of the categorical assistance plans. Although never a simple one-to-one proposition, the relationship between state per capita income and welfare standards was too powerful to be dismissed.

But public assistance is only one, narrow way of measuring the role of social welfare. In fact, means-tested programs targeted at the poor, such as AFDC, old-age assistance, general assistance, public housing, and food stamps, made up only 10 to 19 percent of social welfare expenditures between 1965 and 1975. Other programs—especially old age pensions, unemployment compensation, and Medicare—affected roughly four times as many nonpoor as poor, but their impact on the poor was enormous. These programs, in fact, proved that "throwing money at problems" works.

The growth in all social welfare programs was staggering. Expenditures rose between 1965 and 1976 at an annual rate of 7.2 percent in constant dollars, compared to 4.6 percent annually between 1950 and 1965. In 1960 such spending was 7.7 percent of the GNP; in 1965, 10.5 percent; in 1974, 16 percent. By far the largest sums went for non-means-tested programs like Social Security, unemployment compensation, and Medicare. But public aid also rose during these years, accounting for 1.3 percent of the GNP in 1950, 1.9 percent in 1968, 2.8 percent in 1974. Public assistance payments per recipient increased both in constant dollars and in comparison to average wage rates. These figures reveal that the war in Vietnam, however draining, did not prevent vast increases in domestic spending. On the contrary, social welfare expanded to dimensions that would have been unimaginable in 1960 and continued to do so during the early Nixon years. One careful overview concluded that the nation had a "system within sight of assuring at least a poverty threshold standard of living for all citizens."

In-kind welfare payments (as opposed to cash) jumped especially during these years. Medicaid, a federal-state health program targeted mainly at the welfare poor in 1965, provided $9 billion in benefits to 23 million recipients by 1974. The value of public housing during those same ten years rose from $236 million to $1.2 billion. Food stamps, which in 1965 was a small, virtually unnoticed program that spent $36 million on 633,000 people, was by 1975 outlaying $4.3 billion to 17.1 million recipients. Unlike Social Security, which helped the nonpoor as well as the poor, Medicaid, public housing, and food stamps went almost exclusively to the poverty population. Other in-kind benefits, notably Medicare, raised the total spent for such purposes even more astronomically. The sum doled out in in-kind benefits leaped from $1.2 billion in 1965 to $10.8 billion in 1969 to $26.6 billion in 1974.

A RAND study of AFDC recipients in New York City during 1974 demonstrated the vital help that in-kind benefits gave to people on welfare. It estimated that the average family on AFDC received the equivalent of $6,088, of which only 38 percent was cash, the rest in food stamps, Medicaid, public housing, and social services. Even discounting a little the actual cash value of such benefits, the income of these families was well above the $4,160 that a person could earn laboring full time at the minimum wage of $2 per hour. No wonder conservatives believed there was no work incentive for the welfare poor.

No program, however, expanded so much absolutely as the old age and survivors' insurance plan set in motion by the New Deal. In 1965 this provided $16.6 billion to 20.8 million recipients. Nine years later it cost $54 billion and went to 29.9 million beneficiaries. During those years benefits went up almost twice as fast as personal incomes on the whole. With other insurance programs, such as unemployment compensation and Medicare, Social Security accounted for more than four-fifths of public income maintenance in the United States in 1974. Though much of this money went to people above the poverty line, Social Security programs had a moderately equalizing effect on income distribution and a decisive role in shifting income from the young to the aged, historically one of the most deprived groups of the population.

This growth of social welfare expenditures, broadly defined, was effective in reducing poverty in the United States. Experts who attempted to isolate the impact of social welfare laws distinguished between the "pretransfer" poor (the number left in poverty by the market) and the "posttransfer" poor (those who remained poor after social insurance, public assistance, and in-kind benefits were added to incomes). The impact of such programs was considerable in the mid-1960s and grew dramatically in the next ten years. Cash payments alone pulled about 33 percent of the pretransfer poor, or 5.1 million households, out of poverty in 1965. By 1972 the number of households was 7.7 million, 44 percent. If the impact of in-kind benefits is added, 60 percent or more of the pretransfer poor were removed from poverty.

The decisive role of social welfare in reducing poverty is clear from a snapshot of pre- and posttransfer poverty in 1974. Without any public programs, 20.2 million American families, more than one-quarter of the total population, would have been poor. With social insurance and public aid added to their incomes, 9.1 million remained poor. Adding Medicaid, food stamps, and the other in-kind benefits, the number fell to 5.4 million, or 6.9 percent of all families. Moreover, despite the regressive taxes that supported Social Security and other insurance plans, public programs overall, combined with the moderately progressive income taxes that financed some of them, had what one careful scholar called a "highly egalitarian effect on income distribution." When Harrington blasted welfare as "socialism for the rich, free enterprise for the poor" in 1962, he was already exaggerating. By 1975 such a statement was downright misleading.

These gains managed to bring the United States a little closer into line with other industrialized nations in the field of social welfare. This had not seemed to be the case in 1965, when one expert concluded that America was "more reluctant than any rich democratic country to make a welfare effort appropriate to its affluence." The United States spent a smaller percentage of its GNP on social welfare, broadly defined, than did other comparably advanced countries. Indeed, the nation ranked twentieth (ahead only of Japan) of twenty-one industrial nations in this respect during the mid-1960s. Other critics emphasized the unusually harsh and stigmatizing quality of American public aid, in part resulting from the categorical nature of American legislation, which singled out specially needy groups. In part, critics argued, it stemmed from the power of a poor-law philosophy rampant in a country that glorified success.

By 1975 the American way of public assistance still seemed especially harsh. Where countries such as Sweden—the most advanced welfare state in the West—looked for ways to bring the needy under the umbrella of social welfare, Americans tried to keep them off the public payroll. Where Western European nations moved in the direction of placing a floor under income, the United States adhered officially to the war-on-poverty idea of opening up doors. Americans steadfastly rejected the view that all citizens had a right to a minimum income. As ever, prevention remained the highest priority.

But in strictly monetary terms, the United States moved slightly ahead between 1965 and 1974, to a point where its spending for social insurance plus welfare as a percentage of GNP was close to that of other Western countries. By 1974 it still ranked only seventeenth (ahead of Japan, Australia, New Zealand, and Switzerland), but that was progress of a sort. Moreover, in nations with comprehensive systems, the percentages of people officially defined as poor were probably as high, or higher than, in the United States. England, for instance, had a poverty population that ranged between 4 and 14 percent (depending on placement of the poverty line) in the early 1970s.

America's overall system also came more and more to resemble those of other nations. Until the 1960s, some pioneering countries, such as England and Sweden, had featured collectivist, egalitarian social insurance programs that used general revenue funds to pay equal benefits to all recipients. America, by contrast, relied heavily on wage-based Social Security: the more paid in, the higher the benefits. By the late 1970s Sweden and England were adding wage-based programs to their existing plans, while the United States—thanks in part to the spread of in-kind benefits—moved further away from strictly insurance principles. As one scholar put it, a key development throughout the West was the "progressive blurring of the line between social insurance and public assistance." He added, "Entitlement to income security has become less individually earned and more a social right of citizenship."

One of the many forces that prompted this revolution in social welfare was demographic. By far the largest increases in social spending between 1965 and 1975 occurred in old age insurance; America's population was aging, and ever higher percentages of old people had been in the program long enough to qualify for coverage. By 1975, 93 percent of elderly Americans got Social Security, as opposed to but 20 percent in 1940. Old people as a group also commanded more political respect than they had in the 1930s. At that time, old age lobbies such as the Townsendites had seemed a little zany to younger Americans. By the late 1960s, old people began to be called senior citizens. Their "gray lobbies," increasingly well organized and financed, reflected "senior power." Without the force of such lobbies, Medicare, the other area of great increases in social spending, would not have been passed in 1965. Nor would a range of subsequent amendments have passed that dramatically liberalized benefits—20 percent in the election year of 1972 alone—and that in 1974 indexed them so that they kept pace with the inflation of the 1970s. The leap in spending for Social Security and Medicare continued to depend on the faith among experts as well as in Congress that "insurance" would "prevent" poverty and put a lid on the outpouring of money for welfare.

The maturing of the social welfare system also abetted the increases in spending of the late 1960s and early 1970s. Before then in the United States, a Johnny-come-lately to the field, many old people lacked the required amount of covered time under Social Security to qualify for pensions. No wonder that the most generous countries in the early 1960s were those, like Germany and Austria, that had pioneered in old age insurance and that had high percentages of old people in their populations. By the mid-1960s, America had been expanding its social insurance for thirty years—long enough to move closer at last to the leaders in the field.

Political forces further contributed to the rise in social welfare spending. Passage of Medicare revealed the role of these forces in the area of aid to the aged. They accounted also for the unheralded but vitally important liberalization of food stamp legislation, a liberalization that began in 1968, when a TV documentary on hunger in America dramatized the problem of malnutrition. The following year Senator George McGovern of South Dakota picked up the attack in an investigation of hunger and malnutrition. President Nixon, anxious not to be outflanked, in August 1969 called for a vast expansion of the food stamp program, a change that appealed not only to liberals but also to conservatives, who preferred to give food instead of cash to the poor and who recognized that the program could be administered locally, thus simplifying and decentralizing welfare administration. The food stamp program also received important political support from well-organized producers and retailers. For all these reasons it developed great momentum in both parties, and Congress gave Nixon what he wanted in December 1970. Its response showed that certain kinds of welfare spending had become part of a bipartisan consensus, in spite of the rhetorical flourishes of conservatives. By 1974 food stamps were available to all poor families that passed certain means tests, not just to those on welfare. Without exaggeration, one expert later hailed the expansion of food stamps as "the most important change in public welfare policy since the passage of the Social Security Act."

Bureaucratic pressures added to these demographic and political imperatives. By the 1960s Social Security officials were experienced, self-assured, anxious to enlarge their domain. As one study said, "With the passage of time, administrative routines become established, consensus grows on what has already been accomplished, and administrators acquire an interest in further piecemeal expansion." Another expert observed, "Expansion of the program appears to occur independently of change in social conditions . . . or of party regimes. . . . Policy making and program extension have a continuity, momentum, and political logic of their own . . . aggrandizement is inherent in the modern welfare state."

A partial case in point was Medicaid. In other advanced nations, there was widespread popular consensus that health care for the poor was a fundamental right of citizenship. But that consensus did not exist in America. Rather, Medicaid grew quietly and incrementally out of existing programs that were not working very well. Chief among these was the Kerr-Mills Act of 1960, which set up a matching grant program of medical care to the aged. By 1965, when Congress took up the legislation that resulted in Medicare, the deficiencies of Kerr-Mills were obvious. Reformers complained that it did nothing for people under sixty-five and that the matching grant method resulted in wide state-by-state variations, with the poorer states ignoring the program altogether. Governors and lobbyists for the wealthier northern states, meanwhile, grumbled about its escalating costs.

In the course of passing Medicare, Congress paid special heed to these governors and state lobbyists. It approved Medicaid, which eased the burden on states by obligating the federal government to provide between 50 and 85 percent (for the poorest states) of funding for medical care to the needy blind, disabled, and aged, and to members of poor families with dependent children. States were also permitted to use Medicaid funds to help the "medically indigent"—certain people who did not technically qualify for public assistance but who faced impoverishing medical bills.

The passage of Medicaid, like that of food stamps, testified to three important aspects of welfare legislation since 1960. The first was the role of pressure groups, including state and local officials seeking federal aid. These pressures contributed to the gradual nationalizing process that had characterized the welfare state since the 1930s. The second aspect may be stated as a kind of dictum about welfare bills: the less heralded they are at the time, the fewer potential opponents they arouse, and the more likely they are to slip through Congress. The third follows from the second: such legislation may have totally unforeseen consequences. Few people at the time thought that Medicaid, a sleeper, would become such an expensive program. They expected only that it would offer some fiscal relief to states or that by dealing with illness it would actually help keep people off the welfare rolls. So did preventive thinking lead unexpectedly to largess.

The jump in welfare spending resulted finally from the nation's increased ability to pay. Until the 1960s the United States was the richest nation in the world per capita, but the economic growth of the 1960s and early 1970s was impressive. So was the all-important belief held by many people that America could afford increased social spending, that poverty could be abolished without depriving the middle classes. The rediscovery of poverty, and the war against it that began early in the decade, were but early manifestations of these perceptions. In 1966 Shriver said that in ten years the United States "virtually could eliminate" poverty. His faith reflected a great underlying change that had developed slowly but powerfully over a generation of prosperity: the widespread conviction that the age of Malthusian scarcity had vanished forever.

A pervasive egalitarian ideology accompanied this perception of abundance. As people reached the stage where absolute need was rare, they grew hungry to share what the better half had. They felt deprived relatively, and they grew restless. In the United States, the civil rights revolution first exposed this egalitarian longing. Indians, ethnics, the aged, women, the handicapped—practically all groups that felt deprived—later joined in the demand for rights. Poor people inevitably benefited when public officials responded to the clamor of such groups. The revolution in social welfare in the United States depended finally on the revolution of expectations that was gathering momentum throughout the Western world.

INDEX